"**A**n exciting story of a dedicated hiking club and its fifty-year devotion to the Appalachian Trail... A club that has never swerved from its stated purpose of maintaining the Trail so that others might enjoy."

– Edward B. Garvey, 1994
Author of *Appalachian Hiker*

"**T**he past is only the present become invisible and mute; and because it is invisible and mute, its memoried glances and its murmurs are infinitely precious. We are tomorrow's past."

– Mary Webb, 1924

Friendships

of the

Trail

The History of the
Georgia Appalachian Trail Club
1930 – 1980

Revised edition
1995

Library of Congress Cataloging-in-Publication Data

Friendships of the trail : the history of the Georgia Appalachian
    Trail Club, 1930 - 1980. – Rev. ed.
        p.   cm.
    Written by the GATC History Committee.
    Includes bibliographical references and index.
    ISBN 0-87797-268-0 (acid-free paper)
    1. Georgia Appalachian Trail Club—History.   I. Georgia
Appalachian Trail Club. History Committee.
GV199.43.G462G463   1994
917.4—dc20   94-27312
                                                                 CIP

This book is printed on acid-free paper which conforms to the American National Standard Z39.48-1984, *Permanence of Paper for Printed Library Materials*. Paper that conforms to this standard's requirements for pH, alkaline reserve and freedom from groundwood is anticipated to last several hundred years without significant deterioration under normal library use and storage conditions.

Manufactured in the United States of America

Revised Edition
ISBN: 0-87797-268-0

Edited, Designed and Produced by Harold Arnovitz

Index by Alexa Selph

Cover Photography by Robb Helfrick,
Woodstock, Ga

Cover Design by Richard J. Lenz,
Lenz Design and Communications,
Decatur, Ga

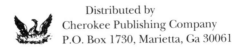

Distributed by
Cherokee Publishing Company
P.O. Box 1730, Marietta, Ga 30061

Dedication

To the hundreds of loyal GATC members who have been a part of the friendships of the Trail during the past 50 years, this book is dedicated. Like the mists hanging over the mountains, many have vanished in time, but the memories of their joyous outings on the Trail they built and loved will remain like the mountains — forever.

Much of the rare, early material in this book was preserved through the dedicated efforts of long-time Club Historian, Marene Snow. Memorial gifts made to Marene's memory were used to defray a portion of the publication cost.

The major portion of the cost of the book was borne by a generous GATC member who wishes to remain anonymous.

Acknowledgments

GEORGIA APPALACHIAN 19 TRAIL CLUB, INC. 30

THE GATC History Committee gratefully acknowledges the contributions of a number of people in the production of this volume: Marene Snow for collecting and preserving the historical materials over the years; Whit Benson for suggesting and encouraging their organization and compilation into this history; current and former members who furnished information and insights into past events and personalities; the past Club presidents and other members who read the manuscript and made helpful suggestions.

The illustrations [in the first editon but replaced by a section of halftones in this edition] included: drawings by Dory White . . . ; contributions by Janet Cochran, student at Southern Technical Institute; GATC yearbook covers by John Myers and others unknown, and other sketches by Mary Eidson and unknown sources from the Club files.

Grace Rogers cheerfully assumed the arduous task of typing the ever lengthening manuscript.

Nancy Shofner, Historian
Joann Ayoubi
Helen Boyd
Judy Galphin
John Krickel
Grace Rogers
Rosalind Van Landingham

Two years ago Nancy Shofner and I were discussing what the GATC and especially the Historian should do in preparation for our Golden Anniversary.

The general theme of our celebration was to focus on the Club's activities during the first fifty years and the personalities that had developed the GATC into the organization which we know today. The History Committee, comprised of Nancy, Judy Galphin, John Krickel and Rosalind Van Landingham, and later expanded to include Helen Boyd, Grace Rogers and Joann Ayoubi, was responsible for sorting through the many boxes containing the Club files and selecting material for the bulletin "Footprints in History" and for the 1980 Multi-Club display. It seemed a shame that the wealth of information contained in old bulletins, minutes, letters and photographs couldn't be condensed into an accessible and usable form for the GATC membership to enjoy.

During 1980, as the Club became involved with management plans, trail construction, preparation for Multi-Club, and the Golden Anniversary party, the idea of a GATC history was apparently forgotten. However, I had discounted Nancy's dedication and determination. In addition to spending many hours actually working on the Trail, she met with the History Committee several evenings a month for several months to sort through the files in preparation for Multi-Club and for indexing them in preparation for permanent storage at the Georgia Department of Archives. When plans for the Golden Anniversary party seemed to flounder because of unexpected complications, Nancy volunteered to take over as chairwoman of the Golden Anniversary committee. Everyone who attended the party is aware of its outstanding success due largely to Nancy's coordination of the efforts of the many people involved. While all of this preparation proceeded, Nancy still found time to scout and lead a reminiscence hike to Mount Oglethorpe the day after the party.

I was, therefore, quite surprised last spring when Nancy forwarded several hundred pages of typed draft text for me to review. She had obviously been writing ferociously in her spare time. I hope that each of you enjoys reading about the GATC's first fifty years. I think that the GATC owes Nancy a well deserved "thank you" not only for producing this history but for her dedicated efforts in behalf of the Club.

—*Whit Benson, President*
September 1981

Acknowledgements
Revised edition

SINCE THE FIRST EDITION of *Friendships of the Trail* was published in 1981, the membership of the Georgia Appalachian Trail Club has almost tripled. The traditions of the GATC, dedication to the AT, desire to be involved in the various and expanding programs of the Club, and camaraderie among members are as evident today as at any time. Also prevalent is the interest in "our" history, the desire to know how the AT in Georgia and GATC were founded, the fun of knowing some of the tales of earlier Club members as they worked on the Trail and enjoyed other Club activities together.

The first edition of *Friendships of the Trail* was only 250 copies. These copies were sold before our membership started growing rapidly. For about five years, no copies of the book have been available. Also, the original edition, which was graciously made possible by an anonymous donor, was not durably bound, and use has left most of our copies more of a loose-leaf edition than a bound copy.

For some time the need for *Friendships of the Trail* to be reprinted has been discussed. Most of us discussed the possibility, but fortunately, there was one among us with talent and with interest in the project. Harold Arnovitz, who earlier as Bulletin Editor reformatted our newsletter and for many years published the Club's yearbook, voluntarily undertook the project. Typical of Harold, he spared no effort, researched all phases involved in publication of a book, made numerous contacts with individuals, explored every facet that would lead to a quality, affordable reprinting of *Friendships of the Trail.*

For this revised edition, we are indebted to the efforts of a true volunteer, Harold Arnovitz, for his persistence, patience, and for the vast amount of time spent to make this edition of *Friendships of the Trail* a reality.

– Rosalind Van Landingham, President
November 1993

My journey from Springer Mountain in Georgia to Mt. Katahdin in Maine began when I joined the Georgia Appalachian Trail Club in 1974. The difficult trek, which culminated in 1990, was wrought with obstacles — physical, mental, logistical — that, on occasion, tested my desire to hike the entire Appalachian Trail. But each time, when I thought that I had reached my limits, someone gave me that "push" to continue.

My fascination with a computer optical character recognition program enticed me to convert the original typewritten manuscript of *Friendships of the Trail* into a computer text file. That was the beginning of another journey — the book's revision and reprinting. But, like hiking the Trail, many obstacles appeared that had to be conquered. Again, there was always someone there to open yet another door.

I would like to thank some of the many people who contributed and cooperated in this project for their support in helping me complete this journey:

President Rosalind Van Landingham and the 1993 GATC Board of Directors, for their faith in my ability to bring this project to fruition. A sizable amount of money was committed to this endeavor — a first in the Club's history.

Nancy Shofner, the prime author of the first edition, for sharing her knowledge of the Club's history to substantiate questions of accuracy about people and events. Her captions added timeliness to the halftones in the photo section, which were from the Club's files in the Georgia Department of Archives, along with slides from Joe Boyd, Jim and June Engle, John Krickel, and Marianne Skeen.

Judy Galphin, Grace Rogers, and Sandi Still, for spending endless hours correcting errors, not only in the conversion, which at best was 95% correct, but also typos and other mistakes in the original edition.

Darrell Maret and Marianne Skeen, for the epilogue, which summarizes the history of the Club's growth and what transpired beyond its first fifty years.

Hillrie Quin, for introducing me to talented and knowledgeable individuals, who in turn opened some of "those doors."

Margaret Drummond, for being there whenever I needed that "special ear."

As Chair of the Appalachian Trail Conference's Board of Managers and a long-time member of the GATC, I could always count on her for sound advice and guidance.

Brian B. King, the ATC's Director of Public Affairs, and Kay Bresee, Brian's assistant, for their help in obtaining printing price quotes, and information on book design and marketing.

Frank Logue, Carolina Graphics Group, Inc., Rome, Georgia, who, at ATC's mention of the revision, graciously offered advice on book design and marketing, and provided me with additional insights into my task.

Richard J. Lenz of Lenz Design and Communications of Decatur, Georgia, who donated much time and creative expertise to the design and production of the cover. I sincerely appreciate his patience with my impatience as a novice. And his friend, Robb Helfrick of Woodstock, Georgia, who contributed the outstanding color photo for the cover.

Alexa Selph, a very talented and professional indexer, for building the excellent index for this revision. The wealth of historical reference in the original edition could not be easily accessed due to its lack of an index.

Bert Martin, an art director at BellSouth Advertising and Publishing Corporation, for his guidance and help in the layout of the text and the photo section. Also, to BAPCO for its assistance in printing the text and photos to film.

Ken Boyd of Cherokee Publishing Company of Marietta, Georgia, for helping me through the nitty gritty of getting this book to print and his assistance in its marketing.

– Harold Arnovitz
January 1995

Contents

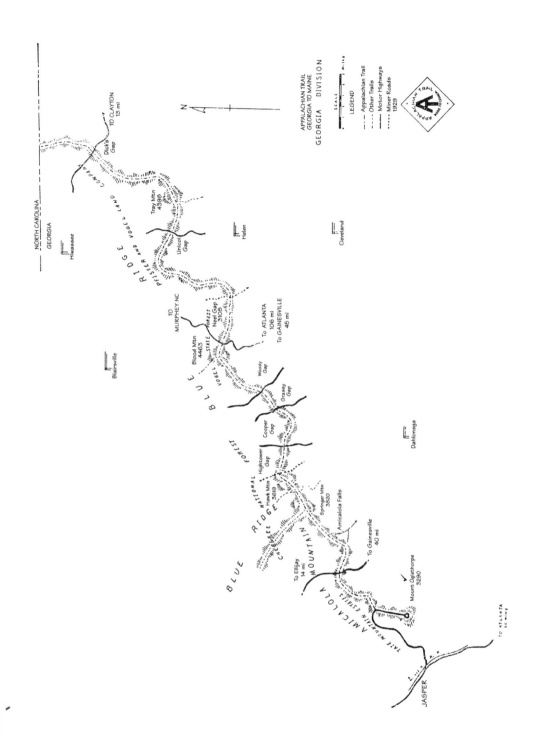

APPALACHIAN TRAIL
GEORGIA TO MAINE
GEORGIA DIVISION

SCALE
MILES

LEGEND
———·— Appalachian Trail
———— Other Trails
········· Motor Highways
Miner Roads
1929

N

NORTH CAROLINA
GEORGIA

Hiwassee

TO CLAYTON
13 mi

Dick's Gap

COWPANA

RIDGE AND VOGEL LAND
PFISTER AND VOGEL LAND

Tray Mtn
4398

Unicoi Gap

Helen

TO MURPHEY NC

Forest
Neel Gap
3108

TO ATLANTA
106 mi
To GAINESVILLE
45 mi

Cleveland

Blairsville

Blood Mtn
4463

BLUE

STATE

VOGEL

Woosy Gap

Grasey Gap

Cooper Gap

RIDGE NATIONAL FOREST

Hightower Gap

Hawk Mtn
3619

Springer Mtn
3820

Amicalola Falls

Dahlonega

BLUE RIDGE MOUNTAIN

CHATTAHOOCHEE

To Ellijay
14 mi

To Gainesville
40 mi

AMICALOLA

Mount Oglethorpe
3290

TATE MOUNTAIN ESTATES

JASPER

TO ATLANTA
60 mi

Beginnings

**GEORGIA
APPALACHIAN
19 TRAIL CLUB, INC. 30**

"A WHIFF OF WOOD SMOKE and coffee along the forest trail hurried the pace of the last stragglers; the hikemaster and advance guard had reached the noon rendezvous and now the hot brew was a-making."[1] On the Georgia Appalachian Trail much had preceded and much would follow this typical scene centered around "Snelly Bo," the old GATC coffee pot, as it, dressed in its canvas jacket, passed from hand to hand and jogged over more trail than any single hiker.

In 1921 Benton MacKaye, forester, regional planner, and conservationist, had presented an idea for "a new approach to the problem of living" in an article in the *Journal of the American Institute of Architects* entitled "An Appalachian Trail: a Project in Regional Planning." He outlined his unique plan for an Appalachian Trail, "a long trail over the full length of the Appalachian Skyline, from the highest peak in the north to the highest peak in the south—from Mount Washington to Mt. Mitchell."[2] It would be a footpath which would be "the backbone of a primeval environment, a sort of retreat or refuge from a civilization which was becoming too mechanized." MacKaye writes later: "The Appalachian Trail indeed is conceived as the backbone of a super reservation and primeval recreation ground covering the length (and width) of the Appalachian Range itself, its ultimate purpose being to extend acquaintance with the scenery and serve as a guide to the understanding of nature."[3]

The "suggested location," with map, included "branch trails" and railway lines to transport to it the "toilers in the bee-hive cities along the Atlantic seaboard." The work on this trail was to be done as far as possible by volunteers, for "volunteer work is really play." MacKaye took his idea to many people and places, promoting it among existing trail organizations, National Park and Forest Service officials, and many other people of influence. Several early hiking clubs—the Appalachian Mountain Club (formed in 1876), the Green Mountain Club, the New England Trail Conference, the Palisades Interstate Park Trail Conference (which soon expanded and became the New York-New Jersey Trail Conference)—had laid the foundations for this long trail, having built regional and state trail systems in New England and the New York area, and urged a merging of many of these trails to form larger ones.

Among the early enthusiastic supporters of MacKaye's idea were Raymond Torrey, journalist and botanist; Major William Welch, then Director of the Bear Mountain Interstate Park; L. F. Schmekebier, economist; and Arno Cammerer, then Director of the National Park Service. Many other active and influential people were involved all along the proposed route.

In 1922 a group of about a dozen people formed the Appalachian Trail Committee of Washington, D.C., to further the Appalachian Trail. Various persons and organizations immediately began to scout and locate portions of the trail. About 350 miles of existing trails in New England and New York were to be incorporated into the Appalachian Trail. The first section of trail was opened in 1923 in Palisades Interstate Park in New York. For the opening Major Welch designed the AT marker/monogram—the distinctive A over T still used today. Trail work was soon begun in Pennsylvania also. In the South, Clinton Smith and Verne Rhodes of the Forest Service and Paul M. Fink of Tennessee took measures to route the trail in Virginia, North Carolina, Tennessee, and Georgia.

In 1925 the Appalachian Trail Conference was formed in Washington, D.C.; a provisional constitution was adopted dividing the Trail into five sections of responsibility, from New England to the "Carolina Highlands." Major Welch was elected chairman; Benton MacKaye, field organizer; and Miss Harlean James, secretary. After this great occasion, the momentum lagged. It was set in motion again in 1926 by Arthur Perkins, a retired Connecticut lawyer, with the aid of Myron Avery, a prominent federal lawyer and one of the founders of the Potomac Appalachian Trail Club.

Work began in earnest all along the Trail. In the South, the Smoky Mountains Hiking Club had existed since 1924 and, until this time, had been the only club south of Pennsylvania. In 1927 the Potomac Appalachian Trail Club was organized and, quickly building a reputation for hard work, had constructed some 260 miles of trail by 1932. The PATC stimulated the formation of a number of other clubs, and work progressed in the South.

Arthur Perkins replaced Major Welch as Chairman of the ATC in 1927, and in 1928 the second ATC conference was held in Washington, D.C. A constitution was adopted and a more permanent organization effected. It was reported that a total of 500 miles of the AT in several segments could be traveled at that time.

The final (but not static) route of the AT took some time to materialize. It was extended in the North from Mt. Washington to Katahdin, although for a time it was considered impossible to build a trail through the Maine wilderness. In 1929 the route south of Virginia remained to be decided upon. It was agreed that it should include the Great Smokies—then a new national park—but not until 1932, after it had been earlier scouted by Roy Ozmer and later by Myron Avery, was a final decision made on the route between the Smokies and central Virginia, bypassing Mt. Mitchell. In 1929 very little was known of the mountain areas in the South, the route having been chosen mostly from maps.

The complex structure of the Appalachian Mountains in the South made these decisions difficult. The Blue Ridge forks below southern Virginia, and the eastern and western ranges come together again at Springer Mountain. Transverse chains connect the two ranges. Either fork of the Blue Ridge might have been utilized, but the western range from southern Virginia through the Smokies was chosen.

This entire southern portion from Georgia to southern Virginia was scouted by Roy Ozmer in 1929. Ozmer, an enthusiastic and accomplished woodsman, was officially enlisted by the ATC in 1928 to scout much of the Trail. He lived in Virginia at the time, but he and his wife moved to Georgia in 1930. He was quite an individual, loving the out-of-doors and seeming to view life as a real adventure—"a most delightful person." He had intended to walk the entire Trail in 1929, but a back injury stopped him in Virginia.

The southern terminus of the Trail is another story. The Trail was definitely to go through the Smokies, but the route on the western end of the park became a matter of dispute. Because of the very loose organization of the Appalachian Trail Conference, Ozmer had been given only general directions and he probably felt that he was empowered to place the Trail wherever he saw fit south of the Smoky Mountains. Also, Ozmer had worked in Georgia as a forester and had a reasonably good knowledge of its mountains—a knowledge which was lacking in Myron Avery and Arthur Perkins.

The original plan of the Conference was to follow the crest of the Smokies to the Nantahalas and on through the northwest tip of Georgia to the Cohutta Mountains. By contrast, the route laid out and scouted by Ozmer began at Mt. Oglethorpe in Georgia and followed the Blue Ridge over Springer, Blood, Tray and into North Carolina at Rich Knob (the route followed today), through the Nantahalas and into the Smokies up Forney Ridge to Siler's Bald. The Smoky Mountains Hiking Club strongly favored the route following the entire length of the Smokies to the Little Tennessee River, necessitating, to them, its eventual end in the Cohutta Mountains.

In Georgia, Roy Ozmer had been working with Everett [Eddie] B. Stone, Assistant State Forester in Gainesville, and his assistant, Charles N. Elliott, in mapping, routing, and scouting the Trail through the state. Stone had come to Georgia from Virginia to work with the Forest Service. He was a quiet, practical man, strong of purpose, "slight of build and active as a mouse on store-bought cheese" according to Elliott. He was a single man and lived at the Dixie Hunt Hotel in Gainesville. Stone was determined that the route world follow the Blue Ridge in Georgia from Rich Knob to Oglethorpe and he was perfectly willing to take on the entire Conference single-handedly if need be.

Stone's dedication to having the Georgia section of the Trail bisect the heart of the then Cherokee National Forest (soon renamed Chattahoochee National Forest) needs some explanation. From his early letters, it is apparent that Stone had a uniquely modern concept of the national forest system. In 1929 the national forests were managed almost exclusively for the benefit of the lumbering interests—in effect, a government subsidy to timber companies. Stone realized the potential for recreational use of the forests—a concept which was later to find an eloquent national voice in Bob Marshall. To Stone, the Appalachian Trail would attract visitors to the national forests, and he further realized that the *quality* of these hiking visitors would include influential people who would build popular support for multiple forest use. Once launched on what he believed to be the "right" course, Stone would stand up to his superiors in the Forest Service, the Appalachian Trail Conference, or anyone else who stood in the way of what was to become "his" trail in Georgia.

Charlie Elliott, described as "the debonnaire [sic], the raconteur—the tongue-in-cheek type" and "a real live wire"—always with pipe in his mouth—was seemingly the opposite of Stone, although equally as devoted to the concept and actuality of the Trail. His devotion does not shine through strongly in this deliberately humorous account he wrote in later years of those early days:

One of my first jobs after I came back [to Georgia from Montana] was as Assistant to Assistant State Forester Eddy Stone. An Assistant to an Assistant is like being a corporal in the Army. He gets all the dirty work that's handed down from above and all the cussin' from below. Many a Sunday morning, when I would have chosen to clutch the blankets around my ears and pass that day as the Bible says all laboring gentlemen should, Eddy dragged me out for a cup of coffee served by sleep-drugged employees in the little restaurant down the street. Although the skies were black, the wind howled like a banshee . . . we'd crawl into his galloping jalopy and point its nose toward places where not even the gods would be caught on a day like that. I've seen the bulging crest of the Blue Ridge when it stood so stark and vast against the sky that I'd feel like an ant plodding down the tomb of eternity. I've been so cold that when I walked, my frozen toes would rattle like castanets in my leather boots. Sometimes I felt my hands grow hot to choke off his ceaseless babbling about the 'Appalachian Trail should terminate at Tate,' or 'the Appalachian Trail goes over Tray' or 'the Appalachian Trail tops Blood.' I often thought, as we crouched on our haunches by some tiny fire while the wind congealed our blood and the trees beat at the ridge tops like witches sweeping off the mountain, that the man should be in some institution for mental derelicts.[4]

Other routes for the Trail through Georgia had also been proposed. Ozmer later gave this account:

At the time I first became interested in the movement it was impossible to find anyone south of Washington who knew whether the Appalachian Trail was a liquid or solid. Even in the North, where the idea had been brewing for some time, few and far between were those who knew much of the movement, much less anything at all of the factors influencing the actual location of the proposed 'highroad for hikers.' Correspondence with MacKaye, Major Welch, . . . Myron Avery, Allen and others finally gave me enough data to start the movement going here in the South.

It was here that E. B. [Stone] and Charlie [Elliot] came in, and without their actual and moral support, it is doubtful if I would have had the hardihood to have carried on. At that time, I was residing in Tennessee, far from the field of action. . . .

Before actually beginning the trail-blazing venture, I held three or four conferences with Horace Kephart, Stone and Elliott, sometimes all of us together and again with any one or two, just as we could arrange things. According to the first plans, as formulated by the AT groups in the North, the Trail was to enter Georgia along the Blue Ridge and follow it throughout the State and then pass into the Cohuttas, or Tennessee, or 'by some route, obscure and only [sic], guarded by ill angels only' swing westward into Alabama, ending at some remote corner in the cotton fields on the Piedmont—the gods alone knowing where—or why!

Another alternative route was to take a plunge downward out of the mountains near Frogtown [Neel] Gap and cross those interminable cotton fields west of Gainesville and finally stagger to a dead stop on the top of Stone Mountain! Knowing that neck o' the woods pretty well, having gadded about among them chasing smokes for the U. S. Forest Service, I felt that the only logical, appropriate and *humane* place for the southern terminus was Oglethorpe and proposed that idea to E.B., Charlie and Kep. It seems all three were acquainted with that section and all gave me their hardy support.[5]

On his attempted walk of the entire—and non-existent—Appalachian Trail in 1929, Ozmer casually planned to lay out and blaze at least the first 700 miles as he walked! He had the full support and actual assistance of Stone and Elliott on part of his walk through the Georgia section.

He later gives this brief account of the first part of his trip through Georgia:

Leaving Boling, at the summit of Mt. O. in mid-afternoon of May 2nd, 1929, I headed north toward the faintly visible Falls of Amicalola. Nightfall found me near Southern's Store, where I pitched camp and spent the first of many nights on the Trail. Next day I made poor progress, having considerable difficulty in locating the desired route through such a confusion of abandoned roads and faint cattle trails between Southern's and the Falls. Reaching the Falls late in the afternoon I made camp in an abandoned apple-orchard (the first above the Falls) and spent the most miserable night on the entire journey. First it rained, sheets and torrents. Having a balloon-silk tent with a sewed-in floor, I was actually obliged to cut holes in the floor-cloth to let out the rain that had been driven in at every crevice. (That darned tent cost twenty-odd dollars, too!) After the first and, fortunately, the worst, of the rain passed on, the winds came! Howling like ten thousand demons on the loose, that wind came swooping down off the 'high-tops' and uprooted the ancient apple tree to which I had made the forestay of the tent fast to! Luckily I happened to pitch the tent on the windward side of the tree and, in falling, it missed the tent. But, and it gave me a scare I'll tell you, in falling, the tree carried the tent with it, leaving me stripped before the howling heavens except for my Duxbak breeches and a sweat-shirt! Everything was soaking wet so I spent the night 'just tol'able, thank you'! The next day I scouted the route over Big Frosty, Springer Mtn. through Winding Stairs Gap, to Hawk Mtn. where I spent the night. E.B. and Charlie were to have met me in Winding Stairs but, on arriving there, I found a note saying they had given me out and returned to Hawk. While climbing Hawk, going North, I met a light snowstorm heading South! This, coupled with black darkness, made me spend the night alone on the howling crest of Hawk, rather than go the last long mile down to the Hightower Gap Ranger Station where E.B. and Charlie had retreated. Calling them by phone from the summit, I found them delighted to know I had neither froze nor had been blown away!

The next day the three of us together hiked over to Woody Gap where they were obliged to leave me and return to their posts in Gainesville. . . .[5]

But by following the Blue Ridge north out of Georgia, Ozmer had missed a fairly sizable portion of the Great Smoky Mountains.

A fight was inevitable, with the Smoky Club determined to have the route extend the entire length of the Smokies and thence west to the Cohuttas in Georgia. Eddit Stone and Roy Ozmer in Georgia strongly favored the Trail's entrance into Georgia at Rich Knob and ending at Oglethorpe. This would necessitate bypassing the western portion of the Smokies. The following letter from Myron Avery to Arthur Perkins, Chairman of ATC, had stated the problems:

The . . . problem relates to the route of the Trail in the south and affords, I think, an opportunity to label as completed a considerable and troublesome section of the trail if the route suggested is agreed upon. First I want to outline Ozmer's route. To understand it, a copy of the Cherokee National Forest map is needed. . . . It will be recalled that someone, I think the State Geologist, told Torrey that a Burnt Mountain [near Oglethorpe] rather than Cohutta was the logical end of the range. This was at the Conference on State Parks. Well here is just where Ozmer started. He started from the railroad town of Jasper. From here it is 8 miles by motor to the top of Burnt Mountain. Here a million dollar development [Tate Mountain Estates] is taking place. He followed along the Pickens-Dawson county line . . . crossing the following places: Amicalola, Bucktown Mt., Black Mt., Winding Stair Gap, Hightower Mt., east to Sassafras Mt. and Crane Gap, Grass Gap, Woody Gap, Baker Mt., Henry Gap, Blood Mt., Frogtown Gap, Cow Rock Mt., Strawberry Mt., and Horsetrough Mt. (on west edge of eastern section of forest). Here he was forced to stop. He says that from Frogtown Gap the Forest Service has an appropriation for a trail north and east partly over private lands to the existing trails on the Nantahala in North Carolina. It is expected that work will be started in July. This will be a standard graded forest trail. Once on the Nantahala, forest trails will be followed by Ozmer until he reaches the Little Tennessee. The route is on the east side of the Nantahala. Then he expects to come up Forney Ridge to Siler's Bald and then east along Smoky. But if it were thought desirable to include all of Smoky in the trail he could leave the Nantahala (near Leadbetter Creek . . .) and follow the Snowbird chain along on the Graham and Cherokee County line and meet the end of Smoky. Stone, whom Torrey met at Clifty Falls and others went with Ozmer for part of the way. They are enthusiastic over the project and Ozmer says could raise enough money for the markers for this section if it is *officially* determined as the route.

The advantage of the standard government trail from Frogtown Gap to Nantahala Forest is obvious. There might be some objection to hitting Smoky at Siler's Bald rather than at the Little Tennessee. But as Fink pointed out, the trail could fork at Siler's and one end run out to the west. I have long wondered who designated Cohutta as the end of the trail and nobody seemed to know. Fink says that long ago Kelsey and others asked him about it. He said that he didn't know the country from actual travel in it but in view of their anxiety to have Lookout Mt. the terminus he studied the maps, etc., to work out a route. So he got them down to Cohutta which has the disadvantage of being not so accessible as Burnt Mt. . . . No one of us know that country and I think in the final analysis we should be governed by the views of Fink and Ozmer. But why let the pot simmer any longer. If we want to mark a route from Burnt Mt. to the Little Tennessee at the mouth of the Nantahala River we can get it done and accomplish something that seemed far away, that is mark the southern portion of the trail. . . . Perhaps the Board of Managers can express their views and this organization down there can get under way. At any rate we should not let their enthusiasm die out. . . . My personal view is to have the route followed by Ozmer marked as the A.T. trail at least as far as Snowbird Mts. at their junction with the Nantahala. We know of no interest over toward Cohutta. . . . Let's at least finish the southern end while we can. (July 24, 1929)

Stone, however, had not waited for the slow wheels of the ATC Board of Managers to grind out a decision. He shrewdly realized that there was no Georgia group seeking to put the Trail anywhere. If Georgia was to get the Trail actually built and blazed, it was up to him. And Eddie Stone seized the opportunity to get the Trail located where he wanted it. As Assistant State Forester he knew the north Georgia mountains perhaps better than anyone else at the time. And, he undoubtedly reasoned, why should the Georgia section of the Trail be located by a group of outsiders who had never even visited Georgia. So Stone set out on a campaign to finalize the southernmost section of the Trail.

On January 16, 1930, Ozmer wrote the following to Stone:

. . . I was immensely pleased over the news of your splendid progress. Right here and now I want to say that you, though having become interested but recently, have accomplished more actual work of value to the Trail than any person in the South to date!. . . By the way, Kephart, George Masa, Jim Thompson, the Knoxville photographer who is the head of the Smoky Mts. Hiking Club, and I spent the past weekend with Paul and held an informal conference on the AT. Thompson, representing that disgusting Knox. bunch, was pulling hard for the Trail to extend to the southern end of the Smokies, where it breaks off into the Little Tenn. Riv. and for it to continue thence southward along the Unaka Mts. to Mt. Cohutta, Ga. Did we change his mind! Well, it would have done your heart good to have heard the oration that Kep put up for Georgia and Mt. Oglethorpe. Seriously, there was no chance of the route which I scouted being changed, but we had to pacify that Knox. bunch some way, therefore, the 'conference.' Thompson, knowing that I was a Georgian, thought that mere prejudice on my part had led to the decision to end the Trail at Oglethorpe. Kep soon convinced him of the folly of his ways! To think that the Knox. crowd had the nerve, though, to ask us to re-route the entire southern section of the Trail in order to traverse the southern end of the Smokies. . . . Well, their nerve beats that of the proverbial Army mule! The conference closed when we stated to Thompson that it was O.K. to fork the Trail in the Smokies and let one branch extend to Cohutta . . . IF HIS BUNCH COULD FINANCE AND BUILD AND MAINTAIN THE BRANCH LINE! . . . It would be mighty nice if the Trail could be so routed to cover the Smokies, but it cannot be warped all over the world to reach every place of beauty and interest in the Mts.! The logical thing for that bunch to do is to construct a side-trip trail from the place (Siler's Bald) where the Trail turns away from the main crest of the Smokies and carry it through the remainder of the Park area, for there is no logical route to follow from the south end of the Park back eastward to the Nantahalas. Doubtless they will see the unreasonableness of their request and content themselves with a side-trip trail, for it is sure that bunch has neither the active interest nor the finances to pull the main trail to the Cohuttas!

There is strong evidence that Stone was actually blazing and marking the Appalachian Trail in Georgia in late 1929 along his favored route. This completed, he composed an article for *Mountain Magazine*, which acted as the semi-official publication of Conference news.

In the article, entitled "Following the Appalachian Trail Through Georgia," Stone outlined his route and extolled its beauties. (At the AT Conference in 1929, Stone had demonstrated that Oglethorpe was the terminus of the Southern Appalachians, and pointed out that existing Forest Service trails through the then Cherokee and Nantahala National Forests would connect with the Smokies.) This article was forwarded by the editor to Arthur Perkins for comment. Perkins wrote to Stone:

I read the article with a great deal of interest, and which is made stronger by the beautiful photographs which you enclose, but I feel that the article itself should be modified somewhat before it is printed in the Magazine. The reason is because there will probably be two branches of the main trail at the southern end—one of them terminating at Cohutta Mountain in Georgia, and the other at Mt. Oglethorpe in the same state. . . . The reason for a branching of the Trail in this way is that the first plan contemplated the western route terminating at Cohutta, but there was so much interest in the east side of the mountain that the Committee in charge of the route have practically decided on an eastern branch also, though the exact location of the same has not been determined officially. (January 31, 1930)

As Elliott said: "Eddy flung a fit." He replied to Perkins as follows:

I have your letter of January 31st in regard to location of the Appalachian Trail. It was my understanding that the route of the Appalachian Trail in Georgia had been definitely settled and it was a surprise to me to learn that there is any question about it. The trail as now recognized follows the main Blue Ridge from the North Carolina line and has its southern terminus at the most logical point within the state. This route is also the one blazed out by Mr. Ozmer who was commissioned the official trail blazer by the Trail Conference. The eastern route is obviously the most desirable for the following reasons: . . .

He listed eight reasons, saying that it follows the main Blue Ridge, a well-defined, clear-cut divide; elevations are greater; Springer Mountain, over which the trail passes, is the southernmost peak of the Blue Ridge; the Mt. Oglethorpe terminus has historic associations and is easily accessible from Atlanta; the trail is readily accessible at numerous intervals; the Blue Ridge is visible from great distances; the trail traverses the National Forest and Vogel State Forest; the trail has been constructed and marked for approximately ninety miles. Then he listed the disadvantages of the Cohuttas terminus: no well-defined divide or great elevations; would be in Georgia for only twenty miles, all on private land; inaccessible for the whole length of the trail. He continued:

I know of no one in Georgia who would be interested in the western route and there is no possibility of creating any interest in it. So far as the State of Georgia is concerned, the route would never be recognized as the main trail. The Trail as now located along the Blue Ridge has been given a great deal of publicity recently, and plans are under way to have a party of Boy Scouts make the hike over its entire length upon its completion. This will be in connection with the dedication exercises at Mount Oglethorpe during May. It is unfortunate that any controversy has come up as to the location of the main trail, and I strongly recommend that the Trail Conference recognize the eastern route. (February 4, 1930)

Stone also wrote to Horace Kephart to enlist his aid, having learned from Ozmer of his interest. He also wrote to others in Georgia who supported the Trail.

Kephart saved the day in his reply:

I will send you a full answer within a few days, enclosing copy of a suggestion I am making to Judge Perkins of a route for the AT in North Carolina-Tennessee that I think will satisfy the Tennesseans and not change the route in Georgia to Mt. Oglethorpe. Briefly, my suggestion is to continue the trail westward along the Smokies from Siler's Bald, through the whole length of the National Park, cross Tennessee River at Rhymer's Ferry, skirt Santeetlah Lake in Graham County to Robbinsville, turn south to Nantahala Station, up the Winding Stairs at head of Nantahala Gorge, out to Near

Burningtown, thence along trail of Nantahala National Forest to Standing Indian, and so on as already plotted in Georgia to Mt. Oglethorpe. This would be a more scenic route than Ozmer's provisional route from Siler's Bald down Forney Ridge to Bushnell, N.C., and via Wesser to the Nantahalas. The latter course will be impracticable, anyway, when the big dams of the Aluminum Co. are built on Tennessee River, as they will form a lake entirely covering the Bushnell territory and with no crossing. . . . As I understand it, the only people interested in the Cohutta route are the Knoxville Hiking Club, and they favor it simply (so far as I know) because it would include the western part of the Smoky Mountains National Park. All that is accomplished by the route I suggest above. I quite agree with you that there is no merit in a trail to Cohutta and that the only trail needed in Georgia is to Mt. Oglethorpe. (February 15, 1930)

He then wrote to Perkins of this plan, saying:

I am thoroughly convinced that Mt. Oglethorpe is the natural and most fitting southern terminus of the AT, as I wrote you some time ago. Cohutta Mt. is isolated and gets one nowhere. Neither is it the true southern end of the Appalachian Mountain system, which Oglethorpe really is. The scenic attractions of Oglethorpe and its surroundings are superior, its accessibility from everywhere in Georgia is all that could be desired, and both the State authorities and the local people heartily support the AT project, whereas, if there is any corresponding sentiment for Cohutta I have not heard of it. Anyway, it is up to Georgia to make the choice, as the opening and maintaining of the Trail in their state requires their support and is their own affair. (February 21, 1930)

Horace Kephart was the most respected outdoor writer of his day. With this solution, which gave both sides their main wishes, Perkins and Avery undoubtedly breathed a sigh of relief. No one would dare speak up against the venerated Kephart, and the reasonableness of the plan made it hard for either side to argue against it. The middle section of the Trail—which was later to become the responsibility of the Carolina and Nantahala Hiking Clubs—took a long time to work out, and it was the Smoky Mountain Club which was to finally lay out the Fontana to Wesser link in its present form.

Perkins replied to Kephart's letter:

. . . you evidently sensed the difficulty in the situation same as I have for the Knoxville club has written me many letters insisting on the westerly route, at least through the Great Smokies, and saying just the same sort of thing about the easterly route as Mr. Stone did about the westerly one. Therefore, your letter suggesting a compromise was exceedingly welcome and I think probably by this change we will be able to satisfy everybody, as I am sure the Knoxville people do not care anything about the route south of the Little Tennessee. I suppose in order to make this change legal, so to speak, there will have to be a modification of the constitution of the Trail Conference, which, as perhaps you remember, fixes the southern terminus at Cohutta. I happen to know, however, that this was done before anybody up here knew much of anything about conditions at the southern end, or how the people in Georgia would feel about it. . . . Thanking you for your interest and assistance in this matter. . . . (February 28, 1930)

He wrote to Stone saying much the same, adding:

I note what you say in regard to Cohutta Mountain as one of the two suggested termini of the Appalachian Trail at the south end, and the reasons for substituting Mt. Oglethorpe as the sole terminus. The matter has given me considerable trouble for the route that you suggest extends southward from about the middle of the Great Smoky range so that the Trail does not follow the whole range to the Georgia State line. The Smoky Mountain Hiking Club of Knoxville, as perhaps you know, is very desirous to have the Trail extend the whole length of the Great Smokies and have taken formal Club action recommending this location, but from what I can learn of their desires, they have no particular interest in the extension of the Trail beyond that point, and if the two routes can be reconciled, I think they will be perfectly satisfied, which you can appreciate is a desirable situation, for we do not want to have the people interested in the Trail at the southern end, or anywhere else, dissatisfied. A short time after my return to work, however, I received a letter from Mr. Horace Kephart which seems to reconcile the ideas of the two interested parties in what, I should think, would be an entirely satisfactory manner.

I sincerely hope that [his] suggestion may recommend itself to you and your friends, in which case, if the Knoxville Club approves, it can be informally adopted as the final location of the Trail in that neighborhood. As the constitution of the Trail Conference provides for a terminus at Cohutta Mountain, I suppose it will have to be amended eventually, but this can probably be done without trouble at the meeting at Skyland on Memorial Day. You will remember that your very interesting article on the Appalachian Trail in Georgia, which you wrote for the *Mountain Magazine*, was sent to me to look over, and that I wrote you about it referring to the two locations for the Trail in that state which you objected to in your letter of February 4th. I am very anxious to have this article with some of the photographs printed in the next number of the Magazine, which will go to press about the 1st of April, and be issued during the latter part of the month, and if you approve of Mr. Kephart's suggestion I would like to have the new route incorporated in the article which I think can be done in a very few words. (March 11, 1930)

Stone's article was finally published in the May, 1930, issue of *Mountain Magazine*.

On March 26 Perkins wrote to Stone:

A few days after I received your letter, I received another letter from Mr. Carlos Campbell of the Smoky Mountain Hiking Club saying that the change in the route of the Appalachian Trail suggested by Mr. Kephart would be entirely satisfactory to that Club; and, therefore, I think we can assume that the route of the Trail will be as suggested by Mr. Kephart and approved by you, with the terminus at Mt. Oglethorpe. I am very glad that this matter has turned out so, for it is very important that everybody interested in the Trail should be harmonious. Of course, we will probably have to get some formal action and approving at the annual meeting, as the Cohutta route was named in the constitution, but I think there will be no difficulty in doing so as the opinion of those locally interested is very important.

To Avery he wrote the following:

I do not think there will be any objection to the change in the constitution as to the southern end of the Trail from Cohutta Mountain to Mt. Oglethorpe except, perhaps, from Ben MacKaye who selected the former location from a map and has always had it in his mind. You can tell him if you want to that I think Oglethorpe is very much preferable because it adds a good many miles to the length of the Trail and brings it down to a point much more accessible near Atlanta, though I would not say anything to him about the proposed hotel development in that location unless you have to. (May 27, 1930)

An interesting aside on the selection of Mt. Oglethorpe as the southern terminus of the Trail: Stone had apparently interested the influential marble quarry owner, Colonel Tate, in having the Appalachian Trail begin at and traverse Tate's newly developed mountain-top resort area, Tate Estates. No one was exactly sure what the Appalachian Trail would evolve into, but real estate developers saw it as a desirable "plus" for the Trail to go near or through their property. The promoters of Chattanooga's Lookout Mountain, for instance, had expressed strong interest in the Trail ending there for reasons which were most likely purely commercial. At any rate, Colonel Tate was prepared to use the Trail's terminus in all of his advertising and promotions. One of the Tate family—Luke Tate—even donated money for the Club's first trail shelter at Amicalola Falls. The Mt. Oglethorpe terminus would also route the Trail past Connahaynee Lodge, an impressive mountain resort fully equal to any of those in the north. The Trail's very beginning would be at an impressive marble monument (sculpted, of course, at the Tate Marble Works) dedicated to Georgia's founder, General James Oglethorpe. (Many in the GATC did not approve of this desecration of wilderness at the beginning of their Trail, and quoted Benton MacKaye as saying the monument was like putting a cap on God.) Colonel Tate had had little trouble in getting the legislature to change the name of Grassy Mountain to Mount Oglethorpe as part of his whole mountain-top development. Benton MacKaye's wilderness concept of the Trail would not become dominant for nearly 40 years; in 1929 Eddie Stone correctly assessed the value of a resort area—and its politically influential developers—as a strong "drawing card" for Georgia's Trail terminus.

The fourth Appalachian Trail Conference was to meet at Skyland, Virginia, in May, 1930. Stone was asked to prepare a talk for the meeting on the "Georgia division" of the Trail, in which he presented all of his arguments for the Oglethorpe route. He was unable to attend the meeting, but Roy Ozmer went in his stead and presented their case.

Ozmer wrote later of the talk he gave:

Even though I was determined to move everything moveable to get Oglethorpe for the terminus I'm afraid I would not have been able to change so many pre-determined minds without the positive and unmistakable emphasis EB gave the matter in that report. To give his report weight and substance (and I've a sneaking idea EB had *that* angle in mind all along) I needed only to cite the Conference to the actual constructive work done by EB. Just as 'Faith, without works, is dead' so are 'proposals, without results accomplished.' The assembled Conference could see from my report of what had actually been accomplished by EB that he was sincere and in dead earnest about the whole movement and so his dictum as to where I thought the Trail should go carried weight enough to turn the tide.

One other thing I feel should be mentioned in connection with the final selection of the southern terminus. I had a series of most lordly and most excellent photos made of, and from, Oglethorpe by George Masa, the Japanese artist of Asheville to display. George, the dear old pagan, was with me and his brief talk in behalf of the Carolina section of the Trail and of Oglethorpe, given in his very, very broken English, was duly impressive. Since, as the Chinese say, 'One picture tells more than ten thousand words,' it was his photos that were so invaluable to us.

Also, Horace Kephart, who was unable to attend, sent a strong letter endorsing me on the Oglethorpe question, and that carried great weight because of Kep's unimpeachable knowledge of the Southern Highlands.[5]

The amendment passed by "unanimous vote of a full assembly." Ozmer wrote to Stone afterward:

At last I am home again from the Conference. Had a most splendid time there, the only thing lacking was your presence to tell that bunch what you have been doing on the southern end. I had to substitute for you, and while it was but poorly done, I feel that I let them know you was on the map, if not at Skylands! When I briefly reviewed your work they drownded me out with applause. They never dreamed that so much had been done in the South. The proposed change in the constitution was made without a hitch. I had to get up and tell them about the local lay of the land and illustrate with a map and answer dozens of questions but the matter went through unanimously at the end. So there can never more be any question involving Cohutta and Mt. Oglethorpe. It was voted that the Conference meet in Gatlinsburg, Tennessee (Smoky-country) next year and all signs indicate that such will be the case.

I sure did hate to see you miss the meeting, but as I know from experience how those things go, I know that your heart was with us, regardless of where you were yourself. The whole gang was disappointed over you not being there and many of them told me to tell you of the appreciation felt for your efforts for the trail. (June 6, 1930)

Avery wrote to Stone on June 2:

Your report and map, as well as your article in *Mountain Magazine*, were received by the Conference with tremendous interest. Roy Ozmer summarized in his talk your work in Georgia. It hardly seems possible that an individual working single handed could accomplish so much. I would like to ask you if you could let me have a blue print of the map which you sent to the Conference. Please let me know the cost.

Harold Allen of the ATC wrote Stone:

You will be gratified, I know, to hear that the Conference was a complete and enthusiastic success. The presence at considerable personal expense of 159 delegates from all up and down the Atlantic seaboard, the fine spirit shown by all, and the bids already received for location of the next year's Conference, show clearly the permanency of the Appalachian Trail appeal as a public movement and the rapidly growing interest in it. I wish you could have heard the enthusiasm of the talks and discussions and the pleasure expressed in the reports and prophesies from all along the route. It is not too flowery to describe this Conference as a big love-feast from start to finish, among some of the finest people in the United States. The members of the local Club who endeavored to make it a success all feel their efforts more than repaid in the pleasure and satisfaction which seemed to be shared by all. The next Conference should be bigger and better and it is to be hoped you will be able to attend. While your personal presence was much missed . . . we wish to express to you our appreciation of your assistance in sending the excellent map and photographs, which were used and referred to in the discussion of the southern terminus of the Appalachian Trail. Roy Ozmer paid you high compliment in his talk, and astonishment was expressed by many persons present that one man could have accomplished what you have done alone, without any organization behind you, to further the Trail in your State. It [Georgia] is worthy of a good [trail] organization, and surely that will follow your individual efforts now that you have made such a splendid start. (June 4, 1930)

And so did follow the organization of the GATC.

Getting the Trail blazed had been the kind of job that Stone could handle well, but he may have felt somewhat ill at ease talking large groups of people into joining together in forming a club. So he turned to his personable young assistant, Charlie Elliott, who could sell refrigerators to the Eskimos.

Charlie Elliott later wrote:

Stone said to me, 'I want you to organize the Georgia Appalachian Trail Club.' Just like that. Just like I could go out into the street and round up fifty people who would walk with me up the summit of a mountain. Most of the folks I knew had never seen a mountain.

But orders were orders. We worked out a plan. Sectional clubs were to be formed in every town that sat in a cradle made by the twisting Blue Ridge. Clayton, Blairsville, Hiawassee, Helen—all should be full of folks who simply could not wait for us to lead them tripping up some mountainside. To get experience in the processes of organization, we decided to first organize in Gainesville.

That should be simple. Everybody—almost everybody—in Gainesville could walk. We called a meeting for the next Tuesday night. [Apparently this was early in the summer of 1930.] During the remainder of the week, I talked to everyone I knew, and a lot of folks I didn't know. They all gave me the same promise, that they would drive down in their cars to the Boy Scout hall to organize a hiking club. I got a hundred promises. I secured the promises of news reporters and photographers that they would be there to give this vast assemblage the recognition it deserved.

On the evening of the meeting I debated for a long time whether I should wear my tux or my boots. Ordinary clothes would not suffice for such a gathering. I polished up my boots, put on my best wool shirt and went forth to the organization meeting.

I was the only living individual who stepped across the threshold of the door that night. Not even Eddy came.

But orders were orders. I tried again. I went to the leading bankers, and asked them to request the presence of all who owed them money. The Chamber of Commerce president promised the attendance of his association to a man. The Boy Scouts all had instructions to appear.

That second night I approached the hall in fear and trembling. I was not alone. That night the janitor kept me company. Eddy had other plans.

After that we decided perhaps the idea of the individual clubs was not the type of organization we wanted. We then tried an organized hike, inviting by letter a number of men and women whom we thought should be interested. This also failed. After much consideration we saw that our only solution lay in dealing with individuals rather than with groups, and in letting the Trail sell itself rather than trying to sell it.

Accordingly, we invited one or two persons at a time to take trips with us into the mountains. These persons accepted for various reasons; scenery, fishing, Kodak pictures, and some for the real joy of hiking. But all were shown the Trail site, some of the interesting spots along the Trail and all were given much information about the possibilities of having a real trail club in Georgia. One by one they became interested.[4]

The mountains of north Georgia were, at this time, a real wilderness area. Much timbering and farming had been going on for years, but establishment of the (then) Cherokee National Forest had by now allowed the area to begin to restore itself. Only one paved road crossed the mountain range—at Neel Gap—and the existing dirt roads were hazardous at best. Moonshining was still a fairly popular pursuit, and cattle, sheep and hogs were allowed to roam free over the hills. In 1930, major unpaved roads crossed the crest of the mountains at Dick's Gap, Unicoi Gap, Woody Gap, Grassy Gap, Cooper Gap, and just south of Amicalola Falls.

In the spring of 1930, Stone and Elliott had asked three Eagle scouts—Byron Mitchell, John Newton, and Jim Brewer of Gainesville—to hike the Georgia Trail in order to see if it could be followed, and to try to get some publicity for the Trail. The Scouts would be the first to hike the whole Georgia AT (other than the scouting parties). Elliott's account of this was:

We talked three unsuspecting boy scouts into hiking down the Blue Ridge from the North Carolina line to Mt. Oglethorpe in Tate Mountain Estates. We released them on the state line, and they headed south—three innocent boy scouts in their early teens. Eddy walked with them a portion of the way. I led them many miles across the weary trail. Back at home my son was born while I toiled, grimy and sweating, up the side of Tray. A portion of the trail they hiked alone. Their food gave out and they lived for one day on berries. There are only a few stunts in my life for which I hope the good Lord will forgive me. That is one. But the boy scouts came through, as boy scouts do, and completed the proposed AT in Georgia.[4]

This had been part of Stone's "master plan" for building popular support for the Trail in Georgia. It was timed to cash in on the publicity attending [the] official dedication of the marble monument to General Oglethorpe, Georgia's founder, on top of newly-renamed Mount Oglethorpe in the midst of Tate Estates, and now the official southern terminus of the Appalachian Trail. In 1930 Boy Scouts rated equally with Motherhood and the Flag as sure-fire news items; what could be more impressive than three of the cream of American youth completing a 100 mile hike through the wilderness in time to salute their country's flag at the dedication of a monument to the state's founder? It would make the Sunday rotogravure section of every newspaper in the state.

The following article appeared in the local paper in November, 1930:

BOY SCOUTS MAKE HIKE OVER
GEORGIA DIVISION OF THE APPALACHIAN TRAIL

E. B. STONE, JR.

In order to tie together, as it were, the two ends of the Appalachian Trail in Georgia, three Boy Scouts were selected to make a continuous hike over the route. The Scouts and their equipment were transported by motor car to a point on the Trail near the North Carolina line. They were accompanied to the starting point by the Scout Executive and a member of the Georgia Forest Service. A hike of about three miles was made to the point where the Trail enters Georgia from North Carolina, and the official start made here.

Each Scout carried a pack with full camp equipment and one blanket. A regulation army shelter tent was also a part of their equipment. Provisions were delivered to them at three points on the Trail: Unicoi Gap, Neel Gap and Hightower Gap. That the boys thrived on the food and the open air is endorsed by the fact that they all gained from one to eleven pounds.

The entire distance was approximately 130 miles, and the time in covering the distance was 13 days, an average of 10 miles per day. The hike was timed so that the Scouts reached Mount Oglethorpe during the ceremony at which the monument to General Oglethorpe, the founder of Georgia, was unveiled. The end of the Appalachian Trail is now marked by a tall marble shaft, and may be reached over a well graded road.

The hike demonstrated the feasibility of the Trail as a travel route and showed that a Scout training prepares a boy to take care of himself in the open.

The three Scouts, Jim Brewer, Byron Mitchell, Jr., and John Newton are natives of Gainesville, Georgia, and were selected from a large number of Scouts in the Gainesville area council.

The boys were to be among the founding members of the Club, and at least two of them remained active for some time.

Elliott, Stone, and Milton Hardy of the *Gainesville News* continued to work toward establishing a trail club and securing members in various towns in North Georgia. Elliott wrote to Stone:

Your letter came this morning. Now get busy and give me some advice on the AT proposition I asked you about. I have got a darn good thing lined up and ready to go, awaiting your word. I may ask you to be temporary Pres. of the darn thing until the first meeting somewhere to elect officers.

I thought I'd start the thing and just a few members, consisting of people I know over the state. I have already sent off to get the cut made. I meant to draw it in the 1st letter I mailed to you, but as I remember now, I forgot it, so I'll use this one to give you an idea. The card will look something like this. We made it up in Gainesville the other day and perhaps you have a suggestion. I thought we would get members all over the state among people I know and later, when they got interested enough to organize separate clubs, let them go to it.

I got one of the AT tree signs of copper in the office and put it on the front of my car, on the radiator. It is attracting lots of attention. It might be a good idea to get a supply of these and sell them to members to put on their radiators, or even give them away. We'll talk about that later. (September 1, 1930)

The membership card he designed began the use of the Club's motto— "Ours is a friendship of the trails that lead to faraway places." The card was sent to all who "signed up," upon payment of two dollars.

Stone became acting president, Elliott acting secretary and Hardy acting treasurer. Stone wrote to Elliott:

We missed you last Sunday when we made a hike across from Woody Gap to Neel Gap. It was an ideal trip and I think we made some more converts for the trail club. I am mailing you some membership cards and wish you would sign the blank ones as acting secretary and return them to me as soon as possible. You should also sign the ones which I have already signed and keep them for use there.

It looks like the best thing we can do is to go ahead and secure members and hold a meeting at some early date and complete the organization. I suggest that for the present that we select only those persons who have shown enough interest to indicate that they are really going to do some hiking. We want as little dead wood as possible in the organization. (October 15, 1930)

The meeting was arranged for November 1 at Zimmer's Mountain Lodge in Dahlonega. Publicity was set up, and many influential and interested persons were invited, including Forest Service and Park Service officials. Elliott wrote to Hardy:

I am making plans and am inviting everyone I know who is likely to be interested. I believe that this meeting has got to go over and go over big or it will just about be our finish and that will never do. I don't know what you and Eddy Stone have planned for Gainesville, how many you have asked there, or what is what. You had better go around and check up and find out what has been done, how many people are planning to go up there and send me all the dope. We've got to do a lot of planning, we've got to inform the Whitners up there how many they can expect and above all, we've got to get plenty of publicity out of that meeting. So write me at the Hartwell Hotel, Hartwell, Ga., as soon as you get this and let me know something. I'm arousing interest everywhere about this meeting and for the sake of the club it can't fall through. (October 20, 1930)

The meeting, according to Charlie Elliott, "was in the nature of an 'experience,' as well as an organization meeting—and I only wish I could remember all the wild tales told."[4]

The minutes read:

Mr. E. B. Stone, Jr., presiding, called the meeting to order. He opened the meeting with an address of welcome in behalf of the club. He then explained the purposes of the club which he divided into two units: (1) To interest the public in nature and the out-of-doors and to set up congenial companionship between lovers of wild things. (2) To construct, maintain and tramp the Georgia section of the Appalachian Trail and preserve it as a retreat from civilization. Mr. Stone then gave a short history of trails and went into detail about the entire Appalachian Trail from Mt. Katahdin in Maine to Mt. Oglethorpe in Georgia. He cited various places of interest in the different states.

Mr. Chas. N. Elliott, acting secretary, made a short talk upon the Georgia section of the trail, describing it and relating a few interesting experiences during hikes over sections of the trail.

Mr. R. R. Ozmer, who looked out and blazed a large portion of the trail, made an interesting talk on his trail experiences from Georgia to Pennsylvania.

Three boy scouts, Byron Mitchell, Jr., Jim Brewer and John Newton, from Gainesville, Ga., told amusing tales of a ten days hike over the Georgia section of the trail, talking in the order named.

Mr. Bonnell H. Stone of Blairsville, Ga., told of the development of the Blue Ridge country north of the trail.

Miss Mary Cresswell, of the Georgia State College of Agriculture, made a short talk on the mountains of yesterday.

Dr. C. R. Hursh, director of the Georgia Mountain Experiment Station, told of an experience in the Smoky Mountains and said that he was very much interested in the development and growth of the club. He predicts a great future.

Officers were elected by the club as follows: E. B. Stone, Jr., Gainesville, President; Henry Estes, Gainesville, Vice President; Secretary and Treasurer, Milton Hardy, Gainesville; Historian, Chas. N. Elliott, Jr., Covington. These officers were all elected unanimously. A discussion on the office of historian revealed that Chas. N. Elliott, Jr., was only four months old. The nomination stood and was carried with the amendment that Chas. N. Elliott, Sr. fill the office of Historian until the elected became of age.

An advisory committee was elected as follows: 1. Bonnell H. Stone, of Blairsville, Ga.; 2. The existing president of the club; 3. To be chosen by the first two officers and decided by the existing vice president in case of a tie.

The motion was made and carried to allow the executive committee, consisting of the advisory committee and the officers of the club, to select committees and chairmen of committees. A tentative list of committees was read as follows: 1. Publicity. 2. Photographs. 3. Trail signs. 4. Equipment and tools. 5. Geographical nomenclature. 6. Activity and transportation.

Through a question, the president brought out the fact that we automatically became a part of the Appalachian Trail Association, which consists of about 30 clubs in the eastern states.

By popular vote, Miss Mary Cresswell of the Georgia State College of Agriculture and Mr. C. A. Whittle of Atlanta were elected to attend the next annual meeting of the Appalachian Trail Association in Gatlinburg, Tenn.

A letter from Mr. Rex Beach, popular novelist, was read to the club by the president. Mr. Beach said in the letter that he was interested in the mountains of north Georgia and that he would visit them in the near future. A nomination was made and carried that the president of the club, in behalf of the club, extend him an invitation to visit our mountains.

Motion was made and carried to wire Arthur Perkins of the Appalachian Trail Association and tell him of the organization of the Georgia Appalachian Trail Club.

A motion to appoint honorary members was made. This motion was vetoed by the club. A second motion that the honorary members be appointed by the executive committee was carried.

Mr. Whittle was appointed as temporary chairman of the publicity committee and Mr. Hardy was named as local correspondent.

A trip for Sunday to the top of Blood Mountain was planned.

A motion was made and carried to adjourn.

Later Elliott wrote:

During the meeting I sat close to the door to guard against any escapes. One portly gentleman arose and left. I followed him determined to sandbag him if necessary and bring him back.

'Don't you like the meeting?' I asked, out in the hall.

'Hell yes,' he replied. 'I'm going after my family. I want them to hear this, or they'll never believe it.'

Elliott continues:

The meeting was a success. And I sat back to rust [sic] upon my laurels.[4]

But, as Elliott was to say:

The job was only just begun. Under Eddy's driving guidance, I marked out trail, cut brush, until my hands were like the bony paws of any other ape. I followed cow trails down wrong ridges and stumbled on moonshine stills where my life was not worth a scrap of schist.

Bonnell and Eddy, the team of Stones, joined forces and talked the Vogels into setting aside twelve acres in Neel Gap as a state park, principally in order that I might leave my warm hotel room and guard this winding, twisting, tortuous, footpath that led down the backbone of the highlands. That was really the origin of the state park system in Georgia.

By the time the first annual meeting of the Georgia Appalachian Trail Club was held at Helen, I had pictured myself as a white-bearded old man, with worn-out shoes, and a crooked stick, plodding wearily up and down the Appalachian Trail in Georgia, praying that when I turned to dust on the parched mountain ridges, the feet of all those innocent people to whom I had preached the joys of Appalachia would not grind my dust too viciously into the trail.[4]

About 25 people joined the club at the meeting. After the Dahlonega meeting a telegram from Arthur Perkins (who was at that time ill with a malady from which he would not recover) welcomed the new club to "the Appalachian family which is getting bigger and more vigorous every day."

Stone wrote to Perkins of the meeting:

The number attending and the general interest shown was much greater than we had expected, and the enthusiasm seems to indicate that the club is organized on a permanent basis. (November 4, 1930)

Among those present at the meeting was Warner Hall of Decatur. Warner, a former school teacher and now helping his father run the *DeKalb New Era* newspaper, made an instant impression. Elliott wrote to Stone:

I had a nice trip with Roy Sunday and a nice visit Sunday night. I went on up and got those two fellows as members, Warner Hall and Professor Johnson from Decatur. They seem to be real fellows and we want that fellow Hall as our Regional vice-president in Decatur. I almost wish we had elected him Sec. & Treas. after I had learned him better. (November 4, 1930)

Hall and Elliott immediately became good friends, and Hall was soon appointed to office and rapidly became an indispensable member.

Miss Nancy Bowly was welcomed by letter as the "first girl member of our club as well as the first girl scout to join us." Shortly after the meeting Elizabeth White and Caroline Greear of Helen, Ga., joined the club. Elizabeth was to become, by 1980, the longest-standing member of the club.

The second official hike was scheduled for November 16 to Hawk Mountain, Hightower Gap and the Game Refuge there (Ozmer had been sent to this refuge as "caretaker" in September of 1930). The hike was rained out.

The first "bulletin," undated, was sent out in November, 1930, in the form of a letter from E. B. Stone, and written by him on the club stationery. It announced the second club hike—to Hightower Gap—gave directions, and stated, "Each person should bring his own lunch, but hot coffee will be served by the club."

During 1931 similar bulletins were sent "To the members of the Georgia Appalachian Trail Club and Their Friends," from E. B. Stone, and were solely for the purpose of announcing the next hike, although sometimes the previous hike was mentioned.

For a time after he became president, Hall also wrote each announcement, imparting to them his lively personality. By 1932, they were more in the form of a bulletin, with an account of the previous trip included in each, and with someone other than the president responsible for the meeting. *The Georgia Mountaineer* first appeared on May 29, 1933, with the exact masthead that is used today. In the early years, announcements of activities were often sent on a postcard in lieu of a bulletin.

In a letter to Elliott on November 8, 1930, Stone wrote:

I have been doing a lot of thinking on the organization details and find that there are many of them. I am going slow before completing the organization and have a few changes to suggest. I am still determined to keep things in our hands and not let any publicity hounds run off with it.

I am going to designate or appoint you as Secretary and change Milton's title to assistant secretary and treasurer. You can help us a lot in your travels around the state and should be an executive officer. Milton will have to do most of the work here and keep the records so you can do more writing.

We held a meeting one night during the week—Henry Estes, Renshaw and Milton. I suggested that we elect or appoint Dr. Strahan as the third member of the executive council and Henry agreed. I wrote Bonnell to that effect but have heard nothing from him. But Dr. Strahan is elected if he will serve as two of us have voted in his favor.

Henry Estes made some good suggestions and I am giving them consideration. We both think that from now on that there should be some restriction as to membership and that prospective members should have to qualify in some way. He suggested that we ask desirable persons to take a hike with us and if they show enough interest and make application to become members that we admit them. We do not want to ask any and everybody but pick our company. So in your publicity please keep this in mind. We want a real organization and not a lot of names on paper.

This last statement would begin a policy which lasted for many years of trying to have no dead wood among active members (except for a few influential or "honorary" members), and an understanding that a member would drop out if he or she would not be able to be active. Hall wrote to a friend in New York telling him of the organization of the club and saying:

I'm sort of afraid of one step forward which they seem to be taking. It makes me a bit uneasy at the way they took in the charter members and I just hope that they are not too low in their requirements for membership. Their desire to get it going encourages such, but my little experience with the A.D.K. trouble makes me realize what may be the effect of letting in a lot of 'bridge players and dancers.' Since we will have no lodge for week-end parties, just merely hikes, there isn't so much danger in that respect as there might be. (November 25, 1930)

Stone decided that the position of historian would be "a permanent one, or extend over a period of years at least"—a practice which continued for over 30 years. Other committee assignments for the year were: Publicity: C. A. Whittle; Photographs: J. M. Hardy; Trail Signs: T. N. Renshaw; Equipment and Tools: Byron Mitchell, Jr.; Activities and Transportation: Warner Hall; Geographic Nomenclature: Roy Ozmer.

Aluminum trail markers were ordered from Conference, signs and a sign plan made, and permission requested from the Forest Supervisor for their installation. Plans were made to erect them on club outings.

Hall plunged into his new job which Stone "poked off on" him—Chairman of Activities and Transportation. He began his intense involvement in the club which is revealed in his many lengthy and open letters written to club members with whom he worked.

Another "organized hike" (one wonders how many "unorganized hikes" there were) was planned for December 13 to Dick's Gap.

Early in December, Stone reported "finances in sight" for the construction of a "comfortable" shelter at Amicalola Falls, and plans for two more cabins "somewhere on the Trail." New stationery was being printed. Things were looking good.

1931

GEORGIA
APPALACHIAN
19 TRAIL CLUB, INC. 30

IN JANUARY, 1931, came the first of many similar crises which were to come throughout the years: A road was being planned "along or near" the crest of the mountains from Woody to Hightower Gaps. It would eliminate twelve miles of trail if built. Stone wrote to Clinton Smith, Forest Supervisor, in Tennessee, for details. Upon receiving his reply that the road would be built along the trail route, Stone started another campaign. He wrote a long letter of protest to Smith, claiming, among other things, that the road would "set a dangerous precedent" which "would eventually destroy the value of the Appalachian Trail. . . . There are many places where roads can be built, but there is only one Blue Ridge." He appealed to Avery, Perkins, and others he knew to be concerned. Smith wrote back that the road would be built although he agreed with the principle involved, saying "it is not always possible to achieve our ideals."

Stone wrote to Elliott about it saying, "Smith is a harmless old soul and I think he . . . let this road project slip past him." Stone wrote another long letter of protest to the regional forester. The matter was considered by him, and finally the route was changed somewhat so that it would only "occupy" about five miles of trail (between Gooch and Cooper Gaps). But this was only the beginning, and the fight was not over. Arthur Woody was the forest ranger for this district at the time, and it is said that he was pushing the building of the roads along the ridge-top.

Stone wrote to Avery about the matter:

Enclosed is copy of a letter received from the regional forester in regard to the Hightower Gap road. While the Forest Service now has apparently somewhat changed the route of this proposed road, it will still occupy some five and one-fourth miles of the Blue Ridge, to which we still object, but it is not so serious a matter as the first proposal to follow the crest of the ridge all the way from Woody Gap.

I still think that they could easily have followed the Mauldin Creek route and that they are building an unnecessary piece of road. I understand that they propose to extend the road along the Blue Ridge to Springer Mountain and probably over into the Amicalola Falls country.

At any rate, we should keep tab on their activities and oppose any further construction of roads along the crest of the Blue Ridge unless there is more urgent reason for it than they were able to show in this case. I presume that this will be thoroughly discussed at the Trail Conference next summer and hope that some definite action will be taken to insure the permanency of the Trail. (February 10, 1931)

It was said that Stone's ideas and feelings about the Trail and the out-of-doors were similar to Benton MacKaye's, although Stone lacked the eloquence to put them across so well. But Stone had the drive and tenacity to go after what he wanted, and was fortunately in a position of influence so that through the early years of the Trail and the Club, his was the will and the practical know-how that made the dreams become a reality, and kept the club and the Trail on the path to success.

Woody, at the time the forest ranger of "one of the largest districts in the Forest System"—in North Georgia—was to become a legend in the Chattahoochee National Forest. He was called "the barefoot ranger;" a photograph in the GATC archives testifies to the authenticity of the following description of him:

At his best he was no prize winner for looks or dress, being six feet tall and 250 pounds, with a low center of gravity. He wore wide galluses to hold up his work pants but the top button, slightly south of center, was usually open for breathing space. Although he owned a pair of shoes, he would put them on only when the mountain trail was rocky or when he went to town. [6]

The GATC photograph includes a gun stuck in the belt of his trousers.

Woody, called Ranger even by his wife, loved the land he "tramped," and often told young foresters, "We should look at forests as a source of 'good' as well as 'wood.'" The following was adapted from Michael Frome's book, *Whose Woods These Are*, printed in the October 22, 1962, issue of the Bulletin of the Metropolitan Atlanta Family Campers, and reprinted in a 1962 GATC bulletin:

Arthur Woody started working for the Forest Service when the Chattahoochee National Forest was first established and stayed with it all his life. Woody didn't always conform to every rule and regulation in the book. He had an idea that an expert was just 'an average boy away from home' so he sort of went his own way. But unorthodox as he was, his district did an outstanding job of fire prevention, timber management, and game protection. When asked how he was able to do such a good job, Woody is reported to have said, 'Well, you have just got to know your people. I fish with the men, buy candy for the kids, and tell each and every woman if I wasn't married I'd sure like to make love to her. '

Woody had a hand in restoring the wildlife of north Georgia, especially deer. Out of his own pocket he bought fawns and bottle fed them. He kept doing this until it got to be fashionable for folks around Suches, Georgia, to raise and look after deer. The herd grew and finally in 1941 the area was opened for a limited deer season. Woody was always sad when he saw a kill. He had several ways of discouraging hunters though. He hauled the cast of a big bear track around in his pickup truck, and whenever he thought there was too much hunting he made bear tracks everywhere. 'That bear track,' he said, 'is about as effective as three game wardens.' Woody had another method of control. He ran a loan and cattle business on the side. If the local folks hunted out of season, he foreclosed their loans. This way he gradually picked up parcels of private land within the Chattahoochee boundaries.

Woody talked the Forest Service into buying back Sosebee Cove—about 152 acres of land covered by a magnificent stand of yellow poplar—in 1915 for $1,520, a big price in those days.

He believed it was the best stand of poplars in the state; some foresters judged it to be the best stand of second growth yellow poplar in the country. Still . . . there are no plans to cut this $300,000 worth of timber. Sosebee Cove was set aside as a memorial to Woody, the barefoot Ranger, who did so much to preserve the north Georgia we all enjoy.

Although Woody was at least a sometime friend of the GATC, and a member for a time, his reputation in the Club was a bit tarnished. One early Club member has said that he wanted roads built along the crest of the mountains because he had become too fat to walk the ridges.

The Club had about 50 members during 1931, although a few of these were merely "supporting" or honorary members, and took no part in the activities of the Club.

Various projects and activities concerning the Club kept Stone, Elliott, Ozmer, Hall and other active members busy.

Hall and Elliott designed an emblem, or patch—"to be worn on the sleeve"—in the shape of a tomahawk, and a button, with the AT monogram. After much discussion it was finally agreed to have the button made for identification purposes, so that it could be pinned on any clothing, since "every member doesn't have an [hiking] outfit." The patch was suggested by Hall as an achievement award for hiking, exploring, or trail building. The depression economy was deepening, however, and the patches were never made.

The first official hike of 1931, on February 1, to Helton Falls, was a success.

Twenty-five people made the trip, "representing four towns and cities and Brenau and Agnes Scott Colleges. . . . Everyone wanted to know when the next hike would be." The next trip was to the Indian Mounds near Cartersville, and other hikes were made to Amicalola Falls, Tallulah Falls, Hightower Gap, Blood Mountain, and a Christmas celebration at Connahaynee Lodge and hike to Mt. Oglethorpe.

The correspondence suggests that Stone took a far broader view of the function of the Trail Club than simply establishing a trail. Some of the sites chosen for club trips were for their possible interest as a prospective state park. At the time Georgia had no state park system, and Stone appears to have seen the Club as an instrument for getting influential people (and their support) to points of interest in the north Georgia mountains.

Stone generally suggested where the hike would be, and Hall, as activities chairman, was usually successful in rounding up around 20 or 30 people to attend. Most hikes were planned for some time ahead, but others were carried off with only a short notice to members and friends. A number of hikes were postponed or cancelled because of bad weather or conflicts of the leader.

Plans were being made for a trail guide—or "bulletin"—to be published, giving "information of interest, both historical and geographical, trail notes and instructions for reaching various points of interest to hikers throughout the state. . . and a schedule of organized hikes."

The booklet was completed in May and distributed to everyone thought to have an interest in the mountains (including Will Rogers). Reviews of it were published in *Appalachia, Mountain Magazine,* and Raymond Torrey's column, "The Long Brown Path" in the *New York Evening Post.* After this wide publicity, orders for the book came in from far and wide. The schedule of hikes did not materialize, but the booklet contains a foreword and brief description of the Trail in Georgia by E. B. Stone, an historical sketch of the mountains by Charlie Elliott, a list of important gaps and mountains, a brief description of various points of interest in north Georgia and "how to get there," an article on walking entitled "A La Sainte Terre" by Roy Ozmer, a bibliography, a list of Cherokee words furnished by Roy Ozmer, a list of the officers of the Club, and a fine aerial photograph of Mount Oglethorpe and vicinity.

In February, 1931, at the request of Avery, Stone sent the following "Activities of the Georgia Appalachian Trail Club" to him for inclusion in *Mountain Magazine,* which published articles about the activities of the clubs along the AT route:

The Trail Club took its initial hike of the year to Helton Falls, one of the most picturesque waterfalls in the State. This fall is located about two miles off of the main Blue Ridge and a side trail has been blazed to it. Approximately twenty-five hikers made the trip, none of whom had ever visited this section before.

The Club has recently posted wooden trail signs at several points along the trail, this being part of the program to thoroughly mark the trail and all important gaps so that the hiker will have ample information as to the distances between various points and his attention will also be called to points of interest to which side trails have been constructed.

The section of the Blue Ridge between Tray Mountain and the North Carolina line has recently been taken over by the United States Forest Service as part of the Nantahala National Forest, and the United States Forest Service expects to begin the construction of the trail from the North Carolina line to Tray Mountain.

With the completion of this trail the Forest Service will have constructed a continuous trail from Springer Mountain to the North Carolina line, which covers most of the Appalachian Trail in the State. This means that the Appalachian Trail Club will be relieved of the necessity of maintaining these trails since the Forest Service will see that they are properly maintained.

The Club also has plans for the immediate construction of an overnight shelter in the form of a one pen open front cabin at Amicalola Falls. This will be the first shelter to be actually constructed on the trail for the convenience of overnight hikers.

And a few months later Elliott wrote, also upon request, some of the accomplishments of the Club during the year for publication in *Appalachia*:

Since its first semi-annual meeting last November, the Georgia Appalachian Trail Club has undertaken and completed the following projects:

1. *Properly marking the Trail.* Thirty-two trail signs, painted with the official colors of the Georgia Club and giving directions and distances, have been located in all important gaps and on many of the mountains along the Trail. These signs were made especially conspicuous in the gaps on the Blue Ridge where highways are located.

2. *Blazing and clearing Trail.* Much of this work has been done by the U.S. Forest Service and by Boy Scout organizations who have an interest in the Club. Some sixty miles of the Trail has been marked in the last five months with the little square standard markers, completing the marking and blazing in the Georgia section of the Trail. In the same length of time, approximately twenty miles of the Trail has been cleared of brush. More than half of the hiking distance is clear, open trail.

3. *Shelters.* Several weeks ago a small log cabin shelter was completed above Amicalola Falls in Dawson County. Plans are now under way for the erection of another such shelter in the Vogel State Forest Park at Neel Gap. These cabins will be open at all times for hikers of the Trail.

4. *Hikes.* Since its organization, the Club has taken a number of hikes to various interesting and historic spots. One of these was to the nationally known Indian mounds near Cartersville, Georgia. Another hike was made to study the flora on Enotah Bald, Georgia's highest mountain. Still another hike was made through the famous Nacoochee Valley and to the wildest region in the state near Tray mountain and through the gold fields near Dahlonega. Near this town the United States Mint was once located.

5. *Publicity.* While we do not want to over-advertise, we believe that a certain amount of publicity is necessary. An account of each hike finds its way into several Georgia papers. Any other publicity of the right sort is used. At present an official publication of

the Trail Club is in the hands of the printers. We hope to have it off the press in a few weeks.

Printed invitations to all hikes are also issued to members of the Club with the request that they bring their friends. These invitations give the place, time, place of departure, hiking distance and a short item about the spot to be visited.

In conclusion I wish to add that we always welcome the opportunity of showing visitors from other clubs as much of the Georgia section of the Trail as they care to see. I shall make this statement in the form of an invitation to be issued through the pages of *Appalachia*. We are sincere in the belief that we have a very desirable section of the Trail down here and dare say that a great many ideas about Georgia will be changed on a hike through its mountainous portion. (April 11, 1931)

The shelter referred to was completed in March of 1931, and was built by a local mountaineer and his sons contracted by the GATC, at a cost of $57.00. The money was contributed by Luke Tate of Jasper.

Stone wrote to Tate:

The log cabin shelter which you so kindly agreed to finance has been constructed on the Appalachian Trail near Amicalola Falls. Enclosed is a blue print and copy of the contract made with the builder which fully describes the cabin. If you will forward me a check for $57.00, the cost of construction, I will see that it is delivered to Mr. Head. This cabin has been erected near a spring about thirty yards from the main trail a short distance above the falls. As soon as possible we will put up suitable signs so that anyone in that vicinity will have no trouble in locating the cabin. As soon as I am in that section again, I will secure photographs of the cabin and send you one. (March 29, 1931)

The cabin was a large open shelter with "bunk space for 12 persons, and shelter for a much larger number." It had a "low log fence in front to keep out the free-running hogs that seemed to delight in taking over the shelters and wallowing in the springs. "[1]

In the spring of 1931, Avery, who was at this time president of the Potomac Appalachian Trail Club, was making plans to visit Georgia "to become as well acquainted as possible with the geography of the Blue Ridge and the mountainous section of Georgia." He planned to come to Georgia in June and hike the entire Georgia Trail, then go on to the fifth ATC conference which was to meet in Gatlinburg. His coming was a red-letter day for the GATC. Plans and schedules were worked out for his hike; Ozmer, Stone and/or Elliott were to hike part or all of the Trail with him. George Masa, of the newly formed Carolina Mountain Club, was to meet him at the end of the hike and take him to the ATC. Avery's intended hiking companion was unable to come with him, so Ozmer, who was to meet him at Amicalola Falls, tried to persuade Hall and/or Elliott to accompany him on the rest of the hike, saying: "I will guarantee that you'll go far and search long before you will find a more splendid trail-buddy than [Avery]. Then, too, I'd be having the one grand and glo-ri-ous

jamboree of my life if I could only run into you two, plus Myron. Try your
damnedest to make the grade. Don't say it can't be done, hang it, it can be
done! Harder things than that have been managed already for the sake of the
old trail." (May 17, 1931) So Hall, eager to see the Trail, much of which he had
not been on, met Avery at Woody Gap and hiked with him for the last five
days—a "record run," as he says, since they covered 115 miles in these five days.
The hike extended into the Nantahalas to the Little Tennessee River. Avery
wrote a fine account of the region and the trip for the December, 1931, issue of
Appalachia magazine.

The fifth Appalachian Trail Conference was held in Gatlinburg on June 12-
14, 1931. A number of GATC members attended. Avery wrote to Major Welch
of the conference: "There was an attendance of over 200 and it seemed to me
that the conference was extremely successful. The most valuable thing was the
opportunity for the southern representatives to become acquainted." (June 18,
1931) Elliott said: "The Georgia delegation . . . came away very pepped up and
with much determination to make the 'tail end' of the Trail first in a great many
other ways." Hall, among others, stayed afterward for hiking in the Smokies,
and later wrote to a friend:

There were almost two hundred people at the AT conference at Gatlinberg and, in
addition to the valuable information which we secured about the trail all along its way,
we had plenty of fun in connection with our . . . dances, banquet and hikes. I climbed
Mt. LeConte and followed the top of the ridge from Newfound to Indian Gap. I hope
to go back up there again this summer. The Smokies are still quite inaccessible in the
northern portion, it requiring 5½ days for two experienced hikers to come 35 miles
over the range just before the conference. They are mighty attractive though, and there
are some good trails in the south end. I hope you can come down sometime soon and
make a trip in them. (June 12, 1931)

The conference meeting produced friendships between the Georgia and the
Smokies clubs that soon led to the planning of a hike together, and the
beginning of a long and close association of the two clubs. After the meeting,
Elliott wrote to J. M. Tinker: "I want you to meet all of those fellows and *girls*
who belong to the Smoky Club. They have one peach of an organization." Guy
Frizzell, at the time treasurer of the Smoky Mountains Hiking Club, wrote to
Elliott: "We are looking forward with a great deal of pleasure to having you on
at least one of our hikes this year. Bring some of your friends along too. Any
friends of yours are welcome." And he ended the letter: "With hearts bustin'
with love, I am . . . ."

Stone, whose job demanded most of his time, seemed to have little time—or
desire?—for frivolities such as annual meetings. So back to work. He wrote to
Hall in July:

In order to insure the proper maintenance and marking of the Georgia division of the

Appalachian Trail it is necessary to establish some systematic program of operation. I am planning to ask different members of the club to take over a section of the trail and make it his special job to see that it is properly maintained and marked at all times. The trail in Georgia is not nearly completed as there are many wooden signs needed and some metal markers; there is also the question of additional water locations and shelters. These new features will all be discussed at our fall meeting. (July 6, 1931)

Accordingly, assignments were made to nine men, dividing the Trail into something over ten mile sections. Instructions were:

1. Placing of additional markers and replacing of markers as needed.
2. Placing of trail signs and replacing of trail signs as needed.
3. Maintenance of trail, keeping tread clear of fallen logs, brush, etc.; and gradually improving treadway of trail by removing rocks and in some places by actually grading of the trail.
4. Locating sources of drinking water and properly marking of same.
5. Complete survey of trail, including securing accurate measurement of your section, together with facts and full notes to be later used in compiling an accurate detailed trail guide.
6. Undertaking the construction of some form of overnight shelter where this is needed and is possible to work out.
7. Miscellaneous. Improvement of the trail in any way that you may be able to work out. This will give you a chance to devise some unique features for your section.

The enclosed trail manual should be followed as nearly as possible in marking and maintenance of the trail. This manual has been approved by the Appalachian Trail Club and is a well prepared treatise on this subject.

Markers may be secured upon application to the Assistant State Forester. The colors for the trail signs are light cream background with black letters, but, as yet, no paint has been selected. However, this will be done later. (July 22, 1931)

Hall's reply to these lengthy instructions was: "I'll try to get up there sometime during the late summer or fall and fix it up."

In June, S. G. Brinkley of Emory University and a friend planned and completed a hike on the Trail from Neel Gap to Oglethorpe. Extended trail hikes were unusual at this time, and Mr. Brinkley's interesting account was of value to the Club:

We left Neel Gap Monday morning and reached Mr. Ozmer's [at Hightower Gap] Wednesday afternoon, traveling slowly and stopping often to rest and enjoying the scenery. We found Mr. Ozmer a most delightful person to meet. His hospitality I shall never forget. We reached the AT shelter Friday noon, and spent the afternoon at the falls. The shelter is a fine place indeed. We spent a comfortable night there. It was very kind of you to extend us the privilege of using it.

Saturday we pushed on to Burnt Mountain, meeting Mr. Southern and having a pleasant hour's talk with him at noon. We did not go out to Mount Oglethorpe, but found a Mr. Manning who drove us down to Jasper Sunday morning.

The wonderful scenery with its many variations delighted us all along the way. It seems to me that we Georgians do not know the beauties that nature has for us right here at home. The mountainsides covered with laurel, the densely wooded ravines, the magnificent oak and chestnut groves, the narrow ridges with views out over the surrounding territory on both sides, the panoramic views from Blood Mountain, Hawk Mountain, and Buck Knob, and the Amicalola Falls—these are some of the sights I shall take pleasure in recalling again and again—and, I hope, in revisiting.

The Trail Club is doing a fine thing in opening up and making known this section of Georgia to the public.

We were never *lost* on our trip, though, like Daniel Boone, we were several times quite *bewildered*. The points where we were confused were on the back side of Black Mt. near Woody Gap (here a stone pointer happened to catch my eye and saved us), and near Ward Gap where the trail just about plays out. We took a left fork at King Creek Gap and went two or three miles down Long Mountain before we discovered our mistake. We spent a night far over there on the end of the ridge half way down into the valley, and retraced our steps the next morning. Just a short distance beyond Amicalola Falls on the way to Southern's we got off the trail and made a detour to the North, but did not have to turn back. These experiences were part of the game for us; we shall probably remember the night at the end of Long Mountain longer than any other part of the trip. (June 15, 1931)

In October of 1931, Stone listed in a Forest Service memorandum under "Activities of the GATC, November 1930-October 1931":

1. Number of trail markers posted – 400
2. Number of trail signs posted – 34
3. Number of hikes held – 10
4. Points visited – 10
5. Number of persons making hikes – 220
6. Condition of Trail – ___
   A. Miles marked – ___
   B. Miles needing markers – 25
   C. Number of wooden signs needed – 15
7. Number of shelters constructed to date – 1
8. Number of points on or near trail where shelter can be secured overnight – 5
9. Points where provisions can be secured – 2
10. Additional number of overnight camps needed – 4

The annual meeting for 1931 was planned for November 7-8 at Mitchell Mountain Ranch, with lodging at Greears Lodge, in Helen. Stone enlisted Hall, Ozmer, and W. D. Young, member and district forester, to make short talks, and wrote to Cecelia Branham, the Club's corresponding secretary, "We are very anxious to have some lady member of the Club to make a short talk . . . and wonder if we can get you to do this."

Hall wrote to Stone of the upcoming meeting:

... I believe that you were opposed to having any sort of a banquet, that you said that anybody could have a banquet. That is true, but anybody can, likewise, have a meeting, can't they? I've seen a lot of meetings which, as such, would have been dull and unattended put over in good fashion by converting them into a banquet. That was the scheme which they followed at Gatlinberg and the Smoky Mountains folks used at Montvale a month ago. In both cases it went over fine. I don't mean to have any swell or formal affair, but merely to have everybody eat dinner in the same room at the same time in an organized way. Then we can go right ahead with some hiking songs, announcements and into the meeting. Charlie agrees with me in that respect and, incidentally, I think Charlie could handle that in good fashion as toastmaster if you didn't want to take charge until the business meeting began with the minutes by the secretary. . . . (October 21, 1931)

Stone replied:

... In regard to your suggestion for a banquet, I am not in favor of this as this is a conventional idea and is, in my judgment, not best suited to our type of meeting. As to the square dance, we hope to have some mountain musicians and if there are enough people there that care to dance, we will be able to indulge in this also. It is my opinion that there will be no large number of people there who care especially for this, and I do not intend to feature it as one of the attractions. . . . (October 23, 1931)

Officers for the coming year were to be elected at the meeting. In the same letter Hall wrote to Stone:

... There's just one more thing. I've heard something about you folks planning to put me into the job of president for next year. It has me quite up in the air. You see, I have an awfully heavy schedule for this winter. They've put more work on me at the Tech Evening School and we've just put in a new fellow as news writer at the paper. It has kept me at an awfully stiff pace. I've tried to get a letter off to you ever since Sunday and, in spite of all I could do, I couldn't get to it until tonight.

I shall possibly be able to go on as many outings this year as last, but I'm absolutely afraid to take on anything which requires my time to think and plan because it is all taken up now. I can, knowing there's going to be an outing on such and such a time, work right up to that time and then dash off to join the crowd. I am too interested in seeing this club grow and move along to take any chance which might cause it to make a back slide. I certainly don't want to see it die on my hands. It has made wonderful progress during the past year and the good work should go on. If I were to become president I could only serve as a figure head president and the club doesn't need that kind. It would not be due to lack of interest, you know that, but when a fellow has about 14 hours of work for every 12 hours available he just can't get around to it all. My folks are opposed to me taking it because they know that I wouldn't have to time to do justice to it and my father, like myself, thinks too much of this undertaking to see it handicapped by someone getting into the presidency who can't do what should be done of it. How about Charlie? I know you fellows want to get it out of the Forest Service, but it is not wise to put a bird out of its nest until it is quite strong enough to fly. . . . (October 21, 1931)

Stone's reply was:

... In regard to the probability of your taking over the presidency of the Club, this is
something that you should be willing to do, and lack of time, of course, is no excuse. I
do not know a single person who is not tied up with their own affairs and will put up the
same plea as you do.

I am strongly opposed to anybody connected with the Georgia Forest Service having
charge of the activities of next year, as I have been criticized and abused for my part in
it, and I think it absolutely essential that we secure somebody outside of the Georgia
Forest Service.

Since you have taken more interest than most anybody else, and have had contact
with other organizations, you would probably take more interest in activities than
anyone else, and we will continue to count on your filling this office. (October 23,
1931)

(In many ways through these years, Stone had risked his career for the sake
of the Trail and the Club, opposing policies set up by the Forest Service, and
taking time and manpower to try to complete trail projects.)

A hike to Tray Mountain was planned for the Sunday of the annual meeting.
The announcement of the weekend stated: "All members, especially the
women, are reminded to be sure to bring their hiking clothes."

The meeting was a success. A "dinner" was held, and a square dance
(beginning another long-standing and much enjoyed practice). Over 70
people attended, with a number of members of the Smoky Club present. Later
Guy Frizzell wrote to Elliott:

The members of our Club who attended your meeting last week have talked of nothing
else much since their return. We surely did have a good time and I want to commend
you folks for the way you handled the meeting. I do not know where one could go to
find more gracious hosts than you people. If this is an example of what you intend to
do for the ATC in 1933, I think you may rest assured it will be a success.

Thanking you for your kindness in allowing me the honor of appearing on your
program, and urging you and any other members of your club to meet with us any time
you can, I am.... (November 12, 1931)

The headline for an article in the Knoxville newspaper read: "E. Tennessee
hikers meet with Georgians; had big time."

Hall wrote to Stone a few days after the meeting:

Now that the big event is over and the opportunity has come for me to reflect on the
occasion I have come to the conclusion that, taking everything into consideration, it
was a 'howlin' success. Several difficulties arose and there were some genuine obstacles
to be overcome, but I think that every one of them was met and handled in remarkable
fashion, much to your credit. Fellow, I think that you've done a wonderful job and can
only feel that the good work can go on if you are going to continue your active part.

I was well pleased with the size of the crowd, but couldn't help but think about what a different crowd it was. There were but a mere handful of those who attended the meeting last year, but I'm sure that these new ones represent a much higher quality of true hiking type. I'm sure that we've discovered about half a dozen new ones here in Atlanta who are the genuine articles and I feel that through them we shall be able to reach as many more who can be depended upon to carry on their part of the job in good fashion. (November 9, 1931)

This meeting is sometimes referred to as the first annual meeting, and the meeting in 1930 at Dahlonega as the "organizational meeting." However, the minutes of the 1931 meeting are headed "Second annual meeting of the GATC," and future meetings are counted from this.

Among those present at the meeting were Marene W. Snow and Chester Elliott, who were to remain active members for many years. Snow was a member until her death in 1981, and Elliott until his death in 1978.

Warner Hall as president and Lewis Johnson as treasurer were the only two new officers elected. The others remained the same.

1932

GEORGIA
APPALACHIAN
19 TRAIL CLUB, INC. 30

T HE YEAR 1932 began the long presidency of Warner
Hall, the man who would, to a great extent—for better or
worse—*be* the GATC for its formative years. As Marion Morris
put it: "Red-headed, effervescent, where Warner led, the Club
rollicked after." Someone wrote rather lavishly of him later:

Warner W. Hall: How reminiscent his very name of the keen enthusiasm, high spirit
and good fellowship in the GATC of which he was so much a part! A name to conjure
forth such lasting memories—of good long hikes over unexplored territory and into
the mysterious wilderness—overnight camps—singing around the camp fire—
incomparable mountain scenes which many of the old timers will long continue to
associate with Warner.

Warner was the Club's second president, and for four consecutive years—1932-
1935—he gave most unstintingly of his energy, talent and money.

As a leader he was second to none.

His enthusiasm highly contagious—twas necessary only that he conceive an idea,
express it aloud—like a flash it would spread through the Club—a committee was
appointed and pronto! the work was well under way.

Truly he was a genuine inspiration to all with whom he worked.

Let it further be recorded that many fine lifelong friendships had their beginning in
those years.

Much of the life and spirit the Club still enjoys is due largely to the foundation stones
laid during the administration of Warner. (Unknown)

Hall lived in Decatur with his parents. His father, James Hall, was publisher of the *DeKalb New Era* newspaper. Warner, formerly a school teacher, had recently returned to Georgia from New York, and was helping his father run the newspaper.

Hall began immediately to collect information on the organization and activities of other hiking clubs. Early in the year he asked Marene Snow and Olivia Herren to "write up a set" of by-laws "which will best fit our needs." This they did, and the first constitution was adopted by the Club in March of 1932. Article I stated the Purpose of the Club:

The purpose of this club shall be to create a love of, and a desire for, the out-of-doors; to make accessible the mountain regions of our state by constructing and maintaining trails, shelters, and camps for walkers; to cooperate with departments of the state and to enlist the support of the public in the conservation of our forests and other natural scenic resources; to teach and to foster public appreciation of out-of-door ethics; and to gather and publish authentic maps and information concerning regions of interest to Georgia hikers.

Article II on Membership contained a lengthy pledge which each new member must take. It included the statement that "the membership of the Club shall also be limited to the extent that not more than 25% of the total membership at any one time may be individuals holding common business, social or professional interests tending to restrict the cosmopolitan atmosphere of the Club." It also stated that "not more than 65% of the total active membership of the Club shall be of one sex." This stipulation was to remain in the by-laws for 40 years.

In the first years of the Club, membership requirements and standards of conduct were established which were to prevail at least throughout the first 50 years of the Club's existence. The "pledge" to be taken by members included the following (briefly): to be thoughtful and considerate of others, to refrain from the use of intoxicants and conduct oneself properly, to attend as many functions as possible and help in any way, to refrain from destroying plants and be careful of the environment, to conduct oneself so as not to decrease the enjoyment of others. It is said that the prohibition against alcoholic beverages was controversial in its very beginnings. Stone, who liked a little nip now and then, strongly opposed a rule prohibiting it, and Hall was strongly in favor of having such a rule, mainly, it is said, for the safety of all concerned on the long drive back to Atlanta over primitive roads. The prohibition rule was adopted and remained in effect until 1980.

Also in the early 1930's, the membership committee, headed by Marene Snow, issued a statement which reflected the feelings of at least some of the members regarding the quality and quantity of Club members:

The constantly increasing popularity of the Georgia Appalachian Trail Club and its activities is very definitely revealed by the number and type of inquiries which are now coming to the president and secretary. These are coming not only from people in Georgia who are interested in our mountain region, the Appalachian Trail and our own activities, but inquiries from other Clubs along the Appalachian Trail have indicated that the activities of our own organization have attracted attention along its entire route.

Although we are one of the smaller clubs, we are, in many respects, one of the most active, and within our own state we are undoubtedly the most active organization of adults devoted to outdoor activities and studies as a hobby.

If there has been any one thing which has put our Club in this enviable position it is the quality of its membership. Our members have been hand picked after consideration which has been conducted to a degree of care that can hardly be appreciated by anyone who has not served on the Executive Council. There has been no effort, no desire, to build up the size of the membership rapidly and with any sacrifice to quality. This has been conducted not without serious problems, but they have been handled carefully and tactfully.

If the quality and standing of the Club is to be maintained, our practice of picking new members most carefully must continue. This is steadily becoming a more difficult task, due to the ever increasing popularity of the Club. It has appeared wise, therefore, to appoint a Membership Committee with the sole duty of promoting a slow but steady growth at a maintained quality,

It is the duty of every member to keep a close vigil over prospective members and, through the cooperation of the Membership Committee, see that no desirable person is overlooked and that no undesirable individual is admitted. . . .

Remember that one undesirable person in our group can seriously jeopardize the service and pleasure which the Club can afford its membership. . . .

Inquiries about the Trail and the Club began to come in at a rapid rate. In January, Hall wrote to one inquiree: "The Club has recently found it necessary to adopt a policy of being rather particular with its membership, receiving only those people who have been with us on several outings." This was to be set forth in the new constitution. He continues in the same letter:

For a time it seemed difficult to find enough people interested in the sort of activities which the Club sponsored to make it possible to put over some of the things which we desired to do. The tide seems to have changed, however, and it now seems to be a problem of keeping it from outgrowing itself. I received the names of nineteen prospects this past week. (January 16, 1932)

The GATC "busted out all over with activity," according to Marion Morris.[1] As Hall put it, it "is growing rapidly in size, reputation and the scope of its activities." Stone had written to Hall in December, 1931: "You certainly are taking serious hold of the Club activities, and you may be sure that we are all with you."

On New Year's Eve, 1931, Elliott and Hall had gone to Knoxville to join the Smoky Club in their New Year's Eve party. Here they talked of a stand of magnificent "big trees" along Big Santeetlah Creek that would soon be timbered. On New Year's Day, Hall and Elliott drove over to the area to see the trees. They had "one of the finest trips of my experience," according to Hall. They spent the night with a mountain family living up the creek "where we got a true sample of the life and philosophy of Southern Appalachian Highlanders." The next day they "examined" the forest. As Elliott tells it many years later:

Warner and I spent a snowy day in this magnificent forest, making pictures and measurements of the almost unbelievable trees. It was like seeing a segment of America as it must have been when the first white men came to our shores. We arrived back at our car after dark.

After this, Hall began a campaign to save these trees. Elliott continues:

Warner was one of those responsible for helping to spread the story of this virgin forest and of enlisting the help of several conservation organizations to save it. His campaign was bitterly contested by the Forest Service and lumber company that had bought the timber, but the conservation forces eventually won and the virgin stand was saved. Today it is known as the Joyce Kilmer Memorial Forest.[7]

Upon their return, Elliott wrote an interesting and detailed account of the trip, which is contained in the GATC archive files.

Early in 1932 the Club, through Stone, began negotiations with Mrs. M. E. Judd, a member of the Forestry and Geological Development Commission and friend of the GATC, to buy a lot at Neel Gap for $25.00. They planned to build a cabin here to rent, and a trail shelter. After some time, the money was promised from various Club members, and an offer was made to Mrs. Judd. The project, however, evidently fell through, for there is no record of its actual purchase.

It was about this period that an association between the GATC and the Atlanta Bird Club was begun. From the Bird Club would come many future GATC members and officers: the Hoben family (Marion, Lou, and Rainnie), Carter Whitaker, Berma Jarrard, and others. For several years in the early 1930's the two clubs extended invitations to each other's Christmas parties and socials.

The first hike of 1932 was a day trip to Neel Gap, with part of the group hiking up Blood Mountain and the rest going to Helton Falls.

It was soon evident that the most popular type of outing was a trip beginning late Saturday with a drive to one of the mountain hotels or lodges where the group would have dinner, perhaps songs and square dancing, and spend the night. The next day they would proceed to the hike. Hall writes of these hotel visits:

It is inspiring to have reactions as we have received from the people whom we have visited, and the parting remarks of Mr. Jones at the hotel are, I think, typical of the feelings of most of them. He said, "This is, indeed, one of the finest bunches of people I have ever seen, and whenever a group of you can come up this way, we will certainly be glad to have you stop by and see us." I think that everywhere the Club has been the people have been very well impressed and not only made sympathetic but enthusiastic about the purposes and activities which the organization is trying to carry on. (April 11, 1932)

The "longest hike yet taken" was to Brasstown (Enotah) Bald, of which the bulletin reports:

Last Sunday, October 8, we conquered Georgia's highest mountain, Mrs. Snow and Miss Annabel Horn were joint hostesses to the group which went up to Blairsville Saturday afternoon. Following a fine chicken dinner at Mrs. Caldwell's summer hotel, the party went over to the summer home of Mrs. Snow and Miss Horn where, before two large open fireplaces, they popped corn, sang songs and each member of the group tried his hand at painting trail markers. The hike on Sunday to the summit of Enotah Bald was the longest scheduled hike of the Club's history. It was 4.8 miles from where we left our cars to the cabin and spring where the group stopped for lunch. The lookout tower on the summit, 0.4 miles beyond, afforded a splendid view. It was an ideal hike, over a splendid forest service trail, and the weather was ideal. As a result of this trip, the trail is now fully marked from the highway to the summit with both trail markers and wooden signs giving distances. It has been measured (thanks to Roderick Taaffe, Olivia Herren, Mrs. Snow, and others who pushed the bicycle wheel), and detail trail notes are now in the Club's files.

A trip to Yonah Mountain with an overnight stay at Greear's Lodge in Helen brought rave notices from the bulletin:

That famous trip to Yonah! The trip to Yonah Mountain has been heralded as one of the most enjoyed outings of the Club's history. On that trip it rained hay rakes, and it turned off cold as two whistles. More than twenty people went up Saturday afternoon to Greear's Lodge at Helen, where they spent the night, and more than twenty climbed Yonah the next day. The wind whistled free from Georgia's icey mountains, but—just ask anybody who went on that trip whether they had a good time. Saturday night we had a business meeting and a two ring square dance at which real cowboys from the nearby hills flashed their long spurs prominently in the whirl. Around the big fire we sang just about every song anybody could suggest; in fact, it looked like we simply couldn't quit. Fully three times the gentlemen's quartet chimed out "Goodnight Ladies" before the group could be disbursed. A little harmonizing on "Three o'clock in the Morning" would have exactly described the time of the breaking up.

The following account tells of a scheduled trip to Neel Gap:

What do you think was the outcome of that trip on December 18? After the big sleet and snow storm hit us, it seemed best to call off that hike from Woody to Neel Gap because roads were so treacherous. There were loud howls of disappointment on the part of several, but transportation proved a problem. Modern cars were afraid of the slippery, icey roads. Finally, a group of six left Atlanta at daylight in a touring car which got its first smell of gasoline more than ten years ago. Passing several wrecks along the way, the old bus stayed in the ruts and reached Gainesville without mishap. There it found the snow and sleet about six inches deep and got stuck six feet from a garage. Chains overcame the difficulty, and the party journeyed on to Neel Gap, where a short hike in the ice and snow was greatly enjoyed.

The first real difficulty arose on the way home that night. Frost kept accumulating on the windshield, affording a real problem for the driver. Numerous stops were made, gasoline was tried, a plug of tobacco was purchased at a roadside store and later an onion was secured from the restaurant at Buford—all without satisfactory results. Finally, Cynthia Ward, the driver, wrapped her face with about all the scarfs in the party and brought the old buggy in home by peering around the side into the icey air. That group didn't envy anybody at home and they assumed that the feeling was mutual.

Other hikes during 1932 included Fort Mountain, with an overnight at the DeSoto Hotel in Chatsworth, and the Indian Mounds near Cartersville and saltpeter caves at Kingston.

The trips usually attracted between 20 and 40 people. A small fee was charged each person on the trip, to cover "incidental expenses." Often the Club would hire (for four to six dollars) a truck and driver from the locality of the hike to transport them over the long, rough roads to and/or from the trailhead. Marion Morris writes: "On those narrow, snaky mountain roads there was quick response to the call, 'All lean to the left' or 'All lean to the right.' Sometimes it was 'All out and push.'"[1]

On trips to the Helen area the group usually stayed at Greear's Lodge in Helen, which was run by John and Caroline Greear. Caroline had been a member of the Club since its organization, and was very helpful in a number of ways, giving discounts for lodging, planning hikes in the vicinity, and she even offered to donate a piece of land to the Club "near our falls" to build a cabin on. (There is no further record of this offer.)

A tentative schedule of trips was made up at the beginning of each season, but trips were often cancelled or changed to another date because of bad weather and impassable roads, or other reasons. The more active members got together for other outings, quite often joining the Smoky Club for hikes, and usually for their annual meeting and Christmas party.

In August of 1932 Hall joined several members of the Smoky Club on a "vacation" hike through the eastern half of the Smokies. This was to be the first "end to end" hike of the AT in the Smokies. Hall writes of the trip: "I will have to admit that that was one of the toughest and roughest camping trips I have ever been on . . . an adventure and experience which I would not have missed for a whole lot."

An article in the *Knoxville Journal* gave the following account:

Back from a nine-day hike through the wildest parts of the Great Smoky Mountains, Carlos Campbell, member of a party of nine which made the hike, last night described trials and tribulations comparable to those which confronted the trail-blazers of old Western days.

The party—which consisted of Campbell, Harvey Broome, president of the Smoky Mountains Hiking Club, Guy Frizzell, Walter Berry, Charles Gibson and Charles Cornforth, Jr., all of Knoxville; Warner Hall, of Decatur, Ga., president of the Georgia Appalachian Trail Club; Carter Whittaker, of Atlanta, and Herrick Brown, of Greeneville, Tenn.—left Knoxville about 7 a.m. Sunday, August 7, headed for Deal's Gap. They went through Newport, leaving the highway between Cosby and Waterville, N.C. Evidently, the hikers made their mistake in leaving the highway at all, for they immediately ran into trouble.

They were forced to climb nearly 5,000 feet of steep and rugged countryside with their heavy packs—averaging around 60 pounds—bearing down heavier with each step. Before nightfall they had run out of water. They pitched their first camp about halfway between White Rock and Lowe's Gap.

Monday they continued on to Lowe's Gap where there is a spring and they had breakfast, afterwards starting westward along the state line. Soon they ran into some of the roughest country that any of the members of the party had ever trod upon.

Tuesday the hikers named a ridge. Hell's Ridge, they named it, because, said Campbell, laughingly, 'that's what it was to travel.' The timber on the North Carolina side had all been burned away and huge snags and roots and briars impeded their progress. Again the party ran out of water after having made but little progress. They were forced to hike ten minutes and rest about three. Nearly famished, and unable to continue, the hikers pooled their money and paid Herrick Brown, the Greeneville man, to bring water.

Brown climbed down the rugged hillside and brought water. They figured out that Brown had been paid two dollars a gallon for the water. 'But if we had not gotten it we would have had to abandon the hike at that stage.' said Campbell.

Broome killed a rattlesnake there. It was the highest altitude Campbell had ever seen a rattler, the benchmark registering the height at 5,916 feet. Finally the party came to the trail from Cosby to Mt. Guyot, got into the Virgin Forest and camped near a spring. It was difficult finding springs as some of the most dependable ones were dried up.

Wednesday the party mounted Mt. Guyot, seeing several good views. They climbed Mt. Chapman, but it was raining atop that peak and the party was forced to eat lunch in the rain.

Thursday rain again delayed them. They found two more beautiful views from Laurel Top after one of the hardest climbs of the trip. They camped at False Gap.

Friday opened as a beautiful day but later turned into a nightmare. The party was hiking along Sawtooth Range, which gets its name from the fact that the country is so rough and rocky, when a terrible storm arose.

The party donned their ponchos but to no avail, the rain came driving uphill, borne by a stiff wind. Sheets of water were washed up under the ponchos and all the hikers were drenched to the skin. It was cold; so cold that some of the party were unable to eat when they reached the Jump Off at noon. They continued and found the first trail since they had left Lowe's Gap.

[The original plan had been to stop at Newfound Gap, but the group decided to push on to Deal's Gap.]

Saturday they climbed Mt. Collins, Clingman's Dome and Siler's Bald. On Clingman's Dome they saw the first people besides their party that they had seen on the trip.

Sunday it rained hard, almost all day, but the hikers went to Hall's Cabin, Briar Knob, Thunderhead, Spencefield and Russellfield and camped at Ekaneetlee Gap.

Monday rain again greeted them and views from Gregory's Bald were obstructed to such an extent that they hardly could see over 100 yards. They arrived at Deal's Gap about 2 p.m. and were met by a bus.

Campbell said that it rained four out of the nine days; that they saw numerous signs of bear; they snapped about 100 pictures at various stages of the hike. There was no sickness or casualties, he said, and the greatest trouble was with blistered feet, caused by the forced hikers in wet shoes. (August 16, 1932)

According to the Smoky Mountains Hiking Club *History* (1976), after Newfound Gap "food became a major problem. . . ."

Herrick, having made travel arrangements, left the party at Buckeye Gap. The others pressed on, managed to talk some herders out of a meager supply of food at Russell Field, and the eight completed the hike on August 15, after nine days. From the 1957 Handbook, Harvey's account of the trip, we quote: 'As we neared the Gap, Frizzell picked up a club and forced everybody to stay together. He was determined that no one would be able to brag that he was the first to hike the whole length of the Smokies. As we came to the edge of the road, those in front waited for the others to catch up and we limped into Deal's Gap eight abreast.'

A long article appeared in the January 10, 1932, issue of the *Atlanta Journal* telling of many of the activities and adventures of the Club. It was entitled "How the Sun Rose in the West," and told, among other stories, how Stone and Elliott "recalled an occasion when they had hiked all day and after a night's rest were astonished next morning to find the sun rising in the west." They "were forced to conclude that they had traveled a whole day in the wrong direction." (Even so, the article resulted in at least four applications for membership in the Club.)

In December a special trip took a number of Club members on a scouting hike to locate the source of the Chattahoochee River. The trip was successful, according to a newspaper account. It stated:

APPALACHIAN CLUB DISCOVERS SOURCE OF CHATTAHOOCHEE

The scouting party of the Georgia Appalachian Trail Club which departed Sunday on a hiking trip into the fastness of the Blue Ridge mountains, seeking the actual springhead of the Chattahoochee returned here late Sunday evening. They report that the highest and most northerly stream source of the Chattahoochee is a bold spring, or fountain, rising within 75 feet of the actual summit of the Blue Ridge at an elevation of about 3,100 feet above mean sea level, in the extreme northwest corner of White county. The geographical location is approximately 34 degrees, 49 minutes north latitude and 83 degrees, 48 minutes west longitude.

The party was under the guidance of Paul Colwell, of Blairsville, a well-known woodsman, and Warner W. Hall, president of the GATC. The party numbered about 10 of the hardier members of the outdoors organization, including Mr. and Mrs. J. M. Tinker, of the University of Georgia; Phil Hoben, of Nova Scotia and Atlanta; Misses Fricken, Ward and Hoben and Mrs. M. W. Snow, all of Atlanta.

The ATC Board of Managers reported in February 1932 that "there has been a developing sentiment that annual meetings . . . are unnecessarily frequent and that a biennial meeting will be more effective. . . ." Therefore, the 1932 meeting scheduled for Vermont was postponed until 1933. (But in 1933 there was again "an almost unanimous opinion [among the clubs] in favor of postponement" until 1934, because of the "financial embarrassment" of members, clubs and Conference, and because, according to Avery, as in 1932 "Trail work is progressing very satisfactorily," and "there is no pressing matter before the Conference." The one remaining problem of trail work in 1933 was in Maine, where the difficulties of building a trail were great, and "trail construction is beyond the scope of volunteer labor.")

Since there would be no ATC meeting, Elliott suggested that the Southern clubs plan a meeting in the spring. A "get-together" with the Smoky Club had already been planned, so they could expand it to include the other southern clubs. Warner was delighted with the idea of a regional meeting, and wrote to Harvey Broome of the Smoky Club, George Masa of the Carolina Club, and Fred Davis of the Natural Bridge Club, urging them to come and bring their members. He outlined a program and various common problems and interests that could be discussed. Considerable time and thought was given to planning for the meeting, which was to be held in May at Connahaynee Lodge. Elliott sent Hall a suggested general program of events for the meeting. At the end of the program was listed "Songs, dances, love making, etc." Those were the good old days!

"At least fifty" members of the Smoky Club and a large delegation from the Carolina Club were expected to come. The conference, however, was not a success—as such. The expected large number of out-of-state people had dwindled down to four Smoky members and George Masa. (Evidently they were not sent Elliott's tentative program.) Hall's letters to some of the participants afterward tell some of the story:

While it was our original intention to have a regional conference and have a larger representation from both the Tennessee and the Carolina Clubs, the depression cast its spell over them, and we were able to get only five from the two neighboring states. That leaving practically an entire Georgia representation accounted for the change in the general attitude and conduct of the affair and the entirely informal and more or less frivolous manner. I say this by way of explanation to visitors who, having not attended some of our former gatherings, would fail to understand and fully appreciate the manner in which it was conducted. (To I. G. Greer, May 24, 1932)

I am afraid that the few non-hiking visitors who were at Connahaynee Saturday night put us down as a regular bunch of drunks, but I want to assure you that there was nothing of the kind back of our crazy way of conducting the meeting. I don't know what Charlie had, but I am sure that it would take something more than a lot of Georgia corn to make him get the way he did, because that fellow could drink a quart of kerosene and go on smoking his pipe without being the least bit affected. He seems to be getting harder and harder, and the only thing that keeps me from being afraid to go out on hiking trips with him is that I have an added feeling of security in case there should be any wild animals or people anywhere in the vicinity. (To Harvey Broome, May 27, 1932)

Hall wrote to Elliott: "Somebody asked me if you had a few drinks before the dinner Saturday night. Did we act like that?"

I am truly sorry that I . . . did not have the time to see more of you folks and introduce you to more of our Georgia crowd. You will have to blame the latter on Charlie, because you will recall that he busted up the meeting with his loud howls for adjournment before I had an opportunity to introduce you and Miss Elvie Manley to the assembly and call on you for a speech or a solo. I wish that you would explain that to Miss Manley. Due to the noise made by the animals from McDonald's farm, which seem to have gathered in your vicinity near the close of our meeting, I do not think you people particularly cared for any more speeches, even though you made them yourselves. I am sorry that you did not have the opportunity just the same. (To Sallie Lou Newcomb, May 27, 1932)

And again to Broome:

I hope that Myron Avery won't be too disappointed with the outcome of the 'conference.' I had truly hoped to bring up two or three matters of permanent business before the main gathering broke up, but I suppose that it is just as well and that so far as a permanent organization is concerned, if we find a real need for it, we can elect or appoint individuals to carry on the duties by mail about as well as we could have done it there. So long as our three southern organizations can cooperate and work together harmoniously, I think we will be carrying out our principal purpose. (May 27, 1932)

But this was not to be the end of Southern regional meetings.

The membership of the Club by the end of 1932 was about 65 people. Generally the Club members were an enthusiastic bunch, eager to hike and enjoy the sociability of any and all activities. There were no regular meetings.

Members of the executive council lived in various cities, and were called together to meet only for special matters. Regular business matters were taken up with the members on hikes or during the evening before a hike at the lodging.

At the beginning of the year, Hall had appointed Stone to head the Trails Committee, but Hall himself seemed to handle almost everything that came up. He wrote to Harvey Broome, "I will certainly be glad when our Club gets large enough to have more committees. As it is now, in spite of our best efforts to delegate various duties, most of the work falls on two or three of us. . . . " In July he wrote, "I . . . hope to divide responsibilities and organize activities for the fall program in such a way as to carry on a pretty full program with the minimum amount of work for any single individual."

The pursuit of fun may have unintentionally been somewhat at the expense of the Trail as well as the workings of the Club. The Trail in Georgia had been scouted and located, and a number of markers (metal diamond-shaped AT signs) had been put up all along the route, but the Trail was not well traveled or really well marked. The maintenance system established by Stone was not 100 percent successful. Often hikers became lost or "bewildered" as S. G. Brinkley put it.

Early in 1932, Myron Avery, by now Chairman of the ATC, suggested to Hall that, rather than trail work being done by "small parties," as had been the practice, the entire Club be called together "for the purpose of working and clearing in some particular section such as Amicalola, which needs paint the entire distance." He further suggested to all the southern clubs that they have more hikes on the AT, saying, "I strongly urge that the Appalachian Trail idea be made more prominent in each club's program."

Preparations for a guidebook for the entire Trail were announced by Avery in February 1932. It was to be in four sections: New England, New York to the Susquehanna River, Maryland to the Unakas, and the Southern region. (The Nantahala route was still to be settled at this time; George Masa had been scouting various routes. Avery was urging a decision on the route, suggesting two official routes, generally the same two through the Nantahalas that were discussed in 1930.) Avery suggested to the clubs that they get busy on measuring and writing up the Trail data for their sections.

Hall was unable to get any help on detailing the Georgia section, and by late spring had himself done only a few miles. Avery continued to prod him, offering suggestions on the gathering and organizing of the data, and urging him every month or so to get it done.

Finally in the fall of 1932, Hall and Stone began in earnest the long task of measuring and writing up the Trail data. The work continued off and on into the summer of 1933. During this year, regular Club hikes were scheduled on the AT so that the work could be done then. Marion Morris wrote: "Volunteers . . . were not so difficult to round up because no one wanted to miss anything."[1]

Stone finally decided to turn the chore of measuring over to Carter Whittaker, a new member who was stationed in north Georgia at a CCC camp. By October, 1933, the measuring was completed, the data written up and submitted to Avery. He returned it for revisions and for "a bit more careful perusal" of the data, thinking it would take only a short time to perfect. Hall appointed a committee to complete the job, and work continued into 1934.

The annual meeting of 1932 was held at the Cloudland Park Club Hotel at Cloudland, Georgia. The bulletin report states:

Sixty-four people attended the banquet and annual meeting at the Cloudland Park Club Hotel November 5 and 6. Highlights of our past year's activities by Annabel Horn; solos by Vaughan Ozmer and Richard Smoot; combined with group singing and some peppy remarks by Harvey Broome and Guy Frizzell, president and president-elect, respectively, of the Smoky Mountains Hiking Club were a few of the interesting features of the banquet. Folks joined into the square dance who were never known to have danced before and an hour of singing before the huge log fire to the accompaniment of 'Brigham' Young's guitar finished up the evening in perfection. We had good weather on the following day and visited several points of interest, including High Rock and DeSoto Falls.

Hall was reelected president and Tinker vice president; Rod Taaffe was elected treasurer and Olivia Herren secretary.

1933

GEORGIA
APPALACHIAN
19|TRAIL CLUB, INC.|30

BY 1933 THE CLUB was running on all four cylinders. Hall wrote to Avery in January: "This is the first year that our Club has been able to function as a real organization, and we are starting off fine. . . . It has at last become large and strong enough to actually stand on its own feet as a club."

Besides a trail committee under Stone, there was an activities committee under Marene Snow, and activities for the year were stepped up and were running smoothly. This year, and for many years to come, members were furnished with a pocket-sized schedule of the year's events. Marion Morris says of the work of the activities committee: "It involved much scouting and planning, appraisal of approach roads—roads of red clay that could dissolve into a sea of mud, or narrow woods tracks with streams to ford."[1] Often a local guide had to he obtained to lead the group into an unknown area.

The first hike of the year was one that would be remembered. It was to be the longest hike yet—from Woody Gap to Neel Gap. The following account (not published in the bulletin) was written by Hall, and tells the story of the hike as well as the typical evening before:

OUTING TO GREEAR'S LODGE AND HIKE, WOODY TO NEEL GAP
January 14 and 15, 1933

The twenty-two people who went up to Greear's Lodge on Saturday afternoon found a different reception from that which they had met on the last trip to this place almost a year before. Instead of overcast skies from which came a downpour of rain, followed by high winds and cold weather, we found clear skies and crisp, invigorating air.

Grace Ficken, Chester Elliott, and Cynthia Ward, in making arrangements for the program, had adopted the ingenious method of numbering each seat at the table and then giving each member a number from the shuffled stack of cards as they entered the dining room. This mixed up the crowd in good fashion. Plates of turkey, baked ham, and all the other things which go along to make up a big dinner kept going around the table often enough to keep the crowd busy and rather quiet for a considerable time.

A little singing, the reading of a poem about Yonah Mountain by Grace Ficken and the passing around of enough chewing gum to keep all present from talking excessively preceded the turning over of the meeting to Warner Hall for the first club business meeting to be held in almost a year. The first treasurer's report in fourteen months, a secretary's report by Olivia Herren of activities during the past year, and an outline of proposed activities during the coming year by Mrs. Snow were the three most important matters. The group adjourned from the dining room to the vicinity of the huge log fire in the front room, where other incidental items of interest were taken up, and the new officers installed.

Warner Hall, both the retiring and the incoming president, installed himself. Mrs. Snow said a few words in expression of the appreciation for Mr. Hall's activities in the club's behalf during the past year and in evidence of such, he was presented with 'four time' a large green alarm clock, delivered by Chester Elliott.

There followed a square dance directed by Llewellyn Wilburn and participated in by just about everybody present. At midnight the crowd left for a short hike in the bright moonlight up to a nearby waterfall, returning for more than an hour of song around the large log fire. It was almost three thirty before the last of the group had helped Jack Bagwell into a sleeping bag which had to be used in lieu of his hidden blankets.

The school bus driven by Mr. Sims was waiting for us at the junction at 10:00 o'clock the next morning in accordance with arrangements made by Mr. Johnson on the previous day. There we left our cars and all climbed into the bus, which carried us up into Woody Gap. Singing, chatter, and a lot of racket made by Warner Hall imitating a radio announcer caused a steady uproar in the bus while the crowd jolted up the mountain. The day was clear and cool, ideal for hiking.

Following moving pictures made by Carter Whittaker and a large photograph by Chester Elliott immediately after arriving in Woody Gap, the crowd started out on the trail. It was 11:00 o'clock when we left. There was not much steep climbing and the ground followed a well defined forest service trail for the entire hike. Several splendid views, both to the east and west, particularly of Old Black Mountain and the fire tower behind us were afforded from time to time.

All went well with occasional stops to enjoy the scenery and rest until the majority of the crowd reached a spring near Slaughter Gap at 1:30, where a stop was made for lunch. Shortly after the stop, Mr. Johnson came up, stating that one member of the party, Mrs. Miller, had given out on the trail, and it would be necessary for two or three men to go back and help her, either go down a trail to some road or bring her on up with the crowd. Chester Elliott and Mrs. Cooke were behind with her and Roderick Taaffe, Eddie Stone, and Frank Abercrombie went back to help. With their assistance, Mrs. Miller was able to overtake the group before they had finished their lunches and coffee.

With the assistance of two people, she was able to continue the quarter of a mile on to Slaughter Gap, where an improvised jinrikisha, consisting of two poles and Warner Hall's Bergan's pack sack was constructed. Here it was necessary for Cynthia Ward, already suffering from a sprained ankle, to dash on ahead along the trail which branched off to the left to overtake Llewllyn Wilburn, Elizabeth White and the young Greear boy, who had gone ahead on the long trail. Mrs. Snow, suffering from two Charlie horses—the first of her experience—went on slowly up the hill, accompanied by Mrs. Johnson. The remainder of the crowd went along in a group picking fallen limbs from the trail while two men at a time carried Mrs. Miller up the steep trail to the summit of Blood Mountain. The crude jinrikisha proved to be very practical for this purpose.

At the summit a splendid view in all directions was afforded and a halt of several minutes was made for resting. From here, Mrs. Miller was able to make the two mile hike down the mountain to Neel Gap on foot. We arrived at the Gap just at dark and found our bus waiting for us. It was a rather quiet group that bounced along down the mountain back to the junction where our cars were waiting. There were no reports of drivers going to sleep and running out of the road on the return trip home, but, according to all information, the chief amusement for the passengers in the cars on the journey home was that of slumber. The hiking distance had been exactly ten miles with one or two steep climbs in addition to the principal one to the summit of Blood Mountain.

Of this hike the bulletin merely reported: "Splendid views, new experiences and wonderful weather were among the highlights of the trip." But it devoted two long paragraphs to the good time had at the lodge the evening before.

In February another memorable trip was taken. The newspaper published the following account:

20 ATLANTA YOUTHS TAKE LONG HIKE

Tate, Ga., Feb. 7.—Twenty members of the Appalachian Trail Club, composed of boys and girls from Atlanta, spent a part of the weekend here on a hike to the Amicalola gap.

Two members of the party, both girls, fell out, one with a sprained ankle, and waited seven hours for the boys to blaze a path over a seldom used road and come back with an automobile. Extreme cold weather and fallen timber endangered the progress of the hike but the boys and girls, en route back to Atlanta, were the picture of health.

The bulletin explained: "This was one of the longest hikes ever scheduled by the Club, and the party was handicapped by a late start, which caused them to be pushed to get back to the cars before dark."

Before the next hike, Hall wrote to John Byrne, supervisor of the Nantahala Forest, for information on the condition of the Trail between Dick's Gap and Rich Knob ("A section into which, so far as we know, only two or three of our members have ever been"), saying "[The previous hike] has made quite a number of [people] a bit skeptical about going on this next trip for fear that they will get into the same difficulties." Therefore, this hike was a little less eventful, according to the bulletin account:

There is a little handful of hikers who can sit back in their easy chairs at home, shut their eyes, and see beautiful mental pictures of mountain ranges and valleys, clear blue sky and sunshine, a rosy sunset behind purple hills, and a mountain trail illuminated by the faint light of a new moon. These are only a few of the rewards for the eighteen people who made the weekend trip to Clayton and Dick's Gap on February 25th and 26th.

On Saturday evening, while seated around a dinner table which had been decorated with unique trail marker placecards by Marian Hoben and Olivia Herren, the group listened to Earle R. Greene tell about Georgia birds. So much interest was shown that the entire group assembled for further discussion after the finish of the square dance at midnight.

The group started out from Dick's Gap Sunday morning over an excellent forest service trail, which followed the crest of the main Blue Ridge toward the North Carolina line. One group pushed ahead, and, despite being held back by frequent temptations to stop and enjoy the views, by lunch time the coffee pail found its place over a fire near the spring of a long abandoned mountain homesite six miles up the ridge. Grace Ficken, Carter Whittaker, Tom Collins, Eddie Stone, Mr. Burrel, Dr. W. H. Miller and Warner Hall pushed on to the North Carolina line to erect two signs to greet future hikers along this trail. It put them an hour after dark getting back to the cars with a hike of almost 18 miles to their credit, the longest yet made on an organized club outing.

There were difficulties, of course. One person was attacked by two wild horses from the herd of old Charlie himself, one automobile had an attack of appendicitis, and another member lost his car keys, to find them later sticking in the door of his car, but everybody got home in time for a good nap before going to work Monday.

This is undoubtedly one of the finest sections of trail in the Georgia mountains and is recommended to hikers, both for the wonderful views and the splendid open trail.

One might gather from the bulletin reports that often the hike was incidental to the dancing, singing, etc. of the evening before.

Another real adventure was announced for April: the Club's "first real exploring trip." A newspaper announcement stated:

APPALACHIAN TRAIL CLUB WILL SCALE PEAK SUNDAY

Members of the Appalachian Trail Club will make their first determined trip of exploration Sunday when they attempt to scale the summit for Tickanetley Bald, in Gilmer County, about ten miles north of Ellijay. The peak has an altitude of 4,054 feet.

Hikers will meet at 9:30 o'clock Sunday morning in Ellijay and leave at 10 o'clock for the ten-mile hike during which an investigation will be made of forest growth and the feasibility of marking a new trail. E. B. Stone will lead the hiking party.

As the bulletin said, "Heretofore small parties have gone out to investigate a certain trail or section, but such [exploring] trips have never been on the schedule of the regular outings of the entire Club."

The next trip was to Jack's River Falls, the first visit for most members. The bulletin reports:

The trip to Jack's River Falls on April 23rd was rich in new experiences for the ten people who went along. . . . The hike on Sunday, led by W. D. Young, carried the party through forests of blooming azalea, along the logging railroad and by the lumber camp of the Connasauga River Lumber company, and over the crest of a high, sharp ridge, with Jack's River flowing close below on both sides, to a final climb down an almost precipitous mountain side to the falls. The most interesting event of the return hike occurred when three of the party decided to take a short cut. This necessitated wading across Jack's River, which is cold, rocky and deep. Strange to say, those who went a half mile around and crossed on the railroad bridge got ahead of the waders, but the latter three had a novel experience and they finally got across without mishap.

The first of trips to the Dillard Farm which were to continue for many years was held in October. It was to be a "straw ride" in a truck to near the top of Rabun Bald. The bulletin report read:

WE CLIMBED RABUN OCTOBER 29

What an outing for the first hike of the fall season we did have two weeks ago! Punkin lanterns winked at us as we drove up to the Dillard farm Saturday night and welcomed us to about the biggest dinner these hikers ever sat down to since the GATC has been organized. The writer lost track of the number of courses after the ninth, but he does remember that even the chicken was prepared two or three ways, one of which was the most popular 'southern fried.' And pitchers full of cider were still sitting around begging when the gang finally quieted down for the night, after a short moonlight walk down to the Little Tennessee River.

Thirty-one of us planted our feet on the summit of Rabun Bald the next morning. There we had visions of a new trail project comprising a great Georgia loop; heard friendly arguments as to which of the many peaks that pierced the horizon were Picken's Nose, Standing Indian, and Enotah; waved greetings to our old friend, Whiteside Mountain in North Carolina, and sympathized with Mable Abercrombie as she stirred her wits to find the best way of getting down off the lookout tower, where she had followed a few steeplejack men of the party for a better view.

The journey back was down hill for all of the six or seven (or did we hear someone say it was eleven) miles to the truck. First on an open trail, then off down the mountains through the rough to another faint trail, which finally brought us out into an old orchard. Though weary enough to drop, we shook down enough red apples to remind us of that cider back at the farm and spur us on with renewed vigor. Most of us agreed that we must have gotten out of practice during the summer. Some had limbered up and were themselves by Tuesday; others say it was the middle of the week before their joints were working freely again.

A newspaper story written on the 25th anniversary of these Dillard trips stated:

Twenty-five years ago, the Georgia Trail Club discovered the Dillard House. Mrs. Dillard, whose place at that time was in its beginning stages, was a little dubious about catering to such a large group, but decided to try anyhow and called in the neighbors who helped quilt, etc., so the Club members could be warm and comfortable. The late Arthur Dillard went with the Club and was one of the most enthusiastic hikers.

The Club was so charmed with the Dillard hospitality and the surrounding scenery that they decided to make this an annual event. (November 26, 1959)

Of a trip to Helton Falls in November, the bulletin reports:

Our trip to Helton Falls on November 12th was a bit different from most of our outings in the past. Twenty-two of us were along and we ate about as many pounds of steak, deliciously prepared by Gertrude Reiley and Mary Dallas. It was unanimously agreed that this, our first time to attempt cooking our noon meal on a hike, was a great success. Hence the decision to repeat it at the cabin next week. The weather was perfect and the fall foliage stood out in colorful contrast. Five trail signs were erected on the trip.

Other trips were planned to Tray Mountain, with overnight at Mitchell's Mountain Ranch in Helen; Highlands, North Carolina, and Whiteside Mountain—a joint hike with the Carolina and Smokies Clubs; Lake Burton with accommodations at the Cherokee Lodge on the lake; Lake Rabun, with overnight at Press Haven cabins; gold mining in Dahlonega; and a trip to the newly built cabin on Tray Mountain. This year also saw the first of the annual Christmas parties held by the Club in Atlanta—at the Agnes Scott cabin at Stone Mountain.

An "extracurricular" hike of note was taken by six Club members: two men and four women. The women had acquired the title of "FFF's: Four Foolish Females"—Marene Snow, Grace Ficken, Cynthia Ward, and Olivia Herren. (The friendship between these four was to endure for fifty years, and included vacations together, parties, and much of the credit for the Club's social events until marriage and World War II sent them on different paths.) Their hike was from the Little Tennessee River to Wallace Gap in the Nantahalas. (Hall wrote Avery of the hike, saying they were "allowing four days to make the trip that we made in a day.") A bulletin report on the trip read:

You should have been at Wallace Gap the second Sunday in June to see that enthusiastic party of "Full Fledged Freaks of the Forest" come strolling in from their five-day walk through the Nantahala Mountains. Leaving the Little Tennessee River on Tuesday, they were to be met in Wallace Gap the following Sunday morning at 10 o'clock. Lewis H. Johnson and Warner Hall were there with a car and trailer to meet them and were wondering whether they should have brought some emergency rations for a two or three days' wait when, exactly at the agreed time, the hikers emerged from the wilderness, waving bouquets at each other.

In interviewing the party concerning their experiences on the hike, it was impossible to get two stories which checked, so we are having to leave it to you to let them tell you about the trip. We agreed that the trip was certainly made through nature's flower garden, because azalea and laurel were in full bloom. When one of them said something about resting better during those four nights of sleeping out on the ground than at home, it made us wonder just what sort of a bed she has at home.

The party consisted of Marene W. Snow, Cynthia Ward, Olivia Herren, Grace Ficken, Paul Caldwell and Carter Whittaker. It was heard in a very round about way that the latter two spent most of the nights keeping ferocious wild animals, like field mice, out of the camp. Incidentally, we hear that in recognition of their ability, Uncle Sam sent for these two men and that they are now stationed at the government reforestation camp near Hiawassee.

In May, Hall wrote to a friend: "This last weekend a crowd of us went to Neel Gap and climbed Blood Mountain in the moonlight at midnight. We stayed on the summit to watch the sun come up at 4:15. It was a glorious spectacle."

A "booklet" to be published by the Club was being planned by Hall, "giving a complete set of the Club's constitution and by-laws, a list of standard instructions to hike leaders, a code of ethics for the true sportsman and other simple instructions which should be clearly understood by every member . . . [and] transportation instructions or policies."

When the booklet was published in the fall, it actually contained short articles on "The Lure of the Mountains," the history and activities of the Club, membership requirements, the AT as a whole, and a brief account of the route of the Georgia Trail.

The effects of the depression were evident in many ways throughout these early years. Many people were out of work, and most had little money to spare. Hall wrote to Avery in 1933, in response to a request for a contribution to Conference:

I will take up the matter of our contribution of $15.00 to the Trail Conference when we hold the next meeting of our Executive Council. We had not figured on anything like this; in fact, I had forgotten that the Conference needed any money for operating purposes, so we will have to do a little figuring and see what can be done.

You see, our active membership is less than forty, and a large percentage of these are school teachers. The City of Atlanta is away behind in the payment of its teachers, with the result that several of them have stopped going on our hiking trips for the lack of funds to pay transportation costs, and a number of them have not yet paid their 1933 dues.

We are endeavoring to publish a small pamphlet this spring, containing a log of the Georgia section of the AT, and have been trying to muster all financial resources to make this possible. I am beginning to get requests from outsiders for information about the Trail and, on this account, we are trying to get something ready for those people who will attempt to hike the Georgia Trail this coming season. Signs and markers are needed at places, but these won't cost so very much.

I have not the authority, of course, to say just how we will spend the few dollars that we have in our treasury, but I can assure you that we will do our best to do our share in carrying on the work of the Conference. (May 24, 1933)

During these years CCC (Civilian Conservation Corps) camps were established by the federal government to give work to the unemployed. There were a number of such camps set up in north Georgia. Carter Whittaker later wrote:

Farsighted Eddie Stone . . . immediately saw a golden opportunity to start many of the Trail projects that he had dreamed of when large quantities of money, men and machines were dumped into his forestry district with the urgent request that they be put to use as soon as possible. At once Eddie envisioned a project consisting of a string of trail shelters ten miles apart the length of the Trail in Georgia and set to work to make this dream a reality. Difficulties were encountered in getting the project approved but undaunted Eddie went ahead; plans were drawn up and Carter Whittaker was hired to do the job.[8]

Stone wrote to Hall in April of 1933: "[The CCC project] is the biggest thing forestry has ever encountered and a wonderful opportunity for us. We will be able to build a real trail system for the entire mountain region and I am going to ask you to help me map out this trail development program. We can build camps and develop water resources and put up monuments and markers." So plans were made to carry out a number of these projects. But others had plans for the CCC to build the roads that had threatened the Trail in 1931 and that would eventually cover many miles of the Georgia AT.

Hall was far from thrilled over the prospects of the CCC work. He wrote:

There is considerable concern on the part of several of our members over reports that within the next two years the CCC activities will have placed roads along the top of the Blue Ridge in many sections now covered by the AT, with the inevitable results that these sections will lose much of their charm and attraction. On this account, they are quite concerned over what this would mean to the life and enthusiasm of our organization, as well as the influence on the advisability of placing permanent bronze markers on trails which will soon be replaced by road. I wish that you would write me a letter telling about the situation, so that I might have some definite information to pass on, and possibly some authoritative information to publish in our bulletin concerning the possible outcome of CCC activities. (August 18, 1933)

And Stone replied:

As far as I have been able to learn, they plan to construct a narrow truck trail along or near the top of the Blue Ridge for much of its distance from Springer Mountain to the North Carolina line. This road will not be continuous, but will be tied in to cross roads at various gaps.

While I hate to see this road constructed, and realize that it may eventually be turned into a paved road, there seems to be little we can do about it. As you will probably recall, we bitterly opposed the construction of the road between Woody Gap and Hightower Gap. However, this road development is not as serious as first it might appear to be. I don't think we should consider abandoning the Appalachian Trail, but think we should consider the development of a system of lateral trails which will be made more accessible by a road of this kind.

There are plenty of trails of this type and we have already constructed several and have projected a number of others. I will be glad to receive suggestions from you as to additional trails which you think would be desired. (August 21, 1933)

This did not comfort Hall. He was very concerned about the roads destroying all the Club had been working for.

The roads, like cancers, continued to cover sections of the Trail. By 1934 the road would run on top of the Trail from just north of Springer Mountain all the way to Gooch Gap, and would appear at numerous other places along the Trail.

In January 1934 Hall wrote to Avery:

CCC activities in the Georgia mountains have the Trail project quite uncertain. They have been working on a road in the vicinity of Tray Mountain which follows the direct course of the Trail for some distance, going very near the summit and passing directly through the site of the old cheese factory. We have heard of other projected plans to extend road work along the crest, but this is the only one which has actually gone forward. I think that within another few days we can definitely determine just how this road on Tray Mountain and any other such construction work will affect the write-up. You wrote me that there was no particular rush about returning the data, and that is why we have been waiting to make final corrections. (January 3, 1934)

A more favorable project (to the GATC) was the building of four trail shelters (or cabins) by Whittaker, who had earlier been engaged to complete the measuring of the Trail. Whittaker, as he wrote later,

. . . took a crew of 12 CCC men and necessary supplies to the Rocky Knob cabin site, pitched camp and began to work on the first cabin.

The plans for the new type cabin called for a completely enclosed cabin except for an open door, a fireplace and an extended roof in the front. Slat bunks, a half log table and a cattle fence were accessory features.

Most of the work was done entirely by hand and only on the last cabin was a mule used to snake logs to the site. With the construction of the other cabins the heavy work of snaking logs was done by hand power. All the shingles used were hand hewn, mountain style. A crew of from four to twelve men was used. These men were isolated for weeks at a time. Provisions were brought in from the main camp. All of us lived in tents. A CCC cook was assigned to the outfit. In spite of the hardships all of us on this project had a glorious time.[8]

It is said that the cabin was modeled after a bird house at Marene Snow's cabin "Butternut" near Blairsville, where the Club spent a good deal of time. Hall wrote to Stone in September of 1933:

Ever since I got home Monday I have been trying to write you a note. I want to congratulate you, Mr. Oliver, Carter Whittaker, Mr. Roosevelt and everybody else who had anything to do with the building of that cabin up above the CCC camp two miles from Unicoi Gap. The fellow who went up there with me has been in the White Mountains, the Adirondacks and other mountains and we both agreed that both from the standpoint of the design and construction of the building and its setting the whole thing was about the best we had ever seen. Barton said that they were fortunate in having a genius in charge of the construction and location of it and now I must admit that he is right.

The cabin is well built—I think that it will stand and be serviceable after the CCC activities have long been forgotten. I think the design is superb. . . . All of us were absolutely amazed, because the whole business so completely exceeded our greatest expectations. If you haven't been up there since it has been finished, do so by all means. Carry the governor, Mr. Oliver, send a picture to the president.

Carter said that it took him five weeks with ten men, but better to have taken his time and done something that perfect than to have cut the time down and had something that wasn't serviceable when finished. I am sure that now that they have passed the experimental stage he can build the next one in much less time if they will give him the same crew.

I must admit that I have been a bit skeptical about the CCC activities, but that cabin changed the whole attitude. With a set of those cabins we can get more people into the Georgia Mountains to where they can see and appreciate our best mountains than anything in the way of road building that can be done. All of us said that it was one of the most enjoyable outings we have ever had in the Georgia mountains and all are anxious to pay another visit to the cabin. With the completion of the trail write-ups, I see a chance to offer to the Georgia people something new, something which they never realized was available to them and which many of them, like Barton, have gone to the Whites, the Adirondacks and the Sierras to find.

I wish you would let me know whether it will be alright for me to write Mr. Oliver and tell him what we think of the shelter. I know we must be careful, for political and other reasons, but I think that I can put it to him and any others in a way that they will appreciate that these cabins are a really valuable service to the Georgia people, filling a deeper need than that of a lot of roads. I would like to know if there are any others I can write to. (September 7, 1933)

Whittaker and his men went on that fall and winter to build three more cabins—at Tray Mountain, Snake Mountain, and Rich Knob. CCC crews also began construction in 1934 on the stone shelter atop Blood Mountain.

Great plans were made for the 1933 annual meeting, which was to be held again at the Cloudland Park Club Hotel. The Club bulletin announced: "The Biggest Meeting in History Almost Here," and continued: "Present prospects are that the annual meeting at Cloudland on October 14 and 15 will considerably excel anything in the Club's history.... Committees and individuals have been at work for some time on plans and arrangements."

Hall wrote to W. D. ("Brigham") Young:

The occasion shows every prospect of being a howling big one. It is too early to tell how many people we will have at Cloudland this weekend, but rumors drifting in from all directions indicate that it will certainly be on par with last year, with a strong probability of a bigger and better crowd.

Everybody around here was busy this past weekend—Elliott and Taaffe were making enlargements for the photographic exhibit and Mrs. Snow has five people at her house all day, working on the favors and name cards. Those Smokies folks are going to find something here that they never thought of in any of their big affairs.

And one thing surely—get that old guitar tuned up. We are certainly depending upon you. That singing around the fireplace was one of the star attractions. I have heard many enthusiastic references to that feature last year, and many are looking forward to it again. (October 10, 1933)

A newspaper account read:

Cloudland, Ga., Oct. 13.—Mountain climbers, ornithologists, naturalists and foresters from three southern states will assemble at the Cloudland Park Club Hotel this weekend, October 14 and 15, for a meeting which is bringing together one of the widest variety of interests in conservation and outdoor life ever assembled in the state.

The occasion is the fourth annual meeting of the Georgia Appalachian Trail Club, which is bringing together, in addition to the regular membership of the Club, large delegations from the Smoky Mountains Hiking Club of Knoxville, the Atlanta Bird Club, the Georgia Society of Naturalists and the Georgia Forestry Service.

And Hall wrote to Charlie Elliott:

Hey, you old hermit—what have you got to say for yourself? You 'flu' out on us last year, but if you don't show up this time, you are going to be the main loser. I wouldn't be surprised to see 125 people up there, judging from the rumors and inquiries that are coming in. I am telling you that we are going to have some things up there that the Smokies folks never thought of before....

Of course, Guy Frizzell will have some inspirational remarks, and if we could depend on you, I would like to have you there to say a few words in front of the big fireplace about fellowship around the campfire before Brigham tunes up his old guitar and we all join in singing the old songs. If you are coming, let me know immediately, so I will know how to fix for you. If you are not coming, I almost feel like the jealous sweetheart who said 'Don't ever let me see you again.'

I was up at Tate Estates and scared up a drove of wild turkeys on the road to Oglethorpe—the first I had seen since that trip to Santeetlah. I think that a condensed and very atmospheric relation of that Santeetlah trip would make a swell fireside story for that crowd. (October 9, 1933)

Several of the officials of the CCC camps were invited to the meeting, but Hall wrote in a letter to the Cloudland Hotel:

I understand that a CCC camp is located down in that unfinished hotel. If those boys have the same habit of wandering off and getting drunk on weekends, like those in the eastern section, I am sure that they would prove quite a problem to us if they get the news that this affair is coming off up there. Since we expect a larger crowd than last year, and since there is such a feeling in our organization against outsiders at our affairs, I am sure that you will make every effort to help us out in this respect by either keeping information concerning the dance from getting out into the neighborhood, or by letting it be understood that it is a strictly private gathering. I am sure that we will have a larger crowd than we can conveniently handle without any extra ones. Otherwise, there would be no objection, except for the fact that most of them get the wrong idea about the type of good time that we are trying to have. (October 6, 1933)

Afterward the bulletin report on the meeting related:

GREAT TIME AT CLOUDLAND

There is not much use of going into details about the annual meeting at Cloudland, since all but four of the active members living within the state were present. Led by Jim Thompson of the Smoky Club, the spirit of the seventy-six rang forth in hiking songs at the banquet Saturday night. Yes, every one of the seventy-six people present seemed to get the old mountain climbers' spirit from the start. Nothing would have seemed right had not the ten folks come down from the Smoky Mountains Hiking Club and, despite the fact that Guy Frizzell and Harvey Broome weren't there to give us a few random remarks about the life of a 'Smoky' hiker, as they did last year, George Barber told us enough to convince us that the Smoky Club is as active as ever.

We enjoyed having with us members of the Georgia Society of Naturalists and the Atlanta Bird Club and appreciated the words of greeting from their presidents. A masterpiece was the letter to us from Benton MacKaye, nestor of the Appalachian Trail, who was confined in a Knoxville hospital and unable to be present.

Most outstanding in the exhibit was the partially finished plaque being modeled by Dr. George H. Noble for a marker to be erected on the Appalachian Trail in Georgia at gaps where it is crossed by highways.

The weather Sunday could not have been finer, and afforded wonderful views from Rock City, where we went for the morning outing and where Earle Greene, of the Bird Club and Naturalist's Society, discovered some rare duck hawks. Several of the group, filled with the desire to explore, were led by 'Brigham' Young and Mr. Forrester on a crawling, climbing and neck craning expedition through some peculiar rock formations. The result was that we were two hours late for lunch and had to cut the noon program short, but we still had time to enjoy an unusually interesting talk by Dr. Ralph Wagar on the Okefenokee Swamp.

Hall was elected to a third year as president, Chester Elliott was elected vice-president, W. Miller treasurer, and Marion Hoben secretary.

Soon after the annual meeting, a special business meeting was called to discuss "frankly and critically some of the plans, as well as the policies which the Club is to follow in the future." It was the "first meeting at which all outsiders are excluded . . . in a good many months." This meeting proved popular, and a similar one was held the next year at the same time.

A few days after the meeting, Stone sent Hall a list of "projects which I believe we should undertake during the coming year."

1. Complete marking the Appalachian Trail and secondary trails.
2. Complete construction of shelters.
3. Erect large markers in principal gaps.
4. Prepare complete map of Trail.
5. Assemble and properly file AT photographs.
6. Publish guide book.
7. Secure new members distributed over north Georgia.
8. Prepare list of hikes.
9. Establish system of inspection of work undertaken on Trail.

Of course, the only way in which we can accomplish this is by appointing committees and charging them with definite duties. I suggest that you appoint the committees and outline as definitely as you can what they are to do. And I suggest that you place Carter Whittaker in charge of seeing that the Trails are marked and shelters completed. (October 27, 1933)

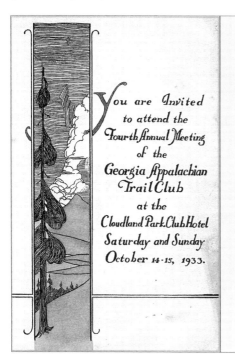

You are Invited to attend the Fourth Annual Meeting of the Georgia Appalachian Trail Club at the Cloudland Park Club Hotel Saturday and Sunday October 14-15, 1933.

This is the big annual event of the Georgia Mountain climbers, and is the occasion when they assemble to swap yarns about their summer outing experiences and make plans for the fall and winter hiking season.

Our friends of the trail from Tennessee and North Carolina will be present as usual, and with the naturalists and bird lovers of Georgia well represented, the meeting promises to be one of the finest gatherings of nature lovers ever assembled in Georgia.

At seven o'clock Saturday evening the banquet begins with music, hiking songs and a few highlights from our outdoor activities of the year. Next follows the old square dance, with a finish of favorite songs to the accompaniment of "Brigham" Young's guitar.

Following breakfast Sunday morning there will be trips to Look Rock, DeSoto Falls and other points of scenic interest. There will also be a special hike for those who must have their little walk. We will reassemble promptly at noon for a short luncheon meeting before permitting those who came farthest to depart for their homes.

The cost of the entire week-end, including the banquet, lodging and the two meals on Sunday will be $2.85. Please send a dollar, or check for full amount, with your reservation to Grace Ficken, 1068 Oglethorpe Ave., S.W., Atlanta, phone Ra. 8667 (evenings), Wal. 0220, Ext. 377 (day). Registrations must be in by Thursday, October 12. If you have no means of transportation or extra room in your car please notify Miss Ficken.

The Cloudline Park Club Hotel is 50 miles from Chattanooga, 40 miles from Rome and 105 miles from Atlanta. Go by way of Summerville and Menlo.

1934

GEORGIA
APPALACHIAN
19 TRAIL CLUB, INC. 30

IN THE SPRING OF 1933 Hall had discussed with G. H. Noble, an Atlanta physician and sculptor, the possibility of modeling a plaque "of some appropriate design to go on the bronze markers to be erected at Neel Gap, Mt. Oglethorpe, and other places." Noble agreed to do it, designs were drawn, and Hall was persuaded to pose for the photograph from which the plaque was modeled.

The plaques were to cost the Club about $20.00 each, "a rather large amount," according to Stone, but considered worth it by Hall. He wrote to Myron Avery:

Enclosed is a check for $10.00—a contribution to the AT Conference about which you wrote me some time ago. The Club voted this contribution at its last business meeting. We are now in somewhat of a sweat trying to figure out a way to raise a goodly little sum of money for the erection of some rather elaborate permanent markers at Tate Estates and in some of the principal gaps, such as Neel Gap, where important highways cross the Trail. We feel that we at present have a wonderful opportunity to, at comparatively little expense, erect some markers which will make the motorists passing through these gaps appreciate the importance and purpose of the AT in a way that would hardly be possible by any other method. (November 15, 1933)

Hall wrote later:

We are extremely fortunate in having an amateur modeler and sculptor as a member of our Club. . . . For a long time we have realized the importance of an artistic marker to gain respect, dignity, and prestige to the Appalachian Trail. The best we could do through some commercial concern would have cost us more than three hundred dollars . . . so we took it upon ourselves, and after almost a year's work by Dr. Noble and a few of the members, we made the bronze tablet. . . . It is needless to say that we are quite proud of it. We now have an aluminum master pattern which is used in casting [the] plaques. (October 30, 1934)

The first plaque was completed in January of 1934. An installation ceremony was planned at Neel Gap for February, but was postponed when the erection of the plaque was delayed. The plaque was on display at the lodge at Neel Gap until it was finally installed in May by CCC personnel.

An article in the *Atlanta Journal* quoted Hall as saying: "This is one of the most outstanding marking projects ever undertaken by any mountaineering club." He wrote at greater length in May, 1934, of the purpose in erecting this "elaborate marker":

Our original purpose . . . was to give added prestige to the Appalachian Trail in our section. In that respect we are meeting with considerable success. People who have heard of the Trail are inquiring about it. Local forest and park authorities, who had looked upon our activities as rather juvenile and the Trail as unimportant are asking us to tell them more about this Trail which deserves such an elaborate marker. This is only one of the steps which we are taking to gain for the Appalachian Trail such recognition that it must be taken into consideration whenever a question of road building or other changes which may affect its course may come up. (May 23, 1934)

A number of plaster casts were made and "finished in imitation bronze for hanging in buildings." One of these was sent to Myron Avery. Requests came from one or two other clubs for copies, and a plan was developed for making money on the sale of them. An aluminum pattern could be made with a plain base, and "stock lettering found in practically any foundry" could be added with another club name. There is no record of any sales, but a similar marker was made by the Blue Mountain Club of Pennsylvania and erected in 1936 at the Delaware Water Gap. (This marker disappeared from its place in 1958.)

Hall sent Benton MacKaye a picture of the plaque and received a rather effusive letter in return:

The photograph has come—with your good letter. It is seldom that I've been hit between the eyes with utter and instantaneous delight as I was on viewing this real work of art. Here in vigorous embodiment is (to my mind) the spirit of the Appalachian Trail. The conception appears to be complete, omitting nothing relevant and including nothing irrelevant. (And I understand that the idea is your own.) 'A footpath for those who seek fellowship with the wilderness.' This (to my mind) is a masterful definition of the Appalachian Trail.

The design carries out the thought. The action is a living thing: here is a man equipped and eager, starting out for Maine. . . .

Your words keep coming back to me: 'fellowship with the wilderness.' The last word cannot too often be repeated—*wilderness, Wilderness, WILDERNESS!* Not man but nature; man's relation not to man but nature (what Harvey calls Earth). And thereby— incidentally—the man-to-man relation finds its place.

This tablet is so *very* appropriate that I wish it might stand at the extreme southern terminus of the Appalachian Trail. This is Mt. Oglethorpe. Is there some real *Wilderness* place thereon (if not on top then at the base or slope)—some place not man's but nature's—that you have in mind, or that might be found, to make the end (and the beginning) of this wilderness footpath?. . . .

I had not expected to rattle on like this but your picture (with its vista of the kind of folks you are) has got me going. (November 3, 1933)

Raymond Torrey called the plaque "a beautiful thing, one of the handsomest markers the Appalachian Trail will have."

Two more plaques were completed in early 1934, but there were no funds to have them erected. The bulletin reported that one of the plaques was on display for several days in the window of Maier and Berkele Jewelers on Peachtree Street in downtown Atlanta. There is some evidence that Dr. Noble may have paid for the plaques himself rather than the Club.

Hall's plan to bring publicity and prestige to the Trail with the plaques, the new cabins, the guide book data (copies of which were made to furnish to anyone planning to hike the Trail) included the erection of several hundred fine chestnut board signs all along the Trail. These were installed by Carter Whittaker and his CCC workers as well as Trail Club members on regular hikes. Hall wrote to Avery of some of the projects and his overall purpose of trying to attract people to the AT. Avery replied:

I am very appreciative of the kindness of my friends in Georgia in having the plaque made for me. . . . I understand your project and what you seek to accomplish. However, it necessarily brings with it the requirement for intensively marking the route. For it won't help much to lure people on the Trail and lose them in half a mile. You will have to consider this seriously. Paint is the only solution. (February 5, 1934)

And a month later Avery wrote again:

In the last issue of your always interesting bulletin, I noticed a reference to the putting up by Carter Whittaker of over 100 chestnut board AT markers. This interested me. Is it something new? Are you making blocks of wood and burning in the AT insignia? If so, let us have one or two to add to our AT museum collection.

Have you people on hand now any of the AT markers? Experimenting is lots of fun and useful but much can be learned from the years of experimenting up here since 1923 in marking. Too novel or attractive markers attract souvenir hunters. Only the galvanized iron markers with long nails are proof against vandalism and to a greater extent shotguns.

After all, the only absolute reliance in marking is judiciously placed paint blazes.

These stay. Even if your trail is overgrown, it can be easily followed. For new trail galvanized markers or your board ones would have to be used so extensively as to be most expensive. (March 5, 1934)

The Trail in Georgia was to become somewhat notorious for its lack of adequate marking. Throughout the thirties, Avery prodded and lectured the Club to *paint* blazes and get it done soon and well. It seemed that it was a remarkable achievement for someone to hike the Georgia Trail and not get lost.

Great consternation struck the GATC in the spring of 1934 when Stone resigned his position as Assistant State Forester to accept a position with the National Park Service. The *Forestry Geological Review* announced the change and stated:

By reason of the resignation of Everett B. Stone, Jr., district forester, Gainesville, to accept a position with the National Park Service, some changes in the staff of the Georgia Forest Service take place May 1.

The resignation of Mr. Stone removes from the staff the oldest employee in point of service of the Georgia Forest Service except the State Forester, B. M. Lufburrow. The National Park Service offers a larger field of usefulness for which Mr. Stone's education and training have well fitted him. A part of his time in recent years has been devoted to Indian Springs and Vogel Park, his work attracting favorable attention of National Park authorities. His headquarters, it is understood, will be in Washington. (May 1, 1934)

W. D. Young, district forester in Rome, Georgia, and also a Club member, would take Stone's place. The staff changes also involved Carter Whittaker, about whom there had evidently been a complaint, possibly concerning his work on the AT. Hall wrote immediately to Avery:

E. B. Stone has resigned as district forester in charge of the Appalachian Trail section of our state to take a post with the Federal Park Service. Immediately following his resignation, the state forester sent a letter to the district calling for the dismissal before May 10 of three foremen, one of whom is Carter R. Whittaker. Whittaker, a former vice consul to Japan, a member of our Club, and a member of the Smoky Mountains Hiking Club's nine day vacation hike year before last, has been in charge of the cabin crew and the erection of trail signs, and has proved himself a rare find for this type of work. He had worked closely under Stone's supervision. The foreman of his camp has always been an engineer and highway builder. To him the march of progress consists only in replacing trail with roads.

The state forester, who is making the change, has never looked upon trail building as of much importance or interest, except possibly to a few boy scouts. He thinks our Georgia AT group is merely a small group of fanatics. I wonder if you would write to him and tell him of your visit to the Georgia mountains; of your, and other people's, interest in the work which has been carried on along the Trail here during the past few months; and your plans for returning to Georgia this spring to see this work. Urge the continuation of this part of the CCC work, and call his attention to the increasing popularity of the AT. A lot of us here are kicking up a racket, but we feel that you in Washington can put an emphasis upon it that is impossible for us to do here in the state. The state forester is B. M. Lufburrow, State Capitol, Atlanta. (May 2, 1934)

Hall also wrote to R. H. Martin of the Tate Estates, telling him of the work of the Club and the uncompleted plans for erecting cabins and signs and compiling information for the guide book, and saying:

The state forester, apparently failing to appreciate the importance of this work, is planning to take off the man who has been in charge of this, and center the entire force of the camp on the construction of truck trails, unsuitable for tourist travel, and other work. That will mean that there will be no permanent signs erected from Springer Mountain to Mt. Oglethorpe because our Club does not have resources sufficient to carry on this extensive program without some sort of aid. We are sure, however, that if only a part of those who are interested in this project will take the matter up with him, he can be shown that this work is as important to the people of Georgia as is the growing of fine grain timber for use in high grade furniture and other places where appearance is important. Several organizations are already planning to approach him and urge that the work be continued to completion. We are comparatively few at best, however, and it will take all who are interested to convince him. I am sure that you people at Tate Estates would be willing to cooperate by at least writing a letter. I would be glad to go more into detail with you, if you so desire. (May 2, 1934)

Whittaker, in charge of the trail work and also again the job of correcting the data for the guide book, sent a report to Hall in April, 1934, with the completed data. In his letter accompanying the material, he added a P.S.: "E. B. manipulated the mileages shown in the mileage list in such a way as to give the Georgia Trail 100 miles plus—when the actual addition is a fraction less. I leave that situation to you, E. B., Myron, your respective consciences and to God. However the books should not be juggled in spots but all through or it might lead to confusion."

The outing schedule for 1934 was full: hikes or other events were planned for twice a month except in the hot summer months. The first hike of the year was to Sweetwater Creek, where the champion woman hiker—Grace Ficken— sprained her leg, and the improvised carrier was once again put to use to carry her out. According to the bulletin:

By virtue of being the only woman who went the full distance of the Club's longest organized hike, Grace holds the title of being about the champion hiker among the girls of the Club, although there are others who say that they can walk just as far if given enough time. We believe it, too. Although she was on the job all last week, her doctor decided it best for her to stay at home and keep quiet (imagine any of the red-headed members of the Club keeping quiet) for this week. We trust that she will be out on the trail with us to defend her title again soon.

Having discovered the Dillard Farm last year, the Club looked forward to returning, so a trip was made to the Farm and then by truck to the Trail to Picken's Nose.

An unscheduled trip to the Smokies was arranged early in February when word came of a heavy snow fall. The bulletin related:

The wires were certainly 'hot' for two nights week before last after we got a telegram from Tennessee that a heavy snow had blanketed the Great Smoky Mountains. It is understood that over seventy telephone calls were made, some to Gainesville, Tennessee and other distant points as the news spread among the membership and plans were made for a trip to the 'Canadian Woods.'

In spite of all sorts of difficulties and conflicts, one carload of six enthusiasts left Atlanta shortly after noon Saturday, February 3, with the sun shining from a clear sky and the thermometer standing at 62 in the shade. By seven that night they were rolling up to the Mountain View Hotel at Gatlinburg, Tennessee, where they were greeted by Guy Frizzell and 'Dutch' Roth, of the Smoky Mountains Hiking Club. Next, followed a big dinner and a drive to Cherokee Orchards, where the climb began.

The group started out promptly at nine o'clock and trudged through snow from three to twelve inches deep along the eight-mile government trail toward the summit of Mt. LeConte. Shortly before midnight the moon came up. By three o'clock Sunday morning they had reached Jack Huff's cabin near the summit, where Harvey Broome and other members of the Smoky Club had made a roaring fire.

The group awoke Sunday morning to find themselves in a new world. The forest growth was exactly that of the Canadian woods—balsam and spruce. A hike was made out to Myrtle Point before breakfast, where many pictures were snapped. Following a good meal, the hikers started shortly after noon back down the mountain. At Gatlinburg another big dinner awaited them, together with much enjoyable chatting with friends from Knoxville and the Smoky Club—Jim Thompson was there. It was seven o'clock before they were on the journey back to Atlanta.

The next trip was announced in the bulletin as follows:

Come with us for a dreamy day in a far-off wild craggy corner of the Blue Ridge where a little trickling spring starts Georgia's greatest river, the Chattahoochee; and where, on a little mountain bench surrounded by virgin woods and rocky crags, there is set a little log shelter, Rocky Knob, which is our ultimate destination. On the way we pass a spot known as Robber's Roost. Tradition has it that a few men used a rocky shelter here as a hideout. Parts of a wall they built may still be seen. Many will be interested in riding over the new CCC road up Soapstone Creek, in seeing CCC Camp P73, and in walking over one of Roy Ozmer's trails. Carter Whittaker will be hike leader. By the way, if you want a real thrill come up Saturday afternoon to CCC P73 and spend the night in the Rocky Knob Shelter and be lulled to sleep by a big log fire, and that is the real stuff.

"Roy Ozmer's trail" was, of course, the Jack's Gap trail, newly constructed.

The bulletin report on the trip began:

Warner Hall missed the trip to the cabin at Rocky Knob February 24. With the exception of the gold mining trip last fall, when he went to the annual banquet of the Smoky Mountains Hiking Club instead, this was the first regular outing of the Club which he had missed in three years. He has constantly said that he was going to have to skip some trips, but it seems that he continually postponed these skips through fear that he would miss something of interest. Well, when he awoke at home on Sunday morning, February 24, and heard the rain pouring down outside, he was sure that he had missed something. He had missed the second rainy outing which the Club has had in more than two years.

A March trip was planned for Yahoola Lodge near Dahlonega with a day hike from Cooper Gap to Woody, of which the bulletin stated: "This is quite an unfamiliar section of the Georgia Trail, in fact, less than half dozen of our members have ever been over it. The hiking distance is approximately ten miles, but most of it will be quite easy going along a well constructed truck trail."

It turned out to be another wet time, according to the bulletin:

Although the seventeen (a rather exclusive party, eh!) of us who journeyed forth from Atlanta on the weekend of March 25th to join our two members from Helen at Yahoola Lodge, found ourselves in a fog during the entire occasion, we had one of the slickest times ever experienced.

Although the sky was heavily overcast on that Saturday, things went well until we left the pavement beyond Dahlonega and started on the last three miles of our journey over a slippery mountain road. One car went into the ditch while another thought it was going well until a voice from the darkness informed its occupants that they were off the road and headed for a man's barn. Going became so slick near the last that some of us had to make the last quarter of a mile to our destination on foot. Although late and tired, immediately upon arriving at our destination, we found hope. And our host, W. Al Hope, stayed with us and gave us the best care and attention until we were back on the pavement headed for Woody Gap the next day.

A trip to Amicalola Falls had the highest attendance of the year, and prompted the bulletin to conclude:

It has long been known that most of us don't particularly mind the rain, but not until our last trip did it become evident that, as a whole, we apparently have quite an affection for the rain—we love it. If that is not true, then why is it that, aside from our annual meetings, the largest attendances have been on those outings which were conducted on rainy days.

A planned overnight hike to Rich Knob on the North Carolina line was changed to accommodate a large crowd, and ended up with the group spending the night at the new Snake Mountain shelter. This was one of the first times the Club had used the shelters for overnight, and was something of a novel experience for most. The *DeKalb New Era* reported on the trip:

THREE LOCAL PEOPLE SLEEP IN TENTS ATOP GEORGIA'S HIGHLANDS

Two Decatur people, Warner W. Hall and Lewis Dogette, and an Emory Professor, Dr. W. Lloyd Adams, were among a group of 15 members of the Georgia Appalachian Trail Club who spent Saturday night in a little cabin and tents on the crest of the Blue Ridge Mountains about ten miles south of the North Carolina line.

The cabin is located at Snake Mountain and the tents were pitched near it when the cabin was found to be too small to accommodate the entire party. Despite the rain and the cold, several members of the party, including some of the women, preferred the tents, and, equipped with heavy blankets and sleeping bags, spent a very enjoyable and comfortable night.

In commenting on the outing Mr. Hall said:

'Getting cold and wet camping out in winter is torture, camping comfortably in the warm sunshiny summer is enjoyable, but sleeping warm and dry in a little tent which you have pitched for the night somewhere way up on a mountain, with a cold rain blowing down outside, is indeed a thrill.'

The party left Atlanta Saturday morning, parked their cars at Dick's Creek Gap and hiked a considerable distance to the cabin at Snake Mountain. Sunday was spent hiking in the Blue Ridge. (May 3, 1934)

Another day hike was planned to the Rocky Knob cabin, since the earlier trip had been rained out. The bulletin announced:

It will be unnecessary to bring your lunch for the noon meal on Sunday. Mary Dallas and her crew of helpers will give us another steak dinner like the one which she and Gertrude Reiley prepared for us at Helton Falls. Just bring your Trail Club cup and the price of your pound of steak, together with the trimmin's.

Thirty-seven people responded to the invitation.

A "pre-Thanksgiving dinner" was held at the Dillard Farm again and "was just about all anyone could ask for." Following the dinner, according to the bulletin, "our library committee introduced us to the large collection of books and exchanges from other clubs, so we spent the remainder of the evening quietly sitting around reading."(!)

The bulletin reported on the Christmas party:

The Christmas party, thanks to Mrs. Martha Noble and her committee, was simply superb. On the night of December 20, the majority of the active members in the state sat down to our Christmas feast. Snowballs were lying around everywhere and a battle ensued which finally broke up the meal—after everyone had eaten his fill. There followed Christmas music, a brief installation of officers and a visit from Santa Claus, who brought toys for everybody except Rainnie Hoben. Rainnie disappeared from the room a few minutes before Santa arrived and didn't show up again until sometime after he left. Far from being the least exciting was the sleigh ride which a part of the group took. The party, equipped with a large set of real sleigh bells, made the neighborhood ring with tinkles of Christmas. At least one member who arrived pretty low in spirit, left the meeting 'with bells on.'

Other outings for the year 1934 included: a visit to Burns Cottage in Atlanta; the Indian Mounds near Macon; a Mother's Day breakfast at Bluebonnet Lodge near Newnan; Greears' Lodge and Mt. Yonah; Hawk and Springer Mountains; and Jacks River Falls.

Although the 1932 meeting of the Southern clubs was not really a success, great plans were made for another such meeting in 1934, to be called the Southern Appalachian Trail Conference. A planning meeting for the conference was held two months before the actual meeting, and an intriguing report appeared in the bulletin:

Olivia Herren, Lou Hoben, Grace Ficken, Marene Snow and Warner Hall went to Highlands, North Carolina, this past weekend, where they joined delegations from the Nantahala and Smoky Mountains Clubs to make preliminary plans for the Southern Appalachian Trail Conference to be held at Highlands on the weekend of May 26th and 27th. For details of this trip you are referred to those who went, because it is too long a story to be repeated here. Since we maintain that it is the unexpected that almost always bobs up to make our outings rich with romance and adventure, may it be merely added here that this trip certainly had nothing lacking—no, indeed!

Elliott, having moved to Augusta, was making himself scarce. Hall wrote to him about the conference:

You got one of the enclosed announcements, didn't you? Well, why haven't I heard from you? Hang it, don't you know what it all means? Guy Frizzell, well, and plenty of others, will be there. I am not planning on getting any sleep Saturday night. I don't know what will be happening, but I know that something will happen, particularly if you are along. How about coming over Friday night and going up with me Saturday? (May 22, 1934)

The "condensed report" of the meeting indicates that it was quite a success. "All clubs south of Virginia which were affiliated with the Appalachian Trail movement were represented. Attendance report: Carolina Mountain Club, 30; Nantahala AT Club, 8; GATC, 40; Smoky Mountains Hiking Club, 80. This large attendance grew from an anticipated 75, and taxed all the hotels and inns in Highlands to care for the crowd."

The highlight of the meeting was the presence of Benton MacKaye, who was, of course, the principal speaker. Reports of progress in trail work were made by each club as follows:

Marcus Book reported that the Carolina Club has scouted and located all of its section of Appalachian Trail and that the marking and painting will soon be completed.

Carl Campbell reported that the Nantahala AT Club has completed its section of the Trail and that it is in first class condition.

Carter Whittaker reported that the Georgia AT Club has almost completed its section and that three shelters have been built, with another soon to be constructed. He also told of the striking bronze plaques which they are placing at major road crossings.

Carlos C. Campbell reported that markers have been placed on the 42 miles of western Smoky, and that as many markers as were thought advisable had been placed along the eastern half of Smoky, most of which must be replaced upon the completion of the Class A trail now being built by the National Park Service, and that the 23 miles between the Great Smokies and Cheoah Bald has been cleared and marked, and some of the painting has been done.

The future guidebook was discussed, and it was agreed that three chapters on side trails in the Smokies, western North Carolina, and Georgia should be included. It was estimated "that the data could not be compiled, edited, and the book published earlier than the first part of 1935." (It actually did not come out until 1937). The report concluded:

About 75 hikers made the long hike—from Highlands to Whiteside. Approximately 45 more hiked from the highway at the foot of Whiteside to the top. All were most enthusiastic about the scenery—and the Conference as a whole.

Everyone hoped that this could be made an annual event.

At this meeting began a lifelong friendship between the light-hearted, fun-loving GATC and the venerated Benton MacKaye. Others may have regarded MacKaye as the Creator of the Trail, only a little removed from the earlier Creator; the GATC locked him out of his room for the night as a joke! And MacKaye loved it. He corresponded with Marene Snow and others until his death, and seemed to regard the Georgia club as his special friends. Later he was to address an annual GATC meeting and received an invitation regularly for many years afterward.

After the meeting. Stone wrote to MacKaye, who was at the time in Knoxville, Tennessee, with the Tennessee Valley Authority:

From your visit to Highlands over the last weekend you no doubt learned how much interest is being taken in the Appalachian Trail wherever hiking clubs have been organized and publicity given to this movement. I enjoyed very much meeting you and I am sorry that I did not have an opportunity to discuss this matter more fully with you.

Here in Georgia we find an ever increasing interest in the development and use of the Appalachian Trail and believe that it will be a center of recreational activities in the mountain region of northeast Georgia. It has already become a very definite thing in the minds of many outdoor loving people and will be coordinated with the development of state parks and other areas of this nature.

It occurred to me that we might work out some more comprehensive plan of development of the Trail, especially in the Southern Appalachians from Virginia south, and I have been wondering if it would not be possible to have it recognized as a worthwhile recreational project with the idea of securing federal funds for its more comprehensive development. We have had a very definite plan of development for the Georgia section and have had assigned to this work a foreman in one of our CCC camps who has done a splendid job in carrying out our ideas. If the various Appalachian Trail Clubs could be recognized as cooperating agencies, it seems to me that some of the relief money could be spent in this manner. I am not thinking so much of the need of this work on the Georgia section as I am for that portion of the Trail from the Georgia line north, at least to Virginia and possibly to the Natural Bridge National Forest. Since you are in a better position to further the interests of the Trail than anyone else, I hope you will give this your serious consideration, and if it seems feasible, I will be glad to let you have some of our ideas as to what can be done to bring about the wider use of the Trail. (May 28, 1934)

MacKaye replied:

. . . I need not tell you that I am intensely interested in your suggestion about the Appalachian Trail, and especially as to its relation to the various federal activities; and what I say in response is of course wholly unofficial as regards the TVA. It is my personal opinion that, as you suggest, the various Appalachian Trail Clubs should be recognized as cooperating agencies—just as are the several Mountain and Outing Clubs in New England and elsewhere. But in this as in all things, it is persons and not agencies that do the real cooperating, and the basis of it all is mutual understanding. You are kind enough to offer to send me your ideas more fully about the use of the Appalachian Trail; please send them along for I should be delighted to have them. Meantime let me now send you some notions that occur to me.

The Appalachian Trail from the Virginia line southward lies within the Tennessee River basin or in 'adjoining territory;' it would be a distinct aid in fostering the social 'well-being' of said territory's people; in location and function then the AT Clubs come clearly within the scope of the TVA program as stated in the organic Act of Congress. Such is my personal opinion. But with all the TVA now finds upon its hands it might very likely defer, officially, taking up at present any projects in this line. This need not prevent us, unofficially, from laying our plans and formulating our ideas.

Another point—while we are on officialdom. The definite purpose of the Appalachian Trail (to foster the wilderness environment) should not be confused with the purposes, varied and sundry, of the federal government. In any dealings of the AT Clubs with the government as 'land owner' the Forest Service as well as the National Park Service is involved. In dealings with the government as 'developer' the TVA would seem to be one at least of the branches involved. In any case the AT Clubs should not allow themselves to be diverted from their sole and simple objective above stated.

All this applies especially in the matter of obtaining federal funds. Therein lies danger. If the government spends money it demands—reasonably enough—to have 'something to show for it.' What do we mean by 'something'? If it is something merely physical then it must be very physical—and the tendency will be to manicure the wilderness. This is the opposite concept of the Appalachian Trail. If it is something chiefly mental (such as a nature trail) then the physical aspects should be carefully delimited. In any case the project should be precisely formulated and thoroughly understood. Perhaps already you have met and solved these dangers in your experience in Georgia with the CCC camps; and it may be just a matter of extending your methods. (June 7, 1934)

Very few people from the Southern clubs, and none from GATC, were able to attend the Appalachian Trail Conference in Rutland, Vermont, that year. A report on the progress of the GATC was sent in to be read. William Welch, honorary president of the ATC, wrote to Hall after the Conference:

Mr. E. G. Frizzell, President of the Smoky Mountains Hiking Club, presented to the one hundred delegates of the Trail Conference at Rutland your detailed report on the accomplishments of the Georgia Appalachian Trail Club. This report was received by the Conference with much interest and is a record of very remarkable achievement.

I wish you would convey to your Club members our appreciation of the very real assistance to the Trail project which they have contributed. (July 19, 1934)

Raymond Torrey, in his column in the *New York Post*, reported that the GATC report to Conference proclaimed the Georgia Trail to be "one of the best provided with shelters at convenient intervals of any in the 2,000 miles of the Trail, not excepting such older parts of the route as the Green Mountain and Appalachian Mountain Club trails. . . ." These "accommodations" included, besides the five shelters, Hightower Game Refuge Station and Hawk Mountain Lookout Tower, a partially burnt cabin at Ward Gap, Ranger Station at Woody Gap and Black Mountain Tower, and cabins at Neel Gap.

In the spring of 1934, the following article appeared in the *Forestry Review* magazine:

Much work has been accomplished by the CCC boys in the northeastern part of the state as a result of a comparatively mild winter, and with the opening up of spring, plans are being rushed with the contemplation of accomplishing even more work with milder weather.

Many beautiful trails have been constructed through the mountains, all of these being well and fully marked with rustic signs so that any hiker can now find his way through the mountains quite easily. Also the Georgia portion of the Appalachian Trail which reaches from Maine to Georgia has been greatly improved and well marked. Nature lovers all agree that the full beauty of the mountains can be better enjoyed and appreciated by hiking over these trails than any other way. Fire lookout towers are being constructed on the highest peaks, and for sightseers who really want to see, these will prove a center of attraction.

The improvement of numerous truck trails through the mountains will enable motorists to pierce them to the inner regions where rainbow and speckled trout are found in abundance in the streams. Many other forms of wildlife can be found in these mountains which many 'City Fellers' have never looked on before.

These "truck trails" were still taking their toll on the AT. In June, Carter Whittaker sent in a detailed report on the Trail in Georgia. He gave the condition of each section of trail and stated:

Although most of the trail has been cleared of the debris left by the ice storm of several years ago (excepting that section between the Amicalola Shelter and Bucktown Bald), much of the trail in the Cherokee Forest is overgrown or otherwise indistinct. Maintenance during the last year has largely been abandoned on account of the road building program of the Cherokee Forest to be discussed later.

He reported on "roads and road projects affecting the Trail," listing almost 24 miles of completed roads replacing the AT, and almost 20 more to be built in the summer of 1934, summing up:

So we can count on at least 42% of the Trail in Georgia being replaced by road by the fall. Work from Low Gap to Indian Grave Gap and from Nimblewill Gap to Amicalola Falls has actually started.
I understand from Mr. Woody, Chief Ranger of the Cherokee Forest in Georgia, that only such sections of the Trail that are short cuts over the road will be maintained.

He listed the "lead-in" (or crossing) roads at ten gaps along the Trail. His "suggestions for maintaining the integrity of the Trail" were:

1. Persuade the Cherokee Forest to maintain old Trail where it is still distinct from the road; to build new trails circumventing the road.
2. Relocate trail that has been replaced by road and assign each member of the Club a section for which he will be responsible. It will be found generally that the road has taken a lower level than the Trail and that a trail keeping near the top or going to the other side of the mountain from the road will suffer but little interference from the road which will be deserted most of the time.

He also reported on trail signs and shelters, saying 275 chestnut board signs were erected, and recommended that more be placed on "non-ridgetop" sections. He reported that the four recently built shelters were in good condition, and listed 12 shelters of "all types" along the Trail, including Connahaynee Lodge, deserted cabin at Ward Gap, and other buildings that could be used. His conclusions were:

There is not much that can be done about the Trail until the road building program is definitely through. When the Trail is readjusted to new conditions we will be 'sitting pretty.' We would be now if it were not for the new road projects. At least the Trail is more accessible than it has ever been before.
Interesting fact: Blood Mountain is not only the highest peak and has the best view on the Georgia Trail but also is almost exactly midway between Oglethorpe and the state line. From Blood one can easily see both ends of the Trail.

In late summer, Colonel and Mrs. John H. Stutesman, who were then living at Fort Benning, wrote to Conference for information on the AT, and eventually to Hall. They planned to walk the entire Georgia Trail in August of 1934. Plans were made, and the time of the hike approached, but Colonel Stutesman was unable to go. Mrs. Stutesman and her 13-year-old son started out from Mt. Oglethorpe and, after many difficulties, finally gave up at Hightower Gap. Colonel Stutesman returned with them after a few weeks and they all completed the trip to Bly Gap. Mrs. Stutesman became the first woman to hike the entire Georgia Trail. She wrote interesting accounts of the trip for the Trail Club and for the Fort Benning and Columbus newspapers. (See Appendix)

The Club had apparently failed to notice or heed Carter Whittaker's trail report which stated the intention of the CCC to build a road all the way from Low Gap to Indian Grave Gap, in addition to other places. On their hike, Mrs. Stutesman discovered, and wrote to Hall about, surveyors' stakes leading from Chattahoochee Gap, which is the end of the existing road, right up to the Rocky Knob shelter and beyond. She also reported seeing a tractor on Blood Mountain, and said that the Chattahoochee spring had been "destroyed" by the road builders. A Club hike was made to the Rocky Knob area, and afterward Warner wrote to Mrs. Stutesman: "We found the surveyors' stakes running right by the cabin and about one mile beyond came upon the grading work. . . . We were all in an uproar." The bulletin reported:

A depressed feeling came to the souls of many of us when we reached Rocky Knob cabin on our last trip and found surveyors' stakes for the new CCC Chattahoochee service road running right through the front yard. Less than half a mile over the mountain in each direction was the advance work of the grading crews, which were pushing their way, with this road, into one of the very, very few remaining little regions in which still prevailed the spirit of the wilderness.

On Tuesday, requests were made to the U.S. Forestry Headquarters, and they were met with the greatest cooperation and understanding. The matter was immediately taken up by them, referred by long distance telephone to the offices of the Cherokee National Forest at Athens, Tennessee, and an investigation started. Reports Friday were that the work on the road has been discontinued for some time; that a survey is being made to determine whether the road can be changed to the south side of Rocky Knob, thus leaving this little section of trail and the environs of Rocky Knob cabin, between Red Clay and Henson Gaps, with its wilderness atmosphere.

Of course, the building of this CCC service road has destroyed much of the attractiveness of this entire region, but the splendid cooperation of the Federal Forest Service, thanks to Mr. Kircher, Mr. Stabler and others, brings new hopes to the numbers of us who are planning to spend a week or more of our vacation next year on a wilderness trail far from highways and habitations, tramping and camping in the Georgia mountains.

The road was stopped, as was reported in the bulletin:

It was announced this week from the Atlanta office of the U.S. Forest Service that the road project begun by them last fall to connect Robertstown with Unicoi Gap, by way of Chattahoochee Gap, has been definitely abandoned because of the conflict of the road with the Appalachian Trail in that vicinity and particularly in the region of the Rocky Knob cabin.

Today the old road remains at an abrupt end at Chattahoochee Gap.

The annual meeting of 1934 was to be the biggest and best yet. The bulletin said: "It promises to excel any of those held in the past by a considerable extent." The outstanding attraction was to be the presence of Benton MacKaye. A number of special committees were appointed to handle all of the preparations.

Two other distinguished speakers were to be present: J. C. Kircher, Federal Regional Forester for the southeast, and Colonel Richard A. Gilliam, executive secretary of the Conservation and Development Commission of Virginia. Club members had assembled exhibits of hiking equipment, trail signs, photographs and maps. The bulletin gave the following account of the meeting:

'BEST MEETING I EVER ATTENDED' JUST CLOSED

Since all of our active members except six attended the biggest event in GATC history, there is little real news which we can give about the fifth annual meeting at Cloudland on October 13 and 14. Of these six who failed to attend, three were out of the state and another was sick with flu.

There were so many outstanding features in connection with this meeting that to do justice to them all would require a large booklet. For the first time we passed the hundred mark in attendance and filled all available lodging accommodations in the hotel. Considering the fact that all those attending came from points more than 100 miles away, the gathering was, indeed, significant.

According to the impressions of several people present, the music, exhibits and speeches all harmonized into what our guest of honor termed a 'great symphony.'

Following an invocation dedicated to the Club by Mr. D. M. Therrell, the first address of the evening program was by Mr. J. C. Kircher, who inspired us with his relation of the activities of the Federal Government in the restoration of large wilderness areas in our state through the program of the U. S. Forest Service. As a fitting portion of the introduction to Benton MacKaye, Vaughan Ozmer sang 'The Hills of Home,' a song written by a native Georgian and inspired by the Georgia mountains.

Mr. MacKaye's address was appropriately summed up by Congressman Robert Ramspeck the following morning when he said: 'Philosopher MacKaye has given me a new conception of our modern civilization.' His address was indeed an inspiration and revelation to everyone present.

The banquet gave way to the whomp! whomp! of the big base viol, beating time to the melodies of the fiddle and banjo as the group swung into a 'Four Hands Across' and 'Paul Jones.' As the clock approached two o'clock in the morning everyone sang 'Juanita' around the huge open fire to bring to a close an hour of fireside singing to the accompaniment of 'Sonny' Morris and Dick Smoot with their harmonicas and Bill

Young and his guitar.

The long rattle of a cowbell stirred all guests out Sunday morning for a breakfast at eight, presided over by Eddie Stone. Then Colonel Gilliam, of Richmond, spoke of the restoration and marking of natural and historic points of interest in Virginia, and complimented Georgia on its vast resources in this respect. Several other brief talks, incorporating both humor and seriousness, were enjoyed before the group adjourned, many of them making a trip to 'Rock City,' where R. W. Smith, state geologist, explained the origin of the peculiar rock formations there.

A number of resolutions were passed favoring the establishment of a parks division in the State government, favoring wilderness areas, recreation areas in the national forests, maintenance of the AT as a footpath by the Forest Service, and preservation of its wilderness character, establishment of a landscape unit of the Georgia Highway Department, bird sanctuaries and wildlife refuges in state parks.

Hall was reelected president; Ross Glover, vice president; Rainnie Hoben, treasurer; Cynthia Ward, secretary; and Maude Sewell, corresponding secretary.

Even Stone seemed enthusiastic about the meeting, as he wrote to Hall afterward:

Think everyone who attended the meeting at Cloudland were delighted with the entire meeting and you certainly are to be congratulated on the manner in which it was conducted. Col. Gilliam was very much pleased and very favorably impressed with the people who attended and the manner in which the whole meeting was conducted. It was far better than anything he expected and he told me he enjoyed it more than any meeting of any kind ever attended anywhere, and I know he really meant what he said.

I feel sure everyone enjoyed his talk, and by having people like him and Benton MacKaye, the interest in our activities is very much advanced and more fully brought to the attention of the general public. (October 15, 1934)

Hall wrote to a friend later:

I suppose that others have written you how splendid our annual meeting went off. It was by far the biggest thing we have ever put across and the response was wonderful. We had a capacity crowd, having sent some of the people home Saturday night because we did not have enough beds for everybody. All in all, I think we have a wonderful year ahead of us. (October 22, 1934)

MacKaye's speech seems to have re-hardened Stone's attitude toward road building. He wrote to MacKaye after the meeting:

This meeting was none too timely as we have reached the point even in Georgia where the country is fairly sparsely settled and where the truly wilderness areas are becoming more and more liable to destruction every day.

Enclosed is some correspondence we had with the U. S. Forest Service when they first proposed to start road construction along the Blue Ridge in the Cherokee National Forest. I am sending this correspondence to you as general information on this subject. I wish to call your attention to one paragraph in which the Regional Forester stated that 'The Forest Service will not parallel the Appalachian Trail except in clear cases of public necessity.' Since that day they have constructed a considerable mileage of roads along the Trail and apparently have projected a road over practically the entire length of the Trail through the National Forest in Georgia. We propose to continue to bring pressure to bear and do everything we can to save the Trail from further encroachment regardless of the opposition we may meet. You may retain the enclosed material as I have copies of it in our files.

We certainly appreciated your attending our meeting and hope you will visit us from time to time. (October 18, 1934)

At the meeting the Club presented to everyone present (and sent to others not able to attend) a small bronze pin, or "name badge," a miniature of the hiker figure on the plaques which were erected on the Trail. Many weeks had been spent by numerous members in making these pins. They were poured with newspaper type lead in the *DeKalb New Era* offices, copper plated, antiqued with liver of sulphur, and waxed and polished. Much of the work was done at Chester Elliott's photography studio. Hall wrote of the pins, "Things like these and the plaque have done as much to impress some of the key people in the state and cause them to listen to our plea for the retention of the Appalachian Trail as a footpath through a wilderness territory as anything we have done."

1935

GEORGIA
APPALACHIAN
19 TRAIL CLUB, INC. 30

A S WARNER HALL was to write to Benton MacKaye later in the year of 1935, his and/or the Club's momentum seemed to lag during this year. There are only a few letters of Hall's on record to indicate much activity by him, and he seems to have been busier than ever at his job of running the *DeKalb New Era* newspaper and serving as secretary of the Georgia Press Association. From the vantage of almost fifty years later, one can speculate that Hall had been *too* successful in making the GATC a rollicking, fun-to-be-along kind of group. Hall, in the eyes of many Club members, had *become* the spirit of GATC. When he could no longer devote the time necessary, there was no one who could quite fill his shoes. Too, the Great Depression was worsening, and the type of weekend at a country lodge with meals and an incidental hike was becoming beyond the reach of most members—even at costs of $1.85 per person!

Hall wrote to MacKaye:

Our group has had a good rest for the last six months. . . . We have been somewhat on the wane, principally because our president has slackened his efforts and activities along the wilderness trail. Truly, he has been awfully busy with his newspaper work, but his neglect of his Trail Club duties has served as a brake to such activities in this section. Had his vanity not got the better of his common sense he should have got out of the way and let the others carry on the good work in the fashion it deserves. (August 2, 1935)

Also in the summer of 1935, Stone moved to North Carolina, and his absence no doubt left another large void in the leadership of the Club.

Other Club members were carrying on, however—planning trips under the leadership of Lou Hoben, and carrying out the other routines that kept the Club functioning. The guidebook committee appointed in 1934 to finish the work of getting the trail data in proper order was still struggling with the task. Avery, evidently fed up with the lack of activity concerning the guidebook and the marking of the Trail, wrote Hall a long letter in January, as follows:

There are a number of things in connection with the Trail at the southern end which give me a good deal of concern and I want to take them up with you rather frankly, with a hope that we can work out something definite. The first relates to the marking at the southern end. You have spent, as I know, considerable effort in the way of getting publicity and ornamental signs and highway markers to draw attention to the Trail. I appreciate the necessity for this in the south, but I have a feeling that to some degree you have overlooked the very important essential element of having in existence a well-marked route which the person, whose attention has been drawn to the Trail by the signs, can follow. One becomes discouraged in very short order if he finds that this featured thing is impossible to follow.

I have suggested rather mildly a number of times the desirability of including in your program some of the trail work trips which the Clubs in this region find so popular. This will emphasize the trail aspect of the name of the organization. I have particularly urged that the section from Oglethorpe north should be properly marked, particularly with paint blazes. I have just spent a good part of an hour explaining and apologizing for the lack of any markers at Mt. Oglethorpe. The man who has charge of the Trail in Connecticut drove there but was unable to see the slightest indication of any marking. In fact, he reports a great change in conditions from what I last observed. The road to Oglethorpe is seldom traveled and in one place is scarcely passable. This, of course, makes it all the more satisfactory as a trail and we can even hope that it will not be put in too good condition.

Apparently there is no agency to care for the Mt. Oglethorpe Monument and the Tate Estates are not assuming this burden. Certainly at the shaft there should be some sort of a sign to the effect that this is the southern terminus of the Appalachian Trail. Along the road, metal markers should be placed at such frequent intervals as to be very conspicuous. The continuous paint blazes should carry the route to the Forest Service Trail at Amicalola Falls.

I wish you would discuss this situation at your Council meeting and see if some action cannot be taken to remedy it. It seems to me that it is most essential and I hope that the Club will not be disposed to permit the present situation to continue.

The second matter is this chapter on the guidebook which has been retained in Atlanta for over a year. In fact, I would not be surprised if it had been lost by now. It seems to me that it should be corrected and sent in. Carlos Campbell is arranging to measure the new trail in the Smokies as fast as it is completed and then we will be in a position to issue this book. The Trail Conference budget provides for it. Further, you will remember that someone was to write the chapter on the mountains of northern

Georgia. You will appreciate that if we permit all of these things to wait until the last minute, it will involve a very considerable difficulty and delay. Therefore, it seems to me that this Guidebook Committee which has this manuscript should be told to finish up their task and get the material in shape. We are setting April 1st as a limit for the completion of these side chapters. . . .

You will have noticed how the program of the other Clubs provides for trail work. I appreciate the uncertainty resulting from the Forest Service program, but to make this thing worthwhile in Georgia, we *must* have an adequately marked route, even if some portions are not what we desire. This could be worked out on a series of Club trips. However, instead of the 200 markers which I have sent you from time to time, nearer 2,000 would be required. The Trail Conference could help supply these so as not to make an unnecessary drain on the Club's finances.

No one appreciates more than I the splendid work you have done in Georgia but I do feel that you are overlooking a very important essential, and, as it is my job to point out things of this sort, I am prodding the Club in this connection. If my remarks and suggestions are considered amiss, they can be attributed to a convalescing invalid. . . .

With regards to a chap whose gameness in traveling with completely blistered feet is a thing I will never forget. (January 11, 1935)

The bulletin, published fairly regularly twice a month, except in the summer, gave the account of the various Club activities, notably the record of hikes.

The first hike of the year was supposed to have been from Gooch Gap to Hawk Mountain and the Cherokee Game Refuge at Hightower Gap, with an overnight stay the night before at Zimmer's Lodge in Dahlonega. The day was rainy, and the trip report stated: "Reports of beautiful trees, three members of the group seeing a deer when coming over the mountain, and a statement that there is quite a lovely night club in Dahlonega were gathered from those who went along."

A special invitation was issued to the Club from the Stutesmans at Fort Benning to visit them for the day. This turned out to be a very enjoyable outing, as the bulletin reports: "Has the Club ever made a one day outing which contained so much—such variety?" The variety was: breakfast, a tour of the post, an eight-mile hike, and a "genuine Army dinner." An account of the trip was written for the *Columbus Inquirer:*

The Georgia Appalachian Trail Club made its first tramp in this section of the state Sunday, coming at the invitation of Colonel and Mrs. J. H. Stutesman for a day at Fort Benning.

The trip began, as most of their hiking trips do, with a motorcade to the point of departure. Sunday it was the home of Colonel and Mrs. Stutesman where they were received with the gay comradely greeting one felt certain was reserved for members of the tribe. Here breakfast awaited them, such a breakfast as real hikers enjoy, fried chicken, scrambled eggs, hominy, rolls, coffee with such delicious additions as baked apples, marmalades, preserves.

And between mouthfuls one listened with open eyed amazement to their talk of eight, ten, twelve mile hikes in rain, sun, snow. Snow, it seems, is the piece de resistance of the GATC program for when scouters from the mountains wire their chief, one 'Red Hall,' that snow is falling a veritable grapevine system carries the word along. Then off they go for a day of tramping in the snow, not over straight roads, but up mountains and down hills. And then if things go well, and they are lucky, there is a night on the trail! Such amazing tastes people have, but the strangest part of it was that listening you were filled with a longing to strap a pack to your back, to get one of the much talked-of new sleeping bags and try it yourself! Did I tell you they were a fascinating lot of people?

The author relates the events of the day, and ends the article:

Vivid, charming people these GATC folk are with an enviable zest for life and an amazing youthfulness. One hated to see them leave after breakfast for their hike and return to Columbus, to spend a conventional Sabbath.

In March the Club joined the Smoky Club and the Benton Trail Blazers for a hike to Benton Falls. A highlight of the trip was the presence of Benton MacKaye. The bulletin reported:

PRIMITIVE WOMEN AT BENTON FALLS

'It takes real he men and sort of primitive women to make that climb at Benton Falls,' said one of our gang who went, saw, survived and returned from our trip on February 24. Other reports state that possibly, with one or two exceptions, those in our group were the first women to make that hike to Benton Falls. It was reported by several to have been one of the stiffest hikes we have ever made—steep climbing right up the sheer side of rocky ledges by the aid of ropes, traveling through dense undergrowth with blazes as the only means of keeping to the course, and pushing through briars 'as big as your arm.' The hike might well have been termed a hike up a waterfall rather than up a creek to a fall, since Falls Creek actually consists of twelve important waterfalls.

More than one hundred people assembled at the top falls for lunch. These consisted of more than thirty of the Smoky Mountains Hiking Club, twenty from our own Club, seventeen from the Benton Trail Blazers and the remainder from 'round about.' All of these didn't make the stiff climb up the creek. Much praise was expressed for Al Mills and Rosalie Edmondson for pushing and pulling to keep the crowd together, while the Benton Trail Blazers escorted and lifted the hikers up the mountainside. To be on another hike with Benton MacKaye was the cause for much delight for us Georgia hikers.

A planned trip from Neel Gap to Tesnatee Gap and down the old road south from Tesnatee was rained out, and the group spent a pleasant day at Butternut Lodge.

A camping trip to Head River, near Rock City, elicited the following bulletin report:

ROCK CITY CAMPING TRIP BRINGS DEMAND FOR MORE CAMPS

The best camping and hiking authorities say, 'Modify plans if necessary, but don't cancel a trip, because the weatherproof minority are worthy of consideration.' Though overcast skies greeted the even dozen of us who were planning to go on the spring camping trip on Lookout Mountain last Saturday, not a one backed out on the pretense of Aunt Minnie coming to town unexpectedly or something else of that sort.

You will recall that the weather had been cold and wet for the preceding two weeks, and gave us no encouragement as we journeyed toward our destination Saturday afternoon. We got into a rainstorm on the way, passengers called for their coats and we slipped in the mud. Our only hope was the weatherman's last report—but what was that worth?

At Mentone, Alabama, the first car stopped to make tentative arrangements for the party to get accommodations at a local hotel—'Please quote rates without cover charge. We have our own sleeping bags.' We might not find the camp site or care to stay.

However, after slipping and sliding for several miles and fording three streams we came to a cardboard sign tacked on a tree. 'GATC camp this way.' There were others farther on and, in time, we sighted a campfire through the darkness. Once at that fire, started during the afternoon by our host, everything was all right. In short order the campfire was surrounded by a circle of pup tents and the aroma of coffee and frying potatoes. The moon was shining from a clear sky before we retired.

Although there was heavy frost on the tents and a little ice about camp the next morning, everyone who had a sleeping bag reported a warm night, although extra blankets and thermats were found among the equipment of some of them. There were reports that 'varmints' were prowling around camp during the night, but it took little detective work to disclose that these (and 'varmints' would have really been preferred) were actually Arthur Stokes and Lloyd Adams, whose feet were too big to get into their tent and had to be toasted before the fire at frequent intervals.

Other trips for the year included: Tallulah Gorge; Lookout Mountain—a joint hike with the Cumberland Hiking Club; Yonah Mountain; Lakemont on Lake Rabun; Dick's Creek to Addis Gap and down Moccasin Creek—"through one of the roughest stretches of real wilderness that we have visited"; Grassy Knob in the Cohuttas; the Indian Mounds near Macon; Thanksgiving at the Dillard Farm with a hike to Ridgepole.

In March MacKaye visited the Club on his first trip to Atlanta and, according to the bulletin, "revealed to us a wonderful opportunity." This opportunity was explained to the Club at a special meeting by R. W. Smith, Club member and Georgia state geologist. Benton MacKaye had, in his article, "The Appalachian Trail, a Guide to the Study of Nature," (printed in the *Scientific Monthly*, April, 1932) expounded his theory of a trail that would follow a stream from its beginning to its end in order to study the different "zones": "weathering breakage, grinding, removal and deposit, and ultimate deposit." It was his wish that such a stream could be found near the AT and used as a "geological study trail."

The task of finding the perfect stream was to be the new "and in many respects the most important of our projects," according to the bulletin. Trips were made to examine the stream from Nottely Falls near Neel Gap as it flowed over Helton Falls and out to Choestoe. This stream, as reported, "would have been perfect, physiographically, had it not been cut over" by the Vogel Lumber Company and "tree stumps, sawdust piles, edgings and miles of plank road have spoiled the beauty of this place for the next 25 years."

They then followed a stream out of Wolf Pen Gap, which turned out not to show the different zones clearly. Other streams suggested were Moccasin Creek, High Shoals Creek and Corbin Creek. MacKaye himself was also searching for such a trail, and solicited the help of Dick Smith in checking it out.

A "four-club outing" was held at Standing Indian in July, with the Smoky Mountains Hiking Club, Nantahala Club, Carolina Club, and GATC attending. According to the bulletin: "Because it has so consistently resisted our attempts, a joint expedition . . . is planned for a grand charge to the summit."

MacKaye joined the clubs for the outing. On writing to him afterward and saying that the GATC was "somewhat on the wane," Hall continued:

Our little conference in the rain on Standing Indian worked wonders with us. . . . I thought of another meeting, almost two thousand years ago on the Mount of Olives. It was just a little group, but how great has been the expanse of its influence? I am sure that great things will also come from that meeting of just a little handful of folks on Standing Indian, but all big moments have a small beginning like that. We are all pepped up—raring to go. Just tell us what to do next.

Plans were made for the "First Annual Photographic Competitive Exhibit" to be held at the annual meeting this year. The purpose was "to provide a recreational contest, which will stimulate a general interest in photography among all members and applicants to the Club." Subject matter, awards and rules for entry were published in the bulletin.

In September square dance practice was begun and a "prep" get together held for the annual meet.

The meeting was held on October 12 and, according to the bulletin, "can best be described in superlatives—the most people, the snappiest songs, the liveliest square dance, the biggest moon, the finest exhibits, the warmest sun, the most speeches, the thickest dust." Among the guest speakers was Charlie Elliott, "charter member of the Georgia Appalachian Trail Club," and "our own Benton MacKaye," who gave "an unusually inspiring talk." Officers elected for the coming year were: Carter Whittaker, president; George H. Noble, vice president; Berma Jarrard, treasurer; Grace Ficken, secretary; Maude Sewell, corresponding secretary; and Warner Hall, executive council. William H. Carr from Bear Mountain, New York, was invited to speak at the annual meeting. He was unable to come, although he did visit the following year. In writing to him

Charlie Elliott was trying to give him an idea on what sort of speech to make. He evidently realized the need for rekindling of Club spirits, for he wrote:

As for the speech, this is the situation. The Trail Club members are composed of all sorts and types of people. Few of them are interested in the various sciences, as ornithology, biology, or dendrology as a science, but they are in the Club because they are outdoor enthusiasts. They love the woods for the sunshine and shadows in them, and for the coolness, rather than because they are merely full of birds, or because they have a hundred species of trees. They love the Trail because it takes them into the hills, and not merely because they are going somewhere on it. So your talk should be something along the lines of philosophy, and with soul stirring themes, as well as with a bit of general scientific knowledge and a lot of stories thrown in. That is rather a vague order, but perhaps it will give you something to build on. I want you to move that crowd as they have never been moved before. (September 3, 1935)

The CCC crest roads were still progressing. The bulletin in May reported:

The AT between Southern's Store and Nimblewill Gap was inspected this past weekend by a small party of GATC members, who spent Saturday night in the shelter at Amicalola Falls. The group went up Saturday afternoon, parking its cars at the base of the falls, and followed the steep trail up the right side of the falls to the shelter. The party reported a wonderful trip, Amicalola Falls at its best, but that the trail had been changed considerably by road construction.

A CCC forest service road now follows the general course of the Trail all the way from Nimblewill Gap to Southern's Store. On Sunday the party drove cars by the Amicalola shelter. Several wooden signs were replaced and metal markers erected. The Amicalola shelter and its surroundings were found in good condition except that the fence which protected it from stock had been entirely removed and several trees nearby had been cut down.

The party consisted of Maude Sewell, Grace Ficken, Lou Hoben, Mrs. J. D. Abercrombie, Carter Whittaker and Warner Hall. It is hoped that other trips may be arranged during the near future to inspect the remainder of the Georgia section of the Trail.

The seventh Appalachian Trail Conference was held in 1935 at Skylands, Virginia, but no one from the GATC was able to attend.

MacKaye was invited to the Christmas party that year, but he wrote his regrets as follows:

Merrily I thank you for sending me your attractive invitation to the gathering of the Clan GATC. You have no idea how those four letters GATC affect me. They send a lightening thrill right through my being from northeast to southwest. For me they stand for Gladness, Art, Thought, Culture; they bring a smile to the eye and a song to the ear. Mournfully, however, I must send you my regrets instead of myself and my best Scotch manners. Wouldn't I like to go and help carry in the Yule log? Wouldn't I though! And I'll do it in Thought—which goes with A for Affection to each and every GATC. . . .

1936

GEORGIA
APPALACHIAN
19 TRAIL CLUB, INC. 30

In January of 1936 Carter Whittaker, the newly elected president, was transferred to Balsam Grove, North Carolina. Early in the year Whittaker wrote to Noble, officially giving him the power to act in his absence and carry out all of the duties of the presidency. He gave him instructions and suggestions about a number of things, saying, "I am writing all committee chairmen today to try and create a little more aggressiveness on their part. . . . We are badly in need of less politics in the Club and more outings—less entertainment and more back to nature spirit. I have been so busy up here I have not given these matters proper attention but hope to be more active in the future." He advised that the membership policy be liberalized, executive council meetings be called frequently, and that a strong outing program be instituted. He continues, "Committee chairmen *must* cooperate in spite of personal differences or the Club will perish. I strongly suggest . . . a revision of the constitution. I am going to have to depend on you to keep the . . . Club going full blast."

The Club, however, continued to decline. As Lloyd Adams was to write in 1937, ". . . the failure of one member to function" had paralyzed the Club. One can only conjecture that the "one member" referred to was Dr. Noble.

Although the facts of the situation cannot be verified, several factors were probably at the root of the problem. The Club had almost become inactive in Hall's last year of presidency. Whittaker could not fill the void left by Hall's early years—and it is doubtful that any one could have at this time. Even in the first months of his presidency, Whittaker was stationed in a remote CCC camp in North Georgia, nearly 100 miles of unpaved road from Atlanta and the in-town parties and all the other social functions which had become a tradition in the Club. Further, when Stone left, all the CCC's resentment at work done on the Trail by Whittaker under Stone's direction resulted in his (Whittaker's) being virtually fired. He was fighting for his job. Also, factions had developed in the Club, each probably fighting for the "power" void left by Hall's neglect and Whittaker's absence. Some wanted to put the Club on a more businesslike, structured basis, and others viewed the Club as primarily a social group. Finally, Dr. Noble, vice president of the Club and sculptor of the hiker plaque, was not a strong leader. He was going through a divorce about this time, and was probably unable to carry out the duties of the absent president satisfactorily. His popular wife, Martha, was an active member of the Club, and remained so for over 20 years, but Dr. Noble resigned in August. So the factions continued while membership steadily declined.

A meeting was called by President Whittaker (in town for the occasion) late in August for the purpose of discussing "revival of activities and enthusiasm and particularly to consider holding of annual meeting." A vice president to replace Dr. Noble was also to be elected. At the meeting, which only 18 people attended, Rainnie Hoben was elected to the vice presidency. He served for only two weeks and pointedly resigned over policies with which he could not agree. Also at the meeting a resolution was passed that the constitution be changed to elect officers in September, to be installed and take office in October at the annual meeting. The resolution, however, was not the official means to change the constitution, and some were opposed to officers being elected at the September meeting.

Nonetheless the annual meeting was held in September at Connahaynee Lodge, with the usual speeches, dancing, eating and singing. Officers elected were: Lloyd Adams, president; Lane Mitchell, vice president; Clyde Passmore, secretary; Berma Jarrard, treasurer; Maude Sewell, corresponding secretary; Carter Whittaker, executive council.

But all was not yet well, according to a letter from former secretary Grace Ficken to Whittaker a short time after the meeting. She wrote:

We (Marene S., Chester, Warner, Lloyd and I) held an executive meeting last night. There has been some discussion as to the election of officers at the annual meeting being unconstitutional. While reading from the constitution last night we found that the exec. meeting we had called was also unconstitutional.

So—what?

Anyhow we would like to know if there is any chance of your being in town within the next 30 days to call a business meeting of Club members. Or in case you cannot come down will you appoint a president pro tempore—probably Lloyd since he is elected to carry on next year?

This will enable him to call a meeting to discuss the disorganization there seems to be in the Club. And we can then approve the things that have taken place outside of the constitution and can revise it as the members see fit to take care of such details.

I'm sure everyone accepts the election as it was held, but since going into the details of the constitution, several feel that it would be better to put it before the entire Club. (October 8, 1936)

(There is no doubt in the minds of present-day historians that this was yet another move by one group to discredit the election and somehow to cling to the past "golden years" of Hall's presidency, which were fast slipping away without his charismatic leadership.)

In spite of the difficulties and lack of strong leadership throughout most of 1936, activities continued more or less as usual. Hikes were fairly well attended, and early in the year several well-known personalities visited the Club.

In 1935 Hall had, with the help of MacKaye, tried to interest Stuart Chase, noted economist and writer, and Robert Marshall of the Bureau of Indian Affairs, in coming to Atlanta to speak to the GATC. The correspondence was successful, and in January, 1936, Robert Marshall came to town and gave an illustrated lecture on Alaska. Later in the year—in November—Stuart Chase came for "one of the most thrilling, the most enjoyable and most inspiring functions in the annals of the GATC. . . ."

In February Myron Avery came for a visit to the Club. He had earlier hoped to come to Atlanta for a demonstration of blazing techniques, but had not had an opportunity. He gave "an illustrated talk . . . on trail scouting and building," and "presented final plans for the publication of the southern guide to the Trail . . . [which] should be ready for distribution within the next few weeks." An article appeared in *Forestry-Geological Review* on his visit and his talk and said:

The pictures of the splendid cabins and accommodations maintained by the northern clubs for the travelers were very impressive. When Mr. Avery spoke of the increased interest in skiing and stated that the sport was becoming popular as far south as Washington, D.C., he expected to surprise his audience. The tables were turned, however, when to his astonishment pictures were shown of the Georgia Club engaging in all the winter sports during the recent cold spell.

The lack of pictures of the 100 miles of the Trail in Georgia was a source of some embarrassment to the Georgia Club, for although the Trail is adequately maintained and four overnight cabins have been constructed, pictures of these improvements had not been sent to Mr. Avery as he had requested.

The previous year, Charlie Elliott had invited his friend, William H. Carr, Director of the Trailside Museum at Bear Mountain and Assistant Curator of the American Museum of Natural History, to speak at the GATC annual meeting. He was unable to come at the time, but did come in 1936 and spoke to the Club. He "delighted his select audience . . . with two illustrated lectures"—on the Trail in New York, and on the life of the beaver.

Whittaker, having been primarily concerned in the past with trail work, pushed this aspect of the Club's function. Maurice Abercrombie as trail supervisor organized the first "walk through"—or, as it was called, "trail and shelter reconnoitering trip" in March. The membership was divided into "squads" covering each section of Trail in two weekends, thus carrying out the mandate given them: "It shall be the duty of the sectional maintenance squads to make a reconnaissance of their section of the Trail as soon as possible and report their findings to the supervisor in writing." The bulletin account read:

The month of March has been trail blazing and clearing month. With so many clearing squads at work all along the Trail it is impossible to relate, in detail, the experiences which were had. One interesting revelation was the reaction to these clearing trips by a large portion of the membership. More than one expressed himself as having got a real 'kick' out of the trip, in fact, sort of preferred it to the regular run of outings.

Equipped with forester's long handled pruning shears, trail markers and axes, small clearing parties have removed fallen trees and brush sufficiently from sections of the Trail to make it possible for a person to walk along without going through a series of setting up exercises for every 100 yards. There's a lot of more work to be done, but by the time the city tender feet are ready to hit the trail on their summer vacations it should be ready for them.

The first outing of 1936 was a "snow trip." Because of the bad roads and "at sight of a fine snow bank and an ice-covered lake the cars—et cetera—refused to go further," the trip ended for some at Gainesville. Others who had started on Friday reached Highlands, North Carolina, and "found it to be a little Switzerland." They requested in the bulletin, "Pray for more cold weather, get your ice skates sharpened and be ready to leave on a moment's notice."

A "mystery trip" took the place of an unpopular scheduled hike to Neel Gap, and the bulletin account read:

It seems that the continuous bad weather had finally dampened the ardour of the members; anyway no great enthusiasm was displayed for a camping trip at the Gap on February 14-15.

However, a few of the more intrepid pioneers met at the Bear Pen early Sunday morning and immediately went into a huddle as to where snow might be found, and a decision having been made we again mounted the cars and galloped off in search of hardship.

After considerable driving and considerable hiking thru snow 10 inches deep in places—Warner says 12—and over large sheets of ice, we arrived at a most delightful cabin and the party, divided into three groups, Coffee Cooks, Fuel Gatherers and Housekeepers, under the direction respectively of Berma, Marion and Cynthia, soon had a fire that would have done credit to the Christmas party, coffee as advertised by the Waldorf, although the water had to be provided by melting vast quantities of snow, and a dining room as spotless and well furnished as your own parlor. Soon the crowd was reveling in a sumptuous repast of sandwiches, coffee and other delicacies fit for a king, and a red hot trail club argument was well under way.

The afternoon was devoted to further exploration and we discovered a beautiful lake high up in the mountains which will bear further looking into. It was so inviting and the weather had become so warm that force had to be used to restrain some of the men from throwing off their clothes and plunging in among the ice cakes.

Supper at Cinciolla's during which more minor matters were discussed in a weighty manner completed the day, which was declared a howling success by all.

A planned trip to what is now Providence Canyon was described in the bulletin thus:

With camping on the banks of the Hannahatchee and an exhibition of Georgia's worst soil erosion, the trip should be most interesting and enjoyable. The 'Caves' as they are known locally, or 'The Grand Canyon of Georgia' as they were described in *National Geographic,* have grown from a tiny wash caused by water falling from the roof of a barn, so tradition puts it, many years ago until now the entire business area of Atlanta could be placed in them. The walls of the canyon, composed of innumerable strata of earth, exhibit a riot of color.

Other trips for the year included an outdoor breakfast and hike along the Amicalola River; a hike along Duke's Creek to Hudson's Gold Mine; Rock City and Lookout Mountain; Head River and Sitton's Gulch; Highlands, North Carolina, and Ellicott's Rock; the Dillard Farm; camping at Vogel Park and a hike from Neel Gap to Blood Mountain, with almost 40 people, "one of the largest weekend groups in recent years"; Cheaha Mountain, the highest point in Alabama; Thanksgiving dinner at the Dillard Farm and a hike up Picken's Nose.

The Southern Regional Conference "did not materialize" in 1936. The clubs made an effort to get together in June for a joint hike in North Carolina, but the GATC members were unable to go because of the long car trip involved.

In October Avery wrote to sing his sad refrain once again in a letter to Maurice Abercrombie:

I feel very much in disgrace.

After my trip to Atlanta, I had been proclaiming loud and long that the deficiency of marking at Mt. Oglethorpe had been remedied. Apparently your overseers failed you in this particular. You will remember that visitors to Oglethorpe had commented decidedly unfavorably upon the complete lack of any marking on the southern end and as we were feeling rather sensitive over this, you and I thought that we would be able to get it remedied and put an end to this rather unfortunate publicity. The comment of the Supervisor of Trails of the Mountain Club of Maryland in the enclosed Bulletin speaks for itself. Let's make this the last adverse comment. Won't you take the matter up with the Club officers and arrange to get this cared for immediately? Plaster the section with markers and arrange some sort of sign at the southern end. I would suggest a duplicate of what appears on Katahdin. . . .

I do feel that this is very serious and I hope that you will push the matter vigorously with the Club and see that the trouble is remedied. Warner Hall has a good supply of markers.

I shall be very glad to hear from you and to know what has been accomplished in the way of improving the marking since last spring. (October 12, 1936)

Another letter in October from Avery to the members of the ATC Board of Managers announced plans for the first meeting of this body, saying:

It seemed to me that an opportunity for the members of the Board to get together would be of very considerable benefit in solving our numerous problems. . . . There are many things of long range aspect and of great importance to the Conference which can be discussed at this time. For one instance, I have in mind the possibility of undertaking a campaign to bring areas adjacent to the Trail into some sort of preserve which will protect the Trail region and afford it a sort of public status. We may be very well able, in the areas federally owned, to induce government officials to establish a narrow strip along the Trail as a reservation and this protection can be progressively extended to privately owned areas as the opportunity arises, without involving questions of the establishment of rights of way, etc., which are always stumbling blocks in these situations. (October 12, 1936)

The meeting was held on November 7, and the minutes reported, among other things:

Mr. Avery spoke of his visit to the Georgia Appalachian Trail Club last spring and the improvements in the system for trail maintenance which were being initiated by Supervisor of Trails, Maurice Abercrombie. In view of the criticisms received as to the lack of marking at Mt. Oglethorpe and for a distance of some five miles north along the route, the Board voted that the Georgia Appalachian Trail Club be requested to have a suitable marker placed at Mt. Oglethorpe and other adequate marking on the route north, so as to put an end to comments as to inadequate marking at the southern terminus.

As was also reported in the Board minutes, the activity of the Nantahala Hiking Club had ceased due to the death of its president and Board member George Tabor. As his wife had written earlier in the year, "The club at Almond is not very active and another thing the young men are most all scattered to the four winds." The Board minutes reported: "Mr. Carlos Campbell had been in touch with the very active Balsam Mountains Hiking Club at Waynesville, North Carolina, who are interested in taking over a section of the Trail and it was voted by the Board to request Mr. Campbell to make contact with this group and request them, on behalf of the Conference, to assume responsibility for this region [in the Nantahala National Forest]."

After the ATC Board meeting, a letter came to Abercrombie from the ATC assistant secretary as follows:

Mr. Avery spoke in detail of his visit to Georgia and the very active program which you were initiating in the way of dividing the Georgia Trail into sections with the view of improving the maintenance and condition of the Trail. The difficulties and handicaps experienced in Georgia are fully understood by the Board and your energetic action in connection with these difficulties was very much appreciated.

There is, however, one matter which, in view of the number of communications which have been received, is such that we feel should be immediately remedied. Perhaps it has already been attended to. The Conference has received a number of complaints from visitors to the southern terminus of the Trail that the road from Mt. Oglethorpe monument for a distance of five miles has no marking of the route. We understand that you have an ample supply of Trail markers and the Board requested that you endeavor to organize an expedition to Mt. Oglethorpe as soon as possible for the purpose of marking this road with Trail markers and paint blazes so well that there would be no further complaint. It was suggested that you could arrange to have made for Mt. Oglethorpe a board sign similar to Katahdin. . . .

In view of the interest manifested in the condition of the Trail at the southern terminus, I trust that you will be able to have the suggestion of the Board carried out in the very near future and that you will be good enough to let me know when this has been accomplished so that the Board may be advised accordingly. (November 24, 1936)

In 1936 MacKaye returned to Massachusetts from Tennessee. He wrote in December to Marene Snow:

Your colorful summons has come to 'gather as of old' for the GATC Christmas revelry. Instructions are to 'call Marene Snow for reservations.' How I wish this were such a call! The thought makes me homesick. Those songs and legends and 'crackling flames' tend to lure me from my northern lair and fly to you while those red candles yet light up the joyous faces that form now part of my most festive and most tender memories.

I'm back in the self-same corner of the self-same den where, just fifteen years ago, I wintered and dreamed dreams of the Appalachian Trail and the life thereon and adjacent unto. At times it would seem that some of them might be coming true. One such time was on receiving this Christmas summons. The life imagined was such a one as you folks of Georgia seem to vision.

So much of life falls between two stools: if it's constructive it becomes a cheerless chore; if recreative it becomes a blowout and fails to truly re-create. But you folks ride two steeds—whatever the creative undertaking (on the open trail or in the Christmas hall) the voice of joy rings out. . . .

I'll be thinking of you on the evening of the 18th and expect to feel your wavelengths from this distance. My affectionate greetings to you all. . . .

1937

GEORGIA
APPALACHIAN
19 TRAIL CLUB, INC. 30

AFTER HE WAS NAMED president pro tempore by Carter Whittaker, Lloyd Adams, a professor at the Emory University Medical School, began right away to try to organize and revitalize the Club. He sent to all Club members the following letter, with an accompanying questionnaire:

Over the summer months the activity of the Club gives way to our personal plans for the vacation period. The Trail Club is largely relegated to the back of our minds with mental reservations of resumed interest in the fall. The autumn season is here now, and the inevitable urge to get back on the Trail has become a dominant feeling to many of us. Who can remember the gorgeous splendor of a view from the mountain-top across the carpet of flaming colored trees, to the peaks in the blue haze beyond, without a sense of nostalgia? To many of us the desire to see these panoramas and symphonies in nature is even more urgent than the longing to return home after a protracted absence. In the past year the Club has weathered a number of storms created by disruptions in its organization, and the advent of the hiking season finds the good ship 'GATC,' though somewhat scarred, ready for another voyage laden with a cargo of spirit and enthusiasm taken on at the Tavern meeting of August 29th, the recent meeting at the Tate Mountain Estates, and the more recent barbecue at the Dillard Farm—Um-mm-h!!

Our president, Carter Whittaker, has delegated me, with the approval of the Executive Council, to carry on in his absence as president pro tempore. With your cooperation we should like to see the Club realize what promises to be a very successful year. The *Club* is stronger than its weakest link, but it is able to accomplish its objectives fully only with the interest and help of each and every member. Can we count on you for practical interest and support?

I would welcome from you a letter or memorandum expressing your ideas and suggestions on the policies and activities of the Club for the future. Feel free to discuss any phase you may wish, but unless you hold very little interest in the Club, please lend me the help which your communication will bring in planning the future. Is the Club worth an hour of serious thought to you? I hope to bring together the ideas gathered in this manner and present them to the entire Club for discussion. Do you not think this will be of value? And do you not think that such a meeting will be interesting? On the enclosure I have brought up a number of questions which seem to me to be pertinent at this time for attaining some measure of efficiency in the Club henceforth. Will you not answer these and include them with your suggestions to me?

Shall we all put a little extra effort in building even higher, the spirit, interest and morale of the Georgia Appalachian Trail Club? I know that if we do, we will all be well repaid in the satisfaction which will come in seeing the old exuberance of happiness which will permeate our midst as we gather round the festive board at the Dillard Farm, as we are wont to do each Thanksgiving time. (October 1936)

The questionnaire asked about personal commitment to the Club, suggested changes in policies or activities, and gave suggestions for a proposed revision of the Club constitution.

In his reply to this, R. W. (Dick) Smith told Adams: "I have a feeling that you are going to make the Club a darned good president. Don't be surprised if the members turn to Warner, instead of you, to pass on things; they have been doing it so many years that it has got to be a habit."

A committee was appointed to write a new constitution, and the proposed draft was distributed at the Christmas party in 1936. In a letter in the January bulletin, Adams wrote: "The Committee on Constitution has worked faithfully in formulating a constitution for the Club which will obviate many of the difficulties experienced in our organization in the past. . . . You are responsible now for a critical reading and re-reading. . . . A vote is now called. . . ." A ballot was attached to be returned. Only seventeen ballots were received—14 for and three against. The new constitution was declared adopted at the next Board meeting in 1937.

Adams sent a letter to each member saying:

The purpose of this letter is to attempt to clarify the objective toward which we are working in the reorganization of the Club under the constitution adopted January 27, 1937. You are urged to read over the constitution and by-laws after reading this letter, and ask yourself if you believe that, once in practice, we will be able to conduct the Club with the minimum of red tape possible with a maximum of efficiency and enjoyment. We believe so.

In the letter, Adams described the responsibilities of the committees to meet and submit reports. "Thus, committees, meeting about once a month, are practically the backbone of the organization, and if any committee fails to function properly, the Club is seriously handicapped." He explained the provision for regular council meetings and only occasional meetings of the whole Club. "Each member is not only privileged, but urged personally, to communicate in writing with any officer. . . on any phase of the Club's activity." He went on:

The institution of any change naturally meets with considerable inertia, and until we all understand the plan and objective of our reorganization, there will be misunderstandings, and much work for a few members. However, we are at the point where we can put the plan into effect if each member will do a small amount of work. When the initial load is overcome, the Club should be able to run smoothly and efficiently without claiming more than one or two evenings per month from any member except officers. (January 1937)

Adams wrote "to each committee chairman:"

In order to fulfill the requirements of By-laws Chapter XI, section 3, I would like to see each committee organized with a Chairman, Vice-chairman, Secretary and Assistant secretary. It is especially important that a permanent written record of committee meetings be kept.
   Will you each please let me have the names of those individual members whom you wish to be on your committee? Each member of the Club will be on some committee and in many cases more than one. Thus it may not be possible to give you everybody you want, and on the other hand, some members may want to work on your committee and would be a good worker on such committee, although you would not at this time have such individual in mind. . . .
   To expedite matters, each chairman should obtain all records of activity from last year's committee chairman, and be ready to call a meeting of his or her committee as soon as possible after the committees are completed. I hope to be able to meet with each committee, especially during its first meeting.
   The purpose of committee organization as mentioned above is to prevent the non-function of the committee in case of temporary absence of its chairman or secretary.
   I am counting on each of you to help me have things well organized by the February 25th meeting. That date should mark the accomplishment of the reorganization of the Club under the provisions of the new constitution. At any time a letter or memorandum on some aspect of the Club's work will be most welcome from any chairman. (February 12, 1937)

Adams seemed optimistic about the Club reorganization for a time, and on February 15 wrote to W. D. Young, "I believe that the Club is going places from now on. . . .
   But the minutes of the February 25 Board meeting reveal a different attitude:

The president mentioned that the acceptance of an office and its privileges entailed also responsibilities, deplored the present-day trend to shirk responsibilities. He discussed the opposing views concerning the organization of the Club. Some members prefer the loosest possible organization, others a definite, efficiently functioning organization. The new constitution provides for the latter. The length has been criticized, but only two pages are pertinent to the membership at large, the balance gives in details the duties of officers and committees.

The president was very much disheartened by the apparent lack of cooperation of members. He read a letter sent to the chairman of each committee, requesting a list of the desired membership of the committee to be announced at the business meeting, and suggestions for the better functioning of the Club. There had been no response. The Outing Committee, Cynthia Ward, chairman, seemed to be the only one functioning. There was also dissatisfaction with the continued delay in the publication of the bulletin. The president expressed the view another leader might be able to secure the cooperation of the Club, offered his resignation, and turned the chair over to Lane Mitchell, first vice president. Mr. Therrell immediately made a motion, seconded by Marene Snow, that the president be asked to withdraw his resignation. This was unanimously carried by the Club. On the promise of the members to give him active support, Lloyd agreed to continue to serve as president.

In a letter to Guy Frizzell in May, Adams wrote:

Under a new constitution which was adopted this year, the affairs of this Club are in the hands of a Council composed of its officers and three members-at-large. For several years this Club was only loosely organized and Warner Hall had all responsibility. Press of business forced him to relinquish most of this work and for the past year he has been almost inactive. In the meantime we are trying to direct communications and business of the Club to the Council in line with this change. This Council meets regularly and our objective is to establish the Club on such basis that the failure of one member to function will not paralyze the Club—an experience which we are just past. (May 19, 1937)

Frizzell replied:

We note that your Club has recently gone through a period of reorganization and that the new set-up seems to be doing quite well. We are darn glad to hear this for you have much too fine a group of people there to let the Club play out. More power to you and to all the other Georgia Appalachian Trail Club members. (May 26, 1937)

The first trip of the year was a new one—to Walker (or Wauka) Mountain, near Cleveland. On the damp and windy winter day steaks were cooked for lunch under a large rocky bluff on top of the mountain.

Mable Abercrombie demonstrated her "champion" hiking abilities as noted in the following January bulletin account:

Bob Marshall, who treated us to an Arctic exploration last January, paid a pop call to the Georgia section of the Appalachian Trail the weekend of January 9th. After camping on top of Blood Mountain with Maurice, Mable and Clyde, he set out with Mable early Sunday morning for Hightower Gap. The walking was so good they went on two and one-half miles past Winding Stair Gap. This makes the 36th state in which Bob has made a day's hike of at least 30 miles. . . .

The next trip, in February, was a work trip between Neel and Tesnatee Gaps with the night before spent at Vogel State Park. A truck took them to within two and a half miles of Tesnatee Gap. The bulletin described the trip:

AND SO — FAR INTO THE NIGHT!

Despite lowering skies Saturday afternoon, eighteen Trail Clubbers gathered at Vogel State Park determined to let the rain dampen anything except their spirits. Lieutenant Welborn had built fires in the cabin so that it was quite cozy and cheerful as the cooks felt pioneerish and vied in broiling steaks in the open fireplaces. After everyone had eaten enough for a long hard winter, there was singing and accordion playing in the firelight. Then, miracle of miracles—the rain stopped, the stars shone out, and some of the nocturnal prowlers took a midnight stroll around the end of the lake to the dam and waterfall.

The reveille sounded all too soon Sunday morning. After a hurried breakfast, the group met their open-air truck at the gap and left, nearly on schedule, for an exhilarating ride to the approach to Tesnatee. Everyone was so eager to get started that the truck was dismissed even before the destination was reached, and the hikers gaily disembarked to live up to their name.

In a short time they hiked the two and one-half miles to Tesnatee. After a lively argument, the tools were apportioned, and vigorous trail clearing begun. It was difficult to stop the axe-wielders, the clippers, the bushwhackers, etc., long enough for lunch, but the burden-bearers prevailed at a clearing which overlooks the valley and range after range of mountains—one of the loveliest views on the trail. Alas and alack! Snelly-bo had been brought in vain. The scouts could find no spring. Canteens and fruit juices were produced, however, and only confirmed coffee-drinkers suffered from thirst. During the siesta, an astronomer spied a star, and to their amazement, the other seventeen could see it, too—at two o'clock in the afternoon. How appreciative they were for the light of that same star a few hours later.

The chestnut sprouts, huckleberry bushes, and briars were then attacked with renewed vigor for an hour or two. A few of the workers became uneasy about being in the mountains after dark and began a rapid hegira for Neel Gap. In their headlong rush they lost the trail. The path they made in their flight was the one followed by the workers; so, nightfall found eighteen jolly hikers thrashing around in brush and brambles, far from Uncle Bob's, far from the Trail. The first group eventually reached the highway about four miles from Neel Gap. The hikers were unsuccessful hitch-hikers. Finally they reached the gap, organized a search party (to the amusement of the wayfarers at the lodge), and met the other group, which had found the Trail on Levelland Mountain, but were glad to have lantern light for the descent.

After a happy reunion, and hot soup and coffee, the weary hikers wended their way homeward. Accomplishment: one mile well cleared—Tesnatee to Cow Rock Mountain. Resolve: never again to hike without flashlights. Never again to desert the leader.

(In May a return trip was made through this section and the bulletin caption read: "Hikers go over Levelland, do not get lost.")

Also in February an exploring trip was made to try to find an approach trail to Oglethorpe and to relocate the actual terminus to a spot with a better viewpoint of the valley and foothills. The trip was "not entirely successful," and another trip was planned later in the year.

In May there was a camping trip to Amicalola Falls, with a round-trip hike to Nimblewill Gap, which, according to the bulletin, "was very elusive."

"The largest group ever to attend a camping trip—23, not counting Tinkum, a dog"—made another trip to Sitton's Gulch late in May.

Ten "adventurous Trail Clubbers" in September made the Club's first trip to the Black Warrior Forest in Alabama. According to a newspaper account, headlined "Trail Club Group Here Gets Lost in Big Forest": "A dozen enthusiastic hikers from Atlanta became lost in the Black Warrior Forest near Jasper, Alabama, over the weekend holiday and spent twelve hours wandering without food or shelter before they finally made their way without assistance back to their starting point. The group. . . plunged into the forest to visit some of its more interesting and historical sections. Within two hours the party became lost and wandered without knowing their whereabouts for more than twelve hours. . . . Much of the night was spent in the forest."

But the bulletin did not admit to the "lost" designation. It stated: "The fascination of a primeval forest in the bottom of a boulder-strewn gorge led ten adventurous Trail Clubbers to forget to turn back until too late. The penalty was a 30 hour fast and a night on the damp forest floor. . . . The legends of this trip, with minor alterations and exaggerations, will be handed down to grandchildren."

Other activities for the year included a trip to Greear's Lodge; Helton Falls; Whitesides and Highlands, North Carolina; Lake Phoebe; Lake Burton; Carter's Pool (a large natural pool near Fort Mountain); Enotah Bald; Tray Mountain; Thanksgiving at Dillard's and hike to Rabun Bald; Toccoa Falls; and the Christmas party. By the middle of the year, the Club had only 26 paid and active members, but by September the number had increased to 38.

In February it was announced that the new trail guide the Club had been working on for several years—the first edition of the "Guide to the Southern Appalachians"—would soon be available.

The "trail and shelter maintenance project for 1937" divided the Trail into ten sections, with squads to perform the following duties: "1. Clear overgrown trails—not too much; 2. Blaze new trails, if possible, to relocate around truck trails; 3. Mark trails by frequent paint blazes and occasional GATC markers; 4. Repair and clean cabins—recommend suitable location if there is no cabin on your section."

Outing chairman Cynthia Ward wrote to Elizabeth White in February, "We hope to make all trips on the AT this year work trips, and get some much-needed clearing done."

In response to an inquiry, Whittaker wrote to Adams:

Eddie Stone had always planned a stone shelter at Tesnatee Gap. I believe this is a logical place for one. There is a nice spot for one less than a mile east of the gap on the Trail. A cabin at Tesnatee would be approximately ten miles from the one at Blood and not much over that from the one at Rocky Knob. As for the other side of Blood, I do not know what to say. As you know, there is one at Amicalola. I do not recall any location that you might say would be ideal for one in this section. I never gave it much thought on account of the roads. Around Springer Mountain should be a good location as that is the outstanding peak of that region.

Let me know if I can be of further service. By the way, I would certainly overhaul and de-animalize our present cabins at the earliest moment. Perhaps you could use hillbilly labor to advantage on these projects. (July 6, 1937)

The eighth Appalachian Trail Conference was held in 1937 in Gatlinburg in June, and was hosted by the GATC, Smoky Mountains Hiking Club, and Carolina Mountain Club. The meeting was to mark the completion of the 2,050 mile Trail. Reportedly, Avery called this "the most harmonious meeting yet held." One of the speakers from the National Park Service spoke on "the importance of the acquisition of land adjacent to the Trail for its future protection and perpetuation." Seventeen GATCers attended the conference.

An announcement in the bulletin in July reported a long-needed accomplishment: the erection of a sign on Mt. Oglethorpe marking the southern terminus of the Trail. "The sign, three by four feet, built by members, was carried in sections up an old road from an abandoned dude ranch. . . . The erection of this marker was received with loud acclaim at the conference."

Hall had for a number of years printed the Club bulletin at the *DeKalb New Era* press. Early in 1937 he sold the printing plant, and the Club searched for other methods of printing. The cost was prohibitive, and the practice of typing the bulletin began.

The minutes of the June council meeting noted the following:

Arthur Stokes called attention to the fact that the provision of the constitution that the membership be kept approximately equally divided between the sexes was not being followed. It was proposed that the membership committee take no further applications from women until the proportion of men had been increased. It was also suggested that invitations be extended to more masculine guests. The council agreed to both of these policies.

The annual meeting in 1937 was held at Indian Springs, Georgia, on October 16-17. There were 84 people present. The bulletin reported "it was fun"—but also said, "Benton MacKaye, Warner Hall and our Smoky Club friends sent greetings and regrets." In a letter afterward to the principal speaker, Professor W. Harry Vaughn, Director of the Georgia Experiment Station, Adams wrote:

"Since we were holding the meeting at a place entirely new to us, I hope that you will excuse the lack of more comfortable accommodations and the crowding which were apparent."

At the "election meeting" in November, the following became officers for 1938: Cynthia Ward, president; C. R. Hoben, first vice president; R. W. Smith, second vice president; Martha Noble, secretary; H. R. Donald, treasurer; Maude Sewell, corresponding secretary; D. M. Therrell, historian; and Lloyd Adams, executive council.

1938

GEORGIA
APPALACHIAN
19 TRAIL CLUB, INC. 30

UNDER THE CLUB'S first woman president, Cynthia Ward, events seemed to go on much as usual, but the lagging spirits of the past few years continued to revive. Emphasis was placed more and more on getting the Trail into good shape.

The Trail and shelters committee, with Lloyd Adams as chairman, in January made detailed plans for clearing, marking, and measuring the Trail. The minutes of the planning meeting read, in part:

The conclusions of the committee were as follows:

1. Marking, measuring, and taking data will be begun immediately, at the Oglethorpe end of the Trail, by the committee. Other members of the Club will be conscripted to assist in this necessary work. Four workers and one chauffeur are needed for each trip. (The Club, through the ingenuity of Lloyd Adams, has a new measuring wheel tested and approved by the constructor during a stroll around a city block.)

2. The Outing committee will be asked to cooperate by scheduling clearing trips to follow up those of the group marking the Trail.

3. New sections of the Trail are to be made to take place of the road on this side of Neel Gap. Lloyd Adams is to go over the new territory with the ranger soon.

4. The Club should be divided into squads, each to care for a designated section of the Trail. Every member of the squad should have as his individual responsibility a certain length of that section.

5. The group is to promote enthusiasm for using the shelters, particularly the new

cabin which is soon to be under construction at Tesnatee Gap. This policy will tend to promote greater cooperation from the Forestry Service in the future.

To this end they recommended purchase of a "bush scythe blade and several whetstones," along with a pint of blue paint and four more copies of the ATC Trail manual. At the meeting a "lecture" was given by Lloyd Adams on proper blazing techniques and on the new galvanized iron markers to be erected.

The bulletin announced that the Club planned to have "as many hikes as possible on the AT." Over half of the trips were scheduled for work or to "inspect" the Trail, notably three weekends in March to be reserved for clearing and marking.

By this year the membership was up to about 65 members, and hikes were scheduled twice a month.

The Forest Service had recently relocated somewhat the Trail off of the new road between Hightower and Cooper Gaps. In March a group went up to inspect the new relocation and the bulletin reported:

Sunday, March 20, a group of hikers covered the six miles between Hightower and Cooper Gaps, much of it on a relocated trail blazed by the Forestry Service. The weather was open, views were good, and the only trouble encountered was the difficulty in finding the Trail out of gaps. But we found it! The following Sunday a group picked up where the others left off, hiking from Cooper to Gooch Gap—about six miles. Rain and thick fog obscured all views after the first mile or so. We were able to see the trailing arbutus blooming all along the way.

The old AT, where it has not been completely obliterated by the road, in both sections crosses it many times, or parallels it closely. Since the road has been built, very little hiking, and no work, has been done on the Trail, and in some spots it is practically non-existent. We hope that the end of this year will find this bit of the AT completely relocated and marked. We owe thanks to Mr. Woody, of the Forestry Service, for the work he has already done toward this end, and for his kindness to us whenever we are in his neighborhood.

In May of 1938, R. B. MacMullin of New York state began a hike on the AT at Oglethorpe and hiked as far as Virginia. He used the new guidebook, and as he traveled he made detailed notes on the condition of the Trail and the information in the guidebook. Upon completion of his trip he sent the report to the ATC. In a short report sent to Avery earlier from Georgia, MacMullin said of the new relocation: "Relocation of Trail from [Hightower to Gooch] is energy wasted in my opinion. It parallels the road and crosses many times and goes over so many knobs that the hiker should prefer the road." A copy of his full report was sent to the southern clubs with a letter that read in part:

We felt that the information as to Trail conditions and developments along the route would be welcomed by Club members and would increase their familiarity with this region. But more important, it would serve to impress upon the Club membership as a whole and not merely those on our Trail committees the responsibility of each organization for the proper marking out of the trails. Perhaps we have not sufficiently addressed—because we know how to find our way over not too well marked trails—the appalling problems which confront the stranger. Our Southern Appalachian Region is outstanding. We are luring here hikers from all sections. Mr. MacMullin has written several commendatory newspaper articles about the region. It is obvious, however, that much trail work is IMMEDIATELY required if the Trail is to be a credit to the maintaining organization. It is the Club's responsibility as a whole. People cannot form favorable impressions of our country if they are constantly getting lost. Marking only requires little effort; overgrown trails can be followed if well marked. The Trail Conference has issued a manual, describing standards. At the last Conference, a session was devoted to trail technique problems solely with the view of trying to improve conditions where needed. Unfortunately, this session was not so well attended as we would have liked.

Our section of the Trail must be a credit to our clubs. It is time now to make the Trail into something well worth preserving rather than to be content with deploring truck trail invasion and let the route get into a deplorable condition. It is a real challenge to our organizations to bring the Trail to standard. That is why we want this most helpful document to reach all Club members. We know that they will recognize their responsibilities and rise to the occasion. (May 1938)

Soon from Conference came "Instructions to Appalachian Trail Workers," a brief resume of the Trail Manual. It stated, "Irrespective of personal views and local practices, these standards must be adhered to on the Appalachian Trail. Do not rely upon an assumed familiarity with what good trail practice requires. . . . The Appalachian Trail is an 'open' not a 'hidden' way."

The Trail and shelters committee report for the year shows an attempt was made to remedy the bad trail situation in Georgia. The report began: "The past year has been characterized by attempts to obtain complete data for a sign list and to blaze and measure the Trail." Accomplishments were listed: Lloyd Adams, committee chairman, assembled a new "cyclometer wheel" to measure the Trail; the approach trail to Oglethorpe was measured and blue blazed; sections of the Trail "visited" by the Club were blazed and marked with metal markers; the Forest Service had built a new shelter at Tesnatee Gap—the Club's "best shelter"; data was collected for signs for the northern half of the Trail; a map of the Georgia Trail was in preparation.

The first hike of the year was from Woody to Neel Gap, with the night spent at the Vogel State Park cabins where, according to the bulletin, "the sturdy hikers were exposed to more lessons in camp craft. One of our visitors discovered that an unpunctured bean can will explode if heated in the ashes and that enough beans can't be found for a meal. . . ."

The next hike, from Unicoi to Indian Grave Gap, was announced with the warning: "This section has never been very distinct, so we may be offered the thrills of a scouting party."

In February the group traveled to near Brevard, North Carolina, to visit Carter Whittaker at his CCC camp. The bulletin reported one of the highlights of the trip to be "the complete invisibility of the ten thousand deer and bear offered as a lure to this wildlife refuge."

Of a hike in April to Hawk Mountain and Springer Mountain, the bulletin related: "That frozen mouse Ernest Runyon found in the water bucket at lunch did not prevent him from ordering cherry mousse for dessert at Cinciolla's where the group gathered for the usual Sunday night supper. What a difference an 's' can make!"

In May, a camping trip was planned to Low Gap, but rain on Saturday changed the camping plans to "the commodious four-compartment, concrete-floored garage" of the ranger at Unicoi Gap. This prompted the bulletin headline "Hikers Drive 100 Miles to Enjoy Sleeping on Concrete." The hike was made on Sunday—to Tesnatee Gap to "inspect" the new shelter there. The bulletin read:

All hardships were forgotten and all efforts well rewarded, as the hikers hiked over the well defined Trail and obtained many views of scenic loveliness. Upon reaching Tesnatee they found a sturdily built log shelter with very solid floor and roof, and one open side, nicely situated on a ten foot terrace of logs and enclosed with a beautiful new rail fence. Just outside the shelter is a large stone chimney with an open fireplace on one side which reflects heat into the cabin and a grill on the other large enough for cooking several steaks at once and other food. There are also a table and benches built of half logs. A very swanky shelter! And the trip covered eleven miles. On the way back home, Mrs. Greear of Greear's Lodge in Helen brought a glorious day to a perfect end by serving the hungry hikers great big goblets of fresh buttermilk and homemade cookies.

Other outings not on the Georgia AT in 1938 included: Sitton's Gulch, Wallace Gap to Wayah Gap in the Nantahalas, Carter's Pool, Lake Blue Ridge, Indian Mounds at Cartersville, Lake Burton, Smokies over Labor Day weekend, Dillard House, and several roller skating parties.

Clyde Passmore, outing chairman, wrote to Carter Whittaker before the trip to Sitton's Gulch, "PLEASE arrange to come down the weekend of the 14th and camp with us at Sitton's Gulch. Every camping trip we've planned this year has met with difficulties. We need you."

The annual meeting for 1938 was planned for October 8-9 at Neel Gap. Clyde Passmore wrote to Charlie Elliott (who was by now Director of the Division of State Parks) about arrangements for the meeting. Neel Gap was a part of Vogel State Park at that time. Passmore told Elliott she hoped he could attend the meeting, saying: "It seems that most of you old timers have deserted us entirely—I don't mean it's your fault—but it makes it almost impossible to keep the primary ideals foremost."

The bulletin reported a successful meeting, and a hike up Blood Mountain, adding: "Afterwards lunch at the Inn and a hurried round-up for a picture. Chester Elliott succeeded in making almost everyone laugh so we have gone on record as having enjoyed another annual meeting and according to Lloyd's report on trail clearing and marking we can feel proud of the achievement for the year as well."

An editorial in the *Atlanta Journal* on October 7 announced the meeting, saying:

As the southern terminus of the enchanting woodland trail that winds across the eastern highlands of our country all the way to Maine, Georgia holds a distinctive place on the map of that rich adventure. And her Appalachian Trail Club, now nearing the end of a full decade of usefulness, is a credit to the commonwealth, no less than to the cause for which the Trail was blazed. It is a club whose members combine with their own heart-deep love of nature and their desire to learn more and more of her beautiful wisdom, a generous purpose to help many, many others share such experiences. It has done much to promote both the conservation and the enjoyment of wild life in Georgia and the Southeast, and will continue to serve these vital interests in the years ahead.

Officers elected for the coming year at a meeting in November were Lloyd Adams, president; Clyde Passmore, first vice president; R. W. Smith, second vice president; Loretta Chappell, secretary; R. K. Babington, treasurer; Maude Sewell, corresponding secretary; D. M. Therrell, historian; Ernest Runyon and Cynthia Ward, Council.

In November Lloyd Adams, member of the Board of Managers of the ATC, reported on a new development for the benefit of the Trail. It was applauded in an editorial in the *Atlanta Journal* of November 3:

Lovers and students of nature will heartily endorse the plan, announced yesterday by Dr. W. Lloyd Adams of Atlanta, to insure for all time the distinctive character of the Appalachian Trail, which reaches two thousand and fifty miles through the heart of mountain woodlands from Georgia to Maine. The wonderful footpath now winds through solitudes that are blessedly free from the noise and clutter of civilization. But there is no certainty that it will remain so and will continue its unspoiled service to those who find joy and strength, as well as peace, in communion with the wilderness, unless early precautions are taken. To this end, the Appalachian Trail Conference, of which Dr. Adams is a member, has proposed that there be set apart on each side of the Trail a strip of land one mile wide on which no encroachments shall ever be made. Within this two-mile area no motor routes, no buildings except temporary shelters for hikers, no developments of any kind that would impair the natural beauty and quietness of the long, long footpath will be permitted. The United States Forestry Service and the National Park Service have approved the plan, which is expected to enlist the generous cooperation of State park officials and the owners of private lands concerned. The Appalachian Trailway, as the widened route will be called, is essential to the preservation of the Trail itself.

As the bulletin said: "This affects over 700 miles of the Trail, lying within eight National Forests and two National Parks. The agreement is a major step in the program of seeking to perpetuate and to protect the Trail—a program initiated at the last Gatlinburg conference."

You are Cordially Invited

to attend the

Ninth Annual Meeting

of the

Georgia Appalachian Trail Club

Saturday and Sunday

October 8-9, 1938

to be held at the

Walasiyi Inn

Neel Gap, Georgia

Please Reply

Program for the Ninth Annual Meeting, October 1938

SATURDAY, OCTOBER EIGHTH

Banquet, 7 P. M.
Cynthia Ward, President, presiding.
Welcome to Vogel Park, Charlie N. Elliot, Director
Georgia State Parks.
Welcome to Annual Meeting, Cynthia Ward.
Address by Stanley A. Cain, Ph.D., Associate Professor
of Botany, University of Tennessee.
Announcements
Square Dance
Motion Pictures—H. R. Halsey, Ph.D., Director of Ed-
ucation, C. C. C. 4th. Corps Area.
Fireside Singing.

SUNDAY, OCTOBER NINTH

Breakfast, 8 A. M.
C. R. Hoben, First Vice-President, presiding.
Invocation
Historian's Report, Mr. D. M. Therrell.
The Appalachian Trail Project, W. Lloyd Adams, Ph.D.,
Chairman Trails and Shelters Committee, A. T.
Conference Representative.
Announcements.
Hike—Two mile trip to summit of Blood Mountain on
A. T. in Georgia. (Alt. 4463.)
Luncheon, 1 P. M.

RESERVATIONS

The cost of $3.50 covers banquet, breakfast, lunch and lodging. Reservations must be made not later than Tuesday, October 4th. Room assignments will be made in the same order that paid reservations are received. . . Please make inquiries arrangements for transportation, and reservations through Mrs. R. K. Babington, 968 Williams Mill Road, N. E., Atlanta. Phone WA. 3403.
Dress: Informal.

OFFICERS

Cynthia Ward	*President*
C. R. Hoben	*First Vice-President*
Richard W. Smith	*Second Vice-President*
Martha Noble	*Recording Secretary*
Loretta Chappell	*Acting Secretary*
H. R. Donald	*Treasurer*
Maude Sewell	*Corresponding Secretary*
D. M. Therrell	*Historian*

Members Executive Council
W. Lloyd Adams   Carter Whittaker
Warner W. Hall

1939

IN FEBRUARY OF 1939, Lloyd Adams resigned as president of the GATC. He left Atlanta and the Emory Medical School to go to the Albany Medical College in New York. The bulletin published a letter from him upon his departure, as follows:

To the Council and all members of the Georgia Appalachian Trail Club:

This is essentially the beginning of a new year for the Club, and it may be safely stated that the prospects for a worthwhile organization are as high or higher than at any time in its ten year history. Many difficulties have been surmounted, and there is a spirit of cooperation within the Club which presages much good to come.

During my association with the Club, I have come to have a very deep interest in its welfare and have formed a lasting affection for it and for all its members. You have honored me with the presidency on two occasions even though my intense interest in seeing things accomplished has not always found me as tactful and considerate as I should have been.

It is with a sad heart, therefore, that I must ask that you accept my resignation. . . . Some of our happiest times have been on the Trail, and it is difficult to think of leaving all our associations in this connection.

At his last council meeting, he gave a "Report to the council on the state of the Club," in which he repeated his admonitions of the past and continued to defend the constitution which was passed in his first administration:

At no time in the history of the Club have there been better organization and prospects for continued effective functioning. Several times in the past there has been occasion to feel the inadequacy of our organization when one or several 'key' members have suddenly been prevented from continuing as active members. At the time I first became President this condition obtained, and it was the prime factor in the movement to provide against such contingencies by preparing and adopting a formal constitution. The constitution which was adopted by the Club was an instrument which embodied most of the policies which had been followed by the Club, and went into some detail to delineate the duties of the various officers, committees, councils and procedures. The committee responsible for drafting the constitution sought the advice and aid of all Club members by questionnaire and verbal appeal. The response was disheartening, but when the proposed constitution appeared and was adopted, there was objection.

The present strong position of the Club shows, however, that the fundamental provisions of the constitution are sound. Continued strength will come by close adherence to it, rather than by forgetful non-observance of its provisions. Yet, the thought and interest in the constitution which resulted from many attacks on it, and the experience which time and practice have given, make it desirable and timely to consider revision and ironing out of rough spots in the constitution. I urge a careful study and revision of it in the near future. It may be well to shorten it, by removing much that is instruction and incorporating this part in a separate 'Code of Practices for the Guidance of Officers and Committees.'

My optimism in saying that prospects are better than ever before is justified by reviewing several points:

Firstly – There is a keen interest in the welfare of the Club on the part of every officer and council member. The attendance at council meetings is excellent and meetings are held regularly each month. The latter has been true only in the past several years. It also appears that each officer is well qualified for the position held, and will execute his duties faithfully.

Secondly – Committees, particularly the Outing and Trails and Shelters, which are so important, are doing good work. The enthusiasm and interest with which the work of the Club is being carried out is truly encouraging.

Thirdly – Harmony exists within the Club, a better understanding of the objectives each member is seeking prevails, and there is an apparent willingness among all to work together for the welfare of the Club.

The council should be more mindful of its responsibility as controller of Club property. It is tacitly assumed that each officer or member turns over his or her records, property, etc., to the proper person or successor. This is true only in some cases. An inventory and accounting for records and property, which will come to be valuable, would be advisable. This assumes that proper records are prepared in the first place— a fact by no means true until relatively recently. The membership lists, treasurer's reports, auditing report and minutes of meetings should be carefully preserved.

In regard to the Conference, the Club should realize that this is a body which can do much more effective work in reaching certain objectives than any individual club, and, therefore, deserves wholehearted support. The Trailway Agreement is an example of its work. Now comes the Federal State Club meeting.

Thus in leaving, there should be no feeling of loss, as so kindly expressed, because things are in fine shape.

In viewing Lloyd Adams' presidency today, and in talking to those who were active in the Club at that time, there is something of a parallel to the presidency of Lyndon Johnson following John Kennedy. Lloyd Adams inherited the unpopular task of putting the Club on a business-like basis; for example, he instituted the first regular, formal meetings of the council and the first official minutes of the meetings. The constitution so carefully drawn up by Lloyd Adams was to stand for more than 30 years. There is no question that Warner Hall gave the GATC its personality and "Golden Era," just as Lloyd Adams saw it through its blackest period and saved it from extinction. Adams was opposed at every turn by certain council members of the "Old Guard," but history must recognize the debt the GATC owes him for his methodical moulding of an organization which could survive brilliant leadership, lackluster leadership, or hardly any leadership at all.

Clyde Passmore, as first vice president, was named by the council as the new president.

The first issue of the *Appalachian Trailway News* was published in January, 1939. It contained articles on each section of the Trail from Maine to Georgia. The report on the Georgia Trail read:

Northern Georgia has some magnificent mountain country. The Trail problems here, however, are perhaps more acute than in any other region. In addition to the lack of adequate marking, the maintenance of the crest line Trail in the Chattahoochee Forest is, unfortunately, somewhat below the standard of Trail maintenance in the other National Forests. ATC Board member, W. Lloyd Adams, and the Georgia Club are endeavoring to solve these problems. A material contribution has been made in the development of a satisfactory approach trail to Mt. Oglethorpe, the southern terminus of the Appalachian Trail, and the placing of adequate signs there.

The U. S. Forest Service built in 1938 a new shelter in Tesnatee Gap. There are also several shelters along the Trail in Georgia, built some time ago. Unfortunately, these need repair and protection from stock, which are permitted to graze in the southern Appalachian forests.

Subsequent to the 1937 Conference, there was prepared a list of signs for use on the Appalachian Trail in the southern Appalachians. It was very gratifying, in 1938, to find that these signs had not only been made but had been erected in the field.

The general objectives of the Conference in the way of increased Trail facilities, shelters, signs and improvements in the route have been responded to by the Forest Service in a most encouraging fashion. The problems in the Southern Appalachians now lie in the limited areas under private ownership outside of the National Forests.

And the July issue had more to say:

Trail conditions in Georgia have been a matter of serious concern. Inadequate marking of the route, coupled with trail maintenance somewhat below the standard of other National Forests, has created for travelers from other states a difficulty in following the route, which has detracted from Georgia's superb mountainous region.

These problems have been added to by failure to adhere to the standard form of marking, often resulting from great local familiarity with the route developing an insufficient appreciation of what the stranger requires in a marked trail. During the past year, the Georgia Club, under Dr. Adams' direction, had undertaken a systematic program for remedying these defects. About 40 percent of the entire Trail has been brought up to standard and marked with white paint blazes. The worst sections have been remedied, and Dr. Adams had hoped during the coming year to complete the remarking of the entire Trail in Georgia.

There are five open shelters on the Trail in Georgia. Four of these were constructed by the CCC under the direction of Carter Whittaker, former president of the Georgia Appalachian Trail Club. One, now in a very bad state of disrepair, near Amicalola Falls, the gift of the owners of the Tate Estates, was one of the earliest structures on the Appalachian Trail in the South. Shelter 'pests' vary in different sections. . . . In the far south it is the grazing cattle and the wild pigs or boars (remember the wild boar hunts in the Cherokee Forest) which cause the trouble. The Club recently reached an agreement with the Forest Service whereby the structures would be cleaned up by the Club, then repaired and fenced in by the Forest Service. The northern section of the Trail in Georgia is quite well provided for and, with these repairs, the structures should again be thoroughly habitable. The Conference has urged the Forest Service to fill in the gaps in the southern section.

Already, the meeting of Conference officials with state and federal authorities at Marion, Virginia, in February, 1939, has begun to bear fruit. Unfortunately, the lower portion of the Chattahoochee National Forest has been covered with truck trails for which the ridge crest route seemed a favored locality. The section between Hightower and Gooch Gaps has become, due to road construction, particularly objectionable. This difficulty was discussed with the Forest Service at the Marion meeting. Supervisor Fischer of the Chattahoochee National Forest has advised the Conference of his willingness to undertake a trail relocation in this section as soon as a route, acceptable to the Conference and the Georgia Appalachian Trail Club, can be agreed upon. As this is a major bit of trail construction, and, as the terrain presents some problems, the Service is naturally anxious to make sure that the relocation will be universally satisfactory before undertaking the work. The ready availability of a CCC camp in this vicinity will make the project relatively easy as soon as the exact route can be determined.

It is expected, therefore, that the trail relocation will be soon undertaken. This will be particularly significant. It will represent the first relocation—to obtain a better route—as a direct consequence of the Appalachian Trailway Agreement as well as a manifestation of the wholehearted and thorough-going cooperation which the Conference has received from Forest Service officials. Necessarily, with these cooperative arrangements, there are certain responsibilities and tasks accruing to the maintaining organizations, and it is particularly important that every effort be made to carry out responsibilities and assignments as expeditiously as possible.

A letter was sent to the members of the Board of Managers in February with several announcements. The first concerned the new Appalachian Trailway Agreement, told of negotiations with the various state authorities "to obtain their adherence to a similar form of agreement," and announced a meeting of the ATC Board, the Forest Service, Park Service and state authorities "for the purpose of procuring" this adherence. Avery also put forth for the Board's consideration the development of a system of reports on Trail conditions from the various sections, digests of which would be published in the *Appalachian Trailway News*. He goes on to say: "It seems rather obvious that the requesting of reports of Trail conditions will call attention to sections where the maintenance has been neglected and result in improved conditions. I trust, however, that the efforts in obtaining the desired information through the medium of these reports will be more successful than some of my efforts to obtain responses from the Board on the problems laid before it for its consideration." He had prepared a form for the questionnaire which could be used by the clubs.

In March a list of projects for the GATC for the year was advanced and included in the Board minutes:

1. Every member to participate in activities and work of Club.
2. Hikes: to cover entire Georgia section of Trail; to be varied—long and short, day and overnight, camp and hotel, distant and local.
3. Maintenance: to mark entire Georgia section; to repair all shelters.
4. a. Instruction: before hike and/or lunch time, exposition of region—route, history, points of interest.
   b. In-town classes: local flora, birds, geology, camping technique, woodcraft, picture making, projects and activities of other clubs, history and ideals of GATC, archeology.
5. Monthly local functions, not to interfere with scheduled outings: square dances, skating, suppers, swimming, and allied activities.
6. Attractive advance booklet of 1940 program (similar to Smoky Mountain publication).
7. Revision of constitution (as outlined by Lloyd).
8. Local club room and/or out-of-town club house.

The minutes of a council meeting in September noted the following: "Dick Smith introduced a discussion of the merits of incorporating, and it was decided that this would not be wise. Lovejoy [Harwell] said that unincorporated, the Club could not be sued as a body, and only an individual offending member could be sued; he could be sued as well as the entire Club if the Club were incorporated."

The same minutes also recorded "the Club would be requested in the next business meeting not to invite women on trips with the expectation of admitting them to membership until the quota of men has caught up with the women."

The Outing committee this year planned several "special study" trips–of historical, geological, or other special interest. The first of these was to Kennesaw Mountain Battlefield for a two-mile hike, a lecture on the history of the battles fought there, and a weiner roast around a campfire at sunset. There were 48 people on the trip.

Of a trip from Southern's store to Tate Estates the bulletin related: "On the way, Lloyd tore a hole in the bottom of his oil pan, which might have been disastrous except for the large amount of chewing gum present."

And of a work trip from Amicalola to Southern's Store, the bulletin said:

Lovejoy Harwell and five others drove to the top, and hiked, blazed, and relocated (a part) the five miles of the AT from Amicalola to Southern's Store. They report that this part of the Trail needs a good overhauling. Nature notes: icicles and sunburn at the same time, frog eggs in a pond and fish eggs in every stream, yellow violets, and a glimpse of wild turkeys. Coming back on the road from Nimblewill Gap to the highway they had an exciting time running through forest fires, but all was forgotten when the day ended at Peacock Alley, where Lovejoy surrounded his car with such a pile of chicken bones he had hard work getting out.

Another adventure was provided by the hike from Low Gap to Unicoi:

Ten weary sojourners of the Trail Club and seven guests motored to our Helen rendezvous on April 16, and, with schedule promptness, trekked by truck to low Gap, whence 14 stalwarts struck out towards old 'Horse Trough' with a light fantastic stride.

Following conventionals on Lovejoy's 'new fangled' map, we soon found ourselves 'crying in the wilderness,' a steep, difficult terrain separating us from the official trail. We called from labor to refreshment at this point and upon resuming 'labor' proceeded as before and picked up the Trail at Cold Spring Gap.

Darkness ushered us to the cars (and chauffeurs) at Unicoi and a speedy drive to Grear's, where soap and water placed us in a strategic position to enjoy a delightful meal at the lodge. Thus refreshed, we headed for Atlanta.

On Labor Day weekend the group went to Joyce Kilmer Memorial Forest, and the trip account in the bulletin contains one of very few references to the troubled pre-war years: "The beauty of the big trees and the ferny forest floor appealed to the love of nature in all of us, although the necessity of keeping up with the war news and a little engine trouble scaled the hiking down to a minimum."

Other hikes of note that year were: Sitton's Gulch and Head River; a joint hike of the four Southern clubs at Richland Balsam in North Carolina; Highlands, North Carolina, and Whitesides; another trip to the Dillard Farm; a number of hikes and work trips on the Georgia Trail; a watermelon cutting; and the Christmas party.

An October bulletin carried the following notice: "All future hike leaders are requested to use Kenneth Babington as an example. He scouted his trail the week before the hike, timing each separate operation, and worked up a knot tying contest for the time spent in waiting for the cars and a questionnaire about the Trail for the period of rest after lunch. Thanks a lot, Kenneth."

The annual meeting was held again at Neel Gap, with speeches, food, square dancing, balloon popping, singing, "and an unprecedentedly early retirement for the GATC." Officers for the coming year were elected: Ed Traylor, president; Elizabeth Motsinger, first vice president; Lovejoy Harwell, second vice president; Ross Wilson, treasurer; Loretta Chappell, recording secretary; Maude Sewell, corresponding secretary; D. M. Therrell, historian; Clyde Passmore, council.

1940

THE GATC'S TENTH anniversary year began on a sad (but not unusual) note. According to the bulletin: "As usual, the Trail Club's new president has been transferred." Ed Traylor moved to New Orleans in January, and Lovejoy Harwell, first vice president, was elected by the council to fill the office.

The *Appalachian Trailway News* reported again in January on the Georgia Trail:

GEORGIA TRAIL BEING IMPROVED

ATC Board Member Lovejoy Harwell reports much activity on the part of the Georgia Appalachian Trail Club.

Many hikers go to Mt. Oglethorpe and start north on the Appalachian Trail, usually for a week to two weeks trip. As the Georgia section has never been up to the high standard of the Trail elsewhere, this experience may create an erroneous impression of the entire Trail. Such hikers frequently send detailed accounts of their journeys. 'The GATC appreciates these careful reports made by the various hikers on the Georgia Trail and the constructive criticism given.'

Recognizing the situation, the GATC is making a definite effort to remedy it. Within the past year over forty miles of Trail have been properly blazed. Inaccuracies in the Guide are being listed as rapidly as possible. ATC Board Member Harwell and the GATC are certainly to be commended for the systematic approach being made to the problem.

And the members continued to do needed work on the Trail on regularly scheduled hikes. Except for a few exceptional and traditional trips, all of the regular hikes were on the AT.

In February a trip was planned from Neel to Tesnatee Gap to do Trail work. It was a "double-barreled hike." A "Sunday group" would hike in to Tesnatee and out again for the day. The "Saturday group" was given the following instructions in the bulletin:

SATURDAY GROUP, Kenneth Babington, Hikemaster. This trip is NOT recommended for beginners. Registrations are limited to eight (capacity of the Tesnatee Shelter). Meet at Neel by 10:00 A.M. Half of the group under the hike-master will proceed directly to Tesnatee and set up camp. The remainder under Lovejoy Harwell will follow and perform the Trail work. They will be greeted at the shelter with a warm fire and a hot supper. A camp fire program is being arranged, including some star observations. NOTE: The moon will be waxing to the full. Maybe the hill wind will sing us a lullaby; if not, who cares whether we sleep or not. Hiking distance, Saturday 5.7 miles, return Sunday, total 11.4 miles. Bring lunch for Saturday, lunch for Sunday to be eaten on the Trail. Saturday supper and Sunday breakfast will be cooked at Tesnatee for the group; these meals, with midnight refreshments, will cost 65¢ (please have correct change). Bring *plenty* of Kivver, canteen, flashlight and all equipment necessary for overnight comfort in the mountains. We want several women of pioneer stock to make this trip, women whose grandmams could split a rail or draw a wicked bead on a redskin. They will be crowned queens of the Culinary department and will be given the choice rooms of the Tesnatee Hotel!

But the trip didn't turn out as planned. The bulletin account reads:

I hesitate to tell of our trip to Tesnatee. We made it and suffered no hardships. To say much more would sound like bragging. Irwin (Smitty) Smith, Bill Buchanan and I, with our guest, Hugh Owen, arrived at Neel Gap in a peppery sleet. We warmed at Uncle Bob Furbish's cottage, and then, with his benediction, set out on the Trail over Levelland (3940') and Cowrock (3867') to Tesnatee Gap. The clouds were high enough to afford some fine views and I shall never forget the grandeur of majestic Blood bathed in a blizzard. The old blazes of the Trail were freshened with new paint and many new blazes were added. In this respect this portion of the AT is in good condition. When we reached the summit of Cowrock, the wind had increased to a gale and stinging sleet hit our faces and covered our hats and ponchos with ice. The shrubs and trees had heavy coatings of ice, and our blaze scrapers encountered as much ice as bark when we used them. Descending the declivities of Cowrock, we spied a most welcome sight in the gap below, the Tesnatee shelter, our 'hotel' for the night. No weary travelers were ever more grateful for a sanctuary than we. We found a sturdy shelter of open adirondack style, built of stout chestnut logs with a fireplace, table, log benches and a surrounding rail fence. We made camp quickly, got in enough wood for the night and started supper. Our menu included steaks fried in sizzling butter, with onions, potatoes boiled in jackets, canned peas, kraut, halved peaches in syrup and pound cake. Our coffee was made from snow scooped up from the table and was fit for a king. After supper, we enjoyed the fire of chestnut wood, dried our togs, spun yarns, discussed the latest philosophical sayings of Confucius, pitied our rocking chair friends in Atlanta, toasted marshmallows and ate rosy cheeked apples. At 9:30 we unrolled our bedding, put a hot rock at our feet and sank to our quiet and peaceful sleep. But not long. First a woods kitty straggled in from the storm. Hugh and Bill spotted him with a flashlight but disputed not his presence. He nibbled a boot, sampled the grease in the fry pan, and went back into the storm. At 2:00 A.M. the wind which had played havoc in Atlanta arrived at Tesnatee Gap. It shrieked through the barren trees like banshees of old. Forest monarchs toppled. Sleet changed to driving rain and we wondered what the morrow had in store—but that was another day. Dawn. Low clouds riding a furious wind through the gap scurried tempestuously over Cowrock. A hurried bite to eat. Packs and the back trail. Slushy snow, rain, fog, poor visibility. Slow painful Cowrock climb. Numerous trees across the Trail, mute evidence of the fury of the night's storm. Baggs Gap, Levelland, Neel and finally Uncle Bob's warm cottage. It was Smitty's ebullient spirit which made us bear up under the lashings of the blizzard. When the sleet bit hardest he would burst forth in song, 'Gloria in excelsis Deo.' That was our thanksgiving prayer at the Trail's end. (Kenneth Babington)

A hike to Addis Gap and down Moccasin Creek supplied the following comments for the bulletin:

The materialization of everything scheduled, plus a few extra curricula activities made the April 20-21 outing memorable for 27 campers and hikers. Partial submersion of the Wilson car, dilution of the icy waters of Dick's Creek with gasoline, impromptu camping at this site by the occupants. Bill Buchanan's nine mile hike for assistance, sleet and snow falling in the light of the moon Saturday night, piggyback crossing of Moccasin Creek and the star visible at lunch time Sunday added more than sufficient novelty to the bill-of-fare.

A glowing announcement of the forthcoming trip to Mt. LeConte brought the following report afterward:

Looking back over our announcement of the Great Smoky Mountain trip in the previous issue of the *Mountaineer*, where we promised everything and warned of nothing, we find that at least a part of our promises were fulfilled. The pavement wasn't so excellent in a few spots, the Little Pigeon hurdled and splashed but its soothing music was lost in that of Jupiter Pluvius' vast sprinkling system, the dense rhododendron thickets were more dense than colorful, and at Mt. LeConte the cloud wisps swung so low that, for a time, the ever-changing panorama was changeless and several hungry groping hikers innocently ate their nearest neighbor's sandwiches. However, as predicted, 'Ol Sol' did poke his nose over the Chimney Tops while several breakfasted at the open grate, the cool freshness of Alum Cave Creek was even more stimulating than usual, the purple rhododendron disported itself spasmodically along the trail, and eventually the clouds unfolded to expose the rugged mountain majesty that all had come to see.

Some twenty Knoxville, Asheville, and Waynesville folks were at the Chimneys Camp Saturday evening to greet the absent Georgians who were scurrying for shelter in

Gatlinburg. Some visitors braved the elements to camp overnight while others returned Sunday morning for the hike.

A trip to scout part of a relocation of the Trail between Gooch and Hightower Gaps was an adventure, according to the bulletin:

Nine rough and ready bushwalkers took off into the woods Sunday morning, July 7th, at Gooch Gap and emerged late in the afternoon at the Cooper Gap declaring their safari to have been one of the most pleasant and successful of the year. The hike was the alternate trip scheduled as such, and its purpose, like that of Christopher Columbus, was to find a new and better route to the south by traveling westward. With Gordon Wilson as leader, and following an uncharted course, the party skirted mountain peaks, explored abandoned farm sites, crossed mountain streams on uncertain logs, trod long-forgotten mountain roads, discovered waterfalls and crude grist mills, and rested elbows on rail fences to chat with mountaineer neighbors. To all fair-weather hikers, be it known that not a 'drap' fell.

For the relocation an abandoned road was found which "approximately parallels the present trail . . . about one mile north of it," and "would make a very satisfactory new location. . . . Further exploration is yet to be made."

The same month (July), an announcement was made of a new shelter:

The Trail and Shelters Committee announces the acquisition from the U.S. Forest Service of a locked cabin (or house) for Trail Club use on the summit of Frosty Mountain. This house was used for some time as a residence for the Forest Service fire warden but was recently abandoned for that purpose. The building is approximately 14 feet square, has an exterior of regular house siding painted white, interior walls completely sealed, good roof, hardwood floor, chimney, three windows, porch, lightning rods, and concrete foundation. The keys are in the hands of the GATC. Inasmuch as there is no inside fireplace, it appears that a small stove suitable for cooking in inclement weather would be an appropriate addition. Do you have such a stove packed away in mothballs while you wonder what you will eventually do with it? If so, the Committee will be glad to hear from you.

A memorable "Four-Club Get-Together" was held at Van Hook Glade near Highlands, North Carolina, in July, with 89 people participating.

A different sort of outing was held in November—a possum hunt. The bulletin gives the following account:

ONE EXCITING NIGHT, SATURDAY, NOVEMBER 16, 1940
A DRAMA, by Geraldine LeMay

The scene: Clear, moonlit night; the bare fields and open woods of wintertime in the country.
The actors: Some twenty odd hikers and guides; three trusty(?) 'possum hounds.
The plot: Group of strangely (but warmly) clad individuals meets at lonely country

home. Car after car arrives, but still group seems awaiting someone. Finally another car drives up, a man who appears to be a leader gets out and sets up sign reading 'M. L. Parks Dairy Farm.'

Guides whistle up dogs, and assembled group starts down country road, then turns off into woods. Dogs sent off to hunt 'possum. Bark triumphantly! Group rushes to bag 'possum! No 'possum. Dogs off again! Frantic barking! Frenzied rush! No 'possum. Group makes fire, stands around to warm and forgets 'possum. Then dogs off! Bark! Rush! No 'possum.

Lapse of several hours
Group on road with twenty-three different ideas of way back to cars. One brave guide faces the dogs on a lonely country farm and gets directions. Group starts off jauntily down moonlit road.

Lapse of several hours more
Pathetic little bunch of footsore hikers appears dragging wearily down country road. Then shouts and exultation and new life! Yes! The cars! It is the cars! (Still, no 'possum.)

Climax: The Smitty's residence. A warm fire. Delightful! Oyster stew. Delicious! Myrta May Edmonson's playing on the piano. Delovely!

Moral: Who wanted 'possum anyway?

In the spring Kenneth Babington, chairman of the map committee, prepared "a set of sketch maps" of the Georgia Trail. According to the *ATN*, this was "a splendid piece of work and fills a sad gap in Trail descriptive matter." While not topographic maps, they were accurate and by far the best yet made of the Georgia Trail. Myron Avery wrote to him:

Congratulations are certainly due you. I have just gone through your folder of maps for the Appalachian Trail in Georgia which arrived today. I cannot think of any work which would have been more useful. In view of the situation with respect to the Southern Guidebook and the changes in the route, these maps are of extreme value to users of the Trail in this area. Your program certainly remedies a real deficiency.

I should like on behalf of the Conference to express to you personally and to the Georgia Appalachian Trail Club our appreciation of this most material contribution. I cannot think of anything which would be of more help at the present moment. (April 15, 1940)

Copies of the maps were sent to other clubs. In his letter of thanks, Alfred Percy of the Natural Bridge Club wrote:

To my way of thinking you have certainly done an excellent piece of work and I wish the map-making moguls in our Club would swipe your ideas and put them into practice. This exchanging of the maps of the Trail sectors by the various local clubs is a good idea. I was doubly interested in your maps because I have always wanted to get down in the Georgia Blue Ridge but have never had the chance.

Our own plans for getting out improved maps are up in the air at present. This Blue Ridge Parkway is a menace to the peace and security of our rather easy-going club. The

Government, after making numerous surveys, decided that the Main Appalachian Trail was good enough after all for the highway. This has meant that we have had to relocate three fourths of our trail. This has been interesting work but has made many of us realize that we haven't as much mountain goat blood in us as we had thought. (May 5, 1940)

Babington was also the *Mountaineer* editor that year and published a lively and interesting bulletin twice a month. Often he issued a "supplement," which featured advice on camping equipment, quizzes, special announcements, etc. He received the following commendation in the bulletin (from the president):

Thanks and congratulations to Kenneth Babington for GAT maps! A short while ago he was appointed chairman of map committee—without further instructions or prompting his recent production appeared winning universal approval. He gets a permanent listing on the roll of GATC members who really 'do things'!

F. I. (Smitty) Smith was also a very active and contributing member, having been chairman of several committees. He was the "moving spirit" in the work of clearing and blazing the Trail. He and Harwell, according to the bulletin, often spent the Saturday before a Sunday hike as an "advance party," clearing and marking the trail to be hiked.

The May issue of the *ATN*, in its report on each trail section, had the following to say about Georgia: "It is to be regretted that no report was received for the last seven sections of the Trail in Georgia. The Georgia AT Club has had under way during the past year a program adequately to re-mark all sections in Georgia; this work is about 50% completed. The work has been scattered through the Georgia section. A new blue-blazed approach trail to Mt. Oglethorpe has been constructed. Lean-tos are being renovated."

A report of the Trail and Shelters committee in July announced 41.7 miles of trail blazed and cleared in the first six months of 1940, 64.5 done in the past ten months. Plans were to do most of the remainder by the end of the year.

In October, a registration cylinder was erected on Mt. Oglethorpe "which it is hoped will provide statistical data as to the use of our Trail."

A key to the locked gates across the roads connecting with the Trail was given to the Club in November. This key was used for many years, until the locked gates were removed.

Elizabeth (Bunny) Motsinger, first vice president of the Club in 1940, was also an "aviatrix." Her feats and her purchases of airplanes were reported occasionally in the bulletin, and a report on one incident appeared in the *Atlanta Journal* in October. She was flying her plane while a friend was doing stunts on the wing for an air show. The plane crashed in front of the audience at the LaGrange Airport; Bunny only suffered slight cuts, and her friend was injured slightly.

The annual meeting in October was held at the Bynum House in Clayton, and was, as usual, a rip-roaring success, according to the bulletin. Officers elected were: F. I. Smith, president; W. K. MacAdam, first vice president; Rilla Reed, second vice president; Maude Sewell, corresponding secretary; Elizabeth Motsinger, recording secretary; Carlon Carter, treasurer; Marene Snow, historian; and Lovejoy Harwell, council.

1941

GEORGIA
APPALACHIAN
TRAIL CLUB, INC.

THE FIRST BIG EVENT OF 1941 was the coming of Myron Avery in January. Avery visited all of the Southern clubs, checking on developments along the Trail. Of the trip, the *ATN* reported, "Plans were made to eliminate existing difficulties and for future close cooperation. . . . Interest, enthusiasm and systematic maintenance programs have reached a new high." The GATC gave a dinner in his honor, "after which he showed over 200 colored slides of the AT and spoke most interestingly of that wilderness footpath from Maine to Georgia," according to the bulletin.

The January *ATN* also published a letter from Robert B. Sosman, an ATC member who hiked the whole Georgia Trail and sent in a report to Conference. He reported, "Most of the Trail is well marked with fresh white blazes, and the old carved signs are still in good condition. Somebody has done a lot of good work down there. . . ." But he reported losing the trail at seven places, being annoyed by briars, and he stated, "The Georgia shelters are rather unappetizing."

In 1940, a beginning had been made in getting together and in order past bulletins, outing schedules, annual meeting programs, photographs, etc., for the historical files. In 1941, the history committee, under Marene Snow, made a concerted effort to gather and organize this material, and they solicited firsthand accounts of events in the Club's beginning days from a number of early members. By the end of the year, E. B. Stone, Charlie Elliott, Roy Ozmer, and Carter Whittaker had sent in a written account of their recollections of the beginning days. Also during the year, copies of all materials pertinent to the GATC were acquired from Conference, a complete set of bulletins was assembled, and other historical material was gathered together. With this great effort, Marene Snow began her 25 years as historian for the GATC, and the invaluable files that exist today are due to her care and organization during those years.

In 1940, plans had been made to publish a booklet similar to the one published in 1934, with up-to-date information. The plans were changed somewhat, and the booklet—which came out in May of 1941 and was called "Hiking on the Appalachian Trail in Georgia"—was actually a guide to the Trail, giving a list of needed equipment, suggested one-day trips, and a "log for hiking the entire Georgia Appalachian Trail." In the booklet an item of interest was included in the description of the day hike from Woody Gap to Gooch Gap. The instructions for getting to Woody Gap were to turn left at Stone Pile Gap and go "to the huge totem pole at Woody Gap." This totem pole was carved at the direction of Arthur Woody, and displayed a large bust of Woody on the top. Its erection on the AT did not exactly please some members of the GATC.

F. I. Smith succeeded in finding a Franklin stove for the new shelter at Frosty Mountain, and he announced in February that he had installed a table, benches, shelves, and candles. When the Forest Service installed the stove, the cabin became "the best equipped shelter on the Georgia Trail."

Work on the Trail continued through the winter months. Besides much blazing and clearing, Smith and Harwell scouted the vicinity of the Trail between Gooch and Hightower Gaps for the proposed relocation, and recommended that "as much of the existing trail as possible be used." The Trail at this time still followed somewhat the route of the road through Cane Creek, Ward, and Justus Gaps.)

Finally, in May, a bulletin supplement announced with joy:

THE JOB IS FINISHED

President F. I. Smith and Lovejoy Harwell, Chairman of the Trails and Shelters Committee, announce with pleasure that the 101 miles of Georgia Appalachian Trail— Bly to Oglethorpe—have been paint-blazed in both directions within the last 14 months. That portion of the Trail taken over by the forest road between Gooch Gap and Winding Stair has been relocated and returned to the wilderness. A full realization of the strength, time and devotion of this task cannot be had unless one has accompanied Smitty and Lovejoy on one or more of their numerous work trips. There is yet much clearing to be done on the relocated sections, but the entire Trail is fully blazed and can be followed without difficulty. Of passing interest is the fact that 23 springs near the Trail were located and marked. Smitty and Lovejoy and their assistants are to be congratulated and thanked for this worthy achievement.

The Trail and Shelters Committee reported in March that the cylinder placed on Mt. Oglethorpe last October was found to have 81 signatures representing eight states. And in August, Smith "displayed the new sign to mark the southern terminus of the Trail . . . two feet six inches by three feet nine inches by two inches thick . . . made by the Forest Service and to be erected by F. I. Smith and Bill Buchanan August 9, 1941."

At Amicalola Falls, the State had "started and abandoned a park project," and had left the falls "in ruins," according to the council minutes of May 6. The bulletin commented:

Have you seen Amicalola Falls—they are ruined. Great road scars blasted out of the mountains on both sides have destroyed the beauty. A dam is built at the top and the water is piped to the falls!!! When the dam fills and a hot dog stand is erected and we can hear Bing Crosby, the spoliation will be complete.

During this period, the Club was losing many of its members to the armed forces. As the bulletin related, a number of trips to Standing Indian had "suffered serious interruptions by disappearing leaders. First, Guerard Spratt was appointed leader. Uncle Sam, however, overlooked including such a duty among the valid reasons for deferment and borrowed him for a year. Lamb Johnson was the next volunteer; but while we were watching the Army carefully to prevent his seizure, the Navy rowed up from behind with muffled oars and carried him away. F. I. Smith has now volunteered believing that his luck will hold for a few months."

And, as is usual in wartime, many members were getting married. The Club facetiously formed a "matrimonial committee to keep track of and announce planned marriages." And in December, 1941, the bulletin announced the "first real GATC baby" born to Rilla and Walter MacAdam.

Following in the steps of his predecessors, President F. I. Smith was transferred out of town in August of 1941. Lovejoy Harwell was elected by the council to fill the remainder of his term.

The momentum achieved by the Club after the "low" of 1936 and 1937 was carried on into 1940 and 1941, due largely to the vitality of F. I. (Smitty) Smith. His obvious enthusiasm for trail maintenance at a time when it was needed the most, and his devotion to the Trail, brought the Trail and the Club to a pinnacle—which was, unfortunately, to he toppled by the advent of World War II. As the bulletin stated on his departure, "The Club loses a good friend, an efficient officer and a tireless worker."

The June, 1941, bulletin contained news of several people well known to GATCers: Charlie Elliott, "one of the founders of the GATC," had moved to Richmond, Virginia, to become the Public Relations Director of the National Park Service for the Eastern United States. "The Reverend Rufus Morgan of Franklin, North Carolina . . . has recently assumed the responsibility of maintaining a part of the AT in the Nantahalas." There was also the announcement of the death of Major William A. Welch, the first president of the ATC.

Hikes in 1941 were mostly on the AT, with a few exceptions, notably the "capture of Mt. Mitchell by 18 members and guests," a return trip to the Black Warrior Forest, and a trip not made for several years—to the "Indian Mounds" near Macon, now called the Ocmulgee National Monument.

Of a trip in September on the AT, the bulletin stated, "a fact worthy of note—there were more men than women along."

In September, Kenneth Babington and new member, Lawrence Freeman, "armed with a park permit, heavy packs and much nerve," hiked the western half of the Trail in the Smokies. They met two other hikers on the Trail during the four day hike.

The annual meeting in 1941 was held at Camp Wahsega, near Dahlonega. "Attendance was the greatest in the history of the Club," according to the bulletin. Officers elected were: Glen Edmonson, president; Bill Buchanan, first vice president; James Cragon, second vice president; Margaret Newton, corresponding secretary; Marene Snow, historian; Carlon Carter, treasurer; W. K. MacAdam, council.

The following announcement was made in the December 23 bulletin: "Captain Warner Hall did come all the way from Birmingham to the Christmas party . . . the right place and the right hour . . . but the wrong date. He turned up Saturday instead of Friday. Too bad, Warner. You were missed."

1942

GEORGIA
APPALACHIAN
19 TRAIL CLUB, INC. 30

T HE EVENTS OF DECEMBER 7, 1941, and the days following, as the United States entered World War II, were to have a profound effect on the Trail and the Club, as, of course, they did on all of humanity. In January of 1942, the bulletin stated that it would be necessary to "curtail our program of out-of-town hikes," and that an announcement of changes would soon be made. A few weeks later, a called meeting was held "to consider the revision of our 1942 hiking schedule due to the unforeseen situation caused by the national emergency." The results of the meeting were published in the bulletin in early March:

The Call Meeting of all members to determine an outing policy for the remainder of the year was an overwhelming success.

Sentiment of the entire group was expressed by Dr. Halsey who said, in effect, that even though, as individuals, we might be willing to use our cars and tires for extended trips into the mountains, these cars and tires were not ours to use as we may wish; they must be looked upon as a part of the resources of the nation which must be conserved and utilized only for necessary and essential requirements throughout the emergency.

However, it was agreed that the use of one set of tires, as long as available to the general public on rented transportation, can be justified for the combined use of 15 or 20 people on one trip, but that such trips should be restricted in number to not more than three or four during the remainder of the year. Estimated transportation costs were discussed, and it was found that rented station wagons and trucks can be used satisfactorily.

It was further agreed that interest in the Club should be kept alive by maintaining our present number of scheduled trips, but substituting local outings (those within a short distance of Atlanta) for the longer ones.

Everyone present expressed opinions and offered suggestions which will be of great value to the new Outing Committee in planning a revised schedule for the remainder of the year.

P.S. The 'short hike' did not materialize, what with the pouring rain outside and a cheery log fire in the Girl Scout Lodge to sit around and just talk.

A schedule of local outings was soon published in the bulletin. Trips were made in the spring to Stone Mountain, Soap (Sope) Creek, Bert Adams Camp near Vinings. A relatively small number of people attended the trips. In the bulletin account of the latter hike, the editor stated that he almost deleted, but actually decided to call attention to the first paragraph in the account:

Trail Clubbers surely demonstrated on this trip that nothing less than the AT can lure them out of their mossy old shells. Really folks, it was the prettiest day of the year—to date—and only a round dozen showed up. Think it over GATC members. Those 'mossy old shells' do sound attractive, but let's not settle down in them permanently just yet.

A hike was planned for Neel Gap in May if enough people expressed interest.

The minutes of a council meeting in April noted: The outing chairman "reported that it had been decided to use the present program as a tentative one in order that, if possible, the local trips could be changed to mountain ones later on." The Trail and shelters chairman "reported that nothing had been done this year."

The bulletin was not published between April and September of 1942 but resumed only for the remainder of that year.

A council meeting was called in August "to discuss the future of policies of the Club in view of the present emergency." The following action was taken: Carolyn Allen was elected treasurer to replace Carlon Carter; dues were reduced to $1.00 per person "for the duration of the war, or until further action of the council; this on account of the forced curtailment of activities"; an in-town meeting would be held to take the place of the annual meeting.

A list of Club members who were serving in the Armed Forces was published in the September bulletin and included: Larry Freeman, Warner Hall, Lovejoy Harwell, and Searcy Slack. Bunny Motsinger, the "aviatrix," was working in a bomber plant, and the article stated, "Keep your eye on Elizabeth White; she is on the fence and we don't know which way she is going to jump."

A letter to the Club from Bunny in August said: "I thought for a while that I might be coming down your way but it's all off because there's no room for my plane at the Akron airport."

A day at "La Casita" (the summer cabin south of Atlanta owned jointly by Marene Snow and other members; it had replaced Marene's other summer home, Butternut, as unofficial Club headquarters for picnics, parties, impromptu square dances, etc.) in September brought out 30 members and guests "including a fine representation of THE OLD GUARD." Hiking, swimming, and eating were enjoyed "but perhaps best of all was just getting together again, forgetting for a few hours the stresses and strains of these hectic days, and renewing 'the friendship for the Trails that lead to far away places.'"

The next bulletin noted: "The last bulletin brought you news of many of our silver star members. Here's what a few of our home folks are doing in the way of civilian defense activities," and listed among others: Maude and Chester Elliott—full-time and over-time job taking pictures of "the boys" and their sweethearts; Olivia Herren—nurse's aide; Lou Hoben—canteen aide with Red Cross; Marion Hoben—USO hostess; Clyde Passmore—in Red Cross surgical dressing division; Marene Snow—civilian defense volunteer.

The annual meeting was held in October at Monroe Gardens Restaurant. The minutes read:

Mrs. Halsey, representing the nominating committee composed of herself, Maude and Chester Elliott, Gertrude Reilly and Lou Hoben, commented as follows: The nominating committee felt that since the Club membership had been widely scattered during the year, leaving a comparatively small group to carry on its affairs, and, as further changes were likely to occur; and since the curtailed activities of the Club would not make too heavy demands on anyone, they thought that it would be simpler not to make any changes in the Executive Council, but to retain the same officers who have served during the past year for another year. The Council was assured that the Club members would stand by them in any action, and would serve if called upon to fill any vacancies in the Council if they should occur. It was, therefore, the wish of the nominating committee that the [present officers] continue in office for the coming year. . . .

A general discussion as to future activities of the Club followed, the gist of which was that since there seemed little chance for any out of town hikes, meetings would have to be in town and of a more or less social nature. It was agreed that the Club must in some way be kept together and continue to function until such time as its activities could be resumed on customary scale. . . .

There followed some plain and fancy square dancing directed by Lane Mitchell and Mr. and Mrs. Collette, ably supported by the Monroe Gardens juke box.

1943 - 1945

GEORGIA
APPALACHIAN
19 TRAIL CLUB, INC. 30

I**N A LETTER TO GUY FRIZZELL** in February, 1943, President Glen Edmonson spoke of the problems of the Georgia Club:

Until recently I have been out of town on business too much to attend to any of the AT activities. . . . In connection with the sale of the [new edition of the southern] guides in this section, I called a GATC council meeting this week with the idea in mind of securing their (the council members) approval to order our share of the guide—but that meeting fell through as we didn't have a quorum. . . . So I plan to try to get them together on the 24th of this month. . . . I have noticed with no little surprise and quite a bit of envy, the apparently full schedule of activities of the Smokies Club. As you no doubt know, our activities have dropped off to practically zero—with only an occasional 'social function' every once in a great long while. This is largely due to the fact that most of the members responsible for the Club's activities (including yours truly) have just been too darn busy on our various jobs. Frankly, we sure could use a live wire and sparkplug like our 'gone but not forgotten Smitty.' (February 12, 1943)

Edmonson was evidently successful in getting a quorum for the next council meeting, which was held later in February. The minutes read, in part:

Motion was made and passed that all men in the service be given free membership as long as they are in the service, this motion to be retroactive to cover anybody who is already in the service for as long as they have been in the service. . . .

Motion was made and passed that council be relieved of the requirement of meeting once a month for the duration of the war but that meetings shall be called upon the request of any member of the council as the need arises and that a quorum for these meetings will consist of three or more members.

The above motion was made in view of the unstable conditions at this time and for the purpose of retaining the rights of the group in the Conference and to hold the members together. . . .

Motion was made and passed that an activities committee be appointed with Marene Snow as chairman and Marion Hoben and Elizabeth White on it to arrange outings or functions to take the place of the usual outings at such times as they see fit. They are to use the bulletin in any way they wish as an instrument to keep the group together.

The war, of course, had a great effect on all of the clubs, the Trail, and the Conference. According to the *ATN,* several sections of Trail were closed in New York, Pennsylvania, Virginia, and North Carolina because of military installations close by, or for other security reasons, and other sections were affected in various ways by the war. Relocations in progress, such as those caused by the Blue Ridge Parkway in Virginia, were delayed. Some clubs were able to continue activities—some more and some less—and some were not.

"Characteristic of the spirit of determination on the part of all trail groups," according to the *ATN,* "is the following quotation" (from Mountain Club of Maryland Bulletin, July-September, 1942):

Plan by all means to work your assigned section of the Appalachian Trail come hell and high water, for there will be need of its recreational value when Victory comes. It is an asset of no mean value contributed to those who love the hills and far-off places, by those who labor for the fun and health of it, for those they can never know. . . . There should be no excuse for failure to work your section.

Myron Avery made an announcement in November, 1942, which was published in the January, 1943, issue of the *ATN* "with respect to the next Appalachian Trail Conference session":

For reasons which require no elaboration, unless I am requested to the contrary by a Board or Conference member, I do not propose, for the duration, to take any step looking toward an Appalachian Trail Conference session. Any such step would seem to me to be totally lacking in recognition of the situation we face today. Apart from this, there would be serious doubt as to the availability of ATC officers and key workers at any such meeting.

This will mean that, at the end of our fiscal year, June 30, 1943, the terms of the officers elected in 1941 will have expired. To provide for the necessary administration of Conference activities it is, of course, necessary that these officers continue de facto. . . .

Considerable thought has been given to a program and systematic method of dealing with Conference activities during the war. As far as is compatible with war requirements, it is our intention to keep an organization intact and a Trail route open.

We believe the Appalachian Trail to have a present and permanent value; activity in this connection requires no justification. Trail maintenance and work trips are in quite a different category from extended group pleasure hiking excursions. The latter are subject to limitations which do not exist in the former case. Pleasure trips which consume extensive quantities of critical materials such as gasoline and rubber, if noised abroad, can only serve to discredit hiking organizations generally; the Appalachian Trail does not exist as a forum for such questionable activity.

As Paul Fink reiterated in a letter in March asking for the clubs' regular contribution:

. . . Briefly, the plan of the Conference during this period is to attempt to maintain some sort of organization and, as far as possible, keep the Trail route open and traversable until the return of better days. Conditions which cannot be forecast at this time will, of course, determine the success of this plan. This means that the organization of the Trail Conference must continue to function. The demands upon the volunteers who are carrying out its objectives remain pretty much the same as in past times. While there perhaps would have been greater demands for guidebooks by those traveling the Trail, there has been no diminishing of the inquiries with respect to the Trail which have come to the Conference.

This explanation as to the nature of the Conference activities, which will have to be continued, is made in order that it may be understood that there is a full recognition of the situation which many outing clubs face at this time. It is appreciated that membership in these organizations has been decidedly reduced and many may experience financial difficulties. The Conference, appreciating the past support of these Clubs, hopes that, despite these difficulties, the groups will be able to continue during the war to assist the Conference in carrying forward its program. (March 2, 1943)

"All activities by the Georgia Appalachian Trail Club at a stand-still," reported the May, 1943 *ATN*. "There may be a little maintenance by the Chattahoochee Forest Service." The report in 1944 was: "South of Springer Mountain to Mt. Ogelthorpe is privately owned land. Trail maintenance in Georgia will depend on what is done in the Chattahoochee National Forest. Forest Supervisor, C.K. Spaulding, writes: 'We will do what we can within limits of priorities and labor shortage. The Trail will be travelable.'"

Potomac Appalachian Trail Club member, Samuel Moore, hiked some of the Georgia Trail in October of 1944 and his report sent to Conference was printed in the *ATN*. He pronounced the Georgia Trail "in excellent shape except for a few briars . . . and a few down logs. The marking was very good indeed."

The September, 1945, *ATN* carried the following article:

In the spring, the outlook for Georgia seemed discouraging, for Chattahoochee National Forest Supervisor, C. K. Spaulding, wrote in late March:
'The labor supply to do maintenance work on the trails is very short in North

Georgia. The workers who are left in the area are fully engaged in farming, logging operations and removal of extractwood, all of which are essential activities to aid in winning the war. It is difficult and nearly impossible to interest workmen in carrying on the maintenance of a non-essential recreation trail which is not being used. Therefore, the maintenance of the Trail in the National Forest in Georgia cannot be kept up to the pre-war standard during the calendar year of 1945. Persons who desire to travel the Trail should not expect to find it in good condition. When labor and funds are more plentiful, we expect to again follow our pre-war standards and have this section of the Trail in first-class condition.'

However, Philadelphia Trail Club Supervisor, Charles Hazlehurst, sends word that during the latter part of May, his party covered the Appalachian Trail from Neel Gap, Georgia, to Deals Gap, North Carolina. He states, 'AT easily followed most of the way. Flame azalea, laurel and even rhododendron beautiful.'

While Dr. Hazlehurst is a most experienced and able hiker and therefore may have no difficulty in places where a novice might feel the Trail obscure, his comment shows that the Trail for the northern half of Georgia and in the Nantahalas is at least passable. In passing, it might also be said that a novice in the woods has no business being on the Appalachian Trail in the Southern Appalachians.

The GATC was "dormant but not dead." In December, 1944, "Christmas Greetings" were sent to the members in lieu of a bulletin, as follows:

Certainly the trails our GATC members have traversed in the last few years have been in 'far away places'—scattered as they are to the four corners of the earth. Here at home, the ones who are left gather from time to time to talk about the days that have been and plan for the days that are to come. For while our Club activities are necessarily dormant now, the mountains, the trails, and the friends await all of us getting together again.

Christmas is the special time of year when our thoughts center around friends, especially friends who have followed the trails together. Hence this roll call—that we may share with each other the gleanings of bits of news—where we are—what we are doing—separated as we are one from the other.

Our information is not complete—it is all we've been able to get so far. We would be so pleased to have you help us with the next bulletin. Won't you write us any news of yourself or others?

The "roll call" listed the "at homes" and the news of them, and those in "far away places."

In June of 1945, a letter was sent to members from Acting President Edmonson asking for a donation of $1.00 to cover the ATC contribution that was paid for 1944 and 1945.

1946

GEORGIA
APPALACHIAN
19 TRAIL CLUB, INC. 30

Finally THE WAR came to an end. In the January, 1946, issue of *ATN*, Myron Avery outlined plans for the year for the Trail and for Conference. All efforts were to go into reopening and/or rebuilding the Trail in those areas where maintenance had lapsed. "Old maintaining organizations, as their members return and resume former activities, will be stimulated to Trail clearing activities. Where sponsorship has definitely ceased, new groups or individuals will be interested." (According to Marene Snow, she and treasurer, Carolyn Allen, had seen to it that the Club's annual contribution was made to Conference during the war years, apparently in part out of their own pockets. As Marene declared in later years, "We didn't want some other group to be put in charge of our Trail!") An AT Conference meeting would not be held until 1947, Avery stated, because of time needed to plan it, and because by then "the full effects of the war and attempted reconversion will be clearly apparent. Plans can be predicated upon existing and exact conditions." He went on to say:

This resume of procedure assumes continued and unceasing activity with respect to the major problem before the Appalachian Trail Conference. This is the fundamental and ever-present problem of the protection and preservation of the route. Post-war developments will make serious inroads on what was thought in 1940 to be secure. Trails on privately-held land, as all trail maintainers know, are subject to the vagaries of fluctuating ownership, lumbering and development. One who labors there very much gambles as to the future of his efforts. Fortunately, the Conference has evolved a very workable and practical plan for the preservation of the Appalachian Trail and comparable projects. This is the 'Hoch bill,' now pending before the Committee on Public Roads which will create a National System of Foot Trails. The absorption of Congressional Committees in pressing post-war matters, and the seeming minor importance of this measure, raise obstacles to its consideration. The Appalachian Trail Conference is fortunate indeed to have a member of its Board of Managers in Congress to press this project. Congressman Hoch will wage his battle with courage and discretion. Whatever success attends his efforts, the problem has become unmistakably clear. Any Trail route which is to survive must be in public ownership. Thereon, trail maintaining organizations may carry on, as the Hoch bill will permit, with the assurance that their activities will not be terminated on the morrow.

This objective, that of carrying the Appalachian Trail into public ownership, is the primary and fundamental problem of the Conference. In comparison, maintenance problems sink into insignificance. If this battle is not won, then all else is useless. Those who come after to carry on the torch of progress and hold the gains which have been made are fortunate in having so clearly defined for them the objective and goal to be sought, even though the way may be long and the goal difficult of attainment.

The same issue of the *ATN* carried a list of trail sections which were "known to have received current maintenance and which are particularly recommended" for travel for "those who seek to add in 1946 to their mileage of Appalachian Trail travel." Of Georgia, it stated: "While Forest Service trail, lack of information as to the character of the marking prompts the suggestion that Georgia Trail travel be an item of one's 1947 agenda. The most southerly 12 miles of Trail on privately owned land between the Chattahoochee National Forest and Mt. Oglethorpe should definitely not be attempted at this time."

However, an article in the May *ATN* reported the reverse. A report sent in to Conference by a Lieutenant F. L. Burgess, who walked from Oglethorpe to Frosty Mountain in March, declared, "The Trail at all points can be followed by blazes alone." He continued:

The Trail from Mt. Oglethorpe as far as it follows the road can hardly be improved. As in all portions through the woods, the Trail is here fouled by blowdowns and underbrush. Walking with packs is not difficult.

The pylon on Mt. Oglethorpe has suffered more damage from weather than from mankind. The marble is chipping rather badly. The large sign is sound, but barely legible, while the provision for registration of visitors needs refurbishing.

The cabin at the foot of the firetower three or four miles north is sound and roomy, although dirty. Fireplace looks good. There is a small cabin at the spring a few hundred yards north of the firetower with shelter for about four. Condition of occupancy uncertain.

At the new road crossing near the old golf course there are no signs indicating distance to towns or the spring.

Southern's Store to Amicalola Falls: Directions around Southern's Store require clarification. Signs are particularly needed here since blazes are obscure. This need extends across the new road north of the store and is present at the first stream crossing a few hundred yards farther on. There is no adequate footbridge at a second crossing of the stream a short distance farther north.

A sad note also appeared in the May *ATN:* Connahaynee Lodge, where the GATC had spent many happy times, burned to ground. The article read:

A stopping place for many starting to hike the Appalachian Trail from the southern terminus was Connahaynee Lodge, in the center of Tate Mountain Estates, five miles from Mt. Oglethorpe. This 20 room log structure, lavishly furnished, with marble baths, surrounded by 1,200 acres of grounds, including a 51-acre lake, was a unique hostelry.

On March 23, it caught fire and, as the site was 3,360 feet above sea level, in the mountains, fire fighting apparatus was not available. A high wind was blowing, and the lodge was completely destroyed.

Early in 1946 GATC members began to rally. Historian Marene Snow wrote:

Lawrence Freeman's return to Atlanta after serving Uncle Sam in far flung places and his enthusiasm for trail hiking furnished the much needed rallying point for old GATC members to stage a get-together and revive active trips to our mountains. Some 27 members got together at the Chester Elliott's to discuss ways and means. Lawrence was unanimously named chairman of activities, a tentative program of hikes set up, and not waiting to issue a bulletin, the date of this first hike—a clearing trip over Blood Mountain—was planned and reservations taken on the spot. Subsequent hikes were planned and the bulletin system re-established.

Glen Edmonson continued to function as president during the year of reorganization.

A small version of the *Mountaineer* appeared on May 14, 1946. The account of the Blood Mountain work trip read:

If the first post-war hike of the GATC is any indication of things to come, then the long banked fire of Trail Club activities has been rekindled and has burst forth in flame. This work trip of clearing and blazing—Neel Gap to the top of Blood Mountain and return—was made under ideal conditions. The weather was fine, and, for those who had expected a veritable jungle growth to be cleared from the Trail, the work was rather light.

The hikers rested and lunched at the top of Blood Mountain. A small group of hikers made a short scouting trip southward from Blood to determine the condition of the Trail and found it to be in very good shape.

The next work trip was planned to Unicoi Gap and Tray Mountain, but access to Unicoi Gap was blocked because of the paving of the highway, so work began at Tray Gap. The bulletin declared it a "highly successful trip, considering the enthusiasm with which the work was undertaken and the professional manner in which the Trail was cleared." Further trips were planned to the area.

Once again, regular trips were scheduled every two weeks to get the Trail cleared and marked. On a trip in June to clear between Neel and Tesnatee, it was found that the Forest Service had beat them to it. The next month an announcement in the bulletin read: "The Forestry Service has just completed clearing and marking the whole length of the AT as it crosses through the Chattahoochee National Forest. Some 200 pounds of galvanized iron markers were used. This is tremendously good news as all who participated in the Blood and Tray Mountain hikes will realize."

The *ATN* in September acknowledged the fine work of the Forest Service in Georgia, and quoted from an article in the *Atlanta Constitution* deploring the damage done in the state by a sleet storm the previous winter:

. . . In the mountains the damage was less, though the winter was the worst in the memory of its oldest men. The low-grade hardwoods on the high tops took a terrible beating, but the big trees in the coves and along the lower slopes were protected by the sheltering hills. But hikers who used to follow the Appalachian Trail, that great mountain highroad that begins at Mt. Oglethorpe north of Jasper, and winds north and east along the crest of the Blue Ridge and length of the eastern seaboard, will find their days of fine walking over. The Trail is now a tangle of fallen trees, impassable in places even to a mountain man.

Following this article, a letter had come to Myron Avery from Supervisor Spaulding which read:

I am happy to report that the entire Appalachian Trail on the Chattahoochee National Forest in Georgia has been maintained to standard, except where a fireroad has replaced the Trail. The 300 new signs you sent me have also been nailed on trees at important points.

The windfalls have been cut out, briars and other low shrubs have been trimmed and trail reblazed where necessary.

It has been difficult to accomplish this task. The District Rangers and their assistants are due considerable credit for this task.

The *ATN* concluded: "Thus the 80 miles of Trail in the Chattahoochee National Forest in Georgia may be added to the list of sections recommended for travel."

The annual meeting of the GATC was held in 1946 at the Dillard House. The bulletin account read, in part:

The weather was perfect, the leaves were at their height. It was fun watching people arrive—everyone was in such good spirits. Whole paragraphs ought to be written about Mrs. Dillard's hospitality and that wonderful food. Indeed, stories of some of the past dozen trips there were read aloud and all were alike in their high praises.

The colored slides from Washington were interesting. Myrtle Mae quickened our hearts with songs and a tango solo. The Rev. Rufus Morgan, legendary one-man trail club of the Nantahalas, said grace and told many of us about his experiences along his private AT. . . .

The hike was outstanding. Many of us have viewed Standing Indian from Kelly Knob and Powell and other high points along the Georgia Trail and have longed to climb it. Well, we did! And a better day for a stiff climb can scarcely be imagined. The trees on the upper third of the mountain had lost their leaves and visibility was perfect. It was cool and warm and the sun was shining.

Most of the group went home via Hiawassee and the new road through Unicoi Gap. The mountains fairly sparkled with reds and golds in the late afternoon sun. At least four carloads accidently met up at the Mayflower in Gainesville for Sunday night supper before the long ride back to Atlanta.

This was a small annual meeting as compared with some of the pre-war ones. But it lacked nothing in enthusiasm and good fellowship and an optimistic outlook for the future.

In December, the Club built a footbridge over the creek north of Highway 52. The bulletin report of the trip declared that the Trail needed clearing and working both ways, adding, "Perhaps it would be wise to relocate a short section that goes through the Southern's barnyard."

The year ended with the traditional Christmas party, held at the "Babington Mansion," with music, slides, food, and a good time by all.

Officers for the following year were elected at a business meeting in October: Larry Freeman, president; Searcy Slack, vice president; Lou Hoben, secretary; Elizabeth White, treasurer; Marene Snow, historian; Henry Morris, council member.

1947

BY THE BEGINNING OF 1947, the Club was really rolling again under the energetic leadership of Larry Freeman. A summary of activities for the coming year was sent out in January, activities were scheduled twice a month, bulletins were published regularly (almost) each month, and the membership was growing again.

The plans for January were stated thus:

A great deal of the Georgia Trail has not been traversed (by Club members) for several years. Roads have been changed, the condition of several shelters is doubtful and, at one point, a lake has bisected the Trail.

So during the month of January, an attempt will be made by various members of the Club to gather all possible data concerning the present condition of the Trail and its approaches. Data collecting trips will be undertaken by individuals—no organized hikes are scheduled.

During the year, members on scheduled hikes reported on the condition of the Trail, and a number of scouting and work trips were carried out by individuals and groups. In the summer, the southernmost part of the Trail was divided into sections with a leader who agreed to assume responsibility for the section and organize his own work trips.

The May 1947 *ATN* reported the Georgia Trail in the National Forest to be in good shape, but again declared most of the Trail on private land to be in bad condition.

The February GATC bulletin reported, "The lake above Amicalola, which was completed during the early stages of the war, had submerged one section of the Trail, and it will be necessary to relocate this section in the near future." This relocation was done toward the end of the year. The bulletin reported:

The AT from Amicalola Falls to Frosty Mountain was cleared and reblazed October 4, 1947. Going north the Trail comes in from Southern's Store over an old logging road. It follows the new road around the lake except for one short stretch where it leaves the road to follow the bank of the lake. We strongly recommend this new lake as an addition to the scenic beauty of the AT's southern end. To see Amicalola Falls, it is necessary to leave the Trail and go to the dam; the falls are just below, and a scramble down beside them is well worth while if you like waterfalls and don't mind the long climb back up.

The "first overnight trip of the year" was reported in the May bulletin:

The first overnight trip of the year was made the weekend of April 12-13. Nine people spent the night at Mr. Gene Willis's camp near Porter Springs, and were joined by four others Sunday morning at Woody Gap. Two groups were formed, one commencing at Woody Gap and hiking south, the other driving around to Cooper Gap and hiking north—meeting somewhere on the Trail. The first group digressed from the AT to climb the steep trail and enjoy the beautiful panorama of mountains and valleys to be seen from the summit of Black Mountain.

While it was comparatively easy to follow the AT, some of the blazes have become dim and are not frequent enough, and it is considered desirable to re-mark this section of the Trail. In addition, high winds have blown trees and brush across the Trail in many places, and considerable clearing is needed.

Highlights: Those making the overnight trip arrived at Mr. Willis's camp well before sundown Saturday, and after renewing old acquaintances and relating incidents of the trip up, a short hike was taken in the cool of the evening to a nearby lake. While other signs of spring were still scarce in North Georgia, masses of arbutus in bloom by the side of the road were a rare and beautiful sight.

Some few hardy souls remained at camp and did such chores as mending the water pump, spraying the peach trees, and bringing in wood for the evening fire.

After a sumptuous dinner including baked ham and scalloped potatoes prepared by Lou Hoben (as only she can prepare them), the evening was spent before a cheerful log fire where various questions of the day were properly settled and the group was entertained by Lawrence Freeman and James Proctor swapping experiences of their travels in foreign countries.

By the time the sun began to make pink streaks in the sky over the mountains Sunday morning, everyone was up; and after a delightful breakfast of hot cakes, maple syrup, crisp bacon, Brookfield sausage, and scrambled eggs, everyone felt properly refreshed, energized, and anxious to get on with the hike.

The last, and one of the most memorable experiences of the trip, was a good long draft of ice cold water from the artesian well at Woody Gap.

The first meeting of the ATC Board of Managers since 1941 was held in

December 1947. An attendance of 12 of the 18 members was "gratifying," according to Myron Avery. In his report of the effect of the war on the Trail sections, he said of the southern Trail:

The activities of our southern Clubs were greatly restricted. The Smoky Mountains Hiking Club was, of course, unable to work on its difficult 30-mile section of Yellow Creek-Wauchecha-Cheoah Mountains. With Arch Nichols becoming Captain Nichols of the U. S. Army, little trail work was done by the Carolina Mountain Club. Dr. Coolidge's organization (Unaka Mountain Club) in northern Tennessee ceased to function. The Georgia Appalachian Trail Club seemed literally to have disintegrated. Happily, all of these organizations (except the Unaka Mountain Club) have resurrected their activities with much promise. We have even gained, by the addition of a new Class 'A' organization, the Tennessee Eastman Hiking Club, which will take over the work in northern Tennessee in the vicinity of the Nolichucky River. While we do not have too clear a picture of the Georgia situation, its President attended our 1946 Armistice Day meeting and we have had reports of Trail activities there and feel that a revival at the southern end is under way. Chattahoochee National Forest activity has absorbed some of the slack.

Avery gave credit to Chattahoochee National Forest Supervisor Spaulding for his "interest and activity" in keeping the Trail open in Georgia.

GATC activities during 1947, other than work trips, included a number of in-town activities, trips to Sitton's Gulch, Joyce Kilmer Forest and the Okefenokee Swamp. On the schedule of yearly activities distributed in January, the announcement of the trip from Tray Mountain to Addis Gap stated: "The last time we visited the Addis's (mountain people) they ran inside their house and bolted the doors and windows. We left our surplus food on their doorstep." On the post-trip account in the bulletin it was noted: "Talking with Forest Ranger at Moccasin Creek, it was learned that the Addis family moved from their little valley in 1942."

At a meeting at Dillard in October, the following officers were elected for 1948: Larry Freeman, president; Searcy Slack, vice president; Marion Morris, secretary; Arnold Ingemann, treasurer; Marene Snow, historian; Jimmy Cragon, Henry Morris, Elizabeth White, council members.

Larry Freeman's leadership, personality and ideas were to be a dominant force in the GATC for a number of years. He was a particularly private person; one anecdote is that, for a time, no one knew where he lived and he had no telephone. To contact him, one would write him at his post office box and would receive a call in reply. Also, he is generally credited with putting the Trail on Forest Service roads in many places where it was obscure or impassable after the war, so that the entire Trail in Georgia would be "open for business" quickly.

The "first in-town annual meeting" was held at the Atlanta Women's Club on November 8. It was "conceded a pronounced success by 70-odd members and visiting friends."

1948

GEORGIA
APPALACHIAN
19 TRAIL CLUB, INC. 30

THE EMPHASIS OF THE CLUB on getting the Trail back into shape continued throughout 1948. A report written by Trail Supervisor, Henry Morris, in June for the AT Conference gave a summary of the Club's activities to that date:

During 1947 the Georgia Appalachian Trail Club began getting back into stride by organizing activities more nearly on a pre-war basis, regular hikes being scheduled and carried out as planned, and some trail clearing accomplished.

This year the program has been even better. A complete schedule of hikes and educational meetings was arranged and published at the beginning of the year, and to date the schedule has been carried out, with the exception of one or two cases where extremely inclement weather prevented. In addition, an excellent program of trail clearing has been accomplished.

Previously, trail clearing had been scattered, in order to get the worst spots first, but it was soon realized that as a result of time, plus a winter of severe wind and ice storms, and logging operations, the entire Trail would have to be gone over to put it in first-class condition.

Additional tools have been purchased; and since last spring, an intense program of trail clearing has been carried on, having from one to three groups clearing trail on a single weekend.

One trail clearing group started at Oglethorpe Mountain, where a new registration book and a new metal container were installed on the post supporting the Appalachian Trail sign, and has worked north on the Trail to Amicalola Falls where it joins the section cleared by another group. This extends the continuously cleared section on to Frosty Mountain, a distance of twenty-one miles. All of this is on privately owned land.

This section, plus other parts of the Trail cleared this year and last, puts about one-third to one-half of the Georgia Trail in excellent condition.

Much valuable assistance has been given by Mr. C. K. Spaulding, Supervisor of the Chattahoochee National Forest, in maintaining the Trail in the forest area. This section, where the Trail does not parallel a road, has been cleared to a width of five feet and many metal markers have been nailed on trees along the way.

There are several factors which contribute to the trail maintenance problem of the Georgia Club:

1. The available working time on our clearing trips is rather short due to the long drive necessary to reach any part of the Trail. Most trips average two hundred miles or more, round trip.

2. Some sections of the Trail are impossible to reach in rainy weather.

3. Membership in the Club is relatively small at the present time.

However, considering the progress made to date, the Georgia Trail should be in jam up condition by the end of next year.

From Gooch Gap to Springer Mountain, a distance of 14.7 miles, the Trail zig-zags back and forth across a Forest Service road and there has been considerable debate whether or not to re-route the Trail completely in order to get it away from this road.

Shelters on the Trail have been found in fair condition considering the long period of inattention; however, some of them have been badly used by persons other than hikers, who have no appreciation of their real worth or importance. Considerable repair work will be necessary to put them in usable condition. Shelters encountered on clearing trips are cleaned out and minor repairs made. It is considered more important to get the Trail cleared and well marked first—then recondition the shelters on subsequent trips.

Several meetings of general interest to our membership have been held throughout the year—such as the hike to Hightower Bald near the Georgia-North Carolina line, led by Dr. Duncan, Professor of Botany at the University of Georgia. Dr. Duncan gave a lecture at the campsite accompanied with Kodachrome slides of Georgia wildflowers. Dr. Fattig of Emory University gave a lecture on insects in his laboratory at the University. Dr. Lane Mitchell of Georgia Tech gave a lecture, demonstration and souvenirs on ceramics and Georgia clays. Dr. Kelly gave a lecture on old Indian trails and campgrounds in Georgia. Many square dances have been held.

A quarter-hour discussion of the Appalachian Trail was broadcast over radio station WCON on May 26 of this year.

Almost every hike was used to do Trail work. One trip announcement declared: "It's fun to try to find the original Trail."

Of a trip in February the bulletin wrote:

The overnight trip February 21-22, Woody Gap to Neel Gap, offers evidence without argument that the GATC has in its membership the stamina and urge of the true hiker. If a trip is scheduled, they make it somehow, somewhere. The weather retards and roads impede but they enjoy the double delight of the conquering victors. Nine such defiant souls reached the cabin north of Dahlonega, two miles off the highway—these two miles almost impassable—where they cooked and sang and slept to the rhythm of the raindrops all night. There was plenty of water to catch which proves again 'an ill wind, etc.' as the cabin well was dry (!) and the spring too doubtful to use. No report on *how* they got out over these two miles back to the highway—but Sunday A.M. in rain and fog they proceeded to Woody Gap. They report the Trail in bad shape, obliterated in places, to the extent of party getting lost briefly.

A trip was made to the Mt. Oglethorpe area in April, according to the bulletin:

Perfect weather for a Trail Club trip, and two young fawns sighted Sunday morning. Everybody was in fine spirit for a good old outing, as proven by the work accomplished and the fine spirit of cooperation. The entire length of trail from Highway 136 to Mt. Oglethorpe was cleared and marked; the grounds surrounding the monument, Sassafras shelter, and one other cabin were cleaned and put in excellent condition, and the spring cleaned out. The old post and mutilated cylinder that formerly held the registration book were removed and a new steel cylinder and registration book installed on one of the posts supporting the sign at Oglethorpe Mountain. By pre-arrangement, all workers met at the 'shelter' at twelve o'clock and spent a delightful hour having lunch, followed by sun-bathing. Although the Sassafras shelter has been badly used by unknown persons, and natural growth had crept in upon it, it really presented an inviting appearance as we stopped by for a last look on the way home. It was also discovered that the shelter has one permanent resident. Not by prearrangement, everyone met at the drug store in Jasper and enjoyed 'goodies.'

By October the work was not finished, as reported in the bulletin:

There are still some miles of our Trail that have not been cleared or blazed since 1942. Old blazes have become so dim that in places a traveler is without any guidance whatsoever.

Our greatest obligation to the Club is the maintenance of this Trail. So, next weekend, weather permitting, we will make a supreme effort to blaze the remaining miles.

The Club's "first scheduled Trail Club climb up Hightower Bald" featured Dr. Wilbur Duncan, botanist from the University of Georgia, who was the "guest leader." In the evening, at a "roadside theater," Dr. Duncan gave a "Kodachrome lantern slide lecture" on mountain plants that attracted 250 "mountain folk." Of the hike up the mountain, Ed Runyon reported in the bulletin:

. . . rest stops were none too frequent nor too long! At the cold spring we tanked up and found amethysts. Then 2,000 feet up in less than two miles, Doc Wilbur opened our eyes to a myriad of plants, including many at or near the southern boundary of their range. Northern plants are especially prominent in a cove on the north-facing side of the mountain where a beech, sugar maple, birch forest flourishes. Wilbur says it's colder on that side, but Ed and Phyllis did not look a bit cool on their return from a trip down that side. I was there to witness that Charlie's Bunion is no steeper. On the tip top—only 200 feet lower than Brasstown—we had lunch, repose and grand vistas of Enotah, Standing Indian, Tray and Wayah Bald; all quenchingly welcome and therapeutic. The descent was down a slope not quite vertical. . . .

The January 1948 *ATN* announced new TVA maps covering the entire AT route and pointed out that the Hightower Gap Quadrangle "incidentally discloses an error in the assumption that Bly Gap is exactly on the Georgia-North Carolina line. The map indicates the gap as lying a little north of the state line. Thus, Georgia must cede to North Carolina a small fraction of its 96 miles of Appalachian Trail."

In 1946, a proposal had been made to Conference to re-route the AT in the western Smokies and the Yellow Creek Mountains, so as to cross the Little Tennessee River at the new Fontana Dam instead of at Tapoca. This re-route would eliminate a long dog-leg over Gregory Bald, to Deals Gap and Tapoca and back east again, and would provide a crossing of the river and accommodations at Fontana Village. The area had been scouted, and at a meeting of southern ATC board members, the route was inspected by them, along with Myron Avery, other Smoky Club members, Larry Freeman of the GATC, "a delegation . . . from a new hiking organization at Kingsport, Tennessee," and others. The relocation was subsequently approved by the Board of Managers and was completed by 1948.

The hoped-for 1947 meeting of the AT Conference had been postponed because of the still "abnormal" situation caused by the war, and the inability of any club to hold such a meeting. The Board of Managers had voted in 1947 to hold the next meeting at Fontana Village in June, 1948. At that time, the eleventh AT Conference—the first since 1941—was convened, and Larry Freeman, who was to be elected at the meeting to the Board of Managers, gave the welcoming address. Reports were made by the clubs on the post-war condition of the Trail and the efforts being made to restore it to pre-war condition. Numerous relocations were reported, one by the New York-New Jersey Conference because of a nudist colony established on the Trail.

Sixteen GATC members attended the Conference, and most of them enjoyed the varied hiking afterward. The *Mountaineer* gave an extensive account of the meeting and activities afterward, and included the following paragraph:

Trail Maintenance. 'She discovered, however, to her disappointment, that the Trail had not been maintained and had become impassable in spots so she had to give up her journey.' 'Plagued by mosquitoes, bad weather, and a run down Trail, they made only 37 miles in seven days. Thoroughly discouraged, they decided to give the whole thing up.' No, the above is not unconscious repetition. They are quotes from two articles, appearing in the *Atlanta Constitution* and *Life Magazine* and refer to two widely separated sections of the AT—Oglethorpe and Katahdin regions. But both show the condition of the Trail at the close of the war years and reports at the Conference disclosed that most other sections were in much the same state. These reports though showed something more—the enthusiastic attack and the progress being made to rapidly bring the Trail back to standard. All clubs seem to have much the same maintenance problems as Georgia. We were very proud of the report of progress on the Georgia sections made by our Chairman, Henry Morris. Due to his leadership, the hard work of the members (and guests) participating, and the help from Mr. Spaulding, Supervisor of the Chattahoochee National Forest, Henry's report was acclaimed one of the best made at Conference. Let's all get busy and finish the work still needed on our section to maintain it up to standard. Remember, it will take 'the everlasting teamwork of every blooming soul.'

At the Conference, the ATC constitution was amended to provide for meetings every three years instead of every two.

During the Conference meeting, a message was received from Earl Shaffer stating that he was nearing the Connecticut line on a proposed hike of the entire AT. The September *ATN* announced that he had completed his journey, and he, thereby, became the first known hiker to accomplish this great feat.

The annual meeting of the GATC was held on October 31 at the Dillard House. Among other business transacted was a proposal to investigate buying a lot at the Allatoona Dam site with a view toward building a cabin there for the Club's use.

Officers for 1949 were elected: James Cragon, president; Searcy Slack, first vice president; E. G. Field, second vice president; Arnold Ingemann, treasurer; Pat Gartrell, secretary; Marene Snow, historian.

At the annual dinner in November, according to the bulletin:

Some mighty nice things were said about our retiring president (much to Larry's discomfort), in which he was likened to the fairy tale prince who came along at just the right time and awakened the sleeping beauty. And that is just what did happen. Through his unbounded enthusiasm, tact, persuasiveness and refusal to accept defeat, Larry revived and rejuvenated the Club from its war-time lethargy until now it is again a going concern, and a darned good one.

It was also recorded that at the dinner "Commander Field introduced our speaker who was no less than E. Guy Frizzell himself. We were indeed honored to have Guy and four others of the Knoxville Club as our guests."

1949

GEORGIA
APPALACHIAN
19 TRAIL CLUB. INC. 30

GAIN IN 1949, THE CLUB worked to put the Trail— and the shelters—in "jam up condition." Along with this went the project of measuring and describing the Georgia section in a north-to-south direction for a new edition of the Southern guidebook. All hikes—planned to cover the entire Georgia Trail—were to be made in a southerly direction for this purpose.

In January, scouting trips were begun to locate new shelter sites, one between Dick's Creek and Bly Gaps, and one in the vicinity of Gooch Gap. In February, at long last, a determined effort was made to scout a relocation of the Trail between Gooch and Cooper Gaps. So the Club had its work cut out for the year, and most hikes found them either pushing the measuring wheel or wielding paint brush or clearing tools. But even these work trips provided an abundance of excitement and fun for those who participated.

On one of the January shelter scouting trips, the group camped just below Tesnatee Gap in below freezing temperatures. The bulletin reported that "the sound of chattering teeth could be heard all the way back to Cleveland." The account continued:

While The Braves prepared their respective steaks, potatoes, et cetera, under the able supervision of the noted culinary expert, Pat Gartrell, the Frail Five sat around the edges looking on longingly and devouring their stew ravenously. The campers 'hit the sack' at ten o'clock and soon the camp was merged into the deep stillness of the night. Lou Hoben, sleeping in the edge of the wooded game preserve, reports she was visited by a BEAR who sat down by her and tickled her through the bedding. A call for help failed to reach the bundled-up ears of nearby campers, so after waiting for half an hour for Mr. Bruin to take more drastic action, Lou got disgusted and went back to sleep.

A proposed trip to the Montray shelter was announced in the bulletin thus:

Lost, one shelter! At least the last party over Tray was unable to find it, but Olivia Bagwell allows she will either find a shelter or where one has been if she has a search party large enough to fan out over the back side of Tray Mountain. Seems like we lose MORE shelters this way! The purpose of this trip is to inspect the shelter for future repairs, if feasible, or to determine that a new shelter must be built.

The report of this trip in the next bulletin, written by Larry Freeman, gave a splendid account of the day:

This turned out to be a pleasant and exciting day, proving once again the old contention that the best trips are often started under the most adverse conditions. Most of those who had made reservations rolled reluctantly out of bed into a cold, very rainy, very dark morning—hoping in vain that someone would phone someone else that the trip was off. A timid few and some sick-a-beds did decide to stay home, but sixteen others left Atlanta in the early, gray light of the dawn—driving the hundred-odd miles through a rain-splattered countryside to the base of Tray Mountain. Here the rain ceased but the upper heights of the mountain were blanketed in thick clouds. Numerous trees, fallen across the road, made driving very dangerous.

The hike began at the Pass. Every twig was coated with ice, and from far overhead came the roar of violent wind. At the summit of Tray the hikers saw that rare spectacle of rime, streaking leeward from every branch. Farther along to the north where the wind was more constant, the rime was sometimes a foot long—exceeding any the members of the group had ever seen before. Red galax leaves, glazed in ice, looked like French ceramics. Along the Trail were hundreds of tiny flowers, tragically frozen, as if encased in transparent teardrops. Along a higher slope the hikers came upon a beautiful doe lying dead on the mountainside, with the mystery all around her of how she came to die. And over all came the sound of myriad heavily-iced trees tossing in the wind.

Down the slope on the other side there was less ice, and green moss carpeted the rocks. Carter knew exactly where the Montray shelter was, and led the group straight to it. A fire was built inside, and lunches, vigorously attacked, soon disappeared. There was a nearby spring, flowing strong and clear. After a short rest the hikers climbed back to the top, then down through the clouds to the valley where rain was still falling steadily. The cars were loaded and soon departed. A stop was made at the little restaurant in Cleveland, where coffee and puddin' (spelled that way on the menu) were enjoyed immensely. Then all hands headed south for home.

The relocation of the Trail between Cooper and Gooch Gaps was to be no easy task. Weather, time and the difficulty of the job combined to delay the completion time and time again. The first successful trip, under the direction of Larry Freeman, was made in February and was "one of the most enjoyable hikes of recent date." The account read, in part:

After sorting and assembling knapsacks, lunches and sweaters, the hikers started north from Cooper Gap. The prospect of locating a new, more remote route for the Trail, in addition to the perfect day, was ample reason for the high spirits and enthusiasm evident throughout the group. The first phase of the hike was a stiff climb up Justus Mountain to the 'Vantage Point' near the summit. Here the old Trail route was left behind, with part of the group going on to the top of Justus, and the remainder cutting across to the 'saddle' due east of the mountain. The hikers worked their way through 'unexplored' forest and were now in one of the most beautiful forest regions in Georgia. Windfalls were on every hand—mute evidence of the havoc of the sleet storm two weeks before. But all around, tiny green buds could be seen, pushing through the black rich floor of the forest. Justus Mountain is almost level along the top for about a quarter mile, and would make a perfect setting for the new Trail route. The group dropped down the back side of the mountain through a beautiful stretch of hardwoods, then descended into a snug, secluded cove with a small stream, near Justus Gap, where lunch and sunshine were enjoyed to the fullest.

The afternoon was spent in further exploration by two groups of the territory in the valley between Justus Gap and Horseshoe Ridge and of Horseshoe Ridge adjacent to Gooch Gap, but due to lack of daylight hours that part of the relocation project was not completed and will have to be worked out at a later time.

After this, several of the scheduled trips on this section were rained out. The frustrated leader, Larry Freeman, announced in the bulletin of the proposed May trip, "We're going to finish this job, or else! . . . Let's show the weather man that we can't be bluffed, and have an even larger registration. . . . This building a new five mile trail through the forest on a compass line is one of the most fascinating, and incidentally the most important, activity that the GATC will have for some time to come. . . . It is again planned to establish a camp and have the food prepared by volunteers for the trail workers."

Of this trip the bulletin reported: "This could well be called the 'Cooper to (almost) Gooch' trip. One more carload of workers and the Georgia Trail would be clear and passable from Oglethorpe to the Nantahalas."

But then the report of THAT trip read:

Only thing wrong with this trip was that the re-route just wasn't finished and, furthermore, there is still a lot of work to be done. After getting off to a late start, it was decided that a trip would be made over the completed section first in order to allow everyone to see it before concentrating on the heavy clearing job. Well, you know how it is when you go back over a completed job, here is another tree that needs to come out and the marking is not clear at this turn, etc. So much time was spent before reaching the main clearing job that very little headway was made. In the meantime, the Trail is adequately marked along the roadway so nobody will get lost coming through.

Even though we didn't finish the job, everyone enjoyed the day and it is the general feeling that when completed this will be one of the beauty sections of the Georgia Trail.

In July, the third "finishing up" trip was scheduled, the announcement admitting, "You're right—it is too hot for a work trip, and we have been having too many work trips this year anyway, but how about that swim at Lake Winfield Scott? . . . We do have an obligation to finish this job. . . ." This trip managed to finish all but less than half a mile. A "grand opening" was scheduled for August, with plans for a group to finish up the small stretch the day before. All went as planned (except for a group led by Searcy Slack which—accidentally?— took a wrong turn and got "side-tracked into a picnic") and the bulletin wrote of the opening: "The new Trail from Gooch to Cooper was officially opened on Sunday, August 7. . . .

A solemn ceremony marked the occasion. Jimmy Cragon told of the six work trips necessary to complete this five and a half mile re-route; and the 38 Club members and guests who had helped with its scouting, clearing and marking, on one or more of these trips, undaunted by the bad weather which haunted each effort, the detours, and the roads almost impassable at times.

To Phyllis fell the honor of placing the first blaze as the Trail leaves the road. (You remember the occasion when one of the crests was given her name?) Lou, the oldest present in terms of membership, nailed up the metal marker. And Carter broke the bottle of champagne, dedicating the 'Trail of '49' to the use of all hikers. We all appreciate the efforts of the members and guests of the Club who helped with this undertaking. We are especially grateful to Larry for his vision in scouting this beautiful section of Trail, and Jimmy for his patience and determination in seeing that the job was completed.

In March, one of the in-town activities provided a special treat: a talk and movie presented by Charlie Elliott, "one of the founders and a charter member of the GATC," on the wildlife of north Georgia and on how the Georgia Trail was established.

In June, the bulletin announced, "For the first time in the remembered history of the GATC, a three-day trip on the Georgia Trail by the Club as a group is offered." The trip was planned from Unicoi Gap to Neel Gap, and was led by Searcy Slack and Pat Gartrell. Pat was the only woman making the three-day trip. The account declared it a successful hike "with no more serious casualties than more or less permanent curvature of the clavicle . . . associated blisters, assorted chiggers, and more tales than this or any future issue . . . will find space or censors to publish."

The "four-club meet"—now including the new Tennessee Eastman Hiking Club—was held over the Labor Day weekend near Highlands, North Carolina, at Van Hook Glade. Camping, hiking, swimming, square dancing, and reports of clubs added up to "the most successful and enjoyable" joint meeting yet held, according to the bulletin.

On a hike in September from Dick's Creek Gap to Tray Gap, the Club was joined by three senior scouts "who were rounding out an 80-mile hike from

Wesser Bald." One of the scouts was Whit Benson, who was soon to become a hard-working member, and remains so today. The bulletin noted, "Bob, Frank, Norman and Whit, aided and abetted by Jim Proctor, can and will cook and consume almost anything to produce a seven (or nine) course meal. But they drew the line at Bob's chocolate pudding that failed to 'pud.'"

A letter from Jimmy Cragon to a hiker who had requested advice (printed in the September *ATN*) gave a good picture of the conditions on the Georgia Trail:

...With regard to the keys to the two cabins, the Sassafras is no longer locked as it is not under our control. It is in good condition but probably not very clean. The Frosty Mountain Shelter has a Forest Service lock as there are some fire fighting tools stored in a closet. We recommend the use of these cabins, as well as all of the others in the Georgia section except one, only for bad weather during the summer. The one exception is the Tesnatee Gap Shelter, which is an open type lean-to and stays clean.

A few things which may be of interest or help to you are as follows: The approach to Oglethorpe, described in the Guide, from Jasper is generally correct, except that the Connahaynee Lodge has burned and a Radio FM relay station is being erected at the site. You should be able to arrange transportation from Jasper, drop off your pack at the Sassafras Cabin and ride to the base of Oglethorpe. However, the road is badly washed and overgrown beyond the old Connahaynee Lodge and the driver may object to going all the way. Generally speaking, the Trail is in fairly good condition all the way though Georgia, but there are places where summer growth will make it necessary to watch closely for markers and there is some down timber, which we have not as yet had an opportunity to clear. However, there have been several groups and individuals through already this year and they had very little, if any, difficulty. The one place where the Guide is now wrong is from Hightower Gap (Section 3) to Cane Creek Gap (7 m.), all of which has been temporarily placed on the roadway. A reroute is now under construction between Cooper Gap (3.5 m.) and Gooch Gap (8.1 m.), which follows the old trail up Justice Mountain for a short distance. Last week, a Boy Scout troop followed these old markings into our uncompleted reroute and had to bushwack a mile and a half through the woods to get back to the road. Although the markings were supposed to have been obliterated near the road, they were following the Trail description in the Guide rather than the new markings along the road.

A few other things which may be of help or interest to you that occur to me are: You can get mail at either Suches, in care of the Ranger Station or a general store which is operated by a young couple named H. E. Tritt who take a great interest in AT folk, or at the Ranger Station at Unicoi Gap. About the only supply point near enough to reach on foot from the Trail is Suches. . . .

A brief history and account of the GATC by Cragon, also printed in the September *ATN*, extended the picture of Trail conditions in Georgia:

During the war, when the Forest Service was undermanned and the Georgia Appalachian Trail Club was more or less dormant, the Appalachian Trail in Georgia was of necessity allowed to get into a very poor condition. As soon as transportation was again available, a concerted effort was made to clear and re-mark the Trail as soon as possible. As a temporary expedient, some of the worst sections were rerouted to parallel fireroads. Unfortunately, some through travel was attempted by out-of-state people before this work could be completed, resulting in some criticism. There is no longer any danger of losing the way on the Trail in Georgia. In fact, a group consisting of a father, mother and two children, none of whom had ever been on a trail before in their lives, recently completed a successful week on the Georgia section. The first of a planned series of reroutes to get off the roadways has just been completed. This particular reroute of approximately five miles has opened up an entirely new and beautiful area to the Appalachian Trail.

Shelters have also deteriorated from lack of attention. It is hoped that they can all be patched up enough to be usable by this winter and that at least one can be replaced each year until they are all again in first-class condition. The old, closed cabins, which were constructed of logs in the early thirties by the CCC, will give way to open-type shelters in which as much of the structure as possible will be built of stone and cement.

The Appalachian Trail in Georgia has much to offer in the way of variety and beauty at each season of the year.

"The fine things of life seem all too rare, and it is always with reluctance that we see them pass on into memory," read the bulletin account of the annual meeting in October of 1949. The meeting was held at the Dillard Farm, and featured food, a talk and songs by Rufus Morgan, slides, the business meeting and election of officers. Officers for the coming year were to be: Jimmy Cragon, president; Searcy Slack and Newell Good, vice presidents; Pat Gartrell, secretary; Charlie Gafnea, treasurer; Marene Snow, historian; and Lou Hoben, council.

Toward the end of the year, the Club began to consider the "disposition" of the Frosty Mountain cabin, "which the Forest Service wants to tear down as being beyond repair." On a work trip in November, a survey of needed repairs was made, and the Trail was relocated to pass the spring and go around the side of the mountain. Trip leader, Searcy Slack, reported, "Moving the shelter down by the spring is proposed, but that would take plenty of doing." The bulletin account included the following paragraph: "Driving down by Amicalola Falls we noted a surprising amount of logging activity. The resultant clearing has revealed Amicalola shelter, long lost and hidden in the laurel slicks. It does not look like any spectacular 'find' from the road." (Amicalola Falls had been made a state park earlier in 1949.)

1950

GEORGIA
APPALACHIAN
19 TRAIL CLUB, INC. 50

AS THE NEW DECADE BEGAN, the Club seemed to have completely recovered from the trauma suffered during the war and the struggle to re-establish itself and the Trail. It was firmly settled into a routine of regular twice-a-month hikes, work trips, square dances and in-town get-togethers. The end-of-the-year report of the activities committee reported that for the first time the entire Trail in Georgia was covered by scheduled hikes, and all but a few hikes were on the Georgia Trail.

The January bulletin reported on the first trip of the year:

The Trail Clubbers and a sizable contingent of guests made a 'touchdown on the kick-off' trip for 1950. The day started cold, crisp and clear. By ten-thirty some twenty-four hikers had assembled in Woody Gap. Although the temperature stood at 22 degrees (above) in the early morning, it had climbed to a high of 28 by the time all hands arrived. The hikers divided into two groups—the larger group going up the Black Mountain trail to the lookout tower on top—the small group striking out around the sunny south side of the mountain on one of the most beautiful sections of the AT we have yet seen. The purpose of the side-trip across the top of Black Mountain was for reconnaissance, with a possibility of making this a secondary through trail, by constructing a trail down the back side of the mountain to Tritt Gap. The views from the top of the mountain are superb, but after sliding down the steep back side, which was ice covered at the time, it was decided the main trail should not be taken over the mountain top—at least not this year.

A report of the "Trail Maintenance Boss Lady" Lou Hoben in August stated that "the almost 100 miles have, since the first of the year, been covered completely at least once. . . ." But weeds, downed trees, and deteriorating shelters showed no mercy, and trail maintenance continued to take priority.

The year's first major chore was the refurbishing of the Montray shelter, including new bunks, a porch, and a new roof made from several hundred pounds of metal signs, carried to the site by Club members. The work was done in great part by "our younger contingent and their scout troop," according to the bulletin.

A ten-day work trip was undertaken in June by some of this "younger contingent"—Whit Benson, Norman Batho, and Jim Proctor, with the help of two guests—from Tesnatee Gap north toward Bly Gap. After almost a week of hard work cutting weeds and windfalls, they finally gave up at Addis Gap and hitch-hiked and walked by way of Highways 75 and 76 to Blue Ridge Gap to meet a weekend GATC work group.

Another project was undertaken in July. The announcement in the bulletin read: "Ever since the three-day hike of last July 4 when half of the 'dauntless dozen' got lost on the so-called trail between Poplar Stomp Gap and Low Gap, we have wanted to go back and relocate the Trail by putting it on the fire road. . . . We will also scout the area between Poplar Stomp Gap and Chattahoochee Gap to decide on the advisability of relocating that section of Trail, or part of it, along the fire road. . . ." There had been intermittent problems on this section for many years. The Trail over Horsetrough Mountain was often overgrown, and the road below offered an easy, open way, with the result that many hikers used the road rather than the Trail. The relocation, as the bulletin stated, had "the advantages over the Horsetrough Mountain trail of being comparatively level, having several springs, of being easy to follow, and of affording good views at several points." (In 1979 when it was suggested that the Trail be put back over Horsetrough, these same reasons were given for leaving it on the road.)

Lou Hoben's report to the council in August on the trail work done was considered worthy of reprinting in the August bulletin. It read:

From the miles I have walked myself, and the reports I've received on other sections, I would say that the Trail in Georgia as of this date is in fair to good condition throughout, and would compare favorably with the trails in other States. The almost 100 miles have, since the first of the year, been covered completely at least once and in some sections, several times. On most of the scheduled trips, much was accomplished in the way of repainting blazes and brushing out; and on some, axes and cross-cut saw were used to good advantage. The new Myron Avery signs have been placed at strategic points on the north end of the Trail (from the North Carolina State Line to Dick's Creek Gap). The blue-blaze approach trails by way of Marble Hill, and Lake Winfield Scott to Slaughter Gap are clearly marked. Also, identification markers have been set up on the approach to Mt. Oglethorpe at intersections on Highway 136. On the thirteen days of regular scheduled trips, there was an aggregate of 184 individuals who helped with the maintenance of the Trail. This represents 952 man-miles and 1560 man-hours. In addition, Jimmy Proctor and his cohorts spent ten days (June 9-19) on an intensive work trip, clearing and marking from Slaughter Gap to the North Carolina State Line, giving an additional 250 man-miles and 336 man-hours. (I'll not convert this into ergs, BTU's or foot-lbs., but it is certainly evident how much work has been done by a limited number of individuals.) There remains to be done the clearing out of some 50 fallen trees in several sections, to make for easier walking; placing more signs (Mr. Traylor can tell exactly how many are planned for) and, of course, the continuous job of retouching blazes and cutting the annual growth of small stuff and underbrush. However, anyone in any way experienced should have no difficulty in hiking from Mt. Oglethorpe to the North Carolina line, either from the point of view of following a blazed trail, or actual comfortable walking conditions.

A somewhat more pessimistic view of Trail conditions was expressed by Shakey Shivers after a nine-day hike with three Explorer scouts from Mt. Oglethorpe to Dick's Creek Gap in August. Shakey reported that "We are now in full knowledge of the entire Trail in Georgia. Some of our impressions are not very favorable. Shelters are in a sad state of repair. Water is too far from shelters. There is too much Trail on hard roads. . . . All of the hard work of swing-blading in the early summer has gone for naught as most of the Trail is heavily overgrown. . . . The Trail from Chattahoochee to Unicoi is only fit for rabbits and foxes to play leap-frog over the many, many windfalls. . . . I could go on and on. . . ." But many of these problems were to be tackled in the near future, and progress was slowly made in putting things in good condition.

The annual get-togethers of the Southern clubs were now being called the "Four Club Meet" (GATC, Smoky Mountains Club, Carolina Mountain Club, and Tennessee Eastman Hiking Club), and were beginning to narrow down to Labor Day as the time for the event. In 1950, the meet was held at Lake Winfield Scott (not on Labor Day) and featured again the Rev. Rufus Morgan singing mountain songs and telling stories for the assemblage. The bulletin account noted that a "new" hiking club was being organized in western North Carolina, to be known as the Nantahala Hiking Club. The club that had ceased to function with the death of George Tabor in 1936 was (eventually) to be brought back to life by Rufus Morgan.

The time and place for the election and installation of officers of the GATC had varied somewhat in recent years. For the first ten or so years the elections had been held at the annual meeting, which was held out of town over a weekend in the fall. For the past few years it had been held at a short business meeting during the fall weekend at the Dillard Farm, although this was not always considered the annual meeting. In 1950, the annual trip to the Dillard Farm was not made, having been cancelled in favor of a fall trip to LeConte. The election of officers was held at a special council meeting in October. Officers for 1951 were: Newell Good, president; Guerrard Spratt, first vice president; Chester Elliott, second vice president; Lou Hoben, secretary;

Charles Gafnea, treasurer; Jim Cragon and Searcy Slack, council.

The annual trips to Mt. LeConte were re-established in 1950. The hike up to the lodge (run by Mr. and Mrs. Jack Huff) "in the gold and crimson forests of the Great Smokies" was made by way of either the Boulevard or the Alum Cave Trail. "A sunset trip over to Cliff Top, evening movies, songs and tales around the log fire in the big cabin," and a walk out to Myrtle Point in the morning were reported by leader Larry Freeman.

The Okefenokee Swamp was the setting for a memorable trip in November—not only for the unique and beautiful surroundings, as the group camped on Billy's Island, but memorable for the temperature, which dropped to around 10 degrees. As the bulletin reported, "Everybody had all their clothes on."

For the past four years, the Club had enjoyed a well-planned and well-carried out program of activities—thanks to Searcy Slack, who had been vice president and activities chairman since 1947. At the year-end council meeting, Searcy was extended "a vote of thanks for his long and faithful service."

1951

GEORGIA
APPALACHIAN
19 TRAIL CLUB, INC. 30

Trips and activities in 1951 continued in much the same pattern, but with several more off-the-AT trips, including three to the Smokies. Committees were reorganized under President Newell Go. d, and several new ones were added. Trail work continued, and the *ATN* report from Georgia stated: "We have definite plans for extensive maintenance improvement work on Trail in 1951 and hope to have the entire Georgia Trail in excellent condition before the end of the year."

The infamous "Buckhead Bullet" made its appearance in January, introducing "a new idea in Trail Club transportation." The Bullet was a boy scout bus, and was driven by Shakey (Hot Rod) Shivers who, according to the report of the first trip, "did a very capable (if occasionally disconcerting) job of driving." After the Club had taken several trips in the bus, the March bulletin announced another "glorious opportunity to ride with 'Hot Rod' Shivers in the 'Buckhead Bullet' . . . on a superb new 'ROCKET RIDE,' a 200-mile round trip through the mountains. . . . Those with weak hearts will meet the bus at Suches. . . ."

The bus was temperamental, however, and of a trip in May to the Okefenokee Swamp, the bulletin reported that those taking the trip on the Bullet "had the 'mostest' fun. . . . Of course, it took a little more travel time by bus(t)— eighteen hours going down and thirty-six hours coming back."

Whit Benson early acquired a reputation as a tough hiker. On a Club trip in April in the Chattahoochee Gap area, the group met Whit and "were very much excited by the recount of his exploits." The bulletin related: "After arriving in the vicinity of Brasstown Bald about 6:00 P.M. Saturday by the hitch-hiking route and then scouting this area for a future hike, Whit naturally decided to set out cross-country to the AT to meet Shakey. It was a lovely night—no moon and pitch black—but Whit finally found Shakey at Rocky Knob shelter at 2:30 A.M."

Although the Club had many "overnight" trips, they were still mostly two day hikes, or hiking on Sunday only, with car camping on Saturday night. "Packing everything through" was rare. After attempting to carry out a real backpack trip, from Neel Gap to Low Gap, Searcy Slack declared in the bulletin report: "If all the reasons for *not* making this trip were laid end to end, they would still add up to the fact that the GATC is allergic to spending the night over 50 feet from a car!"

Since the 1948 Conference meeting, the ATC had been looking forward to the day when the Trail would be "once more completed" after the war. The Trail had actually been officially open and complete for only one year—in 1937-38—since its beginnings in the 1920's. In 1951, all work on reworked sections was finished, and a ceremony was planned for June to be held on top of The Priest Mountain in Virginia, where the last link was closed. Myron Avery was to act as Master of Ceremonies, but he fell ill at the last minute, and the ceremony was cancelled. Avery's prepared speech and program was printed in the January 1952 *ATN* "for historical purposes," since it was found impractical to re-schedule the event. The long struggle to re-establish the Trail was outlined in the proposed talk:

We are here, today, to eliminate, after a lapse of some 13 years, the last barrier which has precluded complete realization of the ideal of The Appalachian Trail. That is, that it should be a continuous, unbroken and unending footpath along the crest of the mountain ranges of the eastern Atlantic states. This aspect of continuity of an unbroken trail is of much importance. What strength the Appalachian Trail may have, what attraction and benefit for those who travel it, lies in the fact that it is, for all practical purposes, endless. It is that which we bring about once again here today.

Before we proceed to the final action required to effect the completion of this master footpath, I should say how there developed this situation of an interrupted Trail for some 13 years and to tender due recognition to those organizations which have eliminated this barrier.

Some 14 years ago, there occurred on the slopes of Mt. Sugarloaf, the second highest peak in Maine, a duplication of what we do here today, that is, finishing the through Trail. Originally begun in 1922, the initial completion of the Appalachian Trail had occurred on August 17, 1937. The matter passed then without any particular ceremony or fanfare due to the tremendous drive in finishing various sections of the Trail and the spirit of friendly rivalry to determine whether the last gap should exist in the Maine woods or in the Southern Appalachians. For one year, there was a completed unbroken

2,025-mile Appalachian Trail. Then came the 1938 New England hurricane, obliterating many, many miles and closing extended sections of the Trail. This assault of Nature was well under control when there occurred the major catastrophe in Appalachian Trail history. This was the extension, south from the Shenandoah National Park, of the Skyline Drive, under the name of Blue Ridge Parkway. It is perhaps a tribute to the excellence of the original Appalachian Trail route that the Parkway was superimposed literally upon it. Some 118 miles of Trail disappeared overnight. The alternatives were abandonment of the ideal of a continuous Trail or a major relocation. Applying the principles of the Appalachian Trailway Agreement, the U.S. Forest Service and the National Park Service promised a restoration of the Trail route. Then commenced the search for a superior Trail route, far away from any possible interference by the Parkway. Possible routes were scouted by veteran members of the Natural Bridge Appalachian Trail Club of Lynchburg, Virginia. Eventually, there developed the concept of the new route, far to the east, which would utilize a series of 4,000-foot conical peaks. It would be a trail of much exertion. The U.S. Forest Service, under the direction of then George Washington National Forest Supervisor Howard, with the project spearheaded by Pedlar District Ranger B. A. Eger, constructed much of the new route. The goal of completion was practically attained. Then, with World War II, came complete cessation of all activity.

At the ATC Conference in 1948, at Fontana Village in North Carolina, we set, as one of our two objectives, the complete physical restoration of the Trail. We attain that objective today.

The end of the program was especially significant as it expressed Avery's commitment to, and recognition of, Trail volunteers:

Now we come to the last moment. This is the matter of fixing the last blaze—the blaze which is the insignia from time immemorial of a trail. The Appalachian Trail is very often spoken of as the 'AT,' the abbreviation for 'Appalachian Trail.' These two letters have another significance. This Trail might well, instead of 'Appalachian Trail,' have been termed 'The Anonymous Trail,' in recognition of the fact that many, many people— indeed, thousands—have labored on the Appalachian Trail. They have asked for no return nor recognition nor reward. They have contributed to the project simply by reason of the pleasure found in trail making and in the realization that they were, perhaps, creating something which would be a distinct contribution to the American recreational system and the training of American people. This is, indeed, 'The Anonymous Trail,' and might have become so known. It is, therefore, particularly appropriate that the installation of the final blaze should symbolize and perpetuate this ideal of volunteered and contributed labor to a utilitarian project. Thus, the final blaze will be placed by an anonymous Trail worker—one chosen by lot. That is the person who received, this morning, the numbered slip which corresponds to the Appalachian Trail mileage of 2,025 miles. This anonymous Trail worker will come forward and place the final blaze. Let it remain thus.

If there be any of you who may know this worker, who completes this Trail marking, I charge you to maintain silence. Let not there be divulged the identity of this Trail worker, who is the symbol of countless thousands of workers on the Appalachian Trail.

Thus, we have now, once again, re-attained, after some 13 years, the ideal of a completed, endless Trail. Our problem, our labor, our goal, will be to hold it as such.

The re-formed Nantahala Club was included in 1951 in the now "Five-Club Meet," on Labor Day, which was reported in the *ATN* as an "established custom." Rufus Morgan, acting as a "one-man Supervisor of Trails for the 55-mile section," responded in the *ATN* to hikers' suggestions for improvements on this section thus:

. . . Of course, you realize that I am a backwoods mountaineer. As a result, conditions on the Trail impress me differently from the way they impress those brought up in softer environment. Even at the worst, during the past months, I have not considered the condition of the Trail in the Nantahalas so terrible. However, spurred on by unfavorable reports, the U.S. Forest Service forces trimmed out the Trail pretty thoroughly from Bly Gap to Wesser Creek. They have also put new signs along most of the section. I note that the sign on North Carolina Highway 19 at Wesser Station has already been knocked down. The Nantahala Forest Service has also rebuilt the toilet at Cold Spring Shelter which was crushed by the falling of a tree.

With the help of volunteers, I have been over most of the Nantahala section repainting and renewing markers and doing some trimming of the Trail. On Wesser Creek, where the stream has washed the road and Trail away, I have trimmed and marked a new route for a short distance, in order to get the Trail out of the stream. Recently I marked with blue blazes the detour around Albert Mountain.

You will be interested to know that the Forest Service has improved the facilities at White Oak Bottoms by building shelters and fireplaces within the enclosure there. That is near enough to the Trail (2 m.) to be of use to those using this section. You will also be interested to know that the Nantahala Forest authorities are planning to erect a tower on Albert Mountain. You will probably remember that at one time there was a cabin at that point. . . .

The first reported person to hike the entire AT at once was Earl Shaffer in 1948. In 1951, Eugene Espy of Macon, Georgia, became the second person to accomplish this. An October GATC bulletin reported the following:

Report on the 2050 Mile Club: This past weekend, the Georgia Appalachian Trail Club really hit the jack-pot! After the embarrassing experience of having a Georgia boy from Georgia Tech (our own personal stamping ground) complete the entire Appalachian Trail without any of us ever having heard of him, we fell heir to a couple of young fellows from the North who had just come in from Mt. Katahdin, one having completed non-stop the entire 2050 miles of the Appalachian Trail and the other having covered all except 300 miles which he bypassed by bus.

There has already been some publicity in the papers and magazines regarding the exploits of the Georgia boy, Eugene Espy of Cordele, Georgia. The other two are Chester Dziengielewski (pronounced DINGLEWESKI) of Naugatuck, Connecticut (age 27) and Bill Hall of East Liverpool, Ohio (age 19). They arrived together at Mt. Oglethorpe on October 10 and came down to Jasper where they chanced to meet Andy

Sparks of the *Atlanta Journal* staff who was at Jasper getting some additional information for a story on Eugene Espy. Mr. Sparks brought the boys back to Atlanta with him and put them in touch with the Georgia Appalachian Trail Club. They were invited out to Jim Proctor's home where they stayed until Sunday. Arrangements were made for them to have a telephone call to their homes and also to call Eugene Espy at Cordele, whom they had passed on the Trail. They were also taken to Sears Roebuck where each purchased a new outfit of clothing as theirs were in a sad shape from the standpoint of wear and tear.

Mr. Sparks had already interviewed them for a feature story in the Sunday Magazine section (a combined story about all three boys will be in an early issue); and on Saturday morning, he arranged for them to make a transcription of about 15 minutes 'question and answer' program which was broadcast over WSB that afternoon.

On Saturday afternoon, Eugene Espy came up to Atlanta and had a reunion with the other boys at Jim Proctor's and the three, with Jim acting as interviewer, made a one hour tape recording of their experiences and impressions while on the Trail. As a matter of interest, Earl Shaffer, who was the first person to complete the entire 2050 miles of the Trail in one continuous hike, knew about at least one of the boys and made a short trip along the Trail with him in one of the Northern States. . . . We have invited all three boys to go up to the Smokies with us this next weekend for the trip to Ramsay Cascade and to meet Mr. Benton MacKaye. They have all accepted.

The weekend trip was to the "Cabin in the Briar," and Benton MacKaye met the group for dinner in Gatlinburg. Upon his return home, MacKaye wrote to Marene Snow, thanking her and the Club for the occasion:

At last I have a moment to send you some word of my existence, and the merry life I've led since you got me started on it, at that (for me) superlative occasion with the GATC folks. Not since Cloudland, in '34, have I had such an experience. Indeed, it marked a new era in itself. To sit there with three men who had actually walked a path of fantasy gave me a sense of reality which I never expected to obtain. It gave me a sort of 'destination feeling,' a reaching of the end of a thirty-year journey. Nothing that could be done for me, in the length of the whole AT, could have more deeply touched me than what you and your vital little band did for me that night. Please give each my special and affectionate sentiments. . . . (November 7, 1951)

Officers for 1952 were elected at the council meeting in November: Charlie Gafnea, president; Guerrard Spratt, first vice president; Jim Proctor, second vice president; Cecile Montgomery, secretary; Ruth Church, treasurer; Marene Snow, historian; Newell Good, council. Also at the council meeting, Eugene Espy was "unanimously elected to membership" in the GATC.

Toward the end of the year, Guy Frizzell of the Smoky Club resigned as vice Chairman of the ATC. Jimmy Cragon of the GATC was appointed to take his place.

In early summer, an "ultimatum" had been received from the Forest Service to do something about the Frosty Mountain cabin. It had been condemned as unsafe, and was to be torn down by the Club. A committee was appointed to "decide how it is to be disposed of and go ahead and do it." No action was taken for several months; and finally, in November, the council minutes reported: "The problem of its disposal has become acute. The Forestry Department is demanding that immediate action be taken, feeling we have had time to make some decision in regard to it." The following account in the bulletin shows that, with the help of a few real leaders, the project finally got rolling in December:

. . . We have been talking about doing something with the Frosty Cabin for a long time. Finally, when our good friend, Mr. Spaulding, requested us to take some action, we brought it up for a decision in the November council meeting. Here we must give due credit to the courage and foresight of Larry Freeman who single-handed turned a vote to let the cabin go back to the Forest Service into a vote to get up there and get to work. Larry then followed up by contacting Mr. Spaulding to work out the details.

The very first trip nearly fizzled out when the Trail Activity Committee failed to get the trip lined up. However, Newell took over from there and, with the aid of Jim and Searcy, got things organized and got a representative group up to Frosty on Sunday morning, December 2. Jim and Newell had expected to do no more than make a definite decision as to what disposition to make of the cabin and where to put the shelter; but, as usual, we reckoned without Shakey. Within about a half hour after arriving at the site, we had (1) agreed to dismantle the cabin and use the material for the new shelter, (2) agreed that the shelter site was to be the very attractive and practicable site beside the spring on Frosty, and (3) already started to dismantle the old cabin in a very efficient and businesslike manner. Searcy had brought a block and tackle which was put to good use in lowering the roof sections. Shakey had a variety of tools including 'papa bar, mama bar and baby bar,' and the others brought various and assorted useful tools. Bob, Russell, and Shakey took to the roof and rafters and the other men did the ground work. The roof was sawed—that's right—sawed into one long and one short section and the two sides of each pried apart and taken down. Russell tried 'catching' one large section after all the others had let go. Fortunately, he landed between two rafters and was only slightly bruised. Arline, Dottie and Jean Ann, and little 'Dutch' Slack too, pulled nails and stacked lumber. Late afternoon found us well along with the dismantling operations. The fire warden, Lou Calhoun, was the only one who felt other than jubilant over the accomplishments of the day as he gazed sorrowfully at the shell of what had been his 'home' for many years. We're sorry, Lou, but it had to be done.

Trips Number Two and Three were made the following weekend, and the account was quoted in part in the *ATN:*

While Searcy and Newell hacked a broad path, later named the 'Frosty Freeway,' to the shelter site by the spring, Shakey and the boys made short work of the remaining intact parts of the cabin and constructed a wheeled frame vehicle hereafter to be known as the 'Shakeymobile.' Sections of the cabin were tied to the Shakeymobile and, with Whit as chief 'workhorse,' four trips were made down the Frosty Freeway to the shelter site. On several occasions, the heavy sections threatened to get out of control going down the steep hill but valiant holding back by the rear rope men plus a patented method of grounding the contraption effectively stopped it. The Sunday group . . . looked at the muddy Nimblewill road through a steady downpour. Could we reach Frosty without getting stuck? And could we accomplish anything if we did make it? A half hour wait failed to produce a change in the weather, so—you are wrong—we went on up! The lumber was soaked and twice as heavy as before; but, nevertheless, four trips were made with the Shakeymobile to the edge of the hill. Some of the lumber was carried on down to the shelter site on our shoulders and the rest stacked at the top of the hill. . . .

Historian Marene Snow had announced earlier in the year that big plans were being made for the celebration of the "coming of age" of the GATC, to be held at the end of this 21st year. A "Coming of Age" party was held in December. The bulletin account began:

Twenty-one years ago, the Georgia Appalachian Trail Club came into being, and on the evening of December 15, 1951, its coming of age was commemorated by a double-barrelled celebration: namely, a dinner at Emory University and a party at the West End Women's Club. A list of past members of the Club, now widely scattered throughout the country, was compiled by Lou Hoben. Early notices, followed by invitations, were sent, requesting them to join us in celebrating the Club's birthday. Practically all replied—some sending regrets due to distance and difficulties of travel. Many others accepted—several coming from faraway places.

The evening was highlighted by the "thrills experienced" in meeting old friends. "One of the greatest of these thrills came with the arrival of Elizabeth (Bunny) Motsinger, who flew to Atlanta from the Canadian border to meet again her GATC friends. . . ." A feature of the evening was "two skits representing the Georgia Appalachian Trail Club 'then and now,' and showing that equipment, costumes, and personnel may change but that the same 'reasons for being' continue through the years."

Other features of the evening were singing, showing of slides, square dancing, refreshments, a brief installation of officers, the singing of Christmas carols. Other highlights as listed in the bulletin were: "verbal expressions of regret . . . that Benton MacKaye . . . could not be present. . . . A message from him was read. . . . The presence of Charles Elliott, one of the founders of the GATC. . . . Disappointment that Warner Hall's plane flight from Washington was cancelled due to weather conditions."

1952

GEORGIA
APPALACHIAN
19 TRAIL CLUB, INC. 30

T HE FROSTY SHELTER work trips continued into 1952.
The first January trip reported:

> . . . we decided to concentrate on the actual building of the new
> shelter instead of attempting to move the large roof section from the
> old cabin down to the shelter site. Soon several crews were hard at
work clearing the site, digging and leveling the space for the foundation, bringing large
rocks from the adjacent site of a long disintegrated and forgotten cabin and bringing
the rest of the lumber from the cache at the top of the hill along the 'Frosty Freeway'
where the group on the #3 work trip had had to leave it on the rainy, slippery day in
December. The 'master minds' made final a check of shelter plans and staked out the
corners of the new shelter. Somehow or other, both Shakey and Newell had neglected
to bring three very essential tools which both had brought on previous trips when they
were not used; i.e., a square, a level, and a compass. The compass was to be used to
orient the shelter to face due south. Since it was a very cloudy day we could not get our
directions by the sun, so if the shelter faces a few degrees away from due south we are
'so sorry, please.' Our resourceful engineers soon devised a homemade square on the
9-12-15 principle, and a level was manufactured out of a bottle filled with water to the
point where only a bubble of air remained—yes, sir, it will take more than that to stop
us!

Under Shakey's direction, the foundation soon took shape and a professional
looking wall was the final result. Shakey's chief 'helper' was little David Dolan, age 3,
whose boundless energy made all the rest of us feel very old and decrepit.
Unfortunately, David raked dirt the wrong way as often as vice versa so that the net
profit was rather low. The agreed quitting time found us in the middle of constructing

the framework and we just did not want to stop until the 2 X 8's were cut, fitted, nailed in place and braced, so it was nearly dark when we gathered up our tools, restacked the lumber to protect it from the weather and headed home.

Evidently very little work was done on the shelter after this until the fourth of July weekend, when a three-day "base camp" was planned to hike in the area and do some work on the side. But according to the bulletin account:

The leisurely fourth of July trip didn't turn out quite as expected. True, we swam twice in the beautiful mountain-top lake at Amicalola, and a few made the late afternoon hike over to the yet-unnamed waterfall near the base of Mt. Springer. The trip along the Blue Ridge to Tickanetly Bald, however, was postponed by popular request.
It was planned to spend some little time building the shelter on Frosty Mountain. But somehow the crowd (31 all told) got in the spirit and put in three of the hardest days of concentrated labor seen on the Georgia Trail in many a year. Our guests worked like Trojans—thanks! You should have seen Butch (age five) with a crowbar as tall as he was, pulling big nails out of the old studs. The ladies did their share, too, Lou and Lalia carrying heavy timbers half-a-mile down the mountain side to the cove where the shelter was being built, Marene nailing on the weatherboarding, Mildred gathering rocks out of the brook for landscaping, etc. . . . When Sunday afternoon came along, the shelter was nearly complete. It needs a few more boards here and there; a coat of paint and a fireplace will just about see it done. The design is excellent, the carpentry neat, the whole structure is very strongly put together. It is beautifully located, has a good spring at the door-step and we hope it will be a welcome stopping place for foot-travelers for a long time to come.

At the August council meeting, it was voted to use money from the Benton MacKaye fund to complete work on the shelter and to rename it the Benton MacKaye Shelter. It was further voted that "if it is definitely established that the fund cannot be used for the original purpose of bringing Benton MacKaye to Georgia to meet with the GATC, any balance remaining in the Fund be used for building and maintenance of trail shelters."

The January, 1952, council meeting minutes recorded that "Jim Proctor suggested that the bulletin, which is a lot of work and also a headache, be given a larger committee." The committee would divide up the various chores, and "each session would be a fun party as well as a work party and would be held in Jim Proctor's basement darkroom."(!)
In the spring, two "benefit square dances" were held to finance a mimeograph machine. A 50¢ entrance fee, food and bake sales, and chances on cakes brought in $80.00 at the first party, and $25.00 at the second, leaving only about $25.00 to achieve the goal.
Most members seemed still allergic to camping "more than 50 feet from a car," as two more planned backpacks were cancelled or "postponed" due to lack of registration.

In May, the bulletin announced "a bit of news: a shoulder patch for the Georgia Club—a long felt need. . . . It's a beautiful patch . . . done in Swiss embroidery, designed by our own Club members. . . ." The same patch is still being used today, with only slight changes in color and size.

The twelfth Appalachian Trail Conference was held in May at Skyland in the Shenandoah National Park in Virginia. Reportedly, six GATC members attended. The bulletin recorded: "Our shoulder patches arrived in time for display at the Trail Conference . . . and we understand the reversal of the order of the words—for us—'Georgia to Maine' instead of the usual 'Maine to Georgia' caused many eyebrows to raise!"

Newell Good reported to Conference on the Georgia Trail, saying that it

. . . is reasonably passable and recommended for travel. 'We have the usual quota of down logs, weeds and other summer growth. . . . Short segments of the Trail are assigned for maintenance to individual members. We have only about twenty active, ambitious men in the Club. That means that either you do it yourself, or make a trade with someone to help him and then try to get him to help you.'

Myron Avery had been ill for the past year, and had resigned as chairman of the Conference; Murray Stevens, a vice-chairman, was elected to take his place. Avery was also unable to attend the Conference meeting, but his report as chairman was printed in the September, 1952, *ATN*. He reviewed his past "stewardship" and, "resisting stoutly any tendency to reminisce," he talked of the future of the Trail and stressed the problems to come:

The Appalachian Trail, long ago, developed its program for the protection of the Trailway, which, as an ideal solution, may be impossible of actual accomplishment. Approximately one-half of the Trail lies in the publicly-owned lands where the Trailway Agreement with the National Park Service and U.S. Forest Service assures the perpetuation of the route. The problem lies in the connecting units of privately-owned land, much of which will soon become subject to intense development. Protest against Federal or State domination is, of course, a popular theme these days. However, the unexpected penetration and development of areas in private ownership, when fully realized, will serve to fortify our conclusion that some form of public protection must be extended to the Trail system if it is to survive as a through, continuous recreational unit. The problem is very real. Its solution and an ability to make effective that desired solution present to our successors an issue and labor in comparison with which the efforts of the past two decades are indeed minute.

A resolution was passed at the meeting stating that,

WHEREAS, throughout the history of the Appalachian Trail, no other person has been more closely identified with the project or has made a comparable contribution to its completion and maintenance;
NOW, THEREFORE, BE IT RESOLVED, That this Twelfth Appalachian Trail

Conference, held at Skyland, in the Shenandoah National Park, May 30 to June 1, 1952, acknowledges that no words are adequate to express the feelings of the Conference but that all who know the story of the Appalachian Trail will cherish in their hearts the privilege which was theirs in being associated with Myron in the common objective and accomplishments of our Appalachian Trail.

A week after the Conference meeting, the GATC bulletin announced a trip to "cover the entire Georgia section of Trail in two days . . ."

Of course, we will have to split up in small groups to do it!

Our Activity Program called for a trip to LeConte this weekend, but this was before the AT Conference delegates returned with a challenge that we make Georgia the best maintained section of Trail in the system. So we are calling off our favorite trip to the Smokies (at least for the time being) and every Trail supervisor who has assumed responsibility for a portion of the Trail is urged to cover his or her section this weekend.

On July 26, 1952, at age 53, Myron Avery "came to the end of his trail" at Annapolis Royal, Nova Scotia, thus bringing to an end the long era of this man who, more than any other, was responsible for the building of the AT and the organization of the ATC. The *ATN* said of him that his work

stands as a monument to all those anonymous and other workers whose labors for twenty-five years brought it into existence [and] to the one who acted as the catalyst, who coordinated all efforts, the 'skipper' who brought the venture through its perilous early days to completion and who has left behind him the pattern for its maintenance and existence.

Mention has been made of but a few of his many activities. His passing leaves a great void. Workers in many fields of endeavor will miss the keen intelligence, dynamic energy, ever-fresh enthusiasm, and the selfless and kindly spirit which inspired everyone to carry through his or her appointed task. Those who knew him have lost a friend who can never be replaced.

A "Five-Club Meet" was announced in the bulletin for the Labor Day weekend, but the report afterward declared it the "Six-Club Meet." It included a new club from Chattanooga—the Tri-State Trail Club. The meeting was held at Cataloochee Cove in the Smokies, with 143 people present.

For some years, it had been planned to take the Trail off of the road between Big Stamp Gap and Cooper Gap. At the April council meeting several routes were considered, all of which had been scouted. Newell Good, who was spearheading the project, had aerial photos and maps to illustrate the sections. Except for the alternative of returning the Trail to the ridgetop above the road, the routes included going down northwest of the ridge along Mauldin Creek.

During the next few months, Good continued to scout the area, reporting on his progress at each council meeting, and in July reported on "two re-route possibilities"—between Cooper Gap and Hightower Gap, and between Hawk

Mountain and Big Stamp Gap. In September, a scouting trip was arranged, with part of the area to be scouted on Saturday and part on Sunday. The bulletin described the plans:

The Saturday hike will be a circle trip starting and ending at Mauldin Gap so that the two alternative routes can be surveyed. The first part will be down through the valley along Mauldin Creek on old trails and logging roads with the return trip along the other route up Greasy Mountain Ridge—sans trail—back to Mauldin Gap.

We will camp on Hawk Mountain (the home of Gene Espy's and Earl Shaffer's wildcats). The road to it is in good shape now.

On Sunday morning we will drive past Winding Stair Gap and start the hike from Big Stamp Gap. The route will be down Silvermine Ridge (slightly brushy) to and across Chester Creek, then along a dirt road to Three Forks where three creeks unite to form Noontootla Creek, then along an old trail near Long Creek with stops to view several cascades and a waterfall (don't forget your camera), then along a logging road up Hickory Flats Ridge and then just follow the ridge back to and up and over Hawk Mountain.

The scouts reported of the Saturday trip:

The ridge was brushy and uninteresting, the climb up Greasy Mountain was definitely on the steep side and, although the long, broad upper ridge of Greasy Mountain was open and more interesting, much work would be required to make and maintain the ridge trail. On the other hand, the Mauldin Creek valley route will require a negligible amount of clearing and maintaining, is interesting and attractive, and its traverse requires very little climbing. All hands present voiced definite approval of rerouting the Trail over this route.

On Sunday, the planned route was successfully followed to Three Forks, and the bulletin reported of the remainder of the trip:

It was nearing noon when we started down Silvermine Ridge and along the dirt road beside Chester Creek. Deer tracks and other animal tracks were plentiful. The roar of a small cascade lured us down through the rhododendrons to a pretty spot where we paused for lunch. After a few snapshots, we pushed on to Three Forks where the creek suddenly started running the wrong way and we were informed by our leader that we had left Chester Creek and were heading up Long Creek. The old trail paralleling the creek was delightful, the giant hemlocks, white pines, rhododendron, and moss covered rocks giving us a strange feeling of being transported to the Smokies. Disregarding the roar of several cascades and small waterfalls, we headed for the waterfall which Newell has been bragging about all summer. It surpassed expectations and proved to be a really beautiful spot. After pausing here, we started our climb up the ridge. Reaching the top, somewhat winded, we headed due east along it passing three large piles of stones which probably marked the graves of long departed Indians. Arriving at the base of Hawk Mountain, each set his own pace toward the top. The view from the fire tower could not be passed up, of course, and this provided a fitting end to the day's hike.

Newell Good, still carrying the ball on the project, declared at the October council meeting that he "would like for more members to show their interest in this project by going on some of the trips and thus helping iron out some of the problems involved in the overall job."

During the year, Mrs. Martha Noble, former Club member and former wife of Dr. G. H. Noble who had modeled the bronze plaques at Neel and Unicoi Gaps, gave the GATC the third of the original plaques. The October council minutes recorded: "There was some discussion as to where the plaque should be placed, and it was decided that probably Woody Gap was on the most widely traveled highway and, therefore, would be the best place for the plaque." (Records do not indicate that it was ever erected at Woody Gap, but instead is said to have been the plaque which was placed on Springer Mountain when the terminus was changed in 1958.)

As decided by the GATC council, the election of officers for 1953 was done by mail. Ballots were sent to all members, to be returned by mail, with a slate of officers and space for write-ins. The resulting officers for the coming year were: Larry Freeman, president; Norman Batho, first vice president; Henry Morris, second vice president; Jo Gambrell, secretary; Ruth Church, treasurer; Marene Snow, historian; James Cragon, Charles Gafnea, Newell Good, council.

The annual jaunts to Mt. LeConte and the Dillard's were made in October and November, and the year ended with the traditional Christmas party held at Olivia (Herren) and Joe Bagwell's new "country house."

1953

GEORGIA
APPALACHIAN
19 TRAIL CLUB, INC. 30

IN FEBRUARY OF 1953, the bulletin announced plans to publish only one *Mountaineer* each month instead of two, changing the long-standing custom of one bulletin per trip. The announcement warned: "This means that you must PRESERVE YOUR BULLETIN and keep it in a prominent place. . . ."

Late in 1952, the council had voted, upon the suggestion of Jim Cragon, "that a brief write-up of trips be made at the beginning of each year and published in a small book, which could be done at very little expense." This resulted in the first GATC yearbook (or handbook) which was announced in the March, 1953, bulletin. According to Whit Benson, this booklet was produced by Whit and Larry Freeman in Whit's father's basement—at very little expense, no doubt. It contained a list of officers, the year's activities schedule, with commentary, a complete list of members' names and addresses, and a profile map of the Georgia Trail.

A long-planned and "much needed" re-route was made in March, with permission of the land owners, of about a mile of Trail north of Southern's Store, in order to avoid two stream crossings. As the bulletin stated: "No one should again have to wade a knee-deep cold mountain stream because the log crossings have washed away." Rain on the Sunday following the new trail clearing prevented blazing the section, so a planned hike up to Amicalola Falls was postponed in order that everybody could "hike back and forth over the re-route in order to establish it as a footpath through the forest." (The exact location of this new piece of Trail is not specified, although a later hike refers to hiking alongside the stream.)

Several trips to north Georgia were made during the year in search of a suitable spot for the Six-Club Meet, which the GATC was to host on Labor Day. One of these trips was to the Cohuttas, where the Lake Conasauga area was inspected. The Club had not been to Jack's River Falls for a good many years, and the trip leader, Whit Benson, reported, " . . . The following morning we searched for Jack's River Falls and again *failed* to locate the falls . . . but we believe we have [it] cornered at last, and will actually reach our goal with one more effort!"

The Frosty Mountain shelter work was still in process, and another trip was planned for April. Leader Henry Morris wrote in the bulletin announcement:

Spring pilgrimage to Frosty Mountain: According to reports, rearrangement of shelter facilities at Frosty Mountain has provided some of the most enjoyable trips of the last couple of years. The shelter now is well-nigh complete, and the plan is to put on a few finishing touches, or raise it slightly above the level of what the government would classify as 'sub-standard,' by providing a front porch and bath facilities, as well as a seat of some kind. It already has running water, so no plumbing will be necessary.

His account afterward read:

If you don't believe fourteen people working on a project will cause it to take shape movie fashion, you should have been there. Saws sawing, hammers flinging, dirt flying and a certain amount of green paint on everything and everybody, including both inside and outside of the shelter. It really looks nice. Same color green, all over, bank graded behind, rock terrace in front, nice comfortable broad path to the East for nature walk.

After a rainy night and morning, the Sunday group "accomplished such work as could be done with everything soaking wet, such as cleaning up and burning trash and planting flagstones and grass on the newly constructed terrace in front of the shelter."

Hoping for more successful surveying of the Trail for maintenance purposes, the trail maintenance chairman divided the Trail into sections of ten miles each to be checked and reported on in the early spring by volunteers. Assignments and a list of needed chores were sent to each participant.

The *ATN* reported in its September issue on Trail work in Georgia, and commented:

The Georgia plan of arranging for a survey of all sections of the Trail within one month, early in the year, with exact details as to conditions, is one that might be adopted to advantage by other Trail maintaining organizations. Under this system, the Overseer of Trails is able to plan the work trips so that the sections in worst condition are covered first, that workers go to the sections that really need work, and it also insures that they have the suitable tools for the conditions they find.

This year, the section selected for the first work trip was Unicoi to Bly Gap. The bulletin listed the condition of each portion of the Trail, the worst being Addis Gap to Dick's Creek, with 50 logs to be removed, briars, and poor blazes. Armed with "cross-cut saw, large ax, clippers, heavy grass blade, and lunch," several groups spread out along the Trail for a weekend of hard work, and had, according to the bulletin, "somewhat amazing success," leaving the Trail in "excellent condition."

Two weeks later a group set out from Poplar Stamp Gap "with grim visages and firm-set jaws . . . toward the dense tangle of windfalls and blackberry jungles that were reported to have choked this section of Trail" only to find that some unknown Boy Scout troop had beat them to the work. "Imagine our abject disappointment." The group camped at Low Gap after driving up the dirt road from Robertstown and declared the highlight of the trip to be "shooting the rapids in the cool waters of the upper Chattahoochee with an inflated air mattress for a craft."

By February of 1953, 4.1 miles of the proposed Trail between Big Stamp Gap and Cooper Gap had been cleared, leaving 3.8 miles to be done, according to Newell Good. By May, he reported to the council that 66 "man-days" had been spent on scouting and working on the new section, and that 20 people had hiked over it. The new Trail would increase the AT by 1.8 miles. An "inspection" trip was planned for the end of the month. According to the bulletin, on the trip the group followed the established route beginning at Cooper Gap, over Sassafras Mountain (on the "old, original trail"), down to Horse Gap, then down into the Mauldin Creek valley on old roads and trails, upstream to Mauldin Gap, "over a low ridge," and down to Hightower Gap "along the general route of the original trail." It then went over Hawk Mountain, down the ridge past Hickory Flats to Long Creek, to Three Forks, and back to Winding Stair Gap. The original plan was to come down Silvermine Ridge from Big Stamp Gap to Three Forks, but the very long account of this particular hike was cut short by the bulletin editor, and it is not recorded where it went at this date; however, the following year a hike was recorded as following the new Forest Service road from Three Forks to Winding Stair Gap, which is where the Trail was established and remained for several years.

This seemingly straightforward attempt to re-route a monotonous section of Trail along a dirt road between Big Stamp and Cooper Gaps, carried out with the full knowledge and consent of the GATC council, was somehow to cause dissention in the Club. It is said that Good, who had spent many, many hours on, and devoted much interest to, this project, had, without formal approval of the Club, gone ahead and white-blazed the new Trail before the Club's "inspection" trip. This angered some of the members and resulted in the council's refusing to approve the section as the official AT. The June council minutes record only the following:

Newell Good gave a brief history of the re-route and made the motion that the proposed re-route be made an official part of the Georgia Appalachian Trail upon completion of markers and other finishing touches. This motion was seconded. It was voted on by the five attending members of the council but was not carried by a majority. Jim Cragon made an amendment to Newell's motion as follows: That we adopt the section between Cooper Gap and Horse Gap as an official part of the Trail. That we designate the proposed re-route from Horse Gap to Mauldin Gap as an alternate or blue-blaze trail. That Mauldin Gap to Hightower be adopted as a permanent Trail. That Hawk Mountain to Big Stamp Gap be an alternate or blue-blaze trail. That the beforementioned blue-blazed trails be maintained as such until that time the Club feels that it can take on the responsibility of maintaining them as a permanent part of the Trail. This amendment was voted on and carried by the majority of council members present.

This beautiful section of Trail was to remain a blue-blazed side trail for two years before finally being declared a part of the Georgia AT.

A rather unusual-for-the-time hike was made in June to Thunderhead Mountain in the Smokies, and led by Whit Benson. The group of six hiked up to the Spence Field shelter from Cades Cove, spent a rainy night in the small shelter with eleven others, and returned to Cades Cove the next morning—except Whit and Larry Freeman, who "decided to climb Gregory Bald and get pictures of the azaleas."

On another rainy weekend in June, more "explorations" were made in search of a site for the Six-Club Meet. After checking out Camp Pioneer and Enotah State Park, the group proceeded to the upper valley of the Tallulah River, where camp was made. Larry Freeman, leader, continued his report:

Still raining. However, Whit is a master hand at camp fires—in wet weather or dry; and the rain turned into only occasional showers during the night and on Sunday. We explored the various trails, springs, waterfalls and camp sites, visited in Arnold's new tent, looked over our fellow campers' shoulders and into their pots and skillets, as we watched with amazement, what, and how, and sometimes, even why! Anyway, rain or shine, it was a fine trip, with objective accomplished. . . . It was agreed by all that this last location most nearly meets our requirements—in fact, is about ideal!

A trip was planned for August to get the area ready "for making our Club the 'hostess-with-the-mostest.'"

The Meet over Labor Day weekend was a big success, and actually claimed representatives from eight hiking clubs ("if we let our visitor from Washington take credit for two clubs.") The weekend featured hikes in the area, a square dance, a speech by Guy Frizzell, and a "Kodachrome show depicting 'The Georgia Trail from Mt. Oglethorpe to Bly Gap,' which ended with a picture of our neighboring 'one-man hiking club,' the Reverend Rufus Morgan, waiting at the North Carolina line. . . . Also there was a camp fire with a brief business meeting and singing until the wee hours."

When the re-route between Cooper and Gooch Gaps was made in 1949, it had been planned to return one day and "put in some switchbacks to lessen the steep grades in two places." A trip for this purpose was planned in November, but cancelled because of hunting season in the area.

The trip to LeConte, "not originally scheduled for 1953," was added "by popular request"; the annual Dillard trip was made in November; and another memorable Christmas party highlighted December.

Officers for 1954 were elected at the December council meeting: Searcy Slack, president; Pat Gartrell, first vice president; Cecile Montgomery, second vice president; Jo Gambrell, secretary; Ed Traylor, treasurer; Marene Snow, historian; Charles Gafnea, James Cragon, Larry Freeman, council.

1954

GEORGIA
APPALACHIAN
19 TRAIL CLUB, INC. 30

THE YEAR 1954 SEEMED to be a relatively uneventful, perhaps with some of the members somewhat in the doldrums. There seemed to be some fewer participants on many of the hikes, and, especially during the later part of the year, only a handful of council members attending the monthly meetings. The minutes of the May council meeting recorded that President Searcy Slack "reported communication from Frank Gordon apologizing for inactivity. In view of above discussion (on attendance on Club meetings and outings) the group thinks that Frank is doing as well as most of us."

As usual, most hikes were made on the Georgia AT, with some clearing and blazing work done on regular hikes, and two trips specifically to work. The regular trip to LeConte was made in May; over the July 4 weekend, a group camp was held at the Deep Gap campground near Standing Indian; the popular Panther Creek hike was repeated; and a trip to Providence Canyon was substituted for the proposed Okefenokee Swamp trip, cancelled because of drought and fires in the swamp.

The "bad condition of Mt. Oglethorpe," which had been of concern to the Club for some time, was discussed at the March council meeting. A trailer, which had been used by Georgia Tech personnel in connection with the radar tower on Oglethorpe, was now "in shambles and is an eyesore," and the entire area was covered with litter.

Permission was sought and given by Mr. Tate "to clean up the area but not to tear down the old building there." It was reported that "Georgia Tech no longer has any right to the building, but Mr. Tate said that he would like to investigate the condition of it and see for himself what he wants done with it. . . ." The May council reported "contact with Mr. Steve Tate re Mt. Oglethorpe including offer of material to build observation tower if Club will furnish labor. President instructed to write Mr. Tate declining offer. . . ."

An overnight trip to Oglethorpe was planned in April to remedy the "unsightly state" by cleaning away the rubbish and litter. Pat Gartrell, leader, reported on the trip:

Sundown Saturday found a baker's half-dozen of GATCers hustling about the Sassafras shelter area making preparations for the night. Tents were pitched, the night being clear and the floor of the shelter dusty; and a small mountain of potatoes, onions, carrots, etc. was prepared for the stew-pot which was presided over by at least two accomplished cooks, one of whom toted a bay leaf all the way from Atlanta to insure the success of the ragout. Russell, the Signs Chairman, and his deputy, Bob Berry, arrived just as the first pot full was done and later, about the time the strawberry shortcake appeared, Liz White hove into view, unheralded but very welcome. A pleasant evening passed before the fire.

Sunday the crew marched on Oglethorpe and set about policing the area. A bonfire was built to consume the scattered brush and rotten lumber and the quantities of tar paper. Two Sunday hikers meanwhile arrived. Some 50,000 (conservative estimate) beer and oil cans were bashed in while various members took turns working in the 'diggins'; and after lunch, an awesome pile of tin was interred below the rock wall behind the shack. The registration cylinder was checked (there are two Georgia-to-Maine hikers now on the Trail) and the condition of the sign noted. . . .

An overnight hike was made in May on the re-routed AT between Cooper Gap and Hightower Gap (on Saturday) and on what was still referred to as the "proposed blue trail" between Hawk Mountain and Winding Stair Gap (on Sunday).

The (again) Five-Club Meet was held at the foot of Mt. Mitchell with "three days of memorable camping, hiking, sunning, riding, swimming, talking, singing, dancing, and eating for 175 people." (The former sixth club—the Tri-State Club from Chattanooga, was not present.) The reorganization of the Nantahala Hiking Club in 1950 evidently did not "take" since Rufus Morgan was still referred to as the "one-man hiking club."

Six people participated in a successful backpack trip led by Pat Gartrell from Low Gap to Neel Gap in October. Gartrell reported:

Falling ice crystals. Scarlet maples on the hill. A roaring fire casting six shadows in Tesnatee Gap Shelter. Frosty, star-sprinkled night and warm down bags, sizzling breakfast bacon, smoky vistas gold and crimson splotched, six rosy-cheeked hikers puffing over Levelland (one was puffing at any rate). A leisurely lunch at Walasiyi Inn. These were the things of which the Low to Neal pack trip was made.

A few challenging obstacles (such as an enormous oak down across the road to Low Gap and a reluctant spring at Tesnatee) just added spice to the outing and were quickly overcome. It was a fine trip with everyone cooperating to make the most of a bright October weekend. Searcy renewed all the blazes between Low and Tesnatee.

Officers for 1955 were elected at an "annual business meeting" in October which was followed by a square dance. Officers were to be: Searcy Slack, president; Bob Scott, first vice president; Lou Hoben, second vice president; Jo Gambrell, secretary; James M. Davis, treasurer; Marene Snow, historian; Pat Gartrell, council.

Lou Hoben reported in November on the perennial trip to the Dillard House and the attempted hike to Scaly Mountain:

We tried to repeat the trip we had across the top and over the bluff (you remember we tried last year, too) and that, along with Jack's River Falls, just isn't there! We engaged a guide—a good one who had grown up in the region, as did his daddy and grand-daddy before him—and in his opinion, Scaly itself has in some way shifted!

But it was a good trip. Never was there finer cooperation from the autumn foliage. There were breathtaking views down into the vivid-hued valleys below us—and in the distance the snow-capped ranges of the Smokies. Part of the way we followed along an old sunken road, the very first 'highway' between Dillard and Highland; then a leaf-filled footpath, next 'through the rough'; a bit of back-tracking to the point where the trail missed us, winding up in a picnic area with Mrs. Dillard's fried chicken and biscuits; scalding coffee and frozen fingers.

Saturday night the singing, Pat with her well-trained guitar leading in all the well known ballads and even composing new ones when the old gave out, revealed an unexpected wealth of talent and enthusiasm. Do let's make this a regular thing.

1955

GEORGIA
APPALACHIAN
19 TRAIL CLUB, INC. 30

THE FEBRUARY, 1955, COUNCIL meeting minutes reported: "It was brought up that $842.62 has been allocated for Trail maintenance from Southern's Store to North Carolina line to be used for removing logs, brush, making signs, etc." This evidently referred to Forest Service funds, for the May *ATN*, listing trail conditions, reported from Georgia, "Chattahoochee National Forest will clear winter damage; GATC will handle blazing and light clearing on all scheduled trips." So again the Forest Service would contribute to the upkeep of the Trail in the national forest.

On many of the Club hikes, Searcy Slack—and others—carried along a paint brush and a bucket of paint and "left a trail of bright, new, white blazes" on the Trail. Slack also might "just happen to have" clippers and saws in his car for light clearing of the Trail.

For a number of years, there had been periodic discussions (as there would continue to be in future years) of the feasibility of having boy scouts help in trail maintenance. This was generally discouraged unless under the close supervision of leaders or Club members, and it was agreed that the work "shall consist only of brushing out the Trail and doing light clearing work."

A trip to Pickens Nose in February, with overnight camping in an abandoned granite quarry in the area, was highlighted by a hike over to Albert Mountain "to explore the new, all-steel fire tower with 360 degree visibility. . . ." A variety trip to the Smokies over the Memorial Day weekend included hikes to Clingman's Dome, Fontana, and Shuckstack.

Another trip on the new trail between Cooper and Winding Stair Gaps through Three Forks brought more praise for this beautiful area; and later in the year, the council finally voted unanimously to "adopt" this portion of trail as the official AT.

Dartmouth College's Moosilauke Ravine Lodge, near Warren, New Hampshire, was the scene of the 13th Appalachian Trail Conference on May 30-31, 1955; 123 people attended. No one from the Georgia Club was able to go except former member Dewey Scadin, who reported to the Club on his trip. At the meeting, Searcy Slack was elected to the Board of Managers for the Southern section.

A very popular return trip was made in July to Tallulah Gorge, site of the 1954 Six-Club Meet; and on Labor Day, the "Four (Five? Six?) Club Meet" was held in Cades Cove in the Smokies, with a record-breaking attendance of 254—75 of which were GATCers.

Foreshadowing things to come was a letter in April from a member of the Cumberlands Hiking Club to Conference complaining about the condition of the Trail near Mt. Oglethorpe. The writer was very upset, declaring the Trail difficult to find, signs defaced and unreadable, blazes poor. She continued:

When we reached the shelter it was in complete disrepair. The roof was a sieve, the floor had holes in it and the door had been torn off. To make matters worse, for about an acre surrounding the so-called shelter, the ground had been used as a dumping ground for manure, the stench of which could be smelled for a quarter of a mile. The place was a filthy shambles. Wonderful maintenance!

We proceeded along the crest of Oglethorpe Mountain amidst glorious scenery. Our next encounter was with a chicken ranch, acres in extent which sat astraddle the Trail. There was no way around it, so we again waded through filth, this time of thousands of chickens. It was so slimy that one of our group fell flat on her face in the stuff.

We finally reached our objective, the statue of General Oglethorpe, only to have the same disagreeable return trip. We returned home completely disillusioned as to the Southern terminus of the Trail and its maintenance. . . . never have I encountered anything to match the conditions on the Southern end on this Trail. (April 18, 1955)

Jean Stephenson replied with a long letter of regret, and President Searcy Slack did the same, saying he would personally check the situation. He did so, and declared, "There was some truth in her letter and a great deal of exaggeration." But the chicken ranch was there, as well as the manure, signalling a further decline in conditions in the area.

At the same time, Slack sent Jean Stephenson a "personal" estimate of the Georgia shelter situation, "official and otherwise." Some of his comments:

Sassafras Mountain shelter: Club will probably abandon altogether. Clearing piled high with manure and shavings from nearby chicken ranch. Southern's Store: OK in emergency. Blood Mountain shelter: Used for many years by goats (not at present) . . .

All movable gear destroyed and used for firewood. . . . Neel Gap: Walasiyi Inn. Vogel State Park offers regular tourist court plus meals. . . . Rocky Knob shelter: A bootleg CCC job. It was never much . . . might be better than nothing. . . . [In only 20 years since it was built, the Rocky Knob shelter had deteriorated from the 'pride of the GATC,' which had elicited letters praising it sent to Franklin Roosevelt (!) to 'better than nothing'! Time, indeed, takes a heavy toll on trailway structures.] Montray shelter: Noisiest roof on the AT. . . . Addis Gap: Old Addis homestead in poor condition. Barn has best roof. Snake Mountain shelter: Condition hard to keep up with. Variously used as home by highway, logging, and other transient laborers.

"Woman Walking the Trail" was the headline in the September *ATN* as it reported on Emma Gatewood's progress toward Katahdin. "So it is possible by the time this issue appears, the newspapers will carry the story that a woman has now made a continuous traverse of the Appalachian Trail, from Georgia to Maine." She did make it all the way, and the *ATN* reported on her unconventional—and her first—trip in the January, 1956, issue.

In October, an "annual business meeting and election of officers" was held, with the following being elected for the coming year: Bob Scott, president; Ralph Ramsey, first vice president; Lou Hoben, second vice president; Cecile Montgomery, secretary; Ross Wilson, treasurer; Marene Snow, historian; Searcy Slack, council.

The new Buford Dam was the site of a trip in November, and a brief talk was given to the group "in explanation of the project, its features, and future use." The lake was to start filling in February, 1956, to be completed by 1958.

The following announcement appeared in the January, 1956, A*TN*: "Due to the development of a 'chicken ranch' farther down the mountain, with 'free range' extending to the area surrounding the shelter, the Georgia Appalachian Trail Club has announced the abandonment of Sassafras Cabin as a Trail shelter. As this shelter was but three miles from the end of the Trail at Mt. Oglethorpe, and on the usual access route, the situation gives rise to numerous problems, but it has arisen so recently that there has not been time, as yet, to work out alternative plans for substitution or replacement."

1956

GEORGIA
APPALACHIAN
19 TRAIL CLUB, INC. 30

T HE PORTION OF TRAIL between Mt. Oglethorpe and Southern's Store, being outside of the National Forest and on private land, was becoming more and more of a headache. As reported in the May 1956 *ATN* Trail report:

Logging, poultry raising and other private property usage makes maintenance of Trail very difficult. Southern's Store (burned recently) to Golf Course, 6.7 miles, has been heavily logged and blazes have suffered in proportion. Section was painted in 1955. Golf Course to Mt. Oglethorpe, 5.1 miles, is mostly on a road where poultry raising has increased recently. Trail terminus sign at Mt. Oglethorpe in bad condition. Sassafras Mountain Cabin is no longer usable.

As President Bob Scott wrote to an inquiring hiker: "As a wilderness trail, this stretch had become more unsatisfactory every year." A decision would soon have to be made on what to do about it.

The January, 1956, council meeting minutes recorded:

Larry Freeman suggested that the President appoint a committee to make a study as to whether or not we would like to change the end of the Trail from Oglethorpe. Committee was appointed, Larry Freeman, Chairman; with members Bob Scott, Jim Cragon, and Henry Morris. This Committee is to study the southern terminus of the Trail and submit recommendations to the Club for the purpose of making recommendations to the National Conference. Perhaps send the Conference pictures of the chicken houses.

In January, the re-route from Hawk Mountain via Three Forks to Winding Stair Gap was (again) white blazed, and the "old ridge road trail" from Winding Stair to Hawk Mountain was blue blazed as a side trail, "and now all travelers on the main AT will pass this way." Then in March, the other half of the re-route, over Sassafras and down into Mauldin Creek Valley, was white blazed, finally completing this long-planned route (although it was to be changed again in the not-too-distant future).

All of the work done on the Trail in the past few years was paying off. A letter from a hiker in April (quoted in the May, 1956, *ATN*) declared Georgia "one beautiful section of Trail, and it is a shame more people from up north cannot get down to appreciate it. . . . One great surprise to me was the magnificent condition of the Trail. You fellows have done a wonderful job and perhaps only those of us who walked in Georgia and North Carolina in 1935 to 1938 can really appreciate what you have done. I wanted to find the bad spots so I could tell you about them, but I was disappointed; there weren't any!"

The May council minutes recorded: "The President reported that our signs are all gone." A discussion resulted in the decision to begin a "sign program." A list was to be made, the Forest Service would be asked to make routed signs, and "failing in this, the Club would undertake the work." The bulletin reported later:

Fred Newnham has agreed, on behalf of the Forest Service, that approximately forty routed redwood signs showing Trail mileages will be furnished to the Georgia Club for erection. Our signs subcommittee selected the principal road crossings for marking this year. A list of these has been submitted to the Forest Service. Next year we can request a similar number to fill in intermediate points.

Stan Murray, Board of Managers member from the Tennessee Eastman Club, was conducting a survey for Conference "in order to determine the present condition of all existing lean-tos on the Appalachian Trail, as well as the status of the proposed lean-tos." He wrote to Searcy Slack about the survey and listed six proposed lean-to sites in Georgia which would complete the chain there. (One of these sites was the "Devil's Kitchen," but no one in the GATC claimed any knowledge of this area.) The site plan was news to the Club, but they proceeded to form a shelter committee and come up with four somewhat different sites to propose: Plumorchard Gap, Addis Gap, Gooch Gap, and Hickory Flats. These were to be added to the existing shelters at Tray Mountain, Rocky Knob, Tesnatee Gap, Blood Mountain, and Frosty Mountain. In reporting to Murray on the plan, President Scott said, "These are definitely only a plan in that there is no action on foot to perform construction. . . . You will note that our plan does not extend beyond the Chattahoochee National Forest. At the present time, private encroachment is a serious problem south of the Southern's Store site; and the matter of Trail location in this section is being studied actively right now."

In his report on the "Status of Lean-Tos," published in the January, 1957, *ATN*, Murray said of Georgia:

In some respects, the situation in Georgia is encouraging, in other respects somewhat discouraging.

Five lean-tos are in existence in the 96 miles of Georgia that the Trail traverses, all of these being on U.S. Forest land. One, Frosty Mountain, was built by the Georgia Appalachian Trail Club in 1952 and is in excellent condition and has a cleanliness rating of 1. The other four, however, dating back to the thirties, are in fair to very poor condition and rate from 2 to 4 on cleanliness. There are no latrines, no tin can dumps.

Of the seven sites that have been proposed, four are satisfactory as lean-to locations, although no campsites have been developed and there are no immediate prospects of lean-tos being built on them. The remaining three are no longer recommended for lean-tos because of easy access and commercial developments. These include the two sites closest to the southern terminus of the Trail.

It should be noted, however, that in spite of the difficulties in finding suitable sites, the Georgia Appalachian Trail Club appears definitely interested in the lean-to program and, in view of the excellent work at Frosty Mountain, it may be safely expected that the Club's interest and contribution to the program will continue.

The report declared the Frosty Mountain shelter one of only five lean-tos "south of Vermont" to receive a rating of Class I.

The "Five-Club Meet"(actually Six-Club since the Roanoke AT Club joined the group this year) was held at Roan Mountain, Tennessee. "An invitation was extended in behalf of Rev. Rufus Morgan and the GATC for next year's meet," according to the bulletin.

The condition of Mt. Oglethorpe and the last few miles of the AT began to receive a bit of unwanted publicity. The January, 1957, *ATN* reported on "The Oglethorpe Story":

Those who have visited or tried to visit the southern terminus of the Appalachian Trail in the past three or four years will not be surprised at what follows. Those who remember Mt. Oglethorpe in Georgia when the gleaming white marble monument to the founder of Georgia on this southernmost point of the Blue Ridge was reached only by a long journey on the Trail through the woods from the north, or from the south by dirt roads definitely not suitable for automobile use, followed by a climb afoot through the woods, will be shocked to hear what has happened there.

As the situation developed, effort was made to halt it; but, due to numerous circumstances too involved to be recounted here, such efforts were unavailing.

The condition of the area is lightly touched on in the following item by Harold Martin, quoted from the July 18, 1956, issue of *The Atlanta Constitution*:

OGLETHORPE SUFFERS SCARS OF VANDALISM

Mt. Oglethorpe—For 20 years or thereabout, the tall white marble shaft has stood, a lonely finger pointing at the sky on the top of this great peak. Only a few Georgians ever made the journey to look upon the shaft and read the inscribed tribute to James Edward Oglethorpe carved upon it. Only an occasional deer hunter passed this way, to stand on the great bald top and look away where the blue hills rolled endlessly east and north and west.

Now and then at night, dwellers in the lowlands saw the wink of camp fires on the peak and dim figures moving in the flickering light. This was a natural thing, for the big mountain marked the southern end of the Appalachian Trail. The wilderness route winds along the ridgetops all the way to Mount Katahdin in Maine.

It was the natural and normal starting point for those adventurous souls who walked the southern segments of the Trail. But hunters and hikers are men who love the woods and nature as God made it and they felt no wanton urge to deface or destroy. So the tall shaft rose undamaged from the grassy mountaintop, as white and smoothly beautiful as it was the day it was dedicated years ago.

Now, though, the story is different. The state, moved by a laudable desire not only to serve the great chicken industry which has grown up along the shoulders of the big hills which nuzzle Oglethorpe but to open up to public use one of the great scenic drives in Georgia, has cut a wide, hard-graveled all-weather road from the Jasper-Dawsonville highway far below to the peak of Oglethorpe. It is a route where beauty lies on every hand. It follows the ridgetops, dipping and swinging with the curves on the spine of the hills.

Only when the goal is reached is the eye offended. For the opening of the road has brought the type of citizen who fouls every spot he finds. The map of Georgia, carved in marble on the eastern face of the shaft, has been blasted with shotgun and pistol bullets. Some earnest idiot has used a rock or hammer to break off the nose of Gen. Oglethorpe, carved on the western face. Names have been scrawled, in lipstick and in pencil, upon the monument. Horses have been tethered to the shaft and have left their tribute on the pedestal on which it stands.

And all about is the litter that careless people leave—beer cans, old sandwich wrappers, sardine cans and broken bottles. Time and the wind and the rains eventually would rust and rot and hide these desecrations of course, but there is little hope of that. Too many will come to replenish the litter until all around the place will look, as it is beginning to look already, like a garbage dump.

Time and wind, snow, frost and rain, would eventually wear and chip and melt the great shaft, too. But that would take perhaps a thousand years. The memorial will not last that long, not even a tenth that long. At the rate the visiting vandals are going now, they will have it hacked and chipped and shot away before another decade has passed.

Actually, this does not begin to tell the story. Photographs show the monument defaced by shot to an unbelievable degree. Due to such misuse, cracks have developed in the shaft and it may fall soon. Photographs also show the 'developments' farther on beyond the monument at the Trail terminus. And this is worst of all. Since the road provides free and easy access to the mountaintop, and it is on private land, so the owner may do as he pleases with it, chicken shacks and roosts have been built on both sides of the Trail for some distance, but the chickens are not fenced in. They have 'free range.' The result is that even if a hiker is willing to brave the debris and odor of the resulting ground-cover and walk through a 'chicken yard,' the lightest rain makes such a slippery mass under foot that walking can be dangerous.

For the past year, various steps have been initiated in the endeavor to remedy conditions there, but with the road and the lack of cooperation by the landowner, it has become apparent that the wilderness that once was Oglethorpe has gone forever.

The GATC "Trail's End" Committee came to a decision in the early fall, and made its recommendations concerning the southern terminus of the AT to the general membership at the October annual meeting. The minutes of the meeting recorded:

Larry Freeman took up the problem of changing the end of the AT in Georgia and strongly recommended that we abandon the present site at Mt. Oglethorpe. Members of his committee shared in presenting the views of the committee. Henry Morris reported on the present condition of Mt. Oglethorpe. Hugh Chase described and gave background on the northern terminus at Mt. Katahdin, after which Larry drew a comparison between the two. Marene Snow recalled the problems and ideas of the men who originally planned the terminus at Mt. Oglethorpe. Jo Gambrell discussed the various possible sites for the new terminus and explained the committee's choice of Springer Mountain. Ralph Ramsey described Springer, showed charts of the approaches and led a discussion of the advantages of having the Trail end at this point. A general discussion followed, ending in this motion stated by Searcy Slack:
    'That the GATC recommend to the AT Conference that the southern terminus of the Appalachian Trail be located at the summit of Springer Mountain, and that the present Trail running north from Amicalola Falls State Park to Springer, which passes the Benton MacKaye shelter at Frosty Mountain, be retained as a blue blazed trail, while that portion of the Trail extending south from Amicalola Falls be abandoned.'
    Some discussion followed and a suggestion was made that further exploration of Springer and further study of the problem be done. This was overruled, however, and the motion was seconded and carried with one dissenting vote.

The bulletin account of the meeting recapped the whole story:

This evening climaxed years of wrestling with the problem of the southern terminus of the 2,000 mile Appalachian Trail. For some time, we have all stood by watching encroachment of private interest to the very edge of the Trail in its southern-most eleven miles outside of the National Forest. No wilderness—this section has been excessively logged; and on the very slopes of Mt. Oglethorpe, hikers must pass chicken coops and butane tanks.
    Recognizing that the time had come for a decision, the Trail's End Committee was appointed last January. During the year, that group studied the possibilities. There were many different opinions. One by one, the differences began to fall away. It is recognized that to preserve the original concept of the Appalachian Trail, the route should follow the wilderness and end in the wilderness, that it is not to be simply an efficient way of getting from one place to another. The Committee recommended that the terminus be the summit of Springer Mountain, which is approximately 21 miles north on the Trail from the present end on Mt. Oglethorpe. Alternate ends considered were Amicalola Lake and Frosty Mountain which are in between Springer and Oglethorpe. These were abandoned because of easy access and increased public use of both places. It was recalled that Mt. Katahdin—the northern end—was in a great wilderness.
    Springer is a long loaf-shaped mountain with rock outcrops to make excellent view

possibilities and no roads ascend its summit. It is the spot where the Appalachian ridge divides—one branch following down to Oglethorpe—the other taking a more northerly direction to Fort Mountain. As a matter of fact, Fort was seriously considered as a possible end but constructing some 40 miles of trail was out of reason at this time.

The motion that Springer be recommended to the Appalachian Trail Conference in Washington as the southern terminus was passed. Another motion that the present portion of Trail from Amicalola Falls to Springer be maintained as an approach trail and blue blazed was also passed. This means that approximately 14 miles from the Falls to Oglethorpe will be completely abandoned. A full account of the presentation is to be distributed later.

In its report on the "Oglethorpe Story," the *ATN* quoted the minutes of this meeting and continued: "A formal recommendation as indicated above is being made by the Georgia Appalachian Trail Club to the Appalachian Trail Conference. As this involves a change in the constitution, formal action to change the southern terminus will await the 1958 Conference session. The Board of Managers will meanwhile prepare the recommendation to that session. . . . There is little doubt that the familiar 'Katahdin to Oglethorpe' or vice versa, will soon give way to 'Katahdin to Springer.'" And it added at the end of the article: "This situation emphasizes again the importance of bringing the Trail route into public ownership, so that weight of public opinion can insure its preservation when it is threatened."

The Club would continue to maintain the Trail until approval was received from Conference, but it did not recommend its use to hikers.

Officers for the coming year were elected at the annual meeting and installed at the Christmas party in December: Bob Scott, president; Ralph Ramsey, vice president for activities; Jo Gambrell, vice president for membership; Margaret Roddy, secretary; Tom Aderhold, treasurer; Marene Snow, historian; Ed Traylor, council. At the end of the year, a report announced 109 members, "84 of whom live in Georgia."

1957

A TREAT OF SOME "brand new 'freeze dried' meats" was the highlight of an overnight trip to Frosty Mountain in January of 1957. The canned meats had been sent to the Club by the Armour Company on a trial basis. The bulletin report on the trip began: "The GATC includes two kinds of people: (1) the 'go ifs' (2) the 'go no matter whats.' One outnumbers the other to a marked degree." Three "go no matter whats" made the hike, and feasted on the new meats. Bob Scott reported back to Armour and Company on the results: "We found that an eight ounce can was required to satisfy the hiker appetites of four persons. When the cans were opened after puncturing under water, some were disappointed at the gray color. These same people were delighted at the flavor and appearance after cooking."

Jean Stephenson, editor of the *ATN*, read in the *Mountaineer* of the meats and wrote to Scott inquiring about them. This resulted in an article in the May *ATN*, which explained that, although "there are available dehydrated vegetables, fruits, and milk, for meats one still has to use the salted, cured or canned variety, all weighty! Thus the possibility of good dehydrated meat is of great importance to hikers."

A trip in February featured "something new and highlight in this year's calendar": a trip to Greenbriar Cabin in the Smokies. The cabin was built in Greenbriar Cove in the 1930's by the Smoky Mountains Hiking Club, and was used by courtesy of that club. The trip featured a variety of hikes: Charlie's Bunion "from below ... the young and brash taking the trip. . . . The indefatigables, the 17 mile long climb to Ramsey Cascades and return; the sissies, the Porters Flats Creek Trail; and the nonconformists covering Brushy."

The long wait for the approval of Conference on changing the Trail's terminus and the abandonment of this section by the GATC continued to result in problems with lost hikers and more publicity. The May, 1957, *ATN* included the following article:

The January 1957 *Appalachian Trailway News* reprinted an article by Harold Martin from the July 18, 1956, *Atlanta Constitution* on Mt. Oglethorpe and reported the action of the Georgia Appalachian Trail Club with respect to the situation there.

For the past several years, out of state visitors to Mt. Oglethorpe have been complaining about the deterioration of the area, orally to friends, in interviews in their home town newspapers, to conservationists in general, to the Appalachian Trail Conference and the GATC, and to various officials in Georgia. It seemed to be considered a matter of interest only to a few outdoor enthusiasts, and complaints 'got nowhere' and received no publicity.

But one such hiker, an active Rotarian at home, apparently felt that if hikers could do nothing, businessmen could, so he wrote to the Rotary Club of Canton, Georgia. From there it reached the State Parks Department and from there the newspapers.

In the March 2, 1957, *Atlanta Constitution*, Leo Aikman discussed the matter:

Trail's End is on Shaky Base

(He begins with the story of the suggestion that the marker to General Harker, halfway up the slope of Cheatham Hill in Kennesaw Mountain National Battlefield Park, be moved to the highway at the top of the hill. . . .)

"But, Mr. Jones," I protested, "he wasn't killed at the top of the hill."

"I know that," said B. F., a practical man if not a historian, "But nobody sees the monument where it is now."

It's that way with the Gen. Oglethorpe monument and the south end of the Appalachian Trail on Mt. Oglethorpe in the Tate Mountain range.

Some think the Trail terminus should be moved to North Carolina.

Cantonians don't agree.

The fuss started over a letter from L. D. Snyder, a Littlestown, Pa., hardware dealer and hiker, to Clayton Reid, secretary of the Canton Rotary Club.

The man up north says he doesn't understand why Georgia doesn't make more fuss over such an important thing as the take-off on the Appalachian Trail and the Oglethorpe monument. He says there is no marker, no nothing to show where the Trail starts. He bets a hat (Alpinist?) Maine has its end of the Trail marked.

Bro. Snyder thinks Georgians should push a twofold project—marking of the Appalachian Highway for Hikers and a decent setting for the Oglethorpe memorial.

George F. Blackburn, secretary of the Appalachian Trail Conference, told Mr. Snyder the complaint is not unusual. Says Mr. Blackburn, "so unsatisfactory is the situation that abandonment of Mt. Oglethorpe as the southern terminus is seriously considered."

Recognizing Mt. Oglethorpe as slightly out of its territory, but the problem as within

·

its field of interest, the Rotary Club of Canton has reported the situation to the State Parks Department.

The *North Georgia Tribune* has dared north Georgians to go out this spring, see for themselves and help put the Georgia section of the Appalachian Trail back on the map.

Move the southern terminus of the Trail from Georgia?

I should say not.

Let's all go out and blaze, with indignation.

GATC President Robert C. Scott promptly wrote Mr. Aikman and gave full information on the subject, also saying—

'Since the last eleven miles of the Trail and Oglethorpe itself are private property we could do nothing but stand by through the years and watch a beautiful wilderness disintegrate into a tin can dump and chicken yard. In recent years, we gave up trying to paint the familiar white blazes to guide hikers along the footway of this eleven miles, since trees were removed as fast as we blazed them. Oglethorpe and the Trail End was marked by a beautiful rustic sign with routed letters a few years ago. But Oglethorpe was accessible by road and the sign fell to target practice; it is no more. No road ascends Springer Mountain and we ask the Canton Rotary Club and all others to help keep it so to maintain its wilderness character. It is too late to save Oglethorpe, but we can save Springer by starting now.

It is much more pleasant to think of the charm—mountain by mountain and gap by gap—of the remaining 78 miles of Georgia Appalachian Trail. These are in the National Forest and we know the men who administer the Forest. They are behind the Appalachian Trail, dedicated to keep it "A Footpath through the Wilderness."'

Mr. Aikman's column in the March 8, 1957, *Atlanta Constitution* brought readers up to date:

'Trail Club Says "Move Terminus"

There's a long, long trail a-winding—from a peak in Pickens County, Ga., to Mt. Katahdin in Maine. The suggestion that it may be made shorter has urged Atlantan Robert C. Scott, president of the Georgia Appalachian Trail Club, to expression. Says Mr. Scott, by letter:

"Your Saturday 'Trail End is on Shaky Base' was a surprise on a couple of counts: (1) That there was general enough interest in the Appalachian Trail in Georgia to warrant news treatment, (2) That there could be such mis-information suggesting a responsible opinion that the terminus be moved to North Carolina."

President Scott enclosed an article from the January 1957 issue of the *Appalachian Trailway News*. It says in substance what the man from Pennsylvania wrote to Canton Rotarians—Trail's End and the Oglethorpe Monument have deteriorated through lack of maintenance and vandalism to a degree that is no credit to Georgians.

Civilization has reached the peak. Broiler raising has pushed back the frontier. Say the Georgia ATC members, " . . . on the very slopes of Oglethorpe, hikers must pass chicken coops and butane tanks."

So a committee from the Club has made a recommendation based on the original concept, that the Trail should start in wilderness and end in wilderness.

The committee wants to move the southern terminus not to North Carolina, but to Springer Mountain, 21 miles north of the present southmost station on Mt.

Oglethorpe. No road ascends Springer, a long, loaf-shaped mountain with rock outcrops to make for good overlooks. Springer is at the place where the Appalachian chain in Georgia divides, one range continuing into Pickens County, the other going to Fort Mountain.

The way to Mt. Oglethorpe would be "blue blazed," which means it would be an approach trail, but no longer be a part of the Appalachian Trail.

The Georgia ATC is dedicated to keeping the remaining 78 miles of the Trail in this state what it was intended to be, "A Footpath Through the Wilderness."

Each year members of the Club walk the Trail in Georgia—cutting entangling briars, applying white paint (12 qts.) to the blazes and removing tree falls. Only those who hike are sought as members. The Club wants no armchair conservationists, the president says.

Bona fide ridge-running pedestrians might like the address: GATC, P.O. Box 654, Atlanta 1.

By the way, this weekend's trek will be from Tray Mountain to Unicoi Gap.'

This cooperation by Mr. Aikman and the newspapers in spreading the word of the 'ruination' of the mountain dedicated to the founder of Georgia, the southern end of the Appalachian Trail, and a beautiful wilderness area, is much appreciated. It may help in preserving the remaining wilderness aspects of north Georgia's little known but extremely interesting mountainous country.

Keeping Jean Stephenson up to date on the matter, Bob Scott wrote: "These developments are at least bringing interest in the Trail to light which we did not know existed down here."

In corresponding with Percy Prescott of the AMC, a prospective through hiker, Scott told him:

Keeping on the Trail from Oglethorpe will not be easy. We fought a losing battle trying to keep paint blazes through there. Logging and chicken ranching outran us. Watch your step, that chicken ---- is right slippery. Don't expect to find Southern Store, much less do any trading there—the moonshiners who occupied it got burned out last year.

Prescott replied to Scott, asking, "Think I should bring my skis to traverse the Trail from Oglethorpe?"

In April "one of two pack trips on this year's calendar" was announced in the bulletin thus: "Those waiting for a 'back pack' trip need wait no more. Here it is—and the call goes out to one and all who long for the thrill realized by packing the bare essentials into remote and otherwise inaccessible areas." The trip, led by Tom Aderhold, was from Deep Gap to Dicks Creek, with eight participants.

Dorothy Laker, of Tampa, Florida, became the second woman to walk the entire Trail, walking into Katahdin Stream Campground in September, ten days after Emma Gatewood finished her second trip. Laker's hike through Georgia and North Carolina was memorable for another would-be through hiker, Mr. Melvin Hodgkin from Maine. A GATC group had met Hodgkin and Laker, who were hiking together at the time, on the Trail, assumed they were married, and commented on meeting "Hodgkin and his wife" in the bulletin account. Bob Scott later wrote to "Mr. and Mrs. Hodgkin," sending the bulletin excerpt and saying, " . . . While we were approaching Wallace Gap in North Carolina, it was good to see your names on the register. . . . Let us hear from you." Scott heard from Hodgkin, who said, "I have a bone to pick with you and you will know what I mean when I say that I quit the Appalachian Trail when I got through the Great Smoky Mountains at Waterville, North Carolina, and my hiking companion, who *was not my wife*, continued on. . . . My hiking companion was a Miss Dorothy Laker. . . . Your letter was opened and read first by my wife and she wanted to know how I signed the register that you refer to. I don't believe I signed it Mr. and Mrs. You don't know how *near* you caused a family breakup!"

In the spring, the Club inaugurated a three-year blazing program, which, as reported in the *ATN*, "provided for 31 miles to be painted each year . . . based on need, accessibility, coordination with Club work trips and hikes, and other factors. . . . Renewal of blazes regularly every three years on an orderly basis should make the Georgia section of Trail one that is a joy to follow."

Van Hook Glade in North Carolina was the scene of the Six-Club Meet, with hosts the Rev. Rufus Morgan and the GATC. It was a "memorable occasion," with hikes, square dance, music, campfires, slides, and singing. One major chore performed by the GATC was maintenance of the large generator hauled to the spot to provide electricity.

The Tesnatee Gap shelter developed a leaky roof during the year, and the Forest Service obligingly repaired it, refusing an offer of some funds and labor from the GATC. Forest Supervisor Paul Vincent explained:

The shelters on the Appalachian Trail were originally constructed by the Forest Service and were maintained until the late 30's. Since that time funds have been too limited to maintain them to a desirable standard. This year, however, funds have been increased and the maintenance of the Appalachian Trail shelters is included in our regular recreation program.

At the October annual meeting, held at the Atlanta Waterworks Lodge, the recommendation was made by the council that "the constitution be amended" to add the office of bulletin editor to the slate of officers, and that "the bulletin editor be a member of the council." The motion was carried. Officers elected for 1958 were: Henry Morris, president; Tom Aderhold, first vice president (activities); Margaret Roddy, second vice president (membership); Carolyn Huey, secretary; Hugh Chase, treasurer; Don Dolan, bulletin editor; Marene Snow, historian; Bob Scott, council. The report of the activities committee proudly announced that "All outings during the year were held without respect to adverse weather."

The regular trip to Dillard and the annual Christmas party and installation of officers finished the activities for the year.

1958

THE YEAR 1958 WAS TO SEE the official declaration of Springer Mountain as the southern terminus of the AT. In the early spring, Murray Stevens, AT Conference chairman, visited Atlanta, attending a GATC council meeting and making a trip to Springer to see the proposed new terminus. He declared it "one of which we can all be proud," and suggested a shelter be built at the spring just north of the summit.

At the council meeting which he attended, the minutes reported, "Mr. Cragon discussed the possibility of changing the name of Springer Mountain, possibly to Cherokee Mountain. Henry Morris moved that 'we adopt the name Cherokee Mountain for the terminus of the Trail with the idea in mind of presenting the change to the legislature after usage has been established.' Marene seconded the motion, which was carried."

The following "recommendation for changing the southern terminus" of the Trail was presented to the Conference meeting in May by Henry Morris:

By reason of the fact that the last few miles of the Appalachian Trail approaching Mt. Oglethorpe in Georgia, and the mountain itself, due to modern development, have become no longer suitable as a part of a wilderness trail, the Georgia Appalachian Trail Club, after much thought and consideration, has resolved to submit the following proposal to the Appalachian Trail Conference:

'That the southern terminus of the Appalachian Trail be changed to Springer Mountain, which is not accessible by road. That the trail from the summit of Springer Mountain south to Amicalola Falls (approximately 7 miles) be maintained as an approach trail with blue blazes, and that the section from Amicalola Falls to Mt. Oglethorpe (approximately 16 miles) which is on privately owned land, be abandoned.'

At a meeting of the council March 21, 1958, a motion was made and carried that the name of Springer Mountain be changed to a suitable Indian name, one suggestion being Cherokee Mountain. Several members and friends of the Club who are students of history and Indian lore are working on the selection of a suitable name but, at the present time, have not reached a decision.

The September *ATN* reported on the new southern terminus:

The change in the past 25 years in the character of the surroundings of Mt. Oglethorpe, the southern terminus of the Appalachian Trail, was described in *ATN* for January and May 1957. Notice was duly given of the proposed amendment to the constitution to change the southern terminus.

In accordance with such notice, it was moved by Henry Morris, President of the Georgia Appalachian Trail Club, that the constitution be amended to change the southern terminus from Mt. Oglethorpe to the mountain referred to in the guidebook as 'Springer.' This was seconded by ATC Board Member Arch Nichols, of the Carolina Mountain Club, and passed without a dissenting vote.

While many present deplored the situation, all realized it was 'a fact and not a theory that confronted' the group and in view of the fact, such action was necessary.

As soon as the name of the 'mountain called Springer' has been determined, the words 'Mt. Oglethorpe' will be stricken from Article 3 of the constitution and the name of the new terminus inserted.

Following the Conference meeting, the GATC took immediate action to eliminate such white blazes as remained on the abandoned section south of Amicalola and blue blazed the approach trail to the new terminus. Trail data for the approaches to the new southern terminus are being prepared and will be published in the January issue.

The Appalachian Trail is now approximately 2,000 miles, determination of the exact distance awaiting information on certain 'minor relocations' which, it developed at the Conference meeting, had not been reported by the maintaining groups concerned.

At the July GATC council meeting, it was voted to rescind the motion made in March to adopt the name Cherokee Mountain for the Trail terminus. The problem of the name of "the mountain called Springer" was summed up by President Henry Morris at the Christmas party at the end of the year:

Henry took up an old matter of business concerning the investigation of a new name for the new terminus of the Appalachian Trail, Springer Mountain. He read a letter from the council which, after investigating many possible new names and studying the situation thoroughly, suggested that the name Springer be left as it now stands. Discussion on this question was asked from the membership. Arnold Ingemann stated his position as being completely satisfied with the name left as Springer Mountain and that he thought the name to be beautiful and satisfactory. Jean Dolan asked what names were considered. Henry explained that several Cherokee Indian names were suggested [Tickanetly, among others]; but, due to the harsh tones of the

Cherokee language, none were deemed phonetic enough to make a pleasant sounding name. He also explained that action on this name was delayed at the annual meeting so that an investigation could be made with the help of two Indians, Mr. and Mrs. George Owl who would be at Dillard. A thorough discussion was held with the Owls at Dillard and the council's investigation that the Cherokee language is a harsh one was confirmed. Therefore, the council decided to bring up this item of business at tonight's gathering. Don Dolan suggested a committee be appointed to study the history and folklore of Springer Mountain. Henry advised that this would be taken up at the next council meeting. Charlie Smith made a motion that the GATC leave the name of the new terminus of the AT as Springer Mountain. This motion was seconded by Tom Aderhold and carried unanimously by the membership.

A committee was appointed in the fall "to design a terminus sign for the end of the Trail."

The blue blazing of the new approach trail between Amicalola and Springer was completed on an overnight trip in late June—by a "lucky 13" under "ideal" camping conditions at Frosty Mountain shelter.

A notice in the March bulletin announced the death of Carter Whittaker, long-time GATC member and former president of the Club.

As Henry Morris explained in a letter to the membership in April, "There has been no printing of the constitution and by-laws of the GATC for a good many years, and practically all copies of the last printing have ceased to exist." In fact, it had been 20 years since the last revision. A new version, with only "minor changes," was produced by a committee, printed, and a copy sent to each member, to be studied and voted on at a meeting in May.

In the spring, a "new development" was reported to the Club concerning the activities of the Army rangers training in the area between Gooch Gap and Winding Stair Gap. The rangers were using mock mine explosions, booby traps, etc. A notice printed in the bulletin and reprinted in the *ATN* warned hikers not to "poke at" strange objects along the Trail in this area.

Mountain Lake, Virginia, was the scene of the 14th Appalachian Trail Conference in May. The *Mountaineer* reported "more than two hundred in attendance and a greater number of Trail organizations represented than at any previous meeting." Besides the big news of changing the Trail terminus, the bulletin also reported on other happenings, saying:

There were many interesting reports given indicating that people in general are getting more conscious of the meaning of wilderness areas and of the existence of the Appalachian Trail. There were, unfortunately, reports of trouble on some sections in the north caused by the encroachment of housing projects where the Trail is on private land.

Bob Scott was elected to the Board of Managers from the Southern district.

Jimmy Cragon resigned as vice chairman, a post he had held since 1950, and Stan Murray was elected to fill this vacancy.

In a report in May to President Henry Morris on Trail conditions, Bob Scott declared that "I think we have the best blazed and cleared trail north of Springer Mountain that we have had in the last five years." Reporting on shelter conditions and proposed shelters, he declared Rocky Knob and Montray shelters in poor condition and the old Snake Mountain shelter in ruins. Scott proposed to the Forest Service that shelters be built at Hickory Flats, Gooch Gap, Addis Gap and Plumorchard Gap (according to the decision made in 1956), as well as a new shelter at Rocky Knob. Paul Vincent of the Forest Service replied:

We are very happy to advise that we have included the construction of four shelters in our FY 1959 Programs of Work. Our tentative selection of sites for these four new shelters included Springer Mountain, Gooch Gap, Addis Gap and Plumorchard Gap. We note that this is in line with your proposed shelter program with the exception of 'Hickory Flats' which should probably be substituted for our Springer Mountain location.

Would you please send us a copy of your Appalachian Trail Guidebook, as well as the latest revised map of the Appalachian Trail in order that we might correct our records and pinpoint the area which you know as 'Hickory Flats'?

We are very much interested in the Appalachian Trail program and we hope that funds will be forthcoming in FY 1960 to complete the entire job of shelter restoration on the Georgia section of the Appalachian Trail.

The Springer site met with the approval of the Club, and construction was to start "immediately," with materials to be "dropped" by helicopter. Priorities for building the other shelters were set in this order: Plumorchard, Gooch, and Addis. If money was forthcoming in 1960, new shelters would also be built at Springer, Rocky Knob and Montray. Scott wrote to Stan Murray: "I am very much encouraged by the splendid spirit of cooperation we are meeting in the Forest Service." All of the shelter sites had been staked out by the Club and "direction to face established" well before the construction began.

In his May report, Scott concluded:

Although we have no way of measuring use of the Appalachian Trail in Georgia, it is my opinion that interest in it is ever increasing. This is based upon telephone inquiries and conversations in North Georgia. Also the footway seems to remain well established indicating considerable traffic. We must go after the active participation of more outdoor people in preserving and maintaining the Trail.

A suggestion was made at the general membership meeting that maps "with the AT well marked" should be "prepared for display at selected places." This suggestion resulted in the fine detailed 21" X 26" maps made by Henry Morris, some of which were framed and "installed" at Neel Gap, Dillard and Dahlonega. The maps were later reduced in size "for distribution to interested members," and have been used since in various ways.

The (again) Five-Club Meet was held at Deep Creek campground near Bryson City, North Carolina. Rufus Morgan was still the "one-man club," although he brought along a guest—Jim Maddox. In November, it was announced in the bulletin that the membership of Rev. Morgan's club had doubled with the addition of Maddox as a member.

Keeping up with one of the GATC's most "flighty" members, the bulletin announced that Aviatrix Bunny Motsinger "will make a trip around the world and afterwards hopes to visit Atlanta."

The annual meeting was held in October at the DeKalb County Federal Savings and Loan Association building. Committee reports were made and officers were elected for 1959: Henry Morris, president; Tom Aderhold, first vice president (activities); Charlie Smith, second vice president (membership); Carolyn Ramsey, secretary; Hugh Chase, treasurer; Marene Snow, historian; Lou Hoben, bulletin editor; Margaret Roddy, council (upon her resignation in December, Ralph Ramsey was elected to fill the vacancy).

At the meeting, activities chairman Tom Aderhold presented a detailed report of the year's outings, with an accounting of the number of people attending each activity, and a comparison of the average attendance with the past three years: the average number of members participating in 1958 was 13, guests 11; compared to 1955, with an average of 10 members and 10 guests. Only one activity out of the 20 planned "failed to materialize" during the year. Tom also reported on several members who had exceptional attendance records—Henry and Marion Morris and Bob Scott—and one guest, Roger Losier, who attended all except one trip.

The trip to the Dillard Farm was made in November, Thanksgiving was celebrated by a four-day trip to Jekyll Island, and the Christmas party and installation of officers ended the year.

1959

GEORGIA
APPALACHIAN
19 TRAIL CLUB, INC. 30

THE FIRST MAJOR ORDER of business for 1959 was to remove the blazes from the former Trail south of Amicalola Falls. The bulletin recounts the first trip—in January—on which 15 hikers

. . . proceeded from the 'store' toward Amicalola removing white blazes as they hiked along the abandoned trail. The wanton destruction of trail blazes, even along this portion, brought a tear to the eye of Bob Scott, who, for so many years, has dedicated himself to bigger and better blazes. After a few practice strokes, even he discovered the thrill all hunters in the Cooper Gap section have known since we first painted blazes along the Trail.

Later in the year, the proposed trip to deblaze the rest of the section was announced as "our farewell to Mt. Oglethorpe," and as Tom Aderhold reported afterward:

Even though advertised as primarily a work trip, this outing attracted 23 members and guests who rendered final tribute to Mt. Oglethorpe as the AT terminus. Left behind for more scenic and colorful surroundings, this faithful mountain served admirably for many years until industry necessary to the State's economy began rapid encroachment of lands on and about the Trail.

The plaque—similar to the ones at Neel and Unicoi Gaps—that had been given to the Club by Mrs. Martha Noble, wife of the sculptor, was to be installed on the new Trail terminus. A trip was planned for April to install

194

the plaque along with the new terminus sign and a Trail register, and for "possibly scouting for new Trail locations." Whit Benson, leader, reported for the bulletin:

This was to be the momentous occasion for installing the terminus sign and bronze marker on Springer, but the keynote of the weekend was "RAIN." Fifteen people left Atlanta beneath dismal, rainy skies Saturday morning. After lunch at Winding Stair Gap, came the job of transporting the sign, bronze marker, register, and their associated 4 X 4 posts and tools to the top of Springer Mountain. The work on Springer was partially completed as dusk began to set in and the group headed for Hawk Mountain to set up camp. While cooking supper, the skies cleared, the stars came out and the prospects were promising for a beautiful Sunday. The fire had long since died out and everyone was asleep when in the first few minutes of Sunday morning (approximately 1:00 A.M.) the wind picked up, and the "RAIN" came. By 8:00 A.M., fifteen wet people had a common thought, "HOME." After meeting at the Smith House to change into dry clothes and extend goodbyes, we headed for home, and another retreat from the weather.

"Sure the weather would not stage a repeat performance," another group made a return trip the following weekend. They were mistaken, however, and the rains came again as the group headed for Nimblewill Gap. Henry Morris reported:

Ninety minutes later, the summit of Springer was reached and the plaque, tools and even the cement were found just as they had been left. BUT it was still raining—only harder. In no time at all, expert hammer wielders, Hugh and E. G., had holes down in the rock for the bolts in the plaque and although we could get no wetter, continually being soaked at such a fast and furious rate was wearing on our patience. The plaque was buried under the turf, tools gathered up and the procession started down—still raining—only much more heavily. . . . Since the weather did not look promising even for the next day, after a brief conference, it was decided to go on to the Smith House for supper and return home.

In May, "with a prediction of fair weather," another trip was made, and finally the job was finished, and the bulletin announced: "Springer Mountain is now properly and officially the southern terminus of the Appalachian Trail, so designated by sign, register, and plaque."

The September, 1959, issue of the *ATN* featured on the cover a picture of the plaque, the sign, and a view from atop Springer. One article reported on the successful attempt to erect the markers, and another article on the approaches, by road and Trail, to reach the new terminus.

1959 was a very good year for the activities committee. The AT was becoming more popular, and attendance on all Club trips was growing. In May it was reported that 196 people had attended seven trips, "and that the guests have outnumbered the members." By the end of the year, according to activities chairman Tom Aderhold, the average number of people attending hikes was 16, with activities scheduled every two weeks; "no activity failed to materialize for 1959 and all leaders performed with enthusiasm, interest and careful planning."

Hiking trips were mainly on the Georgia Trail, but other hiking and camping trips were scheduled. The regular trips were made to the Greenbriar Cabin, LeConte, and the Dillard House (where they celebrated the 25th annual "weekend party" held there), plus the standard Five-Club Meet and Christmas Party. A "first for the Georgia Club" was a backpack into "a remote section of the North Carolina AT": Wayah Bald to Wesser Creek. Other camping trips took large crowds to Round Bottom in the Smokies, Cloudland Canyon, Lake Lanier on the Emersons' property, and the Okefenokee Swamp.

An announcement in the June bulletin declared: "Eligible for membership!! Roger Losier . . . attained the age of 18 years, June 6th. Qualified?? He has been present as a guest on almost every trip during the past two and one half years."

The Forest Service lived up to its promise to build four new shelters on the Georgia Trail, but someone in the Forest Service evidently had ideas of his own, for the location of at least one of them came as a surprise to the Club. In a letter to Jean Stephenson in June, Henry Morris sent her several pictures of the new terminus, and another picture of which he said: "The other picture is what we discovered at Big Stamp Gap June 14, approximately 1.7 miles north of Springer Mountain. I suppose it is the cabin the Forest Service had planned to put at Springer Mountain."

All of the four new shelters were completed by July: Big Stamp Gap, Gooch Gap, Addis Gap, and Plumorchard Gap. It was reported at a council meeting that the Forest Service felt that prospects for additional shelters were poor due to cuts in appropriations.

The work of the membership committee and trail information chairman was growing rapidly, and the need was felt for form letters to answer inquiries about the Club and the Trail. A Committee to Draft Form Letters presented to the council five letters giving information about the Georgia Trail in general, more detailed information about the southern half and the northern half, membership information, and general information about the Club.

The balance in the treasury was slowly growing, and at the May council meeting it was decided to open a savings account with $400 of the $630 balance.

A letter from Benton MacKaye was read at the July council meeting "extending greetings to the GATC, expressing keen interest in the program outlined in the 1959 yearbook, and again voicing his pleasure resulting from our naming one of our shelters (Frosty Mountain) the Benton MacKaye shelter."

The unpaved roads leading to several sections of the AT had been gated for many years. The Club had been given keys to these gates, and on occasion the locks would be changed, necessitating new keys. In the summer of 1959 the locks were changed again, and among a series of letters to various officials in an attempt to get a new set of keys, Henry Morris received a letter from a district forest ranger who said that it was their desire to have all of the gates removed. This would be a welcome relief to the GATC, although the gates actually were not removed until more than ten years later.

The end of the year brought news—good and bad—of members old and new. The December bulletin announced that Bob Scott and his family were moving to California. The Scotts had been very popular and enthusiastic Club members, and Bob had led the Club during one of the times when activity and interest were at a peak and all seemed to be going well. He would be fondly remembered as a hard worker and good friend. As the bulletin said, "The Scotts ... have contributed much to the benefit and pleasure of the Georgia Appalachian Trail Club and we will miss them, greatly."

The same bulletin issue related the return of our favorite aviatrix, Bunny Motsinger, to Georgia, saying that she was in the process of building a home "in the Blue Ridge."

Roy Ozmer, who originally scouted and marked the entire Georgia Trail, was discovered to be living as a "hermit" on an island in the Everglades National Park in Florida. An article in the *Miami News* of November 1, 1959, described Ozmer's situation, saying: "Bearded and wearing a beachcomber outfit of beret, slacks, sport shirt and sandals, Ozmer (a university-educated, former merchant seaman) surprises tourists with his excellent English and scholarly dissertations."

Officers for the coming year were elected at the annual meeting: Tom Aderhold, president; Charlie Smith, vice president-activities; Gannon Coffey, vice president-membership; Barbara Deane, secretary; Norman Brendel, treasurer; Marene Snow, historian; Henry Morris and Hugh Chase, council.

1960

GEORGIA
APPALACHIAN
19 TRAIL CLUB, INC. 50

THE NEW DECADE OF THE 1960's began on the rising tide of "outdoor fever" suffered by masses of American people. Camping areas in the mountains and elsewhere were booming. This interest in outdoor activities would, of course, have a great and lasting effect on the Trail and the Club.

The average number of people attending a GATC hike or camping trip in 1960 was 34—equally divided between members and guests. In February, a trip to Russell Cave drew 73 people. The smallest number of people on a trip was 19 on a work trip to Tray Gap. At the May, 1960, council meeting there was a discussion "on the increased attendance on Club trips and whether it was real or illusory. It was pointed out that . . . attendance is swelled by guests . . . that guests are necessary to attract new members . . . that scouts' presence should be soft-pedaled, since some council members felt they discouraged members from attending." It was decided that arm bands would be furnished the leaders to distinguish them from the crowd.

"Two tasks of Herculean proportion," according to President Tom Aderhold, "became an unexpected part of the agenda" for 1960. One of these tasks was "the mammoth trail clearing necessitated by the most severe winter in 30 years." The Trail report in the May *ATN* reported, "Excess rainfall for several months, with severe ice and snow storms, accompanied by high winds and low temperatures during early March stopped all highway travel and isolated mountain communities for weeks. Trail result is numerous windfalls." As Aderhold wrote to Jean Stephenson:

As you likely noticed in a recent issue of our bulletin, we called attention to the extreme severeness of our winter and the damage it inflicted to the Trail in tree-falls, washouts, etc. At the same time, we called for volunteers to begin clearing trips and work parties, along with our regular Trails and Shelters committee. The response was amazing. Work parties have been organized almost every weekend and the job of clearing is progressing wonderfully well. (May 3, 1960)

Stephenson replied to his letter, in which he also expressed appreciation for several articles in the *ATN* on the Georgia Club and Trail:

Sometimes it almost seems that there is an undue quantity of space given to Maine and to Georgia, but it is because those are the two groups that really get out and 'do things.' And the others, whether they emulate them or not, like to read about them! . . . So I am always glad to have word of what goes on in Georgia for I know that the readers like to hear of what goes on there.

Speaking now, not as editor but as a Board Member, I do want to congratulate the GATC on the energetic way in which it took steps to remedy the results of the past winter's storms on the Trail. It sets a splendid example for other clubs, and mention is going to be made of it at an appropriate time—when it will do the most good in encouraging others! (May 11, 1960)

In planning a course of action for the Trail clearing, Aderhold announced that "one definite action will be a request for an individual(s) to volunteer for certain specific sections they would clear." A number of people volunteered for sections, and by the end of May most of the clearing was completed.

The second "Herculean" task of the year was the "packing-in of materials required to construct two of the three new shelters." With funds limited, the Forest Service had said early in the year that they would be able to furnish "materials but not labor" for the shelters to be constructed at Hawk Mountain (decided upon instead of Hickory Flats), Rocky Knob (next to the remains of the old shelter), and Montray (next to the spring). Several months later, it was indicated that funds would be available for the entire operation. An attempt would be made to borrow "mechanized mules" from the Army Ranger camp to transport the materials to the shelter sites. The "mules" were "unable to negotiate the Trail," however, and the Club was called upon to help out by carrying the materials in. In September, cement, sand and stone in sacks, weighing 2,700 pounds for each shelter, was left at Tray Gap and Henson Gap to be hauled to Tray Mountain and Rocky Knob. A postcard was sent to each member calling for HELP:

Want to contribute some labor toward building a new shelter? Well the time is right. Material for shelter has been transported in as far as possible by Forest Service jeep. Help is needed from every member to pack it in the balance of the distance. Sand and crushed stone will be sacked in ten 50 lb. bags; cement is in 94 lb. unbroken sacks. There are 2,700 lbs. total. Needed badly are pack boards with rope lashings. Also necessary are packs with integral frames and any other type.

. . . This is the first of two shelters which the Forest Service will call on Club members to assist. Let's show them we appreciate their efforts in obtaining these shelters. Y'all come.

The bulletin reported on the results:

Answering the short-notice postcard call for help, an enthusiastic group of members and guests made themselves available for work Saturday and/or Sunday. From around noon Saturday until after 5:00 P.M., approximately 2,700 pounds of sand, cement and gravel were moved by wheelbarrow, pack frame, pack, shoulder and hand, the necessary 0.6 miles to the new shelter site.

The following weekend, the load was hauled from Tray Gap UP to the Montray shelter site. Within two weeks the shelter foundations were completed by the Forest Service, the lumber for the superstructure was trucked to the same gaps, and another call for help went out. The bulletin account of the first lumber-hauling trip read:

The human mules and their guests gathered at Tray Gap Saturday morning and formed into a very effective relay team stretching one and a half miles up to the shelter. Each person was assigned a sector of 150 to 200 paces, and relayed load after never-ending load through his sector to the next in the chain. Late in the afternoon, hopes of finishing the first day were buoyed by a report relayed from the bottom of the hill that all the lumber was on the Trail; however, shortly thereafter, a setting sun and collapsing workers called a halt.

Sunday morning, the group assaulted the mountain again like eager turtles and found the mountain had somehow gotten higher. But happily, the last load was deposited at the shelter location in only one hour and 15 minutes after starting up the mountain. Everyone ate lunch at the shelter site, then began struggling back toward home.

The last weekend in October saw the completion of the "shelter work trips," as reported by Tom Aderhold:

For those who labored so arduously and almost beyond the call of duty at Tray Mountain on a similar work trip earlier this month, this effort proved to be much easier than expected. Arriving bright and early so as to accomplish the task in one day, thirty-two stalwarts lent themselves to the project of transporting by back, shoulder, hand and head a mammoth stack of lumber, roofing, nails, etc., some 0.6 mi. Piece by piece the material moved from relay station to relay station until it had completed its journey from Henson Gap to the site of the new shelter. By early afternoon, the project had been successful. Everyone then gathered at the new site for picture taking and a cheer of victory. Shortly thereafter, the hike was begun back over Blue Mountain and down to Unicoi Gap with each person knowing he had contributed toward the enjoyment and pleasure of many hikers for years to come.

To the veterans of the Tray Mountain lumber work party, let it be sufficient to say that it just ain't quite as hard when you go downhill.

By the end of December all three of the new shelters were completed. As Tom Aderhold said of these tasks in his message for the 1961 yearbook:

These two monuments of labor, of course, only augmented the usual yearly Trail work, but certainly all those who shared so cheerfully in their successful termination will long remember the companionship and congeniality exhibited by all who aided in these endeavors.

Once again we render many thanks to Paul Vincent and his staff, particularly Phil Archibald of the U.S. Forest Service in Gainesville, for their neverending cooperation in procuring the new shelters and numerous other instances of assistance to the Club. A complete chain of shelters has now been built on the Georgia section of AT.

The following was quoted in the May, 1960, *ATN* from a January issue of the *Knoxville News-Sentinel:*

Mt. LeConte Lodge, the mountain-top inn started by Jack Huff in 1926, finally has passed from the hands of the Huffs to those of another who loves the misty high country of the Great Smokies.

Herrick B. Brown, a Knoxville businessman and past president of the Smoky Mountains Hiking Club, bought the Huff interests in the Lodge and concluded a five-year lease agreement with the National Park Service.

Hikers will receive a warm welcome from the hosts, who are ardent hikers of long standing. Requests for information or reservations should be addressed to Herrick B. Brown, LeConte Lodge, Gatlinburg, Tennessee.

In March, the bulletin extended congratulations to Henry Morris on his election to the ATC Board of Managers, "replacing the resigned Bob Scott."

Once again, the Trail between Big Stamp Gap and Three Forks was to be relocated. As the bulletin reported in May:

Once upon a time, a seldom-used sawmill trail meandered north from Winding Stair Gap to Three Forks, dodging in and out of trees and well shaded. Anyone who has walked from Three Forks to Winding Stair in bright sunlight recently knows that something happened to this woodland trail since the AT was blazed along it some ten years ago. As a preliminary to elimination of sweat for tired hikers in this well-traveled road, it is proposed that Silvermine Ridge will be used as a new Trail location. This weekend is devoted to scouting a usable route and to possibly start on clearing and marking IF it works.

Searcy Slack was in charge of this relocation, which was to be on "old logging trails" he had found. The trail he proposed would turn sharp west from Big Stamp Gap and soon pick up an old road which would eventually tie in with a new "timber access" road to Three Forks along Stover Creek. As Slack declared,

"It may or may not add to the Trail's length, but it sure would add to the beauty." The council voted at its July meeting to relocate the Trail in this area, "the relocation to be blue blazed for a period of one to two years."

The council had decided early in the year to incorporate into the next year's yearbook "some of the rules of the Club, rules for leaders, etc." Barbara Deane was asked to draw up a list of rules for leaders. This was done, revised, and beginning with the 1961 yearbook, these rules were printed every year, with only minor changes.

In the summer of 1960 a familiar bugaboo raised its ugly head: a road. An article in the *Atlanta Constitution* in July reported a $500,000 appropriation announced by Senator Richard Russell for a road to be built "up Dukes Creek" to Tesnatee Gap. "As far in the wilderness as a man can go . . . too magnificent to hide any longer under its barely penetrable screen of forest and stream and mountain growth," declared a lengthy *Journal-Constitution* article later in the month, as it urged readers to write to their congressmen—"Old Logan Turnpike . . . must live again!" The bad news was discussed at the July council meeting, and letters to Senators were urged objecting to the road.

Seven clubs were represented at the "Five-Club" meet on Labor Day, the seventh and newest being the Mt. Rogers AT Club. The minutes of the October council meeting recorded:

Tom reported that at this year's Five-Club meet, the host club extended membership to the Roanoke Club. He pointed out some of the drawbacks of this and the need to set some limit on member clubs before the meet gets too big to handle. Marene suggested that at the next meet, for which the GATC is host, a policy for admitting member clubs be formulated.

Officers for the coming year, elected at the October business meeting, were to be: Tom Aderhold, president; Charlie Smith, vice president-activities; Gannon Coffey, vice president-membership; Elizabeth Wilson, secretary; Norman Brendel, treasurer; Marene Snow, historian; Barbara Deane, bulletin editor; Hugh Chase, council.

The year ended with two parties in December: the Club's 30th-anniversary party and the Christmas party. The anniversary party was held at Marene Snow's "country" home in north Fulton County, and featured displays of historical material from the Club's archives files, a "fireside chat" relating some history of the Club, a birthday cake, and films from the early days.

A note from Benton MacKaye to Marene Snow made the occasion complete. He wrote:

I note by my 'Georgia Mountaineer' just received that GATC is about to celebrate (November 30) her thirtieth birthday. Keenly I wish that I could be with you, and renew the comradeship of my looking in on you during your budding years. I recall especially a weekend with you on the Trail about the good year '34, one that stays with me as a kingpin experience untopped by any other in my long lingering life.

Few beings, I presume, ever live to see their dreams come true, but if such beings be, I count myself among those thus fortunate. As I view the world from my present ancienthood, I note two sound waves vying—one the primal melody of nature, the other the cacophonous clang of mechanism; one fun-bent for somewhere, the other hell-bent for nowhere. Nine tenths of all outdoors seems cluttered by the 'nowheres,' but their din can't stay the exploits of your lusty crew of 'somewheres.' And the likes of you are what has made my own dream come true. (November 27, 1960)

1961

IN 1961, THE POSSIBILITY of the destruction of most of the Georgia Trail by the proposed Blue Ridge Parkway extension cast a cloud over the GATC which was to last for many years. At the same time the Club had to resign itself to a smaller disaster in the form of the future Richard Russell Highway through Tesnatee Gap. This road—referred to in early 1961 as the Richard Sims-Dukes Creek Falls Road—was almost a reality before anyone could lift a hand to protest.

In February, Paul Vincent, Forest supervisor, wrote to GATC president, Tom Aderhold, informing him officially of the route of the road and of the Forest Service's role in making the survey of it, saying:

Survey crews were aware of our Cooperative Agreement and our policy on the Trail Zone. This was the only possible location in order to stay within allowable engineering standards and reach Tesnatee Gap. It certainly wasn't where we would like the road, as far as you folks are concerned, but there was no other choice.

We have many conflicts on our national forests between various resource uses. Sometimes, in cases such as this, there are conflicts of use in a single resource management. Here it is in recreation use. This road will open, to the general public, many acres of scenic country unsurpassed in Georgia. On the other hand, we recognize your dedicated group and certainly try to protect your interests.

It may be several years before this upper section of the road is completed, because of lack of funds. However, since the Trail now leaves the top of the mountain and swings north from Tesnatee Gap to Hogpen Gap, we feel that, if necessary, your Club might consider relocating the Trail to the top of the mountain rather than contouring around to the north. This would mean that the road would cross the Trail rather than parallel it.

We would be glad to work with you on this matter when the time comes. In the meantime, we felt you would like to know how things stand on this road. (February 10, 1961)

Aderhold replied, in part:

I certainly do not visualize as does Mr. James Davidson, Editor of the distinguished *Cleveland Courier*, that this road is going to help develop Cleveland into a mecca for tourists. (This is what he informed me during a conversation several weeks ago, shortly after I learned of this impending project.) Also that this particular area of North Georgia is rapidly on its way to becoming (once again with the drawing power of this road) a 'winter resort'! Well, my family has been in Georgia some six generations and has yet to see a North Georgia winter resort, and I rather expect it will take another six, plus the return of the Ice Age before anybody else will either. . . .

I am fairly well acquainted with the problem and necessity of tourists, and what attracts and does not attract them to an area. These ideas I was delighted to pass on to Mr. Davidson and point out that Cleveland itself is certainly not attractive to any tourist at this time. (March 7, 1961)

Aderhold then informed Murray Stevens, ATC chairman, about the impending road:

A couple of days before [a visit to Forest Service headquarters] I read of an impending 'scenic' road (paved) which would be built up to Tesnatee Gap, location of one of our most remote and best shelters and one of our best pack-thru sections. At the meeting, I discussed this road with the Forest Supervisor. He had just been informed of it himself only a few days before, and was as displeased with the project as were we. By the time anyone of responsibility around his office became acquainted with this effort, the $500,000 had been allocated by Congress and the project almost begun.

After the meeting, our organization wrote Senator Russell of Georgia, who was instrumental in making the money available, and many others. We talked with everyone possible and even made extended trips to see persons of influence to attempt to help stop this project. But most unfortunately, the seed was too well rooted by this time for us to pull it out. (March 7, 1961)

Stevens replied:

I wish to bring you up to date on my correspondence with Senator Russell. Since there was nothing more we could do to stop the —— road I wished to insure the provision of funds to relocate the Trail. My understanding is that it will be quite expensive and the Forest Service does not have the funds available.

In answer to my letter of March 23rd, I received a polite typed answer, undoubtedly from an assistant, and then in his own hand the following: 'Please give me the name of

[the] person in Georgia who asked you to intervene or get information on this,' signed R. B. Russell. I have endeavored throughout to make no mention of the Forest Service at the request of their Washington headquarters since the Senator can cause them a lot of anguish. (April 26, 1961)

The GATC bulletin urged members

to continue to write to Senator Russell protesting the paved road into Tesnatee Gap that received so much publicity last fall. Also write letters to newspapers whenever the road receives mention, in either case not as Club members but as individuals. We may not be able to stop this one, but we can make 'em think twice before they do it again!

Some months later, Jean Stephenson commented in a letter to Henry Morris: ". . . It was all done so suddenly and without anyone knowing it, that nothing could be done. I really think all concerned are pretty sorry about it now, but it is too late for it to be stopped. Once Congress has acted, that is that!"

And so, one of the most beautiful and remote sections remaining on the Georgia Trail was to be desecrated by a totally unnecessary road.

In mid-year the big blow came: an article in the *Atlanta Constitution* stated: "A House-passed bill for a $35,000 survey of a proposed extension of Blue Ridge National Parkway into Georgia received approval of a Senate public lands subcommittee Friday. Involved is a 170-mile extension from Tanasee Bald or Beech Gap southwest to the vicinity of Atlanta."

Two surveys were actually to be made: one which would bring the parkway through Cashiers and Highlands, North Carolina, across Rabun Bald and south by Tallulah Falls and Toccoa to Interstate 85. Another would bring it right down the crest of the Blue Ridge to a point near Atlanta. The first route was, of course, favored by the GATC, if any must be built.

In a discussion of the proposed parkway extension at the July GATC council meeting, it was said that it "could possibly wipe out all but approximately eleven miles of the Trail in this state." A suggestion was made that the Club contact the Nature Conservancy and the Wilderness Society to enlist their aid. Conference would, of course, be contacted for help. Gannon Coffey suggested that members get together to suggest an alternate route for the parkway.

The Nature Conservancy's help was enlisted, and their Georgia representative wrote to Rep. Phil Landrum with a plea at least for time to hear others' opinions, and for information on the status of the plans. Landrum replied: ". . . I am interested in doing everything I can to bring this parkway into Georgia and extend it down across the mountain chain as far west as Jasper if possible; but in doing so, I will use every opportunity to preserve those things in which you have expressed an interest." (September 13, 1961)

Stan Murray wrote to Henry Morris of the matter saying he felt that the Trailway Agreement might be the best defense "at a high level," and that he would ask Jean Stephenson to "see what she can do in Washington to block the survey appropriation by means of the Agreement." Tom Aderhold was to try to talk with the North Georgia Mountain Association, which was pushing for the route, but, as Murray said, it would be best not to mention the Agreement now, "lest they get busy to circumvent it." So the lines were drawn and the long task begun of fighting and/or adjusting to the impending disaster.

Back on the Trail, an "open house" was held in January at the new Montray shelter—in the rain—to reward all of the workers who carried "every grain of sand and every stone for its construction." The Club furnished a spaghetti supper and oatmeal breakfast for the 35 participants.

An attempt in January to blue blaze the new re-route between Big Stamp Gap and Three Forks was cancelled because of icy roads; but, finally in May, the job was done on this 4.6 mile section which would "in due time be converted to official AT."

At the April council meeting, activities chairman Charlie Smith reported "attendance was off over last year on most trips." The average was now 30 people per trip. A trip to the old gold mining towns of Auraria and Dahlonega in April drew 61 people; a hike from Cooper Gap to Woody Gap in March, 35. There were 22 functions during the year, with six backpack trips, and only one trip cancelled "due to impassable roads . . . but was rescheduled and completed at a later date."

The Trail was beginning to show the effects of all of these feet. The Trail report in the May *ATN* reported work needed on some sections included reworking of the treadway.

The fifteenth Appalachian Trail Conference was held in June at the Delaware Water Gap in Pennsylvania. Four GATC members attended. Henry Morris reported in the bulletin:

All reports by officers of the Conference were good reports and encouraging. Of particular interest to the Georgia Appalachian Trail Club is the fact that Georgia and Maine were first to get their chain of shelters completed. Others are making good progress toward completion of their shelters but are encountering some problems, especially where the Trail is not on public land. The new length of the Trail is now 1,995.31 miles.

Stan Murray, vice chairman and member of the Tennessee Eastman Hiking Club, was elected chairman to succeed Murray Stevens, and Henry Morris was re-elected to the Board of Managers.

In June, a press release from the Forest Service declared that a 28-acre area on Blood Mountain, "which was once the site of one of Georgia's most famous Indian battles, has been set apart and reserved for recreational purposes" and "dedicated as an Archaeological Area."

The GATC sponsored the Six-Club Meet this year, and selected Lake

Winfield Scott as the location. The bulletin report began:

Campers began arriving Thursday and continued to arrive, and arrive, and arrive, and arrive until at final tabulation 197 persons had registered for this unique outing. By virtue of having complete use of one entire camping area to ourselves, everyone, amazingly enough, found adequate space. Each Club was well represented with the exception of the Nantahala, which, due to circumstances, was unable to attend.

The meet was a big success, and President Tom Aderhold declared it "one of the best club meets we have had."

The GATC council voted at the October meeting to make the chairman of the Trails and Shelters Committee a voting member of the council, to make the office an elective one, and to change the name to "Trail Supervisor." The amendment to the constitution to this effect was voted on and passed at the Christmas party in December.

Jean Stephenson, editor of the *ATN*, came to Atlanta in October and was the guest of the GATC at the annual meeting and on a hike the following day. She spoke to the gathering at the meeting, saying that "in her estimation, the two most active and most unique clubs are the Maine club and the Georgia club." She said that she was doing what she could to "help fight off proposed changes that affect the Trail."

In his report to the annual meeting, membership chairman Gannon Coffey reminded the membership that "the by-law of the club is still 'to keep membership approximately equally divided between sexes.'" He also stated that "we still need some new guides on how to treat guests properly."

Officers elected for 1962 were: Gannon Coffey, president; John Parsons, vice president-activities; Ann Eidson, vice president-membership; Elizabeth Wilson, secretary; Jim Engle, treasurer; Barbara Deane, bulletin editor; Marene Snow, historian; Tom Aderhold, council. Ernest Sparrow was elected at the Christmas party to fill the new office of Trail Supervisor.

The portion of Trail between Mt. Oglethorpe and Amicalola Falls, abandoned for several years, was almost brought back to life by an ambitious scoutmaster and his troop from Dalton. In October, Henry Morris received a letter from the scoutmaster, who said he had been searching for a project for his troop, and decided to hike the Appalachian Trail. All of the information he could get on the Trail still indicated that it began at Oglethorpe, although, as he said, "a further investigation of the Trail in and around Jasper revealed that the Trail Club had discontinued the Trail" in this area. He continued:

Considering the historical aspects of the Mt. Oglethorpe starting point and the beauty of the surrounding countryside, I could hardly conceive of my scouts or any scout, whose motto is 'Onward for God and Country,' wanting to abandon this portion of the Trail, particularly the scouts of this area. Thus, we decided to start up the Trail from atop Mt. Oglethorpe. However, on our first attempt, we found few markings and missed the Trail several times. I then decided the opening up of this portion of the Trail would be a good *service project* for our troop.

Through map study and information secured from Forest Rangers and others in the area, we have been able to locate the old Trail. We have spent two weekends and three Sundays on this portion of the Trail, clearing and marking it. We now have about four more miles and it will be completely remarked and opened so that anyone can travel it without any hazardous encounters or getting off the Trail.

Other scout troops of this area are vitally interested in this portion of the Trail. . . .

Inasmuch as this is a portion rich in history so dear to the people of this area, Georgia, and the Nation, we see no reason why it should not be kept open and Mt. Oglethorpe remain the southern terminus and deeply feel that it should. (October 23, 1961)

He stated that they "had not run into any complaints or opposition," until they met a local landowner who told them the Trail was supposed to be abandoned, although he would not object to hikers following it once again.

Meanwhile Tom Aderhold had received a letter from the landowner about the scouts' clearing work, and wrote to the scoutmaster explaining the abandonment of the Trail and saying:

If your group is interested in locating a trail for its own use from Amicalola Falls towards Mt. Oglethorpe, I suggest perhaps you secure permission from the landowners as this is private property and be sure they are not under the impression this effort is in any way connected with the Appalachian Trail Conference or Georgia Appalachian Trail Club. Also, we would greatly appreciate it if you would not use white paint for blazes as it might confuse some hiker into assuming it to be part of the official AT.

If perhaps you are just interested in providing outdoor activities of this nature for your boys, we would be happy to have them perform such labors on the AT under the auspices of our Club. (November 6, 1961)

The scoutmaster replied, in part:

. . . Upon receipt of your letter last Wednesday, I immediately made plans for removing all markers put up by my scouts and we spent this past weekend removing them. (November 14, 1961)

At the annual Dillard House trip in November, according to the bulletin account, after dinner and a slide show, Mrs. Dillard and two of her cousins "related stories and folklore of nearby Horse Cove and the vicinity, which had been originally settled by their forebears." Mrs. Dillard told "of the purchase from the Indians in the 1700's of the valley in which the 'Dillard Farm' is located, which included all the land to the top of the surrounding mountains 'as far as one can see.' The price? A pocket knife, a coonskin cap, a musket, a jug of apple jack, an old mule and two dollars in cash!"

The Rev. Rufus Morgan, at the age of 76 and with his sight failing, nevertheless reported, according to the January, 1962, *ATN*, that he had "done the maintenance work on his 55 mile section in the Nantahalas as usual this summer. This included going over the entire length, clearing it of summer growth, . . . blowdowns and woody growth and renewing the marking." Even though the Forest Service helped him a great deal, his continued maintenance of this section of Trail was a remarkable feat.

The January *ATN* also reported on eight new shelters built in the Smokies during 1961: Davenport Gap, Tri-Corner Knob, False Gap, Siler's Bald, Derrick Knob, Russell Field, Mollies Ridge, and Birch Spring; a shelter was also built on Mt. LeConte.

Warner Hall (pictured above) surveys early Trail marker. Hall was present at the organizational meeting at Zimmer's Mountain Lodge in Dahlonega on November 1, 1930. "Hall and [Charlie] Elliot immediately became good friends, and Hall was soon appointed to office and rapidly became an indispensible member."

▲ Warner Hall, Stuart Chase (noted economist and writer) and Lloyd Adams during Chase's visit to the GATC, Frances Virginia Tea Room, Atlanta, 1936.

◄Benton MacKaye and Warner Hall in 1934.

▲Eddie Stone poses by one of the first sign posts installed on the Georgia Trail by Stone and other GATC workers.

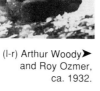

(l-r) Arthur Woody➤ and Roy Ozmer, ca. 1932.

Henry Morris ➤ clears brush from Trail (late 1930's).

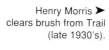

▼Ed Traylor marking the Trail in early 1950's.

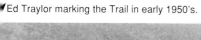

▲A hike from Cooper Gap Gooch Gap, 1950.

(upper left) Whit Benson views the Tusquitee Mountains, 1981.

▼Club members atop tow on Brasstown Bald in 1932

▲GATC group stands beside bus which brought them over mostly unpaved roads to Woody Gap for hike to Neel Gap, January 1933.

▼Warner Hall (left) and other hikers in North Carolina, 1932

The "Four Foolish Females": Club members Marene Snow, Grace Ficken, Cynthia Ward, and Olivia Herren, on their hike in the Nantahalas in June 1933, and (inset)... the same "Four Foolish Females" in 1980 ➤ (r) Cynthia Ward Muise, Marene Snow, Grace Ficken Hawkins, and Olivia Herren Bagwell.

▼Club members carry injured hiker on makeshift seat on hike from Woody Gap to Neel Gap in 1933. Measuring wheel is on right.

▲Club members take a break on top of Tray Mountain in 1949. W Benson, (far left), Pat Gartrell ar Marene Snow (third and fourth from left in back) and Jim Crago (standing far right). Maude Ellio by the wheel.

◄Members of GATC and Smok Club at Greenbriar Cabin.

(lower left) Moonshine still simila to one Lillian and Lloyd Adams ra across near Southern's Store on hike to Amicalola Falls in 1935.

▼Marene Snow (left) and frien with old packs in 1932.

◄Hikers stop for a rest at the Cheese factory on Tray Mountain after the 1931 annual meeting at Greear's Lodge in Helen, Georgia.

Often, the best part of a hike is getting there. A hiker relaxes.➤

(lower right) Club members gather after the War. Larry Freeman is upper right in this picture.

▲Typical dress for a Club hike in 1931.

◄The 1931 annual meeting at Greear's Lodge in Helen, Georgia. Warner Hall (top row on right); Charlie Elliott (bottom row, second from right).

▼Club members at the 1932 annual meeting at the Cloudland Park Hotel, including Eddie Stone (in front with dog), Warner Hall in hat behind Stone, and Charlie Elliott behind and slightly to left of Hall.

▲ The annual meeting at Neel Gap, 1938.

➤ GATC annual meeting at Indian Springs Hotel, 1937.

▼ The 1932 annual meeting of the Smoky Club at Elkmont. More active GATC members got together quite often with the Smoky Club for hikes, and usually for their annual meeting and Christmas party.

▲First shelter on Georgia AT built in 1931 at Amicalola Falls at a cost of $57.00.

◄New Rocky Knob shelter, June 1961. June Engle, Jim Varner and John Parson. Replaced by new shelter on Blue Mountain, 1988.

▼LeConte Lodge in the snow, 1935.

Rocky Knob cabin in 1934. First of CCC-built shelters.

Club members remove original clay roof tiles during renovation of the Blood Mountain shelter in 1981.➤

Rocky Knob shelter, removed in May 1961.

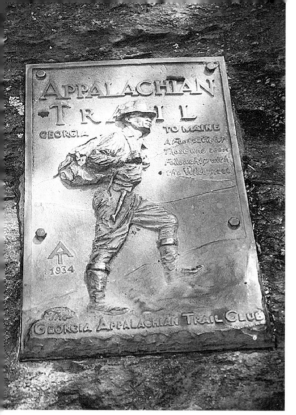

▲Dedication of monument atop Oglethorpe Mountain 1930, southern terminus of the AT from 1930-1958.

◄Warner Hall poses for original plaque on Springer Mountain (upper left) in 1933, sculpted by Club member George H. Noble.

▼First to hike the entire Georgia AT in 1930, three Boy Scouts — John Newton, Jim Brewer and Byron Mitchell Jr. (bottom) The scouts salute the flag at Oglethorpe dedication as they finish the hike.

New plaque on Springer Mountain, installed by GATC in 1993, near original plaque.

(l-r) Lou Hoben, Marene Snow, Henry Morris at dedication of Trail plaque at Amicalola Falls Visitor Center, 1977.

(lower right) Original sign erected by Club members on Mt. Oglethorpe in 1937. Another sign was erected in 1941.

Pat Thomas and Margaret Drummond cut the ribbon at the dedication ceremony officially opening the Toccoa River bridge in 1977 and linking both sections of the Loop Trail.

◄First female Club presiden
Cynthia Ward Muise, place
mantle on incoming preside
Rosalind Van Landingham.

▼Tom Aderhold installs office
for 1976.

GATC 50th Anniversary cake made by ~salind Van Landingham and decorated with ~ures from Club archives.

~50th Anniversary banner made by former ~mber Pat Gartrell Bell.

~GATC officers for 1981.

▲ Marian and Henry Morris, ca. 1958. ▼ Mabel Abercrombie Mansfield, Harold Mansfield and Maude Elliott discu early Club days with history committee members Nancy Shofner and John Krickel, 1980.

1962

GEORGIA
APPALACHIAN
19 TRAIL CLUB, INC. 30

THE ACTIVITIES OF THE CLUB continued as usual during 1962, with most hikes on the Georgia Trail, several hikes and camping trips in the Smokies and the Nantahalas, and the regular trips to the Emersons' property on Lake Lanier, John Mahl's cabin near Dukes Creek, and the Dillard House.

The new Trail Supervisor began the year with "a little different twist to a never–ending job of maintaining our trails." He continued in the bulletin:

This, we hope, will be a good way of getting our work done so when we are on outings our leaders and hikers can spend their time enjoying the trips, except for any emergency work that may arise. Each member of the Trail Committee has chosen a section to put in shape and it's going to be up to the members to support him in marking, clearing and a little work on the shelters. . . . Pick out your trip, call your leader and he will fill you in on final details.

This attempt was only partially successful, but it did succeed in dividing up the work along the Trail. Help was also solicited in measuring and checking the Trail for a new edition of the guidebook.

The division of the Southern guidebook was to be discussed at the six-club meet; the GATC went on record at the July council meeting as not favoring a division into two books unless the Smoky Mountain section could be published in the same book as the Georgia section. (The existing guidebook included the Georgia section, the Nantahalas, the Smokies, the Carolinas and Tennessee to the Virginia-Tennessee border at Damascus.) It was decided at the six-club meet to divide the guidebook into two books and include the Smokies in both books.

The section of Trail between Big Stamp Gap and Three Forks, which was still blue blazed, was to be included in the new guidebook as the official Trail, and the blazes would be painted white when the guidebook was published.

Early in 1962, the GATC and the ATC began to go into a higher gear to try to divert the proposed Blue Ridge Parkway extension. The intention of the Club—and Conference—was not to prevent the building of the parkway, but only to prevent its taking over the route of the AT. Conference seemed for awhile to consider this a problem which could be easily worked out with reasonable officials who had not yet decided exactly where the parkway should be. All of these assumptions were soon proved false.

In January, members of the GATC, Dr. Charles Wharton of the Nature Conservancy, and Miss Carroll Hart of the Georgia Department of Archives mapped a proposed alternative route for the parkway which took it over Rabun Bald (as was planned) and then to lower elevations south of the ridge crest to Tallulah Gorge, Nacoochee Valley, Dahlonega, Mt. Oglethorpe, Chatsworth, and into Alabama. The route featured many points of historical interest as well as views of the mountains and valleys. Dr. Wharton feared that the proposed crest route in Georgia would be a "tedious anticlimax" to the high, level ridges in North Carolina, and praised their proposed lower route as varied and different.

In her strategic position in Washington, Jean Stephenson at ATC headquarters became "coordinator of the Blue Ridge matter." She began her campaign there to try to find an acceptable alternate route and tried to keep up with developments on the parkway in the various federal agencies and in Congress. By studying topo maps, she made herself familiar with the Georgia mountain area and terrain, and then, in February, met with Parkway officials and engineers, showing them the proposed GATC route. She said, "They were more than interested, in fact seemed very grateful for the help . . . ," although they did mention several drawbacks, such as cost of land and possible difficulty of terrain. According to Stephenson it was a "very pleasant discussion." She seemed to feel that, since the surveys had not yet been made and the plans were not definite, the chances were good of getting at least some of "what we want." She said:

I think I made it clear to all concerned that the position of the Appalachian Trail Conference was that we did not want interference with the Trail in Georgia or elsewhere, and that our local members were willing to help work out a route that would be acceptable to the traveling public and yet would not interfere with the Trail. We have done so; we would be willing to cooperate in every way possible; that we knew the Forest Service and Park Service would respect the Appalachian Trailway Agreement but that we also realized that Congress could override it, but that we hoped for the cooperation of the services in preparing recommendations for a route that would maintain the integrity of the Trail, etc. (April 25, 1962)

Forest Service officials in Georgia were not in favor of the parkway at all, feeling that it would add to the difficulties of managing the forest and wildlife. Paul Vincent, forest supervisor, suggested an alternate route which would end the parkway at Dillard and disperse the traffic on to local scenic roads. Wharton wrote to Stephenson that "the Forest Service then is behind us 100%, although . . . their support must not be overt."

Stephenson related to Henry Morris a long telephone conversation in April with Sam Weems, superintendent of the Blue Ridge Parkway, which began to show that the fight would not be easy. Weems and others pointed to what they considered a satisfactory solution of the co-existence of Trail and Parkway in Virginia. According to him, the Trail there "was one beyond amateur construction," and opened up sections previously inaccessible, and seemed to please most people. Stephenson assured him, as did others over and over, that the Georgia situation was different: there was already easy access to the Trail and there was no other ridge on which to relocate the Trail. Stephenson declared Weems a shrewd man, and was unable to figure out what he really thought about the situation.

In May, at the invitation of the Forest Service, a meeting to discuss the parkway was arranged in Atlanta between the GATC, represented by Gannon Coffey, Henry Morris, and Tom Aderhold; the National Park Service with Sam Weems, Superintendent of the Blue Ridge Parkway and Ed A. Abbuehl, landscape architect; the Bureau of Public Roads with J. L. Obenschain, engineer; and the U.S. Forest Service with J. K. Vessey, regional forester, P. H. Bryan and O. W. Hanson of Recreation, and Paul Vincent. Murray stated later that "the only thing accomplished was the solidification of positions."

Each side bargained by appearing to give a little, but promised nothing. Coffey feared that the position taken by the Club was not strong enough and may have given Weems (who seemed to be calling the shots) hope for an easy victory. Vessey declared the GATC-ATC proposed route out of the question, and Coffey was to take marked maps of the Park Service's route back to the GATC council, feeling sure that it would be found unacceptable. Then another route would be worked out and another try made to have it accepted. GATC members agreed to visit Virginia to examine the effect of the Parkway on the Trail there. According to Coffey, the Club was making an effort to be "objective and reasonable."

Vessey wrote to Jean Stephenson of the meeting, saying that several routes were discussed, and possible relocations of the Trail. Any necessary relocations would be done by the Park Service, with the agreement of the GATC, according to Weems.

Parkway officials continued to refer to their route as tentative, while at the same time assuring the Club that the Trail and the Parkway could co-exist happily. As Stan Murray was to say later, Weems was "single-minded in insisting that the Parkway route be a crestline route," and there was only one crest in Georgia. Abbuehl, in a letter to Henry Morris, stated, "We realize that any road along the Blue Ridge will change the wilderness aspect of the Trail, but 'wilderness' is a relative term. . . . Fortunately the Trail is more flexible than our road standards. . . . This might be a good opportunity to make some changes in your Trail at our expense." (May 28, 1962)

With plan number one rejected, Jean Stephenson, still optimistic and feeling that the Park Service was "caught in the middle" and did not want to sabotage a volunteer project such as the Trail, came up with another route higher up on the ridge at roughly 2,200 feet. She also spoke with some of the "higher-ups" in Washington, and wrote that "everyone along the line down was informed that some reasonable compromise should be made, and that it was definitely not the intention to interfere seriously with the Appalachian Trail."

She showed her new route to the Park Service officials who "felt it was definitely worth investigation," but then the route was rejected by Weems "because it does not include the best of the Georgia mountain scenery," and the grades were not suitable. Weems continued, in a letter to Henry Morris, "Our problem, therefore, is basically one of resolving any conflict between a Parkway development and the Appalachian Trail. As you know, we think the two facilities can have peaceful co-existence on the same ridge, as demonstrated north of Roanoke and in Shenandoah National Park. We were hopeful also that in your studies this past summer you might find places where the Appalachian Trail could be relocated (at our expense) without loss of values." (October 2, 1962)

Morris replied to this, "To be perfectly frank, I must say that very little sentiment has developed among members of the Georgia Appalachian Trail Club in favor of relocation." He recounted the Club's reasons for keeping the Trail on the crest:

The fact is, any relocation of the Trail would place it farther north, making it more difficult to reach for maintenance; would place it closer to the edge of the Forest Service holdings, causing it to cross many tracts of land still in private ownership, which would be an insurmountable problem; would add the problem of bridges over streams which would have to be crossed if the Trail were moved from the main ridge; and it would be much more accessible to bulldozers, which are somewhat of a problem even on the ridges. . . .

The route now followed was selected for its wilderness characteristics, because it was away from the main roads, and it was thought that being in the depths of the

National Forest would keep the main roads away from it for all time.

The Trail is described as "A Footpath Through the Wilderness." Today it will be difficult to find much wilderness for a footpath. The word "wilderness" as used here meaning an area where nature is having a chance to develop in its own way after the great devastation inflicted more than a century ago, and a place where a person may have respite from most of the cacophonous noises of modern civilization. . . .

The members of this organization hereby wish to place on record their fervent hope that an acceptable route may be found for the Parkway without disturbing this unique footpath which has been in existence for a third of a century. (October 19, 1962)

Weems replied, ". . . your club's feelings in the matter will be fully considered. . . ."

Meanwhile, the new road through Tesnatee Gap was under way. It was to come onto the AT at Hog Pen Gap and more or less follow the Trail around to Tesnatee Gap. As Henry Morris said: "When the road is graded, the Trail (0.6 mi.) . . . will be obliterated because it is very steep where the Trail is now and the side of the mountain will have to be taken off to make a shelf for the road." A committee of Gannon Coffey, Henry Morris, and Trail Supervisor Ernest Sparrow was to plan a re-route to be presented to the Forest Service, and funds would be sought from a federal agency for its construction. Several routes were considered, including one which would take the Trail through Whitley Gap.

Early in the year, at the request of Conference, and with the aid of the Forest Service, a tabulation and map of "private inholdings" along the Georgia Trail was compiled, along with a list of the owners. It revealed 17 lots or parts of lots totalling 690 acres touching the Trail at eleven places, although the actual miles of Trail on private land was not recorded.

With increasing numbers of people using the nation's forests and wild areas, interest was increasing also in the preservation of these areas by organizations such as the Wilderness Society, Sierra Club, etc. For many years, attempts had been made to pass a wilderness bill in Congress, with no success. In 1962, another bill was introduced, but when issued, was actually "negative with respect to the preservation of wilderness." When called upon, GATC members and the Club as a whole supported these efforts, both with letters to Congress and monetary contributions.

In his message to the Club in the 1962 yearbook, incoming president Gannon Coffey appealed to members "to re-define and re-evaluate our goals." He continued:

While each of us has a special interest in, and mode of enjoyment of, the wilderness and forests, we all have a vested interest in the preservation of the wilderness. If we have a reason for existence, it is because we are persuaded, as were the dedicated conservationists of the nineteenth century, that the wilderness holds physical, cultural, and spiritual values for every age or generation and is, therefore, worth preserving in a civilized society.

To assure that these values are understood and that they will have the necessary precedence to assure the survival of the wilderness, we need to communicate to our generation, as the founders were able to do in theirs, the importance of these values to this and the next generation. Our friends in other organizations or agencies, similarly concerned with wildlife, conservation and wilderness areas, recognize these interests and values. We still have an obligation, however, to constantly re-define our purpose in new ways, so others, who judge us by today's standards and by their images of us, will be confident that our interest encompasses the public interest as well. They should be assured that the 'values' derived from the wilderness are everlasting and that every person and every generation can learn from, and be enriched by, the wilderness.

He renewed his appeal each year of his presidency, as did the two presidents who followed him.

In the fall, at the request of Stan Murray, a committee on Trail Standards was established by Conference, to be headed by Ed Garvey, Trail Supervisor of the Potomac Appalachian Trail Club, and included Gannon Coffey as a committee member. The committee's purpose was "to define and recommend standards of practice and techniques" of trail maintenance, including the "supervision of the contents of ATC Publication No. 1," to handle trail maintenance reports of clubs, evaluate equipment, promote the sign program, write articles for *ATN* on trail maintenance, and coordinate highway crossing signs on the Trail. A newsletter was sent out periodically. The efforts of this committee resulted the following year in large "Appalachian Trail" signs at all of the highway crossings in Georgia.

The GATC annual meeting was held early in November. The membership chairman reported a total membership of 150, and stated that the committee had tried to have one of its members on each hike, "armed with guest cards and a friendly smile."

The activities chairman reported an average of 16.5 members participating in 26 activities during the year, with 152 guests participating throughout the year. Officers were elected as follows: Gannon Coffey, president; J. P. Eidson, vice president–activities; Ann Eidson, vice president–membership; Ernest Sparrow, Trail supervisor; Norma Seiferle, secretary; Jim Engle, treasurer; Marene Snow, historian; Polly Thompson, bulletin editor; Tom Aderhold, Henry Morris, Hugh Chase, council.

The office of Trail information chairman had existed since 1956. Searcy Slack had held the office since 1957, and his work was growing rapidly. Slack reported at the meeting an average of one letter or card a week being written, and numerous telephone inquiries. Slack was complimented several times during the year for the good work he was doing with this task. The many long and personalized letters from Slack to inquirers—and their letters of appreciation—testify to his personal knowledge of the Trail and his diligence in disseminating information.

In December, a letter to Florence Nichol, corresponding secretary of the ATC, told of plans for a "study for a government grant on a Recreation Research Experiment Station . . . close to the point where the Trail crosses Tray Mountain," referring to the area known as the "cheese factory." The five-month study of the northeast Georgia area finally, in early 1963, recommended Unicoi State Park as the site for the experiment station, and a proposal was submitted for a $7 million development there. It was to be a training center for the state's recreation leaders and a "laboratory for essential research in planning and using recreation facilities." The plan resulted in the present development of Unicoi Park.

1963

GEORGIA APPALACHIAN
19 TRAIL CLUB, INC. 30

DURING 1963, THE FOCUS of the GATC—and especially its president, Gannon Coffey—was on the impending Blue Ridge Parkway extension. The normal activities of the Club continued, however, and hikes were made to the usual places, with a sprinkling of the new and different. Attendance on trips was down slightly; the average, reported at the end of the year, was 14+ members per trip, 5.5 members' children per trip, and 6.5 guests per trip. The overall average on each trip was 26.

A "standard" hike from Big Stamp Gap to Cooper Gap in February produced the following unique account in the bulletin, written by Pat Gartrell Bell, leader:

HOW TO BAKE A MID-WINTER HIKER-PIE

Assemble ingredients early on a cold morning and blend at Cooper Gap. Shake well over rough roads for about 45 minutes and pour out onto blue trail at Big Stamp Gap. Allow mixture to run at own pace and absorb brook sounds and spicy woods scents. Mix in a little spring water from time to time. Let set awhile at Three Forks, and, at this point, throw in some sandwiches, sardines, soup, etc. which will be quickly absorbed. Mixture will chill rapidly; to prevent freezing, force it up Hawk Mountain and warm slightly by campfire. Cover well and spread out for the night in a cool place (Hawk Meadow, 24 degrees). When mixture has risen, hustle it over Horse Mountain causing it to simmer in its own juices. Remove from Trail at Cooper Gap and you will have a hearty, bubbling dish with a rosy crust and a woodsy aroma. Trail tested from Big Stamp to Cooper Gap. Pat Bell, Chef. CAUTION: Use only top quality ingredients and season liberally with flavorsome guests.

Trail work seemed to be lagging somewhat; in May a work trip drew only a handful of people. The bulletin carried a "special announcement" from President Coffey, in which he urged a special effort to bring trail maintenance up to date by July. He continued:

Complaints are beginning to come in that certain sections are not clearly, or infrequently, blazed and that blowdowns are all too common. Some sections of the Trail are almost impassable; and after a rain, hikers brushing against foliage would prefer the rainstorm to being soaking wet from the waist down.

Those who are willing to accept a share of responsibility for the Trail, and *all members do have this responsibility*, are requested to telephone Ernest Sparrow and indicate their support by volunteering to clear and maintain a section of their preference, be it a mile, two miles, five or ten, but not more than they will guarantee to do, by themselves, if necessary, by the MIDDLE OF JULY. Members who consider that they have already done their "SHARE" should consider members who have done *MORE* than their share to fill the gap for some who do not.

The new and different activities included a new "twist" to the yearly trip to Mt. LeConte, as announced in the bulletin:

The trip to LeConte this year is to be something different—a backpack trip up LeConte with camping out in the shelter or nearby. This change in plans was decided upon in keeping with the progressive nature of our Club in always wanting to do something new, and also due to the fact that we could not get reservations at the Lodge.

The yearly "trail report" in the May *ATN* cautioned hikers to use care in passing through the Tesnatee-Hog Pen Gap area because of the construction of the Richard Russell Highway. Attempts were being made by the Club to get assistance in relocating the Trail in this area, but because of the difficulty in getting to it, the matter would have to wait until the road was completed to Tesnatee Gap. In the meantime, a "temporary re-route" was blue blazed around the area.

The ill-fated section of Trail between Big Stamp Gap and Three Forks, having only recently been relocated off of an upgraded dirt road—after having been removed from its *original* route on a road—was to suffer another blow. In October, a letter from the Forest Service Ranger in Blue Ridge informed the GATC that they were widening and reworking a section of the Buzzard Roost road between Doublehead Gap and Springer Mountain. This included the mile of AT on that road, and meant that many of the blazed trees would be removed. The Trail, however, was to remain on this road for almost 20 more years.

In the spring of 1962, members of the GATC had begun to compile recipes for inclusion in a campers' cookbook to be issued by the Club. Jean Dolan, Mandy Coffey, and Barbara Deane were responsible for the publication of the booklet which was completed in the summer of 1963 and contained illustrations by Mary Eidson. An article in the September, 1963, *ATN* described the book:

In an attractive golden cover, decorated with a sketch of tall trees and the AT diamond, 40 pages are devoted to outdoor cooking. Subjects treated are shown by the headings: Car Camping; Recipes and Menus; Backpacking; Instant Menus; Recipes; and Stoves. Suggestions are given for packing for car camping, carrying liquids, dry foods, crackers and cookies, reusable tubes, eggs, and on several other subjects.

For several years—until they ran out of copies—the Club received orders for the cookbook from all over the country.

The September *ATN* also featured on the front cover a picture of several GATC members looking at the view from atop Springer Mountain.

In early 1963, Stan Murray had taken over the reins of the "Parkway matter," possibly realizing that it was not to be easily settled, and that it would take more time than the busy Jean Stephenson would be able to give it. He outlined a plan of action for the coming months which included suggesting all possible reasonable routes that might take the Parkway away from the ridgetop, for, as he said, "one of them might work." (That is, be accepted by the Park Service.) His plan also included invoking the Trailway Agreement and preparing to negotiate if Trail relocation became necessary to get the best route and the aid of the government in constructing it.

Although Sam Weems, Parkway superintendent, was holding out for the crest route, other officials gave the ATC and GATC hope that another route could be found. But, as Murray said, "Perhaps they just hope to pacify us as long as possible." In January, Murray suggested two more routes, both avoiding the crest, or only crossing it. But after several months, it was evident that "the Parkway people . . . definitely do not feel that the routes we have suggested . . . would be satisfactory to the Congressmen." Numerous versions of these routes were discussed among the ATC and GATC, including passing near the proposed recreation experiment station at Unicoi State Park, and utilizing the highway in progress up Dukes Creek to Tesnatee Gap (the future Richard Russell highway).

In the spring, Gannon Coffey met with the president of the Georgia Mountains Association, a group which was active in helping out the north Georgia area by political means; Tom Aderhold spoke to the group later, soliciting and receiving their sympathy for the preservation of the Trail, although actual support from the group never seemed to materialize.

The Park Service was approaching its deadline for recommending a route to

Congress, and, as Stan Murray wrote to Coffey, "are obliged to recommend something a fitting character for a national scenic highway." According to Murray, the Parkway route was planned to hit the Trail somewhat south of Dicks Creek Gap and from there south "never stray very far from the Trail." He continued:

I think it is clear to all of us that if this snowball towards a parkway keeps on rolling, we will have to yield to some extent, and should probably do it gracefully, provided we can end up with a fairly decent Trail. On the other hand I feel very strongly that we should try to seek a compromise a little more in our favor in preserving a larger proportion of the route at some greater distance from the Parkway. I told them in particular we would like to see the Trail north and east of Tesnatee Gap remain unmolested. . . . Mr. Stratton (assistant director of NPS) did indicate an open mind. . . ." (July 3, 1963)

Anticipating possible relocation of the Trail, the GATC had located and scouted Duncan Ridge, which led northwest from Blood and Slaughter Mountains, over Coosa Bald and Licklog Mountain, swinging back around to Springer Mountain, and had discussed this with the Forest Service. There was no such alternate ridge north of Tesnatee Gap.

The report of the Park Service "urging the development of a 190-mile national parkway from the Blue Ridge Parkway near Beech Gap, North Carolina, southwest into Georgia" was submitted to Congress on July 11. The recommended route followed the general course of the AT from Dismal Mountain to Springer Mountain, then to Mt. Oglethorpe and Highway 41 near Marietta. Landrum announced that he would introduce a bill to Congress within a week "to provide that the proposed Parkway be built," and on July 23 this was done, and was then referred to committee.

The report galvanized the GATC into action. President Coffey established a parkway committee of GATC members "that may need to have a continuing function for some years." Members of the committee were, besides Coffey, Henry Morris, Tom Aderhold, Searcy Slack, and Jean Dolan. The purpose of the committee was "to establish contacts with all organizations having an interest in the wilderness and the preservation of the AT in an unmolested condition and obtain action from them, or assist them to prepare letters, resolutions, etc. to Landrum or newspapers expressing their concern."

Actions of the committee were to include writing to Landrum, to Congressman Charles Weltner, soliciting help from the Georgia Mountains Association, contacting boy scouts and girl scouts for help in writing letters, contacting the Nature Conservancy for its help, soliciting letters from hunters, fishermen, sports writers and other conservation groups, writing letters to the newspapers. The help of the Georgia Garden Clubs was sought and received in the form of an article in their magazine *Garden Gateways* written by GATC member Barbara Deane on the GATC and the Trail and the necessity for preserving it.

Coffey wrote to Stewart Udall, Secretary of the Interior, detailing the concerns of the Club and inviting him to come to Georgia and hike on the Trail to see for himself its desirable wilderness character. There is no evidence that a reply was received.

One of the arguments used by Coffey—and others—against the Parkway was its detrimental effect on wildlife. This view was hotly disputed in newspaper articles and letters, mostly by officials with an interest in seeing the Parkway built.

In July, Stan Murray visited Georgia to "look over portions of the Trail involved and to look for other possible Parkway routes." He, Coffey, and Henry Morris came up with two more alternatives for the Parkway east of Tesnatee Gap: one would take it above Lake Burton, crossing Hickorynut Ridge, by Unicoi State Park, then follow the Richard Russell highway to Tesnatee Gap, and from there follow the AT route to Oglethorpe; the other route would climb up from Lake Burton, crossing the AT at Indian Grave Gap to the north side of the ridge, recrossing at Unicoi Gap, descending some to cross the Chattahoochee River, rising to Wide Gap and thence follow the AT south. They felt that, as Murray said, "If the Parkway would stay completely clear east of Tesnatee, then we could compromise on the rest. . . ."

The Forest Service had given up its opposition to the Parkway—of necessity—and now favored the crest route because it would interfere the least with their land management operations. They were now advising the GATC to "give up gracefully" and make the best deal possible. The Bureau of Public Roads was also pushing the ridge route from an engineering and cost standpoint. As Coffey wrote to Murray and Stephenson, "There seems to be no concern among the 'people' about where it goes. . . ."

A long article appeared in the *Atlanta Journal/Constitution* in July extolling the beauties of the Parkway and announcing its planned extension into Georgia. At the end of the article the author stated: "Motorists who have enjoyed the present parkway are all for it. The only opposition heard so far came from the small but clear voices of members of the Appalachian Trail Club, who claim that a graded asphalt highway would spoil the rest of the finest hiking route in North America."

Gannon Coffey wrote to Benton MacKaye, telling him of the Parkway threat to the Georgia Trail, saying, "As difficult as it may be to get such a Trail started, we are finding it equally difficult, I'm sure, in keeping it alive." He wonders if it would be more effective to refuse offers of relocation and put the onus of ending the Trail in North Carolina on the National Park Service. He waxes philosophical, continuing:

While we are willing to compromise and be reasonable, there is always that point where principle becomes involved and compromise becomes selling out. . . . We fight this vast bureaucracy and the never-ending desire to satisfy the motorist. But the fight goes on and is part of the challenge; and we find that overcoming obstacles that *man* puts in our path is indeed sordid. The use of the small "M," is intentional, since I wonder if 'he' is really a part of nature or inspired by it. When he is found to recognize his mistake because of what he does now, we may give him a capital 'M,' if repentance results in reform, and a recognition of values in their proper perspective. But you have fought the fight and it is for the new generation to take up the standard. We would like to be inspired by the spoken word, however, and for this reason invite you to our annual meeting . . . all expenses paid. . . ." (July 28, 1963)

MacKaye was unable to come but, as requested, agreed to send a message to inspire the gathering.

When copies of the Parkway bill were received, it was found that it did not appear to specify an exact route, perhaps leaving room for negotiations, but neither did it contain provisions asked for by Murray on relocation and maintenance of the Trail, as the Park Service had led him to believe it would.

So Murray continued to press for one of his new routes to be accepted and for several changes to be made in the wording of the bill: that it should mandate any necessary relocations of the AT by the National Park Service; that maintenance be at least partially the responsibility of the NPS and the Forest Service; [and] that the NPS be responsible for acquisition of any private lands along the route of relocation. He wrote to, among others, the Director of the National Park Service; to Wayne Aspinall, head of the Congressional committee considering the bill; to Stewart Udall, Secretary of Interior; to A. Clark Stratton, assistant and later acting Director of the Department of the Interior; and to Edward Crafts, director of the Bureau of Outdoor Recreation.

Jean Stephenson continued to work on the matter in Washington, and as Coffey wrote to Murray, "It goes without saying that without Jean in her key position, we'd all be floundering around. The ten feet of topographic map she sent just before your visit here was a production which convinced me of the professional character of her office and the variety of skills required." (August 5, 1963)

In August, Murray wrote to Stephenson, Morris, and Coffey, saying, "A day has now passed in which there have been no new developments on the Blue Ridge Parkway extension. . . ." So he summarized the situation and outlined "near-range" and "long-range" strategy, again trying to stop the bill or change it to provide for restoration and relocation of the Trail, and to "work on" Udall to convince him to use an alternate route. He was enlisting the aid of several members of the Board of Managers in contacting Congressmen. In order to keep the good will of Congress and other officials, upon whom the future of the Trail depended, Murray was not yet ready to "make a public issue" of the matter and was very concerned that these people not be "antagonized." Help was to be solicited from the Nature Conservancy and, possibly in the future, from all clubs and Class D ATC members.

In the fall of 1962, Supreme Court Justice William O. Douglas had visited Springer Mountain in the company of the Forest Service. This visit may have prompted the following brief letter to Stewart Udall from Douglas:

Dear Stew:
    Would you mind taking a personal look at the proposed route of the Parkway in Georgia? It follows the Appalachian Trail for all but eight miles in Georgia. I've hiked the Georgia section and know that it is the last vestige of a moderate-sized wilderness in that state. A lower route is feasible. The hiking trail should be preserved; and the ingenuity of engineers is adequate for the task. I wish you could talk with Gannon Coffey, President of the Appalachian Trail Club of Georgia and Leonard E. Foote of the Wildlife Management Institute, both of whom know the details and have an alternate highway route. (September 10, 1963)

Meanwhile, Gannon Coffey, Henry Morris, and others, accompanied for part of the time by the Assistant Regional Director of the Bureau of Outdoor Recreation and Leonard Foote, Field Representative of the Wildlife Management Institute, inspected "in the field" Stan Murray's two proposed routes. Coffey wrote to Murray that "it was the consensus that the Parkway people were being 'bureaucratic' and that they had not really studied alternate routes, that there is room for compromise. "

Even with all of the pleas and letters of explanation received by them, the officials concerned continued to insist that the Trail and the Parkway could co-exist with no problems, while assuring Coffey and Murray that their suggestions would be considered.

Park Service director Stratton replied to a letter from Leonard Foote, saying, "We hope you will agree that our concern for the integrity of the Trail is demonstrated in Section 7 of the report and by our routing the parkway location via Lake Burton to preserve [a] greater length of the Trail undisturbed on the Blue Ridge." (September, 1963)

The GATC council voted in September to "recommend to the annual meeting . . . that the Club be prepared to authorize the negotiation for the relocation of the Trail, south of Tesnatee Gap, if the Parkway stays off the ridge north of the Gap."

Congressional hearings were to be held on the Parkway bill, and a statement was composed from the GATC to be submitted. Coffey planned to attend the hearings.

By October, with no response forthcoming from the Park Service on Murray's proposed alternate routes, things were not looking good. Congressman Weltner wrote to Coffey and Morris, "I feel that it has proceeded beyond the point where substantial alteration is possible." Murray feared that they would simply by-pass his suggestions and give no reason. He was anxious for some decision on the matter and kept searching for ways to tip the scales in favor of one of his proposed Parkway routes, if this was still possible to do.

In late September, in a letter to the officers and board members of the ATC, Murray outlined the Georgia problem and also told of another bill in Congress to survey a proposed parkway in Pennsylvania and New York which would disrupt the Trail there. He continued:

The introduction of the second bill precipitated a change of tack on the part of the Conference officers. It is quite clear that the only chance of survival for the Appalachian Trail as a continuous, wilderness footpath is through Federal protection. Earlier this year, the New York-New Jersey Trail Conference had passed a resolution that the Appalachian Trail Conference pursue negotiations with the Federal Government with a view to securing a permanent right-of-way for the Appalachian Trail in Federal ownership. We now propose to have introduced into Congress legislation in conflict with the two parkway bills: namely, a bill to establish an Appalachian Trailway. On August 20, several other Conference members and I, 'camping' at the Chairback Mountain Camps in Maine, discussed the proposal and drafted a bill. I have already distributed a draft to the Executive Committee and discussed it with the Board members present at the Labor Day Six-Club Meet in the Nantahalas. In essence, it provides that an Appalachian Trailway be established in the Appalachian Mountain region of the eastern United States, consisting of a land area of sufficient width and length to encompass the now existing Appalachian Trail and to provide a wilderness recreation zone and timber resource area, subject to certain restrictive uses. The zone would vary from 200 feet to two miles in width. Ownership would be Federal, state, or private. The only uses permitted would be those compatible with a wilderness recreation zone, wildlife protection, and the production of timber products. We are currently taking steps to secure the best advice as to wording and appropriate provisions, and then, subject to formal Executive Committee approval, we will take the steps necessary to get it introduced in Congress at the earliest practicable date.

A meeting was called—of several Conference members, Walter Boardman of the Nature Conservancy and Howard Zahniser of the Wilderness Society—to firm up the draft bill and discuss its introduction into Congress and plan strategy. Gannon Coffey attended the meeting, in Washington, and at the same time, along with Stan Murray, met with officials of the National Park Service and the Bureau of Outdoor Recreation on the Georgia situation. A Trailway bill committee was formed, and began work on the ideas which Murray presented to them. It was called the Committee on the Preservation of the Appalachian Trail, and its advertised purpose was merely to protect the Trail, since its actual purpose was not yet to be disclosed to the public.

Back in Georgia, Coffey continued to try to get the support of the Forest Service as well as the Georgia Department of State Parks for an alternate route.

Regional Forester Vessey replied to a letter from Stan Murray, assuring him that they were studying the alternate routes, and saying, "I'm sure you folks in the Appalachian Trail Conference realize that this trail conflict has been one of our main concerns in selecting the best parkway route."

Though Murray had been trying to get a mandate for the Park Service to construct any possible new trail in Georgia, Coffey wrote to him, "Paul Vincent has already said he'd rather build the Trail than have NPS making a four foot gravelled tourist attraction out of it . . ." and would "rather get the money from NPS and let the Forest Service do the work."

Despite more correspondence with Stratton, by the end of the year there was no decision, and things were "necessarily marking time until the Park Service completes their new investigation," according to Stephenson. As Murray said, "Right now all we can do is cross a few more fingers."

The Six-Club Meet was held over the Labor Day weekend at the Standing Indian campground in the Nantahalas, and was hosted by the Carolina Mountain Club, the Rev. Rufus Morgan, and the Wayah Ranger District. The spacious campground was still under construction in many places, but afforded a beautiful site for the event.

At the annual business meeting in October, the Club was "enlightened on the problems facing us on the Blue Ridge Parkway." Officers for 1964 were elected: Gannon Coffey, president; J. P. Eidson, vice president–activities; Doug Deane, Vice president–membership; Faye Phipps, secretary; Bob Gibbons, treasurer; Whit Benson, Trail supervisor; Polly Thompson, bulletin editor; Marene Snow, historian; Jim Engle, council,

The two final trips of the year were to the Dillard House, and a special Thanksgiving trip to Fort Clinch State Park at Fernandina Beach, Florida. The Christmas party with installation of officers closed the year.

1964

GEORGIA
APPALACHIAN
19 TRAIL CLUB, INC. 30

Nothing further was heard about the proposed Parkway routes until, in January, 1964, it was discovered that the National Park Service would have another field trip to Georgia in mid-February to examine the area. Gannon Coffey had visited the Forest Service to "feel them out" on their attitude toward the route proposals. He told Stan Murray that they indicated they would have to get with Sam Weems first. "Why they can't make up their own minds I'll never know," Coffey stated.

Later in the month, as Coffey again wrote to Murray, Henry Morris

. . . had seen Paul Vincent this past week and Paul was trying to get us to relocate the Trail instead of taking the Parkway toward Robertstown and Unicoi Park. Henry gave him a going over, since Henry knows the mountains better than Paul and Paul was unable to come up with a concrete route suggestion that wasn't on private land. We've about given up on Paul Vincent. It took him three years or more to get the last set of signs made and then his men put some of them up themselves with arrows pointing in the wrong direction. (February 3, 1964)

The National Park Service was under pressure to submit a report to Congress on the Parkway bill and was pushing for a settlement of the matter. Coffey and Morris met again with Forest Service officials in early March to discuss the routes. A meeting for later in March was tentatively arranged, "if necessary," with NPS and Bureau of Outdoor Recreation people. Paul Vincent was now suggesting that the Parkway get on the Trail route at Cowart Gap instead of

Dismal Mountain, the original NPS suggestion, which would take another eight miles of Trail. Henry Morris wrote to Murray of the meeting, and added:

Another idea advanced by the Forest Service is that we select a route [for the Trail] off on some of the other ridges away from everything and 'of course there won't be any agreement, but we won't do any cutting that will hurt you, just once in a while we will cut some of it out, but that will make a better trail.' Makes me wonder if he is trying to do away with the Trailway Agreement. . . . Of considerable concern to me is whether we can hold together an organization large enough to maintain our section unless we can come up with a good route. (March 7, 1964)

Murray, frustrated at not being able to get any "exact information" out of the government agencies involved, summarized "either the facts or we are pretty sure they are so." These probable facts indicated that the ATC–GATC proposed alternate parkway routes would not be accepted, and that alternate Trail routes should be worked out by the time of the March 23 meeting (which was now definitely scheduled). Murray suggested the possibility of approaching Landrum himself about a "compromise Parkway route."

Coffey and Murray gathered their forces and their thoughts—planning "strategy and tactics" and points for discussion—in preparation for the March 23 meeting, the purpose of which was to "try to arrive at a mutually satisfactory location for the Parkway." Coffey felt that the route of the Trail should be left open "because of probable changes in the Parkway route for engineering purposes," and should be subject only to U.S. Forest Service and ATC agreement. He also stated that the GATC "probably would not provide Weems with a letter ever saying that reroute was satisfactory, only that responsibility done," because it was certain to be an inferior route. As a matter for discussion, he listed several points, one of which was: "Continuation of AT in Georgia if reroute proves too inferior and GATC wants to abandon sponsorship. This hinges in part upon the past history of AT, concept of Trail, need for remoteness, ridge crests, changes in elevation and effect on use."

Present at the meeting were several representatives of the Forest Service and the Bureau of Outdoor Recreation, including J. K. Vessey, Paul Vincent, and Leonard Foote; J. L. Obenschain of the Blue Ridge Parkway; Sam Weems and E. H. Abbuehl of the National Park Service; Jean Stephenson, Stan Murray, Henry Morris and Gannon Coffey.

Abbuehl reported afterward on the meeting, in part:

. . . The report on the proposed Blue Ridge Parkway Extension that was submitted to the Congress in June 1963, recommended following the crest of the Blue Ridge Mountains through the Chattahoochee National Forest. The Appalachian Trail follows the same ridge and the Appalachian Trail Conference protested interferences with their Trail and recommended alternate routes for the Parkway. Studies of the various alternate possibilities were made and, prior to the above meeting, the National Park

Service and Bureau of Public Roads' decision was to keep the location on the ridge with an alternate possibility of leaving the ridge at Addis Gap and rejoining it at Chattahoochee Gap, which would leave approximately 15 of the best miles of the Trail undisturbed. The U.S. Forest Service preferred that the Parkway stay on the ridge as that location provided the minimum interference with their forest service activities.

The U.S. Forest Service Regional Director, Jim Vessey, presided at the above meeting and, at the opening, presented the reasons for the Parkway location to be on the ridge all the way through the National Forest and admitted that the U.S. Forest Service was primarily responsible for insisting on this location after studies had been made of several alternates. The Appalachian Trail Conference representatives then pointed out that they have been subject to considerable pressure to do something about the threatened interference with the Trail. They stated that a meeting of their Conference is planned to be held in New England in June, and they are going to have an answer to what is being done and that it appeared instead of saving some of the Trail, they were actually losing about 8 more miles. (The above Parkway report recommended the Lake Burton route which 'saved' 8 miles of Trail. Further study was made since the report by the U.S. Forest Service, and they find the Lake Burton route very objectionable and asked that the location join the main ridge at Cowart Gap, which takes in 8 more miles of Trail.) After much discussion of several possibilities, the U.S. Forest Service asked the Appalachian Trail representatives if the Parkway took the Addis Gap-Chattahoochee Gap alternate location, would they accept the remainder of the Parkway location being on the ridge from Cowart Gap to Springer Mountain? The Trail representatives were happy to accept this concession by the U.S. Forest Service and they can now make a positive report at their June meeting that they have saved 15 of the best miles of their Trail.

We have now reached a point where the U.S. Forest Service, National Park Service, Bureau of Public Roads, and Appalachian Trail Conference are in general agreement on the location of the Blue Ridge Parkway Extension.

The Appalachian Trail Club wants to retain Springer Mountain as their southern terminus and do not wish to re-establish the location to Oglethorpe as the National Park Service had offered to do.

There still remains sections where more study is required to resolve the conflict of U.S. Forest Service roads with the Parkway location, but the major hurdle has now been cleared in establishing the overall location. (March 1964)

As Murray stated it:

From my notes, the main points upon which all concerned were agreed are:

1. If it becomes the will of Congress that an extension of the Blue Ridge Parkway be built through the mountain region of north Georgia, then the respective routes of Parkway and Trail finally agreed upon represent the best combination of interests of the Forest Service, the National Park Service and the Appalachian Trail Conference.

2. Except for a few short sections (including a minimum of two crossings), it now appears that it will be possible to relocate those portions of the Trail disturbed by the Parkway in such a manner that the Trail will, in general, be at least a mile from the Parkway and will include sufficient scenic features and areas of relative wilderness that a desirable Trail can still be maintained in Georgia.

3. The present route of the Trail will be retained (1) from the North Carolina state line to Cowart Gap and (2) from the vicinity of either Addis Gap or Deep Gap to about a mile east of Chattahoochee Gap. In addition it will probably be desirable to retain the present route a short distance on both sides of Neel Gap, and perhaps on the approach to Springer Mountain.

4. There is no desire on the part of the Georgia Club or the Conference to re-extend the Trail to Mt. Oglethorpe.

The specific route would be "worked out to the satisfaction of the GATC and the Chattahoochee National Forest, the recommendation of the GATC being followed wherever practicable." Murray concluded:

While we are all happy to have arrived at something we can live with, I should restate for the record that these agreements as to respective routes of Parkway and Trail are to the Georgia Appalachian Trail Club and the Appalachian Trail Conference second best to no interference from a parkway at all. Also there will remain personal convictions among some Club members that this north Georgia wilderness area should remain unbroken by a modern parkway regardless of whether or not the Appalachian Trail can be satisfactorily relocated; however, this consideration was beyond the scope of this meeting. (April 13, 1964)

Trail relocations and lean-tos would be constructed by the Forest Service with Park Service funds. Everyone expressed (varying degrees of) satisfaction that a solution had been found, although there remained many details to be worked out.

So the final plan actually gave the GATC only six more miles of trail than the original Park Service plan would have done if the Parkway had come onto the Trail at Dismal Mountain—if from Dismal south the entire Trail route would have been utilized.

Coffey wrote to Murray later:

At the slide show coming up May 22, I'm going to explain the March 25 meeting and agreements to those in attendance. I will also assure the membership that we are confident of provisions for Trail relocation being carried out by USFS and NPS without spelling out in Bill as it will be worded. Assurance that someone will assure follow-up to carry out agreement when department heads change, etc., would make us sleep better nights. (May 2, 1964)

Things had been moving on the Trailway bill: Senator Gaylord Nelson of Wisconsin requested that a bill be prepared—by the Bureau of Outdoor Recreation—following the "general lines" of Murray's suggestions on the protection of the AT; and on May 20, 1964, Nelson introduced the bill into Congress—"A Bill to facilitate the management, use, and public benefits from the Appalachian Trail, a scenic trail designed primarily for foot travel through natural or primitive areas, and extending generally from Maine to Georgia; to facilitate and promote Federal, State, local, and private cooperation and assistance for the promotion of the Trail, and for other purposes."

Murray wrote an urgent letter to all ATC member organizations, informing them of the bill, saying:

I hardly need tell you that passage of this bill is most important to the future of the Trail. Upon reading it, I think you will agree that it is a tremendously important step forward towards lasting protection for the Trail and its environment. While this bill may not provide the complete answer to all our problems, it does provide for Congressional recognition for the Trail, sets the pattern for protection as a primitive or natural recreational facility, provides for certain acquisitions of land, and encourages cooperation among Federal agencies, states, and private owners in promoting the Trail.

Passage of the bill may be greatly affected by the support it gets from the various Trail clubs and their many members. (May 21, 1964)

He asked clubs to contact members to urge them to write to their congressmen, but there was no action taken on the bill in the 1964 session of Congress.

Fortunately, the Land and Water Conservation Bill, introduced into Congress in 1963, became law in 1964. This Act authorized federal grants to aid states in outdoor recreation planning, land acquisition, and development projects. It could be used to acquire land or obtain easements for protecting the route of the AT; if the Trailway Bill passed this would provide funds to carry out its provisions. The Act, of course, was the answer to the ATC plan to try to have the National Forest acquire private land within their area which was crossed by the AT. Figures on the amount of private land and the price per acre had been gathered during 1963 and 1964.

Gannon Coffey wrote to J. K. Vessey, Regional Forester in Atlanta, advising him "of the Trail Club's interest" in the Act, and expressing the hope that the Forest Service would take advantage of it to benefit the Trail as well as "other forms of outdoor recreation." In the name of the GATC, Coffey made the following recommendations:

1. The Forest Service should acquire, or obtain, the necessary interest in all lands located within one mile on each side of the Appalachian Trail.

2. The Forest Service should also acquire, obtain an interest in, or otherwise place under recreation use, all areas of scenic, scientific, historical or cultural value wherever they may be located within or adjacent to the Forest.

Relative to Item 1 above, we would recommend including the proposed re-route of the Trail, assuming the Blue Ridge Parkway extension into Georgia is constructed; and we would consider the application of the restrictions or uses set forth in the Trailway Agreement, Section I, as sufficient, unless clear-cutting is planned or uses of greater benefit to the Trail are permissible or applicable at some future date.

Relative to Item 2 above, the Trail Club would cooperate in locating primitive trails to such areas which would be of interest to hikers and which could be reached from the main Trail. The Club would cooperate, in the public interest, in locating or designating other areas in the Forest which would be of value for outdoor recreation purposes.

In our opinion, the rapid population growth, together with the increasing demand for land in eastern United States, makes it necessary to take full advantage of every opportunity to preserve wilderness or other areas suitable for outdoor recreation. . . .

The Club is . . . aware of the need to protect the Trail and its surrounding environment as well as to provide other opportunities for outdoor recreation. We urge the acquisition or preservation of those lands within or adjacent to the Forest(s) which could contribute, in their recreation use, to the physical, mental and spiritual well-being of our fellow citizens. This, too, would be in the Regional and National interest. (December 8, 1964)

Vessey replied non-committally, expressing an interest in the Fund, and saying that they were studying it.

Scouting of the proposed future route of the AT in Georgia had been in progress since it became evident that the Trail would likely be re-routed away from the Parkway. Usually the scouting trips were made by individuals, or two or three persons traveling together, with topo maps and compasses. Until the Trail relocation committee was set up in 1965, scouting was done by those who maintained sections of the existing Trail in the area to be relocated. Gannon Coffey, Bill Robinson, Whit Benson, Hugh Chase, Henry Morris, and others explored the area south and east of the Trail between Cowart Gap and Neel Gap, the Duncan Ridge area, and back around to Springer Mountain.

The earliest scouting was done primarily to determine the feasibility of relocating the Trail; and, although the exact route could not be determined until the exact route of the Parkway was known, these preliminary trips resulted in the knowledge that a feasible route was possible—especially along Duncan Ridge.

In February, 1964, the bulletin announced an official Club trip to scout part of the area north and west from Blood Mountain:

Have you been lost lately? Well, let's go! I've been told that three fellows were lost in this area, maybe we will find them still wandering around.

The trip was scheduled from Wolf Pen Gap to Cooper Creek area, but because so much of this is actually very near the road we may change it a little. Saturday, plans call for hiking from Mulky Gap toward Wolf Pen until we come back into the forest road leading from Wolf Pen to Cooper Creek. Sunday we will try and go from Mulky Gap to Fish Gap, going south on this part. We will camp in the Cooper Creek area. Let's wish for some dry weather as some of the roads in this area are getting in very bad shape. We will meet at the camp sites by 10:30 Saturday morning. If anyone has any homing pigeons, they may be needed.

Afterward the bulletin account declared:

We didn't get lost but one little ole' time and not for long, . . . There was very favorable comment concerning this section as a possible re-route. From Wolf Pen to Mulky Gap quite a bit actually follows the road, but from Mulky south to Highway 60 is pretty remote except the forest road into Fish Gap with very nice overlooks.

The sixteenth meeting of the Appalachian Trail Conference was to be held in June at the Stratton Mountain Inn in Vermont with the Green Mountain Club as hosts. The GATC arranged for its display at the meeting "a map of the Chattahoochee National Forest showing the present route of the AT, the Parkway location and the proposed re-route (as far as can be presently determined. . . .)." Large photographs of scenes along the new trail, taken by Leonard Foote, were displayed along with the map.

The Conference boasted the largest attendance ever—305 people. Five GATC members attended and volunteered the GATC as hosts for the next Conference in 1967. Henry Morris was re-elected to the Board of Managers.

Anticipating that the shelter at Tesnatee Gap might be removed when the new Richard Russell Scenic Highway came through the gap, the leader of a Club hike in February declared it the "final Club trip to faithful old Tesnatee shelter." Thirty-one hikers came to bid what turned out to be a premature farewell to the shelter. The Club decided that, rather than having the shelter removed at this time, they would try to leave it until the Blue Ridge Parkway was built so that only one move would be necessary.

The completion of the relocation of the Trail in this area was announced in the October bulletin by Trail Supervisor, Whit Benson. The announcement continued: "Some of the new white blazes . . . were put on the trees in the darkness. The Trail, which goes over Wildcat Mountain, has been routed to take the hiker to some of the finest overlooks on the Georgia section of the AT."

Cataloochee campground in the Smokies was the site of the Six (or Seven) Club Meet over Labor Day weekend, with 46 GATCers in attendance.

Generally, activities for 1964 were the usual, with most of the annual trips to the familiar enjoyable spots. A few trips of note included Fontana to Wesser (on two day hikes), Tellico Plains, Tennessee, and Elkmont and the Smokies.

At the October annual meeting, ATC chairman, Stan Murray, honored the GATC with a "special talk" and slide presentation on the origin and development of the Trail and the functions and activities of Conference. Officers for 1965 were, as usual, "duly elected." They were to be: J. P. Eidson, president; Bob Gibbons, vice president-activities; Bill Robinson, vice president-membership; Whit Benson, Trail supervisor; Yvonne Gibbons, secretary; Don Hubbard, treasurer; Amanda Coffey, bulletin editor; Ed Seiferle, historian; Gannon Coffey, council. (Early in January of 1965, Bill Robinson resigned as vice president for membership and the council elected June Engle to replace him.)

Marene Snow had been the historian of the GATC for almost 25 years, as she frequently said because she was the only member with a basement large enough to hold the boxes of Club historical material. In 1963 she gave up the office—possibly because she moved into a smaller home—and turned over to Ed Seiferle a valuable collection of files that she had cared for for those many years.

For the almost 35 years that Marene Snow was on the GATC council, she exerted a strong influence on the workings of the Club. Her devotion to the GATC, along with her definite ideas about its image and its activities, could make her the joy or sometimes the despair of the current president. She remained an interested and faithful member until her death.

1965

GEORGIA APPALACHIAN 19 TRAIL CLUB, INC. 30

THE TRAILWAY BILL was re-introduced into Congress in January, 1965. The text was exactly the same as the 1964 bill. It was co-sponsored by Senators from every state that the Trail passed through except Vermont. Club members were urged to keep writing their Congressmen to express their support for the bill. As Stan Murray said in a message on "Trail Preservation" in the January *ATN:*

Our most concerted efforts these days are not in determining how frequently we should swing the weeders over the Trail (the answer is at least once a year), but in planning how we will preserve the Trail as a single, primitive recreation area. The Appalachian Trail was magnificently laid out through our forests and along our mountain crests at a time when most of the land had little use aside from the production of timber. Now we are finding that it does indeed have other uses, and the need to take positive steps to protect this Trail land for high-quality outdoor recreation experience is urgently upon us.

No action was taken on the bill for some time; hearings were to be held in September. The January, 1966, *ATN* reported on the hearings. Senator Gaylord Nelson opened with a statement in support of his measure, in part:

As Congress finally stirs itself into action to preserve what little is left of this Nation's great misspent heritage of natural beauty, it is only just that special recognition be given to those valiant citizens who have for many years been carrying on this national task from their private resources.

The Appalachian Trail bill would in part do just that. It would provide Federal recognition of the spectacularly beautiful Trail route running 2,000 miles up the Appalachian backbone of the eastern states. It has been maintained for 30 years through the selfless efforts of private individuals banded together in local and regional clubs which in turn make up the Appalachian Trail Conference.

Murray and other ATC people spoke for the bill. Murray stated, in part:

Three things have always characterized the Trail: continuity of route, wildness, and remoteness. Over the years, the Conference has lived with volunteer work arrangements, verbal permissions from land owners, and a very valuable agreement with the Federal agencies. These have served reasonably well up to the present, but it has been clear over the past several years that the Appalachian Trail cannot continue to survive without some legal and binding means for assuring a continuity of the right-of-way, and for preserving the land environment. We have reached the conclusion that the only practical means for achieving permanent protection through 14 states, 2 national parks, and 8 national forests is through Federal legislation. . . .

Murray and others pointed out specific threats to the Trail; many other statements were given by interested persons.

The September, 1965, *ATN* quoted parts of a Department of the Interior press release on Secretary Udall's report to the Senate Committee studying the bill. The report noted that only one-third of the Trail was on Federal land, and 40 per cent crossed private land, usually with only verbal permission of the land owners.

By the end of the year Murray said that it appeared possible the Senate might pass the bill in the next session of Congress. He began to make tentative plans for the implementation of the bill in the event that it was passed.

The Wilderness Act had finally been passed by Congress in 1964, and, continuing the move toward protection of outdoor recreation areas, President Johnson had in February, 1965, requested that the Secretary of the Interior " . . . recommend to me a cooperative program to encourage a national system of trails. . . ." According to the September *ATN*, a study was to be made with the objective to "evaluate present trail programs and recommend a comprehensive plan for the development and use of trails. . . ." The AT and the Pacific Crest Trail were included in the study, as well as numerous shorter trails. In October, a bill to create a national system of hiking trails was introduced into the Senate by Senator Gaylord Nelson.

But roads continued to threaten. Early in 1965, a "feasibility study" was suggested for a new transmountain highway over the Smoky Mountains from North Carolina Highway 28 to Tremont and Townsend in Tennessee. Connecting highways and loop roads were advocated to "improve circulation by automobile." In September, a "sudden announcement" was made by the National Park Service Director that he was "ready to build" the new highway. The fact that the Smokies was to be one of the first national parks to be considered for wilderness may have hurried the road-building decision. The road was to go generally up Forney Creek, on to Welch Ridge almost to the crest, go along the crest and tunnel under it below Buckeye Gap, descend via Miry Ridge and the middle prong of Little River and down to Tremont. Urgent requests were sent out to all interested persons to protest the road.

In Georgia, the Trail relocation committee, headed by Gannon Coffey, reported to the January, 1965, council meeting that it was "looking for scenic spots for Trail relocation." Shelters were to be placed every 7.5 miles, and the type of shelter to be built was being studied. The committee had a goal of having the new Trail laid out by the end of the year. It spent many hours and covered many miles and provided detailed knowledge of the terrain and points of interest for use in the final routing, which actually would not be definitely determined until the Parkway route was final.

By the end of the year, plans were being made to involve all interested Club members on group scouting and flagging trips during the following year. Incoming President J. P. Eidson's advice to those laying out the Trail was, "We have the opportunity to lay out a trail with grades that the backpackers can easily negotiate. . . . If we devote enough careful time to scouting, we will find the natural overlooks, the waterfalls where we must leave the ridge and other points of interest. Let us not concern ourselves too much with how much longer the Trail might be in Georgia, but let us concern ourselves with how much more interesting and spectacular the Trail can be in Georgia." (December 4, 1965)

Outings during the early 1960's were including more and more off-the-AT hikes. In 1965 the annual trips were still made to John Mahl's cabin near Dukes Creek Falls, the Cabin in the Briar in the Smokies, the Emersons' property on Lake Lanier, LeConte Lodge, and the Dillard House. Leader Tom Aderhold's account of the trip to LeConte Lodge was reminiscent of earlier days:

All week, just before this trip, the most asked question was, 'What will be the weather conditions?' And as usual, the answer was, 'Who knows?' As it happened, there was a choice. If you did not find to your liking whatever type was existing at the moment, then you had only to wait awhile, as it was certain to change. Let's see: there was rain (Friday night only), bright sunshine, cold wind, sleet, low humidity, extremely warm air, ice, high humidity, snow, heavy overcast, clear skies, haze, fog, ad infinitum.

Regardless of weather (or perhaps because of it as the fall colors were at their maximum beauty), the trip was most pleasant. The majority of the 36 members and guests who attended hiked up the Alum Cave Trail and by 4:00 P.M. all had arrived at the Lodge. Supper was the usual fare but somehow seemed better than usual. Or were all just hungrier?

The period after supper and until about 9:30 found the big cabin filled with song. Perhaps songs would be more apropos as if there were any which were not sung. No one could think of it at the time. Late in the evening, two of the good members, native Kentuckians, sang some old hillbilly songs most in attendance had never heard. These two could honestly do a good show at one of the Club's annual functions, singing a duet of these colorful tunes. Maybe they can be prevailed upon to do so. We'll let you guess who they were.

Sunday morning found a ground cover of sleet and/or snow, and a 7:30 A.M. temperature of 21 degrees with a strong wind blowing. (Lillian said she knew it was getting colder during the night because Mandy never did keep the fire burning hardily to keep her (Lillian) warm.) After a healthy breakfast and literally gallons of hot chocolate and coffee, or both, the hikes down to the waiting automobiles were begun. Another delightful trip to LeConte had become a memory.

Other trips for the year included Tate City/Standing Indian, Fall Creek Falls, Linville Gorge, Cloudland Canyon, and the Appalachicola National Forest in Florida. Six backpack trips were held this year—they were not the novelty they once had been, as more lightweight equipment was being developed. The entire Georgia Trail was hiked during the year, as well as partially covered on two work trips.

On the first work trip of the year, the workers spread out in small groups along the Trail for clearing and blazing and installing metal markers. In the two days they covered 20.4 miles of Trail, and, as Trail Supervisor Whit Benson stated in the bulletin account, "This leaves only 57.44 miles to be cleared on our next work trip."

From time to time the question had been raised of allowing pets to go along on Club trips. A number of Club members felt that this was not appropriate and would "interfere with the enjoyment of others." At the July council meeting, a motion was made and carried that no pets be allowed on Club outings. This action was to result in the indignant resignation from the Club of at least one couple.

The annual Labor Day event was announced in the bulletin as the "Multi-Club" meet for the first time, the gathering having grown to eight clubs, plus one person from "no place in particular." The meet was to be held near Erwin, Tennessee, and leader, J. P. Eidson, related in the bulletin a bit of local history:

On the scouting trip in June, we found that the city of Erwin had a number of name changes. The first name was Greasy Cove. Before the 1928 blight which killed the chestnut trees, this area was noted for large chestnuts and bears were plentiful. The hunters cooked the fat meat along the stream leaving greasy grounds, thus the name Greasy Cove. The name was changed to the name of Longmire, since the Post Office was located in Mr. Longmire's store. The next name change was Vanderbilt, but this only lasted one year. The people thought that they could entice the Vanderbilts, who were wealthy, to move to the city, but the Vanderbilts did not respond. Since a Mr. Ervin gave the land for the Rock Creek Park, the name was changed to Ervin, but the Post Office misspelled it and thus the name Erwin.

"Some 40" GATCers made the trip to Rock Creek Forest Service Park near Erwin. According to the account of the meet in the January, 1966, *ATN:*

Returning hikers were pleased to find ATC Honorary Member Paul M. Fink wandering around the campground, visiting old acquaintances and reminiscing about old times. In the early days of the AT, Paul worked with Myron Avery and others in putting the Trail through the Southern Appalachians.

The East Point Recreation Center was the site of the October business meeting. A revised edition of the constitution and by-laws was presented to, and accepted by, the members. Gannon Coffey was the entertainment for the evening, providing "a very interesting talk" on the relocation of the Trail and, according to the minutes of the meeting, "After his talk, he demonstrated to the Club members a very entertaining method of clearing the Trail and maintaining it." Officers for 1966 were elected: J. P. Eidson, president; Bob Gibbons, vice president-activities; June Engle, vice president-membership; Jim Rhinehardt, Trail supervisor; Yvonne Gibbons, secretary; Don Hubbard, treasurer; Amanda Coffey, bulletin editor; Ed Seiferle, historian; Ernest Sparrow, council.

Searcy Slack, still holding the position of Trail information director, and writing lengthy letters to each inquirer (one person wrote in reply: "When you sign a letter GATC information, you mean just that."), requested permission at the November council meeting to "prepare a memorandum flyer for information concerning the Club to be used to answer inquiries." Early in the year, President J. P. Eidson, in a note to Slack, said, "I had no idea how much work you have been doing for the GATC until I began reading the file. . . ."

In a lengthy letter of information to club presidents and Board of Managers members in December, Stan Murray announced several recent changes at the ATC headquarters, including: Conference would be moving into a new building in Washington purchased by the PATC; Ed Garvey had replaced Fred Blackburn as Conference secretary; Florence Nichol had taken over the editorship of the *ATN*, with Jean Stephenson having "general guidance" over all publication activity; guidebooks would each now have a separate editor. Murray also brought up-to-date information on the status of the Trailway Bill, hoping for its passage next year, exhorted members to be vigilant in protecting the Trail, discussed major problem areas, including the Smokies, and concluded:

We are in a time of change. Encroachments, both private and public, encouragement of legislation to protect the Trail, planning for implementation of such legislation, and the reorganization and expansion of our headquarters facilities and services: all are taxing the energies and spare time quotas of our officers and staff. Yet, we will do the job because we believe in the Appalachian Trail.

Throughout such times, we try to preserve the Appalachian Trailway *without* noticeable change . . . no change, that is, except for the changing colors, the shifting winds, and the endless progression of animal and plant life that only God has dominion over. (December 1, 1965)

1966

GEORGIA
APPALACHIAN
19 TRAIL CLUB, INC. 50

T HE SEEMINGLY ENDLESS FIGHT for wilderness, against roads, and for Trail protection was to continue into 1966—and beyond. The Georgia Trail was presumed to have lost to the road-builders, and now GATCers turned their concern toward the threatened Smoky Mountains.

The Smoky Club—and all concerned—were fighting at the same time *against* the transmountain highway and *for* the incorporation of the Smoky Mountains National Park into the national wilderness system. GATC members wrote letters to congressmen; Gannon Coffey and Ed Seiferle spoke at hearings on the wilderness proposal in North Carolina and Tennessee; a resolution was passed at the GATC-sponsored multi-club meet condemning the highway, the "commercial lodge" planned to be built at Spence Field on the Appalachian Trail (as part of the road development), and a number of other proposed roads within the park. Also at the multi-club meet, it was "enthusiastically agreed" to hold a protest hike in October from Clingman's Dome to Buckeye Gap, where the road was to cross the crest, and perhaps all the way down Miry Ridge to Elkmont.

The hike—called the "Save-Our-Smokies Wilderness Hike"— was given wide publicity. The day of the hike dawned foggy, with threatening rain, but "the excitement of the occasion was evident." A report on the hike in *The Living Wilderness* magazine declared, "It was the biggest crowd ever to come to lunch at Buckeye Gap. Down the Appalachian Trail they came—men, women, boys, girls, lawyers, brokers, postmen, teachers, scientists, clerks, authors. They were as young as five and as old as 81. They came from 22 states, and among them were visitors from France, Canada, and Japan."

Five hundred seventy-six people had signed the register for the hike, and 234 of them walked the entire 17 miles down to Elkmont, including 81-year-old Rev. Rufus Morgan. The magazine article reported, "He was among the early ones to finish the full 17 miles. In doing so, he walked all over the argument that, without more roads into the wilderness, the elderly are denied sight of the Great Smokies' beauty."

A brief pre-hike ceremony featured a few words from Ernie Dickerman, hike coordinator from the Smoky Club, a message from Benton MacKaye read by Stan Murray, and a brief talk by Harvey Broome, who remembered hiking the area as early as 1917. Eighteen GATCers attended in spite of a conflicting scheduled trip to Mt. LeConte (eight of these hiked down from LeConte before dawn to make it to the protest hike). In his GATC bulletin account of the protest hike, J. P. Eidson wrote:

Standing on the open southern slopes of Mt. Buckley, a continuous line of hikers could be observed hiking from the summit of Mt. Buckley across the open slope and into the trees. From this vantage point, however, one could only observe about one-third the length of the orderly single file of hikers. This was the largest number of people ever to hike together on the Appalachian Trail at one time.

Although in 1965 there had seemed little doubt that the Trailway Bill would be passed by the Congress, the President's proposal for a nationwide system of trails had muddied the waters. Many ATC officials and members felt that this new proposal seemed to call for a more "developed" trail than was desirable. So no bill was passed, and the administration's bill was re-evaluated during the last half of 1966, in close consultation with Conference officials. Murray stated at the end of the year that they "seemed to be in general agreement with" the Bureau of Outdoor Recreation, who had drafted the bill, and new legislation was expected in 1967.

Scouting for relocation of the Georgia Trail was proceeding. Two trips were made early in the year, with four people on each, to cover the section between Springer Mountain and Highway 60 near Margret. Rain, wind, cold, and a small turnout in February kept the distance covered small; the second trip was planned for overnight but conditions were much the same. Leader Gannon Coffey reported in the bulletin:

The scouting hike turned out to be quite different from the forecast made in the announcement. The day was not 'sunny' but rainy. We moved rapidly instead of slowly over the 7 - 9 [mile] route, with bushwhacking at a minimum. We picked up a few old faint trails and some well-used ones along the ridge tops. We crossed barbed-wire barricades (Army) at Bryson Gap before going over the higher of the John Dick Mountains (3,309 feet). The 'suitable place to spend the night—when the time comes' turned out to be Atlanta. The packs were carried, unopened. (We were told this lent realism to the venture, simulating the conditions a backpacker would encounter in traversing this section.) Although we were prepared to spend the night on some lonely ridgetop, we reached the cars by 5:00 P.M., as the rain became heavier. The roads were muddy and deep-rutted, so we got the cars out (slowly) and headed for hot food in Dahlonega. After wringing out the map and wet clothes, we went over the day's work, satisfied (and thankful) that a desirable route was found in half the time predicted.

The GATC was to host the 17th ATC Conference meeting in 1967, and had been searching for a suitable place. Nothing could be found in Georgia, and several places were investigated in North Carolina, including High Hampton near Cashiers and Western Carolina College at Cullowhee. ATC Secretary Ed Garvey, eager to get plans started, wrote to Stan Murray saying, "It is most important that we do not procrastinate" in making arrangements. Murray replied, "The Georgia Appalachian Trail Club has not, of course, been procrastinating. . . ." He and Gannon Coffey had checked out the two locations and planned an announcement in the next *ATN*. The GATC council voted to hold the meeting at the High Hampton Country Club on May 20-26, 1967. As the *ATN* stated, the GATC, "while preferring a site in north Georgia, gave first consideration to the convenience of those who will attend the session."

The GATC was also to host the 1966 Multi-Club Meet. Unicoi State Park near Helen was secured for the event, which drew 163 people—from five clubs. Besides the reports and activities concerning the Smokies transmountain road and proposed wilderness, the program featured a report by GATCers Jim and June Engle, who had successfully completed almost half of their attempted hike of the entire AT, skits, slide shows and reports by the clubs. J. P. Eidson's report on the meet for the bulletin included some "reflections," among which were: "Searcy Slack leading the singing. . . . Bob Taylor, Larry Freeman and Lou Hoben with reminiscent conversation about trips into Tesnatee shelter when Tesnatee Gap was one of the most inaccessible points in Georgia. . . . Gannon Coffey causing tree to disappear with deblazing paint. . . . Charlie and Gail Smith's complete breakfast being eaten by a dog."

Henry Morris had been made responsible for the checking and recording of data for the guidebook, and was following the practice of checking one-third of the Trail each year. He covered the Trail from Springer to Neel Gap in 1966 and sent a detailed report of Trail conditions to Jim Rhinehardt, the Trail supervisor, and recommending "some things I feel we should do to put it in compliance with the best Appalachian Trail standards." Among other things, he noted much evidence in places of jeeps and trail bikes on the Trail, the difficulty of crossing Blackwell Creek except in dry weather, several grades between Cooper and Gooch Gaps being "too steep for comfortable and enjoyable hiking and causing serious erosion," erosion and cutting switchbacks on Blood Mountain, and the fact that the Trail crosses private property at Miller

Gap and Henry Gap. Most of these problems were to remain for a number of years; but eventually, all were recognized as serious enough to warrant corrective action.

A work trip in October to try to correct some of the "smaller" problems found by Morris brought the following bulletin report by Jim Rhinehardt, in part: "Would you believe that 30 members showed up and we completely repainted and cleared more than 22 miles of Trail? Knowing of the enthusiasm our Club shows for work trips you wouldn't, of course. . . . The *real* reason we covered 22 miles is ten hard-working guests. . . ."

In the middle of the year, Bob Gibbons, vice president for activities, and his wife Yvonne, secretary, moved out of town and resigned from the Club. The council elected Hugh Chase to replace Bob and Joyce Rand to replace Yvonne.

Activities for the year averaged about 18 people per trip, and were mostly to familiar places, plus a few somewhat different, including Ellicott's Rock, Roosevelt State Park, Dorothy Thompson Wilderness and Joyce Kilmer Forest.

The weather had a decided effect on a planned trip from Gooch Gap to Jarrard Gap, according to the bulletin account by leader George Shafe:

. . . It was snowing when we left Atlanta and it increased in intensity as we went further north. At Suches, the visibility was zero and the snow was about ten inches deep and getting deeper. We phoned the manager at Lake Winfield Scott (from Suches) and he stated that we might get in, with luck, but was almost certain that we would not get out on Sunday. We turned back. Back at Woody Gap we stopped to take some pictures, at which time three other cars of our group arrived. After some discussion we decided to go back to Dahlonega and eat dinner at the Smith House and then go over to Amicalola Falls to spend the night.

A backpack in October to Bly Gap attracted 27 people, and leader, Larry Freeman, in reporting on the trip, added:

The blazes along this section of the Trail are very neat and the edges have been squared with some kind of a blue-gray paint which matches the tree bark and has a small initial, gc, in the bottom right-hand corner. We all wondered who it is that does such a nice job with their blazes.

At the annual meeting, the new Forest Supervisor, Gilbert Stradt, "gave a witty and informative talk on the goals of the National Forests and the problems facing a conservationist." Officers for 1967 were elected: Ed Seiferle, president; Hugh Chase, vice president-activities; Mary Eidson, vice president-membership; Jim Rhinehardt, Trail supervisor; Frances Shafe, secretary; Bill Shaw, treasurer; Norma Seiferle, historian; Amanda Coffey, bulletin editor; J. P. Eidson, council.

1967

GEORGIA APPALACHIAN TRAIL CLUB, INC. 1930

THE BIG EVENT FOR THE GATC in 1967 was the hosting of the 17th Appalachian Trail Conference at High Hampton in North Carolina in May. A committee under the chairmanship of Gannon Coffey worked diligently to prepare for the event. The Trail was spruced up and hikes, entertainment, and all the many details were planned by committee members who had been working for a year getting ready for the meeting.

The Conference was called "the best meeting ever held north or south" by the ATC secretary, Raymond Gingrich. He continued, "In fact you did such a professional job that no club to date has come forth to volunteer to host the 18th meeting in three years." Three hundred twenty-one people attended, a record number. The September, 1967, *ATN* reported on the meeting with an article from the Carolina Mountain Club bulletin:

Some highlights of a most successful AT Conference held May 20, 21, and 22 at High Hampton Inn included: the excellent and abundant food served by the Inn to some 300 delegates, visitors, campers, hikers, etc.—a most stimulating message to the group by Michael Frome, writer—a charming folk singer (Beth VanOver), who kept one evening's audience absorbed for more than two hours—the illustrated talk by our Forest Service Chief (Edward P. Cliff), who came down from Washington, D.C., for the meet—the well planned programs by the Georgia Club—the numerous informal gatherings of friends— the exhibit of camping and hiking equipment on the Inn's wide veranda—the fascination of seeing the entire AT on plastic relief maps, so many quadrangles that they had to be placed on the lawn for enough space—the gratifying high number of sales by CMC of the book on the Great Smokies, *Strangers in High Places*—the hikes to the rocky, dome-shaped mountains seen from the Inn's lawn and reflected in the lake—the many campers with tents, trailers, and gear on the golf course edge—and last, our rainiest section of eastern America tried to prove itself during our weekend—a night storm and a rainy Monday, but not enough to dampen the enthusiasm of the more than 100 in attendance.

Editor's Postscript. Omitted from this sketch are the delightful exchanges by the official 'greeters' about how Georgia annexed some territory to the north so that the Georgia Appalachian Trail Club could play host to the Conference in its own state; and the official post-Conference hikes, the long drive and short walk to the beginning of the Trail on Springer Mountain, participated in by some 60 people in a misty rain, the hikes over Blood Mountain, the highest point on the AT in Georgia, and over Standing Indian in North Carolina, 'the grandstand of the Southern Appalachians,' and the final jaunt over Tray Mountain and 'The Swag of the Blue Ridge.'

Florence Nichol, editor of the *ATN*, had requested that someone in the GATC prepare an article on the Club, its background, activities, etc., for publication in the May issue, which would announce the Conference meeting. Ed Seiferle asked Marion Morris, as a long-time member, to write the article. This she did, and a very entertaining capsule history was the result, capturing the spirit and flavor of the early GATC days.

A new bill to establish a nationwide system of trails was introduced into Congress early in 1967. The bill had been extensively revised and, according to Stan Murray, provided for adequate protection of the AT. "It represents the culmination of three years of consideration, trial and review on the part of Conference and B.O.R. alike…" stated Murray. "The protection afforded the AT as a wilderness footpath appeared to outweigh by a great measure the risks involved in placing the primary responsibility for the Trail with the Secretary of the Interior. We have been able to give the new bill unqualified Conference support." He declared the prospects for enactment "better than ever before." Daniel Ogden of the Bureau of Outdoor Recreation gave a lengthy talk on the bill to the Conference meeting at High Hampton. But patience was called for once again, since, according to Walter Boardman, ATC conservation chairman, "problems about land ownership" caused some delay, and the bill remained in committee the rest of the year.

The Richard Russell Highway through Hog Pen and Tesnatee Gaps was at last completed, and a dedication ceremony was held in August at Hog Pen Gap by Union and White County officials.

Also in August, a newspaper article announced the "unanimous endorsement" by the House Interior Subcommittee of the bill to extend the Blue Ridge Parkway through Georgia, bringing one step closer the relocation of the Georgia Trail.

A victory was celebrated in December, as huge headlines in the *Knoxville News*

Sentinel declared "Transmountain Road Rejected." Secretary of the Interior Udall had decided not to approve the road which would cross the Smoky Mountains National Park. As usual, work had already begun on the road between Bryson City and the Park, but now this was to be completed only as far as Monteith Branch, about six miles farther.

In March, GATC members were again called upon to support a proposed wilderness area—this time the Okefenokee Swamp. Nine members attended hearings, and many wrote letters in favor of the proposal.

Activities for 1967 began in January with a "daring" hike in the Smokies, from Smokemont to Peck's Corner, led by Jim and June Engle. The successful trip started the year off right, and the activities chairman reported at the end of the year an average of 25 people per trip. The greatest attendance was seen on a February hike scheduled for Woody to Neel Gaps. A reading of zero degrees greeted 52 (count 'em) people at Woody Gap, and sent the group immediately to the reserved cabins at Lake Winfield Scott. Other trips of note during the year included the Pisgah National Forest near Mt. Pisgah, Cades Cove and Gregory Bald, the usual "overwhelming experience of climbing Mt. LeConte," and a Thanksgiving return trip to Cades Cove.

Plans were made during the year to begin relocating sections of the Trail which followed Forest Service roads. The first section flagged for relocation was that between the Cheese Factory and Tray Gap, but by the end of the year had not yet received approval from the Forest Service.

The possibility of incorporating the GATC had been mentioned several times in the past and was brought up for discussion again at the July council meeting. It was decided to bring it before the membership at the annual meeting. Members at the annual meeting voted to appoint a special committee to look into the matter and have the decision made by the council.

The ATC Board of Managers evidently had not held regular meetings before 1966. A report in the January, 1967, *ATN* on a Board of Managers meeting in December, 1966, stated, "The Board of Managers . . . met . . . in three sessions that proved to be so worthwhile that the last act of the Board was to pass a motion to meet at least once a year hereafter."

According to the same report, the ATC Secretary "has long been responsible in large part for the operation of the Washington office of the Conference." Ed Garvey, who had held this position for three years, had written in 1966 to Board of Managers members expressing the wish to have a full-time executive officer for these duties, which had grown considerably. At the December, 1966, meeting a motion was passed to authorize the Chairman "to employ, on a part-time basis, an administrative officer at a remuneration of not to exceed $2,500 a year. . . ." This position was finally filled in late 1968 by Les Holmes, who was to become the first "executive secretary" of the ATC.

Seventeen GATC members and guests attended the 1967 Multi-Club Meet in

Southwestern Virginia, near Marion.

At the October annual meeting the speaker for the evening was former Congressman James Mackay, who was "chairman and principal founding spirit" of the newly-formed Georgia Conservancy. Officers for 1968 were elected: Ed Seiferle, president; Jim Coogler, vice president-activities; Mary Eidson, vice president-membership; Reg Hall, treasurer; Frances Shafe, secretary; Tom Stapler, Trail supervisor; Norma Seiferle, historian; Margaret Drummond, bulletin editor; Hugh Chase, council.

At the meeting, Trail relocation chairman, J. P. Eidson, reported that the decision was made to postpone any relocation of sections of the Trail which the Blue Ridge Parkway would displace "until detail engineering roadway plans and profiles have been approved for roadway construction."

1968

GEORGIA
APPALACHIAN
19 TRAIL CLUB, INC. 30

THIS YEAR WAS TO SEE at last the passage of Congressional legislation so long expected: in effect, one law which would protect the Georgia Trail and another which would destroy it. Throughout the year the signs pointed to the culmination of the efforts of those who had been working for a number of years toward the passage of both of these laws. In January, the House of Representatives passed the bill to extend the Blue Ridge Parkway into Georgia, in September it was passed by the Senate, and on October 9 it became law. In July, the House and Senate each passed a National Trails Act, differences in the two were reconciled, and on October 2 the resulting bill became law.

The National Trails System Act stated its purpose thus:

(a) In order to provide for the ever-increasing outdoor recreation needs of an expanding population and in order to promote public access to, travel within, and enjoyment and appreciation of the open-air, outdoor areas of the Nation, trails should be established (i) primarily, near the urban areas of the Nation, and (ii) secondarily, within established scenic areas more remotely located.

(b) The purpose of this Act is to provide the means for attaining these objectives by instituting a national system of recreation and scenic trails, by designating the Appalachian Trail and the Pacific Crest Trail as the initial components of that system, and by prescribing the methods by which, and standards according to which, additional components may be added to the system.

The national system of trails would consist of: (1) national recreation trails, near urban areas, (2) national scenic trails, which were extended trails in more remote and natural areas, and (3) connecting or side trails, providing access to the scenic and recreation trails. Advisory councils would be established for the AT and the Pacific Crest Trails which would consult with the Secretary of the Interior (for the AT) and the Secretary of Agriculture (for the Pacific Crest Trail). The council would consist of a representative of each Federal agency administering lands through which the Trail passes, a representative of each state through which the Trail passes, and representatives of land owners and "land users," including the ATC. Studies were to be made of the feasibility of designating other national scenic trails.

Stan Murray wrote to Conference members:

The Act will virtually assure a continuous right-of-way for the Appalachian Trail. The power of Federal condemnation has been provided as a 'last resort' measure and there are strict limitations on its use. It is our wish, of course, to maintain our present good relationships with present landowners, many of whom have become our friends through the years. The present Act would appear to make this possible.

The Act also lays a basis for protection of the Trail environment. The purpose of the national scenic trails is stated to be to provide for the conservation and enjoyment of the nationally significant scenic (and) natural . . . areas through which the trails pass. The right-of-way of the Appalachian Trail will include, where practicable, the lands which have been protected by the 1938-39 Appalachian Trailway Agreements.

We expect that most of the present arrangements for maintenance of the Trail by clubs and private individuals will be continued. These arrangements may be made more formal insofar as the Federal trail administrator is concerned. Throughout the history of this bill, it has been clear that Congress and the Federal agencies expect the private participation and personal stewardship that have characterized the AT to continue.

Any law is subject to varying interpretation. One new, vital role that now falls on the Conference is to promote continually the wilderness footpath concept. We have to be always vigilant to be sure that the management of the Appalachian Trail is based on this concept, just as it always has been in the past. The Conference will have its official 'say' on this through the AT Advisory Council provided in the Act. The work of the Conference is perhaps more important now than ever before.

The celebration over the decision not to build the transmountain Smokies road was short-lived. In March, 1968, Interior Secretary Udall was pressured to reconsider his decision, and another study was made of the area. At the end of the year Udall issued a statement saying he had confirmed his view that the road should not be built; however, the new Interior Secretary, Walter Hickel, was asked to *re*-consider, and a final decision was not expected for a year or two.

At the May GATC council meeting, a committee studying the matter of incorporating the Club reported on its findings and recommended incorporation. This was approved by the council members and the committee was to proceed with the mechanics of becoming incorporated. Finally in

December, the work was completed and the Club became the "Georgia Appalachian Trail Club, Inc."

In order to gain more interest on the Club funds (just over $350), in August, the council, at the suggestion of Jim Coogler, authorized the treasurer to transfer the account to Vice President Coogler's mortgage company, to be "personally guaranteed by Jim Coogler."

By mid-year, the Trail re-route between the Cheese Factory and Tray Gap was completed and blue blazed, but had yet to be finally approved by the Forest Service.

The May *ATN* Trail Report from Georgia announced that the Frosty Mountain shelter had been destroyed by fire during the winter of 1967-68.

On a weekend Trail maintenance outing in May, 35 people combined forces to accomplish a large amount of work: renewing blazes and clearing trail on about 26 miles of trail.

A joint "special area clean-up" was planned for October with members of the Georgia Conservancy and the Sierra Club, both organizations having expressed a desire to combine hiking and other activities with the GATC. Litter on the Trail was a great problem during these years, so this special trip was planned to clean up one of the "blighted areas." The public was invited through Bob Harrell's column in the *Atlanta Constitution*, and plans were made to have a number of such "clean-ups" each year. The first "blighted area" to be policed was the Cheese Factory site near Tray Mountain. Randy Bordeaux reported on the trip in the bulletin:

Forty-four people were checked in Sunday morning at the roadside park in Robertstown. In less than two hours we had loaded 50 or more sacks with everything from whiskey bottles to old shoes. A dead cow at Tray Gap was even buried!

Finding we had so much energetic help, we moved to Unicoi Gap, ate lunch and headed for the campground on the headwaters of the Chattahoochee River and picked up about 30 bags of beer cans, etc. Still having excess energy, we moved back to Unicoi Gap and started to clean the mess at the Gap but soon gave up after filling 15 bags . . . and not even seeing a dent made in the pile! It is conceivable that Unicoi Gap will soon be the landfill of north Georgia if corrective active action is not taken . . . SOON.

The first scheduled hike of the year—from Amicalola Falls to Three Forks—was cancelled because of thick ice on the roads, thereby becoming, according to the leader, "one of the few cancelled trips in the history of the Club."

Participants in the winter LeConte trip were treated to a minus four degree temperature on Sunday morning. It had steadily descended from 19 degrees at the parking area, to seven degrees by suppertime, and minus four degrees by morning. Intrepid hikers enjoyed frozen hot chocolate around a COLD blazing fire. A solid sheet of ice gave descending hikers "many, many falls and slides" but no serious injuries.

In March, the GATC provided hike leaders for the monthly outing of the Georgia Conservancy. One hundred seventy-five people met at the Cheese Factory, and from there hikes were made to Tray Mountain and, for some, to Addis Gap.

Among the hikes planned for the weekend at the Greenbriar Cabin in the Smokies was "that perpetually infamous bushwhack (fiasco?) led by the noted G. Coffey along a never-the-same route (NOT by choice!) up to Charlie's Bunion or the Sawteeth or somewhere."

Other trips for the year off the AT were made to Panola Mountain, a return to LeConte in June, Raven Forks Wilderness in the Smokies, Fernbank Forest, and Florida Caverns State Park for Thanksgiving.

The Apple Tree Group Camp west of Franklin, North Carolina, was the site of the Multi-Club Meet, with 223 people representing ten clubs.

At the October annual meeting, the members approved the decision for incorporating the Club, and officers for 1969 were elected as follows: Jim Coogler, president; Al Thompson, first vice president; Randy Bordeaux, second vice president; Tom Stapler, Trail supervisor; Jo Sanders, secretary; Reg Hall, treasurer; Norma Seiferle, historian; Margaret Drummond, bulletin editor; Ed Seiferle, council.

The report of council member Hugh Chase to the meeting was deemed worthy of repeating, in part, in the bulletin "for the membership to read and reconsider," according to President Ed Seiferle:

. . . Originally the Trail clubs were formed to aid in the construction and maintenance of the Appalachian Trail. That policy is still viable and a demanding one upon the Club and all its members. I am of the opinion that most of us are not fully doing our part towards that goal. It should be brought to the attention of all in the Club that they should perform this required participation as a duty to the Club. In other words, the Club ought not to exist as an organization merely for the purpose of scheduling hikes for the pleasure of those so inclined to enjoy the outdoors and as a desire to express their inner self urges. It appears to me that if we attain the help of all the members, the facilities would increase in usefulness and desirability. . . .

Now that the Appalachian [Trail] has become well established, although not entirely free of displacement and improper use by others who are increasing by enormous numbers, another item has come into prominence and might continue in the future . . . protection of the Trail. This will complement the construction and maintenance duties as a third item. As events now move we may get considerable aid in this endeavor by the new legislative enactments of Congress as the National Scenic Trails Bill comes into action. . . .

If the proper amount of attention can be induced toward 'construction, maintenance and protection' in our activities, I believe there is no extreme hazard that will affect the existence of the Trail as a Scenic Wilderness Trail for the future. . . .

The almost simultaneous passage of the Trail Bill and the Blue Ridge Parkway Extension Bill toward the end of the year caused a flurry of activity by the GATC. President Ed Seiferle explained the problem in the December bulletin:

Many of you may be called on during the next two months, even during the holidays, for a rush job on our big Trail Relocation Project. We hope you will respond enthusiastically.

You all know by now that the extension of the Blue Ridge Parkway has been authorized. It will follow approximately some 50 miles of the 76 miles of present AT in Georgia. Consequently, the Club committed itself to a major relocation job, to find a new and desirable route for the Trail so as to minimize the impact of the Parkway upon it. You also know that the National Trails System Act was passed this fall and that the Appalachian Trail was designated as one of the first two National Scenic Trails. The Act requires that the exact route of the Trail and the related right-of- way be selected and published in the Federal Register. The Secretary of the Interior, who will administer the Appalachian Trail, has set his staff to beginning the right-of-way study.

Step one will be a complete aerial photographic survey of the Trail, to be completed by about mid-January. Large plastic X's are to be strategically placed (by us) along the route of the Trail to aid in the photo program.

THE PROBLEM IS THIS! We and the Appalachian Trail Conference have agreed that it would be pointless to describe officially the *present* route of the Trail when, within a relatively short time, we will have a newly relocated Trail route. Therefore, we want to locate, photograph and describe the new Trail. Our Trail Relocation Committees over the past several years have worked hard on the re-routing. They have scouted most of it and have about all of it completed *on maps, but not flagged in the field.* So between now and mid-January, we must get out, find, and possibly flag the whole route, and set out those X's for the photo mission. The Forest Service has volunteered their assistance.

1969

GEORGIA
APPALACHIAN
TRAIL CLUB, INC.

"AMAZING! IS THERE any job this Club can't do?" exclaimed leader J. P. Eidson at the response in January to the call for help in placing the large plastic X's along the route of the Trail. On a cold, foggy, rainy day, 26 members and guests, plus members of the Forest Service and the participants in the regular scheduled Club hike, met to make up teams of three or four, most of whom would venture into the trailless wilderness which they assumed would one day be the route of the AT. Eidson's bulletin account continued:

The weather forecast predicted occasional showers which was correct. There was also fog so at times we could see less than 100 yards in any direction. This was undesirable weather for map and compass work but not one used this as an excuse. . . .

Each team received maps and kits and were asked to note certain information on the maps to be used for future scouting trips.

Saturday night, one team reported that the key furnished them would not unlock the gate on the Low Gap Road. The locks may have been changed; however, another team with another key opened the gate. One team working south of Dicks Creek Gap travelled three miles, with no trails, to reach their first key point and were unable to locate it as a wrong turn had been made. Then, no distance reference point could be sighted in the fog and they were disoriented from then on. The team working out of Hog Pen Gap came out late and spent the night in Helen, Georgia, returning Sunday to place their last panel. The team working south out of Bly Gap placed three panels but darkness overtook them so they will place the last panel next week. The teams working Cow Rock Gap and Swaim Gap, working Unicoi and Red Clay Gap, working

Chattahoochee Gap to the Low Gap Road, working Addis Gap to Indian Grave Gap, completed the panel work.

It is now apparent that this panel work will be completed in time for the January flight. This is a tribute to the GATC and to everyone who had a part in this work. While doing the panel work, some of us recalled the work several years ago when the materials for shelter construction were carried over the mountains on pack frames to the shelter sites, the men packing 96 lb. bags of cement and women packing 50 lb. sacks of sand, then returning to carry lumber. Now we re-route, losing some of these shelters, but the strong team spirit was evident on Saturday with 76 miles of panel work to accomplish. . . .

Our sincere thanks go to the Forest Service for their help and for working with us at meetings in Gainesville. We also thank Len Foote who waited at several key points, sometimes for hours, to make photographs of several teams placing panels. And our deep respect for all those who boldly entered the wilds in the fog, mist and rain, proving truth in one of Goethe's sayings: 'Whatever you can do, or dream you can, begin it. Boldness has genius, power and magic in it.'

There were 35 panels to be put in place; the Forest Service had placed 12 of them on the Duncan Ridge section, and the GATC completed all but two of those remaining.

Clubs all along the Trail responded to the request to help in this "taking a picture of something four feet wide and eleven million feet long," according to Kay Fadner, although heavy snows delayed the project in some areas.

According to Henry Morris in an article in the September *ATN*, "The photographers for Aero Service who made the mapping photos of the Trail expressed great surprise at finding such 'real' mountains" in Georgia.

The regularly scheduled work trips during the year were not quite as popular as the January outing. In April and again in August, small groups spread out along the Trail to renew blazes, clear the Trail, and place markers. In May, another "anti-litter and clean-up demonstration" was held, with help from the Georgia Conservancy, the Sierra Club chapter, the Georgia Canoeing Association, the Boy Scout Area Council, the Bureau of Outdoor Recreation, *The Atlanta Constitution*, and the U.S. Forest Service! The Blood Mountain vicinity was the site of the project; between 300 and 500 pounds of litter was picked up around the shelter and hauled out by the Forest Service.

The Trail Report in the May *ATN* announced that a small creek south of Indian Grave Gap (the Trail at the time followed around the north side of Rocky Mountain and came onto the road to Indian Grave Gap for about a mile) had shifted its course onto the Trail. The Forest service had re-routed the Trail for about one half mile to avoid this section.

Now that the route of the Blue Ridge Parkway was firm, the GATC was faced with the tremendous job of locating and flagging the exact route of the parts of the Trail to be relocated. Shelter sites must be found as well as springs, overlooks, and other points of interest. The Forest Service would construct the

Trail and build whatever bridges were required, the first of which was to be a swinging bridge over the Toccoa River at the foot of Toonowee Mountain.

Henry Morris reviewed the history of this anticipated Trail project in an article in the September *ATN*. He pointed out the problems which would be encountered, one of which would be at Neel Gap, where a proposed four-lane highway would come through as well as the Parkway. The Trail here would be south of the gap, and would probably require at least one, if not two, tunnels to cross the two highways to get over Blood and Slaughter Mountains and onto Duncan Ridge. Morris concludes:

There is one prediction that can be made with certainty: when the road builders finish with these two areas, the mountains will never look the same again. If it can be done without destroying a lot of beauty, it will indeed be a miracle.

By spring, most of the members of the new Appalachian National Scenic Trail Advisory Council, mandated by the new Trail bill, had been appointed by the Secretary of the Interior. Georgia was well represented by Henry Morris, on the ATC Board of Managers, and Robin Jackson, of the Georgia State Parks Department. The first meeting of the body was held in Washington in November.

The *Georgia Mountaineer* sported a new look beginning in August. As editor Margaret Drummond explained:

With the July issue, the printing of the *Georgia Mountaineer* changed from a mimeograph to an offset printing process for the purpose of a clearer, more readable and presentable appearance. Simultaneously almost, our supply of paper with the preprinted masthead (traditionally symbolic of the Mountaineer) was depleted, so now, incidentally at a reduced cost, the masthead, as well as the typing, is being reproduced at the same time, and, of necessity, with the same color ink. And green it is . . . at least on a trial basis.

An all-time record attendance of 326 people was reported for the Multi-Club Meet, which was held at the Smoky Mountains Campground east of Gatlinburg. Eighty-nine GATCers made the trip. Les Holmes, who was now the full-time Executive Secretary of the ATC (his title was soon to be changed to Executive Director) spoke to the gathering at the business meeting.

According to an announcement in the October bulletin, "the interested hiking public" was to be invited to participate in the October 4 Club hike from Tray Mountain to Unicoi Gap. The Board of Directors had "approved the suggestion to make available (to the public) on a temporary experimental basis, this one GATC outing." It was "hoped that many of the members would also attend" to help out. Unfortunately, many of the members did *not* attend, but over 50 guests did. Margaret Drummond, the harried leader, referred to a picture of the crowd published in the bulletin, as she reported on the day, in part:

The Name of the Game Is: where are the GATC members in the photograph? If you look closely, you may see a scant half dozen familiar faces in the throng of more than 50 guests who assembled at the Dell Cliff Restaurant on October 4 at the invitation of the GATC for the Tray Mountain to Unicoi Gap hike. If you do, color them . . . *blue(?)*, because they are longing for the assistance of other Club members with the car shuttle and with keeping the crowd from straggling on the Trail; *white(?)*, because they momentarily paled before the array of 23-odd cars and drivers to be parked and transported respectively; *red(?)*, because, despite rather heroic efforts, they presented to the public an undeserved image of lack of organization and of inefficiency.

But frayed nerves seemed to be the only casualty of the day, as the hike was successfully negotiated.

From the earliest days of the Club, when hikes were taken between Tray Mountain and Unicoi Gap, a stop was inevitably made at the clear spring at a wide flat area along the Trail just south of Tray Mountain. This, perhaps to the puzzlement of newcomers, is called the "Cheese Factory." A first-hand account of the origin of this name was unearthed in 1969 by GATC member Ellen Hanks, and a report of it printed in the May bulletin. As the bulletin states, "The author describes a trip to Tray Mountain in May of 1848, on muleback and in the company of Major Edward Williams, 'principal proprietor of Nacoochee Valley.'" He tells the following story: About 1848 a dairy was established at this site on the side of "Trail Mountain" by Williams, a New Englander, who had come to live in the Nacoochee Valley 20 years earlier. Williams had hired as a dairyman another New Englander who "knew how to make butter and cheese" and had given Williams the idea of establishing the dairy, which was "said to be the only one in the entire state of Georgia." The letter writer and visitor to the area marveled that this dairy was "on top of a mountain, distant from the first farmhouse some fifteen miles, and inaccessible by any conveyance but that of a mule or well-trained horse," where the cattle fed on "the luxuriant weed of the wilderness." Tray Mountain was originally called Trail Mountain, and was "so named by the Cherokees, from the fact that they once had a number of trails leading to the summit, to which point they were in the habit of ascending for the purpose of discovering the campfires of their enemies during the existence of hostilities." [9]

At the annual meeting, according to the bulletin, "President Jim Coogler and historian Norma Seiferle each gave reports on the progress of the Club during the past year." As instructed in the new by-laws, the officers' and committee reports were included in the historian's report. Ralph Russell, the Trail information committee chairman, reported on an "information sheet" on the Club which had been prepared for "prospective members or others interested in the Trail." This would be sent to inquirers, saving the writing of many personal letters, as it answered most questions usually asked about the Club and the Trail. The membership chairman reported an average of ten members and eight guests attending Club activities during the year. He also explained the new system for membership qualification set forth in the new by-laws which was "now on a point system whereby a qualifying member must earn 15 points to be eligible for membership." According to the historian's report, "the strength of the Trail Act may well have its first test here in Georgia as there has been a request to place a relay tower on Springer Mountain." The tower, however, was "disapproved" by the Forest Service.

Although the Club had earlier refused the National Park Service's offer to extend the Trail to Mt. Oglethorpe again, another proposal was made in 1969 through Conference. Henry Morris re-checked the conditions in the area and presented his (unfavorable) findings to the GATC membership, which vetoed the suggestion once again.

The incorporation of the GATC in late 1968 had evidently necessitated a "complete revision" of the Club's by-laws. Jim Coogler, vice president at that time, and a lawyer, was asked to assume the chore. This he did, and in early 1969, as president, he brought the revised by-laws before the council (which was now referred to as the Board of Directors) for discussion. As he announced in the March bulletin: "The proposed by-laws have been agreed upon after two lengthy meetings of the Board of Directors, which were devoted entirely to their consideration. . . . Their adoption will be considered by the general membership at the scheduled . . . meeting."

At the meeting in May, which 22 members attended, the new by-laws, "after some changes," were "voted on and approved."

This was the first extensive revision since 1937, although several minor changes had been made at various times. Major (and/or controversial) changes made this time were:

—The purpose of the Club was changed to read:

The purpose of this organization shall be to educate its membership and the general public in ecological and environmental conservation of natural areas of the state of Georgia; to assist in the construction and maintenance of hiking trails in Georgia, especially the Georgia portion of the National Scenic Trail, known as the 'Appalachian Trail' for the use and enjoyment of the general public; to encourage hiking, camping, and other outdoor recreational activities by participation of its membership and guests in such activities, and to provide such advice and assistance as may be requested by the Appalachian Trail Conference, Inc.

The emphasis was different from the earlier version, which had read for over thirty years much as follows:

The purpose of this organization shall be to bring together persons interested in hiking and camping, and to conduct outings for their recreation and enjoyment; recognizing the mental, moral and spiritual elevation accompanying the climbing of mountains, surrounded by the grandeur and beauty of nature, to make the mountain regions of Georgia accessible by constructing and maintaining trails, shelters and campsites for hikers, especially on the Georgia portion of the National Scenic Trail known as the 'Appalachian Trail,' extending from Georgia to Maine; to create and foster in its members and in the general public a love and appreciation of the outdoors; to teach and to encourage public observation of out-of-doors ethics; to collect and publish authentic information concerning regions of interest to hikers in Georgia; to provide such advice and assistance as may be requested by the Appalachian Trail Conference, Inc.; and to preserve certain wilderness areas unspoiled by the encroachments of civilization; and to conserve our forests and other natural resources through departments of the state and national governments.

—The new document provided for five categories of membership: active, student, honorary, patrons, and friends of the Trail. The last two categories consisted of persons who would contribute an "amount fixed by the Board . . . as an expression of their support."

—The Board of Directors would consist of 11 persons (not to include the bulletin editor) whose titles would be: president, vice president–activities, vice president–membership, vice president–Trails supervisor, vice president–public relations, secretary–Board of Directors, secretary–historian, treasurer, and three directors at large.

—A point system was inaugurated for prospective members, who would be required to earn 15 activity points within a year to become a member.

—The spouse of an active member, upon payment of an additional fee, would be able to "enjoy all of the privileges" of membership except voting.

—The new document would require a two-thirds vote of the Board *denying* membership to an applicant, rather than two-thirds voting for acceptance.

These new by-laws reflected the philosophy and ambitions for the Club of the new president, Jim Coogler, who was very concerned with environmental issues, with the growth and support (or lack of it) of the Georgia Club, and with its seemingly restrictive membership requirements. Coogler had stated his concerns and hopes in his message in the 1969 yearbook, and concluded: "Monumental as it may seem, our goal is to reach the personal conscience and active concern [on conservation matters] of a major part of the general public."

Throughout 1969 Coogler had urged participation in GATC activities by interested non-members and other organizations, feeling that wider interest in the Trail and the Club would be beneficial to both; in November he announced in the bulletin that the Club now had 85 "Friends of the Trail." The large numbers of "guests" who came on some of the hikes, who were sometimes ignorant of Club rules and of proper hiking practices, sometimes caused problems and created potential dangers for the group or the individual. Some

Club members began hiking mostly on their own rather than participating in Club activities.

Though the new by-laws had been discussed extensively over a period of time, and had been finally approved by the Board and the membership, some members were still not happy with them, and evidently felt that they were a threat to some of the traditional ways and purposes of the Club. By the fall of the year, unhappiness with the situation, and with the administration of the Club, had spread among many Club members. Since most of the official records of this time are missing, it is difficult to know all of the facts, or to separate them from the "feelings." There were probably several factors involved: personal, social, "political," and organizational; but the main issues seemed to concern the trend—urged by Coogler and spelled out in the new by-laws—toward becoming basically a conservation organization and toward trying to build a much larger and more "open" membership. Many felt that the Club was heading away from its designated function of maintaining and protecting the Trail, and away from its close-knit "fellowship," and that Coogler was not adequately consulting the Board or the membership on many policies.

Other members felt that the Board *had* been consulted sufficiently on the issues, that conservation and the Trail could not be separated, and that the Club should "change with the times."

The discontent began to come to a head, and discussion among some members resulted in the formation of a "representative group" who wished to bring their concerns before the Board of Directors at the next Board meeting. Henry Morris, who would not be able to attend the meeting with the group, sent in a statement which voiced his concerns. Although his views may not have reflected the opinion of the entire organization, they were indicative of the very strong feelings of many long-standing members about the situation. As a member of the ATC Board of Managers, he spoke of the cooperative relationship of the GATC and Conference, which he seemed to feel was suffering somewhat, and continued:

Local maintaining Clubs, who have been assigned a portion of the Appalachian Trail to maintain, work closely with the local Forest Service and Park Service agencies on matters of concern in their respective areas. Matters of policy and matters of greater concern applying to the whole Trail and its relationship to the various government agencies and private land owners are solely a function of the Appalachian Trail Conference, Inc. and its Board of Managers.

Agreements for maintaining the Trail are made by the Conference with local clubs. These agreements may be changed or withdrawn by the Conference.

One of the principal assets of the GATC has been that it has attracted to its membership a diversity of interested, active, intelligent and compatible people who have respected the privileges and interests of other members and have promoted the enjoyment of this outdoor recreational activity.

The GATC recently was granted a Charter of Incorporation just as a new president was elected to office.

Unfortunately, this new president appears to be obsessed with the idea that the entire structure of the GATC needs changing and that he is the man of destiny to make things over according to his own ideas, disregarding, for the most part, ideas and desires of most of the members.

Under the pretense of being a legal necessity, many ideas have been incorporated into the by-laws which are not in accord with wishes and desires of the membership.

The GATC has apparently become a one-man-controlled organization where no free discussion or reports are allowed without prior approval of the president.

Trail Club trips in the past have afforded the opportunity to its members of carefree trips with friendly, interesting, harmonious and compatible people seeking a relief from the stresses and tensions of everyday living. Inviting great numbers of people on hikes, whether they have a basic interest in hiking or just want a nice outing arranged for them, imposes a great responsibility upon the leaders of hikes; and in most instances, dispenses with any possibility of enjoyment for themselves.

There is much work ahead in selecting a new route for more than fifty miles of Trail which will require people who are interested in this project, have some idea of the method of doing it, specifications to be met . . . and are willing to come again and again to accomplish it. This cannot be done if the leaders are charged with the responsibility of herding a group who are not woodsworthy through the mountains, trying to keep them moving along and seeing that no one gets lost. . . .

He noted with regret the withdrawal of Club funds (in 1968) from the bank used for many years, and the exclusion of the bulletin editor from the Board of Directors. He concluded:

There are many other things, but suffice it to say the GATC has operated very successfully for its members for many years. Many members who have moved away have written back to say that though they had found and joined other hiking clubs, they valued their association with the GATC most of all.

Many members are expressing concern over the course of events and it is entirely possible that demands will be made for the Club to be operated more like it has been for many years past.

A "memorandum to members" after the November Board meeting related the events, and began:

Fifteen Club members attended the November 4, 1969, meeting of the Board of Directors, and expressed concern over some aspect of the recent functions and activities of the Club. Stating that he had been asked by some of these 15 members, and others, to represent them, Tom Aderhold asked for and received permission to read a statement.

Aderhold began his statement:

A representative group of GATC members, which includes some present officers of the

Club, has gathered here tonight to express serious concern over certain recent club activities. Also, to question the possible future direction which the Club may be engaging upon. The numerical size of this group, by necessity, has been limited but it represents a vast cross section of the Club. It has the full and active support of every past president since 1954, excepting Bob Scott who now lives in California, and of past office holders representing over seventy man years of service in office.

On behalf of this group and other members, I have been asked to read a statement:

The year 1969 has been an eventful one for the GATC. Some of the events have been beneficial to the Club; others, unfortunately, not so.

We are here tonight to express our own concern and, at their request, the concern of a sizable number of other Club members, about the direction in which the Club is being taken. The changes, so far, are subtle, but the results are becoming unmistakably evident. We don't like the changes, and we wish to have them reversed.

In discussing this concern with the members, we have made a serious effort to identify, specifically, what points have given rise to it. Rather than any single source, however, this concern seems to be the summation of a wide variety of individualized items making for the overall feeling of distress.

Very disturbing seem to be the efforts recently being made toward bigness, toward throwing the Club open to everyone, toward inviting the general public to participate in any and all Club activities, toward widespread publicity, toward decentralization of Club interest.

The corollary to this is the consequent loss of the sense of fellowship and close friendship that has been so precious to many of us over the years, the loss of the sense of oneness with nature that follows from the tranquillity of a comfortable, happy walk in the wild.

Disturbing also is the importance being placed on money income for the Club, as expressed in the drive for increased membership, the invention of Friends of the Trail, and of Patrons. This all smacks of commercialism, and this certainly is not the tradition of the GATC.

But most disturbing of all are the effects this drive toward bigness, this seeking after money, is having upon the real purposes for which the Club exists and for which most of us joined it—the relationship with the Trail itself, with the Trail Conference, and with nature.

The Trail is becoming only a means to the end of larger membership rolls; maintenance of the Trail but a necessary chore; the Conference an inanimate entity 'out there' that has little meaning and relationship to the GATC; nature itself, as expressed by the Trail and our beautiful Georgia countryside, nothing but a route to publicity.

This may be a bit emotional in expression, but these *are* the emotions many of us feel and many of us have expressed in talking about why we are disturbed, even distressed, by what is happening to our GATC.

Now, what do we recommend? We suggest to you that we revise our program, discontinue our efforts toward widespread recruiting, reduce our public relations efforts to just that needed for advancement of the Trail, minimize our money raising program, and return the Club to that hiking fellowship that it once was and that we find woefully disappearing in recent months.

We therefore propose the following specific actions tonight:

1. The appointment of a special committee, with the approval of the Board, to reconsider the by-laws of the Club and to draft revisions thereof aimed at achieving the objectives of the membership; said revisions to be incorporated into the by-laws under the prescribed procedures.

2. The passage of a resolution by the Board instructing the officers and members to discontinue efforts to raise money and to achieve a broad, effectively non-hiking membership, including promotion of Friends of the Trail and Patron classifications of membership.

3. The passage of a resolution by the Board instructing the officers, especially that officer concerned primarily with public relations, and the membership in general, to discontinue, effective immediately, aggressively publicizing the Club and its activities, and encouraging the general public to participate widely and frequently in Club programs.

4. The passage of a resolution by the Board supporting the relationship of the GATC with the Appalachian Trail Conference and proposing financial, physical and moral support of the Conference by the Club.

5. The passage of a resolution by the Board stating that it is the sense of the Club that the program, activities and efforts of the officers and members of the Club be so directed as to return the Club to its historic role as a group dedicated primarily to hiking, to the love and appreciation of the out-of-doors, to the fellowship and enjoyment of hiking and camping together, and to the support and maintenance of the AT, especially that part located in Georgia.

6. To include immediately the bulletin editor in all Board meetings with full voice, being limited only to a non-voting Board Member due to by-law restrictions.

7. That no officer transact any major business of the Club concerning policy, commitments or activities without first clearly proposing and outlining same before the Board, including defining all possible benefits and repercussions, and then majority support of the Board to be obtained before such action be taken. Highly controversial issues of a major nature should be laid on the table until expressions of opinions can be obtained by Board Members from the membership in general.

It is said that Coogler had not been aware of how widespread was the discontent, or of how strong the feelings. The meeting, held at Coogler's home, was a very distressing and emotional one. In the end the "representative group" prevailed.

The "memorandum to members" related the results of the meeting:

Subsequently, the Board passed two pertinent motions, one implementing point 1, the other implementing points 2 and 3. The second motion deferred for the time being further promotion of and publicity on the concepts of Friends of the Trail and of Patrons, as well as of the more promotional aspects of the Club's recent public relations efforts. The other moved the appointment of a special committee, to be chaired by Tom Aderhold, whose function is to review the by-laws of the Club and to propose revisions thereof. To this committee were appointed the following, in addition to the chairman: Hugh Chase, Gannon Coffey, Margaret Drummond, Ann Eidson, J. P. Eidson, Jim Engle, Ed Seiferle and Al Thompson.

Points 4 through 7 were discussed to some extent but no specific actions thereon were taken by the Board.

The Board wants all the Club members to know of this recent occurrence. It solicits questions, comments, and suggestions from all of them on any pertinent point. Please contact any committee or Board member at once (phone numbers follow), for it is hoped to complete action on the by-laws revision in the near future. . . .

With all comments in hand, the committee, in accord with Article II of the by-laws, will submit its recommendations for amendment, if any, to the Board of Directors. The Board shall submit the proposed amendments, with its own recommendations for action thereon (both majority and minority recommendations are provided for), to the membership at least 15 days prior to the date of a membership meeting to be called specifically to act on the by-laws revision.

It is hoped that all members will give this situation very serious thought and will participate in its resolution.

Not all of the Club members agreed with the statement and recommendations of the "representative group." Ed Johnson wrote to Tom Aderhold in December expressing his views:

. . . First of all, though it may be the result of a brief and casual observation, I would say that most of the difficulties have arisen due to personality clashes rather than a difference in basic creeds. All of us are bound together by the common love of the outdoors, particularly with hiking. It would not seem to be too great a thing for adults joined together by this common bond to sit down and eliminate the difficulties.

Tom, I do not believe that bigness, in itself, is either automatically good or bad. Our organization can be good or mediocre, whether big or small. It is written, and I personally believe, that wilderness will be preserved in direct proportion to the number of people who appreciate its value. This statement would then bring up the idea that we are a hiking club, not a conservation outfit. Again, speaking from a personal standpoint, I do not believe the two can ever be separated. If you love the outdoors, you desire to see it protected for the future.

I would also like to make a statement regarding the loss of the sense of fellowship. The way this statement in the report is presented, it seems to imply that I, as a new member, may have intruded upon someone's private domain. This is certainly not the way I visualized the Club. I do not expect to become very close friends with everyone who is a member of the Club. I do expect to be constantly thrown into association with people who have companion interests, thereby allowing me a broader spectrum from which to select additional friends.

In looking back through publications from the Appalachian Trail Conference, I sense an active desire to increase membership and increase involvement for the use and protection of the Appalachian Trail. With this in mind, I do not think that all of our present trends are in error.

In the interest of time and space, that's all the personal credo I'll burden you with at the present time. There will be additional opportunities for discussion I am sure, or I would be happy to discuss it with you or any other member of the Club at length. I, too, have very strong feelings where my love of the outdoors is concerned.

I look forward to seeing you on the Trail soon.

1970

GEORGIA
APPALACHIAN
19 TRAIL CLUB, INC. 30

T HE NEW BY-LAWS revision committee completed its work by January, and brought their proposed revisions before the Board of Directors. A number of changes were made by the Board, and the revised by-laws were approved and recommended to the membership by a majority of the Board members.

Major changes were: restating the purpose of the Club much as it had been before; deletion of the Friends of the Trail and Patrons membership categories; returning officers' titles to the previous description; returning the bulletin editor to Board member status; returning to the earlier method of denying membership (lack of majority vote *for*); the addition of the stipulation that spouses must meet membership requirements; and the addition of the stipulation that directors must have been a member for five years, the president for four years and other officers for two years.

A "majority report and recommendations" and a "minority report and recommendations" were presented to the membership along with the revised document. The majority report contained the revised sections, and was concurred in by seven Board members and in part by three. The minority report contained the revised sections not concurred in by the three; these sections were: the deletion of membership categories Friends of the Trail and Patrons, the method of voting in denying membership by the Board, the length of membership qualifications for directors and officers, and the stipulation that spouses must meet all qualifications for membership.

264

The April bulletin made the following succinct announcements:

February 27, 1970: A special meeting of the membership was held to consider revision of the by-laws as recommended by the Board of Directors and the By-Laws Revision Committee. Sixty-four members were present and approved the revisions as recommended. [There was no question that the membership was aroused; according to those present at the meeting, the mood was nearly unanimous in favor of ending the Coogler innovations and returning the Club to its former state.]

March 12, 1970: 'Final Memo from the President to Members and Friends: Considering both the provisions of the newly adopted by-laws and the circumstances leading up to their adoption, I do not feel that I can continue in good conscience to serve as President of the Georgia Appalachian Trail Club. Accordingly, I have submitted my resignation to the Board of Directors. Sincerely yours, Jim Coogler.'

March 17, 1970: At the meeting of the Board of Directors, the resignation of Jim Coogler was accepted. According to the by-laws, Al Thompson, vice president, succeeds to the office of president. The Board then elected Jim Engle to fill the position of vice president. The following committee chairmen were approved by the Board: Conservation, Ed Seiferle, chairman; Trail Relocation, Grant Wilkins, chairman. Please make the above changes and additions in your yearbook.

The Board decided in March to refund to each of the three Patrons the $25.00 contribution they had given to the Club, with a letter of explanation. The Friends of the Trail would continue to receive the bulletin for the rest of the year, and would then be informed, if they sought to renew, that the category no longer existed.

In viewing the Coogler presidency, today's historian has to ask the question: was it his ideas that aroused such opposition or simply the way he went about achieving them? The answer is probably both. For almost forty years, since Warner Hall had put his stamp on the personality of the Club, it had remained a group of *friends* who were *dedicated* to an ideal. Jim Coogler believed in the dedication to a goal of outdoor conservation but he failed to understand the importance which members had attached to the friendships associated with the GATC, and the very difficulty of getting into the Club had made it something to be cherished. Were a vote to be taken today, there would probably still be a minority of members who would vote favorably for the *ideas* Jim Coogler espoused, but the vast majority would again vote to keep the sense of intimacy and exclusiveness that have been a trademark of the GATC for over fifty years.

Despite internal strife and organizational changes, activities of the Club, of course, proceeded. The year began with a four-day trip to the Cumberland Gap National Historical Park for a look at some interesting new territory. Tom Aderhold, as usual, led the winter hike to Mt. LeConte, with all but one hiking up in 12 inches of snow. The one—Roger Losier—went up by helicopter with the food and supplies, but, nevertheless, was thanked for his help each year in carrying in supplies and opening and closing up the lodge for the group.

After being unsuccessful the previous year because of heavy snow, John Myers again in April failed to find the trail to Warwoman Dell from Rabun Bald. As he put it:

Sunday morning we headed up into an acreage of laurel—and in the middle of this, the new yellow blazes stopped. . . . In an effort to locate the trail, Leader Myers headed due east and Co-Leader Russell headed due west into the mists. About 15 minutes later, in a display of real compassmanship, they collided in the fog. A decision was made to head south down the ridge we were supposed to be traveling. In a fog, one ridge looks pretty much like another, and shortly before noon, the Leader announced that Alternate Plan #202 would be employed. This meant turning due west and getting the heck out of there. Due west in this case turned out to be quite a trip in its own right. Ask any trip member. Just as we picked up the road into Mountain City, the rain came again to speed us on our way.

Margaret Drummond again attracted a crowd—52 people including 31 guests—on a hike from Blue Ridge Gap down Hightower Creek. Other trips to different places included a Blackburn State Park gold mine trip, the Odum Scout Trail in Alabama, Shining Rock Wilderness and the Crooked River State Park for Thanksgiving.

The announcement in the bulletin of the meeting place and time for each trip had brought unexpected numbers of guests and created difficulties in making arrangements for car shuttles, etc. At the March Board meeting, it was decided to discontinue including the information; participants would be required to call the leader for details.

The lagging participation on work trips called for drastic measures, which came in the form of John Myers in the guise of "Alice." As Trail supervisor, he announced the upcoming April maintenance trip in the bulletin:

It is trail maintenance time again and we will celebrate by the Grand Opening of the North Georgia Branch of Alice's Restaurant, and you can get anything you want just so long as it is spaghetti or chili dinner Saturday night. This is guaranteed to be the best meal in Andrews Cove for 25¢ or your money grumpily refunded. After dinner we won't argue if you insist upon helping with the dishes or even if you don't. Entertainment provided afterwards around a big campfire on a do-it-yourself basis.

We almost forgot to tell you that you can have a full day's work on the Trail before supper at no extra charge. If you insist, you can put in a part day Sunday as well. THERE IS PLENTY TO DO AND WE NEED YOUR HELP.

This, or something, brought out a crowd which incidentally did some trail work. As Myers reported:

. . . On Saturday morning, we met in Robertstown and divided into groups led by Tom Aderhold, Ralph Russell, Mal Sanford, and Gannon Coffey. On the south end of the Trail, a number of our group watched Ed Garvey start a full-length hike of the Trail,

Georgia to Maine, before starting work on that end. The leader and co-leader took Lou Hoben up to the Cheese Factory and gave her four giant sacks and let her pick up trash to fill them while they watched. Roger Losier and Wayne Campbell arrived late in the day and helped Lou. Saturday night we tied on that feed sack.

Sunday morning, those of us able to do so went back to work on the Trail, led by Randy Bordeaux, while members of the Trail Relocation Committee went over to the location of the proposed new trail to do some work. Tom Aderhold had a slight difference of opinion with the Chairman of the Trail Relocation Committee about getting out of his sleeping bag promptly at 6:30. Tom now has the only section of the new Trail that has both an impassable swamp and a 400 foot high sheer rock cliff. Tom also had the air let out of his mattress at 6:31 a.m. . . .

Alice's reappearance in August was not quite as popular, but the small crowd accomplished some necessary chores.

The Forest Service had requested "permanent plans" by early 1971 for the relocation of the Trail off of the Blue Ridge Parkway route. A call went out in April for volunteers to help in the flagging of this route and in exploring the corridor for "springs, shelter sites, views, overlooks, etc." It had been announced at the March Board meeting that "all funding for the Parkway has stopped," so the actual relocation could be as much as ten years away.

The Trail Report in the May *ATN* noted several items of interest: the Trail between Indian Grave Gap and Tray Gap was now completely off of the road; the Tray Mountain shelter was soon to be relocated; a new trail had been built from Jack's Gap to the Brasstown Bald Visitor Center; "extremely active bears" in the area between Unicoi and Tesnatee Gaps had been destroying signs; a re-routed trail from Slaughter Gap to the top of Blood Mountain was being built.

A re-route over Rocky Mountain was planned during the year as a continuation of the effort to remove the Trail from roads—in this case the Indian Grave Gap road. On a Club hike in August, 40 participants followed the proposed new route, enjoying the fine views from the top of Rocky Mountain.

The 18th meeting of the Appalachian Trail Conference was held in May at Shippensburg State College in Pennsylvania, For the first time, the attendance passed the 400 mark. There is no record of GATC attendance at the meeting, although the *ATN* report records attendance "from the 14 Trail states." The principal topic of concern was the National Trails System Act and how it would be implemented by the Conference, the Federal Government and the states. The Conference had been held every three years for many years; but, according to the *ATN*, "the Board of Managers decided that on the basis of what was accomplished at Shippensburg and what will need to be done in the next crucial years, a meeting should be held in 1972."

Later in the year, through an article in the *ATN*, Stan Murray discussed the re-assessment of the role of Conference in view of "the acceptance of responsibility for the Trails' future by Federal and state agencies." The Board of Managers had, in November, adopted six objectives for the Conference, which included: providing information and service to members, Trail users, and clubs; maintaining a public relations program; building the membership; maintaining working relationships with agencies involved in the Trail; and seeing that the AT is a well-maintained and respected natural footpath.

In Georgia, the Forest Service would assume a more active role in the upkeep of the Trail as participation by the GATC in its maintenance seemed to become less active.

Early in the year, Margaret Drummond was appointed editor of the Conference guidebook to the Smokies, Nantahalas, and Georgia. This work had previously been done by Conference staff with the help of various Club members who checked out the Trail. In the future each guidebook was to have a local editor from a Club maintaining a section of Trail covered in the book.

The Multi-Club Meet was held at the Mountain Wilderness Campground near Mt. Mitchell. The GATC was represented by 36 persons. Next year the meet was to be hosted by the GATC.

The bulletin announced in September the death of Larry Freeman, long-time faithful member, who had been active in the Club until shortly before his death.

The annual meeting in October featured a talk by Robin Jackson, assistant Director of State Parks; Charles Hunnicutt and Jim Milner of the Forest Service, also present, presented a plaque to the GATC "in recognition of its establishment and maintenance of the Appalachian Trail." The Club, according to the bulletin account, "presented a framed Expression of Appreciation (done by our artist, Mary Eidson) to Henry Morris for all his years of service and dedication to our Club and to the Conference. For a brief moment, Henry was actually speechless! He received a standing ovation from all present." Committee reports were given and officers elected were: Al Thompson, president; Jim Engle, vice president; Ellen Hanks, secretary; Harry Smith, treasurer; Ralph Russell, membership director; John Myers, Trail supervisor; Bob Taylor, Trails information director (a new office on the Board); Margaret Drummond, historian; Ann Eidson, bulletin editor; Tom Aderhold, director.

Another of the frequent "conservation alerts" was brought to the attention of the GATC in the November bulletin: a road was to be built through the Joyce Kilmer Memorial Forest. A protest hike was planned for late in October.

One of the last of the annual trips to the Dillard House was made in November. Times were changing, the Dillard House had changed, and attendance was dwindling on this trip which had been a favorite for many years.

The Christmas/Birthday party in December celebrated the 40th anniversary of the GATC. Almost 100 persons attended, "including many long-time present and former members." Early members and past presidents were acknowledged, old photographs were shown, and Charles Elliott, one of the founders of the Club, gave a "brief but warm and interesting talk." The party was an "unqualified success."

The year ended on a sad note with the deaths of Marion (Mrs. Henry) Morris, an active member since the earliest days of the Club, and Mrs. E. G. Field, a member for many years.

1971

GEORGIA
APPALACHIAN
19│TRAIL CLUB, INC.│30

T HE BLUE RIDGE PARKWAY was once again the "number one topic of our Club" during 1971. As was noted in 1970, the funding of the project had never materialized from Congress, and as time went by and the conservation movement grew, the public became more aware of the impending road.

In the January, 1971, *ATN*, an article discussed the background of the proposed Parkway extension and stated, "In recent months, as location and design hearings have been held on the extension, there has been considerable public expression of dismay over the fact that the Parkway would displace parts of the AT in Georgia, or even that the Parkway should be built in Georgia at all. . . . There is now a new wave of concern. . . ."

At the January, 1971, GATC Board meeting, the Parkway was "the major topic of discussion." Henry Morris reported on a hearing held in Canton, Georgia, on the Parkway right-of-way, at which "large numbers of people were present." Robin Jackson of the State Parks Department, and a member of the Appalachian National Scenic Trail Advisory Council, attended the Board meeting and spoke about the Canton hearing, urging GATC support for continued opposition to the highway. She reminded the Board that the Club was alone in protesting in 1964, but now "people everywhere are speaking out." Conservation committee chairman, Ed Seiferle, stated that now was the time to renew the discussion on the Parkway and consider at this meeting what steps to take. Board members suggested that a committee be formed of groups who were interested in stopping the Parkway, and a motion was passed to "proceed to develop our objections," leading up to an "official public hearing" on the matter. Ed Seiferle was named to head the committee.

Seiferle reported in March that "quite a bit had happened" since January. The GATC had been instrumental in forming a group of some 20 organizations, including the Izaak Walton League, Audubon Society, Sierra Club, Georgia Parks Commission, Georgia Conservancy, and Wildlife Management Institute, into a coalition—to be called the Georgia Mountains Coalition. As Seiferle reported, "They will work together to try to draw up an acceptable stand . . . and will attempt to bring about reconsideration of the Blue Ridge Parkway and other constructions in the North Georgia Mountains."

The GATC drew up a position paper "to express the feeling of this organization," stating that, while, if necessary, they would honor the 1964 agreement, their participation in the agreement did not signify satisfaction with the situation. The paper called for reopening of the question of the route location, and asked that a thorough study of the impact of the Parkway, as well as a comprehensive study of the whole Georgia mountain area, be made. It called for a moratorium on "all plans for and development of roads" in the Georgia mountains pending completion of the studies. The paper "could be the pattern or statement we could use at public hearings."

Seiferle reported during the year on the "various activities of the Georgia Mountains Coalition," which included writing to Secretary of the Interior asking for a moratorium on road building.

The official route of the Appalachian National Scenic Trail was published, along with maps, in the October 9, 1971, *Federal Register*, as had been mandated by the National Scenic Trails Act. For Georgia, the route, of course, was the *proposed* one to be built to avoid the Blue Ridge Parkway. The declaration of this route as the official AT was to haunt the GATC for at least the next ten years.

Twenty-two GATCers began the year on New Year's Day with a hike in the Smokies from Newfound Gap north on the AT to the Kephart shelter. In March, John Myers again attempted to find the Rabun Bald Trail, but was foiled completely by the weather. Fifty-three hikers headed for Mt. LeConte in October, as reported by leader Jim Coogler:

A heavy fog (some may call it rain) covered the mountains Saturday lending a mystical quality to the virgin forest and intensifying the fresh aroma of balsam in the air. Some hikers, enjoying the new flush facility at the Lodge, reported a brilliantly clear sky around midnight Saturday but the fog returned before sunrise. Fall colors were presented under spots of sunshine Sunday morning in the Alum Cave Bluffs area as the curtain of fog parted for brief periods.

A large number, if not most of the hikers, found ways of going up one trail, down the other and eventually getting back to their cars. So once again, GATC members, family and guests enjoyed, fog and all, a privilege not easy to come by, for it is reported that most weekends at the Lodge are already booked up for next year.

A trip to Alexander Springs in Florida's Ocala National Forest at Thanksgiving featured hiking on portions of the new Florida Trail. The Club was by now generally having two overnight trips and one day hike each month.

By May, 30 miles of the proposed relocated AT had been flagged. Three trips, led by members of the Trail Relocation Committee, had been scheduled in the spring over sections of the proposed Trail between Springer Mountain and Slaughter Mountain. The trips were bushwhacks—for "eager adventurers"— over the rough, uncleared, flagged route. The "first traverse" of the section attracted 29 members and guests. Grant Wilkins reported on the adventures of the day for the bulletin, and added, "I almost forgot about one group who did get to within a quarter of a mile of the river, but they did not finish their hike until 9:30 p.m. Ask Ed Seiferle, Harold Glover, or Lyman Emerson. . . . The whole group did feel that. . . the new Trail is more isolated and can be an even better Trail than our present one." The second trip drew a smaller group, and they pronounced the section between Highway 60 and Fish Gap "a tremendously attractive section of potential AT."

On the third trip, four people covered most of the section between Slaughter and Fish Gaps. J. P. Eidson reported on the day:

'What do you mean, steep?' I asked. Ed Seiferle, retying his bootlace, looked up. 'J. P., surely you are not serious about routing the Trail around here.' 'Well,' I replied, 'the Forest Service road is on the other side of the mountain; this is the only way.' Lyman Emerson, holding on to a tree, said, 'He has followed the contour fairly closely slabbing around the mountain.' 'Yeah,' added George Owen, 'but one leg needs to be shorter than the other.' 'What I can't understand,' said Ed, 'is how are we going to hang the Trail in here?'

After four hours of struggle, we reached Wildcat Knob which ends my three-mile section and begins George Owen's section. As we rested, we tried to identify several plants and agreed with Lyman that we needed our wives along to help with the identification. The clusters of wild iris looked like orchid bouquets.

George Owen took the lead as we switch-backed into Mulky Gap, then began the ascent to the summit of Akin Mountain. Along this slope, Ed and Lyman slipped on the wet moss and slid down the mountain. 'Just stay down there,' yelled George, 'you slid into the next county. We will bring the car around from Fish Gap and pick you up at Mulky Gap.' George and I proceeded up Akin Mountain which is appropriately named, as you are aching when you reach the top. Three hours bushwhack, and we reached Fish Gap. 'What do you think of my section?' asked George. 'Well,' I answered, 'I believe you need to rework several places that are too steep.' George turned to me, 'What do you mean, steep?'

Grant Wilkins stated at the September Board meeting that the Forest Service should be urged to start clearing sections of the new Trail already marked before the tapes were destroyed.

The one Trail maintenance outing of the year was used to "dress up" the parts of the Trail which would be hiked by the participants in the Multi-Club Meet. Alice's restaurant was opened for business at Woody Gap at the end of the day to serve the 23 workers.

Since the passage of the Trailway Bill, which stated that the Trail would be "administered" by the Secretary of the Interior, the Forest Service had been much more involved in maintenance of the Georgia Trail; also, since most of the Georgia Trail supposedly would be relocated, it might be assumed that neither the Club nor the Forest Service felt the necessity for a great deal of work on the existing Trail.

In May, five members of the GATC met in Gainesville with Forest Service officials to discuss the Trail relocation and other matters. Maps of the location of the proposed Trail were furnished the Forest Service, and, according to the Board minutes, "The question of keeping Tesnatee Gap shelter for a historic site was discussed" and agreed to by the Forest Service.

By summer, a new shelter had been built by the Forest Service on Tray Mountain, and the relocation of the one-mile section of Trail over Rocky Mountain into Indian Grave Gap was completed and blue blazed.

Reporting in the bulletin on a trip from Big Stamp Gap to Hawk Mountain, leader Lyman Emerson states, "The leader regrets having promised a view from the fire tower on Hawk Mountain. The Forest Service, who now rely on planes for spotting fires, had removed this old landmark just a couple of weeks before."

The Multi-Club Meet, hosted by the GATC this year, was held at the meadow on top of Hawk Mountain. The Forest Service had agreed to "grade, gravel and work" the road to the top of the mountain, and to furnish generators, public address systems, and portable toilets. The Army Ranger station nearby offered the use, if needed, of the first aid station, wrecker, ambulance, and helicopter. A 500-gallon water tank would be available "to bring water up the mountain." It is said that the help of the Rangers was required to push and haul many of the campers and trailers up the steep road to the meadow.

The 112 participants in the Meet enjoyed the views and the hikes, a film on the training of Army Rangers shown by the Ranger camp commander, and a "comedy skit" by Gannon Coffey and Tom Aderhold on how to scout a trip in the Army Ranger training area, complete with sound effects by the Commander.

Officers for 1972 were elected at the annual meeting as follows: Al Thompson, president; Grant Wilkins, vice president; Mandy Coffey, secretary; Harry Smith, treasurer; Ralph Russell, membership director; Lyman Emerson, Trail supervisor; Bob Taylor, Trail information director; Mary Eidson, historian; John Myers, bulletin editor; Henry Morris and Margaret Drummond, directors at large.

At the Christmas party, in between greetings and conversations among friends old and new, the officers for the coming year were installed and small gifts, brought by all of the participants, were passed out and opened.

1972

GEORGIA
APPALACHIAN
19|TRAIL CLUB,INC.|30

THE GEORGIA MOUNTAIN COALITION continued to work "with no fanfare" to try to get the Blue Ridge Parkway put "on ice" until a land use study of the area could be made, and also to consider the question of whether or not there should be a Parkway at all. By fall the coalition had also, according to GATC conservation committee chairman Ed Seiferle, "undertaken its own recreational analysis of the area and prepared charts showing the impact of the proposed Parkway extension and of Georgia 400 (highway) upon a variety of natural resource characteristics of the region." (Highway 400 was to be a four-lane limited access highway from Atlanta to North Carolina, crossing the mountain crest at Neel Gap.)

A preliminary draft of the Parkway's "environmental impact" study was distributed in August, and it was declared by Ed Seiferle to be a "real whitewash." In fact, the report was merely a propaganda statement in favor of the Parkway, and not a real study of the effects of the Parkway on any aspect of the environment or the AT. Both the Club and Stan Murray of the ATC wrote to Granville Lyles, Superintendent of the Blue Ridge Parkway, refuting or protesting many of the "statements, inferences, errors and omissions" made in the document. The GATC letter declared, "We find in this report . . . very little evidence of any thinking more current than that of the early 1960's." It proposed that the document be "reworked by qualified non-Federal experts so that the nation can benefit by application of modern concepts of its environmental needs and resources."

"The Blue Ridge Parkway: Sunshine and Storm" was the title of an article by Lucy Justus in the September 17 *Atlanta Journal and Constitution Magazine.* The article began, "It has been fascinating to watch the Blue Ridge Parkway storm shape up. First the sunshine, then the clouds, the thunder and the lightning." The article outlined the background of the plans for the Parkway, saying that until early October, 1970, all was sunshine. The clouds began to gather during that month after the announcement of the "open meeting" in Canton, held to "inform the public about the overall plan," and Georgians began thinking what effect this Parkway would have on the beauty of the mountains. "Lightning flashed" at the Canton meeting when many statements of protest were heard. At another meeting in Clayton nearly two years later—in May, 1972—the "thunder crashed" when another huge crowd expressed more opposition. Superintendent Lyles conceded: "You people don't seem to want a Parkway." According to the *Magazine* article, "The proverbial hail and high water had arrived." But unfortunately it had not yet completely drowned the Blue Ridge Parkway.

Under the direction of Trail relocation chairman Herb Daniel, flagging and blazing of the Duncan Ridge Trail was nearly complete. A newspaper article in May, 1972, announced "Appalachian Trail Re-routed in Georgia in Order to Avoid Traffic," saying that the new Trail was "open for public use"—except between Slaughter Gap and Wolfpen Gap.

At the annual meeting in October, Henry Morris suggested that this Trail be referred to as the "Loop Trail." Since the Parkway issue was perhaps dying, but not dead, the Club was trying not to refer to it as the relocated AT for fear that would signal to the Parkway officials the Club's acceptance of defeat in the battle.

On *the* work trip of the year on the AT, a number of sections of Trail, including the two relocated sections between Unicoi and Tray Gaps, were blazed or re-blazed by 18 participants. The bulletin account announced that the beginning of the section of the "new relocation" between Springer Mountain and Three Forks was "now blue blazed and partially cleared," and was shorter by two miles than the white blazed Trail. The shorter route was announced in the May *ATN* Trail report.

Trail supervisor Lyman Emerson had been scouting for a location for the new shelter on Springer Mountain, and recommended a site near the summit close to the present and the future AT. This site was approved by the Board, and, with the help of the Army Rangers in airlifting the materials to the site, the shelter was completed by the Forest Service by May.

According to Emerson's report at the annual meeting:

. . . Relocation of the Trail at Miller Gap took place about the same time. Here, a few miles east of Woody Gap, is one of just a couple of spots in Georgia where the Trail crossed private property. When the owner disclosed plans for another pond and a fenced-in area, the Trail Club directors readily agreed with a Forest Service proposal to relocate the Trail on National Forest land. Harold Glover and I helped Bill Johnson and other Forest Service fellows scout and flag the new route. The Trail was cleared by the Forest Service and white blazed by the Trail Club. We have not measured this relocation but estimate its length to be ⅝ of a mile, about ¼ mile longer than the section it replaces.

Emerson also recommended relocation off of the road of about two miles of Trail between Cooper and Hightower Gaps, and between Amicalola Falls and Nimblewill Gap.

Participation in Trail maintenance was still lagging, and also in his annual report, Emerson stated:

Maintenance of the Trail in Georgia is one of the primary purposes of our Club, and I feel that every active member should have an opportunity to participate. Some progress in this direction was made in 1972 by increasing the number of sections assigned for maintenance from 12 to 16. There are now 20 members sharing maintenance assignments, including 11 named during 1972.

Funds for two new shelters were announced in July, and the sites chosen were Low Gap and Slaughter Gap. (In November, Emerson's report to the Board stated that the Blood Mountain "stone house" would be torn down.) A site also had been selected for a shelter at Whitley Gap. In October, Club members met with the Forest Service at Low Gap to chose a spot for the shelter there.

Weather was the outstanding feature of the first few hikes of the year. On the New Year's hike in the Smokies, freezing rain, ice, fierce winds, cold, and an injured hiker called upon the resources of the group, and they successfully negotiated a treacherous hike from Clingman's Dome to Cade's Cove. A hike from Woody Gap to Neel Gap saw more fierce winds and minus one degree temperature. An accumulation of 14 inches of snow, preceded by high winds and sleet, on Mt. LeConte gave the hikers "the most exquisite covering of snow any of us had ever seen," according to Tom Aderhold, who also mourned, "There were no surprises in the dinner menu . . . although some of us continue to be optimistic. . . . But as always, it tasted good." Even a hike from Cooper Gap to Woody Gap featured "gale force winds" and up to 18 inches of snow.

An overnight hike was scheduled for the section of the new Trail between Three Forks and Highway 60. The bulletin announcement cautioned: ". . . You might want to bring along your Noontootla and Wilscot Quadrangle maps." But, according to June Engle in the trip report, "We made the WHOLE trip! Thought we were gonna die!. . . Thanks to Harry's ingenious device, maneuvered by himself and Herb Daniel, we were pulled across the river in a sling attached to a Ranger's cable. . . . Some got pinched in peculiar places, but as the sun was just setting, there was not a complaint among us." Except for some confusion at the river (". . . we found out later that it was laid out by John Myers. . . .") the trip was "a grand hike."

John Myers *successfully* led the hike over Rabun Bald to Warwoman Road "after a few re-routes, briars, and a very little excitement." As Myers modestly stated, "Magnificent leadership will always tell. . . ."

The bulletin reported on the 19th Appalachian Trail Conference, which was the golden anniversary of the founding of the Appalachian Trail:

Nine GATC members (Hugh Chase, Mandy and Gannon Coffey, Margaret Drummond, June and Jim Engle, Henry Morris, Polly and Al Thompson) were in attendance at the Appalachian Trail Conference in Plymouth, New Hampshire, on June 16 through 18. More than 600 people from at least 26 states, Canada and England registered during this meeting to set an attendance record. Following the three days of business meeting, some hikers divided into two groups to do the range walks while others stayed on for varying periods of day hikes and/or sightseeing.

Wholesale changes occurred in the Board of Managers. Of 24 elected officers, 13 are new. Henry Morris chose not to be nominated for another term of the ATC Board of Managers. Al Thompson was nominated and elected to succeed Henry in this position. Al will also be a member of the Executive Committee of the Conference.

The *Appalachian Trailway News* became a quarterly publication in 1972. It remained primarily a news magazine, with reports on the activities of the clubs, happenings along the Trail, and a few features on hikers, Trail-related problems and events, lengthy reports of Conference meetings, etc.

In August, the Conference headquarters was moved to Harpers Ferry, West Virginia. The move was made because they were about to run out of space on the fourth floor of the PATC building in Washington, and, since office space in Washington was very expensive, took advantage of an available space in a government-owned building at Harpers Ferry. The September *ATN* related the history of the house into which they moved, which was built in the mid-1800's.

Grandfather Mountain in North Carolina was the scene of the Multi-Club Meet. The GATC was represented by 45 of the 166 attendees, with nine clubs represented.

The first "Georgia Trails Symposium" was held in September, with several Club members participating. It was sponsored by the Georgia Department of Natural Resources, and evidently was the result of a Scenic Trails Act, authorizing a system of trails in Georgia, passed by the Georgia legislature in its 1972 session. The purpose of the symposium was to define the trail needs and to "lead in building such a system of trails."

Officers for 1973 were elected as follows at the annual meeting: Al Thompson, president; Grant Wilkins, vice president-activities; Herb Daniel, vice president-membership; Amanda Coffey, secretary; June Engle, treasurer; Lyman Emerson, Trail supervisor; J. P. Eidson, Trail information director; John Myers, bulletin editor; Mary Eidson, historian; Ralph Russell, director at large.

The year ended on a tragic note when GATC member Charlie Runyan died of a heart attack on the first day of a scheduled hike on Standing Indian. As leader Herb Daniel reported in the bulletin, "Immediate effort was made to revive him although all indications were that he died instantly. He was carried by stretcher to a road near Albert Mountain where an ambulance later met us." In an open letter afterward to Club members, his wife stated, "Although I realize how tragic and difficult it was for those involved, please believe that if a time or place could have been chosen by him, this would have been the time and place."

1973

GEORGIA
APPALACHIAN
19 TRAIL CLUB, INC. 30

THE GEORGIA TRAIL saw a number of significant improvements in early 1973 as the Trails and shelters committee, under Trail Supervisor Lyman Emerson, continued to work toward removing the Trail from Forest Service roads. After many years of following the road between Hightower Gap and Horse Gap, the Trail was finally put back up on the ridge where it had been in years past. Steve Swink, who directed the relocation, was surprised to find an old metal AT marker and a faded white blaze on the ridgetop. George Owen directed the work of relocating the Trail between Nimblewill Gap and Amicalola Falls to remove it from the road and onto the ridge top there. The approach Trail in Amicalola State Park was also extended from the top of the falls to the Park entrance behind the pavilion. George Owen reported in the bulletin on the extension of the Amicalola Falls Trail (in part):

That morning, all effort was thrown into completing the approach trail extension from the lake at the top of Amicalola Falls to the Park entrance. Despite not-too-subtle reminders from Henry Morris and Margaret Drummond that the leaders should re-read ATC guidelines as to how steep a trail should be (presumably less than a 90 degree angle), this whole 1.1 mile addition was completed and then blazed by Jim Engle. Woe be unto any hiker who thinks climbs on the AT are a 'snap' and then hits this very first mile of the approach trail!

The new shelter at Low Gap had been completed in late 1972, and the

Whitley Gap shelter in the summer of 1973. The YCC's cleared the Trail from the top of Wildcat Mountain down to Whitley Gap.

Contributions in memory of Charlie Runyan had been put into a special fund to be used "for some worthwhile related cause." A new shelter in his honor was considered, or possibly the bridge to be built over the Toccoa River on the relocated Trail. The estimate of the cost of the bridge was about $7,000, and a shelter about $3,000.

According to conservation chairman Ed Seiferle in his annual report to the Club, the committee had a "relatively quiet year. . . . Most of our work . . . has been of a watchdog nature." Seiferle continued:

The NPS (Blue Ridge Parkway's parent) is required by law to prepare an Environmental Impact Statement for their proposed extension of the Blue Ridge Parkway into Georgia. I reported a year ago on the violent opposition raised to the first two drafts of that Statement. Since then, nothing has come out from them to the public. They report that they are studying a large number of alternate routes or parts of routes to that originally proposed by them along the crest of the Blue Ridge.

But we may expect from them really nothing in the way of seriously proposed alternative routes if one can believe Parkway representatives themselves. . . . A number of other efforts have been made to prevent construction of the Parkway. A most laudable one was the introduction of a bill by State Senator Maylon London, of Cleveland, which would require that approval by a number of State departments be given before the State could appropriate money for the acquisition of right-of-way property for the Parkway extension. . . . Unhappily, this bill made slow progress in the hectic 1973 session of our Legislature and was eventually withdrawn. We are not yet certain whether it will be re-introduced.

The Department of Natural Resources has itself made another move to oppose the Parkway route. It has proposed that a Blue Ridge Crest wilderness/wild area be included in the bills now in Congress to revise or extend the existing Wilderness Act. This area would follow the whole crestline of the Blue Ridge in Georgia and thus would include every bit of the present Georgia section of the Appalachian Trail. . . .

Another step in the direction of insulating the Appalachian Trail in Georgia from possible interference by the Parkway is the proposal that the present Appalachian Trail route be reinstated as the official Appalachian Trail description. . . . This proposal has been advanced by two powerful proponents—the administration of the Chattahoochee National Forest itself, and Chairman Ed Gray of the Appalachian Trail Advisory Committee. . . . Naturally, the Club supports this proposal. We plan to push for it ourselves if, in the immediate future, the Appalachian Trail Conference does not get it going. They have it under consideration now. . . .

Perhaps the best and surest preventive to construction of the Parkway extension would be removal, by some means, of the Parkway extension enabling law from the books. We are pleased to see that just last month the Georgia Wildlife Federation . . . has come out publicly with just exactly that proposal.

We have also kept an eye on the route of Georgia 400, the Appalachian Highway, planned to cross the Blue Ridge at Neel Gap. . . . We have let the Department of Transportation know we oppose the Neel Gap route.

The ATC Board of Managers adopted a "new set of objectives" which "reflected the broadening scope of the Conference program, in particular the establishment of an Appalachian Greenway," according to the February *ATN*. Stan Murray explained the need for the Greenway concept:

... there is reason to be pleased with progress under the National Trails System Act. Vigorously implemented, it will virtually ensure the protection of at least a continuous right-of-way. The National Park Service is aggressively pursuing its coordinating role. The U.S. Forest Service is buying whole tracts along the Trail wherever it can find willing sellers. Most states have at least begun to lay groundwork for right-of-way protection. The real problem is in designating a corridor of such width that the finest qualities of the Trail will be preserved and nurtured. A weakness of the Trails Act, recognized from the start, is that, although it does not preclude protection broader than a 25-acre-per-mile right-of-way (100 feet on each side of the Trail), neither does it effectively encourage it.

To save only a 200-foot strip over the grass bald, or at an untold number of other cherished sites, and leave the rest for development would result in an irrevocable loss. The Appalachian Trail has enjoyed its primeval environment because the privately owned lands have not been subjected to heavy developmental pressures. Now all this is rapidly changing,

To provide a comprehensive statement on the Appalachian Trail environment and to set the stage for what could be a new phase in its protection, the Board of Managers adopted the following objective at its November meeting:

'To seek establishment of an Appalachian Greenway (1) encompassing the Appalachian Trail and (2) of sufficient width to provide a nationally significant zone for dispersed types of recreation, wildlife habitat, scientific study, and timber and watershed management, as well as to provide vicarious benefits to the American public. . . .'

To begin to implement this objective, the Board has authorized an initial planning effort and the employment of such professional assistance within our means as may be necessary. The program may involve broad-scale land-use planning, cooperative undertakings with landowners, possible additional Federal legislation, and the participation of all present stewards of the Trail. The opportunities are exciting, to say the least.

Another hike on the new Trail between Three Forks and Highway 60 was announced in the January bulletin by leader Mary Eidson, "If you don't mind being cold, cold, cold; if you don't mind briars; if you don't mind being wet; if you don't mind being lost; if you don't mind the possibility of being dunked in the Toccoa River in February; if you are in prime physical condition . . . we will welcome you on this . . . trip. The pulley has proved once. Will it hold a second time?" The hikers plunged into the woods on a cold, overcast day, found the river cable gone, camped beside the river near a spring, and walked out on a beautiful sunny Sunday *around* the river to the north on dirt roads and a bridge crossing to Highway 60.

A (presumably) successful hike was made in early spring, led by J. P. Eidson, from Highway 60 to Slaughter Gap on the new Trail.

A small group attempted the scheduled hike to Hightower Bald via Bly Gap, but only made it as far as Hightower Gap. According to leader John Myers, cold and fierce winds all night long sent them down the mountainside the next morning.

Other trips were made to: Wayah Gap to Franklin, North Carolina; another cold but beautiful Mt. LeConte; Fires Creek in the Tusquitee Bald area; an exciting Hiwassee River float trip; Twenty-mile Creek area in the Smokies; rain-swollen Jack's River (the leader declared, "No one escaped total immersion—it was great!"); Raven Fork Wilderness; and another weekend at the Dillard House.

The Board of Directors voted to call a special membership meeting in June "to catch up the membership on what is going on," and "to solicit opinions from the membership in a number of areas." This practice of having a second business meeting during the year lasted for several years, but when attendance became small, it was decided to discontinue it.

The Multi-Club Meet was held at the Apple Tree Group Camp near Franklin, North Carolina, and was hosted by the Carolina Mountain Club as part of its 50th anniversary celebration.

At the annual meeting in October, officers for 1974 were elected; Grant Wilkins, president; John Myers, vice president; Frances Shafe, secretary; June Engle, treasurer; Herb Daniel, membership director; George Owen, Trail supervisor; J. P. Eidson, Trail information director; Tom Aderhold, historian; Ed Seiferle, bulletin editor; Al Thompson, director at large. According to the bulletin account, "To assure that none of us who had dined so abundantly on a delicious barbeque dinner should attempt to sleep through the meeting, Al called on the Club's resident comedian, Gannon Coffey, to expound on the minutes of the 1972 meeting. . . . After Gannon had finished reading the minutes . . . it was moved and passed to accept the minutes 'as written, but not necessarily as read.'"

Al Thompson, who had served as GATC president for almost four years, longer than anyone since Warner Hall, was given "a standing acknowledgment" at the Christmas party for his years of service.

1974

GEORGIA
APPALACHIAN
19 TRAIL CLUB, INC. 30

THE YEAR 1974 was relatively quiet for the GATC if the existing records give a true (if not whole) picture. Fifty-one activities—the most ever—had been planned by the 1973 activities committee under Grant Wilkins' direction. That meant an event every weekend except the latter part of December. The schedule usually included a combination each month of a day hike, two backpack or overnight trips, and a family campout. There were several trips to the Smokies, including, as usual, two to Mt. LeConte; several to the Cohuttas; hikes to Shining Rock, Mt. Mitchell, and the Nantahalas; canoe and float trips; caving; and several bushwhack hikes. As usual, day hikes drew by far the largest crowds. Nine trips were cancelled, mostly for lack of registrants.

In March, Ed Selby led a group of nine stalwarts on a bushwhack in the Dukes Creek-Adams Bald-Whitley Gap area, which was, as he said, "the perfect hike for masochists."

Another rugged but beautiful hike was led by Tom Aderhold and Gannon Coffey in the Balsam Mountain-Mt. Sterling area in the Smokies. Aderhold commented in the trip report, ". . . If you think it requires a big, strong person to backpack, I suggest taking some lessons from little 90-pound (if that much) Judy Galphin, who hung right in there with some pretty capable male backpackers."

The new "Loop Trail," seeing relatively little use, was difficult to keep open for hiking. A scheduled hike from Wolfpen Gap to Fish Gap was changed to

Hightower to Woody Gap because, as the leader stated, "our preliminary hike proved to be mostly a bushwhack."

A bus was chartered for the first time for the Mt. LeConte trip in October and proved to be "successful beyond our wildest expectations," according to the bulletin account. (Maybe it was that poker concession that Grant Wilkins claimed for the back of the bus.)

An interesting adaptation was made on the scheduled trip from Wayah Bald to Wesser in December, as reported by John Myers:

Driving up toward Wayah Gap out of the valley, we passed in sequence through rain, sleet, then snow. At the Gap we found Chip Conner's plush camper van and the news that the four-plus mile road into Wayah Bald was snowed over and impassable. Nobody wanted to go home so we drove to the Standing Indian Campground area and parked Chip's motorized Taj Mahal by the roadside while the less fortunate six of us made the long, hard, 250-yard climb up to the Rock Gap shelter.

After lunch, two members crawled into sleeping bags to stay warm and four started a wild game of Knock Poker and Hearts. One of the participants was a 13 year old who had 'never played before.' By 5:00 PM Greg had won all of our boots and packs. Then to keep warm, an early supper was in order; and afterwards, we picked up Chip at the van and drove into Franklin to see 'The Castaway Cowboy.' After the widow's potato farm was saved and the bad guys were in jail, we drove back by the van where the clinking of glasses, splashing in the built-in pool and wild music told us that Herb and Bill Durrett were still awake. Then up to the Rock Gap shelter again. During the night, a very friendly skunk paid us an inspection visit; but when he saw a tent pitched INSIDE a shelter, he walked away shaking his head.

At 8:00 AM, the leader's wrist alarm went off but everyone pretended not to hear it. Much later, we drove to the City Restaurant in Franklin for breakfast. Bill Davey was heard telling Greg, 'Son, all GATC hikes aren't like this one.' As we drove homeward, to the beat of the windshield wipers, one member kept reading out of the yearbook trip write-up: 'It never rains in December—it never rains—.'

In April, Trail Supervisor George Owen announced, "BIG—no, GREAT NEWS!!! Good ol' ALICE is alive and well and serving supper now in her restaurant at the old Cheese Factory site near Tray Mountain. Come out for a day of maintenance and cleanup, and you'll get to meet Alice and 'her' charmin' sister personally. . . . Oh, do be very careful what you say around Alice and 'her' temperamental assistant. If you tell Alice that 'she' has eyes like John Myers or the assistant that 'she' walks with all the grace of a Grant Wilkins uphill hiking gait, you are liable to be severely whipped with a couple of apron strings!"

The "Trail maintenance outing" brought 11 "eager workers," who collected litter and cleared and blazed portions of the Trail. On an "anti-litter day" in May, only six people met for a clean-up trip to Lake Winfield Scott and Blood Mountain. At the request of the Trail and shelters committee, a floor was put in the Hawk Mountain shelter by the Forest Service.

On an overnight special Loop Trail work trip, seven people worked to clear and blaze the Duncan Ridge section.

Tragedy struck in the GATC "family" again in 1974. Julie Ann Wilson, daughter of long-time members Ross and Elizabeth Wilson, died in a canoe accident on a rain-swollen river in Idaho. Julie had hiked with the Club on many trips during her short life.

A special outing was arranged by the Forest Service in July so that Club members could "get a first-hand look at clear-cutting." The subject had been discussed at length at the last annual meeting of the Club, and subsequently, the Board authorized J. P. Eidson to write a letter to Georgia Congressmen expressing the Club's opposition to clear-cutting. At the spring business meeting, Bob Harper and Charlie Hunnicutt, of the Forest Service in Gainesville, had spoken to Club members about this practice, and this discussion had resulted in an invitation to let them show the Club what it was all about. As the bulletin announcement of the trip stated, "Clear-cutting, all of you are aware, is a forest management practice that has stirred much interest and generated much argument. Our Club has taken a stand in opposition to it. . . . Our good friends and cooperative AT workers in the Forest Service have taken exception to our stand and have asked the Club for a hearing. . . . Pat Thomas, the new Chattahoochee National Forest Supervisor, wants us to see clear-cutting and its effects in several stages. . . ."

Only two members, Mal and Ruth Sanford, attended the Multi-Club Meet at Grayson Highland State Park in Virginia, hosted by the Mt. Rogers AT Club.

Les Holmes, Executive Director of the ATC, spoke at the annual business meeting on Conference history and policies. It was announced at the meeting that "the treasurer's report indicated a deficit for the year." Officers elected for 1975 were: Herb Daniel, president; John Myers, vice president; Judy Galphin, secretary; Frank Baker, treasurer; Steve Swink, membership director; George Owen, Trail supervisor; Ed Selby, Trail information director; Theo Taylor, historian; Ed Seiferle, bulletin editor; Grant Wilkins, director.

The financial deficit called for action, and a called meeting was announced for the Christmas party. Dues were raised to $12 per year for couples and $10 for individual members.

1975

GEORGIA
APPALACHIAN
19 TRAIL CLUB, INC 30

Plans for "GREAT ACCOMPLISHMENTS" within the Club and on the Trail got the year off to a good start and reflected President Herb Daniel's concern for greater and more "educated" involvement of Club members.

At the Board meeting in January, and again in March, Membership Director Steve Swink reported on plans for an orientation program for new members and for an educational program on hiking and the Club, as well as leadership training and educational information to be distributed to the public.

These plans reflected the initiation in 1974 by the ATC of an "On-the-Trail Education Program." Hank Lautz had been employed by Conference to supervise the new program. The May, 1974, *ATN* explained it:

The On-the-Trail Education Program (OTEP) is designed to expand the traditional role of the Conference and the clubs in volunteer trail maintenance to include a volunteer preventative maintenance program through trail-use education. The need for this expansion into trail-use education is readily apparent with the increased numbers of inexperienced people on the Trail from Maine to Georgia; what is yet to be established is whether or not this need for on-the-trail education can be met through the traditional voluntary efforts of the Conference and the clubs.

The focus of the Conference program will be (i) to work through existing Trail club programs where possible, (ii) to encourage clubs that do not have programs to establish them, and (iii) to generally encourage and coordinate volunteer educational efforts on the Appalachian Trail this summer. We believe that a low-key, decentralized program that stimulates informal person-to-person contact on the Trail between experienced and inexperienced hikers can substantially reduce the problems of Trail misuse, litter and vandalism.

The GATC March bulletin announced the first major accomplishment in the general area of education:

At the annual meeting last October, our officers explained their initial plans for upgrading the leadership of our hiking trips, with the eventual objective of having all our trips led by certified trip leaders.

On February 15, the first step was taken in this training program when 21 members attended a five hour, non-certified first aid course. Captains Griffin and Berry of the Atlanta Fire Department presented the course and covered many of the fundamentals of first aid. They also demonstrated the use of the Department's coronary-pulmonary respirator and gave all our members an opportunity to use this valuable equipment.

A second similar course will be given in the near future, and details will be announced in the bulletin when they are finalized. We hope that as many members as possible will participate.

Later in the year, an Education Committee was established by Daniel for the purpose of carrying out the plans for leadership training, on-the-Trail education, first aid, etc.

Trail Supervisor George Owen announced his plans for a "Georgia AT Walk-Thru" for early March, saying:

We did it again! Came up with something very different for this weekend, and as one might thus suspect, John Myers had a hand in the idea. But the Trails and Shelters Committee took his basic suggestion, went with it, and here's what we've got for you.

The entire AT in Georgia will be surveyed by members on day-long hikes. This survey will include: (1) checking each section of the Trail, both north and south, against the latest edition Trail guidebook and noting any discrepancies; (2) observing blazes in both directions and noting any confusion that may be caused by lack of proper blazing—this means we have chosen leaders to hike sections with which they are not too familiar; (3) noting conditions of shelters and Trail in general, such as large trees down on Trail; (4) taking out trash at shelters; (5) establishing compass bearings to distant peaks, lakes, and other landmarks from vistas; (6) noting location of trash barrels at gaps and other locations on or close to Trail. . . .

As Owen reported afterward:

A goodly number of GATC members, prospective members, and guests started the day under calm skies that soon turned to rain and even snow in higher elevations. The task called for small groups to hike short sections of the Georgia AT, with enough people out to traverse the entire Trail in Georgia.

. . . We asked a lot, but here are some things we did *not* ask: (1) for Jim and June Engle to bushwhack in a snowstorm between Tray and Addis Gaps—thanks to unseemly weather and an unbelievable number of downed trees on the Trail; (2) for

Margaret Drummond to bring a car that only operates on flat land and downhill grades (guess who *walked* to the *start* of her hike at Cooper Gap?); (3) for Ellen Hanks and crew to do the 'extra mile' and cut limbs on the Trail—sure am glad you did, though— the GATC *and* the Forest Service thank you! . . .

The regular Trail maintenance outing took place in May, as Owen announced:

We'll be working on several projects scattered along the Georgia Trail. A key project will be relocation of the upper half mile of blue blaze approach trail between the pavilion and the lake at Amicalola. Yep, Henry and Margaret, backed by a solid corps of complaining hikers, have won a victory. George Galphin has just been assigned that section, taking it over from the wild-eyed maniac who once told a fellow: 'Yep, Lyman, we've got a great new trail here!' So George Galphin is re-routing that 'Little Stekoah' and will have it flagged, ready for cutting. Need at least a half dozen helpers there. . . . Members with regularly assigned sections are encouraged to use this day to 'do your thing.'

The work outing was declared a "TOTAL SUCCESS," with a turnout of about 30 people. As Owen reported, "The success is probably due most to the tempting reward offered at day's end: another ravishing spaghetti supper by John and Cynthia Myers. . . ." Owen continued:

One group of seven gathered at the Park to re-route and repair the first and steepest mile of the AT Approach Trail, from the concession pavilion to the lake. By 5:30 p.m. the job was completed, including a thorough re-route of the upper part of this steep trail to allow a much more gradual climb through longer, easier switchbacks. It's so good now, in fact, that when Henry Morris goes up to measure the new route with that wacky one-wheel bike of his, we're promising him a pleasant downhill trip all the way up the ridge to the top of the falls! George Galphin and his chainsaw get the prize for most trees removed, with tree lover Dave Sherman running a close second.

Numerous others worked on various sections of the Appalachian Trail, scattered from Springer Mountain to Bly Gap. . . .

A great deal of work was being done on the Loop Trail, beginning with a work trip in February on which a section over Coosa Bald was cleared by four people, including guest Marty Rubin, of whom the bulletin report declared, "What a worker! We were lucky to have him."

The next bulletin carried a "special notice":

A trip to come and one that's past from our very hard working Chairman of the Side Trail Development Committee, Dudley Eggleston. (Dudley and a band of co-workers are doing a tremendous job and deserve a big hand from the Club. They are giving us and all AT hikers many possible new trips, including some loop trips.)

After the second "side trail development trip" in April, the bulletin announced the next trip, saying:

The new blue blazed trail between Springer Mountain and Slaughter Gap via Duncan Ridge is now 80% complete. We've been working on this trail for over four years and want to complete it quickly so it can relieve pressure on the AT.

By the annual meeting in October, Eggleston could announce that 95 per cent of the Loop Trail had been completed.

Plans for the "Charlie Runyan Memorial Bridge" over the Toccoa River were shown at the March Board meeting by Dudley Eggleston, who also reported that the estimated cost was now $28,491 (considerably more than the $7,000 estimated in 1973). The Board, through Eggleston, had requested that the bridge be named after Charlie, and had also approved the use of the $3,000 donated by Club members and Runyan's business associates to assist in the building of the bridge. The minutes of the GATC-Forest Service meeting in May reported that the Club funds could be used "in landscaping around the bridge, constructing a replica of the Tesnatee Gap Trail shelter and furnishing necessary information plaques." Plans were to begin construction of the bridge by July or August. Bids were put out; and by July, the estimated cost was $35,000. In September, it was announced that the contractor could not get the cable for the bridge, so construction would be delayed until spring.

The Trail through Bly Gap (which is actually in North Carolina) is on private land, and in 1974 it was suggested that the Trail be relocated because the owners would not sell the land to the Forest Service. The GATC was not in favor of relocating away from Bly Gap, but was willing at least to consider an alternative. In February, Lyman Emerson, along with Arch Nichols, ATC Board member and Carolina Mountain Club member, Bill Hazelton of the Nantahala Club, and several Forest Service people spent a long day hiking the proposed and partially flagged re-route. About a mile north of Bly Gap (heading south), the route swung east and down to twice cross Charlie's Creek, and then southwest to a gap almost on the North Carolina-Georgia border. The Georgia section was not flagged, but it was planned to then descend below 3,600 feet to cross Charlie's Creek again, then ascend to about ⅜ mile south of Bly Gap. Emerson declared the proposed route less desirable, and recommended leaving the Trail as it was for the present and continuing to try to obtain the land. The North Carolina people, however, were anxious to make the relocation, and continued to pursue the possibility.

The Forest Service continued to try to obtain rights-of-way across several small pieces of private land along the Georgia Trail. Acquisitions were sought from the owners at Wheeler Knob and at Tritt Gap, but only at the former were negotiations successful.

Although the relocation around Miller Gap had been completed in 1972, a short relocation was necessary in 1975 in order for owner Tom Gilliland to build a fence.

Owners of the land at Henry Gap were also unwilling to sell to the Forest Service, and they (the Forest Service) recommended to the GATC that this section also be relocated. The route was checked out by Trail Supervisor George Owen, who recommended that the decision be delayed pending further study, with the hope that the land could somehow be acquired. A decision was made to try to "stick with the existing location until the land owners object to its use," although the Forest Service continued to recommend relocation.

Historian Theo Taylor reported in March the possibility of the Club's historical files being put on microfilm by the State Department of Archives, and it was recommended that a committee be appointed "to categorize materials and discard duplicate and unnecessary information." The material was turned over to Pete Schinkel of the Archives, who began the task of sorting out the numerous boxes of bulletins, letters, etc.

Also at the March Board meeting "a motion was made and passed that an historical marker about the AT should be placed at Amicalola Falls." By May the wording for the marker had been written by Margaret Drummond, Henry Morris, and George Owen, and approved by the Board. Its erection, however, was to be delayed for various reasons.

George Owen made an unhappy discovery along the Trail in April: in the area around Three Forks, hemlocks were being logged along the Trail. Unknown to the GATC, the Trail in that area was on a Forest Service "system road," which could at any time be opened up for Forest Service use. The Forest Service "admitted they made the mistake of allowing the trees to be cut and also for not letting us know about the systems roads," according to the GATC Board minutes. The May *ATN* reported on the incident:

Following vigorous protests from the Georgia Appalachian Trail Club and the Conference, the Forest Service has stopped its logging operation recently begun on the Appalachian Trail in the Chattahoochee National Forest. What isn't clear is why they ever started.

The logging operation was discovered by the Georgia AT Club in late April along a half mile section of the Trail about 6.1 miles north of Springer Mountain near Three Forks. According to GATC, trees were being cut along the Trail which had been bulldozed into a skidway, and heavy equipment was dragging felled trees down the Trail.

At last report, the Forest Service stated that the halt was only temporary and that they have plans to log the area over the next two years. Future issues of this publication will report more on this incident and its implications.

During the year, Map Committee Chairman Bill Durrett began the long task of making a profile map of the Georgia Trail, and also began mapping the Trail, with nearby private land and Forest Service system roads, on topographic maps. Now being aware of the system roads, the Club wished to know the location of all of them.

The "first annual" (although actually it was not) photo contest was held in August, and Chairman Bartow Cowden reported, "Once again the Club was thrilled, amused and delighted by the world-wide beauty and travel shown through the slides exhibited." Winners received a backpacking stove and a sleeping bag donated by Georgia Outdoors.

The old Tesnatee Gap shelter, which had been described many years ago as "very swanky," was finally removed in 1975 because of vandalism and general disrepair. Once the most remote shelter in Georgia, it was now located only a few feet from the Richard Russell Highway, where it had for a number of years awaited its fate while several GATC "administrations" pondered what best to do with it.

Once again, the GATC was to lose a faithful member: Randy Bordeaux died in March after undergoing surgery a week before.

The 20th Appalachian Trail Conference was held in June at Appalachian State University in Boone, North Carolina. It was the celebration of the golden anniversary of the founding of the ATC. Over 1,000 people attended—the largest crowd ever. Although no report was made in the GATC records, a number of members attended the meeting and enjoyed the hiking afterward.

Stan Murray retired after 14 years as chairman of the Board of Managers, and George Zoebelein was elected to take his place. Les Holmes also retired, and Paul Pritchard was hired as the new ATC executive director.

In March, the GATC Board voted to recommend to leaders that a limitation be put on the number of participants on outings: 15 on backpacking trips and 25 on day hikes. The limit was to be published in the bulletin with the trip announcement.

The February trip to Mt. LeConte was again made by chartered bus. The bulletin report announced that Herrick Brown, who had operated the lodge since 1960, had sold the remaining three years of his lease. A "Citizens' Wilderness Proposal" for the Smokies, as well as a National Park Service proposal, included the phasing out of the lodge operation "as soon as the present lease expires." 1977 was expected to be the last year of operation of the lodge.

The Club's famous (infamous?) duo, Tom Aderhold and Gannon Coffey, led a different kind of trip to the Smokies, the schedule of events having been "agreed to by arbitration." It included canoeing across Lake Fontana and up Hazel Creek a short way (with packs) and backpacking up the Creek to a base camp. The bulletin report continued:

On the second day while the majority proceeded to enjoy (?) the unique day hike, the leader monitored the pursuits of five active young boys. This later so tired him, he relegated this duty to his loyal assistant and modern-day pied piper, Tom Taylor, while he—the leader—retreated to the shade of a large beech tree for a short rest. Meanwhile, the hikers were battling the scourge of all bushwhackers—rhododendron—in a rainstorm complete with lightning and hail, and finding the final stream crossing a bit difficult and perilous in the rain-swollen waters. Gratefully, upon reaching base camp, the hikers found it untouched by rain.

The final day was a full one, reversing the first day's proceedings, but having to make the lake crossing in a thunderstorm, which ironically began with the canoe launchings and ended with their removal. (!!!) Then the drive home.

A "memorable" trip from Wesser to Fontana in March was reported in the bulletin thus by co-leader Judy Galphin:

To Persevere—'To persist in any enterprise undertaken in spite of counter influences; steadfast pursuit.'

In this case the counter influences were one sided mountains, thunderstorms, hail, tired legs, sore feet, wet clothes, cold winds, and an upset stomach.

However, there were some good sides to the mountains and to the story. Friday's weather was beautiful, the terrain was terrible, but you can't have everything. Early Saturday morning a few drops of rain began to fall. By 11:00 a.m. *lots* of rain was falling. Luckily by lunch Saturday things got better. The sun came out, the trail was a bit more reasonable, we dried out slowly, and by camp time things were a little more tolerable, except for Herb's stomach, and we won't dwell on that subject.

Sunday morning was beautiful, the trail continued to be rough but a little easier than Friday and Saturday. The views were fantastic overlooking Fontana. We were all tired but at least we can say we all made it.

Famous quotes along the way were: 'Has anyone ever thought of putting this trail through these mountains?' 'I hike this section every eight years to remind myself how rough it is.' 'A sadist must have cut this thing, or else he was just plain lazy.' 'Just keep persevering.'

Ever-enthusiastic George Owen described a trip to the Shining Rock Wilderness area in glowing terms:

This was surely one of the most scenic and enjoyable trips ever hiked by the GATC.

Ten of us met at Devil's Courthouse parking area at 9:00 a.m. Saturday. Here we were atop North Carolina's majestic Balsam Range, high in a Canadian zone spruce-fir forest. First we climbed to the rock face atop Devil's Courthouse for the 360-degree vista from the Smokies to north Georgia and South Carolina. From here we journeyed over several high spruce-fir-covered peaks with occasional vistas at rock outcroppings. Sometimes the trail virtually disappeared, and your leader, a la John Myers, was accused of 'obscurantism' and simply 'getting us lost.' At this point I was saved by a quote from some old Indian J. P. Eidson conjured up, who said, 'I'm not lost; trail lost.'

At noon we joined the Art Loeb Trail and soon entered the area known as Graveyard Fields. This area is virtually treeless, covered predominantly by grasses and low bushes. Lunch was enjoyed atop 6,214-foot, treeless Black Balsam Knob, complete with a stiff, cool breeze and spectacular views in all directions.

More barren knobs were crossed, and later that afternoon we entered Shining Rock

Wilderness Area and the world of trees again, some of which were changing colors. In late afternoon, the group pitched tents at Shining Rock Gap following a brief visit to the top of Shining Rock. After supper, part of the group journeyed to a vista atop Shining Rock to enjoy a magnificent full moon rise over the mountains. What a way to end the last day of summer!

Sunday morning—a little fall nip was in the air, and it was the first day of autumn. We returned over part of the area traversed the afternoon before, but following the ridges to Ivestor Gap. We entered treeless areas again at Flower Gap, and what a view! Early morning cloud mists covered the valleys, but the higher peaks stabbed their majesties into the bright blue, cloudless skies. We could clearly view the Smokies, Pisgah, nearby Sam Knob, and even extremely distant Mt. Mitchell. Then as we climbed the next almost barren peak with these views, we discovered we were in the midst of a large blueberry field extending for a mile, with all the berries fully ripe. Suddenly the lead bear discovered the rest of the den pack had abandoned him to gorge themselves on blueberries . . . and the view.

Arriving back at Ivestor Gap we dropped off the ridge and followed the Graveyard Fields Trail out to the Blue Ridge Parkway via the second falls of beautiful Yellowstone Prong of the Pigeon River's East Fork. With some brief and easy shuttles, all somewhat sorrowfully departed by mid-afternoon the friendly vistas of the Balsams, thankful to the Creator of all this beauty for its very existence and sustaining powers!

The Multi-Club Meet at Camp Dark Hollow near Roanoke, Virginia, attended by four GATCers, was hosted by the Roanoke AT Club.

At the GATC annual business meeting at American Adventures in Roswell, almost 70 people gathered for a feast, a movie about Sir Edmund Hillary, and the election of officers for 1976, who were: Herb Daniel, president; John Myers, vice president; Frank Baker, treasurer; Judy Galphin, secretary; Whit Benson, membership director; Margaret Drummond, Trail supervisor; Ed Selby, Trail information director; Theo Taylor, historian; Ed Seiferle, bulletin editor; June Engle, director at large.

Two sad events marked the end of the year. In October, the 100-year-old family home of Dr. Rufus Morgan was destroyed by fire, and he lost all of his cherished possessions. Dr. Morgan had just celebrated his 90th birthday two weeks before by climbing Mt. LeConte for the 160th time.

In December, the venerated Benton MacKaye died at the age of 96. He had lived at his home in Shirley Center, Massachusetts, since his return there in 1936. In a letter to Ed Seiferle, long-time member Lou Hoben wrote: "It's strange to have something happen to both of our honoraries at almost the same time. . . . We 'older folk' who knew these unique men personally—have talked with them—and 'hiked' with them—have, of course, a much deeper and more personal feeling for them than the younger members, who are acquainted with them—if at all—only as a name. I read one of Benton's first articles on the subject of a possible Trail, in the Saturday Evening Post, many years ago, long before my family moved to Georgia—and knew I'd someday become acquainted with it." (December 26, 1975)

1976

GEORGIA
APPALACHIAN
TRAIL CLUB, INC.

T HE APPALACHIAN TRAIL Conference, in its attempts to inaugurate programs of on-the-Trail education and Trail protection, held two workshops in Gatlinburg, Tennessee, in January on these subjects for representatives of the southern clubs.

Two members of the newly-formed GATC education committee attended the on-the-Trail education workshop, the purpose of which was "to evaluate the Trail-related educational needs in the region, review what has been done and work out a plan for next year." The meeting initiated several projects for the clubs to carry out, including a count and survey of Trail users, a one-time weekend shelter "caretaker," and the collection of slides for an on-the-Trail educational slide show to be produced by Conference. GATC members gathered information for the Trail survey at various times along the Trail, including during the walk-thru in March; Herb Daniel spent one weekend at the Tray Mountain shelter as caretaker.

In April, the education committee held a leadership "workshop," hoping to inaugurate an ongoing program of leadership education. The workshop was to be an "examination and discussion of the procedures and requirements for leading a trip," according to committee chairperson Nancy Shofner, and it featured various members discussing leadership techniques. Thirty-five people attended. The education committee also developed a list of guidelines and procedures for trip leaders, hoping they would be eventually printed and distributed to Club members.

The Club was also represented at the ATC workshop on Trail protection in Gatlinburg. This project was explained in a letter from Paul Pritchard:

The objectives of what we are calling the 'corridor' project are to first identify the natural, historic, cultural and scenic qualities of the Trail; and second, to identify the degree of protection or lack of protection that the Trail environment has. A detailed list of these qualities and the types of protection is attached.

Maps will be prepared by the joint cooperation of the state and federal agencies which the Conference members will assist in and then verify the information. These two maps will be completed by our Multi-Club meet on Labor Day weekend. (February 4, 1976)

For the project, maps would be prepared by each club, with the help of the various state and federal agencies, of the Trail and surrounding areas, delineating the "natural, historic, cultural and scenic qualities," including such things as botanic sites, scenic rivers, wildlife habitats, archaeological sites, utility corridors, scenic vistas, etc. GATC map committee chairman Bill Durrett, working with Dave Sherman, "state trail planner," of the Department of Natural Resources, completed the data for the maps by the Multi-Club Meet deadline.

The issue of wilderness came closer to home for the GATC during 1976. The Sierra Club had proposed seven areas in north Georgia for potential wilderness designation, five of which would contain parts of the AT. Several areas in the Nantahalas were also under consideration for wilderness, and for some of these areas the Forest Service had revealed a plan ("Unit 22" plan) which included much timber cutting and road building. A special meeting of the GATC Board of Directors was called to discuss these two issues and decide what position the Club would take on them. It was agreed to support a review and reconsideration of the Forest Service plan for the Nantahala area to give time for further action by conservation groups. There was strong feeling on the part of some Board members that the issue of wilderness and its effect on the Trail should be studied further before the Club took a stand in favor of these wilderness areas along the Trail. But finally the decision was made to endorse the concept of wilderness protection of the AT and to join with other conservation organizations in the study of the proposed areas in Georgia.

In order to try to protect the "white blazed" Trail, which was no longer the official AT, the Club, at the suggestion of Ed Seiferle, in mid-year requested of the Forest Service that those portions of the "old" AT not described in the Federal Register as the official Trail be designated "connecting or side trails," which were provided for in the National Scenic Trails Act. The Forest Service "was in agreement with this proposal," and the request was forwarded to the Regional office.

An unpleasant but true picture of the state of the Georgia Trail was revealed by columnist Kent Mitchell in the February 22nd *Atlanta Journal and Constitution:*

People call from time to time, often in bunches, asking how to get in touch with the local Appalachian Trail Club. They want to join and get in on the fun.

The problem is, the Club doesn't particularly want new members. There is no active campaign to discourage hiking the Trail by the Club, but there seems to be a move of 'benign neglect' as far as new membership is concerned.

The reason is obvious once you see the present condition of the Trail. It's horrible. . . .

The Appalachian Trail more resembles a rut than a path from Georgia to Maine. I've seen portions of it in this state and in the Smoky Mountains and it's all the same. . . .

In some places, the Trail is nearly two feet deep. . . .

The hordes of hikers—their numbers doubled since 1970—were taking their toll on the treadway as well as the surrounding areas of the Trail. Columnist Mitchell mentioned the Appalachian Greenway concept as a possible protection for the whole Trail corridor. The Greenway concept, however, was not to be realized, and eventually faded from the scene.

"Before planning on–Trail maintenance activities for the year we first need to know the conditions and problems which exist on the Trail," stated Trail Supervisor Margaret Drummond, announcing the "repeat of last year's success, Georgia AT Walk-thru." Fifty-two participants walked portions of the Georgia Trail on the day of the event, gathering information which was recorded on work sheets and turned in at the end of the day as the group met for dinner at the Smith House and Unicoi Lodge.

A Trail maintenance outing was held in July to work on as many chores as possible that were suggested by the spring walk-thru. A turnout of only 13 people precluded the undertaking of any major projects, but the Trail was cleared and blazed between Tesnatee and Unicoi Gaps. The hot, muggy day was ended at Unicoi State Park, where the group once again enjoyed food prepared by "Alice," who had "agreed to emerge from her temporary retirement to cater the meal and to add her sparkling charm and wit to her now famous culinary prowess," according to leader Margaret Drummond.

The decision was finally made to relocate the Trail at Henry Gap around the private land, and this was completed by the Forest Service by mid-year.

The GATC and the Forest Service agreed that the shelter at Big Stamp Gap, which was on a heavily-used dirt road and was much abused, should be moved to a new location. This was to be done in the fall when a suitable location could be found. The Forest Service also agreed to begin putting floors in all of the shelters. With the help of the Youth Conservation Corps, the Forest Service "worked" much of the white-blazed and blue-blazed trails, clearing brush and blow-downs, installing water bars, and "reworking the tread."

In June, a special work trip was called by section overseer George Galphin to rebuild a section of Trail above Amicalola Falls to remove it from private land and ease the steep climb to the top of the ridge. Six people responded to the call and completed the work.

An "update" on the Toccoa River bridge in the August bulletin stated:

> . . . A couple of years ago the Supervisor of the Chattahoochee National Forest budgeted for construction of a suitable bridge and let a contract on it. Unfortunately, the low bidder went bankrupt during the recent construction recession, before the bridge was started.
>
> The Forest Service is presently negotiating with the contractor's bonding company in an effort to get construction underway. The high escalation rate for construction costs in the last few years has greatly complicated the situation. The Forest Service expects, barring further unforeseen problems, to be able to conclude plans for beginning actual construction of the bridge in the relatively near future. . . .

It was announced in October that construction on the bridge had started, and it should be completed by the next summer.

At the July Board meeting, following considerable discussion pro and con of some of the Club rules and the "hiker's code," a special committee was assigned to "collect, modernize and propose revisions to," the Club rules and regulations. The resulting revision separated the rules and the hiker's code, added a few new provisions, and deleted a few old ones. These new rules were published in the October bulletin, along with a "clarification of procedures for sponsorship of applicants for membership," which spelled out specifically the responsibilities of the sponsor toward the applicant.

For the first time in many years, membership was refused to an applicant by the Board of Directors in August. The feeling of the majority seemed to be that the individual was not compatible with the group. The decision was a difficult one to make, and to many it projected an undesirable attitude of exclusiveness.

The feelings generated by this event apparently lingered in the memories of Board members. When, several years later, a similar question was raised about a prospective member, the sponsor conducted an exhaustive personal investigation, presented his findings, and the Board acted favorably on the application.

A series of articles on "club personalities . . . especially those active in forming and carrying on the Club," was begun in the September bulletin. The series was written by Rosalind Van Landingham in 1976 and featured Henry Morris and Lou Hoben.

In September GATC member Ed Selby completed his hike of the entire AT—"the American way—on the installment plan, 1969 to 1976," as he put it. His climb up Mt. Katahdin came on September 8, 1976.

The Appalachian Trail Conference had to relinquish the building it had been renting from the National Park Service, and in 1976 it purchased another, larger building in Harpers Ferry—its first "permanent headquarters." Funds to aid in the purchase were solicited from clubs and members, and the GATC voted to contribute $200.

The May *ATN* announced some good news for the Trail: the Department of the Interior had set aside $1 million for acquisition of lands along the AT—"a first in the 51 year history of the Trail." The states would match these funds, so it actually would be $2 million.

For the last few years the *ATN* had been developing into more and more of a feature magazine rather than news of the Trail and clubs. Pictures and a more modern layout dressed it up considerably, but its role in the communications process between Conference and the clubs was diminished.

Rough weather was more often than not a factor in the Club hike over the New Year's weekend. The trip in 1976 was to the Slickrock–Joyce Kilmer Wilderness. As leader Whit Benson reported, "The beautiful weather on Friday morning gave little indication of what was to come. . . ." During the evening a cold front moved in and "there was little sleep as the storm raged." Benson's tent collapsed in the early morning hours, breaking and bending the poles and soaking him and his gear. All returned to the cars for dry clothing, but, as he reported, "After hiking for three hours through the rain in the quagmire that the trail had become, and slipping and sliding down Hangover, we all finally arrived at the cars cold and wet" and headed for home.

The February LeConte trip provided a beautiful but cold Saturday climb. Leader Larry Elliott continued his bulletin report:

. . . The temperature held at 15 degrees that night, but by morning we had winds gusting to 35 mph. After Herrick's typical hearty breakfast, we all strapped on ice crampons and made a timely descent down Alum Cave. The never-at-a-loss, always-amazing George Goldman stripped and bathed in the creek at the bottom of the mountains, 'just to freshen up.' How he smiled with the icicle hanging from his nose, I'll never know . . . but that's George. . . .

In March, Harold Arnovitz led a hike in the Moccasin Creek area along trails built by Alan Padgett, the ranger in charge of the Moccasin Creek Wildlife Management Area. Padgett had laid out and cleared a number of trails between Lake Burton and the AT ridge, building foot bridges and hand cables across the streams and opening up a beautiful area to hikers. (Padgett was later transferred to another area, and these trails soon became overgrown and indistinct.)

Reporting in the bulletin on a loop hike from Tesnatee Gap, through Whitley Gap, over Adams Bald into the Town Creek Valley and back up Cowrock Ridge, Ed Selby told of a stop made at the "toll gate" on the old trans–mountain highway in the valley. As Selby reported:

Logan's Lodge, once located at the toll gate, was a major stagecoach stop on the Union Turnpike which 100 years ago ran from North Carolina to Clarkesville, Georgia, via Tesnatee Gap.

A first for the GATC—a bicycle trip—was led by Ralph Russell in June to Hard Labor Creek State Park. A bushwhack through beautiful fall colors, from Cowrock Mountain north down Oak Ridge, was led by Mary Eidson in October. Crawling through thick laurel on this trip led participant John Krickel to remark: 'Now I know what a thread feels like going through a sewing machine.'

Nine GATCers attended the Multi-Club Meet at the Buckskin Boy Scout reservation at Dilley's Mill, West Virginia, hosted by the Kanawha Trail Club.

June Engle reported on the October business meeting:

The trail having been clearly marked, all in the party convened at the designated spot, then continued on thru the entwining of pleasant fellowship, sharing of a meal, and reviewing old trails. We realized how many hours were/are put in by the officers and committee members to keep the trails open and pleasant. . . .

Officers for 1977 were elected at the meeting: Margaret Drummond, president; Whit Benson, vice president; Bill Durrett, secretary; George Galphin, treasurer; Earl Metzger, membership director; Nancy Shofner, Trail supervisor; Ed Selby, Trail information director; Theo Taylor, historian; John Myers, bulletin editor; Herb Daniel, director.

Again the services of Alice were secured—this time for the Christmas party. Planning a covered dish supper, "she" worried that everyone would bring kidney pudding. Reporting on the party under the pseudonym of "John Myers," she declared:

Not one single kidney pudding! One hundred and twelve people and no kidney puddings! . . . The only thing wrong in the cooking department was being faced with bringing charges at the next Board of Directors meeting against two people that I think the world of, but rules are rules and the alcoholic content of two dessert items was over and above that allowed by Club rules. Both desserts were excellent, but illegal. It was my duty to sample these many times to gather evidence.

Then there was the installation of officers. A highlight this year in that for a change it was handled with both decorum and respect for the truth. We missed you Tom, but not too much. Ed Seiferle handled the chore well and I am certain that the other officers felt that they had been installed in office and not merely trampled on.

Then there was an opportunity to sing Christmas Carols and for people who had not seen each other for most of the year to get together and talk. It would seem that we all got away from the parking lot without a single mugging.

1977

YEAR AFTER YEAR, MUCH WORK had gone into the flagging, clearing, and blazing of the Loop Trail, and in 1975 it had been declared 95% complete. However, lack of use and poor maintenance on some sections had allowed it again to become overgrown and indistinct for much of the route.

New Side Trails Development Committee Chairman George Owen announced early in January plans for reopening the Trail and for publicizing it so that foot traffic would help to keep it open. Anticipation of the completion of the Toccoa River bridge made the task even more urgent.

Club work trips on the Loop Trail were scheduled for every available weekend during the winter, spring and summer. Forest Service YCC help also did a good bit of work in clearing and tread work. On a hastily scheduled trip in July, ten Club members spread out along the section between Licklog Mountain and Fish Gap to flag it for a YCC group to clear during the coming week.

The completion of the bridge in September provided the "last major link;" and as Owen then reported, the Trail "can be hiked with no problems from end to end, from Slaughter Gap to Springer Mountain."

Newspaper and magazine articles reported on the new Trail, and it began to be used by groups and individuals eager for new hiking territory. The GATC scheduled several trips on it. Leader John Myers, announcing a hike from Three Forks to Highway 60, declared, "We were admonished *to use the Loop Trail*, so . . . all hikers will be required to shuffle their feet a lot."

In the spring, a brochure was prepared by members Clark Hill, Lyman

Emerson, Margaret Drummond and Herb Daniel, with description and map of the Trail, and was placed in several outdoor shops. The side trails development committee requested that the Club name the new trail for Larry Freeman, much-loved past president of the Club, but inquiries determined that it could not be done, since the Trail was actually the AT.

The now "annual walk-thru" of the Georgia Trail was carried out on a foggy, rainy day in April, with 40 people checking and recording the condition of the Trail and the shelters. An extra work trip in August was scheduled in order to construct a new, more gradual trail down to the spring at Chattahoochee Gap, to replace the old trail that had become a badly-eroded "slide." In October, a maintenance trip saw a variety of tasks completed on sections of both the white and the blue blazed trails. During the year, a floor was put in the Gooch Gap shelter by the Forest Service.

A new location was found for the Big Stamp shelter near the intersection of the white blazed and blue blazed trails about a mile or so north on the Trail from Big Stamp Gap. It was moved by the Forest Service in August (although not on the spot selected by the GATC), repaired, and a new floor installed. At the suggestion of Lyman Emerson, it was named the Cross Trails shelter.

After the shelter was moved, there was no longer any reason to go through Big Stamp Gap (when the AT was relocated through Three Forks off of the road to Winding Stair Gap some years earlier, it left a long dog-leg from Springer Mountain out to Big Stamp Gap and back to Stover Creek and Three Forks), so it was decided to change the new blue blazed trail between Springer Mountain and the Cross Trails shelter to make it the white blazed trail, and make the Trail through Big Stamp Gap a blue blazed side trail. Relocation procedures were initiated, although things were a bit confused because the blue blazed trail was actually the official AT. This change in the Trails was held up for various reasons for several years, and to date, has not been made official.

The May GATC Board minutes noted the following, as reported by President Margaret Drummond:

At the January meeting of ANSTAC in Asheville, North Carolina, a resolution to recommend that the National Park Service restudy the Blue Ridge Parkway Extension into Georgia was tabled. Instead, the AT Project Officer, Dave Richie, was asked to review with the NPS future plans for, and possible termination on a permanent basis of, the Blue Ridge Parkway Extension into Georgia as well as official designation of the actual AT route in Georgia. Margaret Drummond has written Richie to determine who will make the choice as to which route will be used if there is a choice to be made at this time.

At the GATC–Forest Service meeting in June, the question was discussed of changing the Federal Register to make the white blazed Trail again the official AT. According to Forest Service officials, the previous GATC request to have the white blazed Trail designated a scenic side trail was still "in the Regional

Office," and "politics" prevented its being acted upon. Suggestions were made for the GATC and/or the ATC to write to the Department of the Interior to request the "old" AT be reinstated as the official Trail, although earlier requests had been "squelched" by the Park Service. It was also noted that a law on the Georgia books authorizing the Blue Ridge Parkway would have to be removed before anything could be done. President Drummond continued attempts to find out what it would take to resolve the issue.

In late 1976 and early 1977 the GATC had joined with other conservation groups in forming the Southern Highlands Coalition, the purpose of which was to save the Standing Indian area from the "Unit 22" plan of the Forest Service. An appeal was filed by the group with the Regional Forester, contending that the plan was "arbitrary, capricious, unreasonable and unlawful," according to the GATC Board minutes. As a part of the Coalition, the Club voted at the January Board meeting to solicit funds from the membership to help support the appeal. President Drummond was able to report in the May bulletin:

Regional U.S. Forester, Lawrence Whitfield, has responded to the appeal, filed by the Southern Highlands Coalition, by granting a stay of management in the Standing Indian Basin until the area can be studied for possible wilderness designation, sometime within the next 3-5 years. The action culminates almost two years of work by the SHC and represents a major victory. . . .

Many GATC members—and the Georgia Trail—became deeply involved in a new study, the second Roadless Area Review and Evaluation (RARE II)— mandated by the President and to be carried out by the U.S. Forest Service. This study would inventory "roadless areas" in the Eastern United States which were on federal lands with the intent of considering them for wilderness designation, or for categories of special or limited management. It was said that this was the "last chance" for these lands to be considered for wilderness. The study was to receive input from groups and citizens, who would identify particular areas which met the requirements and propose them to the Forest Service for inclusion.

Workshops were held all over the South and East to explain the RARE II process; several GATC members attended one in Dahlonega in August. The Club was asked for their input into the study, and several members outlined a number of areas which included the entire white blazed and blue blazed trails. Each of these areas was assigned to small groups of members to study for the purpose of gathering information on the terrain, biological and science features, elevation, size, etc., and see that the areas met the criteria for "roadless areas." As Margaret Drummond reported in the December bulletin, the groups "did the necessary map and field study and submitted the necessary information. As a result, most of the lands through which the Georgia AT and Loop Trail pass not only were submitted, but met the necessary criteria and were included in the final inventory."

The RARE II issue was highly controversial, and caused many protests from citizens in the mountains near the proposed wilderness areas. It was said by some that the Forest Service personnel (who were not in favor of wilderness for the national forests—although they claimed neutrality) misrepresented the issue, and stirred up even more opposition.

Several especially memorable hikes were made during the year by the Club. New Year's Eve was celebrated by seven GATCers with fireworks at Betty's Creek Gap on the snow-covered Standing Indian loop trail. Perhaps disturbed by the unusual noise, a friendly little mouse found friendly Herb Daniel's tent a welcome respite from the eight-degree weather during the night.

Another memorable trip was led by Harold Arnovitz in his favorite area of Moccasin Creek. He reported for the bulletin:

The day was crisp, clear and cold. Snow and ice covered the Wildcat Creek Road from the Fish Hatchery to Fuller Gap as Ranger Allen Padgett hauled us in his four-wheel drive truck. The hearty souls rode in the open deck with the cold mountain air whipping through them while the others sat cozy in the cab.

The gentle climb up Pigpen Ridge warmed us enough to shed a couple of layers of clothes. The bright snow-capped landscape silhouetted itself against the clear dark blue sky. We intermingled our own tracks amid those of deer, bear, raccoon and wild turkey as we crossed the ridge to Moccasin Creek. The steel hand cable made crossing the icy log over the cascading waters almost enjoyable. . . .

John Krickel boiled a mouth-watering, stomach-warming meal-in-a-bag of ground steak and vegetables, which we all enviously eyed. . . .

As the day wore on, we hiked along Chastain Creek and up to Deep Gap where the wind belted us and made our ascent of Kelly Knob all the more difficult on the four inch deep snow-covered AT. The descent into Addis Gap was punctuated by the pounding of our backsides on the icy patches on the Trail. . . .

After twelve hours in the sack, morning finally arrived. We downed a quick breakfast in the eight degree shelter and headed to Round Mountain and over spectacular Bramlett Ridge to our rendezvous with Allen and Carin Padgett at Fuller Gap. They were waiting for us with their truck and two sleds. After Harry and Sally exhibited their sledding expertise, Allen attached two lines from the truck to the sleds and we all took our turn being pulled down the road back to the Fish Hatchery. John Martin and Harry were crowned the capsizing duo while Roz and Harold took their first-time-ever on sleds in stride. Sally rode alongside Allen as he displayed his acrobatic talents and John Krickel did exceptionally well free-wheeling it down a steep stretch.

Ed Selby, in reporting on his "Double Trouble Hike: Compass and Bushwhack," in March, declared, "Word about my annual bushwhack hikes must be spreading." Only one person (a newcomer) signed up for this adventure in the Dukes Creek–Cowrock area, which, from all reports, lived up to its name.

Then in July came THE BEAR STORY (until a better one comes along). Of a night on Bolos Creek on a loop hike to Hughes Ridge in the Smokies, participant Rosalind Van Landingham reported:

We were not alarmed when Harold said he had seen a bear up on the trail. After all, we were in the Smokies and everyone knows bears are there. We *were* a bit surprised when we saw the bear ambling over to our campsite where breakfast preparations were underway. Most surprised, however, was John Martin who, unaware that a bear had been seen, announced clearly, 'There's a (expletive deleted) bear over here. Get the food!' We quickly gathered all the food, we thought, and left the area—John first, Roz a close second, Sally with bowl of cereal in hand, and David and Bobby with less haste. When we reached the trail, we stopped and watched while the bear made his rounds of the campsite, and Harold bravely moved in close for pictures. The bear discovered Bobby's abandoned breakfast, ate it, sniffed the packs, and then found his prize— Sally's food sack which we had overlooked. Quickly, the bear picked up the food, gracefully crossed the creek, and climbed up the hill to eat. While he ate, we hastened to pack up and move on to the next campsite where we told our bear story to the ones there. No sooner had we finished when Hillrie notice something moving up on the hill, and Gail exclaimed, "I see a bear!' The bear had followed us up the trail. This time he was frightened away by Bobby who charged up the trail blowing his whistle, and by David who wildly waved his hands and shouted.

Leader John Krickel announced the first Club hike of the entire Georgia Trail, saying, "Most of us have covered the AT in Georgia in bits and pieces over the years, but here is the opportunity to see it all at one time exactly as viewed by the hundreds of through-hikers who leave Springer Mountain each year." Thirteen people began the hike at Springer Mountain; on the third day, the trip was "washed out" by torrential rains and the group repaired to the Smith House in Dahlonega where they spread tents on the lawn to dry, and made good use of the dryers at the local laundromat. After a sumptuous dinner to console themselves, and a very unfavorable weather report, the group voted to temporarily halt the hike and return home. Seven of the original participants returned in October to complete the hike to Bly Gap.

A new activity which was soon to become a part of the Club schedule each year was noted in the August bulletin:

The 'Madness' is rapidly spreading, clearly indicating it to be infectious in nature. Legionnaire's Disease? No, the Peachtree Road Race 'madness.' Only a few short years ago, this disease was first spotted in the form of Tom Aderhold. From Tom's initial case, it has spread and is now infecting increasing numbers of GATCers. . . . Our advice? Stay calm; take any indicated preventive precautions. *Maybe* you can escape infection.

What was to become an annual "unofficial" Club trip to the West was begun in 1977 when a group of nine members and one "bear lure" (non-member) traveled to Glacier National Park to hike for a week in that "star-studded wonderland of vistas, including waterfalls, lakes, forests, scree fields, and

achingly high mountains to which cling the inexorable glaciers," as reported by
Marty Rubin.

At the suggestion of Whit Benson, in March the Board created a "pioneer
member" category for Elizabeth White, Marene Snow, Lou Hoben, and Henry
Morris, who had been members of the Club since the early 1930's. The four
were given a life membership in the Club.

The historical marker designating the beginning of the approach to the AT
which was to be placed at Amicalola Falls had finally been completed and
installed, and a dedication ceremony was held in April, hosted by the Georgia
Department of Natural Resources and the Park superintendent. Three of the
four GATC pioneer members, along with President Margaret Drummond,
unveiled the marker for the small crowd, and GATC members Herb Daniel and
Bob Calvert held a backpacking workshop, and George Owen gave a talk on
other trails.

The now biennial Appalachian Trail Conference meeting was held in 1977
at Shepherd College in Shepherdstown, West Virginia, in May. Fourteen GATC
members attended. A fine display featuring the Loop Trail was arranged by
Clark Hill, with an artistic map drawn by Mary Eidson and photographs by John
Krickel. Workshops were given on "Hints and Kinks for Backpackers" by Herb
Daniel, Bill Durrett, and Bob Calvert, and "Drystopping" by John Krickel.
(These workshops were repeated for the Club at a special event in August.)

The outstanding event of the Conference was a "stunning" announcement
by Assistant Secretary of the Interior Robert Herbst that the administration
would seek $90 million for the purchase of private land along the Trail, in
order, once and for all, to provide protection for the constantly threatened
Trail. An article in the *Atlanta Journal and Constitution* reported on the speech:

After 50 years, the federal government has reversed its hands-off policy and pledged to
protect the 2,000-mile Appalachian Trail.

The world-famous Trail, which follows mountain ridges from Maine to Georgia, was
built and has been maintained almost entirely by volunteers. In recent years, private
landowners have barred hikers from hundreds of miles of the original path. Federal
officials have deplored the trend while denying responsibility for reversing it.

'This administration accepts that responsibility,' Assistant Interior Secretary Robert
L. Herbst told 900 cheering members of the Appalachian Trail Conference at
Shepherdstown, West Virginia, recently.

'It is my objective that we will be able to protect at least 300 miles of the Trail's 600
unprotected miles now listed as the most threatened, by your next meeting in 1979,'
Herbst said. 'You have my commitment that we will seek the funds—be they federal or
matching—needed.' He said Interior will seek $35 million for openers.

'It was an about-face if I ever heard one,' said Ed Garvey of the Potomac Appalachian
Trail Club. The speech, delivered in stentorian tones that shook the room and started
tears from some who had thought they'd never see the day, brought Herbst a standing ovation.

The "long awaited event"—the completion of the Toccoa River bridge in mid-September—was celebrated on November 5 with a dedication ceremony at the site. About 50 people—Club members, Forest Service personnel, and friends—gathered in an off-and-on rain to hear brief speeches by Bill Blalock, district ranger, GATC President Margaret Drummond, and Pat Thomas, Forest Supervisor, and to watch as they cut the ribbon to officially open the bridge. A short hike out to Highway 60 by some of the group was led by George Owen.

Historian Theo Taylor and President Margaret Drummond visited the state archives during the year to examine the Club historical files and to make plans for GATC help in organizing them. It was decided that the work could be accomplished with the help of the Club for two days a month for a year. No volunteers were forthcoming for this project.

Hoping to ease the load of traffic on the AT, map committee chairman Lyman Emerson began work in 1977 on the identification of trails in North Georgia other than the AT. As Emerson reported, "Our eventual goal is the publication and distribution of this information to encourage hikers to explore other areas. . . . We are working with the U.S. Forest Service on the project and hope they can put out the information in booklet form."

The first thru-hike of the entire Loop Trail (sans bridge) was made in July by Rosalind Van Landingham and Nancy Shofner. Three other members accompanied them for part of the way, and all were surprised at Mulky Gap in the middle of the night by a mock (it sounded real!) war among Army rangers.

Club treasurer George Galphin began inquiries during the year to try to clarify whether or not the Club could have tax exempt status. He reported in November that the tax exempt status was "almost complete."

Once again the Board of Directors questioned the qualifications for membership of a prospective member; but Hillrie Quin was approved, as the bulletin stated, "in spite of the fact that he was reported to shave regularly on hikes."

A campground near Townsend in the foothills of the Smokies was the scene of the Multi-Club Meet. Forty-one GATCers were among the 200 attendees. Hank Lautz, who had replaced Paul Pritchard as executive director of the ATC, was the guest speaker.

The annual meeting in October featured "a mix of Club business and the usual lively talkathon," according to the bulletin. Officers for the coming year were elected: Margaret Drummond, president; Whit Benson, vice president; George Galphin, treasurer; Bill Durrett, secretary; Bob Calvert, membership director; Nancy Shofner, Trail supervisor; Marty Rubin, Trails information director; Mandy Coffey, historian; Rosalind Van Landingham, bulletin editor; Ed Selby, director.

Although only two work trips had been originally scheduled for 1977, twelve had actually been made—something of a departure from recent years. President Margaret Drummond, realizing that Trail maintenance was the real reason for being of the GATC, had begun during the year to emphasize this function more. In July, the Board had voted to award three activity points to prospective members for each day of Trail work instead of the usual two. As the bulletin stated, the intent was "to provide both greater incentive and recognition for participation in an essential Club function." Also for these reasons, at the annual meeting Drummond initiated an award, "Trail worker of the year," to be given each year to a person who had been an outstanding worker on the Trail and for the Club during the year. The first such award was given to Lyman Emerson. Three other members were given a "Trail worker" patch in recognition of their contributions.

With the approval of the Board—but with dire predictions of failure by some—Drummond also requested the incorporation into the 1978 activities schedule of one Trail maintenance trip per month.

Toward the end of the year the Walasi-yi Inn at Neel Gap was approved for entry into the National Register of Historic Places. The form nominating the building for inclusion was sent by Dave Sherman to the Club, and gives an interesting description and history of the building, as follows (in part):

The Inn is a one-story structure built of native stone on a natural bed and was constructed by the Civilian Conservation Corps . . . during 1934-38. The land on which it stands is part of a parcel given to the State of Georgia by Mr. Fred Vogel, Jr., and Mr. August H. Vogel on May 1, 1927. The original gift was of 16 acres, only two of which are at Neel Gap. . . .

The northernmost portion of the building, which is reached by crossing the Appalachian Trail, is connected to the main building by a covered walkway. This was originally a wooden structure, built by the Pfister-Vogel Land Company. It was used as a tea room and for lodging. During the CCC construction, this structure was veneered with stone to tie in with the other section of the building. The old tea room became the actual lodging quarters of the Inn. . . .

The interior walls are all panelled with chestnut, and room numbers originally used for guest lodging remain on the doors. . . .

The main building originally consisted of a foyer with a concessions counter, a chestnut-panelled dining and lounge area with crossed chestnut beams and rafters. . . .

The State in 1925 completed a highway leading through Lumpkin County into Blairsville in Union County and on to Murphy, North Carolina. The highway at that time was a 20-foot graded road with a ten-foot paved strip. On the 4th of July, 1925, a dedication ceremony was held at Neel Gap, the site of the Inn. The local newspapers reported that between 3,000 and 4,000 people attended the ceremony, said to be the largest number that had ever gathered on any mountain in the area. State Representative Bonnell Stone of Union County had been instrumental in the conception and construction of the highway. . . .

Until the highway was built, the gap was known as Frogtown Gap, a name which had been used since the Cherokee inhabited the area. In fact, one historian says that Walasi was a great mythical frog in Cherokee lore who was the chieftain of the animal council, and made his home high in the gap. Frogtown Gap was changed to Neel Gap about

1924 in honor of the engineer in charge of the highway construction. . . .

Near the turn of the century, the Pfister-Vogel Leather Company of Milwaukee, Wisconsin, bought approximately 65,000 acres of land around what is now Vogel State Park. At that time, tanbark and tanwood from trees were used to supply tannic acid for the leather company's tanning processes. During World War I, however, a synthetic tannic acid was developed, saving some of their Georgia forest land from destruction. But the Pfister-Vogel Company also had five saw mills on their property and participated in logging. . . . Shortly after the Vogels' first gift to Georgia, the State set aside Vogel State Forest Park. . . .

With the beginning of President Roosevelt's Emergency Conservation Work in 1933, a CCC camp was set up on the eastern side of the highway at the bottom of the ridge to the north of Neel Gap. . . . It was used to develop Vogel State Park as a scenic recreation area. At the site of another Vogel grant of 91 acres, an earthen dam was built and water impounded in a 130-acre lake. Cabins were built here, and this area is now the central lodging area of Vogel State Park. A picnic area was developed at Notteley Falls, and an overnight shelter erected at the top of Blood Mountain. A portion of the Appalachian Trail extended from Neel Gap to the crest of Blood Mountain, and a three-mile trail from Notteley Falls to Helton Falls. A system of foot trails was constructed at the park by the CCC. . . .

Most of the development work accomplished by the CCC was concentrated at Neel Gap, where the stone inn was built, along with two log cabins, a 10,000-gallon, spring-fed reservoir and sewerage system. The stone for the Inn's construction came from the highway construction. . . .

The Inn was immediately popular. The year after its completion, the State Parks director recommended that additional bedrooms and servants' quarters be constructed at the Inn. The State leased the Inn to concessionaires from the beginning. . . . Although it was popular, it was never financially successful. . . .

1978

GEORGIA
APPALACHIAN
19 TRAIL CLUB, INC. 30

AS GATC PRESIDENT Margaret Drummond stated in her message in the 1978 yearbook, "... The year ahead appears to hold both new, and renewed, challenges for each of us ... in the form of increased demands on our time and energies for the purpose of Trail protection." She continued, "... At the national level, the picture is exciting. For the first time in nearly ten years, Congress will be considering legislation which directly affects the Appalachian Trail and the Trail corridor.... Each of us will be asked to help by writing to our Congressmen, by urging that others also write and by ... [talking] Trail protection.... At the local level Trail protection, i.e., Trail maintenance, will be needed as perhaps never before...." And so began a year of involvement in, and dedication to, Trail maintenance as hadn't been seen in the GATC for quite a few years.

As was anticipated, in March Congress passed, and President Carter signed, the amendment to the 1968 National Scenic Trails Act, thereby authorizing $90,000,000 for the acquisition of lands along the AT. The Act also re-established ANSTAC for a ten-year period, and mandated a "comprehensive plan for the management, acquisition, development, and use of the Appalachian Trail." As ATC Board Chairman George Zoebelein stated in the March *ATN:*

This new legislation is probably the most significant bill affecting the Trail since its inception. Its passage means a new relationship with AT volunteers in order to maintain a footpath whose corridor will be owned by federal and state agencies. The ramifications are far-reaching. Trail standards will have to be reviewed and revised in conjunction with the National Park Service. A management plan must ensure that the Trail will receive proper maintenance. Plans!!! Rules!!! Are they going to institutionalize the Appalachian Trail as part of the bureaucracy? Without continued involvement of the conference of Trail clubs, and other friends of the AT, this could very well happen.

The ATC Board . . . re-dedicated itself to continue and maintain the spirit and vision of the AT [and] began the process of shaping and redefining its future role: one in which the volunteer traditions remain strong and become even further enhanced.

These, then, are the first steps in a new relationship. For it to succeed fully, the AT tradition must not be allowed to erode. If we retain the sense of volunteerism, the commitment of trail-workers, and the elation of hikers, I am confident that this new federal relationship will serve to strengthen our goals. Thus a challenge lies ahead for us!

The Act would call for new responsibilities and extended commitments from the AT Clubs—including, of course, the GATC. GATC President Margaret Drummond, along with others, commented in the May/June *ATN* on the Act, saying:

The impact of this latest legislation will obviously vary greatly depending upon the section through which the Trail passes. In the east, where much of the Trail is on private land, subject to whims of landowners and developers, the bill and the money it provides will now make it possible to bring these lands under control and protection. In Georgia, however, the entire Trail is already on public lands in the Chattahoochee National Forest, subject mostly to overuse and the vagaries of USFS management. . . .

So, from the southern end (or start!) of the Trail, it appears that although the Appalachian Trail Bill is a cause for jubilation, its direct effects may be greater in areas other than our own. The indirect spinoffs, however, may be more considerable, even for us, and are more difficult to anticipate. It appears that volunteers may be asked for greater involvement in Trail maintenance, a challenge which the GATC enthusiastically accepts; there may be a greater need for organization of Trail management at the Conference and the Club levels; other ramifications would require a crystal ball to determine. Whatever lies ahead, however, the GATC is ready and eager to assume a leadership role in a project to which it has been committed for almost 50 years, the maintenance and preservation of the Appalachian Trail.

With such a large amount of federal money to be used for land acquisition instead of for Trail maintenance, the maintaining clubs *would* be called upon for a greater share of the maintenance of the Trail. In the spring, Hank Lautz, Executive Director of the ATC, visited Atlanta and talked with members of the GATC Board of Directors at a special dinner, as well as with the rest of the Club at the spring meeting. One of the purposes of his visit, according to Margaret Drummond, "was to assess the willingness of the GATC, and its volunteers, to assume this increased responsibility for maintenance. The Board of Directors unanimously voted its support. . . ."

Anticipating that an expanded program of Trail maintenance might very well call for more help, both physically and financially, in May, President Drummond asked Board members to re-examine their thoughts and feelings about increasing the Club's membership and raising money. Many possible alternatives were discussed: other categories of membership, chapters in other towns, soliciting aid in Trail maintenance from other groups, raising dues, etc. But once again, the Board voted for the status quo; and eventually (the following year), the only effort made to publicize the Club or seek aid was a small notice/letter that was placed in a number of outdoor shops in the area. The sale of T-shirts did bring in some money, as did the solicitation of a contribution from members as they paid their dues.

The twelve scheduled work trips for the year were more or less equally divided between the white blazed trail and the blue blazed trail. President Drummond had asked for a commitment from each member to attend at least one work trip during the year. This did not happen, but close to 100 members and guests did participate in at least one trip, with an average of about 17 people per work trip, and an estimated total of almost 1,900 person-hours spent on Trail work for the year. (A bi-monthly tally of Trail work hours was published in the bulletin.) So in spite of predictions to the contrary, this year of greatly increased Trail work was a real success.

Plans had begun in 1977 for several "projects" along the Trail, including the re-routing of a number of very steep and eroded sections of Trail, and the identification of campsites along the Trail to try to relieve overuse of areas around shelters. The latter led to the beginnings of a program to develop off-Trail campsites. The work accomplished on the white blazed Trail, according to Trail supervisor Nancy Shofner in her annual report, included the following:

. . . In April, 37 people participated in the fourth annual 'walk-thru' of the entire Georgia Trail, checking on the condition of each section; in May, work was done on a number of different sections, including blazing, clearing, building a small bridge, and some erosion work; in July, a switchback of about ⅓ mile was constructed on Sassafras Mountain north of Horse Gap to replace a steep and rocky section of Trail; in September, about ⅓ mile of relocated Trail was constructed to slab around the side of Gooch Mountain, cutting off the steep and eroded Trail to near the top (these two sections were suggested by the GATC and flagged by the Forest Service).

In June, before undertaking the Trail construction work, a number of members participated in a field session with several Forest Service personnel on proper procedures for laying out and building a trail, using the Sassafras Mountain and Gooch Mountain relocations as examples.

Trail relocations completed this year other than the two mentioned above are: a switchback on Phyllis Spur on the east side of Justus Mountain was constructed by Forest Service crews at the suggestion of the GATC to replace a very steep and eroded section of about ⅛ mile; the Trail was re-routed by the Forest Service for about ½ mile just north of Long Creek to take the Trail off of an old road and to by-pass Hickory

Flats Cemetery, which is privately owned; a relocation of about ½ mile of Trail between
Grassy Gap and Liss Gap (south of Woody Gap), cleared several years ago by the Forest
Service to by-pass private land, was completed this year by the GATC section overseer.
(There remains only about ½ mile of Trail in Georgia on private land—near Jack's Gap
south of Woody Gap.)

The committee also considered and scouted several alternatives to the badly
eroded Trail from Neel Gap to the top of Blood Mountain, and made plans to
relocate the Hawk Mountain shelter and the Trail over Hawk Mountain,
because of the heavy use and abuse of the shelter area and the very eroded
section of Trail.

Though the Loop Trail had been advertised as having been completed
(again) in 1977, there was some adverse publicity (in columnist Browny
Stephens' column) about the lack of blazing in some areas and lack of sufficient
water sources. Several work trips early in the year attempted to remedy the
situation by again clearing and blazing most of the section between Highway 60
and Slaughter Gap; and in October, scouting parties located several new water
sources in the area between Mulky and Wolfpen Gaps. A section of the Trail
from Wolfpen Gap to the top of Wildcat Mountain was re-routed in June to
avoid a clear-cut area on the east side of the mountain. Much work—on both
Trails—of clearing brush, installing water bars and working the tread was done
by Forest Service YCC crews.

The high point of the year in Trail maintenance was a "Trail Skills Workshop"
held in November. This was developed through the efforts of Rima Farmer
(new southern field representative for the ATC, with the job of coordinating
and helping the southern clubs) and Margaret Drummond. The purpose was
to learn from "experts" the skills necessary for laying out and building trails,
and for proper upkeep through erosion control techniques. The GATC
workshop was to be a pilot for future regional workshops which were planned
by the ATC. The Club secured the services of Bob Proudman of the AMC, and
author of the new book *AMC Field Guide to Trail Building and Maintenance*, to be
the main "instructor." Others assisting in the instruction were Dave Startzell of
the ATC, Jim Botts of the Smoky Mountain Club, Mike Beattie of the Forest
Service in Gainesville, and Dennis Lowell of the Georgia Department of
Natural Resources. The site selected for study and possible relocation was
Blood Mountain. Margaret Drummond reported on the weekend for the
bulletin:

A GATC member and former Trails supervisor remarked recently that Trail work 'is
really pretty dull and routine, splashing paint and hacking weeds.' That member
should have attended the Club's first Trails Skills Workshop and seen the CAPACITY
crowd of energetic participants scrambling all over the side of Blood Mountain,
implementing the skills imparted to them by Bob Proudman . . . and his crew of
experts from Conference, the U.S. Forest Service and Georgia DNR.

The participants were unusual . . . all GATC members, for a change, and mostly Trail crews (6 or 7 non-members on the waiting list had to be turned down!); motivated and enthusiastic; eager to see, to hear, to learn and to do. And what they did was (1) to scout, flag and cut a relocation from the top of Blood Mountain which, when completed, will eliminate 5-6 rocky and eroded switchbacks and will pass undoubtedly the most scenic view in all of north Georgia (a 180° panorama); (2) to dig trenches, fell trees and install water bars; (3) to move rock boulders and build rock cribbing to reinforce the trail; (4) to learn the use of, and to use, firerakes, Pulaskis, pinchbars, Abney levels and clinometers. What they LEARNED would take more space than the Editor allows . . . but was, in part, a heightened self-confidence and sense of accomplishment.

Lest you think the weekend was all work . . . there was fun and fellowship during the overnight at Camp Glisson; dinner at the Smith House; an evening of discussion, remarks by Mike, Jim and Dennis, and a slide presentation by Proudman illustrating trail work in the White Mountains.

For the next three months, on work trips on frigid winter days, the Club was to work on this relocation until it was completed in February of 1979. As leader George Galphin reported in December:

Can you imagine 20 normal people gathering on the coldest day of the season in gale force winds for any type of outdoor activity? To work? For no pay? Perhaps not normal, but 20 members and guests did meet in windswept Neel Gap at 9:30 A.M. with the thermometer reading 18° F. to help construct a re-route of the AT near the top of Blood Mountain. . . .

The discussions during the workshop about the entire Trail up Blood Mountain, and the shelter on top, were to lead eventually to another long relocation and to the complete renovation of the old CCC-built shelter.

Dave Startzell, in writing to Trail supervisor Nancy Shofner after the workshop, declared, "I thought the workshop was very successful—if we had 64 clubs along the Trail like the Georgia ATC our problems would be in control." (November 22, 1978)

The year's hiking schedule had begun with a cold and damp trip to Miry Ridge and Silers Bald in the Smokies, where, as Whit Benson reported, "That night, around a small campfire of wet wood, it was decided to shiver in the New Year at 12 o'clock GMT."

A different sort of winter hike was enjoyed in sunny Florida, as 12 members and guests "motored" (some in Charles Jackson's "rolling party" van) down I-75 for a three-day hike on the Florida Trail. As reported by leader John Krickel, the trail "led high along bluffs overlooking the inky-black Suwanee River . . . past the snowy white sand bars . . . huge live oaks . . . swaying strands of Spanish moss . . . palmetto palm strangely interspersed with groves of beautiful holly and periodically punctuated with enormous sink holes . . . a native red bay tree . . . gentle, clumsy armadillos . . . owls . . . wild hogs . . . and the crossing of flooded creeks . . . on felled logs. . . . The Florida Trail, we agreed, was another world. . . ."

A day of "orienteering" in April was one of several "instructional" trips during the year. A group of energetic members and guests met at Franklin D. Roosevelt State Park at Pine Mountain for a day of map and compass work and running courses planned and set up by leaders Gale Benson and Joe Boyd.

A large crowd of day hikers in early April was unprepared for the unseasonably hot and dry day and the difficulty of the trail, as they struggled along the Loop Trail, some from Mulky Gap and some from Fish Gap, toward Highway 60. It was almost six o'clock as the last of the group gathered at Grizzle's Store, and leader Gannon Coffey's recommendations on the hike were: (1) "censored" and (2) "reroute."

A "whitewater canoe training trip" was led in April by John Krickel and Craig Lyerla, as reported by Krickel in the bulletin:

We had two perfect days and two perfect rivers for our whitewater canoe lessons. The first day on the Hudson River (seems to me there is another river up north by that name) was equally divided between admiring the beautiful stands of wild azalea and learning the strange new ways of wild river running. Our only disagreement of the trip arose on Saturday night when we had to choose between eating at North Georgia's best barbecue stand or at the best catfish restaurant. (Barbecue won on the toss of a coin.) We camped in the backyard of our leader's mother, where we also had a leisurely indoor breakfast on Sunday morning. Later, Sunday found us on a genuine, nerve-tingling whitewater river, shooting over four-foot ledges and speeding down half-mile boiling rapids. Co-leader and expert canoe instructor, Craig Lyerla, looked seven feet tall as he *stood up* in his solo canoe, calmly navigating rapids that had the rest of us gripping our paddles white-knuckled and breathless with excitement. Graduation exercises for the training were conducted at the awesome 'Rooster-tail' rapid, which everyone ran beautifully. Rosalind and Nancy deserve some kind of medal as the only beginners who did not turn over at least once; John Myers deserves some kind of medal for just the opposite.

A four-day hike in the Roan Mountain area on the July fourth weekend provided a variety of activities including beautiful scenery, "a *lot* of uphill, *some* downhill," according to leader Roz Van Landingham, and a thunderstorm atop Grassy Ridge, "an excellent crop of strawberries," lovely Laurel Fork Gorge, popcorn, watermelon carried in by Roz and Hillrie, and a crotchety waitress at a restaurant where somehow the hikers managed to eat several times.

Leader Mary Eidson reported on unusual events on a day hike from Neel Gap to DeSoto Falls:

Was it a mirage?—But the cokes were real! There on a tree on a knoll about two miles into the uncharted woods, we came upon a sign saying 'Welcome GATC.' Underneath was a table with a tablecloth—a tablecloth?!—ice, cups, and cokes, a trash bag to the side and entrepreneur J. P. Eidson waiting to serve a hot, thirsty, surprised throng who had come past three dry (formerly free-running) springs.

It was a lovely trail, mostly open except for several hundred feet just off the AT, up from Neel, past Pointer, Balanced or Council Rock. We trekked in the direction it pointed, found a cave rock overhang, another pointer rock—but as the legend says is there, *no* gold. There are delightful places for overnight camping which would make it a much more leisurely walk than we took—'gold' in itself!

A moonlight hike up Stone Mountain in November was enjoyed by 47 members and guests, who huddled behind the buildings on top for shelter from the wind, and enjoyed hot coffee, chocolate and cookies.

Thanksgiving was observed by 15 members and guests on Cumberland Island, with part of the group at a back-country camp site on the beach, and part at Sea Camp campground. All enjoyed hiking along the beach and around the beautiful island, star-gazing, seeing wild horses, huge live oak trees, old mansions, one armadillo and "one old alligator."

At the GATC–Forest Service meeting in June, the issue of the "official Trail" was discussed once again. It was decided that a "task force" of GATC members and Forest Service personnel would "get together and determine where the Trail should be located in Georgia, whether it be on the old location, the present Federal Register location, or a combination of the two," according to the Forest Service record of the meeting. The group would then recommend the *best* trail for the approval of the Club and the Forest Service. "When this is done," continued the report, "we will propose a major redescription of the Trail in Georgia and try to punch it through the Park Service and get it into the Federal Register." The "other" trail would then be proposed for a national recreation trail. The Task Force met during the year and solicited statements from Club members on what the official trail should be.

Activity continued in the Club's attempts to have areas surrounding the Trail included in the RARE II wilderness proposals. Numerous letters were written by Club members supporting the issue, a position statement was prepared by conservation committee chairman George Goldman, and a strong rebuttal to the "anti-wilderness" draft environmental impact statement on RARE II was prepared by Whit Benson.

Early in the year, the GATC education committee presented for Club members a movie on hypothermia, and in May conducted a "training backpack" for new or inexperienced members and guests. Both were declared a success and left all participants "a bit wiser."

Maps committee chairman Lyman Emerson settled once and for all (?) which section of the Georgia Trail was the toughest to hike. According to the bulletin, Emerson, "using Trail data compiled for a map in preparation and a mathematical formula that incorporates an 'effort' factor, ranks the AT sections (south to north) in order of difficultness." According to his calculations, the most difficult is the Unicoi Gap to Indian Grave Gap section, and the easiest is Low Gap to Chattahoochee Gap. Emerson also measured the Loop Trail with the measuring wheel—for the first time—and declared it to be 35.5 miles long.

Cashing in on the trend of the times, the Board voted during the year to order and sell Club T-shirts. Designed by Ed Selby, the shirts were green or green and white, with the Club hiker emblem and name on the pocket area. They were very popular and provided a "uniform" for Club outings.

In the spring, the ATC began publication of the *Register*, "a newsletter for Trail maintainers and volunteers." It was to take up where the *ATN* had left off—at least in part—in communicating news of the Trail and the clubs to its membership.

Following a discussion at the September Board meeting of guests on outings and possible liability incurred in case of an accident, the Board asked lawyer member Marty Rubin to draft a waiver and release form for use on each hike. Beginning the following year, the form was used, and each participant was asked to sign at the beginning of the hike.

An announcement in the bulletin in June told of the recent death of Warner Hall who almost 50 years earlier had been so much a part of the GATC.

The Multi-Club Meet, held at Roan Mountain, Tennessee, was reported on in the bulletin by Margaret Drummond:

. . . Twelve GATC members and friends represented the Georgia Club at the Labor Day weekend Multi-Club meeting at Roan Mountain State Park which 160 people attended. The weather was superb, warm but with a tinge of fall in the air; hikes over Roan Mountain were challenging; the fellowship was incomparable; AND . . . the blueberries were ripe.

At the annual business meeting, Chester Elliott, GATC member since the early 30's, and who somehow had been overlooked in the designation of pioneer members in 1977, was officially declared a pioneer member. Two other long-time members, Bob and Margaret Scott, were at the annual dinner, and were greeted warmly by many old friends. Trail worker awards and recognitions were made, and officers for the coming year were elected: Whit Benson, president; George Galphin, vice president; John Krickel, secretary; Dudley Eggleston, treasurer; Bob Calvert, membership director; Bob Slater, Trail supervisor; Marty Rubin, Trail information director; Mandy Coffey, historian; Rosalind Van Landingham, bulletin editor; Margaret Drummond and Al Thompson, directors.

"About 100 members and friends gathered at the Northside Y to enjoy the annual Christmas party—the usual good food and fellowship," stated the bulletin account. Chester Elliott, the fifth pioneer member, was present and was recognized. (The Club was very sad to learn in late January of 1979 that Elliott had died earlier in the month.) Special recognition was given to outgoing President Margaret Drummond for her emphasis on Trail maintenance during the year, and, as the bulletin continued, "Whit Benson presented Margaret Drummond the first yearbook for 1979; Gale Benson, artist for the yearbook cover (a picture of Margaret painting a blaze on a tree), presented Margaret the framed, original drawing from which the cover picture was made."

The December bulletin also recognized Drummond's accomplishments, saying:

THANKS, MARGARET!

For the last two years the GATC has moved forward under the leadership of Margaret Drummond. Margaret has been a totally involved president and pursued her duties with her usual enthusiasm and careful attention to all areas of GATC activity. Probably, the most notable of her accomplishments has been to focus our attention on our responsibilities for the protection and maintenance of the Trail. Margaret has spent a vast amount of her time on behalf of the Club and has readily given encouragement and assistance to others involved in the Club's work.

To Margaret we all say, 'Thanks, you did a great job!'

Drummond's contribution to the GATC's renewed commitment to Trail maintenance cannot be overestimated. Her presidency seemed to be a turning point in the direction of the Club, and gave momentum to the trend which was developing, after a lapse of many years, toward a greater responsibility for the upkeep of the Trail. The two years of steady work on the Loop Trail by the GATC had built a cadre of Trail workers and a tradition of Trail maintenance which were now a permanent part of the Club's personality. A prospective member was viewed as much in the light of his contribution to work trips as his hiking ability. None of the light-heartedness of former years was lost, but now the Trail building activities were among the "in" events.

1979

GEORGIA APPALACHIAN TRAIL CLUB, INC.

"**P**LANS! RULES!" ATC's George Zoebelein had exclaimed as he considered the ramifications of the new amendment to the National Scenic Trails Act in 1978. Whit Benson, new president of the GATC, doubtless shared his concern (dismay?) that the Trail and the clubs might drown in red tape and regulations, as he doggedly worked most of the year of 1979 on "plans and rules," namely a "cooperative agreement" with the Forest Service, procedures to follow in reporting Club work plans to the Forest Service, and a "management plan" that was mandated by Conference for each club.

Also of concern to Benson, as expressed in his yearbook message to the Club, was (1) how the Club could effectively work for and encourage conservation or wilderness legislation under its present by-laws, which forbade "influencing" legislation, and (2) the new and growing demands being made on the clubs for maintenance of the Trail. A by-laws committee was appointed to deal with the first issue, and a president's advisory committee to consider the second.

The Cooperative Agreement with the Forest Service grew out of a suggestion the previous year at the Trail Skills Workshop that the Forest Service might be willing to loan the Club tools for Trail maintenance and construction; Forest Supervisor Pat Thomas was agreeable to the idea. From discussions concerning the loan, and also the greater role of the GATC in Trail maintenance, came the drafting of the agreement spelling out the responsibilities of the GATC and the Forest Service in the construction and maintenance of the Trail. (Perhaps, too, Forest Service officials came to realize at the Trail Skills Workshop that the Club was willing and *able* to construct and maintain the Trail as well as—if not better than—they.) The agreement—written by Whit Benson and Bob Slater in conjunction with Forest Service officials—declared that the GATC "shall construct and maintain the Appalachian Trail across the Chattahoochee National Forest, . . . prepare an annual work plan . . . which must be approved by the Forest Service before March 1 each year, . . . take necessary precautions for prevention of fires, and clean up all work areas, . . . promote the public use and recognition" of the Trail, and follow the "Appalachian Trail Relocation Procedures" which had been agreed upon by the two parties the previous year. The Forest Service "shall coordinate with the GATC in locating" the Trail, "furnish supplies and materials," and follow the relocation procedures.

For a time, the Club was very concerned that they would not be able adequately to handle the entire job of Trail maintenance. They had become accustomed to much help from the Forest Service in clearing blowdowns, working the tread of the Trail, building and maintaining shelters, and other heavy jobs. Further discussions were held by the Board on ways to bring in new members or to get help from other groups. But it eventually became clear that the Forest Service would continue to do much of the work when money was available to hire crews, and that the job of keeping up the Trail would continue to be a joint effort. The Club continued to be thankful for, and pleased with, the current administration of the Chattahoochee National Forest.

By early summer, a number of Trail construction tools were loaned (or "transferred," as the form stated) to the GATC by the Forest Service, including swing blades, pulaskis, fire rakes, axes, and eventually a chain saw and a motorized weed cutter.

The mandate in the Cooperative Agreement to furnish a work plan for the year to the Forest Service created another chore for President Benson and Trail Supervisor Bob Slater. The plans for each work trip for the rest of the year were completed by spring and forwarded to Bob Harper of the Forest Service for approval. All of the plans were approved, but with the stipulation that work in several proposed wilderness areas might have to be reconsidered should the areas actually become wilderness.

"Management plans"—from the AT Project Office, from Trail clubs, from Conference, and from the GATC—were to bombard and absorb the time of Club and Conference officials for (at least) the next two years. As required by the Trail Act amendment, a "comprehensive plan" for "management, acquisition, development, and use" of the AT was to be drawn up by the Interior Department and all parties involved within two years. By mid-1979 a "Statement of Management" had been prepared by the Appalachian Trail Project Office (set up to oversee the entire acquisition and management programs for the Trail) under David Richie, which would "serve as a short-term guide to the day-to-day management of the Trail" and was to "provide direction" for the more detailed comprehensive plan. According to the "Purpose" stated in the document, "The result will be overall Trail guidelines insuring the future preservation of the resource, enjoyment of the Trail and compatible cooperative management among all concerned parties." Local club management plans were to be written to "address management and operations issues at the local level."

These local club plans were discussed and explained at the Multi-Club Meet by Hank Lautz; and as the minutes of the September GATC Board meeting stated, "Whit Benson reported that at the Multi-Club meeting, pressure was put on him by the ATC to come up with a management plan for the Georgia AT as a model for other maintaining clubs." Several Board members volunteered to help write the document, and the work was begun. At the annual meeting in October, Benson reported on the plan, and as the minutes recorded:

This plan will probably be presented at one of the next meetings for a vote by the membership. In the course of a spirited discussion, it was pointed out that the National Scenic Trails Act requires such a management plan; if the GATC does not accept the opportunity to draw up such a plan, then Conference or some other organization will do so. The Club endorsed President Benson's agreement to draw up the management plan.

Despite plans and plans for plans, GATC activities went smoothly on. The task force created in 1978 to study the two Georgia Trails and recommend one as the official AT reported in the March bulletin:

The Task Force has begun its work. At a meeting in the fall, it decided that, in order to compare the two Trails, it would be necessary to flag on the ground the undeveloped Federal Register Trail north of Neel Gap. This work has begun. Lyman Emerson has spearheaded a group which is currently scouting and flagging the section north of Bramlett Ridge, over Parks Mountain to Highway 76 and beyond, and has this work almost completed.

On March 3, the Task Force, assisted by the Side Trails Development Committee and the Club membership, will make an all-out, all-day attempt to flag the remote and poorly accessible Chattahoochee Basin section (see first trip writeup in this bulletin). Once the flagging on these two sections is completed, the Task Force, and others interested, will walk and compare both trails. At that time, as well as on March 3, we will need your efforts, comments and recommendation. Although the Task Force has primary responsibility for the assignment, we would like the entire Club membership to share in the final recommendations.

Several four-wheel-drive vehicles were secured for the drive up the old Low Gap–Robertstown road, and on the scheduled day of the flagging, 20 members and guests "braved fog, wind and rain," and essentially completed the tying of flags on the section between Red Clay Gap and Turkeypen Mountain. As the bulletin stated, "Everyone (almost) seemed to enjoy the day in spite of the weather, and found it interesting to explore these off-the-beaten-path areas."

In September an "update" on the task force's work was given by Margaret

Drummond:

. . . the entire undeveloped official Federal Register Trail north of Neel Gap (approximately 35 miles) has been walked by the Task Force, assisted by the Side Trails Development Committee and other Club members, and flagged for the purpose of comparison with the existing unofficial non-Federal Register white blazed Trail.

At a meeting in July following this field work, there was a consensus opinion from the Task Force that *the present ridgetop white blazed Trail is the preferred route for the AT in Georgia*, except for the short distance between Springer Mountain and the Cross Trails Shelter where the blue blazed Trail is recommended. . . .

From Turkeypen Gap (between Neel and Tesnatee Gaps) to Red Clay Gap (between Low and Unicoi Gaps), the route is steep and necessitates many crossings of the Chattahoochee River which would require many bridges; in addition, the route along the river is heavily used by fishermen and campers. The undeveloped Trail north of Bramlett Ridge (near Addis Gap) to Highway 76 (east of Dicks Creek Gap) lies in a more gentle terrain and a beautiful area. However, it was felt that it still is not preferable to the ridgetop, white blazed Trail.

As for the Trail route south of Slaughter Gap, the Task Force voted to recommend the white blazed (unofficial) Trail from Three Forks to Slaughter Gap, the major reason being the undesirability of the close proximity of the blue blazed Loop Trail to the Duncan Ridge Road for much of its length. Between Three Forks and Springer Mountain, the Task Force recommends the blue blazed Trail from the top of Springer Mountain to the Cross Trails Shelter. However, the route between the Cross Trails Shelter and Three Forks evoked much discussion; it appears that any attempts to relocate the Trail off Rich Mountain and closer to its original location along Stover Creek and the stand of virgin hemlocks may run into problems of forest management. This area is under study at present, at the same time that the exact route of the Trail north of Three Forks is being accurately located on topo maps for the first time in many years. By doing these tasks simultaneously, the Task Force hopes to lose no more time in the resolution of this thorny and now longtime problem of TWO AT's in Georgia.

These recommendations were presented to the membership at the annual meeting and, as the minutes stated:

The GATC adopted the following official position on permanent trail location, subject to negotiation with the Forest Service:

1. Springer Mountain to Cross Trails Shelter: Blue blazed Trail.
2. Cross Trails Shelter to Three Forks: The best negotiated route possible, with a side trail to the virgin hemlocks if necessary.
3. Three Forks to the North Carolina line: Present white blazed Trail.

It is understood that the present blue blazed Loop Trail will be maintained but probably change its category to some type of recreation trail.

A redescription of the Georgia Trail was drawn up toward the end of the year by the Forest Service, but the Club found several problems in it which would have to be discussed further.

Conservation committee chairperson Margaret Drummond had reported at the January Board meeting that five areas in Georgia had been proposed for initial inclusion in the RARE II wilderness areas. Two were to include portions of the AT: the southern Nantahalas and Raven Cliffs areas. Several other areas along the Trail were to be in the "further study" category.

The possibility that sections of the Trail might one day be in wilderness areas necessitated re-thinking and re-evaluation of a number of issues. There were questions in the minds of many about exactly what "wilderness" meant, but it was either known or assumed that in a wilderness area there could be, for instance, no structure (shelters), no blazes along the Trail, no motorized vehicles or mechanized tools (chain saws). It was thought by some that these stipulations held for areas under *consideration* for wilderness, which meant—of immediate concern to the GATC—that handsaws must be used to cut blowdowns, no "improvements" could be made on the Blood Mountain shelter, and no side trails (such as the possible development of parts of the flagged Federal Register trail) could be built. However, as time went by, over the next year or so, and no action was taken by Congress on the wilderness issue, the issue became moot.

The first two trail maintenance trips of the year finished up the Blood Mountain re-route begun at the Trail skills workshop in 1978. In January, as leader Whit Benson reported in the bulletin:

Although the trip was officially cancelled as bad weather reports continued through Saturday, eight die-hards refused to give up and insisted on working on the Blood Mountain Trail. They informed the leader that they were going, trip or no trip, so what could he do but follow! As we headed up Blood Mountain, the swirling mist gradually turned to snow. Everyone set to work moving heavy rocks or grading the trail, heedless of the damp cold. After a late lunch, we headed to the top and picked up trash in a very littered shelter. The snow was coming down hard and the temperature was well below freezing as we reached Neel Gap and turned toward home.

The February trip found the group working in rain and fog throughout the day, so painting blazes was left for a later date, and the finishing-up lopping and clearing of a rock vista was done. The new section was opened and the old section closed off on a special trip in April. Everyone agreed that this new Trail was a very "scenic route," and was a vast improvement over the eroded and monotonous switchbacks that it replaced.

The Trail and shelters committee was re-organized in 1979 to include the administration of the Loop Trail as well as the white blazed Trail, with five "district overseers" to aid in the supervision of the two Trails. The side trails development committee was charged with the construction of other side trails, specifically the undeveloped portions of the Federal Register trail. This job, however, was delayed—indefinitely as it turned out, for various reasons— pending the recommendations of the Task Force and the decision on the "official" Georgia Trail.

On Trail maintenance trips during the year, sections of Trail on Wallalah Mountain, Wildcat (between Hog Pen and Tesnatee Gaps), and Cowrock were improved (using the newly-acquired skills) with the installation of water bars, steps, and other Trail-hardening techniques. The annual walk-thru was held in April; some Trail clearing was done, and the overlooks on Springer and Tray Mountains were opened up. The good job done on the overlook at the top of Tray Mountain prompted some to refer to it as Tray Bald.

An attempt was made by the side trails development committee to find and open up trails around the side of Blood Mountain. A trail around the south side was tentatively approved by the Forest Service, but discouraged by the GATC Board on the assumption that the Club did not have the manpower to build or maintain any more trails. This decision, in effect, nullified the purpose of the side trails development committee.

Forest Service crews—especially those of the Toccoa district ranger Bill Blalock—were also busy on the Trail. They re-routed several short sections of the Loop Trail to improve the grade and drainage, relocated the Trail over Hawk Mountain to go around instead of over the mountain (proposed and flagged by the Club the previous year), and moved the Hawk Mountain shelter to a spot along the new portion of Trail. Crews also put a floor in the Addis Gap shelter and re-roofed it.

Again, at the GATC–Forest Service meeting in June the Blood Mountain shelter was discussed at length. It was decided to evaluate possible repairs, and a "condition survey" was to be made sometime during the summer.

At attempt was made early in the year by Whit Benson and Bob Slater to find an effective way to control poison ivy along the Trail. After much correspondence and discussion with the University of Georgia Extension Service and the Forest Service about spraying, which seemed to be the most effective deterrent, the attempt was finally abandoned. The problems involved which seemed insurmountable included environmental concerns, a necessary license for the operator, finding the proper spray, and the necessity of carrying in a considerable amount of water, with which to dilute the spray.

With the exception of the New Year's weekend hike, which, though wet and windy, was relatively warm, the Club's 1979 winter trips were uniformly COLD and wet, as reported in the bulletin. Dudley Eggleston, January 6-7: "We had to put chains on to get to the top of Wayah. . . . I had always wondered what it would be like to hike for two days in rain at 35 degrees; now I know!!" Marty Rubin, January 13-14: "A fearsome foursome set out in the mist from Unicoi Gap on Saturday. . . . On Sunday . . . howling winds and a sharp drop in temperature . . . blast froze the straps on our gear. . . ." Bart Cowden, January 20: "Hike cancelled because 'freezing rain covered north Georgia mountains.'" Marianne Skeen, January 27-28: "Silences in a white world, roaring wind blowing across Albert Mountain, snow covered tents among frozen rhododendrons . . . frozen water bottles, the crisp crunchiness of a 16 degree morning. . . ." Harold Arnovitz, February 3-4: "Wildcat Creek road was impassable to Fuller Gap due to snow and ice patches. . . . Whit, Roz, John and Harry chose to climb Kelly Knob through two feet of snow. . . ." Bobby Goldstein, February 10-11: "Four eager hikers started at Woody Gap on six inches of snow. . . . Ice on the trees looked like crystals and sounded like chimes. . . . Snowdrifts were over our knees. . . ."

Even a return trip to the Florida Trail featured a snow flurry or two, and the hikers returned to a snow-bound Atlanta. Several opted for the Smokies the same weekend, where, according to poet Bob Slater, "the snow looked sorta' thin . . . " but "all night long fell the snow of seventy-nine," and the hikers returned to find their cars literally buried in the snow, and had to ask the help of Park rangers to dig them out.

In the spring, a weekend at High Hampton Inn, in Cashiers, North Carolina, led by Ed Selby, provided a luxuriously different sort of trip.

A new and beautiful area was explored in June as Gale Benson led a group into the Snowbird Mountains, along—and across (23 times?)—Snowbird Creek, over ridges and balds, and back around to cross the creek (river) once more.

George Goldman created another "happening" at Scaly Mountain, North Carolina, as 35 members and guests enjoyed a "wild weekend with wild strawberry eating, Rabun Bald hiking, frisbee playing, creek walking, bathing in the swimming hole for the hardy, clogging or watching clogging at the Mountain City playhouse and a surprise for George for his 50th birthday on Sunday. . . ."

And then another BEAR STORY, reported by leader Rosalind Van Landingham (who could it be that attracts these bears??):

It was an action-packed weekend that didn't exactly go the way it was planned! A hearty five started hiking from Smokemont at 9 A.M. on Saturday headed for McGee Springs via the Bradley Fork, Chasteen Creek, Enloe Creek and Hyatt Ridge Trails. While eating lunch at the Raven Fork crossing on the Enloe Creek Trail, the group began to wonder how the long afternoon would be spent at McGee Springs and decided to take the more time-consuming route, the Raven Forks Manway (which was to be hiked on Sunday), to the campsite for the night, rather than the regular trails as planned. About 6:30 P.M., after crawling over and under logs, thru rhododendron and over rocks, scratched by briars and stung by nettles, the five reached the Big Pool at Three Forks. After a short rest the five ascended Breakneck Ridge and with flashlights in hand the five arrived at the campsite at McGee Springs. Camp was set up and dinner eaten and all settled down for a well deserved rest. About 1:30 A.M. the group awoke to find a bear devouring the food from one of the food sacks (which had been properly hung). The events of the next couple of hours were dominated by the bear, who refused to leave the camping area. Finally, after puncturing two water bottles, one water container hanging on the tree, poking her head in Marianne's tent (Marianne was not inside!)

and getting all five food sacks, the bear left for the night and the weary five again settled down for a few hours rest. On Sunday, the foodless five packed up and headed for the car and town for brunch, then went back to the Park and climbed the Chimneys, a spectacular finish for the outing. This was Darrell's first experience in the Smokies— what a beginning!

Another new area, Little River Canyon in Alabama, was discovered by 18 members and guests in October, and was reported by leader Mary Eidson as being "a good alternative to Tallulah Gorge."

The Thanksgiving weekend for the first time offered a choice of trips: Okefenokee Swamp or Walnut Bottoms in the Smokies. The large crowds which in the past had attended the "family camping" type of Thanksgiving weekend had begun to dwindle—at least one reason being that the children of the families who went were older and had other interests. (The active members of the Club were slowly changing from largely young married couples and families to more single and one-of-a-couple members, and few children.)

The Appalachian Trail Conference biennial meeting in August was reported in the bulletin by Margaret Drummond:

Although the 22nd meeting of the Appalachian Trail Conference at Carrabassett, Maine, was held at the FAR end of the Trail from Georgia, the Georgia AT Club was well represented by 14⅔ delegates (well, technically young George Galphin is still too young to be a member, but he is rapidly gaining hiking skills that will help him to qualify in a few years). Led by President Whit Benson, the Georgia delegation, resplendent in Daniel designed T-shirts, especially made for the occasion, participated in a variety of activities, from symposia to workshops; heard addresses by visiting dignitaries as well as the Conference staff; enjoyed such culinary delights as a Maine bean-hole dinner and also, a lobster and steamed clam dinner; and reveled in the comfortable condominium living at the Sugarloaf Ski Resort. The Education Committee, under Joe Boyd's expert leadership, designed and put up a creatively 'different' Club exhibit depicting the AT and Club activities in Georgia.

As for what happened *after* the Conference meeting, if you ask, you'll get 14⅔ versions (or more!). Most climbed Katahdin (Nancy did it twice); some hiked the White Mountains (in the process, a few hikers were 'lost' and a few were 'added'); most hiked sections on the AT in the Bigelow Range; and two hiked for a week in Baxter State Park. All have tales to tell, slides to show and memories that will last.

As Whit Benson reported of the Conference meeting:

. . . One of the most popular workshops was on bridge building, conducted by Win Robins, a 70-year old friend and former student of Hugh Chase and a member of the MATC. Win presented his topic in a typically dry, New England manner and left at least half of the Georgia delegation convinced that they could bridge either the Toccoa or Chattahoochee Rivers with no problem. . . .

At the meeting, Margaret Drummond was elected to the ATC Board of Managers to replace Al Thompson, and Charles Pugh was elected as chairman of the Board to replace George Zoebelein.

A week after the Conference meeting, several GATCers journeyed half way back to Maine (almost) for the Multi-Club Meet in Virginia. An important feature of the business session during the weekend was the organization of the Southern Regional Management Committee, a group of ATC officials and club presidents which would, according to Whit Benson, "address itself to problems confronting clubs in the Southern region."

Attempts had continued to remove the Trail from the two remaining places where it followed Forest Service system roads: from Low Gap to Cold Springs Gap, and from the Cross Trails shelter to Three Forks. In November, President Benson reported that the Forest Service was willing to permanently close the road from Low Gap to Cold Springs Gap; the Board voted to leave the Trail on the old road rather than move it back to the top of the ridge, as had been suggested by several Club members. The decision of the task force on the official Trail was to settle the problem of the Cross Trails–Three Forks section.

A revision of the Loop Trail brochure and map was completed during the year by the Map committee. It was copyrighted in hopes that this would prevent its being duplicated and sold by others.

Another "colorful and attractive" brochure and map—"Hikers Guide to the Chattahoochee National Forest"—was completed in 1979 and reported in the bulletin:

A cooperative project between the GATC and the USFS has resulted in the attractive brochure enclosed with this bulletin, compliments of Pat Thomas and the U.S. Forest Service. The project was initiated and begun several years ago by members Lyman Emerson and Ed Seiferle who spent many hours in the field researching the trails data; Teresa Moen, then Information Officer for the Gainesville office, who assisted with the writing; and others of the USFS. The result is the colorful and attractive brochure which will be extremely helpful to hikers and campers in the Chattahoochee National Forest.

A Golden Anniversary committee had been organized in 1979 to begin to plan for events to celebrate the upcoming 50th anniversary of the Club.

George Galphin, still working on tax exempt status for the Club, expressed hope in September that it would be completed soon.

Officers for 1980 were elected at the annual meeting: Whit Benson, president; Rosalind Van Landingham, vice president; George Galphin, secretary; Dudley Eggleston, treasurer; Herb Daniel, membership director; Bob Slater, Trail supervisor; Hillrie Quin, Trails information director; Nancy Shofner, historian; Bill Funkhouser, bulletin editor; Grant Wilkins, director.

At the Christmas party—which featured "the usual gourmet feast"—yearbooks for 1980 were passed out. The cover featured drawings by Gale Benson of the four GATC pioneer members, in honor of the coming golden anniversary year.

1980

GEORGIA
APPALACHIAN
19 TRAIL CLUB, INC. 50

NINETEEN EIGHTY was the Golden Anniversary of the Georgia Appalachian Trail Club. It was a busy year, but it was especially memorable to most because of its significance and the various events which commemorated and celebrated the first 50 years of the Club.

The golden anniversary committee organized in 1979 had planned several special events and ways in which to bring to the Club members' glimpses of past years—especially the formative years of the 1930's. These plans were generally tied in with regular Club events, and included: a special feature in each issue of the *Mountaineer* which recounted various incidents and facts of the early years, called "Footprints in History"; commemorative patches in gold and white made similar to the patch planned in 1931; a showing of photographs from the early years at the annual slide show; a display of old photographs, newspaper clippings, bulletins, letters, and artifacts at the Multi-Club Meet, as well as a talk on E. B. Stone and the early days of the Club given by John Krickel; and plans were made during the year for a big birthday party in December (in lieu of the annual Christmas party), with a "nostalgic" hike the following day.

Hoping to *finally* settle the matter of the official Trail in Georgia during this golden anniversary year, President Whit Benson early in the year worked out with the Forest Service the one remaining problem of the location of the Trail: the section between Cross Trails shelter and Three Forks. It was suggested, and approved by all parties, that the Trail follow the former Loop Trail up Rich

Mountain, then turn west down to Stover Creek, and follow the white blazed Trail to Three Forks. This new Trail between the top of Rich Mountain and Stover Creek was to be built by the Forest Service. The re-description of the Trail was re-written to include this section, and in early April was sent "up through Forest Service channels" for approval, to eventually go to the Park Service.

A report by Margaret Drummond on the Southern Regional Management committee and ANSTAC meetings in March stated that Blue Ridge Parkway superintendent, Gary Eberhardt, was in favor of de-authorizing the Parkway extension in Georgia and putting the AT back on the ridge. So there seemed to be no remaining obstacles in the way of final approval. In July, Bob Harper of the Forest Service in Gainesville declared that they were "going on the basis this is now the location of the Appalachian Trail." But by the end of the year, the new description had not appeared in the Federal Register, and uncertainty was to continue.

On the monthly Trail maintenance trips, an average of 12–15 people each time carried out a number of necessary projects, including the following: building a half mile re-route of the Loop Trail just south of Fish Gap; installing water bars and clearing trail north of Unicoi Gap, on Tray Mountain, and various places between Neel and Tesnatee Gaps; clearing a very large number of blowdowns from a winter storm between Springer Mountain and Cooper Gap; clearing weeds and brush south of Addis Gap, between Neel and Tesnatee, and north of Hogpen Gap; and installing water bars and steps on Blood Mountain.

Continuing the improvement of the heavily-used Blood Mountain Trail, workers also flagged and cleared a relocation of about ¾ of a mile just south of Neel Gap, which was to be completed the following year. This would eliminate numerous switchbacks, and opened up a beautiful new section going around the north side of the knoll and coming back into the old Trail just below Flatrock Gap.

Two special events were included in the work schedule in the spring. The Board had agreed early in the year, at the request of Randy Snodgrass, president of the new Benton MacKaye Trail Association, to help in the establishment of a new trail—the Benton MacKaye Trail—which would, when completed, form a large loop with the AT into North Carolina and Tennessee as far as Davenport Gap. Grant Wilkins, of the GATC side trails committee, offered to help supervise the flagging—all in one day—of the 60-mile Georgia section. On April 5, many GATC members and guests, BMTA members and guests, and others met and formed small groups to spread out in pre-arranged sections, and with compass and topo maps, found and flagged the route.

Appropriations of the $90 million for land acquisition along the Trail had fallen short of the authorized level, and the ATC planned to dramatize the Trail and the need for more money by staging a one-day blazing—or "paint thru"—

of the entire 2,000-mile Trail. The GATC agreed to participate on the specified date in May, and combined it with the annual "walk-thru." Fifty to sixty members and guests "met with paint buckets and brushes in hand" and dispersed along the Trail "on what turned out to be a great day for ducks." The day-long downpour prevented blazing, but the Trail was checked and some clipping and trimming was done.

At the GATC–Forest Service meeting in June, the Blood Mountain shelter was once again discussed, and the Forest Service indicated that by the following year funds would be available for a new roof, cement floor, and metal doors and windows. Also at the meeting, the GATC volunteered to assume the task of sign making, with the Forest Service furnishing the material.

Whit Benson and his committee continued to work on the management plan, in conjunction with the Forest Service, and with suggestions from the Board. The final draft was not completed until early 1981. As the introduction stated, "The purpose . . . is to provide a basis for the cooperative management of the . . . Appalachian Trail in Georgia by the responsible parties." It was a detailed plan spelling out the various responsibilities and policies of the Forest Service and the GATC pertaining to all phases of Trail maintenance and use.

The varied schedule of activities for the year included, besides backpacks, day hikes and work trips, canoeing, skiing, caving, rock climbing, family camping, fishing, bicycling, and running. Fourteen of the scheduled trips were cancelled, generally because of bad weather or lack of interest. The cancellations included all but two of the hikes planned for the Georgia AT.

As usual the New Year's trip was an adventure—a wet one this time, according to leader, Whit Benson. Four members hiked in the rain and/or clouds for four days "through Kephart country" in the Smokies, crossing rain-swollen rivers many times each day. Until the last day, when it snowed, the temperatures fortunately remained at least above freezing. All bravely reported that they had a good time.

A more pleasant winter hike in February was reported in the bulletin by leader, Mary Eidson:

It's a beautiful sight to look behind you on a cold winter's day and see 21 people in their colorful parkas and packs, gliding along through the woods in single file. The visibility from 488-foot Picken's Nose was fine and we could see our route for both days. The hike took us from Mooney Gap to Carter Gap for the night, then we ended up at Patterson Gap. John Krickel lived up to his reputation of having unique lunches by having superb homemade summer sausage and hot Leekie soup at Betty Creek Gap. After a good campfire that night, and our late retiring to bed at 8:30, the visit of bears in this bear sanctuary was not the excitement we had expected. . . . The excitement was for Jim Crew, looking down the barrel of a shotgun with a large spotlight shining in his face, from two men and one dog looking for a lost dog. We heard the mournful cry of the lost dog looking for the men. The other excitement was Elinor Metzger's hot water bottle leaking in her sleeping bag. Dillard Jr. probably had to order extra coffee because of having to serve so much to those waiting during the long car shuttle both days.

Another beautiful winter trip, led by Whit Benson, took a small group from Newfound Gap to Smokemont in the Smokies:

A stolen stove, forgotten boots, busted radiator hose, blown out tire, what more would it take to spoil a trip as the four of us left Newfound Gap with a late start in 18° weather. What started with everything going wrong ended up as the perfect winter hiking trip. Charlie's Bunion appeared to be covered with green ice from a distance. The spruce were encased in a frosted cover of whipped cream. The cold air afforded clear views of Mt. Kephart, the Jump Off and the trail over the Saw Teeth. The snow was deep but the cold weather provided easy walking on a frosted layer as we hiked past Ice Water Springs, Charlie's Bunion and started down the Richland Mountain Trail. We reached Cabin Flats just at dark and hurriedly set up tents and cooked supper with the temperature dropping to 10°. Sunday dawned as another crisp clear day and we headed down the trail toward Smokemont and then back to Newfound Gap to try our skill on Hillrie and Roz's skis before heading home.

A cross-country ski trip in February was a Club first, and was participated in by 30 members and guests. Leader, Hillrie Quin, reported for the bulletin:

Friday night we outran the sleet and all arrived safely in Cherokee, North Carolina. Saturday morning we all checked out our skis and headed for Soco Gap where U.S. 19 crosses the Blue Ridge Parkway. The morning was spent in ski school and the afternoon in practice and 'touring.' Roz and Darrell won the long distance award. Nancy lost a fight with a ski pole and Marshall tried to make the cover of Nordic Skiing. Grant won the steepest double pole brake (break). Craig had the neatest Dutch Army pants and Bill Funkhouser wore his new ski goggles to bed. Jim Skeen thinks we are all crazy. Maybe we are but we sure had a good time.

A weekend in June combined work with pleasure, as 30 members and guests participated in all or part of a Saturday "trail maintenance workshop" near Dicks Creek Gap, and an evening and Sunday near Highlands, North Carolina, as Roz Van Landingham reported in the bulletin:

If you didn't come, you missed one of the best weekends of the year! We had breakfast at LaPrade's; a chance to learn trail construction and maintenance techniques and a chance to put our learning into practice by building rock steps and installing some of the Trail's finest waterbars; a great evening at the Cook/Quin cabin with hamburgers, hotdogs and homemade ice cream for dinner on Saturday; a Sally Bauer breakfast on Sunday morning; a walk up Yellow Mountain on Sunday which, for some, ended with a bushwhack back and a chilling swim in Buck Creek. Many thanks, to Mary B., Bev and Hillrie for the use of their cabin; especially to Hillrie for an informative and productive workshop; to Helen and Joe who helped 'get ready' for the crowd; to Sally for her tasty efforts in the kitchen; to the entire group of GATCers and guests who seemed to thrive on hard work, good food and fun.

For several years the historical files of the GATC had been in the state archives awaiting help from the Club in sorting and organizing them. In 1980 President Benson recommended that the historian select a committee to proceed with this task, and also to write a history of the first 50 years of the Club. A history committee was formed, and the dozen or so boxes of bulletins, letters, pictures, etc., were retrieved from the archives building. Meeting once or twice a month throughout the year, the committee had completed the task of sorting the material by the end of the year, and about half of the lengthy history had been written. The work would have proceeded faster if the committee members had been able to resist stopping to read many of the fascinating old letters, trip accounts and newspaper clippings, and had it not been for the often sumptuous dinners they prepared and consumed before getting down to work at each meeting.

A long article entitled "Happy Birthday GATC" was featured in the September *ATN*. Written by ATC Field Representative, Rima Farmer, it told much of the early days of the Club, and was illustrated with a number of old pictures from the files. The cover featured the photograph of Warner Hall from which the Trail plaque was made in 1934, and on the back cover was a reproduction of the plaque itself.

In March, the by-laws committee completed the proposed changes; a membership meeting was called in May for discussion, several changes were made, and the new document was approved by the membership at the annual meeting. The changes, according to President Benson, were made "to delete the unnecessary, to clarify the ambiguous, and in general to 'tighten' and strengthen the document." One change of note was the addition of a "junior" membership category for persons 14–18 years old.

Another change made during the year by the Board was not so favorably received by some members. After much discussion at the July Board meeting, a change was made in the "hiker's code" which eliminated the prohibition of alcohol on Club activities, and changed the prohibition against pets to group activities only. The first was a rule which had existed in the Club for 50 years, and its change brought protests and much concern on the part of a number of members. It was discussed at length at the October business meeting, and when a vote was called for, the change was approved by a two-thirds majority. The Board of Directors felt that the new statement of the rule should be sufficient to cover any ill behavior resulting from a possible indiscretion. The new rule read:

. . . In general, all members and guests of the GATC should conduct themselves at all times in such a manner as not to detract from the enjoyment of the outing for other people.

Also in July, the Board voted to relinquish any "jurisdiction" over, and maintenance functions on, the Loop Trail, in order to concentrate efforts on the AT. At the request of the Benton MacKaye Trail Association, the Benton MacKaye Trail (which had had to be relocated north of Springer Mountain) would occupy the Loop Trail from Springer Mountain to Rhodes Mountain, from which point it would go in a generally northwest direction to the Cohuttas. The remainder of the Loop Trail would probably become a National Recreation Trail under the supervision of the Forest Service.

As photography chairwoman, Marianne Skeen reported at the annual meeting:

The major effort of this committee involved the putting together of two 35mm slide programs, one a presentation for the general public with information on both the Appalachian Trail in general as well as on the activities of the Georgia Appalachian Trail Club. The second was a presentation for other trail maintaining clubs to be shown at the Multi-Club Meeting.

The first mentioned slide show was a very fine production, narrated, with musical accompaniment, and was shown at various events during the year, and would be used for many years to come.

A sad event of this 50th year was the death in May of pioneer member Lou Hoben. Lou had been an enthusiastic supporter of the Club since 1932, but had been in poor health for the past few years.

In mid-year, it was revealed that the Appalachian Trail Conference was "in the red" financially, in part because of a large and rapid increase in expenditures necessary to handle the additional work involved in land acquisition and other matters resulting from the authorization of funds from Congress. The situation ultimately resulted in a "shake-up" in the administration of ATC, but many clubs along the Trail were asked to contribute large sums—$3.00 per member was suggested—to pull them out of the hole. After much discussion pro and con, and questions about how it happened and whether or not it would continue to happen, the GATC Board decided to help by raising money through a special project. It was decided to have a "flea market"; a committee under the direction of Margaret Drummond was formed to plan the event, and members and friends contributed a huge amount of camping and household goods. The day-long event was held in the front yard of member Jennifer Harvey, with the use of Grant Wilkins' house across the street. It was a "fabulous success" and grossed over $1,000, $650 of which was sent to Conference.

Toward the end of the year, Ruth Blackburn was elected new chairwoman of the Board of Managers (until the official election at the next Conference meeting, when she was elected permanently). Hank Lautz had resigned his position as executive director earlier in the year, and Larry Van Meter was appointed by the Board to the position.

Early in the year, George Galphin reported that the application for tax exempt status had been mailed to the IRS, but it "met with a stumbling block"—the IRS questioned the Club's qualifications for the status. The matter was studied further during the rest of the year.

GATC member Darrell Maret became one of a very few GATCers to hike the entire AT, beginning his trip in March from Springer Mountain. He planned to hike at least to Harpers Ferry, and then decided to go the whole distance, climbing Katahdin on August 25. On top of Katahdin he posed for a picture holding up a sign (made by wife Marta) saying "Happy 50th Anniversary GATC."

The Multi-Club Meet in 1980 was to be hosted by the GATC. Several members spent much time searching for a suitable location, and finally settled on Unicoi State Park. An arrangement was made with Park officials whereby the Club would get the use of a large field, a display area, and other facilities for a minimal fee, in exchange for presenting to the public a slide presentation (the new slide show created by the photography committee), and backpacking and day-hiking seminars. As Whit Benson reported in the bulletin:

Multi-Club 1980 was another example of the GATC getting behind a project and turning it into a huge success. Everyone enjoyed and was impressed with the historical display by the Historical, Education and Trails Information Committees, the slide show developed by Marianne and the Photographic Committee, the talk on the history of the southern Trail by John Krickel, and the hiking seminars conducted by Herb and Hillrie. The hikes planned by George Galphin and his hike leaders gave our guests a nice sampling of the Georgia Trail. Even George Goldman managed to pull off a successful campfire program after the heavy rains Sunday afternoon. Practically every GATC member who attended contributed in some way, such as Sally helping with registration, Bill Funkhouser with highway signs, Margaret Drummond with ATC coordination or Grant with clean-up. Grant and his crew scoured the bottoms area on Monday and couldn't find more than a handful of trash. . . .

Over 150 people attended the gathering.

The annual meeting in October was a festive affair with a large crowd in attendance. Annual reports of committees were made, and officers for the coming year were elected: Rosalind Van Landingham, president; Hillrie Quin, vice president; Marianne Skeen, treasurer; George Galphin, secretary; Herb Daniel, membership director; John Krickel, Trails information director; Joe Boyd, Trail supervisor; Nancy Shofner, historian; Bill Funkhouser, bulletin editor; Whit Benson, director.

The big event of the year for the Golden Anniversary committee—and the *biggest* for the entire Club—was the "birthday party" in December. The committee spent many hours planning the program, invitations, etc. Names and addresses of many former members were gathered, invitations were printed similar to annual meeting invitations used in the 1930's, and sent to almost 100 former members, plus all of the current members. Former member Pat Gartrell Bell designed and made a beautiful "banner" to commemorate the

50th birthday of the Club. A beautiful birthday cake was created by Rosalind Van Landingham and committee, using figures made for the cake at the 21st birthday party in 1951. A square dance was arranged, with caller, and table decorations made, featuring the hiker figure and footprints along the tables similar to those used a number of years ago. Two of the displays of historical material used at the Multi-Club Meet were set up again, and a slide show of photographs from the 1930's was created and shown by John Krickel.

Historian Nancy Shofner reported on the affair for the bulletin:

The celebration of the 50th anniversary of the GATC turned out to be the biggest and best party we have had in a while. Approximately 180 members and guests jammed into the Fellowship Hall of the Chamblee Methodist Church for the occasion. The group included almost 40 former members—many from the 1930's—who returned to the 'fold' for the evening. Registration was abandoned when it seemed it was about to take the whole evening. The long line shifted over to the food table, which was creaking under the weight of all that food which came in response to 'bring LOTS.' When everyone had eaten LOTS, the program was opened by President Whit Benson, who greeted everyone and then turned the program over to Darrell Maret, who did an excellent job of 'MC'ing.' A beautiful wooden plaque, featuring our hiker figure and carved by Hillrie Quin, was presented to Whit in appreciation of his hard work and accomplishments as president of the Club for the past two years. A roll call was taken of all the members, past and present, by the year of their joining the GATC, beginning with Elizabeth White, our longest-standing member, who joined in 1930 only days after its organization, and remains a member today. Marene Snow, also a pioneer member, blew out the candles on the birthday cake, which was created by Rosalind Van Landingham and her helpers, and featured figures made for the Club's Coming of Age party in 1951. The centerpiece of the evening was a beautiful banner made by Pat Gartrell Bell in commemoration of the 50th anniversary. This was on display along with the officers' mantles made by Pat some years ago. Officers for 1981 were installed by Al Thompson with the aid of Cynthia Ward Muise, the first woman president of the GATC.

After the program, the room was cleared and the first square dance in about 20 years was under way—slowly at first, but soon the floor was filled with feet going in all directions. It was decided afterward that this was a tradition that deserves resurrecting. The hit of the evening for many of the former members was the show by John Krickel of slides made from Club pictures of the 1930's. Others viewed the excellent slide presentation produced by the photography committee this year and shown at the Multi-Club Meet. A good time was had by all and we were especially pleased to be able to meet so many of the past members and also to get them together again to visit with each other. Thanks goes to the many who helped plan, carry out, and clean up after the evening—and especially to all of our members through the years whose dedication to the GATC made this 50th anniversary possible.

FORMER MEMBERS PRESENT: *From out of state:* Lloyd and Lillian Adams, Lexington, Kentucky; Jean and Don Dolan, Signal Mountain, Tennessee; Cynthia Ward Muise, Lantana, Florida; Ann and Jim Proctor, Birmingham, Alabama; F. I. Smith, Short Hills, New Jersey. *From Georgia:* Maurice and Berma Abercrombie, Frances

Adair, Joe and Olivia Bagwell, Mr. and Mrs. John Ball, Bill and Pat Bell, Loretta Chappell, Mary Collette, Kent Christopher, Lewis and Ann Estes, Grace (Ficken) Hawkins, Hugh and Nell Jordan, Harold and Mable Mansfield, Lane and Mildred Mitchell, Ann and Bill Naff, Lee and Carole Perry, Guerard and Joan Spratt, Rod Taaffe, Llewellyn Wilburn, Gordon and Mickey Wilson. NOTE: We are very sad to report that Rod Taaffe, one of our guests at the party, and a member of the GATC in the early 1930's, died on Monday December 15. Rod had written a very appreciative letter to the Club after the party in which he said in part, 'I only wish that I were able to share the pleasures of the Club and the Trails with you—however, I wish you all the best weather and finest trails forever.'

The day after the party a "golden anniversary hike/drive" was made, and reported in the bulletin by leader Nancy Shofner:

The spirits of the past gave us a warm and beautiful day for our 'nostalgic' hike, which took us back to Mt. Oglethorpe and the section that for many years was the beginning of the AT. We drove down the old road (the former trail) to Oglethorpe and walked up to the top where we took pictures and studied the topo maps of the trail to Amicalola Falls. We then retraced our drive, viewing the remains of the infamous chicken coops, which had been one of the reasons for abandoning the trail, and stopped to walk to the top of Burnt Mountain, just off the road, to have lunch at the ruins of Connahaynee Lodge, where early Club members spent many pleasant hours. After lunch we swapped cars and drove to both ends of the section between Highway 52 and 108 to begin the hike. Ignoring the comments of the timid, who were not prepared to spend the night in the woods, the leaders of both groups managed to find their way successfully over the old Trail route, with everyone helpfully—and hopefully—peering at each tree for evidence of old blazes, many of which can still be found. This scenic ridge—the very end of the Appalachian mountain chain—remains for the most part a pleasant woods walk with numerous views—and numerous tales to be told of the hard work and good times that it furnished the GATC 'way back when.'

The end of 1980 found the GATC at a peak in terms of membership, dedication, and purpose. In its more than 50 years of existence, it had survived crises of war, economic hard times, ever-increasing encroachment on the Trail by civilization, changes in government policy ranging from outright opposition to full cooperation, a partnership with Conference which has ranged from prodigal child to full partner, and square dancing to Trail building. Like the great cathedrals of Europe which were built over a three hundred year period, each member and officer has contributed to the building of the Club to its present form—based on the original plan laid out in 1930, yet modified with the needs of the times. While it is easy to see even today the continuing influence of some of the identifiable "greats" from the past—Everett Stone's dedication to building the Trail, Warner Hall's spirit of friendship and fun, Lloyd Adams' concern for a sound Club government, Larry Freeman's determination that the Trail and Club be resurrected after the war, the fight against almost hopeless odds in stopping the Blue Ridge Parkway—nonetheless, every person who has belonged to GATC has helped shape its present form and personality. And the Club's personality is perhaps what this history has attempted to delineate: GATC is as distinct from its sister clubs in the Conference as the two great national champions of the Appalachian Trail, Benton MacKaye and Myron Avery. Perhaps the easiest way to describe the GATC personality is in terms of what it has meant to its members. Our Club has been a relatively small association of close friends with a common purpose. It has never been easy to become a member, and consequently that membership has been a thing which has been fiercely cherished by its members. That five members would remain active for nearly the 50 years of the Club's existence speaks to this feeling. The Club has always been fun-loving: in the early days the "socials" were perhaps as important as the hikes, but even today a GATC work trip has the same rollicking spirit and joyful gathering at some mountain restaurant for supper that has marked our outings since 1930. Finally, the Club has a dogged determination to shape its Georgia portion of the Trail as it sees fit—come hell, high water, the Forest Service, Conference, or whoever. We fought for this Trail; we built it with our sweat, blisters and laughter; and we're immensely proud of it. To every member, great and small, who has been a part of the friendships of the Trail, the Club and its history owe a great debt. You are our history and we are a cherished part of your life.

May our sons and daughters find health and happiness and beauty up there as we have found it, may they still hold in reverence the sacred peaks of the Cherokees, may they find joy in the strength of the hills and in the secrets that the valleys hold! The unbroken wilderness with a long, tiny trail stretching through it for other generations to know, is our dream!

– Charles N. Elliott, 1931

Epilogue

GEORGIA
APPALACHIAN
19 TRAIL CLUB, INC. 30

DURING THE THIRTEEN YEARS following the original publication of *Friendships of the Trail*, the GATC experienced major changes in several areas. Most notable were the rapid growth in membership and greater responsibilities for management and maintenance of the Appalachian Trail. A formal Management Plan was adopted in 1984 which delineated the roles of the Club and the USFS in the management partnership. Under this plan, major treadway reroutes were constructed at Black Mountain and Springer Mountain, two new side trails were constructed on Blood Mountain, and new bridges were installed at Justus, Blackwell and Stover Creeks. Responsibility for construction and installation of all Trail signs was assumed by the Club. The Blood Mountain shelter was renovated, the Cross Trails shelter was relocated to Stover Creek and repaired, and new shelters were installed at Blue Mountain, Deep Gap, Plumorchard Gap, Springer Mountain, and Hawk Mountain. The old Springer Mountain shelter was relocated to Black Mountain Gap and renovated, and privies were installed at several shelter sites. Much of the shelter work depended not only upon the GATC/USFS partnership, but also involved a North Georgia community business—specializing in timber frame construction—as well as the U.S. Army Rangers, who provided logistical support for materials transfer. These projects resulted in innovative shelter design and provided a model for public/private cooperation. The GATC not only supplied most of the labor for both the treadway and facilities construction projects, but more significantly, assumed the primary management responsibility for their planning and successful completion.

Trail management was also affected by both legislative and administrative actions instituted by governmental agencies during this time period. The USFS established a Visual Management System which, among other things, provided protection for the "viewshed" of the AT such that timber cutting within easy view of the Trail was restricted. An Optimal Location Review was conducted in which the best location for the AT treadway was determined cooperatively by the GATC, ATC, and USFS. Passage of three different wilderness bills resulted in the incorporation of significant portions of the Georgia AT into federally-designated wilderness areas. The management of Trail sections in wilderness areas is a topic of on-going discussions by the various partners.

In 1984, the NPS, in an unprecedented move, delegated management responsibility for the AT to the ATC. This resulted in increased involvement of the ATC in day-to-day management of the Trail. Staffing was increased at the headquarters office, and regional offices were established to help local clubs move into new areas of management responsibility following the delegation agreement. By the end of 1993, more than 95% of AT treadway was in public ownership, including all of the Trail in Georgia. GATC member Margaret Drummond served throughout this period on the volunteer ATC Board of Managers and was elected Chair of the Board in 1989.

Perhaps the single biggest and most sophisticated project carried out by the GATC during this period was Deep South '93, the 29th General Meeting of the Appalachian Trail Conference. ATC general membership meetings are hosted biennially by Trail maintaining clubs. In 1993, the GATC, assisted by the other four southern-most maintaining clubs, served as host for Deep South '93. The meeting was held at North Georgia College in Dahlonega and was attended by 1349 registrants, the largest group ever to attend one of these meetings. It was a watershed event for the expanding membership of the GATC. Countless hours of volunteer effort went into this project which encompassed everything from coordination of 23 working committees, to publication of programs, to processing of sophisticated computerized registration procedures, and even to gathering up used towels and linens from the dormitories at the end of the week. Over 150 hikes were organized, the weekend was filled with workshops and panel discussions, and the evenings were filled with entertainment events. It was a high quality event which involved numerous members and instilled a sense of pride in a job well done. Comments from registrants were overwhelmingly favorable.

The ability of the GATC to undertake a project of the magnitude of Deep South '93 was due at least in part to the approximate three-fold increase in membership to nearly 600 members during this time period. Although the membership expansion allowed increased capabilities, it also resulted in increasingly complex jobs for the Board of Directors and Club members. The Club invested in its first computer in the mid 80's and by 1993 owned five computer systems which supplemented those which were personally owned by Board and Committee members. The number of planned activities was expanded to accommodate the increased membership, and new member orientation meetings provided a more formal presentation of Club operations and goals to newcomers. Committee structure was expanded by the addition of numerous subcommittees in order to divide the labor and to encourage the involvement of a broad cross section of the membership. A committee was formed to begin searching for a permanent facility for the Club in anticipation of a future need for paid staff. The monthly newsletter, a tool for communication with the membership, was upgraded significantly and converted to a desktop publishing operation.

Along with these internal changes, the GATC became more visible in the community at large. In addition to the long-standing partnership with the USFS, the Club negotiated a cooperative management agreement and established annual meetings with the Georgia DNR. The Club joined the Georgia Environmental Council and participated in coalitions that monitored forest management issues. Caretaker programs were instituted in which volunteers provided a presence on the AT on the weekends in order to educate Trail users. Club members cooperated with the USFS in monitoring public use of various Trail sections. In 1993, the GATC took a very firm public stand in opposition to a DOT proposal to widen the highway where the Trail crosses in Dick's Creek Gap.

Throughout this period of growth and change, the GATC was skillfully led by Presidents Rosalind Van Landingham (1981-82, 1991-93), Hillrie Quin (1983-84), Joe Boyd (1985-86), Marianne Skeen (1987-88), and Marshall Cooper (1989-90).

Rosalind Van Landingham, in her final President's Log in the December 1993 *Georgia Mountaineer*, summed it up:

I have always been 'high' on the GATC and GATC members, and at this time, my enthusiasm is as great as ever. I think we have a wealth of interested, capable members (and more coming by virtue of our prospective members) who are eager and ready to work on behalf of the GATC and dedicated to the Club's purposes. I think that the increasing membership we have experienced in the last several years is, in fact, a luxury that will allow us the option of expanding our program while maintaining our same level of commitment to the AT as our primary responsibility. Our Club is bursting with energy and the desire to be involved. With the resources we have among our members, and their willingness to be involved, I know our future is very bright.

—Marianne Skeen and Darrell Maret
February 1994

"Something hidden. Go and find it. Go and look behind the ranges—
Something lost behind the ranges. Lost and waiting for you. Go."
                                                          – Rudyard Kipling

Appendix

References

1. Morris, Marion. "Your Host: Georgia Appalachian Trail Club." *Appalachian Trailway News,* v. 28, no. 2, May, 1967.

2. MacKaye, Benton. "The Appalachian Trail, a Project in Regional Planning." *Journal of the American Institute of Architects,* v. 9, Oct., 1921.

3. MacKaye, Benton. "The Appalachian Trail: a Guide to the Study of Nature." *The Scientific Monthly,* April, 1932.

4. Elliott, Charles N. Account of the organization of the GATC prepared at the request of Historian Marene Snow for GATC archive files, 1941.

5. Ozmer, Roy. Account of the scouting of the Georgia Trail prepared at the request of Historian Marene Snow for GATC archive files, 1941.

6. Frome, Michael. *Whose Woods These Are.* New York, Doubleday, 1962.

7. Elliott, Charles N. "Former *Era* Editor Lauded." *The Dekalb New Era,* April 20, 1978.

8. Whittaker, Carter. Account of the building of shelters on the Georgia Trail prepared at the request of Historian Marene Snow for GATC archive files, 1941.

9. Lanman, Charles. *Letters from the Alleghany Mountains.* Letter VII. New York, Putnam, 1849.

Other:

Avery, Myron. "Along the Appalachian Trail in the Georgia Blue Ridge." *Appalachia,* Dec., 1931.

Avery, Myron. "The Appalachian Trail." Reprint, *American Forests,* March, 1934.

Deane, Barbara. "The Appalachian Trail." *Garden Gateways,* Sept.-Oct., 1963.

Georgia Appalachian Trail Club. *Trail Guide to the Mountains of North Georgia,* 1931.

"History of the Appalachian Trail." *The Appalachian Trail,* Pub. no. 5, 8th ed., Appalachian Trail Conference, 1970.

MacKaye, Benton. *Some Early A.T. History.* Reprinted from *Potomac Appalachian Trail Club Bulletin,* Oct.-Dec., 1957.

"I like a road that wanders straight; the King's Highway is fair,
And lovely are the sheltered lanes that take you here and there;
But best of all I love a trail that leads to God knows where."
— Charles Hanson Towne

GATC Members*
1930 – 1980

Abell, C.A.	1930		Barnett, Crawford	1956
Abercrombie, Mable	1933		Batho, Norman	1950
Abercrombie, Maurice	1933		Bauer, Sally	1976
Abrams, Sylvia	1980		Beavers, J. P.	1958
Adair, Frances	1949		Beck, Charles	1930
Adams, Lillian	1936		Bell, Eugene	1976
Adams, Lloyd	1936		Bell, Pat (Gartrell)	1949
Aderhold, Peggy	1954		Benson, Dottie	1950
Aderhold, Tom	1954		Benson, Gale	1969
Agee, Mrs. Wallace	1955		Benson, Whit	1950
Aiken, Ouida	1950		Berry, Bob	1950
Allemong, Evelyn	1933		Bill, Chip	1970
Allen, Carolyn	1941		Bird, Buford	1954
Anderson, Albert	1976		Bird, Mrs. Buford	1954
Anderson, Lee	1930		Bischoff, Lillian	1950
Anderson, Marge	1976		Bixler, Beverly	1953
Anselmo, Lisa (Eidson)	1975		Black, Mary Ann	1969
Anselmo, Rich	1979		Blackmon, Janet	1980
Aquadro, Betty	1962		Bledsoe, Dick	1954
Aquadro, Link	1962		Bledsoe, Doug	1954
Arnold, Donald	1967		Bledsoe, Yvonne	1961
Arnold, Roy	1978		Bogle, Raymond	1966
Arnovitz, Harold	1974		Bohanan, Jim	1980
Ayoubi, Joann	1980		Boland, Emily	1965
Baber, Orpha	1953		Boland, F. C.	1950
Babington, Elizabeth	1938		Boland, Fay	1965
Babington, Kenneth	1938		Boland, Mrs. F. C.	1950
Bagwell, Joe	1949		Bordeaux, Brooke	1970
Bagwell, Olivia (Herren)	1949		Bordeaux, Randy	1967
Baker, Frank	1971		Bounds, Osborn	1969
Baker, Lathrope	1938		Bowly, Nancy	1930
Baker, Phil	1966		Boyd, Helen	1975
Baker, Susie	1966		Boyd, Joe	1975
Ball, John	1939		Brackman, Philip	1968
Balster, Arlene	1954		Branham, Cecelia	1930
Banick, Bill	1965		Brendel, Margaret	1958
Bankston, Julian	1973		Brendel, Norman	1958
Bardi, Beverly (Runyon)	1972		Brewer, Jim	1930

* with year or approximate year of joining. Includes honorary members.

Dye, Randy	1980	Foy, Bill	1965
Edmonson, Glen	1940	Franklet, Mrs. D.L.	1956
Edmonson, Myrtle	1942	Fraser, Sheila	1963
Eggleston, Dudley	1972	Freeman, Hugh	1940
Eggleston, Susan	1978	Freeman, Jack	1959
Eidson, Ann	1960	Freeman, Larry	1942
Eidson, Bill	1961	Fuerst, Fred	1979
Eidson, J. P.	1960	Fujimori, George	1972
Eidson, Mary	1960	Funkhouser, Bill	1977
Elliott, Charles	1930	Furbish, Robert	1930
Elliott, Charles, Jr.	1930	Furcron, H. S.	1938
Elliott, Chester	1931	Futch, Opal	1933
Elliott, Larry	1971	Gafnea, Charles	1948
Elliott, Maude	1931	Gafnea, Mary	1948
Ellis, Beela	1949	Galphin, George	1971
Elrod, Jack	1957	Galphin, Judy	1971
Emerson, David	1968	Gaskins, Cliff	1978
Emerson, Janet	1976	Gellerstadt, Wright	1958
Emerson, Lyman	1957	Gibbons, Bob	1962
Emerson, Vivian	1957	Gibbons, Yvonne	1962
Emory, Roberta	1960	Giles, Norman	1936
Enders, Paul	1980	Gilland, Betty	1950
Engle, Jim	1960	Gillham, Mrs. William	1949
Engle, June	1960	Gillham, William	1949
Engle, Sherry	1962	Gleaves, Ed	1963
Espy, Eugene	1951	Gleaves, Georgia	1963
Estes, Ann	1961	Glenn, John	1963
Estes, George	1931	Glover, Harold	1964
Estes, Henry	1930	Glower, Ross	1936
Estes, Lewis	1961	Gogel, Ruth	1964
Ethridge, Bill	1972	Goldman, George	1974
Eyles, Don	1936	Goldstein, Bobby	1977
Fambrough, Jack	1958	Good, Dottie	1949
Fambrough, Martha	1966	Good, Newell	1949
Fambrough, Mary	1958	Goode, Betty Jo	1966
Farrow, Bill	1975	Goodwin, Buddy	1953
Ficken, Grace (Hawkins)	1933	Gordon, Franklin	1950
Field, E. G.	1939	Gordon, Mrs. Franklin	1950
Field, Elizabeth	1939	Greear, Caroline	1930
Fink, Harold	1971	Green, W. L.	1930
Finkelstein, Harold	1970	Griffin, Frank	1949
Fitch, Elizabeth	1969	Gunter, Sally	1978
Fitzgerald, W. A.	1936	Haakmeester, Pete	1975
Flowers, Ed	1972	Hall, Reginald	1966
Flowers, Sara	1973	Hall, Warner	1930
Fournace, Louise	1949	Hallock, Roger	1967
Fowler, Peggy	1974	Halsey, H. R.	1939

Pace, Lillian	1959
Parker, Richard	1964
Parker, Richard	1974
Parsons, John	1960
Passmore, Clyde	1936
Peacock, Fred	1957
Penland, Hettie	1959
Perkins, Jean Ann	1950
Perry, James	1960
Pfeifer, Donald	1967
Phillips, Larry	1974
Phipps, Faye	1960
Phipps, Homer	1960
Pierce, David	1969
Pinkerton, Jack	1968
Pinkerton, Susie	1968
Pitman, Keith	1973
Pitts, Beverly	1967
Pitts, Bob	1971
Pitts, Guy	1967
Pons, Edward	1956
Pons, Jennie	1956
Pringle, Bob	1974
Proctor, Ann	1953
Proctor, Jim	1947
Pruitt, Bob	1950
Pruitt, Ruth	1950
Quin, Hillrie	1977
Ramsey, Carolyn	1956
Ramsey, Ralph	1949
Rand, Ed	1962
Rand, Joyce	1962
Rasnick, Marione	1975
Rauber, Albert	1971
Rauber, Shirley	1971
Raulerson, Lynn	1969
Ray, Vivian	1969
Reiley, Gertrude	1933
Reimer, Eugene	1968
Renshaw, Tom	1930
Rhinehardt, James	1964
Rice, Barbara	1980
Rittenhouse, Oliver	1971
Roberts, Mary	1961
Roberts, Mrs. Roy	1947
Roberts, Roy	1947
Robinson, Bill	1963

Roddy, Margaret	1956
Rogers, Grace	1979
Rogowski, A. S.	1958
Roseman, Gary	1974
Rubin, Marty	1975
Runyan, Charles	1973
Runyon, Ernest	1938
Runyon, Laliah	1938
Runyon, Miriam	1950
Runyon, Phyllis	1950
Runyon, Ruth	1950
Russell, Lois	1950
Russell, Ralph	1968
Sanders, Josephine	1959
Sanford, Malcolm	1969
Sanford, Ruth	1969
Sarner, June	1978
Sarner, Russ	1978
Savelle, Leon	1940
Sawyer, Edwina	1979
Scadin, Dewey	1950
Schaeffler, Bernice	1960
Schaeffler, Bill	1960
Schenck, David	1971
Scott, Margaret	1952
Scott, Robert	1952
Seagle, Kent	1950
Searcy, Ash	1959
Seiferle, Ed	1958
Seiferle, Norma	1958
Selby, Beth	1972
Selby, Ed	1972
Sennner, Ed	1949
Sewell, Maude	1933
Shacklett, Knox	1979
Shafe, Frances	1965
Shafe, George	1965
Shaw, Bill	1965
Shaw, Carolyn	1965
Shelton, Rosser	1963
Shenkel, William	1976
Shivers, Robert	1950
Shofner, Nancy	1973
Shuford, Carlton	1972
Shuford, Kathleen	1972
Sichveland, Don	1972
Sichveland, Marsha	1972

Skeen, Emily	1975	Stutz, William	1939
Skeen, Marianne	1978	Sullivan, Gordon	1965
Skorapa, Victor	1973	Summerson, Billie	1930
Slack, Arline	1946	Swartz, Hal	1950
Slack, Ginny	1975	Swartz, Janet	1950
Slack, Searcy	1939	Swift, Mrs. Frank	1942
Slater, Bob	1972	Swink, Steve	1971
Slater, Mary	1972	Taaffe, Roderick	1932
Smail, Jane	1969	Tappey, Dawn	1968
Smail, Ken	1969	Tappey, Ed	1968
Smith, Barbara	1975	Tate, Luke	1930
Smith, Bernice	1940	Taylor, Bob	1956
Smith, C. G.	1931	Taylor, Harrison	1939
Smith, Charles	1957	Taylor, Theo	1956
Smith, Claiborne	1957	Terp, Al	1972
Smith, F. I.	1939	Terp, Anne	1972
Smith, Harry	1966	Therrell, D. M.	1936
Smith, Katharine	1930	Thomas, David	1950
Smith, Kitty	1936	Thomas, Pat	1975
Smith, Milner	1949	Thompson, Al	1958
Smith, Mrs. E. M.	1949	Thompson, Cathy	1969
Smith, Nelle	1957	Thompson, Eleanor	1977
Smith, R. W.	1936	Thompson, Harry	1975
Smith, W. P.	1930	Thompson, Polly	1958
Smoot, Richard	1933	Thompson, Roger	1949
Snow, Marene	1931	Thorpe, Armand	1931
Sovey, Terrell	1949	Thorpe, John	1947
Sparrow, Ernest	1960	Thorpe, Mrs. John	1947
Sparrow, Jean	1960	Timpe, Alice	1953
Spaulding, C. K.	1949	Tinker, J. M.	1930
Spaulding, Mrs. C. K.	1949	Trapp, Mrs. Robert	1950
Sperry, Alexander	1958	Trapp, Robert	1950
Spratt, Guerrard	1939	Travis, Robert	1949
Spratt, Joan	1939	Traylor, Ed	1949
Stapler,Tom	1966	Traylor, Maggie	1949
Steel, Virginia	1954	Tucker, Tecoah	1969
Stewart, Frank	1949	Tull, Al	1974
Stokes, Arthur	1936	Van Landingham, Rosalind	1975
Stone, Bonnell	1930	Vincent, Paul	1958
Stone, Everett B.	1930	Wadewitz, Guenter	1949
Strahan, Charles	1931	Wadsworth, Harrison	1961
Straley, [unknown]	1972	Wadsworth, Irene	1961
Stuckey, Herbert	1950	Walker, Hattie Sue	1938
Stuckey, Mrs. Herbert	1950	Wallace, Anne	1967
Sturmer, Louis	1941	Walter, Marshall	1970
Stutesman, John	1936	Walton, Nina	1980
Stutesman, V. G.(Mrs. John)	1936	Wamsley, Sue	1954

GATC Officers
1930 – 1980

	1930	1931	1932	1933	1934	1935
PRESIDENT	Stone, E.B.[1]	Stone, E.B.	Hall, W.	Hall, W.	Hall, W.	Hall, W.
V. PRES. 1st		Estes, H.	Estes, H.	Tinker, J.	Elliott, C.R.	Glower, R.
2nd		Tinker, J.	Tinker, J.			
TREASURER	Hardy, M.[1]	Hardy, M.	Johnson, L.	Taaffe, R.	Miller, W.	Hoben, R.
SECRETARY	Elliott, C.N.[1]	Elliott, C.N.	Elliott, C.N.	Herren, O.	Hoben, M.	Ward, C.
CORR. SEC.		Branham, C	Branham, C.			Sewell, M.
HISTORIAN		Elliott, C.N.	Elliott, C.N.			
EXEC. COUNCIL		Stone, B.H.	Stone, B.H.	Johnson, L.	Johnson, L.	Johnson, L.
EXEC. COUNCIL		Strahan, C.	Strahan, C.	Snow, M.	Snow, M.	Elliott, C.B.
EXEC. COUNCIL		Stone, E.B.	Stone, E.B.	Stone, E.B.	Stone, E.B.	Stone, E.B.

[1]Acting until organizational meeting in November.

	1936	1937	1938	1939	1940	1941
PRESIDENT	Whittaker, C.	Adams, L.	Ward, C.	Adams, L.[1]/ Passmore, C.[2]	Traylor, E.[3]/ Harwell, L.[2]	Smith, F.[4]/ Harwell, L.[2]
V. PRES. 1st	Noble, G.H.	Mitchell, L.	Hoben, R.	Passmore, C./ Smith, R.[2]/	Motsinger, E.	MacAdam, W.
2nd		Stokes, A.	Smith, R.	Hoben, R.[2]/ Jordan, H.[2]	Harwell, L./ Smith, F.[2]	Reed, R.
TREASURER	Jarrard, B.	Jarrard, B.	Donald, H.	Babbington, K.	Wilson, R.	Carter, C.
SECRETARY	Ficken, G.	Passmore, C.	Noble, M.	Chappell, L.	Hatter, M.	Motsinger, E.
CORR. SEC.	Sewell, M.	Sewell, M.	Sewell, M.	Sewell, M.	Sewell, M.	Sewell, M.
HISTORIAN		Therrell, D.	Therrell, D.	Therrell, D.	Therrell, D.	Snow, M.
COUNCIL	Hall, W.	Hall, W.	Hall, W.	Ward, C.	Ward, C.	Harwell, L.
COUNCIL	Elliott, C.R.	Elliott, C.R.	Adams, L.	Runyon, E.	Runyon, E.	Runyon, E.
COUNCIL	Whittaker, C.	Whittaker, C.	Whittaker, C.	Whittaker, C.	Passmore, C.	Passmore, C.

[1]Resigned in February.
[2]Succeeded or appointed to vacancy.
[3]Resigned in January.
[4]Resigned in August.

	1942	1943	1944	1945	1946	1947
PRESIDENT	Edmonson, G.	Edmonson, G.	Edmonson, G.[1]	Edmonson, G.[1]	Edmonson, G.[1]	Freeman, L.
V. PRES. 1st 2nd	Buchanan, W./ Cragon, J.[2]	White, E.				Slack, S.
TREASURER	Carter, C./ Allen, C.[2]	Allen, C.	Allen, C.[1]	Allen, C.[1]	Allen, C.[1]	White, E.
SECRETARY	Newton, M.	Clanton, K.				Hoben, L.
CORR. SEC.	Sewell, N.	Hoben, L.				
HISTORIAN	Snow, M.	Snow, M.	Snow, M.	Snow, M.	Snow, M.	Snow, M.
COUNCIL	Harwell, L.	Herren, O.				Morris, H.
COUNCIL	MacAdam, W.	Halsey, H.R.				Cragon, J.
COUNCIL						Field, E.

[1]Acting for duration of war.
[2]Succeeded or appointed to vacancy.

	1948	1949	1950	1951	1952	1953
PRESIDENT	Freeman, L.	Cragon, J.	Cragon, J.	Good, N.	Gafnea, C.	Freeman, L.
V. PRES. 1st 2nd	Slack, S.	Slack, S. Field, E.	Slack, S. Good, N.	Spratt, G. Elliott, C.R.	Spratt, G. Proctor, J.	Batho, N. Morris, H.
TREASURER	Ingemann, A.	Ingemann, A.	Gafnea, C.	Gafnea, C.	Church, R.	Church, R.
SECRETARY	Morris, M.	Gartrell, P.	Gartrell, P.	Hoben, L.	Montgomery, C.	Gambrell, J.
HISTORIAN	Snow, M.	Snow, M.	Snow, M.	Snow, M.	Snow, M.	Snow, M.
COUNCIL	Morris, H.	Morris, H.	Hoben, L.	Cragon, J.	Cragon, J.	Cragon, J.
COUNCIL	Cragon, J.	Freeman, L.	Freeman, L.	Freeman, L.	Freeman, L.	Gafnea, C.
COUNCIL	White, E.	White, E.	White, E.	Slack, S.	Good, N.	Good, N.

	1954	1955	1956	1957	1958	1959
PRESIDENT	Slack, S.	Slack, S.	Scott, R.	Scott, R.	Morris, H.	Morris, H.
V.P. ACTIVITIES MEMBER.	Gartrell, P. Montgomery, C.	Scott, R. Hoben, L.	Ramsey, R. Hoben, L.	Ramsey, R. Gambrell, J.	Aderhold, T. Roddy, M.	Aderhold, T. Smith, C.
TREASURER	Traylor, E.	Davis, J.	Wilson, R.	Aderhold, T.	Chase, H.	Chase, H.
SECRETARY	Gambrell, J.	Gambrell, J.	Montgomery, C.	Roddy, M.	Huey, C.	Ramsey, C.
HISTORIAN	Snow, M.	Snow, M.	Snow, M.	Snow, M.	Snow, M.	Snow, M.
BULL. EDITOR					Dolan, D.	Hoben, L.
COUNCIL	Cragon, J.	Cragon, J.	Slack, S.	Slack, S.	Slack, S.	Roddy, M./ Ramsey, R.
COUNCIL	Gafnea, C.	Gartrell, P.	Gartrell, P.	Gartrell, P.	Scott, R.	Scott, R.
COUNCIL	Freeman, L.	Freeman, L.	Freeman, L.	Traylor, E.	Traylor, E.	Traylor, E.

	1960	1961	1962	1963	1964	1965
PRESIDENT	Aderhold, T.	Aderhold, T.	Coffey, G.	Coffey, G.	Coffey, G.	Eidson, J.
V.P. ACTIVITIES MEMBER.	Smith, C. Coffey, G.	Smith, C. Coffey, G.	Parsons, J. Eidson, A.	Eidson, J. Eidson, A.	Eidson, J. Deane, B.	Gibbons, R. Robinson, B./ Engle, June
TREASURER	Brendel, N.	Brendel, N.	Engle, Jim	Engle, Jim	Gibbons, R.	Hubbard, D.
SECRETARY	Deane, B.	Wilson, E.	Wilson, E.	Seiferle, N.	Phipps, F.	Gibbons, Y.
HISTORIAN	Snow, M.	Snow, M.	Snow, M.	Snow, M.	Snow, M.	Seiferle, E.
BULL. EDITOR	Hoben, L.	Deane, B.	Deane, B.	Thompson, P.	Thompson, P.	Coffey, A.
TRAIL SUPER.			Sparrow, E.	Sparrow, E.	Benson, W.	Benson, W.
COUNCIL	Ramsey, R.	Ramsey, R.	Aderhold, T.	Aderhold, T.	Aderhold, T.	Coffey, G.
COUNCIL	Chase, H.	Chase, H.	Chase, H.	Chase, H.	Engle, Jim	Engle, Jim
COUNCIL	Morris, H.	Morris, H.	Morris, H.	Morris, H.	Morris, H.	Morris, H.

	1966	1967	1968	1969	1970[1]	1971
PRESIDENT	Eidson, J.	Seiferle, E.	Seiferle, E.	Coogler, J.	Coogler, J./ Thompson, A.	Thompson, A.
V.P. ACTIVITIES MEMBER.	Gibbons, R./ Chase, H. Engle, June	Chase, H. Eidson, M.	Coogler, J. Eidson, M.	Thompson, A. Bordeaux, R.	Thompson, A./ Engle, Jim	Engle, Jim
TREASURER	Hubbard, D.	Shaw, B.	Hall, R.	Hall, R.	Johnson, E.	Smith, H.
SECRETARY	Gibbons, Y./ Rand, J.	Shafe, F.	Shafe, F.	Sanders, J.	Hungerford, J.	Hanks, E.
MEMBERSHIP					Bordeaux, R.	Russell, R.
TRAIL SUPER.	Rhinehardt, J.	Rhinehardt, J.	Stapler, T.	Stapler, T.	Myers, J.	Myers, J.
TRAIL INFO.						Taylor, B.
HISTORIAN	Seiferle, E.	Seiferle, E.	Seiferle, N.	Seiferle, N.	Drummond, M.	Drummond, M.
BULL. EDITOR	Coffey, A.	Coffey, A.	Drummond, M.	Drummond, M.	Eidson, A.	Eidson, A.
COUNCILOR[2]	Coffey, G.	Coffey, G.	Chase, H.	Chase, H.	Chase, H.	Aderhold, T.
COUNCILOR	Engle, Jim	Eidson, J.	Eidson, J.	Eidson, J.	Wilkins, G.	Wilkins, G.
COUNCILOR	Sparrow, E.	Sparrow, E.	Sparrow, E.	Seiferle, E.	Seiferle, E.	Seiferle, E.

[1]Titles changed per 1969 by-law revision. Returned to former designation in March, 1970.
[2]Called Director after 1970.

	1972	1973	1974	1975	1976	1977
PRESIDENT	Thompson, A.	Thompson, A.	Wilkins, G.	Daniel, H.	Daniel, H.	Drummond, M.
V.P. ACTIVITIES	Wilkins, G.	Wilkins, G.	Myers, J.	Myers, J.	Myers, J.	Benson, W.
TREASURER	Smith, H.	Engle, June	Engle, June	Baker, F.	Baker, F.	Galphin, G.
SECRETARY	Coffey, A.	Coffey, A.	Shafe, F.	Galphin, J.	Galphin, J.	Durrett, B.
MEMBERSHIP	Russell, R.	Daniel, H.	Daniel, H.	Swink, S.	Benson, W.	Metzger, E.
TRAIL SUPER.	Emerson, L.	Emerson, L.	Owen, G.	Owen, G.	Drummond, M.	Shofner, N.
TRAIL INFO.	Taylor, B.	Eidson, J.	Eidson, J.	Selby, E.	Selby, E.	Selby, E.
BULL. EDITOR	Myers, J.	Myers, J.	Seiferle, E.	Seiferle, E.	Seiferle, E.	Myers, J.
HISTORIAN	Eidson, M.	Eidson, M.	Aderhold, T.	Taylor, T.	Taylor, T.	Taylor, T.
DIRECTOR	Aderhold, T.	Aderhold, T.	Thompson, A.	Thompson, A.	Thompson, A.	Daniel, H.
DIRECTOR	Morris, H.	Russell, R.	Russell, R.	Wilkins, G.	Wilkins, G.	Wilkins, G.
DIRECTOR	Drummond, M.	Drummond, M.	Drummond, M.	Russell, R.	Engle, June	Engle, June

	1978	1979	1980
PRESIDENT	Drummond, M.	Benson, W.	Benson, W.
V.P. ACTIVITIES	Benson, W.	Galphin, G.	Van Landingham, R.
TREASURER	Galphin, G.	Eggleston, D.	Eggleston, D
SECRETARY	Durrett, B.	Krickel, J.	Galphin, G.
MEMBERSHIP	Calvert, B.	Calvert, B.	Daniel, H.
TRAIL SUPER.	Shofner, N.	Slater, B.	Slater, B.
TRAIL INFO.	Rubin, M.	Rubin, M.	Quin, H.
BULL. EDITOR	Van Landingham, R.	Van Landingham, R.	Funkhouser, B.
HISTORIAN	Coffey, A.	Coffey, A.	Shofner, N.
DIRECTOR	Daniel, H.	Daniel, H.	Wilkins, G.
DIRECTOR	Selby, E.	Thompson, A.	Thompson, A.
DIRECTOR	Engle, June	Drummond, M.	Drummond, M.

"One touch of nature makes the whole world kin."

– Shakespeare

GATC Members of the ATC Board of Managers
1930 – 1980

E. B. Stone, 1931 – 1935

Warner Hall, 1935 – 1937

W. Lloyd Adams, 1937 – 1939

Lovejoy Harwell, 1939 – 1947?

Larry Freeman, 1948 – 1952

James Cragon, 1952 – 1958 (vice-chairman)

Searcy Slack, 1955 – 1958

Robert Scott, 1958 – 1960

Henry Morris, 1960 – 1972

Al Thompson, 1972 – 1979

Margaret Drummond, 1979 –

"I come here to find myself, it's so easy to get lost in the world."
– John Burroughs

Activities

1930 – 1980

Date	Place	Leader	People
	1930		
Nov. 1	Organizational meeting, Dahlonega Blood Mt. hike		25
Nov. 16	Hawk Mt., Hightower Gap	rained out	
	1931		
Feb. 1	Helton Falls	Cha. Elliott	25-30
Feb. 22	Indian Mounds, Cartersville	H. Estes	
Mar. 22	Yonah Mt.	T. Renshaw	
Apr. 19	Tallulah Falls	W. Hall	22
May 17	Amicalola Falls (5 mi.)	J. Tinker	
Nov. 7-8	Annual meeting, Greear's Lodge, Helen; Tray Mt. hike		
Dec. 19-20	Christmas celebration; Mt. Oglethorpe hike		
	1932		
Jan. 31	Neel Gap - Blood Mt.		
Apr. 9-10	Fort Mountain	W. Young	
Sep. 25	Indian Mounds, Cartersville; Saltpeter Caves, Kingston	M. Crawford (guide)	41
Oct. 2	SMHC banquet, square dance		14
Oct. 8-9	Enotah Bald (5.2 mi.); Butternut	M. Snow, A. Horn	
Oct. 23	Neel Gap - Tesnatee Gap		
Nov. 5-6	Annual meeting, Cloudland Park Hotel		64
Nov. 26	Stone Mt.	O. Herren, C. Ward	
Dec. 10	SMHC Christmas party		9
Dec. 18	Neel Gap		6
	1933		
Jan. 14-15	Greear's Lodge; Woody Gap - Neel	C. Ward	24
Feb. 5	Mt. Oglethorpe - Southern's Store	E. Allemong, R.Taaffe	19
Feb. 25-26	Dick's Creek - Rich Knob		18
Mar. 19	Neel Gap - Levelland Mt.		
Apr. 9	Tickanetley Bald (10 mi.)	E. Stone	20+
Apr. 23	Jacks River Falls	W. Young	10
May 20-21	Tray Mt.	M. Elliott	30
Jun. 3-4	Highlands, Whiteside Mt.		
Jul. 8-9	Lake Burton		
Sep. 16-17	Lake Rabun		
Sep. 30	Gold prospecting, Dahlonega		

Sep. 30	SMHC annual banquet	Mab. Abercrombie	
Oct. 14-15	Annual meeting, Cloudland		76
Oct. 29	Dillard Farm; Rabun Bald (12 mi.)		31
Nov. 12	Helton Falls		22
Nov. 25-26	Greear's Lodge; Tray Mt.	Che. Elliott, etc.	
Dec. 9	Atlanta Bird Club banquet		
Dec. 16-17	SMHC Christmas party	Mab. Abercrombie	6
Dec. 20	Christmas party (1st),	M. Snow	
	Agnes Scott Cabin, Stone Mt.		

1934

Jan. 14	Sweetwater Creek, Factory Shoals	O. Herren	
Jan. 27-25	Dillard Farm; Pickens Nose	L. Hoben	
Feb. 3	Mt. LeConte (1st trip) (8 mi.)		6
Feb. 11	Soap (Sope) Creek		
Feb. 17	In-town meeting, Burns Cottage		
Feb. 24	Jack's Gap	C Whittaker	28
Mar. 11	Indian Mounds, Macon	Mau. Abercrombie	30
Mar. 24-25	Yahoola Lodge; Black Mt. tower	M. Elliott	17
Apr. 15	Amicalola Falls (4 mi.)	N. Noble	36
Apr. 28-29	Snake Mt. shelter	C. Whittaker	15
May 13	Blue Bonnet Lodge, Newnan	M. Snow	
May 26-27	Southern Trail Conf., Highlands		40
Jun. 23-24	Greear's Lodge	R. Mann	
Jul. ?	Lake Burton		
Sep. 16	Hawk & Springer Mts. (4-5 mi.)	Mau. Abercrombie	
Sep. 29	SMRC banquet & square dance	Mab. Abercrombie	
Oct. 13-14	Annual meeting, Cloudland		
Oct. 27-28	Jack's River Falls (6 mi.)	H. Morris	
Nov. 4-5	Tray Mt. - Dick's Creek Gap (11 mi.)		
Nov. 11	Rocky Knob Cabin (7 mi.)	G. Ficken	37
Nov. 24-25	Dillard Farm; Scaly Mt.		
Dec. 8	SMHC Christmas party		
Dec. 20	Christmas party	M. Noble	

1935

Jan. 11?	Hightower Gap, Game Refuge	M. Hoben	19
Feb. 3	Fort Benning, Stutesman's	Stutesmans	35
Feb. 24	Benton Falls, Tenn. with SMHC	Elliotts	20
Mar. 10	Butternut cottage (substitute)	G. Ficken	23
Mar. 14	Business meeting, dinner		
Mar. 24	Tallulah Gorge	A. Horn	22
Apr. 9	Dinner Meeting	G. Reilly	
Apr. 13-14	Rock City Camping trip	H. Forester (guide)	
Apr. 27-28	Neel Gap - Nottely Falls,	R. Smith	
	Helton Falls; Wolfpen Gap		
May 10	Lake Arabia		28
May 17-18	Amicalola Falls; Southern's Store,		
	Nimblewill Gap		

May 25-26	Lookout Mt. with Cumberland Club	B. Jarrard	
Jun. 16	Yonah Mt.		
Jul. 13-14	Four-Club outing, Standing Indian	L. Hoben	
Sep. 14-15	Lakemont	M. Snow	9
Sep. 28-29	Dick's Creek - Addis Gap	C. Whittaker	
Oct. 12-13	Annual meeting, Cloudland; Photo exhibit	C. Ward	
Oct. 26	Grassy Knob, Cohuttas (8 mi.)	C. Whittaker	23
Nov. 17	Indian Mounds, Macon		
Nov. 23-24	Dillard Farm, Ridgepole (8+ mi.)	D. Therrell	32

1936

Jan. 1	Highlands/Gainesville snow trip		
Jan. 11	Amicalola River outdoor breakfast	B. Jarrard	21
Jan. 24	Meeting: Bob Marshall speaks		
Jan. 25-26	Greear's Lodge; Dukes Creek		18
Feb. 15-16	Neel Gap - Woody Gap		
March	Work trips		
Apr. 4-5	Providence Canyon		
Apr. 24-25	Rock City; Head River	H. Forester	20
May 2	Tea for Benton MacKaye, Harvey Broome, Mabel Abercrombie	R. Smith	
May 23-24	Sitton's Gulch		
Jun. 6-7	Highlands; Ellicott's Rock	C. Ward, B. Fitzgerald	
Sep. ?	Annual meeting, Connahaynee Lodge		
Oct. 11	Dillard Farm (substitute)		21
Oct. 12	Meeting: William Carr speaks		
Oct. 24-25	Neel Gap, Blood Mt.; Vogel State Park		40
Nov. 8	"Devil's Den" Alabama; Cheahaw Mt.		
Nov. 16	Dinner: Stuart Chase speaks		
Nov. 21-22	Dillard Farm; Pickens Nose		27
Dec. 18	Christmas party		

1937

Jan. 24	Walker Mt. (4 mi.)	C. Ward	29
Feb. 13-14	Spring cleaning of Trail	C. Passmore	18
Feb. 25	Marble Hill - Oglethorpe	B. Jarrard	26
Mar. 13-14	Greear's Lodge; Unicoi - Rocky Knob		15
Apr. 4	Helton Falls (4 mi.)		7
Apr. 17-18	Amicalola Falls - Nimblewill Gap		12
May 2	Neel - Tesnatee		
May 15-16	Sitton's Gulch	C. Passmore	23
May 27	In-town steak supper		
May 29-30	Highlands, Whiteside Mt.	M. Snow	
Jun. 13	Dude Ranch - Oglethorpe	Mau. Abercrombie	
Jun. 26-28	8th annual ATC Conference	L. Hoben	18
Jul. 10-11	Lake Burton		20
Jul. 25	Lake Phoebe	B. Fitzgerald	35+
Aug. 8	The Shack		28
Aug. 22	Carter's Pool		15

Sep. 4-6	Black Warrior Forest, Ala.	W. Hall	10
Sep. 26	Enotah Bald (10 mi.)		19
Sep. 28	Business meeting		
Oct. 16-17	Annual meeting, Indian Springs, Ga.		84
Oct. 30-31	Tray Mt., Helen		25-30
Nov. 7	Slide Show by Jim Thompson		
Dec. 5	Toccoa Falls		11
Dec. 16	Christmas party		

1938

Jan. 15-16	Woody Gap - Neel Gap	Mau. Abercrombie	18
Jan. 23	In-town meeting, Warner Hall slides		
Jan. 30	Unicoi Gap - Indian Grave (work)	O. Herren	16
Feb. 12-13	CCC camp in Pisgahs	C. Whittaker	17
Feb. 27	Dick's Creek - Tray Mt.(12 mi.)	H. Donald	23
Mar. 20	Hightower - Cooper Gap	E. Cowart	
Mar. 27	Cooper - Gooch	E. Motsinger	
Apr. 10	Hawk & Springer Mt.	C. Passmore	13
Apr. 23-24	Amicalola Falls	F. Hamilton	
May 14-15	Sitton's Gulch	L. Runyon	
May 28-29	Low Gap - Tesnatee (11 mi.)	L. Hoben	14
Jun. 11-12	Nantahalas, Wayah Bald	Whittakers	24
Jun. 23	Business meeting		
Jun. 26	Carter's Pool	L. Adams	24
Jul. 9-10	Lake Blue Ridge	M. Noble	17
Jul. 15	Roller skating party		59
Jul. 31	Indian Mounds, Saltpeter caves		20
Aug. 13-14	Lake Burton		18
Aug. 21	The Shack		29
Sep. 3-5	Smokemont	C. Hoben	7
Sep. 18	Bucktown Mt.	L. Adams	
Oct. 8-9	Annual meeting, Neel Gap; Hike - Blood Mt.		
Oct. 29-30	Dillard Farm, Halloween party		
Nov. 13	Nimblewill Gap - Springer		23
Nov. 29	Skating party	O. Herren	
Dec. 4	Winding Stair Gap - Springer (work)	L. Harwell	8
Dec. 10	Christmas party		

1939

Jan. 15	Mt. Oglethorpe - Connahaynee Lodge	G. Wilson	22
Feb. 4-5	Greear's Lodge; Tray Mt.	C. Ward	21
Feb. 17	Lloyd & Lillian Adams farewell party	C. Ward	31
Feb. 19	Tate Estates - Southern's Store	B. Motsinger	19
Mar. 4-5	Vogel State Park; Neel - Tesnatee		12
Mar. 9	Business meeting		30
Mar. 16	Skating party		
Mar. 19	Amicalola Falls - Southern's Store	L. Baker	
Apr. 1-2	Pine Mt. Park; Providence Canyon	C. & M. Elliott	21
Apr. 16	Low Gap - Unicoi		14

Date	Activity	Leader	Number
Apr. 23	Kennesaw Mt. Battlefield		48
May 6-7	Sitton's Gulch, Head River	H. Donald	17
May 20-21	Four Club Meet, Balsam Mt. N.C.	K. Smith	6
Jun. 17-18	Highlands, Whitesides, Primeval Forest	H. Jordan	22
Jul. 2	Frosty Mt. - Amicalola Falls	C. Passmore	21
Jul. 15-16	Woody - Gooch Gap	C. Carter	11
Jul. 30	La Casita		37
Aug. 13	Carter's Pool	R. Wilson	18
Aug. 26	Watermelon cutting		
Sep. 3-4	Joyce Kilmer		12
Sep. 17	Unicoi Gap - Tray Mt.	K. & E. Babington	31
Oct. 7-8	Annual meeting, Neel Gap		81
Oct. 22	Low Gap - Tesnatee Gap	L. Hoben	31
Nov. 4-5	Dillard Farm; Blue Ridge Gap - N.C. Line	M. Hoben	32
Nov. 19	Neel Gap - Woody Gap	C. Carter	19
Dec. 3	Stone Mt. Geological trip	R. Smith	
Dec. 9	Christmas party		

1940

Date	Activity	Leader	Number
Jan. 20-21	Greear's Lodge; Poplar Stamp-Unicoi	L. Harwell	19
Feb. 12	Ed & Maggie Traylor farewell party		
Feb. 17-18	Neel - Tesnatee Gap	K. Babington	4
Mar. 3	Tate Estates, Marble Quarry		16
Mar. 17	Woody Gap - Ward Gap	M. Sewell	25
Apr. 6-7	Dillard Farm; Dick's Creek - Deep Gap	B. Motsinger	18
Apr. 20-21	Dick's Creek - Addis - Moccasin Creek	C. Passmore	27
May 5	Southern's Store - Amicalola Falls	C. Carter	26
May 18-19	Tray Gap - Addis Gap	E. White, B.Buchanan	22
May 26	Lost Mountain botanical trip		
Jun. 8-9	Mt. LeConte	F. Smith	26
Jun. 23	Amicalola Falls - Nimblewill Gap	H. Halsey	23
Jul. 7	Gooch - Cooper Gap	C. Passmore, F. Smith	9
Jul. 20-21	Four Club Meet, Van Hook Glade		89
Aug. 4	Carter's Pool	L. Baker	34
Aug. 18	Lake Phoebe		16
Aug. 31-S.2	Black Warrior Forest	R. Wilson	9
Sep. 15	LaCasita		40
Sep. 22	Fort Mountain	A. Furcron	29
Oct. 5-6	Annual Meeting, Bynum House, Clayton		73
Oct. 20	Mt. Oglethorpe - Settlement Rd.	H. Jordan	24
Oct. 29	Trail and shelter movies		
Nov. 9-10	Dillard House and hiking	Runyons	35
Nov. 16	Possum Hunt		20

1941

Date	Activity	Leader	Number
Jan. 8	Dinner: Myron Avery		32
Jan. 11-12	Low Gap - Dukes Creek	H. Freeman	13
Jan. 26	Yonah Mt.	E. White	16

Feb. 8-9	Poplar Stamp - Tesnatee - Neel Gap	B. Buchanan	7
Feb. 23	Unicoi Gap - Poplar Stamp	G. Edmonson	22
Mar. 22-23	Nimblewill Gap - Springer	H. Jordan	17
Apr. 6	Dick's Creek - Swallow Creek	E. & R. Wilson	20
Apr. 15	In-town meeting		
Apr. 27	Ocmulgee National Monument	L. Harwel	37
May 3	"Dare Stones" - Brenau College		50+
May 10-11	Sitton's Gulch	W. McAdam	15
May 24-25	Standing Indian	F. Smith	3
Jun. 14-15	Joint outing, Cumberland Club		45
Jul. 4-6	Black Warrior Forest	G. & M. Edmonson	6
Jul. 20	Carter's Pool	M. Brandon	18
Aug. 2-3	SMHC, Cades Cove	F. Smith	20
Aug. 16-17	Tri-State (SMHC, CMC); Lake Winfield Scott		40
Aug. 31	Mt. Mitchell	K. Babington	18
Sep. 7	La Casita	E. Babington	35
Sep. 19	Square dance	A. Ingemann	
Sep. 21	Cooper Gap - Hightower Gap	C. Whittaker	19
Oct. 4-5	Annual meeting, Camp Wasega	L. Harwell	
Oct. 19	Amicalola Falls - Southern's Store	L. Freeman	16
Nov. 1-2	Dillard House	A. Ingemann	20
Nov. 16	Southern's Store - Settlement Rd.	C. Carter	9
Nov. 30	Unicoi Gap - Tray Mt.	J. Cragon	11
Dec. 19	Christmas Party	M. Cragon	

1942

Jan. 3-4	Woody Gap - Gooch Gap	E. Motsinger	5
Jan. 18	Yonah Mt.	E. White	8
Feb. 1	Stone Mt.	B. Buchanan	8
Feb. 15	Called business meeting		
Mar. 8	Soap (Sope) Creek	M. Sewell	5
Mar. 29	Bert Adams Camp	L. Freeman	12
Aug. 17	Council meeting		
Sep. 13	La Casita		
Oct. 24	Annual meeting		

1943 – 45

No activities

1946

May 14	Neel Gap - Blood Mt. (work)		18
May 26	Unicoi Gap - Tray Mt. (work)	Edmonsons	10
Jun. 15-16	Neel Gap - Levelland Mt. (work)	L. Hoben	12
Jul. 6-7	Frosty Mt. - Winding Stair Gap	G. Edmonson	11
Jul. 28	Mt. Oglethorpe - Sassafras Mt.		21
Aug. 11	La Casita	Babingtons	
Aug. 17-18	Sitton's Gulch	G. Edmonson	
Oct. 26-27	Dillard House	Edmonsons	

| Dec. 1 | Southern's Store (work) | | |
| Dec. ? | Christmas party | | |

1947

Feb. 9	Amicalola Falls	S. Slack	3
Feb. 20	In-town meeting		
Feb. 23	Frosty Mt. - Amicalola Falls	S. Slack	29+
Mar. 9	Neel Gap - Woody Gap	J. Proctor	
Apr. 12-13	Woody Gap - Gooch - Hightower - Hawk	H. Morris	9
Apr. 25-27	Okefenokee Swamp	M. Snow	
May 17-18	Sitton's Gulch	L. Hoben	15
Jun. ?	Stone Mt.		53
Jun. 21-22	Robertstown - Cabin		12
Jun. 26	In-town meeting		
Jul. 6	Tray Mt.		16
Jul. 27	Mt. Oglethorpe	R. Hoben	
Aug. 3	Allatoona Dam		40
Aug. 30-S.1	Joyce Kilmer	M. Snow	
Oct. 9	Square Dance		
Oct. 23	In-town meeting		
Oct. 25-26	Dillard House		
Nov. 8	Annual meeting		70+
Dec. 13	Christmas party		

1948

Jan. 11	Amicalola Falls - Southern's Store	S. Slack	11
Jan. 22	In-town meeting		
Jan. 25	Chattahoochee River area	L. Weaver	6
Feb. 5	In-town meeting		
Feb. 8	Woody Gap - Black Mt.	G. Wilson	8
Feb. 21-22	Woody Gap - Neel Gap		9
Feb. 26	In-town meeting	L. Mitchell	
Mar. 4	Practice square dance		
Mar. 21	Tray Mt. - Unicoi Gap	P. Gartrell	13
Apr. 3	Square dance with Folk Dance Group		150
Apr. 11	Unicoi Gap - Chattahoochee Gap	Elliotts	15
Apr. 24-25	Oglethorpe Mt. - Sassafras shelter	H. Morris	14
Apr. 29	In-town meeting		
May 15-16	Golf course - Settlement Rd.(work)	J. Proctor	15
	Dick's Creek Gap - Addis Gap (work)	B. Gillham	7
	Tate Mt. Estates - Frosty Mt. (work)	L. Freeman	3
May 22-23	Hightower Bald	W. Duncan	11
May 30	Golf course - Settlement Rd. (work)		10
Jun. 12-13	Southern's Store - Amicalola Falls (work)	H. Morris	16
Jun. 26-Jl.5	ATC Conference - Fontana, N.C.		16
Jul. 10	Jackson Lake	A. Slack	30
Jul. 18	La Casita	Babingtons	43
Jul. 24	Neel Gap - Woody Gap	S. Slack	6
Jul. 25	Dahlonega - Gold panning		

Aug. 8	Trail clearing		4
Aug. 21-23	Lake Burton	A. Ingemann	13
Sep. 23	In-town meeting		30
Sep. 27	Yonah Mt.	E. White	13
Oct. 17	Winding Stair - Nimblewill Gap	Wilsons	
Oct. 30-31	Dillard House - business meeting		43
Nov. 13	Annual dinner		73
Dec. 18	Christmas Party		23

1949

Jan. 16	Kennesaw Mt.	Bagwells	38
Jan. 29-30	Shelter scouting trips	Traylors	21
Feb. 13	Cooper - Gooch Trail relocation	L. Freeman	
Feb. 24	Fernbank Science Center	C. Elliott	38
Feb. 27	Tray Gap - Montray shelter	C. Whittaker	16
Mar. 12	Woody Gap - Cooper Gap	E. Runyon	8
Mar. 13	Cooper Gap - Winding Stair	B. Gillham	10
Mar. 15	In-town Jamboree, square dance	J. Bagwell	50+
Mar. 26	Winding Stair - Frosty Mt.	C. Gafnea	5
Mar. 27	Frosty Mt. - Southern's Store	C. Elliott	12
Apr. 2	Square dance		
Apr. 10	Allatoona Dam	E. Smith	30
Apr. 23	Cooper Gap - Southern's Store (work)	S. Slack	7
Apr. 24	Amicalola Falls - Southern's Store (work)	C. Elliott	6
Apr. 28	In-town meeting		
May 14-15	Cooper Gap - Gooch Gap	L. Freeman	16
May 21	Square dance		
May 28-29	Sitton's Gulch		17
Jun. 4	Cooper Gap - Gooch Gap	L. Freeman	10
Jun. 5	Tray Gap - Unicoi Gap	L. Hoben	10
Jun. 9	Neel Gap - Woody Gap	C. Montgomery	8
Jun. 23	In-town meeting	A. Furcron	
Jul. 3-5	Unicoi Gap - Neel Gap	S. Slack	14
Jul. 16-17	Cooper Gap - Gooch Gap; Winfield Scott	J. Cragon	7
Aug. 6-7	Cooper Gap - Gooch Gap Grand opening	S. Slack	17
Aug. 21	La Casita	Babingtons	21
Aug. 25	Square dance	E. Smith	25
Sep. 3-5	Four-Club meet, Highlands		21
Sep. 17-18	Dick's Creek Gap - Tray Gap	J. Proctor	26
Oct. 8-9	Southern's Store - Mt. Oglethorpe	Field/Morris	10
Oct. 20	In-town meeting	G. Ruskin	
Oct. 29-30	Dillard House - Annual meeting		34
Nov. 5-6	Tray Mt. shelter (work)	J. Proctor	13
Nov. 20	Frosty Mt. (work)	S. Slack	17
Dec. 16	Christmas Party	Runyons	

1950

Jan. 8	Woody Gap - Gooch Gap	R. Church	24+
Jan. 14-15	Tray Mt. shelter (work)	F. Gordon	15+

Jan. 29	Settlement Rd. - Mt. Oglethorpe	J. Cragon	16
Feb. 12	Cooper Gap - Gooch Gap	N. Good	5
Feb. 19	Square Dance	M. Elliott	
Feb. 23	In-town program	K. Babington	45
Feb. 25	Montray shelter (work)	F. Gordon	20
Mar. 12	Talking Rock	A. Furcron	12+
Mar. 18	Square dance	D. Good	40
Mar. 26	Tray Gap - Unicoi Gap	M. Cragon	18
Apr. 8	Oglethorpe approach trail	H. Morris	9
Apr. 20	In-town program	W. Duncan	65
Apr. 22	Amicalola Falls - Frosty Mt.	D. Dolan	4
Apr. 23	Amicalola Falls - Southern's Store	A. Ingemann	13
Apr. 29	Square dance	M. Elliott	
May 6	Cooper Gap - Winding Stair	C. Gafnea	11
May 7	Winding Stair Gap - Nimblewill	C. Elliott	26
May 20-21	Spring clean-up	L. Hoben	10
Jun. 3-4	Standing Indian	C. Elliott	22
Jun. 9-15	10-day work trip	S. Shivers	4
Jun. 17-18	Dick's Creek Gap - N.C. Line	E. Field	23
Jun. 22	In-town program	C. Elliott	50
Jun. 24	Supper & square dance		40
Jul. 1	Low Gap - Chattahoochee Gap (7. mi.)	N. Good	6
Jul. 15	Robins Nest	Adairs	26
Aug. 6	Carter's Pool	C. Whittaker	25
Aug. 10	In-town meeting	W. Calder	45
Aug. 19-20	Tray Gap - Dick's Creek Gap	B. Travis	10+
Sep. 4	Oglethorpe (work)	S.Slack	5
Sep. 16-17	Four-Club meet; Winfield Scott	J. Cragon	30+
Sep. 30	Square dance		
Oct. 7-8	Neel Gap - Low Gap	N. Good/L.Freeman	17
Oct. 19	In-town meeting		40
Oct. 21-22	Mt. LeConte	M. Snow	18
Oct. 27-29	Unicoi Gap - Red Clay Gap; Scout Trail clearing	N. Batho	22
Nov. 4	Supper & Square dance	Bagwells	59
Nov. 12	Yonah Mt.	J. Proctor	15
Nov. 18	Square dance		
Nov. 23-26	Okefenokee Swamp	N. Batho	17
Dec. 16	Christmas Party		63

1951

Jan. 12	Square dance		40+
Jan. 13-14	Unicoi Gap - Tray Gap	J. McGeever	41
Jan. 20	Jim Proctor's picture party		50
Jan. 29	Neel Gap - Lake Winfield Scott	D. Dolan	29
Feb. 12	Gooch Gap - Woody Gap	L. Hoben	11
Feb. 17	Square dance		40
Feb. 25	Nimblewill Gap - Amicalola Falls	E. Field	24
Feb. 27	In-town meeting		
Mar. 11	Gooch Gap - Cooper Gap	F. Gordon	16
Mar. 18-24	Wesser, N.C. - Newfound Gap	N. Batho	8

Mar. 24	Square dance	D. Good	
Apr. 1	Poplar Stamp - Unicoi Gap	T. McGeever	17
Apr. 10	In-town meeting - "Safety Frolic"	A. Slack	12+
Apr. 14-15	Golf course - Mt. Oglethorpe	N. Batho	30
Apr. 29	Blue Ridge Gap - Dick's Creek Gap	W. Benson	25
			50
May 5	Square dance		
May 11-13	Okefenokee Swamp	S. Shivers	46
May 26-27	Woody Gap - Winfield Scott	K. Seagle	20
Jun. 5	In-town program	R. Ramsey	
Jun. 9-10	Le Conte	M. Snow	
Jun. 23-24	Tray Gap - Dick's Creek Gap	J. Cragon	13
Jul. 7-8	Sitton's Gulch (Cloudland Canyon)	F. Affair	20
Jul. 21	Lake Rabun	G. Spratt	14
Jul. 22	Blue Ridge Gap - Bly Gap	G. Spratt	7
Aug. 4-5	Cherokee Reservation	D. Good	17
Aug. 19	Allatoona Lake	C. Whittaker	9
Aug. 30	In-town meeting	R. Church	
Sep. 1-3	Five-Club meet - Nantahalas	N. Good	25
Sep. 15-16	Cooper Gap - Nimblewill Gap	F. Boland	10
Sep. 29-30	Golf course - Amicalola Falls	E. Traylor	10
Oct. 6	Square dance	D. Good	
Oct. 13-14	Neel Gap - Low Gap	S. Slack	
Oct. 18	In-town meeting	A. Nichols	30+
Oct. 20-21	Smoky Mt., Ramsay Cascades	M. Cragon	31
Oct. 27-28	Jack's River Falls	J. Proctor	
Nov. 3	Square dance		
Nov. 17-18	Dillard House	L. Freeman	13
Dec. 2	Frosty Mt. shelter (work)	J. Cragon	8
Dec. 8-9	Frosty Mt. shelter (work)	L. Freeman	9
Dec. 15	Coming-of-Age Party	M. Snow	100+

1952

Jan. 6	Frosty Mt. shelter (work)	N. Good	17
Jan. 27	Dick's Creek Gap - Blue Ridge Gap	R. Chiselbrook	28
Feb. 10	Tray Gap - Unicoi Gap	A. Nichols	21
Feb. 24	Gooch - Cooper Gap	E. Traylor	18
Mar. 9	Golf course - Mt. Oglethorpe	W Benson	12
Mar. 23	Poplar Stamp - Unicoi Gap	B. Pruitt	14
Mar. 25	Square dance	J. Bagwell	
Apr. 5-6	Golf course - Amicalola Falls	N. Batho	16
Apr. 19-20	Neel Gap - Tesnatee	P. Gartrell	5
Apr. 22	McGauhey's Barn (work)	D. Good	14
May 3-4	Neel Gap - Woody Gap	J. Cragon	22
May 10	Square dance		20
May 17-18	Head River, Rock City	M. Snow	13
May 31-Je.1	ATC Conference - Skyland, Va.		6
Jun. 14-15	Trail clearing	J. Cragon	14
Jul. 4-6	Frosty Mt. (work)	L. Freeman	31
Aug. 10	Allatoona Lake	A. Ingemann	25
Aug.. 31-S.1	Five-Club meet; Cataloochee Cove	C. Gafnea	42

Sep. 14	Woody Gap - Gooch Gap	N. Batho	5
Sep. 27-25	Cooper Gap - Big Stamp Gap survey	N. Good	
Oct. 11-12	Mt. LeConte	C. Montgomery	14
Oct. 25	Square dance		
Oct. 26	Nimblewill Gap - Winding Stair Gap	D. Dolan	19
Nov. 3	Exploring - Ga. Mineral Society	A. Furcron	
Nov. 14	Slide Show	L. Freeman	
Nov. 22-23	Dillard House	L. Freeman	20
Dec. 13	Christmas Party	Bagwells	64

1953

Jan. 11	Unicoi Gap - Tray Mt.	R. Chiselbrook	10
Jan. 24	Square dance	J. Bagwell	
Jan. 25	Woody Gap - Gooch Gap	N. Chew	20
Feb. 8	Southern's Store - Golf course	C. Montgomery	21
Feb. 21-22	Cohuttas	W. Benson	8
Mar. 8	Dick's Creek - Blue Ridge Gap	P. Runyon	15
Mar. 21-22	Amicalola Falls - Southern's Store	J. Cragon	13
Apr. 10	Square dance		
Apr. 11-12	Frosty Mt. shelter (work)	H. Morris	14
Apri 18	Scouting trip	J. Davis	11
Apr. 25-26	Neel Gap - Woody Gap	N. Batho	12
May 9-10	Unicoi Gap - Bly Gap	J. Davis	15
May 23-24	Trail maintenance	J. Davis	20
May 29	Square dance	E. Traylor	
May 30-31	Cooper Gap - Big Stamp reroute	N. Good	1
Jun. 13-14	Thunderhead	W. Benson	17
Jun. 26	Photography exhibit	E. Runyon	
Jun. 27-28	Exploration for Six-Club meet	L. Freeman	8
Jul. 12	Lake Berkeley	A. Ingemann	19
Jul. 19	The Bagwells	Bagwells	22
Aug. 1-2	Panther Creek	J. Davis	25
Aug. 15-16	Tallulah River	Wh. Benson	21
Sep. 5-7	Six-Club meet - Tallulah River	L. Freeman	143
Oct. 3-4	Head River, Rock City	M. Snow	21
Oct. 16	Square dance		
Oct. 17-18	Mt. LeConte	L. Freeman	10
Nov. 8	Kennesaw Mt.	L. Hoben	19
Nov. 21-22	Dillard House	L. Hoben	24
Dec. 12	Christmas Party		

1954

Jan. 17	Woody to Gooch Gap	A. Timpe	16
Jan. 31	Southern's Store - Amicalola Falls	A. Ingemann	28
Feb. 13-14	Tray Mt.	F. Gordon	16
Feb. 27-28	Neel Gap - Woody Gap	P. Runyon	13
Mar. 13-14	Cooper Gap - Gooch Gap (work)	J. Cragon	10
Mar. 16	In-town meeting		
Mar. 27-28	Unicoi Gap - Poplar Stamp	J. Gambrell	11

Apr. 11	Mt. Oglethorpe (work)	P. Gartrell	15
May 15-16	Cooper Gap - Winding Stair	E. Traylor	14
May 29-30	Mt. LeConte	M. Snow	16
Jun. 20	Panther Creek	C. Gafnea	24
July 3-5	Deep Gap, N.C.	B. Scott	22
Aug. 15	Carter's Pool	J. Davis	31
Sep. 4-6	Six-Club meet	S. Slack	28
Sep. 26	Winding Stair - Nimblewill Gap	H. Morris	11
Oct. 1	Annual business meeting		
Oct. 16-17	Neel Gap - Low Gap	P. Gartrell	6
Oct. 22	Slide show		
Oct. 30-31	Dillard House - Scaly Mt.	L. Hoben	18
Nov. 14	Stone Mt. party	F. Adair	35
Nov. 27-28	Providence Canyon	L. Freeman	5
Dec. 12	Christmas Party	M. Morris	60

1955

Jan. 16	Gooch Gap - Cooper Gap	A. Ingemann	9
Jan. 29-30	Winding Stair - Frosty Mt.	E. Traylor	14
Feb. 12	Southern's Store - Golf course	J. Gambrell	9
Feb. 26-27	Deep Gap, Pickens Nose	J. Davis	6
Mar. 13	Southern's Store - Amicalola Falls	R. Church	25
Mar. 26-27	Blue Ridge Gap - Addis Gap	Dolans	14
Apr. 16-17	Cooper Gap - Winding Stair	B. Scott	14
Apr. 30-M.1	Enotah (Brasstown) Bald	R. Ramsey	15
May 15	Neel Gap - Toll Gate	S. Slack	17
May 28-30	Clingman's Dome - Fontana	L. Freeman	3
Jun. 19	Carter's Pool	R. Wilson	14
Jul. 2-4	Tallulah Gorge	H. Morris	53
Jul. 23	Woody Gap - Gooch Gap	O. Baber	
Sep. 3-5	Four (Five? Six?) Club meet	S. Slack	75
Sep. 25	Lake Berkeley	A. Ingemann	26
Oct. 8-9	Tray Gap - Dick's Creek	T. Aderhold	9
Oct. 18	Annual business meeting		
Oct. 22-23	Locust Gap, Bear Paw, Betty Gap	P. Gartrell	18
Nov. 12-13	Dillard House	M. Snow	25
Nov. 20	Buford Dam	E. Field	18
Dec. 10	Christmas Party	J. Dolan	60

1956

Jan. 15	Woody Gap - Gooch Gap	D. Bledsoe	5
Jan. 28-29	Hawk Mt. - Three Forks	B. Scott	15
Feb 11-12	Frosty Mt. - Southern's Store	D. Bledsoe	18
Feb. 26	Gooch Gap - Cooper Gap	S. Slack	17
Mar. 24	Supper and Kodachrome Show		56
Mar. 25	Cooper Gap - Winding Stair Gap	B. Scott	13
Apr. 7-8	Low Gap - Neel Gap	T. Aderhold	5
Apr. 21-22	Dick's Creek - Tray Mt.	D. Dolan	18
May 5-6	Woody Gap - Neel Gap	R. Ramsey	12

Date	Activity	Name	Number
May 19-20	Tray Mt. - Unicoi Gap; Enotah Bald	C. Gafnea	21
Jun. 9-10	Mt. LeConte	L. Hoben	20
Jun. 23-24	Low Gap - Unicoi Gap	R. Ramsey	6
Jul. 7-8	Tallulah Gorge	L. Freeman	
Jul. 21-22	Dick's Creek - Bly Gap	J. Gambrell	9
Aug. 19	Lake Berkeley	A. Ingemann	52
Sep. 1-3	Five-Club meet; Roan Mt.	B. Scott	29
Sep. 22-23	Locust Gap	P. Gartrell	20
Oct. 13-14	Rock City	M. Snow	15
Oct. 20	Annual meeting		
Oct. 27-28	Cades Cove	B. Scott	23
Nov. 17-18	Dillard House	Morrises	23
Dec. 15	Christmas Party	J. Dolan	60

1957

Date	Activity	Name	Number
Jan. 13	Cooper Gap - Gooch Gap	R. Ramsey	6
Jan. 26-27	Frosty Mt. - Winding Stair Gap	B. Goodwin	3
Feb. 10	Woody Gap - Gooch Gap	S. Slack	27
Feb. 22-23	Greenbriar Cabin	L. Hoben	20
Mar. 9-10	Tray Mt.; Enotah Glade	E. Traylor	9
Mar. 23-24	Lake Winfield Scott - Neel Gap	J. Gambrell	57
Apr. 6-7	Providence Canyon	L. Freeman/H.Chase	26
Apr. 20	Arabia Mt.	E. Fields	75
Apr. 27-28	Deep Gap - Dick's Creek	T. Aderhold	8
May 11-12	Betty's Creek - Whiteoak Bottoms	B. Scott	20
May 31	Slide show	L. Freeman	42
Jun. 8-9	Hightower Gap - Winding Stair	R. Ramsey	10
Jun. 21-23	Mt. LeConte	C. Gafnea	23
Jul. 4-7	Deep Gap, N.C.	R. Wilson	19
Jul. 20-21	Low Gap - Unicoi Gap	P. Gartrell	9
Jul. 28	Lake Berkeley	A. Ingemann	40
Aug. 10-11	Van Hook Glade, N.C.	Morrises	31
Aug. 31-S.3	Six-Club Meet, Cliffside N.C.		62
Sep. 21-22	Cooper Gap East (work)	Bob Scott	10
Oct. 5-6	Low Gap - Neel Gap	D. Dolan	9
Oct. 19-20	Deep Creek Campground, Smokies	D. Deane	20
Oct. 25	Annual meeting	N. Smith	
Nov. 16-17	Dillard House	M. Snow	37
Dec. 14	Christmas Party	Slacks	

1958

Date	Activity	Name	Number
Jan. 4-5	Hightower Gap - Three Forks	L. Freeman	24
Feb. 8-9	Dick's Creek - Plumorchard Gap	H. Chase	23
Feb. 23	Cooper Gap - Woody Gap	E. Traylor	25
Mar. 15-16	Blue Ridge Gap - Bly Gap	G. Coffey	24
Mar. 29-30	Low Gap - Unicoi Gap	B. Deane	14
Apr. 12-13	Unicoi Gap - Dick's Creek Gap	W. Gellerstadt	12
Apr. 24-27	Greenbriar Cabin	S. Slack	24
May 17-18	Tesnatee - Neel Gap	R. Chiselbrook	16

May 30-Je.1	Balsam Mt. Campground, Smokies	R. Ramsey	18
May 31-Je.2	ATC Conference, Mountain Lake, Va.		10
Jun. 21-22	Amicalola Lake - Springer Mt.	J. McGraw	13
Jul. 4-6	Linville Gorge	E. Pons	14
Jul. 26	Etowah Indian Mounds	Fields	89
Aug. 10	Lake Berkeley	A. Ingemann	19
Aug. 30-31	Six-Club Meet, Deep Creek, N.C.	H. Morris	68
Oct. 4-5	Woody Gap - Neel Gap	J. Dolan	44
Oct. 18-19	Mt. LeConte	D. Dolan	19
Oct. 23	Annual meeting		53
Nov. 1-2	Low Gap - Tesnatee Gap	D. Deane	22
Nov. 15-16	Dillard House	C. Huey	32
Nov. 27-30	Jekyll Island	L. Freeman	36
Dec. 12	Christmas party	T. Taylor	60

1959

Jan. 10-11	Cooper Gap - Woody Gap	R. Chiselbrook	7
Jan. 24-25	Frosty Mt. - Springer Mt.	C. Smith	31
Feb. 15	Tray Gap - Dick's Creek Gap	F. McCrimmon	6
Feb. 28-M.1	Unicoi Gap - Tray Mt.	H. Chase	30
Mar. 14-15	Neel Gap - Woody Gap	J. McGraw	46
Apr. 4-5	Dick's Creek Gap - Blue Ridge Gap	P. Gartrell	19
Apr. 11-12	Big Stamp Gap - Nimblewill Gap	W. Benson	15
Apr. 18-19	Springer Mt.	H. Morris	8
Apr. 25-27	Greenbriar Cabin	G. Coffey	12
May 2	Arabia Mt.	Fields	46
May 16-17	Wayah Bald - Wesser Creek	B. Taylor	12
May 30-31	Blue Ridge Gap - Bly Gap	D. Deane	14
Jun. 12	Slide Show	H. Morris	85
Jun. 13-14	Neel Gap - Tesnatee Gap	S. Slack	18
Jul. 3-5	Smokies, Round Bottom	B. Scott	66
Jul. 18-19	Mt. Oglethorpe - Southern's Store	T. Aderhold	23
Aug. 1-2	Nickajack Cave, Tenn.	B. Taylor	23
Aug. 22-23	Lake Lanier	Emersons	60
Sep. 5-7	Five-Club Meet, Cosby Cove	H. Morris	80
Sep. 26-27	Cloudland Canyon	A. Coffey	26
Oct. 10	Annual meeting	M. Scott	
Oct. 24-25	Mt. LeConte	G. Meade	24
Oct. 31-N.1	Unicoi Gap - Tesnatee Gap (16 mi.)	D. Dolan	27
Nov. 14-15	Dillard House	L. Hoben	37
Nov. 26-29	Okefenokee Swamp	H. Morris	26
Dec. 11	Christmas Party	E. Wilson	73

1960

Jan. 9-10	Woody Gap - Cooper Gap	H. Chase	36
Jan. 23-24	Greenbriar Cabin	W. Gellerstadt	32
Feb. 6	Slide show	J. Sanders	75
Feb. 13-14	Cooper Gap - Three Forks	J. Dolan	29
Feb. 27-28	Russell Cave	A. Thompson	73

Mar. 12-13	Blue Ridge Gap - Dick's Creek Gap	W. Benson	3
Mar. 26-27	Deep Gap - White Oak Bottoms	C. Smith	36
Apr. 9-10	Neel Gap - Low Gap	J. Mahl	20
Apr. 22	Slide show	M. Snow	
Apr. 23-24	Tallulah Gorge	B. Taylor	56
May 14-15	Deep Gap - Dick's Creek Gap	N. Brendel	31
May 28-30	Mt. LeConte	E. Seiferle	23
Jun. 11-12	Three Forks - Springer	S. Slack	39
Jun. 25	Slide show	C. Gafnea	100
Jul. 2-4	Fontana Lake, Joyce Kilmer	G. Coffey	42
Jul. 16-17	Low Gap - Unicoi Gap	P. Gartrell	45
Jul. 23	Tate Marble Quarry & Mine	Fields	61
Aug. 6-7	Unicoi Gap - Tray Mt.	J. Engle	33
Aug. 20-21	Lake Lanier	L. Emerson	58
Sep. 3-5	Five-Club Meet, Dennis Cove, Tenn.	T. Aderhold	25
Sep. 17-18	Lake Winfield Scott, Woody - Neel	D. Deane	54
Sep. 24-25	Rocky Knob shelter (work)	T. Aderhold	28
Oct. 1-2	Tray Gap - Montray shelter (work)	P. Aderhold	19
Oct. 15-16	Tray Gap - Montray shelter (work)	J. Fambrough	41
Oct. 29	Annual meeting	V. Emerson	60
Oct. 30	Rocky Knob shelter (work)	T. Aderhold	31
Nov. 12-13	Dillard House	H. Morris	30
Nov. 24-27	Cades Cove	G. Coffey	19
Dec. 2	GATC Birthday Party	M. Snow	32
Dec. 9	Christmas Party	M. Brendel	65

1961

Jan. 13-14	Montray shelter open house	R. Losier	27
Jan. 28-29	Springer - Three Forks	P. Aderhold	11
Feb. 11-12	Deep Gap - White Oak Bottoms (18 mi.)	N. Brendel	11
Feb. 25-26	Three Forks - Cooper Gap (12 mi)	D. Dolan	11
Mar. 4	Slide Show	R. Ramsey	
Mar. 11-12	Greenbriar Cabin	P. Gartrell	35
Mar. 25-26	Cooper Gap - Woody Gap	H. Phillips	35
Apr. 8-9	Woody Gap - Neel Gap	F. Lawton	34
Apr. 22-23	Dahlonega Gold Mines	J. Parsons	63
May 6-7	Neel Gap - Low Gap	D. Deane	25
May 21-22	Low Gap - Unicoi Gap	A. Eidson	9
May 27	Springer Mt. - Three Forks (work)	P. Aderhold	32
Jun. 3-4	Dude Ranch	J. Mahl	36
Jun. 17-18	Bankhead Forest	R. Wilson	15
Jul. 1-4	Smokies backpack (10 mi.)	G. Coffey	3
Jul. 15-16	Cooper Creek Scenic Area	Fields	60
Jul. 29-30	Cumberland Caverns	B. Taylor	16
Aug. 5-6	Lake Lanier	L. Emerson	68
Aug. 19-20	Unicoi Gap - Tray	E. Sparrow	27
Sep. 2-4	Six-Club Meet, Lake Winfield Scott	T. Aderhold	103
Sep. 9	Slide show		
Sep. 16-17	Tray Gap - Dick's Creek	J. Fambrough	11
Sep.30-O.1	Dick's Creek - Bly Gap (12 mi.)	H. Chase	10

Oct. 14-15	Wayah - Wesser (13.5 mi.)	D. McFarlan	
Oct. 21	Annual meeting	J. Dolan	65
Oct. 28-29	LeConte Lodge	N. Smith	25
Nov. 11-12	Dillard House	L. Hoben	44
Nov. 23-26	Jekyll Island	A. Thompson	38
Dec. 9	Christmas Party	N. Smith	94

1962

Jan. 13-14	Woody Gap - Neel Gap	E. Sparrow	14
Jan. 27-28	Big Stamp Gap - Amicalola	A. Eidson	21
Feb. 10-11	Greenbriar Cabin	H. Chase	30
Feb. 24-25	Unicoi Gap - Tray Gap	N. Brendel	27
Mar. 10-11	Low Gap - Neel Gap	B. Taylor	10
Mar. 17	Marking crashed aircraft	C. Smith	
Mar. 24-25	Springer Mt. - Cooper Gap	J. Eagle	16
Mar. 31	Slide show	N. Brendel	
Apr. 7-8	Trail and shelters work trip	E. Sparrow	27
Apr. 28-29	Deep Gap - Dick's Creek	B. Hill	8
May 12	Arabia Mt.	Fields	105
May 19-20	LeConte Lodge	J. Fambrough	24
Jun. 2-3	Wesser - Wayah Bald	D. Dolan	10
Jun. 23-24	Blue Valley Primitive camp area	C. Smith	33
Jul. 7-8	Mahl's Cabin	J. Mahl	48
Jul. 21-22	Low Gap - Unicoi Gap	Coffeys	26
Aug. 4-5	Lake Lanier	Emersons	48
Aug. 18-19	Cloudland Canyon	J. Parsons	14
Sep. 1-3	Six-Club Meet, Camp Bethel, Va.	G. Coffey	12
Sep. 15-16	Tray Mt. - Dick's Creek	C. Smith	22
Sep. 29-30	Wocdy Gap - Cooper Gap	B. Gillham	13
Oct. 13-14	White Oak Bottoms	Seiferles	54
Nov. 2	Annual meeting	F. Gillham	
Nov. 10-12	Dillard House	F. Boland	35
Nov. 22-25	Deep Creek, Smokies	J. Parsons	20
Dec. 8	Christmas party	T. Taylor	75

1963

Jan. 12-13	Woody Gap - Cooper Gap	E. Sparrow	24
Jan. 26-27	Nickajack Cave	A. Thompson	18
Feb. 1	Slide Show	R. Ramsey	
Feb. 9-10	Big Stamp - Cooper Gap	P. Bell	33
Feb. 23-24	Kolomoki Mounds;Providence Canyon	J. Parsons	19
Mar. 9-10	Woody Gap - Neel Gap	N. Brendel	20
Mar. 23-24	Greenbriar Cabin	T. Aderhold	27
Apr. 6-7	Tray Gap - Dicks Creek	B. Eidson	17
Apr. 20-21	Low Gap - Unicoi	C. Smith	7
May 4-5	Dick's Creek - Deep Gap	D. Deane	17
May 18-19	Work trip	E. Sparrow	11
Jun. 8-9	Amicalola Falls - Big Stamp Gap	H. Chase	14
Jun. 22-23	Cooper Creek Scenic Area	Fields	57

Jul. 6-7	Unicoi - Tray Mt.	H. Morris	44
Jul. 20-21	Lake Allatoona Camp	H. Phipps	42
Aug. 3-4	Cloudland Canyon; Byers Cave	B. Taylor	25
Aug.31-S.2	Six-Club Meet, Standing Indian	G. Coffey	68
Sep. 14-15	Rabun Bald, Blue Valley, N.C.	C. Smith	14
Sep. 28-29	Neel Gap - Low Gap	J. Eidson	22
Oct. 4	Annual meeting	J. Engle	58
Oct. 19-20	Mt. LeConte	J. Fambrough	10
Nov. 2-3	Mahl's Cabin	J. Mahl	21
Nov.28-O.1	Fort Clinch State Park, Fla.	R. Wilson	60
Nov. 16-17	Dillard House	E. Traylor	24
Dec. 14	Christmas Party	J. Oppenlander	

1964

Jan. 4-5	Amicalola - Big Stamp	E. Gleaves	17
Jan. 18-19	Factory Shoals	C. Smith	31
Jan. 18-19	Mt. LeConte	T. Aderhold	16
Feb. 8-9	Neel Gap - Low Gap	A. Eidson	31
Feb. 22-23	Woody Gap - Neel Gap	D. Gwen	27
Mar. 7-8	Wolfpen Gap - Cooper Creek	E. Sparrow	26
Mar. 21-22	Tray Gap - Dick's Creek	B. Robinson	12
Apr. 4-5	Dick's Creek - Deep Gap	B. Gibbons	7
Apr. 18-19	Tallulah Gorge	L. Freeman	34
May 2-3	Mt. LeConte	J. Fambrough	33
May 16-17	Low Gap - Unicoi	B. Holley	
May 29-31	Fontana - Wesser	H. Chase	10
May 22	Slide show	C. Smith	
Jun. 13-14	Unicoi - Tray Mt.	B. Close	29
Jun. 27-28	Roosevelt State Park	A. Slack	54
Jun. 27-29	ATC Conference, Stratton Mt., Vt.	G. Coffey	5
Jul. 11-12	Nickajack Cave	B. Hardman	14
Jul. 25-26	Lake Lanier	Emersons	47
Aug. 8-9	Blue Valley, N.C.	J. Glenn	26
Aug. 22-23	Float Trip, Chattahoochee R.	H. Phipps	22
Sep. 5-7	Six-Club Meet, Cataloochee Cove	G. Coffey	46
Sep. 19-20	Woody Gap - Cooper Gap	K. Christopher	12
Oct. 3-4	Tellico Plains, Tenn.	J. Dolan	16
Oct. 9	Annual meeting	M. Eidson	59
Oct. 17-18	Big Stamp - Cooper Gap	N. Brendel	35
Oct. 31-N.1	Brasstown Bald - Jack's Gap	R. Losier	14
Nov. 6	Slide show		
Nov. 14-15	Dillard House	J. Engle	42
Nov. 26-29	Elkmont, Tenn.	J. Engle	13
Dec. 12	Christmas Party		70

1965

| Jan. 9-10 | Tate City, Standing Indian | R. Losier | 8 |
| Jan. 23-24 | Three Forks - Nimblewill Falls, Spr. | H. Glover | 9 |

Feb. 6-7	Mt. Yonah, Brasstown Bald, Tray Falls	C. Smith	20
Feb. 20-21	Dick's Creek Gap - Unicoi Gap	B. Gibbons	21
Mar. 13-14	Neel Gap - Low Gap	J. Rhinehardt	16
Mar. 26-28	Fall Creek Falls, Tenn.	E. Gleaves	29
Apr. 10-11	Dick's Creek Gap - Deep Gap	J. Rhinehardt	13
Apr. 24-25	Woody Gap - Neel Gap	H. Morris	35
May 1-2	Work trip	W. Benson	23
May 15-16	Mahl's Cabin	J. Mahl	32
May 29-31	Greenbriar Cabin	G. Coffey	23
Jun. 5-6	Lake Lanier	Emersons	24
Jun. 11	Slide Show		
Jun. 19-20	Lake Rabun	D. Gwen	9
Jul. 3-5	Linville Gorge	E. Pons	20
Jul. 24-25	Work trip	W Benson	18
Aug. 7-8	Case Cave, Cloudland Canyon	B. Taylor	28
Sep. 4-6	Multi-Club meet Rock Creek Area	J. Eisdon	40
Sep. 11-12	Cooper Gap - Three Forks	E. Sparrow	8
Sep. 25-26	Low Gap - Unicoi Gap	E. Rand	14
Oct. 9-10	Woody Gap - Cooper Gap	A. Thompson	12
Oct. 16	Annual meeting	P. Thompson	56
Oct. 23-24	Mt. LeConte	T. Aderhold	36
Nov. 13-14	Dillard House	D. Owen	35
Nov. 25-28	Appalachicola Nat. Forest	J. Mahl	43
Nov. 30	Slide show	C. Smith	
Dec. 11	Christmas Party	Y. Gibbons	61

1966

Jan. 8-9	Wayah Gap - Wesser	J. Engle	9
Jan. 15	AT scouting hike	G. Coffey	4
Jan. 22-23	LeConte Lodge	T. Aderhold	17
Jan. 29-30	Gooch Gap - Jarrard Gap	G. Shafe	12
Feb. 5-6	Tesnatee - Unicoi	A. Thompson	8+
Feb. 12-13	AT scouting trip	G. Coffey	4
Feb. 19-20	Ellicott's Rock	H. Morris	28
Mar. 5	Yonah and Pinky	W. Benson	20
Mar. 19-20	Cloudland Canyon	B. Taylor	37
Apr. 2-3	Roosevelt State Park	N. Seiferle	56
Apr. 16-17	Nimblewill Falls - Three Forks	H. Glover	7
Apr. 30-M.1	Dorothy Thompson Wilderness	J. Molyneaux	34
May 14-15	Unicoi Gap - Dick's Creek	D. Owen	18
May 28-30	Joyce Kilmer	G. Coffey	20
Jun. 11-12	Gooch Gap - Three Forks	B. Shaw	11
Jun. 25-26	Tesnatee - Jarrard Gap	E. Rand	13
Jul. 2-4	Linville Gorge	E. Pons	6
Jul. 23-24	Lake Lanier - Emersons	B. Close	37
Jul. 30-31	Work trip	J. Rhinehardt	7
Aug. 6-7	Oconee National Forest Canoe trip	C. Smith	19
Aug. 20-21	Iron Hill - Lake Allatoona	H. Chase	9
Sep. 3-5	Multi-Club meet,Unicoi State Park	J. Eidson	100
Sep. 17-18	DeSota Falls, Ala.	D. Magruder	7

Oct. 8-9	Dick's Creek - Bly Gap	L. Freeman	27
Oct. 15	Annual meeting	F. Shafe	47
Oct. 22-23	Mt. LeConte	T. Aderhold	36
Oct. 23	Save Our Smokies Hike	J. Eidson	18
Oct. 29-30	Work trip	J. Rhinehardt	30
Nov. 4-5	Dillard House	M. Drummond	22
Nov. 24-27	Okefenokee Swamp	L. Freeman	
Nov. 29	Slide show	R. Losier	
Dec. 3	Christmas party		76
Dec. 17-18	Cochran Falls	J. Engle	26

1967

Jan. 14-15	Smokemont - Peck's Corner, Smokies	Engles	17
Jan. 28-29	Three Forks - Springer - Nimblewill Falls	B. Shaw	22
Feb. 11	Neel Gap - Hogpen Gap	H. Glover	12
Feb. 25-26	Woody Gap - Neel Gap	A. Thompson	52
Mar. 11-12	Standing Indian, Tate City	T. Stapler	14
Apr. 1-2	Three Forks - Hightower	R. Parker	4
Apr. 8-9	Work trip	J. Rhinehardt	9
Apr. 22-23	Pisgah Nat. Forest	D. Scadin	23
May 13	Work trip	J. Rhinehardt	8
May 20-22	ATC Conference, High Hampton, N.C.	E. Seiferle	36
May 27-28	Dorothy Thompson Wilderness	J. Molyneaux	15
Jun. 10-11	Cades Cove - Gregory Bald	L. Freeman	21
Jun. 24-25	Hogpen Gap - Unicoi Gap	Shafes	9
Jul. 8-9	Lake Lanier	Emersons	42
Jul. 22-23	Oostanoula Float Trip	J. Coogler	24
Aug. 19-20	Lake Blue Ridge camping	H. Chase	45
Aug. 25	Slide show	R. Hall	23
Sep. 2-4	Multi-Club meet	E. Seiferle	17
Sep. 23-24	Tray Gap - Dick's Creek	G. Wilkins	29
Oct. 7	Annual meeting	V. Emerson	57
Oct. 14-15	Coleman River - Patterson Gap	J. Engle	10
Oct. 21-22	Mt. LeConte	E. Rand	53
Nov. 11-12	Dillard House	R. Wilson	51
Nov. 23-26	Cades Cove, Tenn.	J. Eidson	17
Dec. 9	Christmas party	A. Slack	78

1968

Jan. 27-28	Wayah Bald - Wesser	G. Wilkins	15
Feb. 10-11	Mt. LeConte	T. Aderhold	23
Feb. 24-25	Dick's Creek - Tray	B Shaw	17
Mar. 9-10	Cooper Gap - Woody Gap	M. Drummond	23
Mar. 23-24	Deep Gap - Dick's Creek Gap	J. Rhinehardt	15
Apr. 6	Kennesaw Mt.	R. Bordeaux	37
Apr. 20-21	Neel Gap - Low Gap	J. Parsons	19
May 4-5	Trail maintenance	T. Stapler	35
May 11	Panola Mt.	N. Seiferle	
May 18-19	Beech Creek Gap, Tallulah River	J. Engle	13

Jun. 1-2	Cooper Gap - Three Forks	G. Shafe	14
Jun. 15-16	Mt. LeConte	Thompsons	30
Jun. 29	Sweetwater Creek, Factory Shoals	L. Hoben	46
Jul. 5-7	Raven Fork Wilderness,Three Forks	G. Coffey	
Jul. 20-21	Lake Lanier	Emersons	69
Aug. 3-4	Woody Gap - Neel Gap	J. Engle	30
Aug. 17-18	Chattahoochee River float trip	J. Eidson	18
Aug.30-S.2	Multi-Club meet	Shafes	30+
Sep.14-15	Low Gap - Unicoi	J. Coogler	12
Sep. 28-29	Indian Grave - Dick's Creek	G. Wetherhold	
Oct. 5	Annual meeting	A. CIose	44
Oct. 11	Slide show	R. Hall	45
Oct. 13	Special area clean-up	J. Coogler	44
Oct. 19-20	Greenbriar Cabin	T. Aderhold	
Nov. 2-3	Dillard House	C. Smith	33
Nov. 16	Fernbank Forest	S. Slack	14
Nov.28-D.1	Florida Caverns State Park	B. Taylor	77
Dec. 14	Christmas party	M. Brendel	

1969

Jan. 18-19	Dick's Creek - Indian Grave Gap	R. Bordeaux	10
Jan. 18	Trail relocation	J. Eidson	26
Feb. 1-2	Unicoi Gap - Chattahoochee Gap	J. Eidson	26
Mar. 1-2	Rabun Bald - Warwoman Dell (16 mi.)	J. Myers	5
Mar. 15-16	Cooper Gap - Three Forks	H. Glover	17
Mar. 29-30	Woody Gap - Neel Gap	A. Thompson	18
Apr. 12-13	Trail Maintenance	T. Stapler	14
Apr. 26-27	Smoky Mt. Wildflower tour	N. Seiferle	43
May 10	Anti-Litter & Clean-up	C. Smith	27
May 17-18	Neel Gap - Low Gap	R. Russell	10
May 30-J.1	Hazel Creek, Eagle Creek, Smokies	G. Coffey	8
Jun. 14-15	Lake Lanier	Emersons	
Jun. 28	Cooper - Woody	L. Hoben	31
Jul. 4-6	Roan Mt. - Elk Park	J. Engle	16
Jul. 19	Float Trip	R. Wilson	34
Aug. 2-3	Trail Maintenance	T. Stapler	13
Aug. 16-17	Low Gap - Unicoi Gap	G. Wetherhold	18
Aug. 30-S.1	Multi-Club meet, Smokies	J. Coogler	89
Sep. 13-14	Wallace - Mooney Gap	J. Engle	22
Sep. 27-28	Deep Gap - Dick's Creek Gap	R. Hallock	22
Oct. 4	Tray Mt. - Unicoi Gap	M. Drummond	50+
Oct. 10	Annual meeting	J. Sanders	40
Oct. 18-19	LeConte Lodge	E. Seiferle	47
Oct. 24	Slide show	H. Morris	40+
Nov. 1-2	Dillard House	L. Pace	13
Nov. 15-16	Fort Mt. State Park	H. Chase	22
Nov. 27-30	Okefenokee Swamp	G. Reiner	57
Dec. 6	Christmas party	J. Hungerford	47

1970

Date	Activity	Leader	Count
Jan. 1-4	Cumberland Gap, Ky.	J. Engle	15
Jan. 17-18	Unicoi Gap - Tesnatee Gap	G. Wilkins	17
Jan.31-F.1	Three Forks - Cooper Gap	J. Rhinehardt	18
Feb. 14-15	Mt. LeConte	T. Aderhold	
Feb. 28-M.1	Addis Gap - Hickory Ridge	J. Eidson	17
Feb. 27	Special membership meeting		
Mar. 7	Cooper Gap - Woody Gap	H. Chase	41
Mar. 14-15	Woody Gap - Neel Gap	G. Shafe	33
Apr. 4-5	Trail Maintenance	J. Myers	45
Apr. 11-12	Blackburn State Park, gold mining	J. Parsons	55
Apr. 25-26	Rabun Bald - Warwoman Dell (18 mi.)	J. Myers	10
May 2	Slide show	E. Sparrow	
May 9	Odum Scout Trail, Ala.	R. Bordeaux	49
May 16-17	Mooney Gap - Patterson Gap	H. Glover	8
May 29-31	Blackbeard Island	G. Reiner	
Jun. 13	Nimblewill Gap - Three Forks	M. Drummond	27
Jun. 20-21	Gregory Bald, Hannah Mt.	G. Coffey	19
Jul. 3-5	Shining Rock Wilderness	E. Pons	41
Aug. 1	Tallulah Gorge	B. Taylor	40
Aug. 15	Unicoi - Tray Mt.	E. Seiferle	40
Aug. 29-30	Trail Maintenance	J. Myers	13
Sep. 5-7	Multi-Club meet, Mt. Mitchell	A. Thompson	36
Sep. 19-20	Tray Gap - Dick's Creek	E. Johnson	17
Oct. 3-4	Kinsey Creek- Frog Mt.	Je. Engle	14
Oct. 16	Annual meeting	F. Shafe	55
Oct. 17	Blue Ridge Gap - Titus Valley	M. Drummond	52
Oct. 31-N.1	Dick's Creek Gap - Deep Gap	R. Hallock	7
Nov. 14-15	Dillard House	N. Seiferle	29
Nov. 26-29	Crooked River State Park	T. Aderhold	35
Dec. 12	Christmas Party	J. Rand	100
Dec. 19	Frosty Mt. - Nimblewill Falls	H. Glover	32

1971

Date	Activity	Leader	Count
Jan. 1-3	Newfound Gap, Smoky Mts.	R Bordeaux	24
Jan. 16-17	Unicoi Gap - Tesnatee	B Cantey	9
Jan. 30-31	Raven Cliffs, Dukes Creek, Mahl Cabin	J. Mahl	22
Feb. 6-7	Mt. LeConte	T. Aderhold	26
Feb. 13	Neel - Desoto Falls	J. Eidson	17
Feb. 27-28	Jack's Gap - Unicoi Gap	F. Menger	7
Mar. 6	Springer Mt. - Toccoa River	H. Glover	29
Mar. 13-14	Woody Gap - Tesnatee Gap	J. Rhinehardt	6
Mar. 27-28	Standing Indian (alternate)	J. Myers	14
Apr. 3	Toccoa River - Fish Gap	T. Aderhold	8
Apr. 10-11	Wallace Gap - Wayah Gap	A. Eidson	14
Apr. 17	Slide show	C. Gafnea	
Apr. 24-25	Cooper Gap - Woody Gap	J. DeVaughn	25
May 1-2	Joyce Kilmer	G. Wilkins	10
May 8	Whiteoak Stomp Gap - Fish Gap	J. Eidson	4

May 16-17	Forney Ridge - Forney Creek	G. Coffey	2
May 29-31	Suwanee River float trip	R. Losier	28
Jun. 5	Hawk Mt. - Big Stamp Gap	L. Emerson	22
Jun. 12-13	Cloudland Canyon, Case Cave	B. Taylor	20
Jun. 26-27	Rock Gap - Big Spring - Standing Indian	M. Eidson	27
Jul. 3-5	Linville Gorge	E. Pons	23
Jul. 17-18	Trail Maintenance	J. Myers	23
Aug. 14-15	Addis Gap - Unicoi	H. Daniel	22
Aug. 21	Ellicott's Rock	H. Morris	19
Aug. 28-29	Dick's Creek - Bly	E. Johnson	7
Sep. 4-6	Multi-Club meet, Hawk Mt.	A. Thompson	69
Sep. 11	Sarah's Creek	M. Drummond	38
Sep. 18-19	Unicoi Gap - Hogpen	R. Russell	9
Oct. 2-3	Lake Burton	R. Hallock	22
Oct. 15	Annual meeting	T. Taylor	46
Oct. 23-24	Mt.LeConte	J. Coogler	51
Oct. 30-31	Tate City, Standing Indian	E. Seiferle	16
Nov. 6	Slide Show	R. Ramsey	
Nov. 13-14	Big Stamp - Amicalola Falls	G. Shafe	17
Nov. 25-28	Alexander Springs, Fla.	R. Losier	29
Dec. 11	Christmas party	M. Orr	
Dec. 18	Cochran Falls	Je. Engle	27
Dec.31-J.2	Clingman's Dome - Cades Cove	J. Eidson	15

1972

Jan. 15-16	Woody Gap - Neel Gap	G. Shafe	17
Jan. 29-30	Kimsey Creek , Standing Indian	H. Daniel	19
Feb. 12-13	Mt. LeConte	T. Aderhold	34
Feb. 19-20	Cooper Gap - Woody Gap	B. Cantey	11
Feb. 26	Stone Mt.	S. Slack	51
Mar. 4	Lake Winfield Scott - Blood Mt.	R. Russell	21
Mar. 11-12	Neel Gap - Turner's Corner	M. Walter	22
Mar. 24-26	Yellow Creek Mts.	G. Wilkins	13
Apr. 8	Trail Maintenance	L. Emerson	18
Apr. 15-16	Three Forks - Hwy. 60	H. Smith	16
Apr. 22-23	Dukes Creek Falls, Raven Cliffs	J. Parsons	25
May 6-7	Tray Mt. - Dick's Creek	E. Metzger	22
May 13-14	Rivermont Cave	R. Bordeaux	10
May 20-21	Etowah Canoe trip	R. Wilson	30
May 27-29	High Rocks. Smokies	G. Coffey	5
Jun. 9	Slide show, tent sale	G. Wilkins	60
Jun. 10-11	Frosty Mt. - Three Forks	E. Rand	26
Jun. 16-18	ATC Conference, Plymouth, N.H.		9
Jun. 24-25	Mooney Gap - Rock Gap	J. Rhinehardt	31
Jul. 1-3	Fall Creek Falls	B. Taylor	20
Jul. 15-16	Cooper Gap - Three Forks	El. Metzger	25
Jul. 29	Sweetwater Creek	M. Eidson	32
Aug. 12-13	Chattahoochee River Canoe	M. Drummond	23
Aug. 26-27	Dick's Creek - Deep Gap	D. Kenney	12
Sep. 1-4	Multi-Club meet, Grandfather Mt.	A. Thompson	45

Sep. 16-17	Unicoi Gap - Tesnatee	B. Mann	23
Sep. 30-O.1	Greenbriar Cabin	A. Coffey	37
Oct. 6	Annual meeting	M. Hubbard	55
Oct. 14-15	Mooney Gap - Patterson Gap	H. GIover	32
Oct. 21	Nimblewill Gap - Nimblewill Falls	P. Aderhold	52
Oct. 28-29	Rabun Bald - Warwoman Dell	J. Myers	19
Nov. 11-12	Mt. Collins, Chimney Tops, Poke Patch	Ji. Engle	25
Nov. 23-26	Ft. Clinch State Park, Fla.	DeVaughns	55
Dec. 2-3	Brasstown Bald	G. Owen	28
Dec. 9	Christmas Party		
Dec. 13	Kennesaw Mt	G. Davy	18
Dec. 30	Standing Indian	H. Daniel	19

1973

Jan. 27-28	Wayah Gap - Franklin, N.C.	Ji. Engle	22
Feb. 3-4	Three Forks - Highway 60	M. Eidson	9
Feb. 17-18	Mt. LeConte	D. Cook	44
Feb. 24-25	Unicoi Gap - Dick's Creek Gap	S. Swink	8
Mar. 3-4	Fires Creek, Big Stamp Mt.	DeVaughns	8
Mar. 17-18	Dick's Creek - Hightower Bald	J. Myers	6
Mar. 24	Trail Maintenance	L. Emerson	23
Mar. 31-A.1	Highway 60 - Slaughter Gap	J. Eidson	5
Apr. 14-15	Coleman River - Beech Creek	Ju. Engle	8
Apr. 21	Tallulah Gorge	A. Coffey	11
Apr. 29	Allatoona Area, wildflowers	N. Seiferle	38
May 5-6	Hiwassee River float trip	D. Kenney	19
May 12-13	Joyce Kilmer	H. Smith	23
May 19-20	Conasauga River	G. Wilkins	12
May 26-28	Smokies, 20-mile Creek	T. Aderhold	17
Jun. 2	Trail Maintenance	L. Emerson	6
Jun. 9-10	Rivermont Cave	R. Bordeaux	13
Jun. 16-17	Jack's River	J. Carter	13
Jun. 30-J.1	Springer Mt. - Three Forks	E. Seiferle	19
Jul. 14-15	Ellicott's Rock	M. Drummond	
Jul. 20	Slide show, Auction	J. Eidson	38
Jul. 22	Sarah's Creek	D. Owen	8
Aug. 4-5	Cooper Gap - Woody Gap	J. Rhinehardt	4
Aug. 11-12	Flat Creek Ranch	J. Coogler	
Aug. 18	Panther Creek	B. Mann	7
Aug.31-S.3	Multi-Club meet, Appletree Camp	A. Thompson	34
Sep. 15-16	Raven Fork Wilderness, Smokies	G. Coffey	22
Sep. 22	Chickamauga Nat. Military Park	C. Gafnea	10
Sep. 29-30	Unicoi Gap - Hogpen Gap	H. Fink	11
Oct. 5	Annual meeting	E. Hanks	50
Octi 6-7	Dillard House	G. Shafe	19
Oct. 13-14	Stecoah Gap - Fontana	G. Wilkins	4
Oct. 20-21	Woody Gap - Neel Gap	H. Morris	10
Oct. 27-28	Wayah Bald - Wesser	R. Russell	13
Nov. 3-4	Mt. LeConte	Sanfords	46
Nov. 10-11	Cooper Gap - Three Forks	E. Johnson	15

Nov. 22-25	Okefenokee Swamp	R. Hallock	40
Dec. 8	Christmas party	El. Metzger	94
Dec. 15	Stone Mt.	Terps	12
Dec. 29-31	Standing Indian Loop	H. Daniel	13

1974

Jan. 12-13	Cohutta Mt. campout	G. Wilkins	16
Jan. 19-20	Hightower - Amicalola Falls	H. Glover	10
Feb. 2	Neel Gap - Lake Winfield Scott	B. Mann	39
Feb. 9-10	Cades Cove	J. Carter	3
Feb. 16-17	Hightower Gap - Lake Winfield Scott	S. Swink	15
Feb. 23-24	Mt. LeConte	E. Johnson	
Mar. 3	Stone Mt.	M. Coffey	46
Mar. 9-10	Blue Mt., Chattahoochee outfall	J. Eidson	6
Mar. 16-17	Lake Winfield Scott - Tesnatee Gap	J. Conroy	12
Mar. 23-24	Dukes Creek Falls - Whitley Gap loop	E. Selby	9
Mar. 30-31	Three Forks - Highway 60	G. Wilkins	15
Apr. 5	Spring meeting	J. Myers	40
Apr. 6	Nimblewill Falls	J. Galphin	17
Apr. 13-14	Ellicott's Rock	H. Fink	6
Apr. 20	Trail Maintenance	G. Owen	11
Apr. 27-28	Unicoi - Hogpen	G. Wilkins	19
May 4	Anti-Litter day	E. Hanks	6
May 18-19	Chestatee & Etowah canoe	R Wilson	
May 25-27	Balsam Mt., Mt. Sterling	T. Aderhold	8
Jun. 8	Canasauga River	M. Grinnell	20
Jun. 14-16	Shining Rock	D. Eggleston	
Jun. 15	The Pocket, John's Mt.	V. Emerson	30
Jun. 22-23	Cloudland Canyon	A. Thompson	15
Jun. 29-30	Jack's River	B. Slater	13
Jul. 14	Mahl's Cabin	J. Mahl	18
Jul. 20-21	Lakeside camping	E. DeVaughn	23
Jul. 27	Clear cutting trip with Forest Service	G. Wilkins	36
Aug. 17-18	Mt. Mitchell	G. Owen	11
Aug. 24-25	Unicoi Gap - Dick's Creek	R. Russell	17
Aug. 31-S.2	Multi-Club meet, Grayson Highlands State Park, Va.	G. Wilkins	2
Sep. 14-15	Wolfpen to Fish Gap	L. Elliott	6
Sep. 20	Slide Show	J. Myers	38
Sep. 22	Neel Gap - Cowrock	El. Metzger	37
Sep. 28-29	Poke Patch, Smokies	G. Coffey	14
Oct. 4	Annual Meeting	P. Thompson	
Oct. 5	Panther Creek	H. Morris	38
Oct. 12-13	Dick's Creek - Deep Gap	R. Hallock	18
Oct. 26-27	Mt. LeConte	M. Walter	42
Nov. 3	Springer - Three Forks	M. Drummond	25
Nov. 9-10	Loop Trail work trip	J. Engle	7
Nov. 16	Brasstown Bald - Trackrock	S. Howard	37
Nov. 23-24	Hightower Cr., Bly Gap, Tallulah R.	Ji. Engle	11
Nov. 28-D.1	Marianna Springs, Fla.	G. Wilkins	13

Dec. 1	Kennesaw Mt.	G. Owen	6
Dec. 7-8	Wayah Bald - Wesser	J. Myers	9
Dec. 13	Christmas Party	P. Aderhold	90

1975

Jan. 4-5	Smokies	D. Eggleston	5
Jan. 11-12	Rabun Bald - Warwoman Dell	B. Slater	8
Jan. 18-19	Unicoi Gap - Dick's Creek Gap	E. Johnson	12
Jan. 25	Springer - Three Forks	H. Glover	33
Feb. 1-2	Mt. LeConte	D. Cook	47
Feb. 8-9	Tesnatee Gap - Lake Winfield Scott	B. Ethridge	6
Feb. 15-16	Dick's Creek - Deep Gap	R. Bordeaux	7
Feb. 22-23	Joyce Kilmer	H. Smith	10
Feb. 22	Side Trails outing	E. Johnson	4
Mar. 1	Georgia AT walk-thru	G. Owen	
Mar. 8-9	Hightower Gap - Lake Winfield Scott	B. Durrett	7
Mar. 16	Headwaters Dukes Creek	L. Emerson	5
Mar. 21-23	Wesser - Fontana	H. Daniel	12
Apr. 5	Spring meeting	F. Shafe	52
Apr. 12-13	Side Trail trip	C. Conner	5
Apr. 19-20	Rough Ridge, Jack's River	G. Wilkins	8
Apr. 26-27	Standing Indian	C. Conner	14
May 3-4	Joyce Kilmer Wildflower	V. Emerson	18
May 10	Panola Mt.	R. Russell	23
May 10	Side Trail trip	D. Eggleston	9
May 17	Trail Maintenance	G. Owen	35
May 24-26	Smokies	T. Aderhold	17
May 31	Blood Mt.	C. Howard	16
Jun. 7-8	Hurricane Creek	M. Eidson	19
Jun. 14	Stone Mt.	H. Morris	8
Jun. 21-22	Tesnatee - Unicoi	E. Metzger	5
Jun. 28-29	Cloudland Canyon	J. Coogler	25
Jul. 26-27	Fires Creek	DeVaughns	14
Aug. 2-3	Cloudland Canyon caving	B. Taylor	24
Aug. 9	Slide show & Photo contest	B. Cowden	
Aug. 16-17	Chattahoochee Float Trip	H. Smith	16
Aug. 23-24	Hogpen - Unicoi	R. Russell	26
Aug. 30-S.1	Multi-Club meet, Dark Hollow, Va.	H. Daniel	5
Sep. 13-14	Moccasin Creek camping	H. Arnovitz	22
Sep. 20-21	Shining Rock Wilderness	G. Owen	10
Sep. 27-28	Hightower Gap - Amicalola Falls	R. Hallock	20
Oct. 4-5	Stone Mt. Camping	Humphries	8
Oct. 10	Annual meeting	M. Black	69
Oct. 17-19	Roan Mt.	Ju. Engle	15
Oct. 25-26	Mt. LeConte	G. Galphin	39
Nov. 1-2	Wolfpen - Fish Gap	E. Selby	8
Nov. 8-9	Wayah Gap - Franklin	J. Burns	14
Nov. 15-16	Kephart Prong, Richland Mt.	S. Swink	15
Nov. 22	Coweta Station, Pickens Nose	E. Seiferle	8
Nov. 27-30	Jekyll Island	A. Thompson	

Dec. 6-7	Titus Valley, Charlies Creek	J. Engle	20
Dec. 12	Christmas Party	T. Taylor	120
Dec. 21	Kennesaw Mt.	H. Arnovitz	29

1976

Jan. 2-4	Slickrock Basin	W. Benson	11
Jan. 10-11	Three Forks - Cooper Gap	F. Baker	14
Jan. 24	Nimblewill Falls	M. Slater	30
Jan. 31-F.1	Three Forks - Springer	H. Smith	9
Feb. 7-8	Mt. LeConte	L. Elliott	38
Feb. 14	Cochran Falls	H. Glover	17
Feb. 21-22	Unicoi - Dick's Creek	M. Rubin	7
Feb. 28-29	Hwy. 60 - Fish Gap	B. Durrett	9
Mar. 6-7	Lake Winfield Scott - Hightower Gap	R. Hallock	7
Mar. 13	Trail Maintenance	M. Drummond	52
Mar. 20	Noontootla Creek	Emersons	24
Mar. 27-28	Moccasin Creek - Dick's Creek	H. Arnovitz	10
Apr. 3-4	Wayah Bald - Wesser	H. Daniel	11
Apr. 10-11	Dick's Creek - Deep Gap	N. Shofner	11
Apr. 17	Panola Mt.	R. Ramsey	24
Apr. 24-25	Hudson & Broad Rivers canoe	C. Shuford	
May 1-2	Cowrock Mt. loop	E. Selby	6
May 8	Panther Creek	C. Newton	19
May 15-16	Wildflower hike	N. Seiferle	13
May 22-23	Unicoi Gap - Tesnatee	E. Hanks	14
May 29-31	Smoky Mt.	G. Coffey	12
Jun. 5	Spring meeting	F. Shafe	35
Jun. 12	Trail Maintenance	G. Galphin	6
Jun. 19	Bike trip	R. Russell	8
Jun. 26-27	Betty's Creek camping	G. Goldman	32
Jul. 3-5	Shining Rock	D. Schenck	16
Jul. 18	Sarah's Creek	J. Galphin	9
Jul. 24	Trail Maintenance	M. Drummond	13
Aug. 7-8	Jack's River	B. Slater	18
Aug. 14-15	Caving trip	B. Taylor	20
Aug. 20	Slide show, photo contest	B. Cowden	20
Sep. 4-6	Multi-Club meet, Dilley's Mill, W.Va.	H. Daniel	9
Sep. 11-12	Tesnatee Gap - Winfield Scott	J. Conroy	
Sep. 25-26	Neel Gap - Mulkey	J. Burns	10
Oct. 2-3	Mt. LeConte	A. Thompson	20
Oct. 9-10	Raven Forks	G. Roseman	10
Oct. 15	Annual meeting	Engles	58
Oct. 17	Oak Ridge Cross country	M. Eidson	13
Oct. 23-24	Standing Indian	C. Conner	11
Nov. 6	Blue Ridge vistas	G. Owen	13
Nov. 20-21	Toccoa River - Three Forks	G. Galphin	9
Nov. 24-29	Okefenokee Swamp canoe	M. Sanford	33
Dec. 4	Panther Creek	B. Cowden	20
Dec. 10	Christmas party	J. Myers	

1977

Date	Activity	Leader	Count
Dec.30-J.2	Standing Indian	B. Bryant	8
Jan. 8	Ellicott's Rock	G. Galphin	15
Jan. 22-23	Hogpen - Unicoi	F. Baker	2
Jan. 29-30	Moccasin Creek	H. Arnovitz	7
Feb. 5-6	Loop Trail (work)	W. Benson	18
Feb. 12-13	Hwy. 60 - Fish Gap	D. Eggleston	
Feb. 20	Kennesaw Mt.	H. Morris	20
Feb. 26-27	Loop Trail (work)	C. Conner	16
Mar. 5-6	Wayah Bald - Wesser	H. Daniel	9
Mar. 12-13	Joyce Kilmer	R. Van Landingham	10
Mar. 19	Tallulah Gorge	M. Eidson	34
Mar. 26-27	Double Trouble hike	E. Selby	3
Apr. 1-3	Wesser - Fontana	M. Rubin	4
Apr. 9	Loop Trail (work)	G. Owen	12
Apr. 16	Univ. of Ga. Botanical Gardens	B. Shenkel	8
Apr. 23-24	Wildflower weekend	G. Benson	
Apr. 30	Walk-thru	N. Shofner	40
May 6	Spring meeting	W. Durrett	46
May 7	Loop Trail (work)	C. Conner	
May 14	Etowah canoe	R. Wilson	7
May 14	Loop Trail (work)	G. Owen	
May 21-22	Lake Winfield Scott - Tesnatee	H. Glover	6
May 27-30	ATC Conference, Shepherdstown, W.Va.	M. Drummond	14
May 28-30	Hughes Ridge, Smokies	B. Slater	16
Jun. 4-5	Wallaby Bye family campout	Durretts	16
Jun. 11	Loop Trail (work)	G. Owen	
Jun. 19	The Pocket	G. Benson	23
Jun. 25-26	Jack's River	G. Wilkins	11
Jul. 2-4	Mt. Mitchell	W. Benson	18
Jul. 9	Loop Trail (work)	E. Seiferle	10
Jul. 10	Chattahoochee raft & tube float	H. Daniel	34
Jul. 16	Bike Trip with So. Bicycle League	R. Russell	
Jul. 23-24	Byers Cave	B. Taylor	11
Aug. 6	Trail Maintenance	N. Shofner	11
Aug. 12-22	Glacier National Park		10
Aug. 13	Tusquitee Bald	J. DeVaughn	2
Aug. 20	Sarah's Creek	G. Goldman	29
Aug. 26	Slide show	J. Krickel	45
Sep. 3-5	Multi-Club meet, Townsend, Tenn.	M. Drummond	41
Sep. 10-18	Georgia AT	J. Krickel	7
Sep. 18	Sweetwater Creek	Humphries	23
Sep. 24-25	Cooper Gap - Lake Winfield Scott	W. Langford	11
Oct. 8-9	Cohuttas	C. Conner	8
Oct. 14	Annual meeting	P. Aderhold	69
Oct. 15	Trail Maintenance	N. Shofner	11
Oct. 22-23	Wayah Bald - Wesser Creek	J. Galphin	11
Oct. 29-30	Three Forks - Highway 60	J. Myers	22
Nov. 5	Toccoa River Bridge dedication	M. Drummond	11
Nov. 6	Brasstown Bald - Track Rock	M. Drummond	18

Nov. 12-13	Tesnatee - Unicoi Gap	R. Russell	13
Nov. 19	Bike trip	H. Smith	4
Nov. 24-27	Alexander Springs, Fla.	G. Coffey	20
Dec. 16	Christmas party	B. Bordeaux	104
Dec. 17	Dukes Creek Falls, Raven Cliffs	S. Bauer	7

1978

Dec. 31-J.2	Smokies - Miry Ridge, Silers Bald	W. Benson	13
Jan. 21-22	Rabun Bald - Warwoman Dell	J. Myers	15
Jan. 28-29	Pine Mt.	E. Butler	6
Feb. 4-5	Odum Scout Trail, Ala.	G. Wilkins	8
Feb. 11-12	Moccasin Creek	H. Arnovitz	17
Feb. 18	Trail Maintenance	F. Baker	25
Feb. 18-20	Fla. Trail, Suwanee River	J. Krickel	12
Feb. 25-26	Woody Gap - Neel Gap	D. Herring	7
Mar. 4-5	Unicoi Gap - Dick's Creek	R. Russell	6
Mar. 12	Tesnatee - Neel Gap	T. Negas	10
Mar. 18-19	Dick's Creek - Bly Gap	B. Davey	9
Mar. 25	Trail Maintenance	N. Shofner	18
Apr. 2	Orienteering	G. Benson	17
Apr. 7	Spring meeting	Ju. Engle	55+
Apr. 9	Mulky Gap - Hwy. 60	G. Coffey	22
Apr. 14-16	Wildflower weekend, Toccoa area	V. Emerson	18
Apr. 15-16	Nantahalas	H. Daniel	15
Apr. 22	Walk-thru	N. Shofner	37
Apr. 29-30	Whitewater canoe training	J. Krickel	11
May 6	Trail Maintenance	N. Shofner	13
May 7	Raven Cliffs	J. Mahl	14
May 20-21	Training backpack	H. Daniel	9
May 27-29	Slickrock Wilderness	B. Calvert	7
Jun. 3	Trail Maintenance	R. Van Landingham	13
Jun. 4	Wolfpen Gap - Lake Winfield Scott	L. Eidson	9
Jun. 10-11	Nantahala River canoe	C. Shuford	2
Jun. 17-18	Cohuttas	D. Eggleston	13
Jun. 24-25	Track Rock Campground family camping	G. Goldman	31
Jul. 4	Peachtree Road Race	T. Aderhold	
Jul. 1-4	Iron Mt. Gap, Roan Mt.	R. Van Landingham	8
Jul. 8	Trail Maintenance	R. Chiselbrook	9
Jul. 9	Panther Creek	S. Slack	12
Jul. 15	Trail Maintenance	N. Shofner	9
Jul. 29	Partly Creek hike	M. Eidson	21
Aug. 5-6	Byers Cave	B. Taylor	26
Aug. 12-13	Lake Blue Ridge camping	J. Boyd	14
Aug. 16	Trail Maintenance	B. Slater	13
Aug. 26-27	Balsam Mt., Round Bottom	S. Bauer	9
Sep. 2-4	Multi-Club meet, Roan Mt.	M. Drummond	12
Sep. 7	Slide show	G. Benson	
Sep. 9-10	Shining Rock	P. Haakmeester	6
Sep. 16-17	Hightower Gap - Woody Gap	G. Galphin	17
Sep. 23	Trail Maintenance	G. Coffey	10

Sep. 24	Jack's Gap - Unicoi Gap	J. Boyd	25
Sep.30-O.1	Amicalola Falls - Hightower Gap	H. Quin	19
Oct. 7-8	Greenbriar Cove	T. Aderhold	7
Oct. 14	Annual meeting	P. Thompson	75
Oct. 15	Trail Maintenance	G. Benson	19
Oct. 16	Stone Mt. moonlight hike	H. Daniel	47
Oct. 21-23	Explorers Rock, Mt. Mitchell	B. Slater	12
Oct. 28-29	Wayah Bald - Wesser Creek	A. Anderson	13
Nov. 4-5	Providence Canyon	B. Mann	13
Nov. 11-12	Trail Skills workshop	M. Drummond	33
Nov. 18-19	Joyce Kilmer	M. Rubin	13
Nov. 23-26	Cumberland Island	Ea. Metzger	15
Dec. 2-3	Fish Gap - Wildcat Gap	D. Langham	8
Dec. 7	Christmas party	P. Aderhold	100+
Dec. lO	Trail Maintenance	G. Galphin	20
Dec. 17	Kennesaw Mt.	H. Morris	37

1979

Dec. 30-J.1	Elkmont - Thunderhead	J. Eidson	14
Jan. 6-7	Wesser - Wayah	D. Eggleston	3
Jan. 13-14	Unicoi Gap - Dick's Creek Gap	M. Rubin	4
Jan. 21	Trail Maintenance	W. Benson	8
Jan. 27-28	Nantahalas hike	H. Daniel	12
Feb. 3-4	Moccasin Creek	H. Arnovitz	16
Feb. 10-11	Woody Gap - Neel Gap	B. Goldstein	4
Feb. 17-19	Florida Trail	J. Krickel	12
Feb. 17-18	Smokemont - Charlies Bunion	B. Slater	6
Feb. 24	Trail Maintenance	F. Baker	7
Mar. 3	Chattahoochee River Basin, flagging	N. Shofner	9
Mar. 10-11	Ellicott's Rock	G. Galphin	11
Mar. 17	Trail Maintenance	R. Chiselbrook	8
Mar. 18	Neel Gap - Hogpen Gap	M. Slater	13
Mar. 24-25	Rabun Bald Bushwack	J. Myers	9
Mar. 31-A.1	Hogpen - Unicoi Gap	L. Eidson	7
Apr. 7-8	Amicalola Falls - Hightower	J. Burns	5
Apr. 14	Walk-thru	B. Slater	
Apr. 15	Predicted Time Race	M. Rubin	16
Apr. 19	Spring meeting	Ju. Engle	36
Apr. 21-22	Big Stamp - Highway 60	M. Drummond	8
Apr. 21-22	High Hampton Inn, Cashiers, N.C.	E. Selby	16
Apr. 28-29	Wesser - Fontana	J. Galphin	5
May 5-6	Cohuttas, Conasauga River	C. Conner	
May 12	Trail Maintenance	G. Wilkins	16
May 19-20	Highway 60 - Mulky Gap	J. Boyd	15
Jun. 2-3	Whitewater canoe training	C. Lyerla	17
Jun. 9-10	Big Snowbird loop	G. Benson	10
Jun. 16	Trail Maintenance	H. Quin	15
Jun. 17	Woody Gap - Dockery Lake	N. Shofner	15
Jun. 23-24	Family campout, Scaly Mt.	G. Goldman	35
Jul. 4	Peachtree Road Race	B. Calvert	23

Jul. 7-8	Slickrock Wilderness family	G. Coffey	8
Jul. 14	Trail Maintenance	M. Drummond	11
Jul. 21	Panther Creek Falls	D. Schenck	10
Jul. 28-29	Art Loeb Trail	B. Davey	11
Aug. 4-5	Raven Forks Manway, Smokies	R. Van Landingham	5
Aug. 10-14	ATC Conference, Carrabassett, Me.	W. Benson	18
Sep. 1-3	Multi-Club meet, Bland, Va.	W. Benson	9
Sep. 8-9	Neel Gap - Desoto Falls	S. Bauer	21
Sep. 15	Cooper Gap - Woody Gap	W. Langford	10
Sep. 16	Trail Maintenance	B. Funkhouser	13
Sep. 20	Slide show	H. Arnovitz	40
Sep. 22-23	Dorothy Thompson Wilderness area	B. Durrett	18
Oct. 4	Stone Mt. moonlight	H. Daniel	16
Oct. 6	Trail Maintenance	G. Benson	6
Oct. 7	Fall bike ride	Ju. Burns	5
Oct. 11	Annual meeting	A. Coffey	62
Oct. 13-15	Standing Indian	M. Skeen	4
Oct. 20	Little River Canyon, Ala.	M. Eidson	18
Oct. 21	Highway 180 - Neel Gap	J. Link	14
Oct. 27-28	Dick's Creek Gap - Deep Gap	R. Russell	25
Nov. 3-4	Orienteering	R. Sarner	10
Nov. 10	Trail Maintenance	G. Galphin	12
Nov. 11	Tallulah Gorge	B. Funkhouser	7
Nov. 17-18	Case Cave	B. Taylor	10
Nov. 22-25	Okefenokee Swamp	A. Thompson	7
Nov. 23-25	White Oak Bottoms, Smokies	H. Quin	5
Dec. 1	Mt. Yonah	R. Chiselbrook	10
Dec. 2	Trail Maintenance	N. Shofner	14
Dec. 8	Christmas party	T. Taylor	85
Dec. 15-16	Brasstown Bald - Unicoi Gap	E. Butler	10
Dec. 22	Kennesaw Mt.	J. Byrd	8

1980

Dec. 29-J.1	Kephart Country, Smokies	W. Benson	4
Jan. 12-13	Nantahala winter hike	M. Eidson	21
Jan. 19-20	Wayah - Wesser	M. Rubin	6
Jan. 26	Nimblewill Falls	J. Boyd	24
Jan. 27	Trail Maintenance	N. Shofner	16
Feb. 2-3	Newfound Gap	W. Benson	4
Feb. 9-10	Cross country ski trip	H. Quin	30
Feb. 16-18	Florida canoe trip	J. Krickel	9
Feb. 16-17	Unicoi Gap - Dick's Creek Gap	B. Goldstein	6
Feb. 23	Trail Maintenance	M. Drummond	9
Feb. 24	Blood Mountain loop	N. Shofner	5
Mar. 8-9	Frozen Head State Park	M. Skeen	3
Mar. 22-23	Shining Rock Wilderness	B. Davey	8
Mar. 29	Trail Maintenance	N. Shofner	5
Mar. 30	Wolfpen - Slaughter Gap	J. Negas	7
Apr. 5	Benton MacKaye Trail, flagging	G. Wilkins	
Apr. 12-19	Loop Trail - AT Circuit	J. Krickel	7

Apr. 19-20	High Hampton Inn	E. Selby	11
Apr. 26	Panola Mountain	H. Boyd	14
Apr. 27	Trail Maintenance	R. Chiselbrook	14
May 3-4	White water adventure, Toccoa R.	C. Lyerla	3
May 6	By-laws review meeting	W. Benson	
May 10	Rock climbing	W. Benson	11
May 17	Paint/Walk-thru	B. Slater	50+
May 24-26	Hazel Creek, Smokies	W. Benson	4
May 31-Je.1	Highlands Fling	H. Quin	29
Jun. 7-8	Moccasin Creek	H. Arnovitz	10
Jun. 14-15	Jack's River	M. Drummond	13
Jun. 20-22	Track Rock campground	G. Goldman	21
Jun. 29	Trail Maintenance	G. Benson	9
Jul. 4-6	Bald River, Tenn.	R. Van Landingham	13
Jul. 12-13	Snowbird Mountains	G. Benson	10
Jul. 26	Big Stamp - Three Forks loop	N. Shofner	15
Jul. 27	Trail Maintenance	A. Anderson	13
Aug. 16-17	Three Forks fishing trip	G. Wilkins	8
Aug. 21	Slide show	M. Skeen	40+
Aug. 23	Trail Maintenance	G. Galphin	9
Aug.30-S.1	Multi-Club meet, Unicoi State Park	W. Benson	
Sep. 27	Trail Maintenance	D. Maret	19
Oct. 4-5	Hogpen - Unicoi	B. Davey	6
Oct. 9	Annual meeting	G. Morris	
Oct. 11-12	Mulky Gap - Hwy. 60	D. Eggleston	5
Oct. 18-20	Dick's Creek - Standing Indian	H. Daniel	11
Oct. 23	Stone Mt. moonlight hike	C. Hill	14
Oct. 25	Wolfpen Gap - Mulky Gap	J. Engle	14
Oct. 26	Trail Maintenance	W. Benson	12
Nov. 8-9	Chattooga River hike	G. Galphin	5
Nov. 14-16	Cumberland Island	S. Bauer	19
Nov. 23	Trail Maintenance	B. Cowden	9
Nov. 22-23	Flea market	M. Drummond	
Nov. 28-30	Smokies	H. Quin	7
Dec. 6	Golden Anniversary party	N. Shofner	180
Dec. 7	Golden Anniversary hike/drive	N. Shofner	25
Dec. 13-14	Joyce Kilmer	B. Funkhouser	11
Dec. 27	Trail Maintenance	R. Van Landingham	7

"Then give me the clear blue sky overhead
And the long trail to my feet."

— *Tincksom-Fernandey*

A Mother's Story

A Mother and Her 13-Year Old Son in the Appalachians[*]

Tempted by the heights, we allowed ourselves to drive up to Connahaynee Lodge from Jasper, instead of remaining in a modest hotel below. Once up in the clouds we stayed, remembering there was a small sum set aside in the home bank for "emergencies." We stayed and gloried in our rashness: in the far stretches of valley, opening out in all but one direction, that in which lies Grassy Mountain, now Mount Oglethorpe, where stands a marble shaft to the Englishman who came over here so long ago to found a colony in a new state. Little did he dream of what the future held, or did his hopes outstrip, perhaps, the reality. We are all proud of our ancestors, but are we living so they would be proud of us?

After a perfect night's sleep, the moon, like a silver thread in the sky, the same turquoise moon that hung over the miraculous sunset of the evening before, we donned our hiking clothes and started out to the proper and fitting beginning place of our trip along the Appalachian Trail to the North Carolina Border. There was nothing sure as to the length of our "safari" as it was our first attempt, and without a guide and only fairly adequate preparation, we looked to bog down at any moment. However, a start must be made, and we were determined to "do" some of the Trail, anyway. And we hoped to make Rich Knob some day.

Arrived at the Monument, we looked around for the beginning of the Trail. No visible signs. No marker. Ye Gods, weren't we even going to begin our hike? Around the monument we walked. Still no sign of egress. So down we plumped ourselves and began to consult the Geographical Survey maps and the typewritten data furnished us by the president of the Georgia section of the Trail. We found we were right: we were at the beginning of the Trail, allright. But it went down the automobile road which we had just come up!

Didn't we feel flat! Walk back down that automobile road four and a half miles to where an arrow would lead us off into the woods? And yet, we were at the beginning of the Trail. We finally all acknowledged that the most sensible thing to do would be to hitch-hike the distance! So back into the car we piled

---

[*] This report, written by V. G. Stutesman of Ft. Benning, Ga., covers the hike made by her husband Col. John H. Stutesman, their son, John, and herself along the Georgia Appalachian Trail in August and September, 1934. It is the earliest existing account of a hike of the entire Georgia Trail.

and asked our husband and father if he would carry us back to the arrow! It was somehow ignominious, but it seemed the only reasonable thing to do, tho' as I look back now, I believe it might have been better had we not. However, one can never tell.

At the sign, a board of treated hard wood with the directions burnt in— not painted on—we slung on our sacks and started. It was hard to say "au revoir" to the third member of the family, who was unable to accompany us, but all things must be finished, and so down a sharp, rocky slope, with thoughts of broken ankles or bruised heels in the offing—and in fifteen minutes a halt, sacks off, down on the ground to lie and look at the fleecy white clouds sailing overhead. Then up, with a fixed schedule of: march twenty minutes, rest ten, change sacks after every two rests, lead turn and turn about, a swig at the canteen every five rests. And so on to the next halt, where we found blackberries, and thought of Boone and Indians and other trailrunners. Later on we had a feast of blue berries. Then the trail directions began to talk of a spring and we began to dream of a long, cool drink. We became irregular as to stops and rests; the packs became heavier; the straps more galling; and in a while we knew we'd missed that blessed spring! But just as we were really growing exhausted, we saw an old deserted sawmill at the bottom of the hill, and then *I* had the thrill of locating the spring. Son went down and dipped me up the first cupfull, and I never tasted anything so good in all my life!

Opened up the sack to get something to eat. Chocolate. Whew! Bitter instead of sweet! What a fool I was not to take the package in my hand and examine it, instead of trusting to that salesman!

We walked a bit after taking the sacks off, and there was the queerest sensation of lightness, of loss of equilibrium. My son remarked it, too. "Did you have a funny feeling when you took your sack off and walked without it? I had to lean forward to keep from falling! Well, it's worth carrying a pack to have the sensation!"

And here we are, sitting on the trail somewhere near Amicalola Falls, a lovely valley spread out below us, Connahaynee Lodge visible far away to the right.

Into the shelter just at twilight. Too late. It is closed on three sides. I threw out a sight of old tin cans and other debris left by our neat and considerate American hikers. John got a fire started while I unpacked, wondering how anyone could sleep on slats. We soon found they were better, perhaps, than hard board, as one's hip could fit between two, and shoulder and elbow between others! Heard an owl hooting in the night and once thought it was raining, but saw a star and was relieved. To cure insomnia, I recommend eleven miles of mountain hiking with a thirty pound pack on one's back.

Up and at 'em at ten minutes after five. Cooked a really decent breakfast. Bacon, flapjacks, coffee, bouillon. Prunes to start off!

Then on the trail at seven-fifty-five, having sewed on a button, fixed a blister, cleaned up everything, packed carefully.

Off on trail, gayly and gallantly, in spite of a drizzling rain and soaking underbrush. Gayly and gallantly, I repeat, to get absolutely and completely lost in about one hour. At present we are still lost. Got panicky and followed a cow bell for a bit, but are all over that now, and are marching on the compass northeast by north.

Now can you imagine Graham NcNamee's voice? And *there* they go, up from the lunch camp, and by the compass on a trail running along the crest—and—yes—the boy shouts "here is a road"—and there it is, what they judge to be a CCC road down the hillside running N.E. by N. The boy says, "We're not going to leave this road, are we?" and the Mother replies, memories fresh of the alder and rhododendron thickets just behind, where her pack caught on every bough and her feet in every vine, "No! I wouldn't leave this road for anything. Not even for a black bear!"

Have just seen an Appalachian Trail sign! And we're hoofing N.E. on another CCC road, with gorgeous scenery to our left. Also thunder on our left! Well, I wouldn't take anything for it! On Black Mountain, we saw a corner Forest Service sign, and felt as comfortable as tho' we had met an old friend. And so down the North side of the mountain, to find three nice cows in the valley, and I was all set to ask the farmer-owner to let us sleep on his front porch. That one blister had multiplied and we were tired from having been lost. John isn't fond of cows, and approached them gingerly, whereupon they turned tail and ran! No sign of a farmhouse, so up Springer Mountain we plugged. Our schedule was all shot to pieces by now, what with being lost, and so John always led, and I plugged behind, my old left knee hurting like sin. That knee certainly surprised me. I never suspected myself of gout or rheumatism, but the twinges in that joint made me wonder if I'd been a high-liver unbeknownst to myself! However, we were finally at the top of Springer Mountain, and I left John sitting on the trail and went to hunt the spring. I was just about giving up, and had turned back, when there on the tree above my head was a blessed Appalachian Trail sign—"Spring 100 ft." Whew! I sat down and yelled for John! While I prayerfully made a fire, he cut wood and prepared a lean-to, with one poncho hung on a rope between two trees as a beginning. With the fire leaping merrily, the lean-to all comfy looking, and supper in the making, we felt pretty happy. Later in the night, when rain began pattering in my face, I admit to qualms, but later still I could see the stars clear in the sky so close above, and I prayed to wake to a sun-shiny morning. Sunshine does help so much! Instead, however, we got up in a drizzle. Couldn't start a fire, tho' I tried every device I knew, not enough, evidently. Finally we ate raisins and that cooking chocolate, tore down the first shelter we ever made (John said "and we haven't a picture of it!") and swung on our packs to get going. John was limping. Too narrow shoes, he thought. I was cutting one heel, too wet sox, low shoes bad, mud and gravel kicking in. But on we went. Finally coming to a truck road, and signs of "Game Refuge." And the prettiest butterflies we've ever seen. Lovely, floating colored things, we saw at least five different varieties. I made up a little song and asked them to send us some one to take us to Woody Gap. I knew we'd never make it on foot. Finally, we saw Hawk Mountain Fire Tower. And at the beginning of the road up I left John sitting on a gravel pile, with the packs, and went up. No one there! I gazed thro' the windows of the Ranger's house at the telephone— and at the kerosene—With one I might call a car, with the other I could have started a fire. But somehow, I could not see our case as so desperate as to warrant my breaking the glass. So down I started, first picking up a good dry stick, and then, in the barn, another. And back to the boy I went, with bad news but dry wood. With which we made a fire at once and cooked pancakes and bacon and hot chocolate and coffee! After seeing the fire safely extinguished, we packed up and started off again. We'd both used what first aid was possible for our feet, but there's not much to do for squdgy shoes and soaking sox, skinned heels and blistered toes. One just realized there's been a big mistake somewhere and definitely vows to rectify it before another trip!

Finally we came to a sign pointing to a Game Warden, and down the road we plugged, to find him, thank heavens, at home. He 'foned Woody Gap, and after some questions, evidently satisfactorily answered, they said for us to start on and a car would meet us on the road. So, up with the packs, adieu and a little Thank-You piece to the warden, and back to the main road, to trudge on up it, wondering if the car *would* come, marvelling at the wonderful views of magnificent mountains and small valleys between. Occasionally to our right long, long vistas of a valley, apparently limitless. Again the lovely, hovering butterflies, and a violet plant *right* in the middle of the road, bearing two perfect blossoms, "to teach us fortitude." And after a while of weary but somehow ecstatic limping—the car.

The Second Venture

A Father, Mother and Their 13-Year Old Son in the Appalachians

Did you ever lie on a wood's trail and gaze up into the foliage? Green, red and tawny leaves against a blue and white sky. Oak, ash and thorn! No, it's not Merrie England, but Georgia, so it's oak of a good many varieties, chestnut, hemlock, and maple and dogwood. A stream tumbles down alongside the trail, a woodpecker hammers on a tree nearby. It's choice, that life.

It's a long pull up Blood Mountain. The name, and also that of Slaughter Mountain, close by, so reminiscent of the last stand made by the Cherokee Indians in this region. We looked for arrowheads, but had no luck. CCC men are building a shelter on top Blood, the second highest mountain in Georgia.

We finally made the summit at 1:30, having commenced our hike at its foot at 11:30, on the nineteenth day of September, 1934.

And what a view from the top! If there is anything to compare with the elation that comes when a height has been attained, I don't know it.

We are three, this time, so the decisions are apt to be wiser, and the final outcome more successful. John sang a little prayer: "Now I lay me down to sleep, I pray the Lord my feet to keep." We all agreed, for an army may walk on its stomach, but it also most certainly walks on its feet, and John and I had vivid recollections of skinned heels and blistered toes.

2d day. 9:10 A.M. A most comfortable night, spent in a cottage of the Vogel State Park Lodge at Neels Gap, where hiking is made luxurious! Also, where there is a most beautiful view of Blood Mountain Gorge, and Brass Town Bald, and far away, unknown blue mountains flat against the horizon. This morning three country boys came up hunting cows. It appears the owners mark their cows' ears and turn them loose in the mountains to graze.—10:50 A.M. On top Levelland Mountain. John stretched out in the sun, hat cocked over his eyes, fanning himself with an oak branch, one leaf of which says, with its flaming red edges, that Fall is coming. The Blue Ridge stretches out to either side of us; a fly buzzes nearby; otherwise all is perfectly calm and quiet. White clouds sail across the blue sky, and the world with its problems seems very far away.

11:20. Levelland Gap. Wild asters, wild phlox, goldenrod, blue bells, harebells, little tufts of a pink straw-flower; long wands of a sort of purple thistle. Oaks, dead chestnuts, twisted pines. We chopped a bit on the trail and broke back long thorn trailers. 12:00. Spring, and *I* found it! We cleaned it out and put a blaze on a tree to mark it, and then lay down on a sunny rock and felt fine! Lovely odour of penny royal. Small daisies. Wild tomatoes. 2:17 P.M. Marvelous view. We lost our canteen at the spring, and had to return for it, as we only had three, and we knew we must have one for each person. We found it, and were very glad. We also heard the eerie sound of boys calling their cows thro' the woods. It is startling at first. We wondered if they would ever find them.

That night. The shelter to which we had looked forward all day didn't exist. So we slept under a rock, and thankful were we to have our sleeping bags, which, with a beautiful poncho and the high laced boots, were the new items of our equipment for the second try for the Carolina border. Our rock was rain proof, but gave us no room to sit up. At first there were two under and one out. But a rain soon drove the third in among the herd, and so, head and heels intermingling, we slept the sleep of the hiker.

7:00 A.M. I like hiking, and the out-of-doors, but I don't like making breakfast and packing packs, etc., on wet ground. We came along from Tesnatee Gap at a fair rate and found the trail particularly beautiful, running along the hillside, the valley and mountains stretching far away to our right. We soon came to a CCC road, and followed it, losing the Appalachian Trail completely soon after Low Gap. We lunched in a hollow, pigs rooting near by, and so on to the

Chattahoochee Gap, tho' we could not find the springs, the CCC work having obliterated the trail to the spring. That was a real disappointment, as we live near the broad Chattahoochee River here, and had looked forward to drinking from its source.

We had a beautiful night in the Rocky Knob shelter, which is far and away my favorite on the trail. John liked the Traymount shelter, as he was much impressed with the view out over the valley and Lake Burton, but I admired the way the Rocky Knob shelter was built: the many places left where one could hang things, the sturdy slats on the bunks, the wild appearance of the glade, the moonlight shimmering on the leaves of the trees, the funny sheep that seemed so startled, the next morning to find the shelter occupied.

We left Rocky Knob at 10:10 the next morning, the 22nd, and about 11:30, while descending Rocky Mountain, were caught in a pretty heavy rain. I don't like rain, with its attendant wet clothes and squdgy shoes, but it seems to cheer my husband up immensely. He catches a good drink in his poncho and seems to feel magnificent.

There is the loveliest trail up from Unicoi Gap, like a park. Violets, rhododendrons, maple, small red oaks. It looked almost artificial in its ordered beauty. We arrived Tray Mountain at 4:50, 8.5 miles. All the world is surely at one's feet there. And from the Montray shelter the view seemed very Swiss in character.

Left Montray shelter 10:05 A.M. Sunday 23/9/34. Arrived Snake Mountain shelter 4:30 P.M., 10 miles. 1 mile per 40', 1.3 miles per hour elapsed time. Fifth day. Sunday, Sept. 23, 11:00 A.M. A lovely trail entering Nantahala Forest Reserve. 12:05. Lovely descent, good path, beautiful views to right, long vistas with a lovely lake below. The Blue Ridge is certainly well named. It is Blue as blue.

Each of us three seems to have a day off! As I said, the rain suits the man, but yesterday so dispirited me I wanted (almost) to go home. So when I waked to a heavenly sunny morning on Tray Mountain I felt like singing! And then on the trail we found lovely asters and goldenrod, and, swinging down into a gap, we came upon the most charming little country boy, perched on a stump, wearing blue overalls and a lighter blue denim shirt, his fox-terrier at his feet. And a little later we met three men and two dogs hunting pigs, which completed the total number of six persons seen in the six days on the trail.

2:25. Kelly's Knob! What a "knob"! It took us 50 minutes to ascend it. Rain all the way up. John said he certainly admired the sprinkler system in the country! And then he made up a poor little rhyme, but it showed he was gay:

> Up the hill we go,
> Whether it rain or no.
> It matters naught if we bust
> But up the hill we go!

3:15. We took a good breather on top Powell Mountain. Later raining again.

4:00. My husband remarked there were three kinds of miles: The statute mile, the nautical mile and the Appalachian mile. "Yes," says the son, "and the S mile. which all hikers should have!"

4:20. Jim Hooper Gap. Wonder who he was. The shelter is very nice. Beautiful moonlight, and I sat and looked at it shining on the forest leaves. There was a marvelous sunrise. The shelter faced east, and far away, on the horizon, two mountains joined and made a great dip, the peak of another almost directly in the center of it. Just to the left of this third, the sun rose in all his majesty. It was very dramatic. We left the shelter at 8:05, on a beautiful morning, with marvelous sunlight pouring into the forest glens.

Our bacon was all gone, one or two chiggers had found me, and visions of bath-tubs, full of hot, steaming water, were beginning to dance, occasionally, before us. We hoped to reach the North Carolina border at about three that afternoon.

2:05 P.M. Eureka! Blye Gap, Rich Knob, and the Border! We dumped our packs at the shelter (which was in horrible condition, and glad was I there was no necessity to clean it up) and went up on the ridge to see the state we had been trying so long to reach. And there it was, mountain upon mountain, stretching out before us. I should like to have gone to Standing Indian, but bathtubs and John's school were waiting, so we stood and looked for a little while and then turned and went back to the shelter, made a little fire and some good hot bouillon, and gloated.

Soon we were en route again, starting definitely down at last, toward Tree Post Office, which we reached, after crossing the Tallulah River, in about three hours. John at last saw a big snake when he picked up a stone on the river bank in order to make a stepping stone. He let out a yell that could have been heard in Clayton, and we got across the river without any extra aid!

And so, the end of the Trail in Georgia. For us it has been a wonderful discovery; a marvelously beautiful country right at hand, where people with beer pocket books and champagne tastes may go and be quiet and calm and feel themselves owners of all the beautiful universe. Where they may surmount difficulties and hardships, and so, in turn, feel the moral fibre grow stronger daily.

All this, with the eternal beauty of the mountains brought within our reach, we owe to those who have gone before us on the Appalachian Trail.

"Let us probe the silent places . . . .
Let us journey to a lonely land I know . . . ."

– Robert William Service

Index

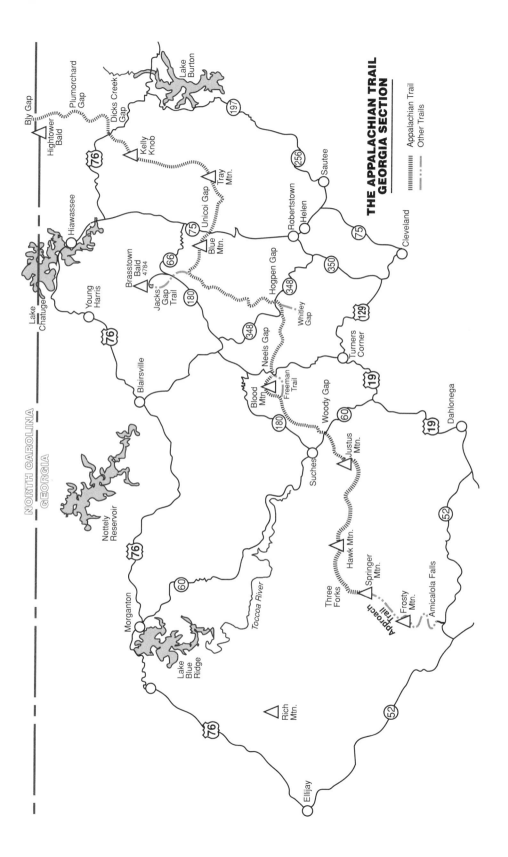

THE APPALACHIAN TRAIL
GEORGIA SECTION

|||||||| Appalachian Trail
-·-·- Other Trails

NORTH CAROLINA
GEORGIA

Bly Gap
Hightower Bald
Plumorchard Gap
Dicks Creek Gap
Lake Burton
197
Kelly Knob
256
Sautee
76
Tray Mtn.
Unicoi Gap
75
Robertstown
Helen
75
Cleveland
Brasstown Bald 4784
66
Blue Mtn.
Hogpen Gap
350
Hiawassee
Young Harris
Jacks Gap Trail
180
348
Whitley Gap
348
Neels Gap
129
Lake Chatuge
76
Blairsville
Turners Corner
19
Dahlonega
Blood Mtn.
Freeman Trail
Woody Gap
60
19
180
Nottely Reservoir
Suches
Justus Mtn.
76
Morganton
60
Hawk Mtn.
52
Toccoa River
Three Forks
Springer Mtn.
Frosty Mtn.
Amicalola Falls
Approach Trail
Lake Blue Ridge
Rich Mtn.
76
Ellijay
52

"One may well feel chagrined when he finds he can do nearly all he can conceive."

– Henry David Thoreau

Order Form

Copies of *Friendships of the Trail* are available from the
Georgia Appalachian Trail Club, Inc.
P.O. Box 654, Atlanta, Georgia 30301

Ordered by:

Name _____

Address* _____

City _____ State ____ Zip _____ - ____

Home Telephone No.   (____)_____

Daytime Telephone No. (____)_____

Ship to (if different from above):

Name _____

Address* _____

City _____ State ____ Zip _____ - ____

* Please use street address, if possible, since parcels over two pounds are generally shipped by United Parcel Service for faster service.

Cost per book: $19.95   x _____   = $ _____

Sales Tax:
Please add 6% sales tax to total for
orders sent to Georgia addresses   Sales Tax   _____

Shipping:
$4.00 for the first book and $1.00 for each additional book   _____
(Please allow two to four weeks for delivery.)

Tax-Deductible Contribution: _____

TOTAL: $ _____

Payment:
❏ Check   ❏ Money Order

❏ I would like to join the Georgia Appalachian Trail Club, Inc.

❏ Please send information on other GATC publications.